Why Do You Need this New Edition?

If you're wondering why you should buy this new edition of *The Contemporary Reader*, here are five good reasons!

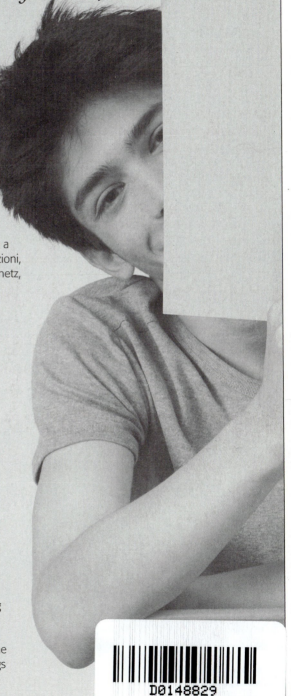

1. **Three brand new thematic chapters,** Chapter 3, "Generation Debt: The Financial Challenges We Face," Chapter 4, "Carbon Footprints: It's Not Easy Being Green," and Chapter 5, "Look at Me!: Celebrity and Our Fifteen Minutes of Fame" give you a rich source of ideas for writing about some of today's most important topics.

2. **With more than 50 new readings,** the tenth edition features fresh selections from a variety of notable writers such as Amitai Etzioni, Margaret Atwood, Roger Ebert, Anya Kamenetz, Joseph Epstein, Joe Queenan, and William Deresiewicz. The new perspectives explore a wealth of contemporary subjects to provide you with an array of writing ideas.

3. **Every chapter includes a new feature, "Perspectives: Editorial Cartoon."** These cartoons show you how to analyze and think critically about visual arguments—a key skill in today's image-driven world.

4. **Many new visuals have been added to the frequently assigned advertising chapter.** Chapter 2, "Consumer Nation: Wanting It, Selling It" now presents a range of new ads, all accompanied by critical thinking questions that ask you to take a closer look at the effects of advertising on our culture.

5. **Updated introduction to critical thinking** emphasizes the relationship between reading, thinking, and writing to help you read critically and write effectively about the topics you'll encounter in academic settings and beyond.

The Contemporary Reader

The **Contemporary** Reader

TENTH EDITION

Gary Goshgarian

NORTHEASTERN UNIVERSITY

Longman

Boston Columbus Indianapolis New York San Francisco Upper Saddle River
Amsterdam Cape Town Dubai London Madrid Milan Munich Paris Montreal Toronto
Delhi Mexico City Sao Paulo Sydney Hong Kong Seoul Singapore Taipei Tokyo

Executive Editor: Suzanne Phelps Chambers
Editorial Assistant: Erica Schweitzer
Senior Development Editor: Katharine Glynn
Senior Marketing Manager: Sandra McGuire
Senior Supplements Editor: Donna Campion
Production Manager: Stacey Kulig
Project Coordination, Text Design, and Electronic Page Makeup: Pre-Press PMG
Cover Designer/Manager: John Callahan
Cover Images: Monk at video console (Getty); Hands with light bulb (Getty); Scissors cut
credit card (Getty); Woman composting (Getty); iPhone (Corbis); Guitarist love music/hate
racism (Corbis)
Photo Researcher: Rebecca Karamehmedovic
Senior Manufacturing Buyer: Alfred C. Dorsey
Printer and Binder: R.R. Donnelley and Sons
Cover Printer: R.R. Donnelley and Sons

For permission to use copyrighted material, grateful acknowledgment is made to the
copyright holders on pp. 515–521, which are hereby made part of this copyright page.

Library of Congress Cataloging-in-Publication Data

The contemporary reader / [edited by] Gary Goshgarian. — 10th ed.
    p. cm.
  Includes bibliographical references and index.
  ISBN-13: 978-0-205-74144-1
  ISBN-10: 0-205-74144-4
  1. College readers.   2. English language—Rhetoric—Problems, exercises, etc.
3. Report writing—Problems, exercises, etc.   I. Goshgarian, Gary.   II. Title.
  PE1417.C6523 2009
  808'.0427—dc22

                                                          2009038349

2 3 4 5 6 7 8 9 10—DOC—13 12 11

Longman
is an imprint of

www.pearsonhighered.com   ISBN-13: 978-0-205-74144-1
                             ISBN-10:   0-205-74144-4

Contents

Introduction: How to Read and Write Critically   1

1   Fashion and Flesh: The Images We Project   41

What I Think About the Fashion World   43
Liz Jones

"We decided to publish two covers for the same edition [of *Marie Claire*]—one featuring Sophie Dahl, a size 12; the other, Pamela Anderson, a minute size 6—and we asked readers to choose. . . . You would think that we had declared war."

Culture Shock: Get Real Ad   49

Out-of-Body Image   50
Caroline Heldman

"What would disappear from our lives if we stopped seeing ourselves as objects? Painful high heels? Body hatred? Constant dieting? Liposuction? It's hard to know."

The Natural Beauty Myth   54
Garance Franke-Ruta

"Only in America do we think that beauty is a purely natural attribute, rather than a type of artistry requiring effort."

My Hips, My Caderas   57
Alisa Valdes

"In Spanish, the word for hips is *caderas*—a broad term used to denote everything a real woman carries from her waist to her thighs, and the bigger, the better. In English, hips are something women try to be rid of."

Weight of the World   61
Niranjana Iyer

"In India, I'd been above average in height. In the States, I was short (so said the Gap). From a tall, thin Women's, I had morphed into a petite, plump Misses'—without gaining or losing a smidgen of flesh."

How Men Really Feel About Their Bodies   63
Ted Spiker

"I'm not the only man who wishes his body looked more like Michael Jordan's and less like a vat of pudding."

Culture Shock: Mr. Olympia   67

2 Consumer Nation: Wanting It, Selling It 79

Grow Up? Not So Fast   140
Lev Grossman

"Today there is a new, intermediate phase along the way [between adolescence and adulthood]. The years from 18 until 25 and even beyond have become a distinct and separate life stage . . . in which people stall for a few extra years, putting off the iron cage of adult responsibility that constantly threatens to crash down on them. They're betwixt and between. You could call them twixters."

Culture Shock: Boomerang Statistics   151

Maxed Out   153
James D. Scurlock

"As they carried [her son] Sean's belongings across campus, [his mother] noticed a number of tables advertising credit cards. 'But I didn't worry,' she recalls. 'Sean was 18, he didn't have a job. Who would give him a credit card?' Not only would they give him a credit card, they would practically shove it down his throat."

Strapped   156
Tamara Draut

"About a quarter of students report using their credit cards to pay for tuition and books. What about the other three quarters? Visa and MasterCard have no doubt funded a great many pizzas, kegs, and spring breaks. The problem is that after graduation, the need for credit often morphs into a whole new category: survival debt."

Debtor's Prism   161
Margaret Atwood

"The hidden metaphors [of debt] are revealing: We get 'into' debt, as if into a prison, swamp, or well, or possibly a bed; we get 'out' of it, as if coming into the open air or climbing out of a hole. If we are 'overwhelmed' by debt, the image is possibly that of a foundering ship, with the sea and the waves pouring inexorably in on top of us as we flail and choke."

Investigating the Nation's Exploding Credit Squeeze   166
Danny Schechter

"There is a credit divide in America that fuels our economic divide. Put another way, the globalization of our economy is about more than the outsourcing of jobs. There is a deeper shift underway from a society based around production, with the factory as the symbol of American economic prowess, to a culture driven by consumption, with the mall as its dominant icon."

Perspectives: Empty-nesters   171

► Twentysomething: Be Responsible, Go Back Home After College   172
Ryan Healy

"When you look closely, it is glaringly apparent that moving back in with parents is one of the most responsible things a new college grad can do. By sucking it up at home for a year or two, young people give themselves the opportunity to take control of their career, take control of their

just below the surface. We are not lawyers, executives, and managers. We are female lawyers, female executives, and female managers."

Perspectives: What She Wore 302

Has Male Bashing Gone Too Far? 303
Jake Brennan

"The backlash against male domination in our society has reached the point where we expect a father in a sitcom or TV commercial to be an oafish, grunting Neanderthal, as in Tim Allen's famous caricature of the "typical" male. Take the male leads in *Everybody Loves Raymond* or *The King of Queens*, for example: blundering nitwits, most of the time."

The New Girl Order 307
Kay S. Hymowitz

"Carrie Bradshaw is alive and well and living in Warsaw. Well, not just Warsaw. Today you can find her in cities across Europe, Asia, and North America. Seek out the trendy shoe stores in Shanghai, Berlin, Singapore, Seoul, and Dublin, and you'll see crowds of single young females (SYFs) in their twenties and thirties, who spend their hours working their abs and their careers, sipping cocktails, dancing at clubs, and (yawn) talking about relationships."

The Men We Carry in Our Minds 316
Scott Russell Sanders

"When the women I met at college thought about the joys and privileges of men, they did not carry in their minds the sort of men I had known in my childhood."

The Science of Difference 320
Steven Pinker

"The belief, still popular among some academics (particularly outside the biological sciences), that children are born unisex and are molded into male and female roles by their parents and society, is becoming less credible."

Hip-Hop: Beyond Beats and Rhymes? 326
Byron Hurt

"When you think about American society, the notion of violent masculinity is at the heart of American identity." From the outlaw cowboy in American history to the hypermasculine thug of gangster rap, violent masculinity is an enduring symbol of American manhood itself."

Culture Shock: 50 Cent 329

► He's a Laker; She's a "Looker" 330
Jennifer L. Knight and Traci A. Giuliano

"Coverage of women's sport is inferior to that of men's not only in quantity but in quality. Sport commentators and writers often allude or explicitly refer to a female athlete's attractiveness, emotionality, femininity, and heterosexuality (all of which effectively convey to the audience that her stereotypical gender role is more salient than her athletic role)."

Rhetorical Contents

Preface

Like its predecessors, the tenth edition of *The Contemporary Reader* comprises many new readings and several new issues. The nature of the subject matter covered necessitates constant updating to keep abreast of trends in popular culture, media, and society. However, despite such changes, the book's foundation remains the same: It continues to provide a collection of well-written, thought-provoking readings that students can relate to, readings that stimulate classroom discussion, critical thinking, and writing.

The Contemporary Reader, tenth edition, is contemporary in more than just the selections. The introduction includes strategies for critical writing. Likewise, the apparatus reflects the latest and most effective rhetorical theories and practice. Preceding each reading is a headnote that helps orient the student to the topic and the reading. The critical thinking and writing questions following each essay help students process the text, encourage the flow of ideas, and promote class discussion. Where appropriate, we have included a directional cue in italics before certain writing questions, such as "Personal Narrative" or "Research and Analysis," to help students focus their critical writing. In Viewpoints articles, a feature continued in this edition, authors explore different aspects of the same issue.

What's New in the Tenth Edition?

- **Three new chapter themes**—Chapter 3, "Generation Debt: The Financial Challenges We Face"; Chapter 4, "Carbon Footprints: It's Not Easy Being Green"; and Chapter 5, "Look at Me! Celebrity and Our Fifteen Minutes of Fame," encourage class discussion and writing about today's important topics.
- **More than 50 new readings** explore a wealth of contemporary subjects, including selections from James D. Scurlock, Tamara Draut, Margaret Atwood, Roger Ebert, and Kay S. Hymowitz.
- **A new feature, Perspectives: Editorial Cartoon,** is found in every chapter. The cartoons, which connect to the chapter's topic, ask students to consider how visual arguments express their point of view.
- **New images have been added to the widely taught advertising chapter,** "Consumer Nation: Wanting It, Selling It." Chapter 2 includes a range of new ads. Each ad is supported with critical thinking questions that ask students to closely analyze the affects advertising has on our culture.
- **The introduction has been updated.** The revised introduction emphasizes the relationship between reading, thinking, and writing.

Chapter Topics

While we have repeated or retooled the most popular chapters from the previous edition—and added three new chapters—the themes of all the chapters were chosen to reflect a wide spectrum of issues that affect us all. Most importantly, they capture some of the conflicts and paradoxes that make our culture unique. From fashion and advertising to the cult of celebrity to education and family, ours is a culture caught in conflicts. We are a people who crave the modern yet long for nostalgia. We harness technology to the hilt, and reminisce about how things used to be simpler. We are as much a society steeped in traditional values and identities as we are one that redefines itself in response to trends and subcultures.

A Closer Look at Chapter Themes

The nine thematic chapters in this edition span issues that encourage students to consider their place in the world and their impact upon it. In many cases, topics in different chapters overlap an issue with another perspective. For example, some readings in the celebrity culture chapter address issues connected to gender, and pieces in the new chapter on debt connect back to essays in the chapter on consumerism. A description of the contents, themes, and issues addressed in each chapter is featured at the beginning of the section.

Variety of Readings

In addition to extensively revising the chapter themes, we include many different types of readings. Expository communication comes in all shapes and models. This book includes newspaper stories, editorials, political cartoons, advertisements, academic essays, magazine articles, television interviews, Internet articles from "e-zines," student essays, humor columns, and a lot more. Students will read academic articles, personal narratives, objective essays, position papers, political arguments, and research reports.

Advertisements

Chapter 2, "Consumer Nation: Wanting It, Selling It," one of the most popular chapters in previous editions, has been updated with many new images. Each ad is accompanied by specific questions to help students closely analyze how advertising—and the particular ad at issue—affects us. The questions should spark lively class discussion about the art and craft of advertising. Beyond that, they encourage students to increase their visual literacy and critical thinking by closely focusing on particular print ads and making new associations and discoveries.

Viewpoints

The Viewpoints articles bring the traditional pro–con debates to a more focused level and aim to help students explore the different sides of a focused issue, such as body stereotyping, human cloning, or a particular aspect of advertising. The questions following these readings aim to help students consider multiple sides of an issue and move toward a collaborative discussion rather than a heated debate.

Culture Shock

Images are everywhere—and more and more, all of us need to be able to understand and evaluate those images critically. Images sell, they amuse, they provide information. The Culture Shock features found throughout this book reflect the kind of images that confront us every day—cartoons, advertisements, statistical maps, and charts—and the questions that accompany them encourage students to analyze the arguments being made visually and rhetorically.

Updated Introduction to Critical Reading and Writing

The premise of the new edition of *The Contemporary Reader* is that effective writing grows out of effective thinking, and effective thinking grows out of thoughtful reading. We intertwine these three concepts in the new Introduction, featuring sections that discuss both critical reading and critical writing. The introductory chapter illustrates the process in a detailed, sample analysis of John Leo's essay, "Now Cut That Out!" The sample analysis demonstrates systematic approaches to critical reading and then continues this exploration into the Critical Writing section.

Critical Thinking and Critical Writing Considerations

Following each reading are critical thinking and critical writing questions that help students connect to the reading, analyze its points, and place themselves within the context of the issue. Writing assignments encourage students to expand their critical thinking, respond to the text, and research issues in greater depth.

Group Projects

Active communities work together, accepting multiple points of view and interacting with different identities, values, ideas, races, social outlooks, ethnicities, and educational backgrounds. In an effort to develop students' skills for working and learning together, and to expose them to different points of view, group projects accompany each reading. These exercises emphasize collaborative research, topic exploration, group writing, and problem solving. They also may encourage students to incorporate resources outside the classroom—to search the Internet, explore pop-culture sources, interview people, and conduct observations—to explore further what they have read.

Supplements

MyCompLab is Pearson's all-in-one online site for composition, with a wealth of interactive resources for writing, research, and grammar. Access to this site is available packaged with this Longman text at no additional cost, or it may be purchased at http://www.mycomplab.com. Longman's open access Web site for composition resources, http://www.longmancomposition.com, includes an array of materials about writing and research. Pearson English also offers many other supplementary items—some at no additional cost, some deeply discounted—that are available for packaging with this text. Please contact your local Pearson representative to find out more.

Instructor's Manual

The *Instructor's Manual* includes suggested responses to the critical reading questions in the text and offers ideas for directing class discussion and eliciting student response.

Acknowledgments

Many people behind the scenes deserve much acknowledgment and gratitude for their help with this edition. It would be impossible to thank all of them, but there are some for whose help I am particularly grateful. I would like to thank all the instructors and students who used the first nine editions of *The Contemporary Reader* and have remained loyal to its concept and content. Their continued support has made this latest edition possible. Also, I would like to thank those instructors who spent hours answering lengthy questionnaires on the effectiveness of the essays and who supplied many helpful comments and suggestions for the preparation of this new edition. For this edition, these include Sydney Brown, Grossmont College; Susan Callender, Sinclair Community College; Emily J. Lamb, West Virginia University at Parkersburg; Zachary Locklin, California State University, Long Beach; Andrew J. Manno, Raritan Valley Community College; Cheryl Novins, Nassau Community College; Amisha Patel, Arizona State University; Christy Tidwell, The University of Texas at Arlington; Tara J. Timberman, Community College of Philadelphia; and Shirley Wachtel, Middlesex County College.

Foremost, I would like to thank Kathryn Goodfellow for her invaluable help in locating material, writing the apparatus, and putting together the *Instructor's Manual*. Her keen ability to identify topics and pieces that matter to today's students helped make this edition extraordinary. Thanks also to Kristine Perlmutter for her assistance with some of the questions for this edition. I would also like to thank Amy Trumbull for her help in securing permissions for the readings featured in this volume. Finally, my thanks to the people of Longman Publishers, especially Suzanne Phelps Chambers and Katharine Glynn, who helped conceptualize this edition as its editors, and Teresa Ward for her assistance in coordinating the *Instructor's Manual*.

Gary Goshgarian

Introduction
How to Read and Write Critically

What Is Critical Thinking?

Whenever you read a magazine article, newspaper editorial, or a piece of advertising and find yourself questioning the author's claims, you are exercising the basics of critical reading. You are looking beneath the surface of words and thinking about their meaning and significance. And, subconsciously, you are asking the authors some of the following questions:

- What did you mean by that?
- Can you back up that statement?
- How do you define that term?
- How did you draw that conclusion?
- Do all the experts agree?
- Is this evidence dated?
- What is your point?
- Why do I need to know this?
- Where did you get your data?

You are also making some internal statements:

- That is not true.
- You are contradicting yourself.
- I see your point, but I do not agree because. . . .
- That's a poor choice of words.
- You are jumping to conclusions.
- Good point. I never thought of that.
- That was nicely stated.
- This is an extreme view.

Whether conscious or unconscious, such responses indicate that you are thinking critically about what you read. You are weighing claims, asking for definitions, evaluating information, looking for proof, questioning assumptions, and making judgments. In short, you are processing another person's words, rather than just accepting them at face value.

1

Why Read Critically?

When you read critically, you think critically. Instead of blindly accepting what is written on a page, you begin to separate yourself from the text and decide for yourself what is or is not important, logical, or right. And you do so because you bring to your reading your own perspective, experience, education, and personal values, as well as your own powers of comprehension and analysis.

Critical reading is an active process of discovery. You discover an author's view on a subject, you enter into a dialogue with the author, you discover the strengths and weaknesses of the author's thesis or argument, and you decide if you agree or disagree with the author's views. By questioning and analyzing what the author says with respect to other experiences or views of the issue, including your own, you actively enter into a dialogue or a debate and seek the truth on your own. The result is that you have a better understanding of the issue and the author.

In reality, we understand truth and meaning through interplay. Experience teaches us that knowledge and truth are not static entities but the by-products of struggle and dialogue—of asking tough questions. We witness this phenomenon all the time, recreated in the media through dialogue and conflict. And we recognize it as a force for social change. Consider, for example, how our culture has changed its attitudes concerning race and concepts of success, kinship, social groups, and class since the 1950s. Perhaps the most obvious example of changed attitudes regards gender: Were it not for the fact that old, rigid conventions have been questioned, most women would still be bound to the laundry and the kitchen stove.

The point is that critical reading is an active and reactive process that sharpens your focus on a subject and your ability to absorb information and ideas; at the same time, it encourages you to question accepted norms, views, and myths. And that is both healthy and laudable, for it is the basis of social evolution.

Critical reading also helps you become a better writer, because critical reading is the first step to critical writing. Good writers look at another's writing the way architects look at a house: They study the fine details and how those details connect and create the whole. Likewise, they consider the particular slants and strategies of appeal. Good writers always have a clear sense of their audience: their reader's social makeup, gender, and educational background; their political or religious persuasions; their values, prejudices, and assumptions about life; and so forth. Knowing your audience helps you to determine nearly every aspect of the writing process: the kind of language to use; the writing style, whether casual or formal, humorous or serious, technical or philosophical; the particular slant to take, appealing to the reader's reason, emotions, ethics, or a combination of these; what emphasis to give the essay; the type of evidence to offer; and the kinds of authorities to cite.

The better you become at analyzing and reacting to another's written work, the better you will analyze and react to your own. You will ask yourself questions such as the following: Is this argument logical? Do my points come across clearly? Are my examples solid enough? Is this the best wording? Is my conclusion persuasive? Do I have a clear sense of my audience? What strategy should I take: an appeal to logic, emotions, or ethics? In short, critical reading will help you to evaluate your own writing, thereby making you both a better reader and a better writer. Although you may already employ many strategies of critical reading, the following text presents some techniques to make you an even better critical reader.

How to Read Critically

To help you improve your critical reading, use these six proven, basic steps:

1. Keep a journal on what you read.
2. Annotate what you read.
3. Outline what you read.
4. Summarize what you read.
5. Question what you read.
6. Analyze what you read.

To demonstrate just how these techniques work, we will apply each of them to a sample essay, "Now Cut That Out!" by John Leo, which appeared in the June 30, 2003, issue of *U.S. News and World Report*. This piece works well because, like all of the pieces in this book, it addresses a contemporary issue, namely, the impact of politically correct language in textbooks, and presents opportunities for debate.

Now Cut That Out!
John Leo

1 Which of the following stories would be too biased for schools to allow on tests? (1) Overcoming daunting obstacles, a blind man climbs Mount McKinley; (2) Dinosaurs roamed the Earth in prehistoric times; (3) An Asian-American girl, whose mother is a professor, plays checkers with her grandfather and brings him pizza.

2 As you probably guessed, all three stories are deeply biased. (1) Emphasis on a "daunting" climb implies that blindness is some sort of disability, when it should be viewed as just another personal attribute, like hair color. Besides, mountain-climbing stories are examples of "regional bias," unfair to readers who live in deserts, cities, and rural areas. (2) Dinosaurs are a no-no: they imply acceptance of evolutionary theory. (3) Making the girl's mother a professor perpetuates the "model minority" myth that stereotypes Asian Americans. Older people must not be shown playing checkers. They should be up on the roof fixing shingles or doing something vigorous. And pizza is a junk food. Kids may eat it—but not in a school story.

3 That's what's going on in schools these days. Diane Ravitch's new book, *The Language Police*, documents "an intricate set of rules" applied to test questions as well as textbooks. A historian of education who served as an assistant secretary of education for the first President Bush, Ravitch offers many eye-catching cases of subjects vetoed: peanuts as a good snack (some children are allergic), owls (taboo in Navajo culture), and the palaces of ancient Egypt (elitist).

4   Back in the 1980s and 1990s, lots of us chuckled at the spread of the "sensitivity" industry in schools. Words were removed from tests and books lest they hurt someone's feelings, harm the classroom effort, or impair morals. Most of us assumed that this was a fad that would soon disappear as grown-ups in education exerted the rule of reason.

5   But ridicule had little effect, and grown-ups either converted to the sensitivity ethic or looked the other way. Textbook publishers, with millions of dollars at stake, learned to insulate themselves from criticism by caving in to all objections and writing craven "guidelines" to make sure authors would cave, too.

6   No, no, no! Ravitch warns that these guidelines amount to a full-blown form of "censorship at the source" in schools and "something important and dangerous" that few people know about. She blames both the religious right and the multicultural-feminist left. The right objects to evolution, magic and witchcraft, gambling, nudity, suicide, drug use, and stories about disobedient children. The left objects to "sexist" fairy tales, Huckleberry Finn, religion, smoking, junk food, guns and knives, and what some guidelines call "activities stereotyping" (blacks as athletes, men playing sports or working with tools, women cooking or caring for children).

7   What started out as a sensible suggestion—don't always show women as home-makers or minorities in low-level jobs—developed into hard reverse stereotypes (women must not be shown in the home, maids can't be black). "In the ideal world of education-think," Ravitch writes, "women would be breadwinners, African Americans would be academics, Asian Americans would be athletes and no one would be a wife or a mother."

8   Whites are a group, perhaps the only group, not protected by smothering sensitivity. This follows multicultural dogma. One set of guidelines (McGraw-Hill) "express[es] barely concealed rage against people of European ancestry" as "uniquely responsible for bigotry and exploitation," Ravitch notes.

9   What can be done? Ravitch recommends eliminating the current system in which 22 states adopt textbooks for all their schools. She says it results in cartel-like behavior that allows extremists to manipulate textbook requirements, particularly in the two big states that matter most—California and Texas. Opening up the market, she thinks, would free teachers to choose biographies, histories, or anthologies, rather than sensitivity-laden textbooks.

10   Panels that analyze tests and texts should include teachers of the subjects, not just diversity specialists, Ravitch says. She insists we need better-educated teachers and an end to secrecy about sensitivity: State education officials must put bias and sensitivity reviews on the Internet, listing the reasons that passages and test items were rejected.

11   Unsurprisingly, *The Language Police* has gotten the cold shoulder from our education establishment, which usually limits discussion to three topics: promoting diversity, reducing classroom size, and increasing funding. Ravitch speaks for parents more concerned about something else: substituting censorship and propaganda for actual learning. ◆

Keep a Journal on What You Read

Unlike writing an essay or a paper, journal writing is a personal exploration in which you develop your own ideas without set rules. It is a process of recording impressions and exploring feelings and ideas. Journal writing is a freewriting exercise in which you express yourself without restrictions and without judgment. You do not have to worry about breaking any rules, because in a journal, anything goes.

Reserve a special notebook just for your journal—not one you use for class notes or homework. Also, date your entries and include the titles of the articles to which you are responding. Eventually, by the end of the semester, you should have a substantial number of pages to review, enabling you to see how your ideas and writing style have developed over time.

What do you include in your journal? Although it may serve as a means to understanding an essay, you are not required to write only about the essay itself. Perhaps the article reminds you of a personal experience. Maybe it triggered an opinion you did not know you had. Or perhaps you wish to explore a particular phrase or idea presented by the author.

Some students may find keeping a journal difficult because it is so personal. They may feel as if they are exposing their feelings too much. Or they may feel uncomfortable thinking that someone else, perhaps a teacher or another student, may read their writing. Such apprehensions should not prevent you from exploring your impressions and feelings. If you must turn in your journal to your teacher, do not include anything you do not want others to read. Consider keeping a more private journal for your own benefit.

Reprinted below is one student's journal entry on our sample essay:

John Leo's essay on Diane Ravitch's book helps support his personal opinion that "language police" are controlling the content of texts and tests in American schools and hurting students. Apparently, Ravitch feels that multicultural-feminists AND the religious right have distorted what material is presented in the classroom. The feminists and the religious right are demanding that the language used in textbooks and tests be "sensitive" and "unbiased."

Ravitch and Leo seem to think that the revisions made in the '80s and '90s have gone too far. At first, it seems as if Leo agrees that the original desire to be sensitive was a good idea, but he then agrees with Ravitch's opinion that the panels that decide what language to use on standardized tests have a cartel-like hold on our educational system. Leo often quotes Ravitch, and it is clear that he agrees with her. His fourth paragraph particularly reveals his position.

I think that both Ravitch and Leo are missing a very important point. Language can hurt. And it can influence how we think. They don't seem to acknowledge this. Maybe they have never experienced biased writing. I know from personal experience that it can affect students. I even remember stopping to think about how a question seemed biased on the SAT. I probably didn't need to waste my time thinking about that.

If language policing has gone to an extreme, like Leo says, there must be a happy middle, right?

Annotate What You Read

It is a good idea to underline or highlight key passages and to make margin notes when reading an essay. If you do not own the publication in which the essay appears, or choose not to mark it up, make a photocopy of the piece and annotate that. You should annotate on the second or third reading, once you have an understanding of the essay's general ideas.

There are no specific guidelines for annotation. Use whatever technique suits you best, but keep in mind that in annotating a piece of writing, you are engaging in a dialogue with the author. As in any meaningful dialogue, you hear things you may not have known: things that may be interesting and exciting to you, things with which you may agree or disagree, or things that give you cause to ponder. The other side of the dialogue, of course, is your response. In annotating a piece of writing, that response takes the form of underlining or highlighting key passages and jotting down comments in the margin. Such comments can take the form of full sentences or shorthand codes. Sometimes "Why?" or "True" or "NO!" will be enough to help you respond to a writer's position or claim. If you come across a word or reference that is unfamiliar to you, underline or circle it. Once you have located the main thesis statement or claim, highlight or underline it and jot down "CLAIM" or "THESIS" in the margin.

The Leo essay is reproduced here in its entirety with sample annotations.

Now Cut That Out!
John Leo

1 Which of the following stories would be too biased for schools to allow on tests? (1) Overcoming daunting obstacles, a blind man climbs Mount McKinley; (2) dinosaurs roam the Earth in prehistoric times; (3) an Asian American girl, whose mother is a professor, plays checkers with her grandfather and brings him pizza.

Are these examples from a real test, or did Leo make them up?

2   As you probably guessed, all three stories are deeply biased. (1) Emphasis on a "daunting" climb implies that blindness is some sort of disability, when it should be viewed as just another personal attribute, like hair color. Besides, mountain-climbing stories are examples of "regional bias," unfair to readers who live in deserts, cities, and rural areas. (2) Dinosaurs are a no-no—they imply acceptance of evolutionary theory. (3) Making the girl's mother a professor perpetuates the "model minority" myth that stereotypes Asian Americans. Older people must not be shown playing checkers. They should be up on the roof fixing shingles or doing something vigorous. And pizza is a junk food. Kids may eat it—but not in a school story.

Oh, come on!

Loose interpretation of evolutionary theory. Isn't evolutionary theory related to humans connection to apes? Look up this issue.

3   That's what's going on in schools these days. Diane Ravitch's new book, *The Language Police*, documents "an intricate set of rules" applied to test questions as well as textbooks. A historian of education who served as an assistant secretary of education for the first President Bush, Ravitch offers many eye-catching cases of subjects vetoed: peanuts as a good snack (some children are allergic), owls (taboo in Navajo culture), and the palaces of ancient Egypt (elitist).

Check out this book in university library.

Whose rules?

Who "vetoed"?

Why is this word in quotes?

4   Back in the 1980s and 1990s, lots of us chuckled at the spread of the "sensitivity" industry in schools. Words were removed from tests and books lest they hurt someone's feelings, harm the classroom effort, or impair morals. Most of us assumed that this was a fad that would soon disappear as grown-ups in education exerted the rule of reason.

Well, many words did hurt—especially ones that were racist or sexist.

5   But ridicule had little effect, and grown-ups either converted to the sensitivity ethic or looked the other way. Textbook publishers, with millions of dollars at stake, learned to insulate themselves from criticism by caving in to all objections and writing craven "guidelines" to make sure authors would cave, too.

This is a sweeping generalization as to motivation of teachers and publishers.

look up

6   No, no, no! Ravitch warns that these guidelines amount to a full-blown form of "censorship at the source" in schools and "something important and dangerous" that

Check source for context

few people know about. She blames both the religious right and the multicultural-feminist left. The right objects to evolution, magic and witchcraft, gambling, nudity, suicide, drug use, and stories about disobedient children. The left objects to "sexist" fairy tales, Huckleberry Finn, religion, smoking, junk food, guns and knives, and what some guidelines call "activities stereotyping" (blacks as athletes, men playing sports or working with tools, women cooking or caring for children).

[margin note: look up]

[margin note: Says who?]

7   What started out as a sensible suggestion—don't always show women as homemakers or minorities in low-level jobs—developed into hard reverse stereotypes (women must not be shown in the home, maids can't be black). "In the ideal world of education-think," Ravitch writes, "women would be breadwinners, African Americans would be academics, Asian Americans would be athletes and no one would be a wife or a mother."

[margin note: So author approves that changes were made?]

[margin note: What about white women?]

8   Whites are a group, perhaps the only group, not protected by smothering sensitivity. This follows multicultural dogma. One set of guidelines (McGraw-Hill) "express[es] barely concealed rage against people of European ancestry" as "uniquely responsible for bigotry and exploitation," Ravitch notes.

[margin note: What exactly is "multicultural dogma"?]

[margin note: Ravitch's interpretation of the guideline's tone?]

9   What can be done? Ravitch recommends eliminating the current system in which 22 states adopt textbooks for all their schools. She says it results in cartel-like behavior that allows extremists to manipulate textbook requirements, particularly in the two big states that matter most—California and Texas. Opening up the market, she thinks, would free teachers to choose biographies, histories, or anthologies, rather than sensitivity-laden textbooks.

[margin note: She wants to overhaul the way 22 states choose their textbooks. Doesn't that go against what seems to be an approved consensus? What about the other 28 states that don't use such guidelines?]

[margin note: examples?]

10   Panels that analyze tests and texts should include teachers of the subjects, not just diversity specialists, Ravitch says. She insists we need better-educated teachers and an end to secrecy about sensitivity: State education officials must put bias and sensitivity reviews on the Internet, listing the reasons that passages and test items were rejected.

[margin note: They should be! They aren't now? Is this really true?]

[margin note: This is another issue entirely.]

11   Unsurprisingly, *The Language Police* has gotten the cold shoulder from our education establishment, which

usually limits discussion to three topics: <u>promoting di-</u>
<u>versity, reducing classroom size, and increasing funding</u>.
Ravitch speaks for parents more concerned about something else: <u>substituting censorship and propaganda for</u>
<u>actual learning.</u>

> *Censorship, maybe.*
> *But is Leo concerned*
> *that presenting*
> *blacks as academics*
> *or women Asians as*
> *athletes is actually*
> *propaganda?*

Outline What You Read

Briefly outlining an essay is a good way to see how writers structure their ideas.
When you physically diagram the thesis statement, claims, and supporting evidence,
you can better assess the quality of the writing and decide how convincing it is. You
may already be familiar with detailed, formal essay outlines in which structure is
broken down into main ideas and subsections. However, for our purposes, a brief
and concise breakdown of an essay's components will suffice. This is done by simply jotting down a one-sentence summary of each paragraph. Sometimes brief paragraphs elaborating the same point can be lumped together:

- Point 1
- Point 2
- Point 3
- Point 4
- Point 5, etc.

Such outlines may seem rather primitive, but they demonstrate how the various parts
of an essay are connected—that is, the organization and sequence of ideas.

Below is a sentence outline of "Now Cut That Out!" It identifies the points of
each paragraph in an unbiased way. The purpose of summarizing is to better understand the author's point and how this point is constructed.

Point 1: The author provides three examples of stories that
would not appear on a standardized test because they may use
insensitive or biased language.

Point 2: Diane Ravitch has written a book titled "The Language
Police," in which she discusses the language used in school textbooks
and tests.

Point 3: The author notes that some people may have viewed
the language "sensitivity" movement in schools during the 1980s
and 1990s as a passing "fad." He states that instead of passing,
the movement became entrenched in schools, and publishers
followed suit in order to please their buyers.

Point 4: Ravitch feels that the guidelines developed to encourage language sensitivity in textbooks and tests is a form of censorship. She claims that people who hold extreme viewpoints are controlling the content of school materials.

Point 5: The author concedes that language sensitivity was based on a good idea, but that it has reached extremes.

Point 6: Ravitch advocates eliminating the current system used by 22 states to adopt textbooks in order to loosen the "cartel-like" hold extremists have on the educational system.

Point 7: Ravitch also supports the idea that textbook selection panels include teachers who use the adopted texts and tests, and that the panel should publicly explain its reasons for using certain questions on tests while rejecting others.

Point 8: The author concludes that Ravitch's observation "speaks for parents," while the education establishment focuses on other issues, including diversity, class size, and educational funding.

At this point, you should have a fairly solid grasp of the points expressed in the essay and the author's position on the issue. This exercise prepares you to critically evaluate the essay.

Summarize What You Read

Summarizing is perhaps the most important technique to develop for understanding and evaluating what you read. This means reducing the essay to its main points. In your journal or notebook, try to write a brief (about 100 words) synopsis of the reading in your own words. Note the claim or thesis of the discussion or argument and the chief supporting points. It is important to write these points down, rather than passively highlighting them with a pen or pencil, because the act of jotting down a summary helps you absorb the argument.

Now let us return to the sample essay. In the following paragraph, we offer a summary of Leo's essay, mindful of using our own words rather than those of the author to avoid plagiarism. Again, you should approach this aspect of critical reading impartially: summary is not your opinion, that will come later. At times, it may be impossible to avoid using the author's own words in a summary; but if you do, remember to use quotation marks.

In this essay, John Leo discusses a book by Diane Ravitch, "The Language Police," in which she asserts that language sensitivity in textbooks and tests is controlled by extreme groups, such as the religious right and the "multicultural-feminist left." These groups have, in turn, influenced the language publishers use to better appeal to the panels that select the textbooks. Leo and Ravitch are in agreement that this control is a form of censorship and must stop. Panels that choose textbooks and test questions should include teachers and should also explain the reasons behind language choices.

Although this paragraph seems to do a fairly good job of summarizing Leo's essay, it took us a few tries to get it down to under 100 words. Do not be too discouraged when trying to summarize a reading on your own.

Question What You Read

Although we break down critical reading into discrete steps, these steps will naturally overlap in the actual process of reading and writing critically. In reading this essay, you were simultaneously summarizing and evaluating Leo's points, perhaps adding your own ideas or even arguing with him. If something strikes you as particularly interesting or insightful, make a mental note of it. Likewise, if something strikes you the wrong way, argue back. For beginning writers, a good strategy is to convert that automatic mental response into actual note taking.

In your journal or in the margins of the text, question and challenge the writer. Jot down any points in the essay that do not measure up to your expectations or personal views. Note anything about which you are skeptical. Write down any questions you have about the claims, views, or evidence. If some point or conclusion seems forced or unfounded, record it and briefly explain why. The more skeptical and questioning you are, the better reader you are. Likewise, note what features of the essay impressed you: outstanding points and interesting wording, clever or amusing phrases or allusions, particular references, and the general structure of the piece. Record what you learned from the reading and the aspects of the issue you would like to explore.

Of course, you may not feel qualified to pass judgment on an author's views, especially if the author is a professional writer or an expert on a particular subject. Sometimes the issue discussed might be too technical, or you may not feel informed enough to make critical evaluations. Sometimes a personal narrative may focus on experiences completely alien to you. Nonetheless, you are an intelligent person with the instincts to determine if the writing impresses you or if an argument is sound, logical, and convincing. What you can do in such instances, and another good habit to get into, is to think of other views on the issue. If you have read or heard of experiences different from those of the author, or arguments with opposing views, jot them down. Similarly, if you agree with the author's view, highlight the parts of the essay with which you particularly identify.

Let us return to Leo's essay, which is, technically, an argument. Although it is theoretically possible to question or comment on every sentence in the piece, let us select a few key points that may have struck you, made you question, or made you want to respond. Refer to your point-by-point outline to assist you in this exercise.

Paragraphs 1&2: While I understand Leo's point here with these examples, are they real examples from actual tests or ones Leo just made up to support his argument? If they are real, it would greatly support his position. However, these examples probably represent extreme illustrations of test questions. Furthermore, I wonder why certain adjectives are used at all. The stories could stand up on their own without the story being about a blind man, or an Asian American professor. Couldn't the story just be about a girl whose mother is a professor and who also plays a game with her grandfather? Why is omitting the adjectives so controversial anyway?

Paragraph 3: Leo states that there is "an intricate set of rules" that Ravitch cites in her book. His essay would be strengthened if he cited these rules and their sources. That way, we would have more hard evidence, rather than what seems to be opinion.

Paragraph 4: In this paragraph, Leo states his own position on language sensitivity by admitting he is one of "us" who "chuckled" at the "sensitivity industry" in schools during the '80s and '90s. As such, he admits that he thought that the movement was frivolous, and he calls it a "fad". However, he seems to admit in paragraph 7 that it wasn't entirely a bad idea.

Paragraph 6: Leo takes quotations from Ravitch's book to support his assertion that the language police are out of control. While it is good to quote sources, Ravitch herself seems questionable as a reliable source.

Paragraphs 7&8: It seems as if Leo admits that at one time unbiased language was a good idea—"a sensible suggestion." And he may have a point, if things have really swung to an extreme. But why is he so against the idea that blacks not be portrayed as maids? Who does it hurt? Maybe more importantly, who does it help? Leo's comment on whites being the only group not "protected" by the language police is revealing. Elsewhere in his essay, he comments on the "rule" that women cannot be shown in the home or as mothers. Well, what about women who are white? What Leo really meant to say here was "white males." Another point about paragraph 8 relates to the last sentence. Is this Ravitch's interpretation? Can she really interpret "barely concealed rage" in a set of guidelines prepared by a textbook company? Quoting this material would help the readers decide for themselves.

Paragraphs 9&10: Leo relays Ravitch's suggestions for changes, and he clearly endorses these changes. This helps his essay, because it isn't just a long complaint; the essay actually advocates something. Whether these solutions are possible, or even necessary, is up to the reader.

Paragraph 11: Most of Leo's concluding paragraph could be read in a neutral way. Educators aren't really reacting to Ravitch's book. Rather, they are responding to more pressing issues. Leo's final sentence might make the reader pause—while influencing language may seem like a form of censorship, does he really feel that depicting women as professionals, blacks as academics, and Asians as athletes is equal to propaganda?

Analyze What You Read

To analyze something means to break it down into its components, examine those components closely to evaluate their significance, and determine how they relate as a whole. In part, you already did this by briefly outlining the essay. However, there is more. Analyzing what you read involves interpreting and evaluating the points of a discussion or argument as well as its presentation—that is, its language and structure. Ultimately, analyzing an essay after establishing its key points will help you understand what may not be evident at first. A close examination of the author's words takes you beneath the surface and sharpens your understanding of the issues at hand.

Although there is no set procedure for analyzing a piece of prose, there are some specific questions you should raise when reading an essay, particularly one that is trying to sway you to its view:

- What kind of audience is the author addressing?
- What are the author's assumptions?
- What are the author's purpose and intentions?
- How well does the author accomplish those purposes?
- How convincing is the evidence presented? Is it sufficient and specific? Relevant? Reliable and not dated? Slanted?
- What types of sources were used: personal experience, outside authorities, factual references, or statistical data?
- Did the author address opposing views on the issue?
- Is the perspective of the author persuasive?

Using the essay by Leo once more, let us apply these questions to his article.

What Kind of Audience Is the Author Addressing?

Before the first word is written, a good writer considers his or her audience—that is, their age group, gender, ethnic and racial makeup, educational background, and socioeconomic status. Writers also take into account the values, prejudices, and assumptions of their readers, as well as their readers' political and religious persuasions. Some writers, including several in this book, write for a target audience of readers who share the same interests, opinions, and prejudices. Other authors write for a general audience. Although general audiences consist of very different people with diversified backgrounds, expectations, and standards, think of them as the people who read *Time, Newsweek,* and your local newspaper. You can assume general audiences are relatively well informed about what is going on in the country, that they have a good comprehension of language and a sense of humor, and that they are willing to listen to new ideas.

Because Leo's essay appeared in his column in *U.S. News and World Report,* he is clearly writing for a general audience—an audience with a vast racial and ethnic makeup, an average age of 35, possessing a high school education and some college, and politically middle of the road. A close look tells us more about Leo's audience:

1. The language level suggests at least a high school education.

2. The references to attitudes in the 1980s and the concerns of parents suggest an older audience—certainly at least 30 years old.

3. The references to politics, academic and political movements, and panel policies for textbook selection imply that the readers are culturally informed.

4. The slant of Leo's remarks assumes a more conservative view toward educational trends, perhaps one opposed to the "new" trend of multiculturalism.

5. The language level addresses an audience that will see the absurdity of the language situation, and this audience presumably does not belong to the groups criticized by Leo.

What Are the Author's Assumptions?

Having a sense of the audience leads writers to certain assumptions. If a writer is addressing a general audience, as Leo is, then he or she can assume certain levels of awareness about language and current events, certain values about education and morality, and certain nuances of an argument. After going through Leo's essay, the following conclusions might be drawn about the author:

1. Leo assumes that his readers have a basic understanding of the concept of political right and left.

2. He assumes that his audience is as exasperated as he is that extreme groups are controlling the content of textbooks and test questions in public schools.

3. He assumes that his readers believe that the claims of these groups (the religious right and the multicultural-feminist left) are questionable.

4. He assumes that his readers have a basic understanding of multiculturalism and that they suspect these principles have gone too far.

5. He assumes his readers will agree that the issues the educational establishment are most concerned with—diversity, class size, and school funding—are not as important as stopping "censorship and propaganda" in schools.

What Are the Author's Purposes and Intentions?

A writer has a purpose in writing that goes beyond wanting to show up in print. Sometimes it is simply the expression of how the writer feels about something; sometimes the intent is to convince others to see things in a different light; sometimes the purpose is to persuade readers to change their views or behavior. We might infer that Leo intends:

1. To alert people that extreme interest groups are controlling the content of textbooks and tests in American schools.

2. To urge people to demand changes in their schools and in the way books and materials are selected, especially in the 22 states that currently use this system.

3. To raise public awareness that apathy toward this trend is detrimental to education and harmful to students.

4. To urge people to stop "turning a blind eye" to the "language police" and say "enough is enough."

5. To encourage people to demand reform from the education establishment to focus on issues that matter most.

How Well Does the Author Accomplish Those Purposes?

Determining how well an author accomplishes such purposes may seem subjective, but in reality it comes down to how well the case is presented. Is the thesis clear? Is it organized and well presented? Are the examples sharp and convincing? Is the author's conclusion a logical result of what came before? Returning to Leo's essay, let us apply these questions:

1. Leo keeps to the point for most of his essay, although he sometimes blurs his opinion with that of Diane Ravitch.

2. He offers many examples of the situation, presents his view clearly, and cites Ravitch's book.

3. Because Leo focuses on a book expressing the opinions of one person, the examples he uses to express his point need more support, perhaps from the original sources Ravitch uses.

4. Leo's essay is well constructed and entertaining. He holds his reader's attention through his strong writing style.

How Convincing Is the Evidence Presented? Is It Sufficient and Specific? Relevant? Reliable and Not Dated? Slanted?

Convincing writing depends on convincing evidence; that is, it depends on sufficient and relevant facts along with proper interpretations of facts. Facts—such as statistics, examples, personal experience, expert testimony, and historical details—are pieces of information that can be verified. A proper interpretation of the facts must be logical and supported by relevant data. For instance, it is a fact that SAT verbal scores went up in 2003, and that students from Massachusetts had the highest national scores. One reason might be that students are spending more time reading and less time watching TV than in the past, or that Massachusetts has many colleges and universities available, prompting students to study harder for the test in that state. But without hard statistics that document the viewing habits of a sample of students, such interpretations are shaky: the result of a writer jumping to conclusions.

Is the Evidence Sufficient and Specific? Writers routinely use evidence, but sometimes it may not be sufficient. Sometimes the conclusions reached have too little evidence to be justified. Sometimes writers make hasty generalizations based solely on personal experience as evidence. How much evidence is enough? It is hard to say, but the more specific the details, the more convincing the argument. Instead of generalizations, good writers cite figures, dates, and facts. Instead of paraphrasing information, they quote the experts verbatim.

Is the Evidence Relevant? Good writers select evidence based on how well it supports their thesis, not on how interesting, novel, or humorous it is. For instance, if you are claiming that Barry Bonds is the greatest living baseball player, you should not mention that he was born in California, had a father who played for the San Francisco Giants, or that his godfather is Willie Mays. Those are facts, and they are very interesting, but they have nothing to do with Bonds' athletic abilities. Irrelevant evidence distracts readers and weakens an argument.

Is the Evidence Reliable and Current? Evidence should not be so dated or vague that it fails to support your claim. For instance, it is not accurate to say that candidate Jones fails to support the American worker because 15 years ago she purchased a foreign car. Her current actions are more important. Readers expect the information writers provide to be current and specific enough to be verifiable. A writer supporting animal rights may cite cases of rabbits blinded in drug research, but such tests have been outlawed in the United States for many years. Another may point to medical research that appears to abuse human subjects, while it fails to name the researchers, the place, or the year of such testing. Because readers may have no way of verifying the evidence, the claims become suspicious and will weaken your point.

Is the Evidence Slanted? Sometimes writers select evidence that supports their case and ignore evidence that does not. Often referred to as "stacking the deck," this practice is unfair and potentially self-defeating for a writer. Although some evidence presented may have merit, an argument will be dismissed if readers discover that evidence was slanted or suppressed. For example, suppose you heard a classmate state that he would never take a course with Professor Sanchez because she gives surprise quizzes, assigns 50 pages of reading a night, and does not grade on a curve. Even if these statements are true, that may not be the whole truth. You might discover that Professor Sanchez is a dynamic and talented teacher whose classes are stimulating. Withholding that information may make an argument suspect. A better strategy is to acknowledge counterevidence and to confront it—that is, to strive for a balanced presentation by raising views and evidence that may not be supportive of your own.

Let us take a look at the evidence in Leo's essay, applying some of the points we have just covered.

1. Leo quotes information from Ravitch's book without documenting her sources. This may make the reader wonder if the information is fact or opinion.

2. His use of quotes from Ravitch's book without verifying his own position may make it appear that he is hiding behind her words, rather than supporting his argument on his own.

3. He makes many assumptions about how the general public feels about the language sensitivity movement in schools.

4. Leo assumes that the reason the "fad" of language sensitivity did not "go away" was because people looked the other way. He does not allow for alternative reasons, such as the possibility that people thought the idea was a good one.

5. His argument is emotional rather than logical. Likewise, his presentation of the facts is clearly one-sided.

6. He makes statements without qualifying them, such as "Ravitch speaks for parents more concerned about something else: substituting censorship and propaganda for actual learning." He does not prove that the language sensitivity movement has harmed education, or that parents are indeed concerned that it is hindering the learning process.

What Types of Sources Were Used: Personal Experience, Outside Authorities, Factual References, or Statistical Data?

Writers enlist four basic kinds of evidence to support their views or arguments: (1) *personal testimony* (theirs and others'), (2) *outside authorities,* (3) *factual references and examples,* and (4) *statistics.* In your own writing, you should aim to use combinations of these.

Personal testimony cannot be underestimated. Think of the books you have read or movies you have seen based on word-of-mouth recommendations. (Maybe you learned of the school you are attending through word of mouth.) Personal testimony, which provides eyewitness accounts not available to you or to other readers, is sometimes the most persuasive kind of evidence. Suppose you are writing about the rising abuse of alcohol on college campuses. In addition to statistics and hard facts, quoting the experience of a first-year student who nearly died one night from alcohol poisoning would add dramatic impact. Although personal observations are useful and valuable, writers must not draw hasty conclusions based only on such evidence. The fact that you and a few friends are in favor of replacing letter grades with a pass-fail system does not provide support for the claim that the student body at your school is in favor of the conversion.

Outside authorities are people recognized as experts in a given field. Appealing to such authorities is a powerful tool in writing, particularly for writers wanting to persuade readers of their views. We hear it all the time: "Scientists have found. . . ." "Scholars inform us that. . . ." "According to his biographer, Abraham Lincoln. . . ." Although experts try to be objective and fair-minded, their testimony may be biased. You would not expect scientists working for tobacco companies to provide unbiased opinions on lung cancer. And remember to cite who the authorities behind the statements are. It is not enough to simply state "scientists conducted a study"; you must say *who* they were, *where* the study was conducted, and even who paid for it.

Factual references and examples do as much to inform as to persuade. If somebody wants to sell you something, they will pour on the details. Think of the television commercials that show a sports utility vehicle climbing rocky mountain roads as a narrator lists all its great standard features: four-wheel drive, alloy wheels, second-generation airbags, power brakes, cruise control, and so on. Or cereal "infomercials" in which manufacturers explain that new Yummy-Os have 15 percent more fiber to help prevent cancer. Although readers may not have the expertise to determine which data are useful, they are often convinced by the sheer weight of the evidence, like courtroom juries judging a case.

Statistics impress people. Saying that 77 percent of your school's student body approves of women in military combat roles is much more persuasive than saying "a lot of people" do. Why? Because statistics have a no-nonsense authority. Batting averages, polling results, economic indicators, medical and FBI statistics, and demographic percentages are all reported in numbers. If accurate, they are persuasive, although they can be used to mislead. The claim that 139 people on campus protested the appearance of a certain controversial speaker may be accurate; however, it would be a distortion of the truth not to mention that another 1,500 people attended the talk and gave the speaker a standing ovation. Likewise, the manufacturer who claims that its potato chips are fried in 100 percent cholesterol-free vegetable oil misleads the public, because vegetable oil does not contain cholesterol, which is found only in animal fats. That is known as the "bandwagon" use of statistics, appealing to what people want to hear.

Now let us briefly examine Leo's sources of evidence:

1. Leo draws much of his support from one source: Diane Ravitch. Although her qualifications as a former assistant secretary of education may elevate her authority, she still represents only one opinion. Leo's argument might be stronger if he had quoted some of the groups that held extreme views.

2. He provides examples of biased stories deemed unacceptable for tests without explaining whether these are real examples and without identifying who rejected them.

3. Leo's citing of Ravitch's examples of vetoed subjects—peanuts, owls, and palaces in Egypt—may support his point to his target audience, but some readers may agree that these subjects were indeed unacceptable.

4. His statement that "women must not be shown in the home, maids can't be black" fails to support his premise that this "control" of language is harmful to students. He also fails to show the other side of the issue, such as the idea that some students may be hurt by certain stereotypes.

Did the Author Address Opposing Views on the Issue?

Many of the essays in this book will, in varying degrees, try to persuade you to agree with the author's position. But any slant on a topic can have multiple points of view. In developing their ideas, good writers will anticipate different and opposing views. They will cite alternative opinions and maybe even evidence that does not support their position. By treating alternative points of view fairly, writers strengthen their own position. Failing to present or admit other views could leave their perspective open to scrutiny, as well as to claims of naïveté and ignorance. This is particularly damaging when discussing a controversial issue.

Let us see how Leo's essay addresses alternative points of view:

1. Leo does not introduce alternative points of view into his editorial. It is, after all, an editorial, based on his opinion as he can best support it.

2. Although it is an editorial, and therefore his own point of view, his discussion would have been stronger had he approached the issue more fairly. For example, if he had admitted the possibility that biased language can be harmful, or that some sensitivity is desirable, he might have reached a wider audience.

Is the Perspective of the Author Persuasive?

Style and content make for persuasive writing. Important points are how well a paper is composed—the organization, logic, quality of thought, presentation of evidence, use of language, tone of discussion—and the details and evidence. Turning to Leo's essay, we might make the following observations:

1. On the surface, Leo presents his argument well. A closer reading, however, raises more questions about his presentation of the material. He bases his argument primarily on generalizations and personal opinion.

2. Leo appears to be "pushing buttons" rather than presenting a well-formed, logical argument. He relies on an assumption that his audience shares a common view that the influence of multi-cultural feminists and the religious right on language is ridiculous and should be curtailed.

3. He makes many statements without qualifying them and presents his own assumptions about the opinions of parents and teachers, rather than providing proof of these assumptions.

By now you should have a fairly clear idea of how critical reading can improve your comprehension of a work and make you a better writer in the process. Make critical reading part of your daily life, not just something you do in the classroom or while studying. For example, as you wait for the bus, look at some billboards and consider how they try to hook their audience. While watching TV, think about the techniques advertisers use to convince you to buy their products. Try to apply some of the elements of critical reading as you peruse the articles and editorials in your favorite magazine or newspaper. The more you approach reading with a critical eye, the more natural it will become, and the better writer you will be.

What Is Critical Writing?

Critical writing is a systematic process. When following a recipe, you would not begin mixing ingredients together haphazardly. Instead, you would first gather your ingredients and equipment and then combine the ingredients according to the recipe. Similarly, in writing, you could not plan, write, edit, and proofread all at the same time. Rather, writing occurs one thoughtful step at a time.

Some writing assignments may require more steps than others. An in-class, freewriting exercise may allow for only one or two steps: light planning and writing. An essay question on a midterm examination may permit enough time for only three steps: planning, writing, and proofreading. A simple plan for such an assignment need answer only two questions: What am I going to say and how am I going to develop my idea convincingly? For example, suppose you are asked to answer the following question: Do you agree with Leo's assertion in "Now Cut That Out!" that the "language police" are controlling language in schools to the detriment of students? You might decide to answer with the statement, "The words we use in textbooks and tests should reflect reality while also being sensitive to student's feelings." Or you could decide to answer, "Leo makes an interesting point in his essay that language sensitivity has gone too far. When textbooks no longer reflect reality because words are so controlled, education suffers." You would then develop your idea by comparing or contrasting your own experiences in school with the examples Leo gives in his essay, or by presenting data or information that challenges or supports his argument.

A longer, out-of-class paper allows you to plan and organize your material and to develop more than one draft. In this extended version of the writing process, you will need to do the following to create a strong, critical paper:

- Develop your ideas into a focused thesis that is appropriate for your audience.
- Research pertinent sources.
- Organize your material and draft your paper.
- Proofread your paper thoroughly.

These are the general steps that every writer goes through when writing a paper. In the following sections, the use of these strategies will be discussed to help you write most effectively.

Developing Ideas

Even the most experienced writers sometimes have trouble getting started. Common problems you may encounter include focusing your ideas, knowing where to begin, having too much or too little to say, and determining your position on an issue. Developmental strategies can help promote the free expression of your ideas and make you more comfortable with writing.

Although your finished product should be a tightly focused and well-written essay, you can begin the writing process by being free and sloppy. This approach allows your ideas to develop and flow unblocked onto your paper. Writing techniques such as brainstorming, freewriting, and ballooning can help you through the development process. As with all writing strategies, you should try all of them at first to discover which ones work best for you.

Brainstorming

The goal of brainstorming is to generate and focus ideas. Brainstorming can be a personal exercise or a group project. Begin with a blank sheet of paper or a blackboard and—without paying attention to spelling, order, or grammar—simply list ideas about the topic as they come to you. You should spend at least 10 minutes brainstorming, building on the ideas you write down. There are no dumb ideas in brainstorming: the smallest detail may turn into a great essay.

Let us assume, for example, that you decide to write a paper supporting Leo's assertion in "Now Cut That Out!" Brainstorming for a few minutes may provide something like this:

> language sensitivity may be getting out of hand when NO women are
>
> allowed to be depicted as mothers and NO blacks may be presented
>
> as athletes—it could imply that there is something wrong with
>
> these choices
>
> get a bunch of textbooks written after 1995 to see if such languge
>
> bias is prevalent, get real examples
>
> read Ravitch's book—how does it connect to this essay? what
>
> sources does she site?
>
> explore other multicultural issues
>
> get other people's opinions on this issue, especially parents of
>
> school-age kids
>
> locate the textbook-adoption system in place in the 22 states that
>
> Leo/Ravitch cite
>
> check out the McGraw-Hill guidelines (see Ravitch book?) Leo cites in
>
> paragraph 8

You may notice that this brainstorming example has little structure, no apparent order, and even spelling errors. Its purpose is to elicit all the ideas you have about a subject, so you can read your ideas and identify an interesting topic to develop.

Freewriting

Like brainstorming, freewriting is a free expression of ideas. It helps you jump-start the writing process and get things flowing on paper. Freewriting is unencumbered by rules—you can write about your impressions, ideas, and reactions to the article or essay.

You should devote about 10 minutes to freewriting, keeping in mind that the goal is to write about the topic as ideas occur to you. If you are writing on a particular topic or idea, you may wish to note it at the top of your paper as a visual reminder of your focus. Structure, grammar, and spelling are not important—just focus on the free flow of ideas. Above all, do not stop writing, even if you feel that what you are writing is silly or irrelevant. Any one idea, or a combination of ideas, can be developed into a thoughtful essay. The following is an example of a freewriting exercise:

> In this essay Leo is presenting his opinion and the opinion of
>
> Diane Ravitch. In my opinion, I think Leo could actually make a good
>
> point if his information wasn't so skewed and his bias so apparent.

I guess it doesn't help matters much that he is a white male, and so may be viewed as less likely to suffer from language insensitivity. In one place in his essay, he begins to admit that language sensitivity started out as a "sensible suggestion," but he never elaborates, and that could be where his essay could be most helped, because it is on this point that he could balance his view. For example, he could have admitted that presenting women as mothers at the expense of presenting men as caregivers was insensitive to women and girls, as well as to men and boys. He could have advocated for balance—sometimes women could be shown as both. The same could hold true for athletes and academics, when nationality has to be expressed at all. I sort of wonder about that. Why do you need to say that someone is blind or that a girl's mother is Asian American and a professor at all? Just say a guy climbed a mountain or a girl's mother went to work (this actually allows the woman to be a mother AND a working woman). I guess the other thing I wonder about is whether this language policing is really hurting anyone. Maybe it sort of upsets white guys like Leo, who are left out in the cold, but everyone else seems to be ok. I mean, it isn't as if there are no texts or tests anymore. Why all the fuss?

Ballooning

There are many names for ballooning, including *mind mapping, clustering,* or *grouping.* These techniques all provide a more graphic presentation of ideas, allowing writers to visualize ideas and the connections that stem from them. Ballooning is particularly effective if you already have a fairly clear idea about your topic and wish to develop it more fully.

Write your main topic in the center of a large sheet of paper or a blackboard and circle it. Using the circled idea as your focus, think of subtopics and place them in circles around the center circle, connecting them to each other with radiating lines; remember to keep the subtopics short. Continue doing this until you feel you have developed all the subtopics more fully. When you have finished this exercise, you should be able to visualize the connections between your main topic and its subpoints, which will provide a starting point for your essay.

Narrowing the Topic

Although brainstorming, freewriting, and ballooning help list and develop general ideas, you still need to narrow one idea down to something more manageable. Narrowing a topic can be quite a challenge: you might like more than one idea, or you may be afraid of limiting yourself to only one concept. Nevertheless, you must identify one idea and focus on developing it into an essay. Choose an idea that will interest you and your audience. Remember that if you do not like the way one idea begins to develop, you can always go back and develop another one instead. Once you identify your topic, you are ready to develop the thesis statement for your essay.

Based on the freewriting exercise described earlier, and additional idea development using ballooning techniques, we will follow a student who has decided to write his paper on the idea that language sensitivity is a good idea and that it helps more students than it harms. The idea stems from a response to Leo's essay, but it will develop into a thesis that uniquely belongs to the student.

Identifying Your Audience

Identifying your audience is one of the most important steps in organizing your essay. Knowing what your audience needs and expects from your essay will help you compose a convincing, effective paper. The following questions can help you identify the expectations of your audience:

- Who is my audience?
- What do they already know about my topic?
- What questions do they have about my topic?
- What do they need to know to understand my point?
- What is the best order in which to present information?
- How do they feel about this topic?
- Why would they want to read my essay?

Based on these questions, our student determined that her audience would be her teacher and fellow expository writing classmates. All of them would be familiar with Leo's article and would have discussed it to some extent in class. As members of an academic institution, they should be familiar with the basics of multicultural theory, feminism, and politics, but they may need some additional background on these theories. The intended audience may also have different opinions on the issue, so supporting evidence—from both Leo's article and some outside research—would be necessary to help our student make his or her point effectively. Because the essay would be about an issue that directly concerns both teachers and students, it should generate some level of personal interest to engage readers.

Developing a Thesis

A **thesis** is a type of contract between the writer and reader. It makes a claim or declaration and tells your audience exactly what you are going to discuss. It should be stated in the opening paragraph with the rest of the paper developing and supporting it.

As you write and develop your paper, your thesis should guide you as clearer and more precise thoughts evolve. Do not be constrained by your first thesis: If your paper is changing as you write, your thesis may change. Remember to go back and revise the thesis so that it matches the points made in your essay.

Although the thesis represents the last step in developing the topic for your essay, it is only the beginning of the actual writing process. For her paper, our student worked out the following sentence to help develop her thesis:

> The language sensitivity movement of the 1980s and 1990s grew out of a belief that stereotyping and racial or cultural bias could offend or negatively influence students' self-esteem. As a result, publishers and test panels began to carefully consider the language they used. While language sensitivity may sometimes seem extreme, it ultimately benefits students and the society of which they will later become a part.

Understanding Your Paper's Objective

Before determining how to research or organize your paper, consider what you are trying to achieve by writing it. Your objective may be *to inform*, *to describe*, or *to persuade*. To define your purpose, you should first determine your objective and then identify what you need to do to accomplish this objective. This helps you determine what you need to put in the body of your paper.

Writing to inform involves anticipating the questions your audience may have regarding the topic and how much background they will need to understand it. Once you have developed a list of questions, you can determine what order will best present the information that will answer these questions.

Writing to describe also involves answering some questions. First, you must identify what is important or relevant about the topic you intend to describe. Then you should determine what information is vital to conveying what is important. List these elements and order them in a way that presents a clear view of the experience to the reader.

Writing to persuade presents a perspective on an issue and attempts to convince readers to agree with it. You must provide reasons and supporting evidence to persuade your audience that your perspective makes sense. Although you might not sway all readers to your point of view, you should make enough of a case to allow them to understand your argument, even if they might not agree with it.

The first step in persuasive writing is to determine your position and to identify the objections others might have to it. Remember that there are many different reasons readers may not agree with you. By identifying the arguments against your position, you are better able to address them and thus support your own argument in the process. Three primary kinds of arguments are used in persuasive writing:

1. *Arguments based on disputed facts or consequences*, such as the claim that the building of a gambling casino generated revenue for a bankrupt town, created jobs, and improved the quality of life there.

2. *Arguments that advocate change*, such as arguing for a lower drinking age or changing how the penal system punishes juvenile offenders.
3. *Arguments based on evaluative personal claims*, as right or wrong, ethical or immoral, or favoring one thing or idea over another—such as arguing that physician-assisted suicide is wrong or that supermodels contribute to the development of anorexia nervosa in young women.

The key to effective persuasive writing is to support your perspective with statistics, factual data, and examples. Although your opinions drive the essay, your supporting evidence is what convinces your audience of the validity of your main point.

Researching

Research can involve a few or many steps, depending on the type and length of the paper you are writing. In many cases, simply reviewing the article and applying the steps of critical reading will be the final step you take before organizing your paper. For longer research papers that require outside sources, you will probably need to tap into library resources or look for information online.

Research may even involve taking surveys and conducting interviews. For her paper on language sensitivity in education, our student decided to speak to children and their teachers to determine their opinions on language policing and on Leo and Ravitch's claims.

Selecting Sources for Your Paper

The best place to look for sources for your paper is the library, either at your local library or online. Most libraries have their holdings archived on electronic cataloging systems that let you look up books by author, title, and subject. Although books are a rich source of information, they can be dated and are sometimes inappropriate for essays addressing contemporary issues. For such papers, journals and periodicals are better. With all the different ways to do research, gathering useful and appropriate information can be overwhelming. Do not be afraid to ask the librarian for help.

For many people, the Internet has become the first avenue of research on a topic, and it can be an extremely useful way to locate information on contemporary issues. In addition to Web sites, newsgroups and bulletin boards can aid your research process. Remember that the Internet is largely unregulated, so you should surf the Web with the careful eye of a critic. Simply because something is posted online does not mean it is accurate or truthful. Whenever possible, take steps to verify your sources. When you do find a good source, write it down immediately. Many students lament the loss of a valuable resource, because they forgot to write down the title of the book or Internet address. A good technique is to write down your sources on index cards, which allow you to add sources, and to arrange them alphabetically, without having to rewrite, as you would with a list. You can also write down quotes for your paper on these cards for quick retrieval, and use them to help write the Works Cited section at the end of your essay.

Documenting Sources

Sources help support your ideas and emphasize your points. It is very important to cite any sources you use in your essay. Whether you quote, paraphrase, or use an idea from another source, you must identify the source of information. Documenting sources gives credit to the person who did the work, and it helps locate information on your topic. Even if you rewrite information in your own words, you must still document the source, because it is *borrowed* information. Failure to document your sources is called **plagiarism,** which is presenting someone else's work as your own, and it is considered a form of theft by most academic institutions. The following checklist should help you determine when to document your sources:

- When using someone's exact words
- When presenting someone else's opinion
- When paraphrasing or summarizing someone else's ideas
- When using information gathered from a study
- When citing statistics or reporting the results of research that is not your own

It is *not* necessary to cite dates, facts, or ideas considered common knowledge.

Organizing Your Paper

There are many ways to organize your paper. Some students prefer to use the standard outline technique, complete with Roman numerals and indented subpoints. Other students prefer more flexible flowcharts. The key to organizing is to define your focus and plan how to support your thesis statement from point to point in a logical order.

Drafting Your Essay

When writing your essay, think of your draft as a work in progress. Your objective should be to present your ideas in a logical order; you can address spelling, grammar, and sentence structure later. If you get stuck writing one paragraph or section, go on and work on another. Depending on how you write, you may choose to write your draft sequentially; or you may choose to move from your thesis to your body paragraphs, leaving your introduction and conclusion for last. Feel free to leave gaps, or write notes to yourself in brackets, to indicate areas to develop later when revising. Do not make the mistake of thinking that your first draft has to be your final draft. Remember that writing is a process of refinement—you can always go back and fix things later.

Writing Your Introduction

For many students, the hardest part of writing an essay is drafting the first paragraph. Humorist James Thurber once said "Don't get it right, get it written." What Thurber means is just start writing, even if you do not think it sounds very good. Use your thesis statement as a starting point and build around it. Explain what your essay will do, or provide interesting background information that serves to frame your points for your audience. After you have written the first paragraph, take a break before you revise it. Return to it later with a fresh outlook. Likewise, review your first paragraph as you develop the other sections of your essay to make sure that you are meeting your objectives.

Turning back to our student paper, an introduction might look like the one that follows. Note that the introduction works with the thesis statement developed earlier, and it builds in a few more ideas.

> The language sensitivity movement of the 1980s and 1990s grew out of a belief that stereotyping and racial or cultural bias could offend or negatively influence students' self-esteem. As a result, publishers and test panels began to carefully consider the language they used. Some people fear that language sensitivity has gone too far and no longer reflects reality. Others are concerned that panels are focusing too much on not offending anyone at the expense of education. While language sensitivity may sometimes seem extreme, it ultimately benefits students and the society of which they will later become a part.

Developing Paragraphs and Making Transitions

A **paragraph** is a group of sentences that support and develop a central idea. The central idea serves as the core point of the paragraph, and the surrounding sentences support it. There are three primary types of sentences that make up paragraphs: *topic sentences, supporting sentences,* and *transitional sentences.*

The core point, or the **topic sentence,** is usually the first or second sentence in the paragraph. It is the controlling idea of the paragraph. Placing the topic sentence first lets the reader immediately know what the paragraph is about. However, sometimes a transition sentence or some supporting material needs to precede the topic sentence, in which case the topic sentence may appear as the second or third sentence in the paragraph. Think of the topic sentence as a mini thesis statement; it should connect logically to the topic sentences in the paragraphs before and after it.

Supporting sentences do just that: they support the topic sentence. This support may be from outside sources in the form of quotes or paraphrased material, or it may be from your own ideas. Think of the support sentences as proving the validity of your topic sentence.

Transitional sentences link paragraphs together. They make the paper a cohesive unit and promote its readability. Transitional sentences are often the first and last sentences of the paragraph. When they appear at the end of the paragraph, they foreshadow the topic to come. Words such as *in addition, yet, moreover, furthermore, meanwhile, likewise, also, since, before, hence, on the other* *hand, as well,* and *thus* are often used in transitional sentences. These words can also be used within the body of the paragraph to clarify and smooth the progression from idea to idea. For example, the last sentence in our student's introductory paragraph sets up the expectation that the paragraphs that follow will explain why language sensitivity in educational materials is a good idea. It forecasts what will come next.

Paragraphs have no required length. Remember, however, that an essay comprised of long, detailed paragraphs might prove tiresome and confusing to the reader. Likewise, short, choppy paragraphs may sacrifice clarity and leave the reader with unanswered questions. Remember that a paragraph presents a single, unified idea. It should be just long enough to effectively support its subject. Begin a new paragraph when your subject changes.

Use this list to help keep your paragraphs organized and coherent:

- Organize material logically, and present your core idea early in the paragraph.
- Include a topic sentence that expresses the core point of the paragraph.
- Support and explain the core point.
- Use transitional sentences to indicate where you are going and where you have been.

Let us see how our student applies these ideas to the second paragraph of her essay.

> To better approach this issue, we must first understand a little bit more about the "language sensitivity" movement. For much of the twentieth century, textbooks taught primarily from a white, Anglo-Saxon, Protestant Christian, male-centered perspective. Stereotyping was common: girls played with dolls, boys participated in sports, and mothers and fathers were depicted in traditional roles as homemakers and wage-earners. By the 1980s, however, publishers began to listen to the concerns expressed by academics and outside interest groups, who suggested that educational material be more inclusive, more sensitive, and include the perspectives of women and racial, ethnic, and religious groups [*topic sentence*]. The hope was that through such language awareness, students would learn to avoid stereotyping, to be more tolerant of others, and to feel pride in their own social and cultural backgrounds [*supporting sentence*]. Considering the fact that America is often called the "Great Melting Pot," it is surprising that it took so long to institute this inclusionary approach

to language. Not everyone, however, has embraced this new academic approach [*transitional, "forecasting" sentence*].

Concluding Well

Your conclusion should bring together the points made in your paper and reiterate your final point. You may also use your conclusion as an opportunity to provoke a final thought you wish your audience to consider. Try to frame your conclusion to mirror your introduction—in other words, be consistent in your style. You may wish to repeat the point of the paper, revisit its key points, and then leave your reader with a final idea or thought on your topic.

Conclusions are your opportunity to explain to your reader how all your material adds up. In a short essay of about three to four pages, your conclusion should begin around the penultimate paragraph, winding down the discussion. Avoid the temptation to simply summarize your material; try to give your conclusions a little punch. However, it is equally important not to be overly dramatic, which can undercut your essay. Rather, conclusions should sound confident and reflective.

Notice how our student concludes her essay, making references to her final point as well as to the paper against which she is arguing, the essay by John Leo. Based on her conclusion, we may infer that she has supported all of her final points within the actual body of her essay.

The key to language sensitivity is to create a balance between maintaining the principles of tolerance and maintaining reasonable expectations. Simply because the language sensitivity ethic is relatively new does not make it a "fad" or passing fancy. It means we are progressing as a culture. The saying "You can't please all of the people all of the time" holds particularly true for this issue. Understanding and tolerating alternative cultural, religious, and social points of view through language sensitivity does not mean that students are missing out on a good education. Moreover, language sensitivity ensures that children are not alienated by what they read. Rather than arguing that Asian-American athletes are not a realistic norm, or questioning why panels avoid casting black women in the role of maids, we should instead consider how language sensitivity affords children more possibility, hope, and acceptance. It will help nurture future generations of children to be more tolerant and accepting of different viewpoints and ways of life.

Editing and Revising

Once you have drafted a paper and, if possible, spent several hours or even a day away from it, you should begin editing and revising it. To edit your paper, read it closely, marking the words, phrases, and sections you want to change. Have a grammar handbook nearby to quickly reference any grammatical questions that may arise. Look for things that seem out of place or sound awkward, passages that lack adequate support and detail, and sentences that seem wordy or unclear. Many students find that reading the essay aloud helps them recognize awkward sentences and ambiguous wording. This technique may also reveal missing words.

As you read, you should always ask if what you have written refers back to your thesis. Keep the following questions in mind:

- Does this paragraph support my thesis?
- What does my reader need to know?
- Do my paragraphs flow in a logical order?
- Have I deviated from my point?

As you revise your paper, think about the voice and style you are using to present your material. Is your style smooth and confident? How much of yourself is in the essay, and is this level appropriate for the type of paper you are writing? Some writers, for example, overuse the pronoun *I*. If you find that this is the case, try to rework your sentences to decrease the use of this pronoun.

Using Active Voice

Although grammatically correct, the use of the passive voice can slow down the flow of a paper or distance the reader from your material. Many students are befuddled by the active versus the passive voice, confusing it with past, present, and future tense. The active voice can be used in any tense, and, in most situations, it is the better choice. In the active voice, you make your agent actively perform an action. Consider the following examples:

Passive: In "Now Cut That Out!" in order to describe how extremist groups are controlling language, examples of rejected subjects are provided by John Leo.

Active: In his essay, "Now Cut That Out!" John Leo provides examples of subjects that language extremist groups have vetoed.

Passive: The control of textbook content by the "language police" is feared by Ravitch.

Active: Ravitch fears that the "language police" are controlling textbook content.

In both of these examples, using the active voice makes the sentences cleaner, stronger, and more engaging.

Grammar and Punctuation

You probably already have a grammar handbook; most first-year composition courses require students to purchase these invaluable little books. If you do not have a grammar handbook, get one. You will use it throughout college and probably throughout your professional career. Grammar handbooks can help you identify problems with phrases and clauses, parallel structure, verb-tense agreement, and the various forms of punctuation. Most have useful sections on common usage mistakes, such as when to use *further* and *farther* and *effect* and *affect.* Try not to rely on grammar-checking software available in most word-processing programs. You are the best grammar checker for your essay.

Proofreading Effectively

The final step in preparing a paper is proofreading, the process of reading your paper to correct errors. You will probably be more successful if you wait until you are fresh to do it: Proofreading a paper at 3:00 A.M immediately after finishing it is not a good idea. With the use of word-processing programs, proofreading usually involves three steps: *spell checking, reading,* and *correcting.*

If you are writing your paper using a word-processing system, you probably have been using the spell checker throughout the composition process. Most word-processing systems highlight misspelled words as you type them into the computer. Remember to run the spell checker every time you change or revise your paper. Many students make last minute changes to their papers and neglect to run the spell checker one last time before printing it, only to discover a misspelled word as they turn in their paper—or when it is returned to them. Keep in mind that spell checkers can fix only words that are misspelled, not words that are mistyped that are still real words. Common typing errors in which letters are transposed, such as *from* and *form* and *won* and *own,* will not be caught by a spell checker, because they all are real words. Other common errors not caught by spell checkers include words incompletely typed, such as when the *t* in *the* or the *e* in *here* are left off. Reading your paper carefully will catch these errors.

To proofread correctly, you must read slowly and critically. Try to distance yourself from the material. One careful, slow, attentive proofreading is better than six careless reads. Look for and mark the following: errors in spelling and usage, sentence fragments and comma splices, inconsistencies in number between nouns and pronouns and between subjects and verbs, faulty parallelism, grammatical errors, unintentional repetitions, and omissions.

After you have proofread and identified the errors, go back and correct them. When you have finished, proofread the paper *again* to make sure you caught everything. As you proofread for grammar and style, ask yourself the questions listed above, and make corrections on your paper. Be prepared to read your essay through multiple times. Having only one or two small grammatical corrections is a good indication that you are done revising.

If your schedule permits, you might want to show your paper to a friend or instructor for review. Obtaining feedback from your audience is another way you can test the effectiveness of your paper. An outside reviewer will probably think of questions you had not thought of, and if you revise to answer those questions, you will make your paper stronger.

In the chapters that follow, you will discover dozens of new and updated selections, both written and visual, that range widely across contemporary matters; we hope you will find them exciting and thought provoking. Arranged thematically into nine chapters, the writings represent widely diverse topics—from the ways we construct beauty, to what makes us want to buy something, to the way the Internet is changing our lives, to the ethical issues surrounding human reproduction and gene technology. Some of the topics will be familiar, others you may be encountering for the first time. Regardless of how these language issues touch your experience, critical thinking, critical reading, and critical writing will open you up to a deeper understanding of our culture in the twenty-first century.

Approaching Visuals Critically

We have all heard the old saying: "A picture is worth a thousand words." Our daily lives are filled with the images of pop culture that influence what we buy, how we look, even how we think. Symbols, images, gestures, and graphics all communicate instant information about our culture.

Now more than ever before, ours is a visual world. Everywhere we look, images vie for our attention: magazine ads, T-shirt logos, movie billboards, artwork, traffic signs, political cartoons, statues, and storefront windows. Glanced at only briefly, visuals communicate information and ideas. They may project commonly held values, ideals, or fantasies. They can relay opinion, inspire reaction, and influence emotion. And because the competition for our attention today is so great, and the time for communication is so short, visuals compete to make an instant impression or risk being lost.

Consider the instant messages projected by brand names, company logos, or even the American flag; or the emotional appeal of a photo of a lost kitten or dog attached to a reward notice on a telephone pole. Without the skills of visual literacy, we are at the mercy of a highly persuasive visual universe. Just as we approach writing with the tools of critical analysis, we should carefully consider the many ways visuals influence us.

Understanding the persuasive power of visuals requires a close examination and interpretation of the premise, claims, details, supporting evidence, and stylistic touches embedded in any visual piece. Just as when we examine written arguments, we should ask ourselves the following four questions when examining visual arguments:

1. Who is the target *audience*?
2. What are the *claims* made in the images?
3. What shared history or cultural *assumptions* does the image make?
4. What is the supporting *evidence*?

Like works of art, visuals employ color, shape, line, texture, depth, and point of view to create their effect. Therefore to understand how visuals work and to analyze the way visuals persuade, we must also ask questions about specific aspects of form and design. For example, some questions to ask about print images, such as those in newspaper and magazine ads, include:

- What in the frame catches your attention immediately?
- What is the central image? The background image? The foreground images? The surrounding images? What is significant in the placement of these images? What is their relationship to one another?
- What verbal information is included? How is it made prominent? How does it relate to the other graphics or images?
- What specific details—people, objects, locale—are emphasized? Which are exaggerated or idealized?
- What is the effect of color and lighting?
- What emotional effect is created by the images? Pleasure? Longing? Anxiety? Nostalgia?
- Do the graphics and images make you want to know more about the subject or product?
- What special significance might objects in the image have?
- Is there any symbolism embedded in the images?

Because the goal of a calculated visual is to persuade, coax, intimidate, or otherwise subliminally influence its viewer, it is important that an audience be able to discern the strategies or techniques employed. To get you started, we will critically analyze two types of visuals: advertisements and editorial cartoons.

Images and Advertising

Images have clout, and none are so obvious or so craftily designed as those that come from the world of advertising. Advertising images are everywhere: television, newspapers, the Internet, magazines, the sides of buses, and on highway billboards. Each year, companies collectively spend more than $150 billion on print ads and television commercials—more than the gross national product of many countries. Advertisements make up at least a quarter of each television hour and form the bulk of most newspapers and magazines. Tapping into our most basic emotions, their appeal goes right to the quick of our fantasies: happiness, material wealth, eternal youth, social acceptance, sexual fulfillment, and power.

Yet most of us are so accustomed to the onslaught of such images that we see them without looking and hear them without listening. But if we stopped to examine how the images work, we might be amazed at their powerful and complex psychological force. And we might be surprised at how much effort goes into the crafting of such images—an effort solely intended to separate us from our money.

Like a written argument, every print ad or commercial has an audience, makes claims and assumptions, and offers evidence. Sometimes these elements are obvious, sometimes understated, sometimes implied. They may boast testimonials by average folk or celebrities, or they may cite hard scientific evidence. Sometimes they simply manipulate our desire to be happy or socially accepted. But common to every ad and commercial, no matter what the medium, is the assertion that you should buy the product.

Print ads are complex mixtures of images, graphics, and text. So in analyzing an ad, you should be aware of the use of photography, the placement of the images, and the use of text, company logos, and other graphics such as illustrations, drawings, sidebar boxes, and so on. You should keep in mind that every aspect of the image has been considered and designed carefully, even in those ads where the guiding principle was minimalism. Let us take a look at a recent magazine ad for Altoids.

Altoids Ad

When analyzing a print ad, we should try to determine what first catches our attention. In the accompanying Altoids ad, the image of the soldier—featured floating on a solid, pale green background—pops from the page. This is a calculated move on

THANK YOU SIR!
MAY I HAVE ANOTHER!
THE CURIOUSLY STRONG MINTS

©2000 Callard & Bowser-Suchard Inc.   www.altoids.com

the part of the ad's designers: The soldier fills the center of the page, and the image is arresting—we stop and look. Ad images are staged and manipulated for maximum attention and effect; the uncluttered nature of this advertisement forces us to look at the soldier and the little tin he is holding in his hand.

The person featured in the ad is almost comic. He is wearing an ill-fitting uniform, he sports thick glasses, and he lacks the chiseled quality of many male models commonly used in advertising. This comic quality, coupled with the text under the ad, appeals to the viewer's sense of humor.

What Is the Claim?

Because advertisers are fighting for our attention, they must project their claim as efficiently as possible to discourage us from turning the page. The Altoids ad states its "claim" simply and boldly in white letters against a pale green background below the central photograph. In a large typeface, the slogan and claim come in two parts. The first two sentences presumably come from the soldier: "Thank you sir! May I have another!" The second statement tells us more specifically what the soldier wants: the curiously strong mints. It is interesting to note that the actual name of the product, Altoids, only appears on the little tin held in the soldier's right hand.

Let us take a closer look at the intention of framing the claim in two sentences and at how the layout subtly directs us. The first statement is intended to tap into our shared cultural expectations of what we know about military service. Soldiers must shout responses to their superiors and thank them even for punishments. For example, after being assigned 20 pushups as disciplinary action, a soldier is expected to not only thank his sergeant for the punishment but to actually ask for more. The ad twists this expectation by having Altoids be the "punishment." In this ad, the soldier is actually getting a treat.

The indirect claim is that the reader should also want these "curiously strong" mints. The word *curiously* is designed to set the product apart from its competitors. *Curiously* is more commonly used in British English, and the parent company for Altoids—Callard & Bowser-Suchard—has its roots in England. Viewers familiar with the mint will enjoy the ad for its comic appeal. Those readers who are unfamiliar with the product may wonder just what makes these mints "curiously strong," and curiosity is an effective hook.

Another possible claim could be connected to the scenario leading to the soldier's receiving the first mint. We know that soldiers are supposed to shout back responses to their commanding officer, often face to face. Perhaps his commanding officer was appalled at his recruit's bad breath and "punished" him with the directive to have a mint. The claim is that even at extremely close range, Altoids fixes bad breath.

What Is the Evidence?

The Altoids tag line, "the curiously strong mints," implies that other mints are simply ordinary and unremarkable. Altoids are different—they are "curiously strong" and thus, presumably, superior to their bland competition. Referring back to the possible scenario that led to the soldier's first mint, viewers might presume that if a commanding officer would "treat" his company's bad breath with this mint, it must be good.

Around the language of advertising, we should tread cautiously. As William Lutz warns us in his essay, "With These Words I Can Sell You Anything" (page 112), we hear promises that are not really being made. The Altoids text does not say that they are in fact better than other mints, just that they are "curiously strong." What does the word *curiously* really mean? According to Lutz, such words sound enticing, but they are really telling readers nothing meaningful about the product.

What Are the Assumptions?

The creators of this ad make several assumptions about the audience: (1) that they are familiar with the phrase "Thank you sir, may I have another"; (2) that they understand who is depicted in the ad—a soldier at boot camp; and (3) that they want to have fresh breath.

Altoids Questions

1. What cultural conventions does this ad use to promote the product? What does it assume about the viewer? Would it work in another country, such as France or China? Explain.
2. This ad lists a Web site. Visit the Altoids Web site at www.altoids.com. How does the Web site complement the print ad? Who would visit this site? Evaluate the effectiveness of having companion Web sites in addition to printed advertisements.
3. Would you try Altoids based on this advertisement? Why or why not?
4. How does this photograph capture your attention? Can you tell at a glance what it is selling? Where is your eye directed?

Deciphering Editorial Cartoons

Editorial cartoons have been a part of American life for over a century. They are a mainstay feature on the editorial pages in most newspapers—those pages reserved for columnists, contributing editors, and illustrators to present their views in words and pen and ink. As in the nineteenth century, when they first started to appear, such editorial cartoons are political in nature, holding political and social issues up for public scrutiny and sometimes ridicule.

A stand-alone editorial cartoon, as opposed to a strip of multiple frames, is a powerful and terse form of communication that combines pen-and-ink drawings with dialogue balloons and captions. These are not just visual jokes but visual humor, which comments on social and political issues while drawing on viewers' experience and knowledge.

The editorial cartoon is the story of a moment in the flow of familiar current events. And the key words here are *moment* and *familiar.* Although a cartoon captures a split instant in time, it also implies what came before and, perhaps, what may happen next—either in the next moment or in some indefinite future. And usually the cartoon depicts a moment after which things will never be the same. One of the most famous cartoons of the last 40 years is the late Bill Mauldin's Pulitzer Prize-winning drawing of the figure of Abraham Lincoln with his head in his hands.

It appeared the morning after the assassination of President John F. Kennedy in 1963. There was no caption, nor was there a need for one. The image represented the profound grief of a nation that had lost its leader to an assassin's bullet. But to capture the enormity of the event, Mauldin brilliantly chose to represent a woeful America by using the figure of Abraham Lincoln as depicted in the sculpture of the Lincoln Memorial in Washington, D.C. In so doing, the message implied that so profound was the loss that it even reduced to tears the marble figure of a man many considered to be our greatest president, assassinated a century before.

For a cartoon to be effective, it must make the issue clear at a glance, and it must establish where it stands on the argument. As in the Mauldin illustration, we instantly recognize Lincoln and identify with the emotion. We need not be told the circumstances, because by the time the cartoon appeared the next day, all the world knew the horrible news. To convey less obvious issues and figures at a glance, cartoonists resort to images that are instantly recognizable and that we do not have to work at to grasp. Locales are determined by giveaway props: airports have an airplane out the window, the desert is identified by a cactus and a cow's skull, and an overstuffed arm chair and TV represents the standard living room. Likewise, human emotions are instantly conveyed: pleasure is a huge, toothy grin; fury is steam blowing out of a figure's ears; and love is two figures making goo-goo eyes with floating hearts. Characters may also have exaggerated features to emphasize a point or emotion.

Mort Gerberg, in his essay "What Is a Cartoon?" (*The Arbor House Book of Cartooning*, HarperCollins, 1989) says that editorial cartoons rely on such visual clichés to instantly convey their messages; that is, they employ stock figures for their representation—images instantly recognizable from cultural stereotypes: the fat-cat tycoon, the mobster thug, the sexy female movie star. These images come to us in familiar outfits and with props that give away their identities and professions. The cartoon judge has a black robe and a gavel; the prisoner wears striped overalls and a ball and chain; the physician dons a smock and forehead light; the doomsayer is a scrawny, long-haired guy carrying a sign that reads "The End Is Near." These are visual clichés known by the population at large, and we get them.

The visual cliché may be what catches our eye in the editorial cartoon, but the message lies in what the cartoonist does with it. As Gerberg observes, "The message is in twisting it, in turning the cliché around."

Graduation Resistance Cartoon

Consider Mike Keefe's cartoon shown here. The cliché is a young graduate on his graduation day. We know that from the familiar props: the cap and gown, the bespectacled professor at the podium, the gowned professors in the background, and the rolled diploma. The scene is familiar to anyone who has attended a commencement ceremony. The twist, of course, is that instead of the graduate walking proudly across the stage, he is dragged by security guards as he begs those assembled to stop the ceremony. He does not want that diploma! The issue, of course, is the harsh reality of the current job market and the uncertainty many graduates face in a turbulent economy.

The cartoon's joke is in the twist—the gap between the familiar and the unexpected. The familiar is the graduation ceremony; the unexpected is the screaming student.

What Is the Claim?

The claim in this cartoon is that students enjoy a special grace period in college and that graduation marks a student's entry into the real world with all of its responsibilities and economic demands. Most of us can understand and sympathize with the student's fears.

What Are the Assumptions?

This cartoon assumes that viewers will know the meaning of a commencement ceremony and what happened before it and what happens after the student receives his diploma. The cartoon also presumes that the reader will be aware of current economic challenges in the United States and why the student would be reluctant to graduate.

What Is the Evidence?

This cartoon was published in June of 2008—during graduation month and during a period of particular economic uncertainty in the United States and in the world. The unemployment rate in the United States was around 7 percent—a rate that continued to rise even months later. Graduates faced the most severe economic downturn since the Great Depression. Clearly, for students comfortable with college life and the respite it affords many of them from financial responsibility, the prospect of entering the job market under such conditions was particularly discouraging.

As you review the various visuals throughout the text, approach what you see with the critical eye of a skeptic. Many of the techniques used in reading critically can be applied to visuals. Consider the ways symbolism, brand recognition, stereotyping, and cultural expectations contribute to how such illustrations communicate their ideas. Try to think abstractly and take into account the many different levels of consciousness that visuals use to communicate. Consider also the way shading, lighting, and subject placement in the photos all converge to make a point. "Read" them as you would any text.

CHAPTER
1

Fashion and Flesh
The Images We Project

Pick up a magazine. Turn on the television. View a film. Every day we are bombarded with images and messages telling us that slim is sexy, buff bodies are the best, and beauty means happiness. The right labels mean success and respect. The right look means acceptance. And overwhelmingly, our culture buys into these messages.

We live in a society caught up in images of itself, a society seemingly more driven by the cultivation of the body and how we clothe it than by personal achievement. In fact, so powerful is the influence of image that other terms of self-definition are difficult to identify. In this chapter, several writers grapple with questions raised by our cultural preoccupation with flesh and fashion: Are we our bodies? Can our inner selves transcend the flesh? Do the clothes we wear express the self we want to be? Where does all the body-consciousness pressure come from? Some essays in this chapter recount people at war with their bodies due to cultural pressure. Other essays are accounts of people rising above the din of fashion's dictates to create a sense of self that is authentic and rooted in personal happiness. And some explore the cultural trends that help direct contemporary fashion.

Many women feel that men are free from the social pressures associated with body image. It may come as a surprise to some people that many men, like women, are concerned with body image. The first section of readings addresses how cultural pressures, especially from advertisers and the fashion industry, are influencing how young men feel about their bodies. First, former fashion editor Liz Jones questions the influence of the fashion industry on women's feelings about their bodies in "What I Think about the Fashion World." Why does the fashion industry continue to promote tall, emaciated models on runways and magazine covers when the average woman is five feet four inches tall and about 160 pounds? Next is an essay by Caroline Heldman exploring the distortions many young women have about their bodies in "Out-of-Body Image." Then, Garance Franke-Ruta disagrees with critics of media-driven ideals of beauty in her editorial "The Natural Beauty Myth," as she challenges the concept of "natural beauty" and asserts that being beautiful takes hard work.

The next two essays address how we, as individuals, feel about our bodies. In a society in which beauty seems to be precisely defined, there is little room for variation from the prescribed parameters of beauty. In "My Hips, My Caderas" Alisa Valdes examines the cultural differences that define beauty, as she tries to balance her sense of body image between her Hispanic and white roots. Niranjana Iyer continues this examination of cultural values in her essay "Weight of the World," in which she explains how she became overweight just by changing time zones.

The readings then explore the connections between male self-perception, body image, and advertising. First, Ted Spiker provides personal insight, as well as critical analysis, of the pressures men face but rarely talk about in "How Men Really Feel About Their Bodies." Then, in "Never Too Buff," John Cloud reports the disturbing trend that many men, and even young boys, are struggling with—the cultural pressure to achieve physical perfection.

Finally, the Viewpoints section ends the chapter by taking a closer look at body art. Beth Janes explains her motivations and regrets regarding her choice of body art in "Why I Rue My Tattoo." Her piece is balanced by Stephanie Dolgoff's perspective, "Tattoo Me Again and Again," in which she explores the meaning and importance of her body art and how this medium is part of who she is.

What I Think About the Fashion World
Liz Jones*

Are thin models part of a fashion conspiracy, or are they merely reflective of what the public wants to see? For many young women, perfect beauty is defined by fashion models: tall, thin, long-limbed, and with sculpted features. In a culture in which women are often measured by how they look, the pressure to be thin can be great. In this article, Liz Jones gives her perspective on the fashion industry's influence on female body image. Jones is the former editor of the British edition of *Marie Claire*, a women's fashion magazine. In June 2000, while still editor of *Marie Claire*, she shocked the fashion world with two covers: one featured a thin Pamela Anderson, the other a voluptuous Sophie Dahl, then a size 12. Many fashion critics spoke out against Jones for using the magazine to forward her own agenda, but consumers voted with their pocketbooks by buying more issues with the Dahl cover.

1 For four weeks last month, I sat in the front row of catwalk shows in London, Milan, Paris, and New York watching painfully thin models walking up and down inches from my nose.

2 Kate Moss, the original "superwaif," was looking positively curvaceous compared to the current bunch of underweight teenagers.

3 For those used to the fashion industry, there was nothing unusual about the shows at all. But for me it was the end; it was then that I decided to resign as editor of *Marie Claire* magazine.

4 I had reached the point where I had simply had enough of working in an industry that pretends to support women while it bombards them with impossible images of perfection day after day, undermining their self-confidence, their health, and hard-earned cash.

5 My decision to quit was partly precipitated by the failure of a campaign I started a year ago to encourage magazines, designers, and advertisers to use models with more realistic, representative body images. Then I could not have anticipated the extraordinarily hostile reaction to my fairly innocuous suggestions from fellow editors and designers. A year later I have come to realize the sheer terrorism of the fashion industry and accept that, alone, I cannot change things.

6 But in the spring of last year, I was full of optimism that we could change. I believed wholeheartedly that we could stop magazines and advertisers using underweight girls as fashion icons. I had already banned diets and slimming advice from our pages, but after meeting Gisele, the Brazilian supermodel credited with bringing "curves to the catwalk," and discovering that she is a tiny size 8, I decided to challenge the status quo.

7 We decided to publish two covers for the same edition—one featuring Sophie Dahl, a size 12; the other, Pamela Anderson, a minute size 6—and we asked readers to choose between the skinny, cosmetically enhanced "perfection" or a more

* Liz Jones, *YOU Magazine,* a supplement of *The London Daily Mail,* April 15, 2001 attainable, but still very beautiful, curvy woman. Sophie Dahl won by an over-whelming majority.

8   But you would think that we had declared war. The reaction was staggering: Newspapers, radio, and TV stations were largely behind us. They welcomed the opportunity to demystify the closed and cliquey world of fashion. Our covers were in the national press for weeks, even making headlines in the *New York Post*. I had requests from universities here and abroad wanting to include our experiment in their college courses. Documentaries were made in the United States and Germany. The response from readers was unprecedented: We received 4,000 letters in two weeks.

9   However, the very people from whom I had expected the most support—my fellow female editors—were unanimous in their disapproval.

10   I was invited to speak at the Body Image Summit set up by Tessa Jowell, Min-ister for Women, in June 2000, to debate the influence of media images on rising problems of anorexia and bulimia among women. One suggestion was that a group—consisting of editors, designers, young women readers, and professionals who treat women with eating disorders—should get together on a regular basis to monitor the industry, bring in guidelines on using girls under a certain body size and weight, and discuss ways the industry could evolve. My job was to gather these people: not one single other editor agreed to take part.

11   Instead most of them were hostile and aggressive. Jo Elvin, then editor of *New Woman*, accused *Marie Claire* of "discriminating against thin women." (As if there aren't enough role models in the media for thinness, from Jennifer Anis-ton to Gwyneth Paltrow to American supermodel Maggie Rizer.) Another fashion editor made the point that there had always been skinny women—look at Twiggy, for example. Jasper Conran absurdly suggested we should be looking at obesity as a serious health problem instead of anorexia and bulimia. I didn't bother to point out that people with obesity were not usually put on magazine covers as fashion icons.

12   The next day, after the summit, I received a fax, signed by nearly all the other editors of women's magazines and some model agencies, stating that they would not be following any initiative to expand the types of women featured in their magazines—one of the topics up for discussion at the summit was how to introduce more black and Asian women onto the pages of Britain's glossies.

I realized that far from being the influential trendsetters I had thought, magazine editors are more often ruled by fear—and advertisers.

13   When I read the list of names, I felt like giving up the fight there and then. I was isolated, sickened to my stomach that something so posi-tive had been turned into a petty catfight by women I respected and admired. They were my peers, friends, and colleagues I sat next to in the front row of the fashion shows. They were also the most important, influential group of women in the busi-ness, the only people who could change the fashion and beauty industry. Why were they so reluctant to even think about change?

14   Like me, they had sat at the summit while a group of teenage girls, black, Asian, and white, some fat, some thin, had berated us all for what we were doing to their lives. I had found it moving to listen to these young women, brave enough to come and talk in front of all these scary, high-profile people. Anyway, to me, it made good business sense to listen to them and address their concerns: why alienate your readers? I could see those teenagers turning away from magazines because we seemed hopelessly outmoded, old fashioned, unattainable. But I was clearly alone.

15   The other editors seemed to revel in the chance to counterattack. Alexandra Shulman, editor of *Vogue,* denounced the whole campaign as a promotional tool for *Marie Claire* and said that suggestions of an agreement to set up a self-regulatory body within the industry was "totally out of order." Debbie Bee, then editor of *Nova*—a supposedly cutting-edge fashion magazine for young women—asserted in her editorial the following month that magazines didn't cause anorexia, as readers were intelligent enough to differentiate between an idealized model and real life.

16   Fiona McIntosh, editor of *Elle*, published a cover picture of Calista Flockhart with the caption, "I'm thin, so what?" [McIntosh] accused me of "betraying the editors' code." Frankly, I didn't even know there was a code; only one, surely, to put your readers first.

17   Some model agencies blacklisted the magazine. Storm, who represents Sophie Dahl and who you would have thought would have been happy that one of their models was being held up as an example of healthy gorgeousness, told us that we could no longer book any of their girls. Several publicists from Hollywood, reacting both to the cover and a feature called "Lollipop Ladies," about women in Hollywood whose heads are too big for their tiny bodies, wrote to me saying their stars would not be gracing our covers—ever.

18   I had clearly put my head too far above the parapet. I realized that far from being the influential trendsetters I had thought, magazine editors are more often ruled by fear—and advertisers. No one feels that they can afford to be different. They are happy to settle, instead, for free handbags and relentless glamour.

19   To be honest, it would have been very easy to give up then. Every time the contacts of a fashion shoot landed on my desk with a model whose ribs showed, whose bony shoulders and collar bone could have cut glass, whose legs were like sticks, we could have published them anyway and said, "Oh well, we tried." But we didn't. We threw them out, set up a reshoot, and eventually, slowly, agencies started to take us seriously and would only send girls with curves in all the right places.

20   I cannot deny the campaign got the magazine talked and written about. The choice of covers got the readers involved and made them have a little bit of power for a change; they got to choose who they wanted on the cover. The Sophie Dahl cover started to sell out, and readers would phone me, frantic, saying, "I could only buy the Pamela Anderson cover, but I want you to register my vote for Sophie." It could never have been a scientific exercise—subscribers to the magazine had to take potluck; but still they would phone up saying, "No, I wanted Sophie!"

A model displays an outfit as part of the Milan Fashion Week in this September 29, 2006 file photo. The Italian fashion capital of Milan has formally barred ultra-skinny and underage models ahead of its February 2007 catwalk shows as the fashion world faces pressure to promote a healthier image.

Photo Credit: REUTERS/Stefano Rellandini

21   But I was dismayed by accusations that this was just another way to boost sales. I suffered from anorexia from the age of 11 until my late twenties and understand firsthand the damaging effect of a daily diet of unrealistically tiny role models gracing the pages of the magazines that I was addicted to. Although it did not cause my illness, the images definitely perpetuated the hatred I had for my own body.

22   I agree with Debbie Bee of *Nova* that young women are intelligent enough to be able to tell the difference between a model and real life, but the effects are often subliminal. One piece of research we did at *Marie Claire* was to ask a group of intelligent professional women about their bodies then let them browse a selection of magazines for an hour, before asking them again. Their self-esteem had plummeted.

23   Never before have we been bombarded with so many images of perfection: more and more glossies on the shelves, Web sites, digital satellite channels, more and more channels showing music videos 24 hours a day. New technology is also removing the images we see of women even further from reality. Just try finding a cover on the shelves this month where the star has not had her spots removed, the dark circles under her eyes eradicated, the wrinkles smoothed, and her waist trimmed. It is common practice nowadays to "stretch" women whose legs aren't

long enough. One men's magazine currently on the shelves, so the industry gossip has it, has put one star's head on another woman's body—apparently, her original breasts weren't "spherical enough."

24 So women have been conditioned to go to the gym and diet, or if they don't, to feel guilty about it, but that still won't achieve "cover-girl" perfection because you can't be airbrushed in real life. I've seen the models close up: believe me, lots of them have varicose veins, spots, appendectomy scars and, yes, cellulite. Only the 16 year olds don't have fine lines.

25 So did I achieve anything with my campaign? I believe so. One newspaper conducted a survey of high street and designer shops and proved how women over size 12 were not being catered to. Stores are now providing a broader range of sizes.

26 In the subsequent issue, we published naked pictures of eight ordinary women and asked readers to fill in a questionnaire telling us honestly how they feel about the women in the photographs and about their own bodies. Interestingly, of the respondents so far, all the women say their boyfriends find the size 16 woman the most attractive. The results will be made into a Channel 4 documentary in the autumn.

27 In the next issue, my final edition as editor, we have on our cover three young women, all size 12, curvy, imperfect, but very beautiful all the same. On the shoot, it was apparent that Suzanne, Myleene, and Kym from Hear'Say were all happy in their own skin. For now. On the *Popstars*[1] program, Nasty Nigel had told the girls they should go on a diet. "Christmas is over," he said to Kym, "but the goose is still fat." How long before the girls start feeling paranoid about their bodies, under the constant pressure of fame, is anybody's guess.

28 In Britain an estimated 60,000 people, most of them young women, suffer from eating disorders, while far greater numbers have an unhealthy relationship with food. Many of them take up smoking or eat diet pills to keep their weight below a certain level. Of all psychiatric disorders, anorexia has the most fatalities—it is very hard to recover from. I refuse to conform to an industry that could, literally, kill.

29 It's time for the industry—the photographers, the editors, the casting directors, designers and the advertisers—to wake up and allow women to just be themselves. From the phone calls and letters I received at *Marie Claire*, I know that women are fed up with feeling needlessly bad about their wobbly bits.

30 I only hope that my successor listens to them. ◆

CRITICAL THINKING

1. Try to picture your version of the perfect female body. What does it look like? Is your image influenced by outside forces, such as the media, your gender, or your age? How do real women you know compare to the image in your mind?

2. In your opinion, is the fashion industry's use of extremely thin models harmful? Has mass media created unrealistic expectations of beauty? Explain.

---

[1] The British equivalent of the American television program *American Idol*

3. By running the two covers, Jones sought to discover whether women wanted perfection and aspiration or something more realistic and attainable. What did sales of the June 2000 cover reveal? Based on your own observations, how do you think American women would have reacted to the same experiment?

4. How did other fashion magazine editors react to Jones's *Marie Claire* covers? What do you think their reaction reveals about the fashion industry?

5. Debbie Bee of *Nova*, another British fashion magazine, argues that young women are "intelligent enough to be able to tell the difference between a model and real life." How does Jones test this theory? What does she discover?

6. Evaluate how well Jones supports her viewpoint in this essay. Does she provide supporting evidence? Is she biased? Does she provide a balanced perspective, or does she slant her data? Explain.

7. Jones is a former editor for a major fashion magazine. Does the fact that she held this position and was willing to risk her career for this issue influence your opinion of her essay or her points? Why or why not?

CRITICAL WRITING

1. *Exploratory Writing:* Do you know someone who seems obsessed with his or her weight or who suffers from an eating disorder? Discuss what you feel are the causes of the problem. Do you agree with Jones that many eating disorders are influenced by the cult of thinness perpetuated by the fashion industry? Why or why not?

2. *Exploratory Writing:* Write an essay exploring the connections among the fashion industry, body image, and self-esteem. Does the fashion industry have a direct role in our feelings of self-worth and acceptance? Support your viewpoint with examples from the text and your own personal experience.

GROUP PROJECTS

1. With your group, gather magazine photographs of several models and analyze their body types. What common elements do you notice? How are they similar or different? How do they compare to "real" people? Based on the photographs, can you reach any conclusions about fashion models in today's culture?

2. Discuss the following question: If you could be either very beautiful or very wealthy, which would you choose? Explain the motivation behind your choice. Based on your group's multiple responses, can you reach any conclusions about the influence of beauty on men and women in today's society?

CULTURE SHOCK

Get Real Ad*

Most people who suffer from eating disorders, such as anorexia nervosa or bulimia, also experience distorted self-perception. The person they see in the mirror differs drastically from their physical reality. The National Eating Disorders Association (NEDA) launched the "Get Real" awareness campaign to portray how distorted the self-image of someone suffering from an eating disorder can be.

THINKING CRITICALLY

1. If you were leafing through a magazine and saw this ad, would you stop to read it? Why or why not? What catches your eye? How long would you spend looking at the ad? Explain.
2. Visit the NEDA Web site at *www.nationaleatingdisorders.org* and read about eating disorders in men and women (look at the "Eating Disorder Info" pages). Who is at risk for an eating disorder? What roles do social and cultural pressures play in exacerbating eating disorders? Explain.
3. What is happening in the photo? What is the woman thinking? What does she see? What do we see? What message does the photo convey?
4. Who is the target audience for this ad? Do you think someone with an eating disorder will be persuaded to follow the advice in the ad? If not, who is likely to respond to it? Explain.

---

* This print ad was created for NEDA in 2005 by Porter Novelli, a public relations firm known for health promotion campaigns.

Out-of-Body Image

Caroline Heldman*

Everyday men and women are bombarded with images of buff and beautiful bodies. Media and advertising in particular present an idealized female shape that few women actually embody. Women begin to think of their bodies as objects rather than seeing themselves as people. The result, explains Caroline Heldman, professor of politics at Occidental College in Los Angeles, is a self-objectification that impairs women's body image, mental health, motor skills, and even their sex lives.

1 On a typical day, you might see ads featuring a naked woman's body tempting viewers to buy an electronic organizer, partially exposed women's breasts being used to sell fishing line, and a woman's rear—wearing only a thong—being used to pitch a new running shoe. Meanwhile, on every newsstand, impossibly slim (and digitally airbrushed) cover "girls" adorn a slew of magazines. With each image, you're hit with a simple, subliminal message: Girls' and women's bodies are objects for others to visually consume.

2 If such images seem more ubiquitous than ever, it's because U.S. residents are now exposed to 3,000 to 5,000 advertisements a day—as many per year as those living a half century ago would have seen in a lifetime. The Internet accounts for much of this growth, and young people are particularly exposed to advertising: 70 percent of 15- to 34-year-olds use social networking technologies such as MySpace and Facebook, which allow advertisers to infiltrate previously private communication space.

3 A steady diet of exploitative, sexually provocative depictions of women feeds a poisonous trend in women's and girl's perceptions of their bodies, one that has recently been recognized by social scientists as self-objectification—viewing one's body as a sex object

> *What would disappear from our lives if we stopped seeing ourselves as objects? Painful high heels? Body hatred? Constant dieting? Liposuction? It's hard to know.*

to be consumed by the male gaze. Like W. E. B. DuBois' famous description of the experience of black Americans, self-objectification is a state of "double consciousness . . . a sense of always looking at one's self through the eyes of others."

4 Women who self-objectify are desperate for outside validation of their appearance and present their bodies in ways that draw attention. A study I did of 71 randomly selected female students from a liberal arts college in Los Angeles, for example, found that 70 percent were medium or high self-objectifiers, meaning that they have internalized the male gaze and chronically monitor their physical appearance. Boys and men experience self-objectification as well, but at a much lower

* Caroline Heldman, *Ms. Magazine*, Spring 2008

rate—probably because, unlike women, they rarely get the message that their bodies are the primary determination of their worth.

5   Researchers have learned a lot about self-objectification since the term was coined in 1997 by University of Michigan psychology professor Barbara Fredrickson and Colorado College psychology professor Tomi-Ann Roberts. Numerous studies since then have shown that girls and women who self-objectify are more prone to depression and low self-esteem and have less faith in their own capabilities, which can lead to diminished success in life. They are more likely to engage in "habitual body monitoring"—constantly thinking about how their bodies appear to the outside world—which puts them at higher risk for eating disorders such as anorexia and bulimia.

6   Self-objectification has also been repeatedly shown to sap cognitive functioning because of all the attention devoted to body monitoring. For instance, a study by Yale psychologists asked two groups of women to take a math exam—one group in swimsuits, the other in sweaters. The swimsuit-wearers, distracted by body concerns, performed significantly worse than their peers in sweaters.

7   Several of my own surveys of college students indicate that this impaired concentration by self-objectifiers may hurt their academic performance. Those with low self-objectification reported an average GPA of 3.5, whereas those with high self-objectification reported a 3.1. While this gap may appear small, in graduate school admissions, it represents the difference between being competitive and being out of the running for the top schools.

8   Another worrisome effect of self-objectification is that it diminishes political efficacy—a personal belief that he or she can have an impact through the political process. In another survey, 33 percent of high self-objectifiers felt low political efficacy, compared to 13 percent of low self-objectifiers. Since political efficacy leads to participation in politics, having less of it means that self-objectifiers may be less likely to vote or run for office.

9   The effects of self-objectification on young girls are of such growing concern that the American Psychological Association published an investigative report on it in 2007. The APA found that girls as young as 7 years old are exposed to clothing, toys, music, magazines, and television programs that encourage them to be sexy or "hot"—teaching them to think of themselves as sex objects before their own sexual maturity. Even thong underwear is being sold in sizes for 7- to 10-year-olds. The consequence, wrote Kenyon College psychology professor Sarah Murnen in the journal *Sex Roles*, is that girls "are taught to view their bodies as 'projects' that need work before they can attract others, whereas boys are likely to learn to view their bodies as tools to use to master the environment."

10   Fredrickson, along with Michigan communications professor Kristen Harrison (both work within the university's Institute for Research on Women and Gender), recently discovered that self-objectification actually impairs girls' motor skills. Their study of 202 girls, ages 10 to 17, found that self-objectification impeded girls' ability to throw a softball, even after differences in age and prior experience were factored out. Self-objectification forced girls to split their attention between how their bodies looked and what they wanted them to do, resulting in less forceful throws and worse aim.

11   One of the more stunning effects of self-objectification is its impact on sex. One young woman I interviewed described sex as being an "out of body" experience during which she viewed herself through the eyes of her lover, and, sometimes, through the imaginary lens of a camera shooting a porn film. As a constant critic of her body, she couldn't focus on her own sexual pleasure.

12   Self-objectification can likely explain some other things that researchers are just starting to study. For instance, leading anti-sexist male activist and author Jackson Katz observes, " 'Many young women now engage in sex acts with men that prioritize the man's pleasure, with little or no expectation of reciprocity.' Could this be another result of women seeing themselves as sexual objects, not agents?"

13   Disturbingly, some girls and women celebrate their object status as a form of empowerment. This is evident in a booming industry of T-shirts for women that proclaim their object status. It would be encouraging if these choices reflected the sexual agency for women that feminists have fought so hard for, but they do not. The notion of objectification as empowering is illogical, since objects are acted upon, rather than taking action themselves. The real power in such arrangements lies with boys and men, who come to feel entitled to consume women as objects—first in media, then in real life.

14   Self-objectification isn't going anywhere anytime soon. So what can we do about it? First, we can recognize how our everyday actions feed the larger beast, and realize that we are not powerless. Mass media, the primary peddler of female bodies, can be assailed with millions of little consumer swords. We can boycott companies and engage in other forms of consumer activism, such as socially conscious investments and shareholder actions. We can also contact companies directly to voice our concerns and refuse to patronize businesses that overtly depict women as sex objects.

15   An example of women's spending power, and the limits of our tolerance for objectification, can be found in the 12-percent dip in profits of clothing company Victoria's Secret, due, according to the company's CEO, to its image becoming "too sexy." Victoria's Secret was not the target of an organized boycott; rather its increasingly risqué "bra and panty show" seems to have begun alienating women, who perhaps no longer want to simply be shown as highly sexualized window dressing.

16   Another strategy to counter one's own tendency to self-objectify is to make a point of buying products, watching programs, and reading publications that promote more authentic women's empowerment. This can be difficult, of course, in a media climate in which companies are rarely wholeheartedly body-positive. For instance, Dove beauty products launched a much lauded advertising campaign that used "real women" instead of models, but then Dove's parent company, Unilever, put out hypersexual ads for Axe men's body spray that showed the fragrance driving scantily clad women into orgiastic states.

17   Locating unadulterated television and film programming is also tough. Even Lifetime and Oxygen, TV networks created specifically for women, often portray us as weak victims or sex objects and present a narrow version of thin, white "beauty." Action films that promise strong female protagonists (think of the women in *X-Men*, or Lara Croft in *Tomb Raider*) usually deliver these characters in skintight clothes, serving the visual pleasure of men.

18   A more radical, personal solution is to actively avoid media that compels us to self-objectify—which, unfortunately, is the vast majority of movies, television programs, and women's magazines. Research with college-age women indicates that the less women consume media, the less they self-objectify, particularly if they avoid fashion magazines. What would women's lives look like if they viewed their bodies as tools to master their environment, instead of projects to be worked on? What would disappear if they stopped seeing themselves as objects? Painful high heels? Body hatred? Constant dieting? Liposuction?

19   It's hard to know. Perhaps the most striking outcome of self-objectification is the difficulty women have in imagining identities and sexualities truly our own. In solidarity, we can start on this path, however confusing and difficult it may be. ◆

CRITICAL THINKING

1. Heldman notes that young girls are taught—through media, toys, images, and culture—to think of themselves as objects rather than agents. If you are female, does this observation ring true? If you are male, what messages, images, and toys encouraged the development of your own identity? Explain.
2. Heldman notes that self-objectification is a state of "double consciousness . . . a sense of always looking at one's self through the eyes of others." How do young women "self-objectify"? What does it mean to self-objectify, and why is it harmful?
3. In paragraph 4, Heldman notes that a majority of women self-objectify, because they have learned through cultural and social messages that "their bodies are the primary determination of their worth." Respond to this statement with your own viewpoint.
4. What do you think of the test administered by Yale researchers, in which two groups of women took a math test, one group fully clothed and the other in swimsuits? What other factors could have contributed to the results? What do you think would have happened if the test had also been given to young men?
5. Evaluate the suggestions Heldman provides at the end of her essay. Would you consider doing any of them? Why or why not?

CRITICAL WRITING

1. *Exploratory Writing:* Vanity and obsessive preoccupation with self-image have historically been connected to women more than men. In your opinion, do men and women approach the issue of fashion and body image differently? If so, in what ways? What social and cultural pressures influence how men and women view themselves?
2. *Exploratory Writing*: In this essay, Heldman explains how self-objectification can harm women in many different ways. Write an essay in which you address how we strive to look a certain way to conform to social expectations. Drawing from this article and others in the chapter, write an essay in which you explore the connection between our personal sense of self and our physical appearance.

GROUP PROJECT

1. Make a list of the most popular prime-time shows on television. After compiling the list, identify the body size of the characters on each program. How many male and female characters could be considered overweight? What is the male-to-female ratio of these characters? Discuss your findings with the rest of the class in a discussion about how actors on television promote or do not promote certain body types as more desirable than others.

2. Heldman notes that women who read fashion magazines are more likely to self-objectify and to be uncomfortable with their physiques. Each member of your group should read a different fashion magazine, and include a men's magazine such as *Maxim* or *Men's Health*. Evaluate how men and women are presented in these magazines; include physical appearance, clothing style, accessories, and how they interact with other people in the articles and ads. As a group, discuss your observations and write a short summary of your discussion. Include any conclusions your group came to regarding the influence of fashion magazines on male and female body image and the messages we send to each gender about self-worth.

The Natural Beauty Myth
Garance Franke-Ruta*

Critics of the beauty industry argue that it attacks women's self-esteem as it raises the beauty bar impossibly high. But journalist Garance Franke-Ruta argues that the fashion industry does not oppress women, but makes beauty accessible to all, because the truth is that there is no such thing as "natural beauty." Is what we have come to recognize as "natural beauty" really the result of chemicals, surgery, and a whole lot of suffering in the name of fashion?

1 Last week, Italy's government and some of its fashion moguls announced plans to crack down on the use of ultrathin models on the catwalk. This decision follows in the wake of Madrid's recently instituted ban on underweight models at its annual fashion show. Let's not rush to celebrate.

2 Pictures of beautiful but undernourished-looking women have led, in recent months, to a round of fashion-industry bashing in the press. One anonymous wit even mocked up satirical pictures of women who looked like concentration camp victims—except that they had masses of glossy hair and wore slinky clothes. As often happens when satire meets a mass audience, lots of people thought that the doctored pictures were real—which is how, one day in November, they wound up in my inbox, courtesy of a women and media list-serv.

3 A predictable discussion followed. Curvy women were praised for their healthy-seeming fuller figures. "Self-acceptance" was praised, too. It was argued

---

* Garance Franke-Ruta, *The Wall Street Journal*, December 15, 2006

that the evil images presented to women by the fashion industry were part of the broader plan of beauty magazines to make women feel bad about themselves and thus buy products for self-improvement.

4   Such a critique, which we hear over and over today, is based on a conceptual error. The beauty industry is not the problem; it is a part of the solution. American women today are the victims of a more insidious idea, an idea that underlies the American obsession with self-esteem: the tyrannical ideal of "natural beauty."

5   Few Americans today live a "natural" life, whatever that may be. The more educated and well-to-do among us may eat organic foods and avoid chemicals as best they can, but such efforts hardly make us "natural." Our society is too complex for that. Indeed, all societies involve such a thick layering of culture over our malleable essence that it is virtually impossible to say what we might be like in a natural state.

6   What is clear is that over the past century, American women have changed their shape. Most noticeably, they have gained so much poundage that today more than half are overweight and a third are clinically obese. The sharpest spike in obesity has come since the late 1970s. There are all sorts of reasons, of course—from the rise of corn syrup as a sweetener to the increased portion sizes of our daily meals and our increasingly sedentary styles of life. And yet the doctrine of "natural beauty"—so favored by the self-esteem brigades of the 1970s and still confusing women today—asks women to accept themselves as this unnatural environment has made them.

7   What the critics of the beauty industry further fail to recognize is that the doctrine of "natural beauty"—and the desire it breeds in women to be accepted as they are or to be seen as beautiful without any effort—is a ruthless and antiegalitarian ideal. It is far more punishing than the one that says any woman can be beautiful if she merely treats beauty as a form of discipline.

8   Only in America do we think that beauty is a purely natural attribute rather than a type of artistry requiring effort. Look at the French: They are no more beautiful as a people than we Americans, but they understand that every woman can be attractive— if not beautiful—if she chooses to be. Yes, we are given forms by nature, but how we choose to present them is a matter of our own discretion. Few people are blessed by nature and circumstance with the Golden Mean proportions that seem to be universally appreciated. Thus, in the end, it is more democratic to think of beauty or attractiveness as an attribute that one can acquire, like speaking a foreign language or cooking well. To see beauty as a capacity like any other—the product of educated taste and daily discipline—is to see it as something chosen: to be possessed or left aside, according to one's preference.

9   The same goes, relatedly, for maintaining a certain size. In contemporary America, becoming thin is a choice that for most people requires rigorous and sometimes painful self-discipline. But so does becoming a lawyer or a concert

Only in America do we think that beauty is a purely natural attribute, rather than a type of artistry requiring effort.

pianist. The celebrity press is wrongly decried for giving women false ideals. In fact, it has demystified the relationship between effort and beauty, between discipline and weight. It opens up a path for noncelebrities.

10   One celebrity glossy recently estimated that in a single year, actress Jennifer Aniston spends close to the average woman's annual salary on trainers and other aspects of a high-level workout. Former tween-queen Britney Spears told Oprah Winfrey that she used to do between 500 and 1,000 crunches a day to perfect her on-display abs. Actress Kate Hudson told one interviewer that to lose post-pregnancy "baby weight," she worked out three hours a day until she lost her 70 pounds: It was so hard that she used to sit on the exercise cycle and cry. Entertainment figures and models are like athletes; it takes a lot of discipline and social support to look like them. Money helps, too.

11   The celebrity magazines also specialize in a genre of stories best understood as tutorials in beauty as artifice: celebrities without their make-up. Makeover shows like "What Not to Wear" and "The Biggest Loser"—even "Queer Eye for the Straight Guy"—show beauty as something created, a condition to which anyone can have access with the right education and effort. This is a meritocratic ideal, not an insistent, elitist one. The makeover shows also help to make it clear that a life of artifice is not for everyone. Once we see the effort and hours that go into making a body more appealing, we may decide not to attempt a labor-intensive presentation of the self. We may decide that other things are more important.

12   Take, for example, U.S. Navy Cmdr. Sunita L. Williams, an astronaut who recently joined the staff of the International Space Station for six months. Since entering orbit she has announced plans to cut her long chestnut tresses and donate them to charity, because all that hair was uncomfortable and hard to manage in a zero-gravity environment. Most of us live in a less exotic environment, but the essence of our choice is the same. Just as it would be difficult for anyone to be a concert pianist and a nuclear scientist at the same time, it can be a pointless distraction for women to strive to maintain the time-consuming artifices of beauty while pursuing their other goals.

13   Ms. Williams spent her time in other ways and today has access to the most majestic natural beauty of all: the vision of our globe from space. But it took a half century of human effort and discipline to put her there. ◆

CRITICAL THINKING

1. Evaluate the author's tone in this editorial. Identify phrases and words in which the author's tone attempts to influence her readers' reception of her point of view.
2. Is the fashion industry exerting pressure on women to be thin? Consider the women featured on the covers of popular magazines for men and women, including *Marie Claire*, *Cosmopolitan*, *Vogue*, *Maxim*, and *Vibe*. Do you think such magazine covers influence how we define beauty and desirability?
3. What does "natural beauty" mean to you? Why does the author claim that natural beauty is a false concept? Do you agree?
4. What is the conceptual error (paragraph 4) underlying critiques that the fashion industry is out to make women "feel bad" about their bodies? Explain.

5. The author points out that the physique of the average American woman has clearly changed its shape, and not for the better. Does this shift in size influence our concept of natural beauty?

CRITICAL WRITING

1. *Personal Narrative:* Write an essay in which you analyze your own feelings about your self-image. What factors do you think have shaped your feelings? What elements of our culture, if any, have influenced your development of body consciousness? Explain.
2. *Research Writing:* In this essay, Franke-Ruta claims that any woman can be beautiful, but it takes work. Does she have a point? Interview at least 10 people, men and women, from different ages and backgrounds, and ask them how much work is reasonable to be considered attractive. Do people who work harder, such as Kate Hudson on the exercise cycle, deserve our admiration? Why or why not?
3. *Reader's Response:* This essay appeared as an editorial in the *Wall Street Journal.* Imagine that you are a newspaper editorialist. Write a response to Franke-Ruta's essay, focusing on how effective you find her argument. Support your critique with examples from your personal observations and external research if necessary.

GROUP PROJECTS

1. With your group, gather magazine photographs of several models and analyze their body types. What common elements do you notice? How are they similar or different? How do they compare to "real" people? Based on the photographs, can you reach any conclusions about fashion models in today's culture and what it means to be beautiful?
2. Select two characters from a recent film or popular television program. Write a description of each character's body type and attire. Discuss with your group the connection, if any, between the physical appearance of the characters you selected and the temperament, personality, or nature of the character. What influence, if any, do the characters, or the actors who play them, exert on the fashion world and on our cultural constructions of beauty?

My Hips, My Caderas
*Alisa Valdes**

The saying "Beauty is in the eye of the beholder" may be better expressed as "Beauty is in the eye of the culture." A feature or characteristic that one culture finds unappealing may be considered beautiful in another. Physical beauty seems to be largely a subjective thing—some

* Alisa Valdes, *UnderWire MSN*, April 2000

cultures artificially elongate the neck, others put plates in their lips, and others prefer tiny feet or high foreheads. As a Latina woman with a white mother and a Cuban father, Alisa Valdes explores the challenges she faces straddling the beauty preferences of two cultures.

1   My father is Cuban, with dark hair, a cleft in his chin, and feet that can dance the Guaguanco.

2   My mother is white and American, as blue-eyed as they come.

3   My voluptuous/big hips are both Cuban and American. And neither. Just like me. As I shift different halves of my soul daily to match whichever cultural backdrop I happen to face, I also carefully prepare myself for how differently my womanly/fat hips will be treated in my two realities.

4   It all started 15 years ago, when my hips bloomed in Albuquerque, New Mexico, where I was born. I went from being a track club twig—mistaken more than once for a boy—to being a splendidly curving thing that Chicano men with their bandanas down low whistled at as they drove by in their low-riders. White boys in my middle school thought I suddenly had a fat ass, and had no problem saying so.

5   But the cholos loved me. San Mateo Boulevard . . . I remember it well. Jack in the Box on one corner, me on a splintered wooden bench with a Three Musketeers bar, tight shorts, a hot summer sun, and those catcalls and woof-woofs like slaps. I was 12.

6   My best friend Stacy and I set out dieting right away that summer, to lose our new hips so boys from the heights, like the nearly albino Tim Fairfield with the orange soccer socks, would like us. In those days, I was too naive to know that dismissing the Chicano guys from the valley and taking French instead of Spanish in middle school were leftovers of colonialism. Taking Spanish still had the stigma of shame, like it would make you a dirty wetback. So Stacy and I pushed through hundreds of leg lifts on her bedroom floor, an open *Seventeen* magazine as a tiny table for our lemon water, and the sound of cicadas grinding away in the tree outside.

7   In Spanish, the word for hips is *caderas*—a broad term used to denote everything a real woman carries from her waist to her thighs, all the way around. Belly, butt, it's all part of your caderas. And caderas are a magical sphere of womanhood. In the lyrics of Merengue and Salsa, caderas are to be shaken, caressed, admired and exalted. The bigger, the better. In Spanish, you eat your rice and beans and sometimes your *chicharrones* because you fear your caderas will disappear.

8   In my work as a Latin music critic for a Boston newspaper, I frequent nightclubs with wood-paneled walls and Christmas lights flashing all year long. I wear short rubber skirts and tall shoes. There, I swing my round hips like a metronome. I become fierce. I strut. In the red disco lights, my hips absolutely torture men. I can see it on their faces.

9   "*Mujeron!*" they exclaim as I shimmy past. Much woman. They click their tongues, buy me drinks. They ask me to dance, and I often say "no," because I can. And these men suffer. Ironically, this makes the feminist in me very happy. In these places, my mujeron's hips get more nods than they might at a pony farm.

10   In English, your hips are those pesky things on the sides of your hipbones. They don't "*menear*," as they do in Spanish; they "jiggle." In English, hips are something women try to be rid of. Hips are why women bruise themselves in the name of liposuction.

11   My mother's people hate my hips. They diet. My aunt smokes so she won't eat. And in the gym where I teach step aerobics—a habit I took up in the days when I identified more with my mother's than my father's people—I sometimes hear the suburban anorexics whisper in the front row: "My God, would you look at those hips." Sometimes they walk out of the room even before I have begun teaching, as if hips were contagious. In these situations, I am sad. I drive home and examine my hips in the mirror, hit them for being so imprudent, like great big ears on the side of my body. Sometimes I fast for days. Sometimes I make myself puke up rice and beans. Usually I get over it, but it always comes back.

12   Sociologists will tell you that in cultures where women are valued for traditional roles of mother and caregiver, hips are in, and that in cultures where those roles have broken down and women try to be like men were in traditional societies—i.e., have jobs—hips are out.

In the gym where I teach step aerobics—a habit I took up in the days when I identified more with my mother's than my father's people—I sometimes hear the suburban anorexics whisper in the front row: "My God, would you look at those hips."

13   So when I want to be loved for my body, I am a Latina. But most Latino men will not love my mind as they do my body, because I am an Americanized professional. Indeed, they will feel threatened, and will soon lose interest in hips that want to "andar por la calle come un hombre" (carry themselves like a man).

14   When I want to be loved for my mind, I flock to liberal intellectuals, usually whites. They listen to my writings and nod . . . and then suggest I use skim milk instead of cream. These men love my fire and passion—words they always use to describe a Latina—but they are embarrassed by my hips. They want me to wear looser pants.

15   In some ways I am lucky to be able to move between two worlds. At least my hips get acknowledged as beautiful. I can't say the same for a lot of my bulimic friends, who don't have a second set of standards to turn to. But still, I dream of the day when bicultural Latinas will set the standards for beauty and success, when our voluptuous caderas won't bar us from getting through those narrow American doors. ◆

CRITICAL THINKING

1. Valdes notes that sociologists conjecture that in cultures in which women adhere to the more traditional roles of housewife and mother, hips and voluptuous forms are considered beautiful. Evaluate this theory and its implied inversion—that in societies in which women hold jobs outside the home, small waists and hips are culturally preferred by both sexes.

2. Does the author view the transformation of her hips from her "track club twig" physique to her more womanly shape as a positive or negative change? How does her writing reveal her feelings?

3. In paragraph 6 Valdes describes how she and her best friend Stacy worked out to reduce their hips. How does she connect these efforts to other practices of her youth, such as taking French in middle school? Explain.

4. Valdes writes, "My mother's people hate my hips." Who are her "mother's people"? Does it seem strange that she would refer to her relatives this way? Compare her description of her mother's side of the family to that of her father's side of the family.
5. How can driving men wild with her hips make "the feminist in [Valdes] very happy"? Why does she consider this ironic?
6. How does Valdes's mixed background create conflict in her life? How does she deal with this conflict?
7. Valdes uses striking, vivid language in her essay to describe the two cultures she straddles. What particular words and phrases work especially well in conveying her message?

CRITICAL WRITING

1. *Exploratory Writing:* Valdes writes, "In cultures where women are valued for traditional roles of mother and caregiver, hips are in." If beauty is a cultural creation, how is it constructed? Write an essay exploring the idea that social politics influence our cultural sense of beauty.
2. *Narrative and Analysis:* Write a short essay describing the parts of your body you find especially appealing and why. Does your culture influence your perception of your body? What outside forces influence your sense of physical identity? What changes would you make if you could? Explain.
3. *Research and Analysis:* In your library, newsstand, or bookstore, locate at least two fashion magazines from cultures or ethnicities different from yours. Compare how beauty differs between the two and from your own. How are the models similar and different? Is beauty based on universal principles with a few deviations, or is it a social construction based on individual cultural factors? Write an essay detailing your conclusions, using your magazine research and personal perspective as support.

GROUP PROJECTS

1. In her article, Valdes implies that white women feel more pressure to be thin than Latino women do, because Latin culture holds women to a different standard of beauty. In small groups, explore the idea that beauty is culturally determined—that is, that what one group may find beautiful, another may not. Can you find any evidence that the all-American image of beauty is changing?
2. Have each member of your group interview a man or woman from another country to ask the following question: "What characteristics are considered physically beautiful in your culture?" Descriptions may be of both men and women or of only one sex. Compare your notes with the group. What traits are universally admired and what traits are not? Report your findings to the class.

Weight of the World
Niranjana Iyer*

Beauty is a cultural construct. In some areas of the world, such as the Pacific Islands and India, a more plump shape is considered healthy and beautiful. In the next essay, Niranjana Iyer explores the definitions of beauty in two cultures and the challenges she faces as a "slimmigrant." And as Western media permeate even the most remote corners of the world, the battle of the bulge has gone global.

1   Like several million people on this planet, I weigh 15 pounds more than I'd like. But my 15 pounds appeared overnight, after an airplane ride from my home in India to Boston.

2   As a child in Chennai, I was considered worryingly thin. My mother sluiced an appetite stimulant down my throat at dinnertime and force-fed me cod liver oil once a week—to no avail. As I grew into a slim teen, Ma would point to my collarbones as evidence that I was wasting away, but I was unmoved. If my figure didn't quite match the voluptuous Bollywood heroine standard, well, my salwar kameezes (flowing tunics worn over drawstring pants) fit me fine. Rare was the woman who wore pants in Chennai, which was far too hot for anything but the lightest and loosest of clothing.

3   Then I moved to New Hampshire for graduate school and began a life in denim.

4   The body that I had considered normal was now revealed to be anything but. My jeans showed no mercy; every untoned millimeter of my belly hung over my waistband like an overbite in search of an orthodontist. Pants widened my hips, shrank my legs and made my waist disappear. In India, I'd been above average in height. In the States, I was short (so said the Gap). From a tall, thin Women's, I had morphed into a petite, plump Misses'—without gaining or losing a smidgen of flesh.

5   There ought to be a dictionary entry for those who enter the Western world to find that their bodies are thin no more. My vote goes to "slimmigrant"—for an immigrant who discovers that he or she needs to shed a dozen pounds to be considered unfat.

> **There ought to be a dictionary entry for those who enter the Western world to find that their bodies are thin no more.**

6   My quest for assimilation began with a whimper. I forswore mayonnaise, peanut butter, cheesecake, and tortilla chips—delicacies I'd never sampled before coming to America. I stopped going to those $9.99 Indian buffets with their unlimited helpings of butter chicken. For the first time in my life, I visited a gym, where my whimpers became shrieks of pain.

7   My extra poundage, however, was like a cockroach; it might disappear for a while, but it could never be eradicated. Potluck lunches, Thanksgiving dinners, and snow days made sure of that.

* Niranjana Iyer, *Smithsonian Magazine,* August 2006

8   Two years ago, on my 30th birthday, I resolved to remain plump forever rather than go on another diet. And to escape my new homeland, which considered me overweight, I resolved to take a holiday in Chennai, where salesgirls would hint that garments would drape better if only I were wider, my aunt would insist that I was scrawny, and my mother would feed me restorative spoonfuls of clarified butter. I booked my plane tickets.

9   Slimmigrants, beware!

10   Satellite television and globalization had changed the city I grew up in: in the five years I'd been away, skim milk had replaced the heavy cream of middle-class India, and those cushiony Bollywood heroines had been supplanted by supermodels whose hipbones could shred lettuce.

11   It seemed that every girl in Chennai was wearing trousers (and the girls' waists seemed no bigger round than a CD). The neighborhood video-rental store had become a fitness center. Even my aunt had bought a stationary bike (which she rode very competently in her sari).

12   My mother said she was glad to see me looking so nice and healthy. Time to go on a diet, I realized. I opted for the Mediterranean one—I love pizza. ◆

CRITICAL THINKING

1. Is beauty a cultural construction? Why are some physical characteristics admired in some cultures but not in others? Can you think of any physical traits that Americans esteem that other cultures do not?

2. How much do the opinions of others influence your personal view of your body and your concept of beauty? Was the author of this piece influenced by her family members? By American constructs of beauty? Whose opinions mattered more, and why?

3. At the end of her essay, Iyer notes that the city she grew up in had changed as a result of "globalization." What does she mean? How does she feel about this change? How can you tell?

4. What decision does the author make regarding her weight and her constant dieting? What words does she use to describe her weight and her struggle to meet the expectations of her new culture?

5. Is body size part of who you are? Do we try to pretend body size doesn't matter, while feeling that it really does? Explain.

CRITICAL WRITING

1. *Exploratory Writing:* Write about a time in your life when you received criticism or praise for your appearance. What did people notice about your body? How did it make you feel? How did you react?

2. *Research Writing:* The author of this piece, who is from India, makes a reference to the actresses from "Bollywood." Research Bollywood on the Web and find out more about famous actors and actresses from India. What similarities and differences do you notice between Bollywood and Hollywood?

3. *Exploratory Writing:* As the author explains, in India plumpness had always been a sign of health and beauty. Write an essay in which you explore the social and psychological aspects of this idea. What would your life be like if the Indian view of beauty and health were embraced by Western culture? Would you be more comfortable in your own skin or, like the author, encouraged to eat more spoonfuls of clarified butter? Explain.

GROUP PROJECTS

1. With your group, select two or three non-Western countries and research the cultural perspectives of beauty and health for each. (You may wish to ask international students for their perspectives on this topic.) How do the standards of beauty in the countries you researched compare with Western definitions? In your opinion—and supported by your research—what role, if any, does American popular culture play on body image in these countries?

2. Research fashion trends from two different cultures, such as the United States and Japan or England and India. Consult popular media online for each culture, including fashion magazines, popular television programs, and movies. What common themes can you find in both cultures? What differences seem distinct to each? Share your evaluation with the class to promote discussion on similarities and differences between each culture and what messages are conveyed to youth about beauty, self-confidence, and self-identity.

How Men Really Feel About Their Bodies
Ted Spiker*

Many women are surprised to learn that many men fret about their bodies. While rarely discussed, many men worry about what they see in the mirror but feel that it is socially inappropriate to admit it. In this essay, author and journalism professor Ted Spiker relates his own experiences with male body image. Uncomfortable in his own skin since childhood, he explains to women why body image really does matter to men.

1 Dressed only in my underwear, I'm eight years old and sitting on the pediatrician's exam table, waiting for my checkup. My mother points to the two mounds of fatty flesh between my chest and belly. She asks the doctor, "Could they be tumors?" "No," he says, "it's just fat." Since that day, my fat has absorbed more darts than the back wall of a bar.

2 At six feet two and 215 pounds, I'm not huge. I just carry my weight where women do—in my hips, butt, and thighs. And I hate it. I hate the way clothes fit. I hate that friends say I use the "big-butt defense" in basketball.

---

* Ted Spiker, *O, The Oprah Magazine,* August 2003

3   I'm not the only man who wishes his body looked more like Michael Jordan's and less like a vat of pudding. A recent survey showed that only 18 percent of men are happy enough with their physiques that they wouldn't change them.

4   While women get there first, they don't have a monopoly on stressing over looks.

5   *One: We have more body angst than you realize...*
...but we'll never have a serious conversation with you about it. Look at the standards we have to measure up to: If we're fat, we're labeled as beer-guzzling couch potatoes. Too thin, and we're deemed wimpy. We can have too

> *I'm not the only man who wishes his body looked more like Michael Jordan's and less like a vat of pudding.*

little hair on our heads or too much on our backs. And maybe worst of all, we can be too big in the backside of our pants yet too small in the front.

6   Now add the fact that our mental struggle has two layers.

7   "A man thinks, 'Not only does it bother me that I'm fat and my hair is thinning. It bothers me that it bothers me, because I'm not supposed to feel this way,'" says Thomas Cash, Ph.D., a professor of psychology at Old Dominion University in Norfolk, Virginia. "The thinking is that it's like a woman to worry about looks."

8   *Two: Instead, we'll joke about our bodies*
We make fun of ourselves to cover up what we're really feeling—frustration, embarrassment, and anger that we're not perfect.

9   But other people's jokes sting. Mark Meador, 37, of Westerville, Ohio, returned from a trip to Disney World with photos of himself.

10   "Man, you look like Big Pun," Meador's friend said, referring to the obese rapper who died of a heart attack. Meador laughed off the comment, not letting on that it hurt. That same weekend, his daughter said, "Dad, you look like you're having a baby." Fortunately for Meador, the gentle pokes inspired him to change. He dropped junk food, started Tae Bo, and lost more than 40 pounds.

11   *Three: We're worried about our bodies because we're competing for you—and against you*
With more people both marrying later and getting divorced, it's a competitive environment for finding mates. And since this generation of women can support themselves, they're freer to pick a man for his cute butt. Lynne Luciano, Ph.D., who has researched body-image issues at California State University at Dominguez Hills, says women are tired of being objectified and have turned the tables on men. "They don't like a man to be overly vain," she says. "He shouldn't care too much about the way he looks, but on the other hand, he should look good."

12   At the same time, men are also shaping up because they're seeing that people who are fit are more successful at work. "Women are very good at using their looks for competition," Cash says. "So men think, 'I'd better clean up my act.'"

13   *Four: We're not just checking you out*
We're a visual gender. We like the way you look. A lot. But that doesn't mean we don't compare ourselves to other men the way women compare themselves to other women. I notice the way men look on the beach, at work, or simply walking by. Maybe it's male competitiveness or primal instincts, but we don't just want to have better bodies to attract you. We want better bodies to improve our position among ourselves.

14 A scary thought that proves the point: When Luciano interviewed doctors who perform penis enlargements, they reported that the main reason men undergo the surgery isn't to improve their relationships, but to be more impressive in the locker room.

15 *Five: We want to look like we're 25*
It used to be that our mythical heroes had wisdom, experience, and maturity. Think Harrison Ford as Indiana Jones. Now our heroes are baby-faced with six-pack abs. Think Tobey Maguire as Spider-Man.

16 "The youth movement has been cruel to men," says Luciano. "The Cary Grants have fallen through the cracks. Today's ideal is younger, buffer, more muscular. A lot of men in their 40s and 50s have trouble trying to emulate that." So men, like women, are swimming against the age current. That might explain why from 1997 to 2001, the number of men who had cosmetic surgery increased 256 percent.

17 *Six: Desperation makes us do desperate things*
Delusion makes us do nothing. I can't remember the last pair of pants that fit me well. If I buy size 38s, they fit around the waist but suffocate my hips and butt. If I go to a 40, they're roomy where I need it but gaping in the waist.

18 Several years ago, I tried on my wife's post-pregnancy size-20 jeans to see if they were cut differently. The jeans fit me perfectly. I wore those jeans for six months, and I felt leaner every day I wore them. My wife asked me why I didn't just buy a big pair of men's jeans and have a tailor alter them. My answer: Why pay for alterations when I know that tomorrow I'm going to start an exercise routine that will change my body shape forever? It's been my mantra for two decades.

19 *Seven: Men's body image problems can be just as dangerous as women's*
For some men, poor body image can lead to anger, anxiety, depression, sexual dysfunction, and steroid abuse. Doctors may fail to recognize eating disorders or muscle dysmorphia (the need to constantly bulk up), even though it's estimated that eating disorders affect one million men.

20 Roberto Olivardia, Ph.D., a clinical psychologist at Harvard Medical School and coauthor of *The Adonis Complex,* says secrecy reinforces the patients' sense of shame. "I've treated men who would tell people they were alcoholics, but they'd never admit they were bulimic," he says.

21 *Eight: We don't blame anyone*
(Except maybe Tiger Woods and Taco Bell.) But we'll be grateful to anyone who makes us feel good about shaping up. We know what it's like to be bombarded with images of perfect bodies. We see the men in commercials and on magazine covers, the bigger-stronger-better mentality that dominates our culture.

22 "Look at Tiger Woods. The best golfer in the world has an outstanding physique. Golfers used to be everyday men," says J. Kevin Thompson, Ph.D., professor of psychology at the University of South Florida. "Basketball players used to be skinny. They're all muscular now." ◆

CRITICAL THINKING

1. Try to imagine the "perfect" male body. What does it look like? Is your image influenced by outside forces, such as the media, your gender, or your age? How do "real men" you know compare to the image in your mind?

2. "The thinking is that it's like a woman to worry about looks." Do you agree with the author's assertion? Give examples to contradict or corroborate the statement.

3. Who is Spiker's intended audience, and what do you think he is trying to achieve in this article? Give a concrete example from the text to explain your answer.

4. When is it right to criticize others for how they look in hopes of eliciting change? Could these "gentle pokes" potentially backfire, or can they inspire a positive outcome? Find the example in Spiker's article in which criticism influenced weight loss.

5. Spiker asserts that men want to have better bodies to "improve our position among ourselves." For men, is physical perfection necessarily related to social stature? Explain.

CRITICAL WRITING

1. *Persuasive Writing:* You have probably heard the expressions "Don't judge a book by its cover" and "The clothes don't make the man." Write an essay in which you agree or disagree with these statements. Be sure to support your position with logical examples.

2. *Exploratory Writing:* Media critic George Gerbner has observed that "what we see on TV and in magazines eventually becomes our standard of reality and desire." Respond to this statement with your own opinion and experience. How has the media, especially TV and magazines, influenced your personal reality of body image? What about your expectations of what you desire in a partner?

3. *Research Writing:* According to Spiker's statistical data, "From 1997 to 2001, the number of men who had cosmetic surgery increased 256 percent." Research the most popular trends of cosmetic surgery for men along with how and why they are doing this. Find at least one male celebrity who has had cosmetic surgery and report your findings.

GROUP PROJECTS

1. Create and administer your own survey regarding the ideal male appearance. As a group, come up with a list of qualities—such as intelligence, body build, facial features, sense of humor, and physical strength—that can be ranked in order of importance. Try to come up with 8 to 12 qualities or characteristics. Distribute your poll among men and women on your campus (indicate whether the poll is given to a man or a woman). Tabulate the results and present your findings to the class. For an interesting comparison, groups may also want to distribute a similar list of female characteristics and qualities.

2. Spiker mentions modern day superheroes being "baby-faced with six-pack abs." As a group, determine the 10 most popular superheroes found on television and/or on the big screen. In a chart, compare and contrast age, size, body shape, gender, race, hair, and facial features. Discuss what might account for the similarities and/or differences.

CULTURE SHOCK

Mr. Olympia

The Mr. Olympia competition is organized by the International Federation of Bodybuilding and Fitness (IFBB). The 2008 Mr. Olympia winner was Dexter Jackson, pictured here.

THINKING CRITICALLY

1. What social messages do competitions such as Mr. Olympia and Mr. Universe convey to young males about the ideal male physique?
2. In your opinion, is this an ideal male body? Why or why not?
3. In what ways do advertising, the media, and professional sports influence male body image?
4. Review some popular men's magazines. How are men depicted in these magazines? Do they resemble Mr. Olympia or Mr. Universe?

Never Too Buff

John Cloud*

We tend to assume that most men simply do not care about their appearance the way women do. But psychiatrists Harrison Pope and Katharine Phillips and psychologist Roberto Olivardia report in *The Adonis Complex* (2000) on a disturbing trend: just as many young women aspire to be supermodel thin, an increasing number of young men yearn for the steroid-boosted and buff bodies typical of today's action heroes and weightlifters. John Cloud reports on this groundbreaking research and what it might mean for boys and men in the years ahead.

1   Pop quiz: Who is more likely to be dissatisfied with the appearance of their chests, men or women? Who is more likely to be concerned about acne, your teenage son or his sister? And who is more likely to binge eat, your nephew or your niece?

2   If you chose the women and girls in your life, you are right only for the last question—and even then, not by the margin you might expect. About 40 percent of Americans who go on compulsive eating sprees are men. Thirty-eight percent of men want bigger pecs, while only 34 percent of women want bigger breasts. And more boys have fretted about zits than girls, going all the way back to a 1972 study.

3   A groundbreaking new book declares that these numbers, along with hundreds of other statistics and interviews the authors have compiled, mean something awful has happened to American men over the past few decades: They have become obsessed with their bodies. Authors Harrison Pope and Katharine Phillips, professors of psychiatry at Harvard and Brown, respectively, and Roberto Olivardia, a clinical psychologist at McLean Hospital in Belmont, Massachusetts, have a catchy name to describe this obsession, a term that will soon be doing many reps on chat shows: the *Adonis complex.*

4   The name, which refers to the gorgeous half man, half god of mythology, may be a little too ready for Oprah, but the theory behind it will start a wonderful debate. Based on original research involving more than a thousand men over the past 15 years, the book argues that many men desperately want to look like Adonis, because they constantly see the "ideal," steroid-boosted bodies of actors and models, and because their muscles are all they have over women today. In an age when women fly combat missions, the authors ask, "What can a modern boy or man do to distinguish himself as being 'masculine'?"

5   For years, of course, some men—ice skaters, body builders, George Hamilton— have fretted over aspects of their appearance. But the numbers suggest that body-image concerns have gone mainstream: nearly half of men do not like their overall appearance, in contrast to just 1 in 6 in 1972. True, men typically are fatter now, but another study found that 46 percent of men of normal weight think about their appearance "all the time" or "frequently." And some men—probably hundreds of thousands, if you extrapolate from small surveys—say they have passed up job and even romantic opportunities because they refuse to disrupt workouts or dine on

* John Cloud, *TIME* magazine, April 24, 2000

restaurant food. In other words, an increasing number of men would rather look brawny for their girlfriends than have sex with them.

6   Consider the money spent: Last year American men forked over $2 billion for gym memberships and another $2 billion for home exercise equipment. *Men's Health* ("Rock-hard abs in six weeks!" it screams every other issue) had 250,000 subscribers in 1990; now it has 1.6 million. In 1996 alone, men underwent some 700,000 cosmetic procedures.

7   At least those profits are legal. Anabolic steroids, the common name for synthetic testosterone, have led to the most dramatic changes in the male form in modern history; and more and more average men want those changes for themselves. Since steroids became widely available on the black market in the 1960s, perhaps three million American men have swallowed or injected them—mostly in the past 15 years. A 1993 survey found that 1 Georgia high school boy in every 15 admitted to having used steroids without a prescription. And the Drug En-

The G.I. Joe of 1982 looks scrawny compared with G.I. Joe Extreme, introduced in the mid-1990s. If G.I. Joe Extreme were a real man, he would have a 55-inch chest and 27-inch biceps, which simply cannot be replicated in nature.

forcement Administration reports that the percentage of all high school students who have used steroids has increased 50 percent in the past four years, from 1.8 to 2.8 percent. The abuse of steroids has so alarmed the National Institute on Drug Abuse that it launched a campaign in gyms, malls, bookstores, clubs, and on the Internet to warn teenagers about the dangers. Meanwhile, teenagers in even larger numbers are buying legal but lightly regulated food supplements, some with dangerous side effects, that promise to make them bigger, leaner, or stronger.

8   As they infiltrated the bodybuilding world in the 1970s and Hollywood a decade later, steroids created bodies for mass consumption that the world had literally never seen before. Pope likes to chart the changes by looking at Mr. America winners, which he called up on the Internet in his office last week. "Look at this guy," Pope exclaimed when he clicked on the 1943 winner, Jules Bacon. "He couldn't even win a county bodybuilding contest today." Indeed, there are 16-year-olds working out at your gym who are as big as Bacon. Does that necessarily mean that today's bodybuilders—including those 16-year-olds—are 'roided? Pope is careful. "The possibility exists that rare or exceptional people, those with an unusual genetic makeup or a hormonal imbalance, could achieve the muscularity and leanness of today's big bodybuilders," he says.

9   But it is not likely. And Pope is not lobbing dumbbells from an ivory tower: he lifts weights six days a week, from 11 AM to 1 PM. (He can even mark historical occasions by his workouts: "I remember when the Challenger went down; I was doing a set of squats.") "We are being assaulted by images virtually impossible to attain without the use of drugs," says Pope. "So what happens when you change a million-year-old equilibrium of nature?"

10   A historical loop forms: Steroids beget pro wrestlers—Hulk Hogan, for one, has admitted to taking steroids—who inspire boys to be just like them. Steroids have changed even boys' toys. Feminists have long derided Barbie for her tiny waist and

big bosom. The authors of *The Adonis Complex* see a similar problem for boys in the growth of G.I. Joe. The grunt of 1982 looks scrawny compared with G.I. Joe Extreme, introduced in the mid-1990s. If he were a real man, G.I. Joe Extreme would have a 55-inch chest and 27-inch biceps, which simply cannot be replicated in nature. Pope also points out a stunning feature of the 3-year-old video game *Duke Nukem: Total Meltdown,* developed by GT Interactive Software. When Duke gets tired, he can find a bottle of steroids to get him going. "Steroids give Duke a super adrenaline rush," the game manual notes.

11   To bolster their argument, the *Adonis* authors developed a computerized test that allows subjects to "add" muscle to a typical male body. Subjects estimate their own size and then pick the size they would like to be and the size they think women want. Pope and his colleagues gave the test to college students and found that on average, the men wanted 28 pounds more muscle, and they thought women wanted them to have 30 pounds more. In fact, the women who took the test picked an ideal man only slightly more muscular than average, which goes a long way toward explaining why Leonardo DiCaprio can be a megastar in a nation that also idealizes "Stone Cold" Steve Austin.

12   But when younger boys took Pope's test, they revealed an even deeper sense of inadequacy about their bodies. More than half of the boys aged 11 to 17 chose as their physical ideal an image attainable only by using steroids: So they do. Boys are a big part of the clientele at Muscle Mania (not its real name), a weight-lifting store that *TIME* visited last week at a strip mall in a Boston suburb. A couple of teenagers came in to ask about Tribulus, one of the many over-the-counter drugs and body-building supplements the store sells—all legally.

13   "A friend of mine," one boy begins, fooling no one, "just came off a cycle of juice, and he heard that Tribulus can help you produce testosterone naturally." Patrick, 28, who runs the store and who stopped using steroids four years ago because of chest pain, tells the kid, "The s__ shuts off your nuts," meaning steroids can reduce sperm production, shrink the testicles, and cause impotence. Tribulus, Patrick says, can help restart natural testosterone production. The teen hands over $12 for 100 Tribulus Fuel pills. (Every day, Muscle Mania does $4,000 in sales of such products, with protein supplements and so-called fat burners leading the pack.)

14   Patrick says many of his teen customers, because they are short on cash, will not pay for a gym membership "until they've saved up for a cycle [of steroids]. They don't see the point without them." The saddest customers, he says, are the little boys, 12 and 13, brought in by young fathers. "The dad will say, 'How do we put some weight on this kid?' with the boy just staring at the floor. Dad is going to turn him into Hulk Hogan, even if it's against his will."

15   What would motivate someone to take steroids? Pope, Phillips, and Olivardia say the Adonis complex works in different ways for different men. "Michael," 32, one of their research subjects, told *TIME* he had always been a short kid who got picked on. He started working out when he was about 14, and he bought muscle magazines for advice. The pictures taunted him: he sweated, but he was not getting as big as the men in the photos. Other men in his gym also made him feel bad. When he found out they were on steroids, he did two cycles himself, even though he knew they could be dangerous.

16   But not all men with body-image problems take steroids. Jim Davis, 29, a human services manager, told *TIME* he never took them, even when training for

bodybuilding competitions. But Davis says he developed a form of obsessive-compulsive disorder around his workouts. He lifted weights six days a week for at least six years. He worked out even when injured. He adhered to a rigid regimen for every session, and if he changed it, he felt anxious all day. He began to be worried about clothes, and eventually he could wear only three shirts—the ones that made him look big. Yet he still felt small. "I would sit in class at college with a coat on," he says. You may have heard of this condition, called *bigorexia:* thinking your muscles are puny when they are not. Pope and his colleagues call it *muscle dysmorphia* and estimate that hundreds of thousands of men suffer from it.

17   Even though most boys and men never approach the compulsion of Michael or Jim, who eventually conquered it, they undoubtedly face more pressure now than in the past to conform to an impossible ideal. Ripped male bodies are used today to advertise everything that shapely female bodies advertise: not just fitness products but also dessert liqueurs, microwave ovens, and luxury hotels. The authors of *The Adonis Complex* want guys to rebel against those images, or at least to see them for what they are: a goal unattainable without drug use.

18   Feminists raised these issues for women years ago, and more recent books, such as *The Beauty Myth* (1991),were part of a backlash against the hourglass ideal. Now, says Phillips, "I actually think it may be harder for men than women to talk about these problems, because it's not considered masculine to worry about such things." But maybe there is a masculine alternative: Next time WWE comes on, guys, throw the TV out the window and order a large pizza. ◆

CRITICAL THINKING

1. Pope, Phillips, and Olivardia report that, in general, men would like to add 28 pounds more muscle to their frames but believe women would prefer at least 30 pounds more muscle. What, in your opinion, accounts for this perception? Does it seem reasonable?

2. Evaluate the comment made by Pope, Phillips, and Olivardia that young men are increasingly obsessed with body image, because they feel that muscle is "all they have over women today." Do you agree or disagree with this statement? Explain.

3. Analyze the author's use of statistics to support his points. Do their conclusions seem reasonable based on the data they cite? Why or why not?

4. According to the author, what cultural messages tell children that steroid use is okay? Describe some of the ways children receive these messages.

CRITICAL WRITING

1. *Analytical Writing:* Write a detailed description of your ideal male image (what you desire in a male or what you would most want to look like as a male). How does your description compare with the conclusions drawn by the psychiatrists and psychologist in the article? Did outside cultural influences direct your description? Explain.

2. *Personal Narrative:* Looking back at your experience in high school, write a narrative about the males who were considered the most buff. What qualities made these particular males more desirable and more enviable

than their peers? How much of their appeal was based on their physical appearance? How much was based on something else?

3. *Persuasive Writing:* Pope, Phillips, and Olivardia comment that media pressure is connected to the emergence of men's new obsession with body image. Write an essay discussing whether this is true or not true. Support your perspective using examples from Cloud's article and your own experience.

GROUP PROJECTS

1. Have everyone in the group bring a copy of a men's magazine, such as *Details, GQ,* or *Esquire.* Different group members may want to focus on different aspects of the magazines, like advertising, articles, fashion, or advice columns. Do the models in the magazine fit the description in Cloud's article? What do the articles suggest men should aspire to look like? How many articles on improving appearance are featured? After reviewing the magazines, discuss your findings and collaborate on an essay about how men's fashion magazines help define the ideal male.

2. Working in small groups, arrange to visit your campus gym or local health club. Split up and take notes about what kinds of men you see working out there. What patterns of behavior do you see? For example, are there more men working out with weights than doing aerobics? Write brief descriptions of the men's workout attire. Do they seem concerned with how they look? Why or why not? After your visit, get together and compare notes. Write a report on your findings and present your conclusions to the class.

VIEWPOINTS

▶ **Why I Rue My Tattoo**
   Beth Janes*

▶ **Tattoo Me Again and Again**
   Stephanie Dolgoff

The next two readings explore the aftereffects of tattooing. The process of tattooing can be traced back 5,000 years, and tattoos are as diverse as the people who wear them. In recent years, however, tattooing has gone from a subversive form of self-expression to a popular form of body art, especially among people under 30. For some of the initiated, the tattoo is a source of pride; however, for others, the tattoo causes embarrassment and regret. In "Why I Rue My Tattoo," Beth Janes explains how her impulsive attempt at body art went awry. Stephanie Dolgoff, however, observes in "Tattoo Me Again and Again" that her choice of body art reflects important moments in her life. Carefully considered, tattoos are reminders of the things we care deeply about. How will this new generation of the tattooed feel in 10, 20, or 40 years? Perhaps they will be as divided as these next two articles.

---

* Beth Janes, *MSNBC*, October 4, 2007; Stephanie Dolgoff, *Self*, October 4, 2007

Why I Rue My Tattoo

Beth Janes

1 I got my second tattoo when I was 19. For two hours, I lay belly down, butt up, with my Levi's pulled low enough to have a good plumber look happening. Doc, the tatted-out, 50-something shop owner, hunched over my bum, his wiry gray hair dusting my skin and his buzzing, needled handpiece imprinting me with what turned out to be a permanent Rorschach inkblot. Not exactly the swirling design I initially had in mind. I wanted an image that was one part delicate, one part strong, like something you'd see on a fancy wrought-iron gate. Instead I was branded with an abstract, somewhat vulgar design with a point directed straight down my crack.

2 "Wow, it's great," I said, lying through my teeth, still gritted from the needle's sting.

3 "Hot. Really hot," Doc said. My friend Jessie, seated next to me and there for moral support, offered similar affirmations. But a little voice inside of my head said, Ugh.

4 It wasn't Doc's fault. He was a pro; I was the amateur, an amateur at thinking things through. I had thought I possessed that skill. It had been present a year earlier when, in the same chair, with Jessie by my side, I got my first tattoo, a good-luck ladybug southwest of my belly button.

5 Jessie and I got our first tats together to spice up our senior year at Catholic school. Three times before the appointment, I drove my 1988 Oldsmobile to the library, where I sat cross-legged in my uniform kilt, thumbing through books, looking for the perfect depiction. The spot I had chosen on my body was a bit clichéd but easily hidden from potential employers and by a wedding dress. (That was my mother's sole wish, which I granted because she was less than thrilled about the tattoo but didn't try to stop me.) When it was done, I loved it. I loved it even after someone pointed out that, thanks to the ladybug's tilt and placement, it looked as if a bug were crawling out of my underwear.

6 But when I got that second tattoo a year later, there was no research involved. I simply made a decision right before the lower-back-tattoo trend took off. To me, the tattoos, and those who sported them at the time, seemed tough—in a good way. If I got one, I thought, I would still be a nice girl, the occasional Ann Taylor shopper and A student, but I'd be drawing out the Sonic Youth–listening, beer-swigging badass I also identified with.

For every tattoo cherished, there's another that brings regret.

7 I gave Doc the picture of the design, which I had found on a friend's T-shirt. He said it wouldn't reproduce with the same detail on my skin but that he'd sketch something similar that would. My critical mistakes came after that: The final design wasn't exactly what I wanted, but I convinced myself that it looked cool enough (mistake one). Not only was I too shy to ask for other sketches (two), but I was so

eager to get the tattoo that I spent 30 seconds thinking it over after seeing the drawing (three). Once I saw the stencil on my skin, I thought, it will be fine. The Ugh voice was there, but I ignored it. Perhaps the voice, likely dressed in a cashmere sweater set, was being smothered by a badass in a concert tee.

8   In the weeks after, I lied to friends about my feelings. I even tried to convince myself that I liked the tattoo, that it conveyed the tough side I was desperate to show off to the world in order to balance my good-girl side. A few months later, though, I started seeing girls everywhere (and not only the tough types that had initially inspired me) sporting lower-back tattoos. Mall rats in belly shirts, cheerleaders, sex sirens, moody emo-girls and preppy blondes all showed off ink when bending over to pick up their pom-poms/mix tapes/polo mallets. I had little in common with these girls before my tattoo, but now we were officially connected. My plan had backfired. Not only might people get the wrong idea about me, they might actually get the worst idea: that I was yet another too-trendy girl who thought tattoos were just, like, so cool. I might as well have asked for a tattoo that said "Trying too hard."

9   Somewhere along the way, though, the regret started to fade. At first it was superficial realizations: I thought, At least I didn't get an ex-boyfriend's name or a Chinese character that instead of meaning beautiful symbolizes harlot. But then, as I graduated from college and began living on my own and flourishing in my career, I started to feel more comfortable with myself at a deeper level. I liked the person I had become and accepted all the decisions I had made along the way, including the tattoo. While at a friend's wedding, reflecting on how marriage would change her life, I began to ponder my own path and realized that I had, in fact, become a real badass. To me, that had nothing to do with listening to the right music, wearing the latest clothes or deciding to get my second tattoo—and everything to do with being fearless about my true self and accepting who I was, inside and out.

10   A decade later, I'm not embarrassed if my tattoo peeks out or friends make a joke. At my grandfather's funeral, for instance, I had to bow at the altar before giving my reading. I was wearing high-waisted pants (thank you, Marc Jacobs, for a rise of more than 8 inches) and a blouse I was certain fell beyond the safety zone. After mass, though, a cousin said, "Father Michael saw your tattoo, and he wanted me to tell you he's very disappointed." He then clapped me on the back and broke into a full belly laugh. I felt good, even honored, that the tattoo could provide joke fodder for my relatives—and that I could laugh, too.

11   When it comes to regrets, my tattoo falls somewhere between a misguided hookup and the time I drove after one too many beers. For it and all my other mistakes, I've forgiven myself—and instead of contemplating laser removal, I choose to look at the tattoo as a reminder of who I was and who I am now. Sure, I'll keep making mistakes, but I'm smart enough now to recognize and avoid those I may later come to regret. Why spend thousands of dollars erasing this bad decision when I could use the money to make good ones: traveling, helping a friend, buying more Marc Jacobs trousers? And as far as worrying about what people will think of me if they accidentally see my tattoo: If they don't also see that I'm a fun and empathetic friend, a smart woman and a kind and responsible person, then f--- 'em ; the badass in me doesn't care.

Tattoo Me Again and Again
Stephanie Dolgoff

1   Anyone who tells you that getting a tattoo doesn't hurt is either lying or lying. Or she may be so hopped up on Vicodin that although the process is torturous, she's too loopy to care. Or it might be like childbirth amnesia: She's so pleased with the results that she's blocked out what it feels like to have an electric needle scraped back and forth over her delicate skin. Any of those would explain why people—like me—get more than one.

2   I went the Vicodin route when I got my third and most recent tattoo six months ago, popping one pill and then later another, which I had saved from my cesarean section a few years ago. This latest tattoo, two lush pink and plum peonies on my left inner ankle, hurt more than the C-section. Like I've never regretted having my twin girls, I've never regretted getting my tats or looked back and thought, What was I thinking? (They don't give

> *Like I've never regretted having my twin girls, I've never regretted getting my tats or looked back and thought, What was I thinking?*

epidurals for tattoos, after all.) That's because I knew exactly what I was thinking all three times.

3   I got my first tattoo—a small line drawing of one of Picasso's doves—above my right shoulder blade when I was 25, right before I quit my job, packed up my life, and moved to Seville to teach English. I'd felt so embraced by the city (and by a guy named Manolo) when I'd visited a few years earlier that I was sure it was my natural home. I didn't wind up staying, but the decision was one of the best I've ever made. I learned that I could fly above life's expectations and rely on myself for all my needs if I had to. (Oh, and that Spanish men who still live with their parents— i.e., most single Spanish men—are a wee bit immature.)

4   Nine years later, I got a second dove on the small of my back, right before my husband and I became engaged. It signified the calm, soaring feeling I had after years of searching for the right partner. It had partly to do with Paul, who made me feel safe and loved, but even more to do with the fact that I'd grown into a person who knew how to include people like Paul in her life. And the third tattoo, the largest and most painful, those dual-colored peonies situated above my foot? They represent my fraternal twin girls, Sasha and Vivian, two very different flowers growing on the same vine. Now they'll always be with me, even when we're apart.

5   Each of my three tattoos represents a major emotional milestone or epiphany and serves as a bodily reminder of the freedom I felt because of my new experience or bit of knowledge. They're like signposts along the road to now, someplace I feel lucky to be. When I look at them, I can feel again the exhilaration of the life-altering shift that pointed me squarely toward personal peace and fulfillment. If I'd gotten Denzel Forever on my butt or Hello Kitty on my inner arm during a drunken moment, I might well regret it. In general, though, I'm not a big regretter. I tend to see even the dumbest decisions as learning experiences ("Google? What a stupid name for a company. No way am I investing!"), as opposed to evidence of what a fool I was when I was younger.

6   My reasons for getting my tattoos make sense to me, and that's all that matters. There are as many reasons to get a tattoo as there are images to express people's personal experiences, memories, emotions or even favorite band, if you feel that strongly about it. The best reasons have this in common: They please the person wearing the body art, not necessarily the person looking at it. One friend got a leafy cuff around her upper arm purely because it made her feel like a hot mama; another went with her best friend and got matching Japanese symbols for happiness, to give their friendship its symbolic due; still another got a C-sized battery on her hip, to remind her that she needs to stop and recharge.

7   Whatever the meaning, you're more likely to be happy with your tattoo if you have a reason—or reasons, in my case—you can live with forever, like the tattoo itself. You can't think of a permanent piece of skin art as a haircut that, once you're tired of it, you can let grow out. And even though it's possible to have a tattoo removed, the process certainly isn't easy. The few people I know who regret their tattoos say they liked them when they got them but now hate what they project to potential bosses or mothers-in-law. It's true that you never know how radically your priorities or career goals (or the names of your lovers—I'm talking to you, Angelina) will change over time. (Case in point: I know a woman who, in her 20s, covered both of her arms in colorful mermaids and ivy vines. She now works with children; the kids think her tattoos are cool, but she wears long-sleeved shirts around the parents, mostly because she doesn't want to lose clients.) But I like to think if I ever forsook writing for, say, holding public office, becoming a trophy wife for a prominent real estate magnate or even turning letters on Wheel of Fortune, I'd be so good at what I did that people would forgive my tattoos as one of the eccentricities that come with creative genius. Clearly I'm not that concerned, though—not least of all because I know many hard-driving female CEOs have secret ladybugs, hearts or lotus blossoms hidden under their posh, tailored suits. These days, Satanic pentagrams, swastikas and symbols of anarchy aside, most tattoos hardly signify rebellion.

8   Although I love my tattoos, I don't plan on getting any more, mostly because I'm running out of spots on my body that will never droop, get stretched out or grow hair—all of which would ruin even the most beautiful, well-thought-out design. After getting the peonies, I told Paul of my decision to call it quits. He said he distinctly remembered my saying that the last time. And he's probably right. So I never say never, except that I know I'll never regret my tattoos. ◆

CRITICAL THINKING

1. Janes's article sets up the audience to believe that she "rues" her tattoo; however, she changes her tone to one of acceptance in her conclusion. Does the author convince you of her acceptance, or do you think she is still trying to convince herself that she likes the tattoo?

2. How were Janes's and Dolgoff's experiences different when getting their tattoos? Do you think this could have led to why they have different attitudes about their tattoos?

3. If you have a tattoo, what image do you think it will project to "potential bosses or mothers-in-law"? If you don't have a tattoo, what have been

your reasons for not getting one? Would you ever consider it? Why or why not?

4. Dolgoff argues, "If I ever forsook writing for, say, holding public office, becoming a trophy wife for a prominent real estate magnate or even turning letters on Wheel of Fortune, I'd be so good at what I did that people would forgive my tattoos as one of the eccentricities that come with creative genius." Do you agree that her tattoos would be "forgiven" in these circumstances? Explain. Also, is getting a tattoo a form of "creative genius"? Explain.

5. In Dolgoff's article, she asserts, "These days, Satanic pentagrams, swastikas and symbols of anarchy aside, most tattoos hardly signify rebellion." Do you agree or disagree with this statement? Explain.

CRITICAL WRITING

1. *Persuasive Writing:* Write an essay in which you argue either for getting a tattoo or against getting one. Use personal experience for your reasoning, and if you already have a tattoo, explain whether you have any regrets or, if you have none, why you would do it again.

2. *Research Writing:* Research the current trend for tattoo removal. Try to find statistics on how many people are getting tattoos compared to how many people are removing them. Also explain the different processes for tattoo removal and which are most effective. Add details on any personal experiences that you may find in your research.

3. *Exploratory Writing:* Write an essay in which you explore the idea of tattoos as a form of self-expression that set you apart from others. For example, when you see someone with a tattoo, what do you think? Is this person a rebel, subversive, trendy, a "creative genius," or something else? Which prejudices are associated with tattoos in our current lifestyle, and which prejudices no long exist?

GROUP PROJECT

1. Explore the reasoning behind getting a tattoo. Is it to be a "badass" as Janes suggests, or is it to give a special memory permanence as Dolgoff suggests? Try to come up with a brainstorm list of as many reasons as you can think of. Summarize all of the reasons given by the authors and then create a more extensive list of your own. You may wish to interview students who have tattoos and ask them to discuss their motivations for their choices in body art.

Perspectives: Dress to Please

I've decided to dress to please men instead. It's cheaper.

THINKING CRITICALLY

1. What issue is this cartoon highlighting for discussion? Explain.
2. Do you think this cartoon would appeal to both women and men? Does it make a connection to one group more than another?
3. Have you ever dressed uncomfortably because you wanted to present a particular image? Explain.

Consumer Nation

Wanting It, Selling It

Advertising is everywhere—television, newspapers, magazines, the Internet, the sides of buses and trains, highway billboards, T-shirts, sports arenas, and even license plates. It is the driving force of our consumptive economy, accounting for $150 billion worth of commercials and print ads each year—more than the gross national product of many countries. Advertising fills a quarter of each television hour and the bulk of most newspapers and magazines. It is everywhere people are, and its appeal goes to the quick of our fantasies: happiness, material wealth, eternal youth, social acceptance, sexual fulfillment, and power. Through carefully selected images and words, advertising is the most pervasive form of persuasion in America and perhaps the single most significant manufacturer of meaning in our consumer society, and many of us are not aware of its astounding influence on our lives.

Most of us are so accustomed to advertising that we hear it without listening and see it without looking. However, if we stop to examine how it works on our subconscious, we would be amazed at how powerful and complex a psychological force it is. This chapter examines how words compel us to buy, how images feed our fantasies, and how the advertising industry tempts us to part with our money.

We begin by taking a closer look at the connections among advertisements, media, and our consumer culture. First, Joseph Turow discusses the ways in which advertisers exploit rips in the American social fabric to target particular products to specific audiences in "Targeting a New World." Although it may seem obvious that advertisers wish to target their ads to the people who will want to use their products most, Turow questions the long-term social impact of this marketing strategy and what it might mean to American culture in general. His piece is followed by an essay by Slate editor Daniel Gross, who proposes a new economic theory based on the frequency of Starbucks coffee houses located in a given area in "Will Your Recession Be Tall, Grande, or Venti?"

The next two articles confirm what parents have long suspected—that Madison Avenue is after their children. Television and the Internet make it easier to target the child market. Peggy Orenstein questions why the marketing moguls at Disney want her little girl to be a princess—with all the frippery princesses encompass—in her essay, "Just a Little Princess?" Are America's little girls being forced to buy pink and wear tutus, or is Disney just giving children what they want and love? "Which One of These Sneakers Is Me?" by Douglas Rushkoff, explains that advertisers have declared an all-out market assault on today's kids, surrounding them with logos, labels, and ads literally from the day they are born. Are we simply giving children more choices, or are we controlling childhood itself?

The American quest for luxury is examined by consumer-culture critic James Twitchell in "The Allure of Luxury." Twitchell argues that while academics like to wring their hands over the materialistic excesses of society, the truth is humans have always loved nice things. We are creatures of luxury—in general, humans prefer comfort, style, and the next new thing. Such materialism is not necessarily bad either; it is all in how you look at it.

This chapter's Viewpoints section focuses on advertising language. By its nature, the language of advertising is a very special one that combines words cleverly and methodically to get us to spend our money. In "With These Words, I Can

Sell You Anything," word-watcher William Lutz explores how advertisers twist simple words so that they appear to promise whatever the consumer wants. In the second piece, "The Language of Advertising," advertising executive Charles A. O'Neill concedes that the language of ads can be very appealing, but that's the point. However, unless consumers are willing, no ad can force them to part with their money.

Targeting a New World
Joseph Turow *

Advertisers do not target their campaigns to universal audiences. Rather, they target specific audiences to market specific products. Communications professor Joseph Turow explains how the techniques of "target marketing" by advertising agencies widen divisions in American society by breaking us up into different target audiences. To advertisers, the catch phrase is "divide and conquer," and the American consumer public is what they aim to divide.

1 "Advertisers will have their choice of horizontal demographic groups and vertical psychographic program types."

2 "Our judgment as to the enhanced quality of our subscriber base has been confirmed by the advertisers."

3 "Unfortunately, most media plans are based on exposure opportunities. This is particularly true for television because G.R.P. analysis is usually based on television ratings and ratings do not measure actual exposure."

4 Most Americans would likely have a hard time conceiving the meaning of these quotations. The words would clearly be understood as English, but the jargon would seem quite mysterious. They might be surprised to learn that they have heard a specialized language that advertisers use about them. Rooted in various kinds of research, the language has a straightforward purpose. The aim is to package individuals, or groups of people, in ways that make them useful targets for the advertisers of certain products through certain types of media.

5 Clearly, the way the advertising industry talks about us is not the way we talk about ourselves. Yet when we look at the advertisements that emerge from the cauldron of marketing strategies and strange terminology, we see pictures of our surroundings that we can understand, even recognize. The pictures remind us that the advertising industry does far more than sell goods and services through the mass media. With budgets that add up to hundreds of billions of dollars, the industry exceeds the church and the school in its ability to promote images about our place in society—where we belong, why, and how we should act toward others.

6 A revolutionary shift is taking place in the way advertisers talk about America and the way they create ads and shape media to reflect that talk. The shift has been influenced by, and has been influencing, major changes in the audiovisual options

---

* Joseph Turow, *Breaking Up America: Advertisers and the New Media World* [excerpt], 1997

available to the home. But it most importantly has been driven by, and has been driving, a profound sense of division in American society.

7   The era we are entering is one in which advertisers will work with media firms to create the electronic equivalents of gated communities. Marketers are aware that the U.S. population sees itself marked by enormous economic and cultural tensions. Marketers don't feel, though, that it benefits them to encourage Americans to deal with these tensions head-on through a media brew of discussion, entertainment, and argumentation aimed at broadly diverse audiences. Rather, new approaches to marketing make it increasingly worthwhile for even the largest media companies to separate audiences into different worlds according to distinctions that ad people feel make the audiences feel secure and comfortable. The impact of these activities on Americans' views of themselves and others will be profound, enduring, and often disturbing.

8   The changes have begun only recently. The hallmark is the way marketers and media practitioners have been approaching the development of new audiovisual technology. Before the late 1970s, most people in the United States could view without charge three commercial broadcast stations, a public (noncommercial) TV station, and possibly an independent commercial station (one not affiliated with a network). By the mid 1990s, several independent broadcast TV stations, scores of cable and satellite television channels, videocassettes, video games, home computer programs, online computer services, and the beginnings of two-way ("interactive") television had become available to major segments of the population with an interest and a budget to match.

9   People in the advertising industry are working to integrate the new media channels into the broader world of print and electronic media to maximize the entire system's potential for selling. They see these developments as signifying not just the breakup of the traditional broadcast network domain, but as indicating a breakdown in social cohesion as well. Advertisers' most public talk about America—in trade magazine interviews, trade magazine ads, convention speeches, and interviews for this book—consistently features a nation that is breaking up. Their vision is of a fractured population of self-indulgent, frenetic, and suspicious individuals who increasingly reach out only to people like themselves.

10   Advertising practitioners do not view these distinctions along primarily racial or ethnic lines, though race and ethnicity certainly play a part, provoking turf battles among marketers. Rather, the new portraits of society that advertisers and media personnel invoke involve the blending of income, generation, marital status, and gender into a soup of geographical and psychological profiles they call "lifestyles."

11   At the business level, what is driving all this is a major shift in the balance between targeting and mass marketing in U.S. media. Mass marketing involves aiming a home-based medium or outdoor event at people irrespective of their background or patterns of activities (their lifestyles). Targeting, by contrast, involves the intentional pursuit of specific segments of society—groups and even individuals. The Underground [radio] Network, the Comedy Central cable channel, and *Details* magazine are far more targeted than the ABC Television Network, the Sony Jumbotron screen on Times Square, and the Super Bowl. Yet even these examples of targeting are far from close to the pinpointing of audiences that many ad people expect is possible.

12   The ultimate aim of this new wave of marketing is to reach different groups with specific messages about how certain products tie into their lifestyles. Target-minded media firms are helping advertisers do that by building primary media communities. These are formed when viewers or readers feel that a magazine, TV channel, newspaper, radio station, or other medium reaches people like them, resonates with their personal beliefs, and helps them chart their position in the larger world. For advertisers, tying into those communities means gaining consumer loyalties that are nearly impossible to establish in today's mass market.

13   Nickelodeon and MTV were pioneer attempts to establish this sort of ad-sponsored communion on cable television. While they started as cable channels, they have become something more. Owned by media giant Viacom, they are lifestyle parades that invite their target audiences (rel-

The new portraits of society that advertisers and media personnel invoke involve the blending of income, generation, marital status, and gender into a soup of geographical and psychological profiles they call "lifestyles."

atively upscale children and young adults, respectively) into a sense of belonging that goes far beyond the coaxial wire into books, magazines, videotapes, and outdoor events that Viacom controls or licenses.

14   The idea of these sorts of "programming services" is to cultivate a must-see, must-read, must-share mentality that makes the audience feel part of a family, attached to the program hosts, other viewers, and sponsors. It is a strategy that extends across a wide spectrum of marketing vehicles, from cable TV to catalogs, from direct mailings to online computer services, from outdoor events to in-store clubs. In all these areas, national advertisers make it clear that they prefer to conduct their targeting with the huge media firms they had gotten to know in earlier years. But the giants don't always let their offspring operate on huge production budgets. To keep costs low enough to satisfy advertisers' demands for efficient targeting, much of ad-supported cable television is based on recycled materials created or distributed by media conglomerates. What makes MTV, ESPN, Nickelodeon, A&E, and other such "program services" distinctive is not the uniqueness of the programs but the special character created by their formats: the flow of their programs, packaged to attract the right audience at a price that will draw advertisers.

15   But media firms have come to believe that simply attracting groups to specialized formats is often not enough. Urging people who do not fit the desired lifestyle profile not to be part of the audience is sometimes also an aim, since it makes the community more pure and thereby more efficient for advertisers. So in the highly competitive media environment of the 1980s and early 1990s, cable companies aiming to lure desirable types to specialized formats have felt the need to create "signature" materials that both drew the "right" people and signaled the "wrong" people that they ought to go away. It is no accident that the producers of certain signature programs on Nickelodeon (for example, Ren and Stimpy) and MTV (such as Beavis and Butt-head) in the early 1990s acknowledge that they chase away irrelevant viewers as much as they attract desirable ones.

16   An even more effective form of targeting, ad people believe, is a type that goes beyond chasing undesirables away. It simply excludes them in the first place. Using computer models based on zip codes and a variety of databases, it is economically feasible to tailor materials for small groups, even individuals. That is already taking place in the direct mail, telemarketing, and magazine industries. With certain forms of interactive television, it is technologically quite possible to send some TV programs and commercials only to neighborhoods, census blocks, and households that advertisers want to reach. Media firms are working toward a time when people will be able to choose the news, information, and entertainment they want when they want it. Advertisers who back these developments will be able to offer different product messages—and variable discounts—to individuals based on what they know about them.

17   Clearly, not all these technologies are widespread. Clearly, too, there is a lot of hype around them. Many companies that stand to benefit from the spread of target marketing have doubtless exaggerated the short time it will take to get there and the low costs that will confront advertisers once they do. Moreover, as will be seen, some marketers have been slower than others to buy into the usefulness of a media system that encourages the partitioning of people with different lifestyles.

18   Nevertheless, the trajectory is clear. A desire to label people so that they may be separated into primary media communities is transforming the way television is programmed, the way newspapers are "zoned," the way magazines are printed, and the way cultural events are produced and promoted. Most critically, advertisers' interest in exploiting lifestyle differences is woven into the basic assumptions about media models for the next century—the so-called 500 Channel Environment or the future Information Superhighway.

19   For me and you—individual readers and viewers—this segmentation and targeting can portend terrific things. If we can afford to pay, or if we're important to sponsors who will pick up the tab, we will be able to receive immediately the news, information, and entertainment we order. In a world pressing us with high-speed concerns, we will surely welcome media and sponsors that offer to surround us with exactly what we want when we want it.

20   As an entirety, though, society in the United States will lose out. One of the consequences of turning the U.S. into a pastiche of market-driven labels is that such a multitude of categories makes it impossible for a person to directly overlap with more than a tiny portion of them. If primary media communities continue to take hold, their large numbers will diminish the chance that individuals who identify with certain social categories will even have an opportunity to learn about others. Offputting signature programs such as Beavis and Butt-head may make the situation worse, causing individuals annoyed by the shows or what they read about them to feel alienated from groups that appear to enjoy them. If you are told over and over again that different kinds of people are not part of your world, you will be less and less likely to want to deal with those people.

21   The creation of customized media materials will likely take this lifestyle segregation further. It will allow, even encourage, individuals to live in their own personally constructed worlds, separated from people and issues they don't care about or don't want to be bothered with. The desire to do that may accelerate when, as is the case in the late-twentieth-century United States, seemingly intractable antagonisms

based on age, income, ethnicity, geography, and more result from competition over jobs and political muscle. In these circumstances, market segmentation and targeting may accelerate an erosion of the tolerance and mutual dependence between diverse groups that enable a society to work. Ironically, the one common message across media will be that a common center for sharing ideas and feelings is more and more difficult to find—or even to care about. ◆

CRITICAL THINKING

1. How can exploiting Americans' social and cultural divisions actually help advertisers market products to consumers?
2. Turow comments that the ways advertisers exploit fissures in American society is "often disturbing." Why is it disturbing? Alternatively, other critics argue that we should not be concerned with this advertising dynamic. Respond to each viewpoint.
3. Turow uses three quotations to begin his essay. How do these quotations contribute to the points he makes in his article? Are they an effective way to reach his audience? Explain.
4. How does packaging individuals or groups of people make them "useful targets" for advertisers? Can you think of any examples of ways advertisers package people or groups of people?
5. According to Turow, what social impact does target marketing have on America? Do you agree with his perspective? Explain.
6. Evaluate Turow's tone in this essay. What phrases or words reveal his tone? Who is his audience? How does this tone connect to his intended audience?
7. What are primary media communities? How do they help advertisers market a product?
8. Why would producers of certain programs actually want to chase away certain viewers? How can audience exclusion actually help improve a market or sell a product?

CRITICAL WRITING

1. *Research and Exploratory Writing:* Locate a few advertisements or write down the details of a few commercials for some popular products. Write about each ad's intended audience. Applying some of the information you learned from Turow's article, discuss the ways your ads are targeted to specific audiences. Do they exploit cultural fissures? Do you think they help contribute to the fragmenting of American culture? Explain your viewpoint.
2. *Persuasive Writing:* Turow comments that "new approaches to marketing make it increasingly worthwhile for . . . media companies to separate audiences into different worlds according to distinctions that ad people feel make the audiences feel secure and comfortable" (paragraph 7). What types of ads appeal to you and why? Do you feel that advertisements that actively target you as part of a particular segment of society work more

effectively on you as a consumer? Explain your perspective in a well-considered essay. Cite specific ads in your response to support your view.

3. *Exploratory Writing:* Write an essay in which you explore the connection between product targeting, audience packaging, and social diversification.

GROUP PROJECTS

1. Turow describes some of the ways advertisers target audiences by exploiting cultural divisions in American society. You and the members of your group are members of an advertising agency developing a campaign for a new cologne. First, determine to whom you will market this new product and then create an advertising strategy for the product. What will your ads look like? If you use commercials, when will they air and during what programs? Explain the rationale for your campaign to the class, referring to some of the points Turow makes in his article about product targeting.

2. Select several advertisements from a diversified collection of magazines (news, fashion, business, music, etc.). With your group, try to determine the ways in which each ad uses product targeting. Based on your results, present the advertisements to a few people that you feel fit the audience profile you linked to the ad. Ask them for their impressions of the advertisement and its overall effectiveness. Discuss the results with your group.

Will Your Recession Be Tall, Grande, or Venti?
*Daniel Gross**

How could coffee, that morning staple on which so many of us depend, also be linked to the health of our economy? While financial gurus argue over the deciding factors of our current recession and the direction it will take, business columnist Daniel Gross has already figured it out. The problem he explains, is Starbucks. In this next editorial, Gross illustrates the correlation between having too many Starbucks and having a financial crisis. Perhaps economists should be counting the number of baristas when they judge the direction the economy will take.

1 Remember Thomas Friedman's McDonald's theory of international relations? The thinking was that if two countries had evolved into prosperous, mass-consumer societies, with middle classes able to afford Big Macs, they would generally find peaceful means of adjudicating disputes. They'd sit down over a Happy Meal to resolve issues rather than use mortars. The recent unpleasantries between Israel and Lebanon, which both have McDonald's operations, put paid to that reasoning. But the Golden Arches theory of realpolitik was good while it lasted.

2 In the same spirit, I propose the Starbucks theory of international economics. The higher the concentration of expensive, nautically themed, faux-Italian-branded

* Daniel Gross, *Slate* Magazine, October 20, 2008

Frappuccino joints in a country's financial capital, the more likely the country is to have suffered catastrophic financial losses.

> **"We haven't heard much about bailouts in Central America, where Starbucks has no presence."**

3   It may sound doppio, but work with me. This recent crisis has its roots in the unhappy coupling of a frenzied nationwide real-estate market centered in California, Las Vegas, and Florida, and a nationwide credit mania centered in New York. If you could pick one brand name that personified these twin bubbles, it was Starbucks. The Seattle-based coffee chain followed new housing developments into the suburbs and exurbs, where its outlets became pit stops for real-estate brokers and their clients. It also carpet-bombed the business districts of large cities, especially the financial centers, with nearly 200 in Manhattan alone. Starbucks' frothy treats provided the fuel for the boom, the caffeine that enabled deal jockeys to stay up all hours putting together offering papers for CDOs, and helped mortgage brokers work overtime processing dubious loan documents. Starbucks strategically located many of its outlets on the ground floors of big investment banks. (The one around the corner from the former Bear Stearns headquarters has already closed.)

4   Like American financial capitalism, Starbucks, fueled by the capital markets, took a great idea too far (quality coffee for Starbucks, securitization for Wall Street) and diluted the experience unnecessarily (subprime food such as egg-and-sausage sandwiches for Starbucks, subprime loans for Wall Street). Like so many sadder-but-wiser Miami condo developers, Starbucks operated on a "build it and they will come" philosophy. Like many of the humiliated Wall Street firms, the coffee company let algorithms and number-crunching get the better of sound judgment: If the waiting time at one Starbucks was over a certain number of minutes, Starbucks reasoned that an opposite corner could sustain a new outlet. Like the housing market, Starbucks peaked in the spring of 2006 and has since fallen precipitously.

5   America's financial crisis has gone global in the past month. European and Asian governments, which until recently were rejoicing over America's financial downfall, have had to nationalize banks and expand depositors' insurance. Why? Many of their banks feasted on American subprime debt and took shoddy risk-management cues from their American cousins. Indeed, the countries whose financial sectors were most connected to the U.S.-dominated global financial system, the ones whose financial institutions plunged into CDOs, credit-default swaps, and the whole catalog of horribles have suffered the most.

6   What does this have to do with the price of coffee? Well, when you start poking around Starbucks' international store locator, some interesting patterns emerge. At first blush, there's a pretty close correlation between a country having a significant Starbucks presence, especially in its financial capital, and major financial cock-ups, from Australia (big blowups in finance, hedge funds, and asset management companies; 23 stores) to the United Kingdom (nationalization of its largest banks). In many ways, London in recent years has been a more concentrated version of New York—the wellspring of many toxic innovations, a hedge-fund haven. It sports 256 Starbucks. In Spain, which is now grappling with the bursting of a speculative coastal real-estate bubble (sound familiar?), the financial capital, Madrid, has 48 outlets.

In crazy Dubai, 48 Starbucks outlets serve a population of 1.4 million. And so on: South Korea, which is bailing outs its banks big time, has 253; Paris, the locus of several embarrassing debacles, has 35.

7   But there are many spots on the globe where it's tough to find a Starbucks. And these are precisely the places where banks are surviving, in large part because they have not financially integrated with banks in the Starbucks economies. In the entire continent of Africa, whose banks don't stray too far, I count just three (in Egypt). We haven't heard much about bailouts in Central America, where Starbucks has no presence. South America's banks may be buckling, but they haven't broken. Argentina, formerly a financial basket case and now a pocket of relative strength, has just one store. Brazil, with a population of nearly 200 million, has a mere 14. Italy hasn't suffered any major bank failures in part because its banking sector isn't very active on the international scene. The number of Starbucks there? Zero. And the small countries of Northern Europe, whose banking systems have been largely spared, are largely Starbucks-free. (There are two in Denmark, three in the Netherlands, and none in the Scandinavian trio of Sweden, Finland, and Norway.)

8   My tentative theory: Having a significant Starbucks presence is a pretty significant indicator of the degree of connectedness to the form of highly caffeinated, free-spending capitalism that got us into this mess. It's also a sign of a culture's willingness to abandon traditional norms and ways of doing business (virtually all the countries in which Starbucks has established beachheads have their own venerable coffee-house traditions) in favor of fast-moving American ones. The fact that the company or its local licensee felt there was room for dozens of outlets where consumers would pony up lots of euros, liras, and rials for expensive drinks is also a pretty good indicator that excessive financial optimism had entered the bloodstream.

9   This theory isn't foolproof. Some places that have relatively high concentrations of Starbucks, such as Santiago, Chile (27), have been safe havens. Russia, which has just six, has blown up. But it's close enough. And so, if you're looking for potential trouble spots, forget about the *Financial Times* or the Bloomberg terminal. Just look at the user-friendly Starbucks store locator. The next potential trouble spot? I just returned from a week in Istanbul, Turkey, a booming financial capital increasingly tied to the fortunes of Western Europe. It has a storied coffee culture, yet I gave up counting the number of Starbucks stores occupying prime real estate. It turns out there are 67 of them. Watch out, Turkey. ◆

CRITICAL THINKING

1. What is the tone of Gross's article? Is it serious, tongue-in-cheek, sarcastic, angry, harsh, or something else? Give at least one example from the text to support your opinion.
2. Does Gross convince you of his "Starbucks theory of international economics"? What do you find convincing or not convincing?
3. In the last paragraph of this article, Gross gives a warning to Turkey. What is the warning?
4. Gross uses interesting vocabulary in his article to support his points. Find unfamiliar words, uncommon vocabulary, or the use of slang and acronyms in his article. Why do you think he chose to use those precise words?

5. What image does Starbucks have? How does this image tie in with the economic health of an area?

CRITICAL WRITING

1. *Expository Writing Compare/Contrast*: Read Daniel Gross's article "Obscure Economic Indicator: Keeneland Thoroughbred Sales: What the Price of Racehorses Signals about the Health of the World Economy" posted on the December 2, 2005, edition of *Slate* in which Gross states, "When the world's economy catches a sniffle, the horseflesh market starts wheezing." Compare the correlation between elite racehorses and the economy to the number of Starbucks and the economy. Explain which article makes the better argument. Can you think of other minutiae of American life that might reveal the health of the economy?
2. *Exploratory Writing*: Consider the thesis of this article: "Having a significant Starbucks presence is a pretty significant indicator of the degree of connectedness to the form of highly caffeinated, free-spending capitalism that got us into this mess." Explore other indicators besides Starbucks that proves we are a consumer-driven nation.

GROUP PROJECTS

1. Look up Thomas Friedman's "McDonald's Theory," described in his book *The Lexus and the Olive Tree,* and then summarize this theory in your own words. As a group, discuss Friedman's theory and its strengths and weaknesses.
2. Research the history of the Starbucks franchise—how it started, how it grew, where it is today, and then predict where it will be in the future. Report the key points of your discussion to the class as part of a larger discussion on how consumer culture is tied to the health of the economy.

Just a Little Princess?
*Peggy Orenstein**

To call the allure of princesses a passing fad among little girls is "like calling Harry Potter a book," explains author and noted feminist Peggy Orenstein in a *"New York Times"* commentary. The Disney media engine has been pushing princess culture since practically stumbling upon its popularity in 2001. Today, Disney sales in princess gear exceeds $3 billion. Is the pitch too intense? What does it reveal about how companies market to children? What messages does it send to little girls, and what impact could it have on American culture overall? In the next essay, Orenstein describes her reaction to the princess onslaught and her helplessness to stop it from drawing in her own little girl.

* Peggy Orenstein, *New York Times*, December 2006

1   I finally came unhinged in the dentist's office—one of those ritzy pediatric practices tricked out with comic books, DVDs and arcade games—where I'd taken my 3-year-old daughter for her first exam. Until then, I'd held my tongue. I'd smiled politely every time the supermarket-checkout clerk greeted her with "Hi, Princess," ignored the waitress at our local breakfast joint who called the funny-face pancakes she ordered her "princess meal," made no comment when the lady at Long's Drugs said, "I bet I know your favorite color" and handed her a pink balloon rather than letting her choose for herself. Maybe it was the dentist's Betty Boop inflection that got to me, but when she pointed to the exam chair and said, "Would you like to sit in my special princess throne so I can sparkle your teeth?" I lost it.

2   "Oh, for God's sake," I snapped. "Do you have a princess drill, too?"

3   She stared at me as if I were an evil stepmother.

4   "Come on!" I continued, my voice rising. "It's 2006, not 1950. This is Berkeley, California. Does every little girl really have to be a princess?"

5   My daughter, who was reaching for a Cinderella sticker, looked back and forth between us. "Why are you so mad, Mama?" she asked. "What's wrong with princesses?"

6   Diana may be dead and Masako disgraced, but here in America, we are in the midst of a royal moment. To call princesses a "trend" among girls is like calling Harry Potter a book. Sales at Disney Consumer Products, which started the craze six years ago by packaging nine of its female characters under one royal rubric, have shot up to $3 billion, globally, this year, from $300 million in 2001. There are now more than 25,000 Disney Princess items. "Princess," as some Disney execs call it, is not only the fastest-growing brand the company has ever created; they say it is on its way to becoming the largest girls' franchise on the planet.

7   Meanwhile in 2001, Mattel brought out its own "world of girl" line of princess Barbie dolls, DVDs, toys, clothing, home décor and myriad other products. At a time when Barbie sales were declining domestically, they became instant best sellers. Shortly before that, Mary Drolet, a Chicago-area mother and former Claire's and Montgomery Ward executive, opened Club Libby Lu, now a chain of mall stores based largely in the suburbs in which girls ages 4 to 12 can shop for "Princess Phones" covered in faux fur and attend "Princess-Makeover Birthday Parties." Saks bought Club Libby Lu in 2003 for $12 million and has since expanded it to 87 outlets; by 2005, with only scant local advertising, revenues hovered around the $46 million mark, a 53 percent jump from the previous year. Pink, it seems, is the new gold.

8   Even Dora the Explorer, the intrepid, dirty-kneed adventurer, has ascended to the throne: in 2004, after a two-part episode in which she turns into a "true princess," the Nickelodeon and Viacom consumer-products division released a satin-gowned "Magic Hair Fairytale Dora," with hair that grows or shortens when her crown is touched. Among other phrases the bilingual doll utters: "Vámonos! Let's go to fairy-tale land!" and "Will you brush my hair?"

9   As a feminist mother—not to mention a nostalgic product of the Garanimals era—I have been taken by surprise by the princess craze and the girlie-girl culture that has risen around it. What happened to William wanting a doll and not dressing your cat in an apron? Whither Marlo Thomas? I watch my fellow mothers, women

who once swore they'd never be dependent on a man, smile indulgently at daughters who warble "So This Is Love" or insist on being called Snow White. I wonder if they'd concede so readily to sons who begged for combat fatigues and mock AK-47s.

10   More to the point, when my own girl makes her daily beeline for the dress-up corner of her preschool classroom—something I'm convinced she does largely to torture me—I worry about what playing Little Mermaid is teaching her. I've spent much of my career writing about experiences that undermine girls' well-being, warning parents that a preoccupation with body and beauty (encouraged by films, TV, magazines and, yes, toys) is perilous to their daughters' mental and physical health. Am I now supposed to shrug and forget all that? If trafficking in stereotypes doesn't matter at 3, when does it matter? At 6? Eight? Thirteen?

11   On the other hand, maybe I'm still surfing a washed-out second wave of feminism in a third-wave world. Maybe princesses are in fact a sign of progress, an indication that girls can embrace their predilection for pink without compromising strength or ambition; that, at long last, they can "have it all." Or maybe it is even less complex than that: to mangle Freud, maybe a princess is sometimes just a princess. And, as my daughter wants to know, what's wrong with that?

12   The rise of the Disney princesses reads like a fairy tale itself, with Andy Mooney, a former Nike executive, playing the part of prince, riding into the company on a metaphoric white horse in January 2000 to save a consumer-products division whose sales were dropping by as much as 30 percent a year. Both overstretched and underfocused, the division had triggered price wars by granting multiple licenses for core products (say, Winnie-the-Pooh undies) while ignoring the potential of new media. What's more, Disney films like "A Bug's Life" in 1998 had yielded few merchandising opportunities—what child wants to snuggle up with an ant?

13   It was about a month after Mooney's arrival that the magic struck. That's when he flew to Phoenix to check out his first "Disney on Ice" show. "Standing in line in the arena, I was surrounded by little girls dressed head to toe as princesses," he told me last summer in his palatial office, then located in Burbank, and speaking in a rolling Scottish burr. "They weren't even Disney products. They were generic princess products they'd appended to a Halloween costume. And the light bulb went off. Clearly there was latent demand here. So the next morning I said to my team, 'O.K., let's establish standards and a color palette and talk to licensees and get as much product out there as we possibly can that allows these girls to do what they're doing anyway: projecting themselves into the characters from the classic movies.' "

14   Mooney picked a mix of old and new heroines to wear the Pantone pink No. 241 corona: Cinderella, Sleeping Beauty, Snow White, Ariel, Belle, Jasmine, Mulan and Pocahontas. It was the first time Disney marketed characters separately from a film's release, let alone lumped together those from different stories. To ensure the sanctity of what Mooney called their individual "mythologies," the princesses never make eye contact when they're grouped: each stares off in a slightly different direction as if unaware of the others' presence.

15   It is also worth noting that not all of the ladies are of royal extraction. Part of the genius of "Princess" is that its meaning is so broadly constructed that it actually has no meaning. Even Tinker Bell was originally a Princess, though her reign didn't last. "We'd always debate over whether she was really a part of the Princess mythology,"

Mooney recalled. "She really wasn't." Likewise, Mulan and Pocahontas, arguably the most resourceful of the bunch, are rarely depicted on Princess merchandise, though for a different reason. Their rustic garb has less bling potential than that of old-school heroines like Sleeping Beauty. (When Mulan does appear, she is typically in the kimonolike hanfu, which makes her miserable in the movie, rather than her liberated warrior's gear.)

16   The first Princess items, released with no marketing plan, no focus groups, no advertising, sold as if blessed by a fairy godmother. To this day, Disney conducts little market research on the Princess line, relying instead on the power of its legacy among mothers as well as the instant-read sales barometer of the theme parks and Disney Stores. "We simply gave girls what they wanted," Mooney said of the line's success, "although I don't think any of us grasped how much they wanted this. I wish I could sit here and take credit for having some grand scheme to develop this, but all we did was envision a little girl's room and think about how she could live out the princess fantasy. The counsel we gave to licensees was: What type of bedding would a princess want to sleep in? What kind of alarm clock would a princess want to wake up to? What type of television would a princess like to see? It's a rare case where you find a girl who has every aspect of her room bedecked in Princess, but if she ends up with three or four of these items, well, then you have a very healthy business."

17   Every reporter Mooney talks to asks some version of my next question: Aren't the Princesses, who are interested only in clothes, jewelry and cadging the handsome prince, somewhat retrograde role models?

18   "Look," he said, "I have friends whose son went through the Power Rangers phase who castigated themselves over what they must've done wrong. Then they talked to other parents whose kids had gone through it. The boy passes through. The girl passes through. I see girls expanding their imagination through visualizing themselves as princesses, and then they pass through that phase and end up becoming lawyers, doctors, mothers or princesses, whatever the case may be."

19   Mooney has a point: There are no studies proving that playing princess directly damages girls' self-esteem or dampens other aspirations. On the other hand, there is evidence that young women who hold the most conventionally feminine beliefs— who avoid conflict and think they should be perpetually nice and pretty—are more likely to be depressed than others and less likely to use contraception. What's more, the 23 percent decline in girls' participation in sports and other vigorous activity between middle and high school has been linked to their sense that athletics is unfeminine. And in a survey released last October by Girls Inc., school-age girls overwhelmingly reported a paralyzing pressure to be "perfect": not only to get straight A's and be the student-body president, editor of the newspaper and captain of the swim team but also to be "kind and caring," "please everyone, be very thin and dress right." Give those girls a pumpkin and a glass slipper and they'd be in business.

20   At the grocery store one day, my daughter noticed a little girl sporting a Cinderella backpack. "There's that princess you don't like, Mama!" she shouted.

21   "Um, yeah," I said, trying not to meet the other mother's hostile gaze.

22   "Don't you like her blue dress, Mama?"

23   I had to admit, I did.

24   She thought about this. "Then don't you like her face?"

25   "Her face is all right," I said, noncommittally, though I'm not thrilled to have my Japanese-Jewish child in thrall to those Aryan features. (And what the heck are those blue things covering her ears?) "It's just, honey, Cinderella doesn't really do anything."

26   Over the next 45 minutes, we ran through that conversation, verbatim, approximately 37 million times, as my daughter pointed out Disney Princess Band-Aids, Disney Princess paper cups, Disney Princess lip balm, Disney Princess pens, Disney Princess crayons and Disney Princess notebooks—all cleverly displayed at the eye level of a 3-year-old trapped in a shopping cart—as well as a bouquet of Disney Princess balloons bobbing over the checkout line. The repetition was excessive, even for a preschooler. What was it about my answers that confounded her? What if, instead of realizing: Aha! Cinderella is a symbol of the patriarchal oppression of all women, another example of corporate mind control and power-to-the-people! my 3-year-old was thinking, Mommy doesn't want me to be a girl?

27   According to theories of gender constancy, until they're about 6 or 7, children don't realize that the sex they were born with is immutable. They believe that they have a choice: they can grow up to be either a mommy or a daddy. Some psychologists say that until permanency sets in, kids embrace whatever stereotypes our culture presents, whether it's piling on the most spangles or attacking one another with light sabers. What better way to assure that they'll always remain themselves? If that's the case, score one for Mooney. By not buying the Princess Pull-Ups, I may be inadvertently communicating that being female (to the extent that my daughter is able to understand it) is a bad thing.

28   Anyway, you have to give girls some credit. It's true that, according to Mattel, one of the most popular games young girls play is "bride," but Disney found that a groom or prince is incidental to that fantasy, a regrettable necessity at best. Although they keep him around for the climactic kiss, he is otherwise relegated to the bottom of the toy box, which is why you don't see him prominently displayed in stores.

29   What's more, just because they wear the tulle doesn't mean they've drunk the Kool-Aid. Plenty of girls stray from the script, say, by playing basketball in their finery, or casting themselves as the powerful evil stepsister bossing around the sniveling Cinderella. I recall a headline-grabbing 2005 British study that revealed that girls enjoy torturing, decapitating and microwaving their Barbies nearly as much as they like to dress them up for dates. There is spice along with that sugar after all, though why this was news is beyond me: anyone who ever played with the doll knows there's nothing more satisfying than hacking off all her hair and holding her underwater in the bathtub. Princesses can even be a boon to exasperated parents: in our house, for instance, royalty never whines and uses the potty every single time.

30   "Playing princess is not the issue," argues Lyn Mikel Brown, an author, with Sharon Lamb, of "Packaging Girlhood: Rescuing Our Daughters From Marketers' Schemes." "The issue is 25,000 Princess products," says Brown, a professor of education and human development at Colby College. "When one thing is so dominant, then it's no longer a choice: it's a mandate, cannibalizing all other forms of play. There's the illusion of more choices out there for girls, but if you look around, you'll see their choices are steadily narrowing."

31   It's hard to imagine that girls' options could truly be shrinking when they dominate the honor roll and outnumber boys in college. Then again, have you taken a stroll through a chil-

When one thing is so dominant, then it's no longer a choice: it's a mandate, cannibalizing all other forms of play.

dren's store lately? A year ago, when we shopped for "big girl" bedding at Pottery Barn Kids, we found the "girls" side awash in flowers, hearts and hula dancers; not a soccer player or sailboat in sight. Across the no-fly zone, the "boys" territory was all about sports, trains, planes and automobiles. Meanwhile, Baby GAP's boys' one-sies were emblazoned with "Big Man on Campus" and the girls' with "Social Butterfly"; guess whose matching shoes were decorated on the soles with hearts and whose sported a "No. 1" logo? And at Toys"R"Us, aisles of pink baby dolls, kitchens, shopping carts and princesses unfurl a safe distance from the "Star Wars" figures, GeoTrax and tool chests. The relentless resegregation of childhood appears to have sneaked up without any further discussion about sex roles, about what it now means to be a boy or to be a girl. Or maybe it has happened in lieu of such discussion because it's easier this way.

32   Easier, that is, unless you want to buy your daughter something that isn't pink. Girls' obsession with that color may seem like something they're born with, like the ability to breathe or talk on the phone for hours on end. But according to Jo Paoletti, an associate professor of American studies at the University of Maryland, it ain't so. When colors were first introduced to the nursery in the early part of the 20th century, pink was considered the more masculine hue, a pastel version of red. Blue, with its intimations of the Virgin Mary, constancy and faithfulness, was thought to be dainty. Why or when that switched is not clear, but as late as the 1930s a significant percentage of adults in one national survey held to that split. Perhaps that's why so many early Disney heroines—Cinderella, Sleeping Beauty, Wendy, Alice-in-Wonderland—are swathed in varying shades of azure. (Purple, incidentally, may be the next color to swap teams: once the realm of kings and N.F.L. players, it is fast becoming the bolder girl's version of pink.)

33   It wasn't until the mid-1980s, when amplifying age and sex differences became a key strategy of children's marketing (recall the emergence of " 'tween"), that pink became seemingly innate to girls, part of what defined them as female, at least for the first few years. That was also the time that the first of the generation raised during the unisex phase of feminism—ah, hither Marlo!—became parents. "The kids who grew up in the 1970s wanted sharp definitions for their own kids," Paoletti told me. "I can understand that, because the unisex thing denied everything—you couldn't be this, you couldn't be that, you had to be a neutral nothing."

34   The infatuation with the girlie girl certainly could, at least in part, be a reaction against the so-called second wave of the women's movement of the 1960s and '70s (the first wave was the fight for suffrage), which fought for reproductive rights and economic, social and legal equality. If nothing else, pink and Princess have resuscitated the fantasy of romance that that era of feminism threatened, the privileges that traditional femininity conferred on women despite its costs—doors magically opened, dinner checks picked up, Manolo Blahniks. Frippery. Fun. Why should we

give up the perks of our sex until we're sure of what we'll get in exchange? Why should we give them up at all? Or maybe it's deeper than that: the freedoms feminism bestowed came with an undercurrent of fear among women themselves— flowing through "Ally McBeal," "Bridget Jones's Diary," "Sex and the City"—of losing male love, of never marrying, of not having children, of being deprived of something that felt essentially and exclusively female.

35   I mulled that over while flipping through "The Paper Bag Princess," a 1980 picture book hailed as an antidote to Disney. The heroine outwits a dragon who has kidnapped her prince, but not before the beast's fiery breath frizzles her hair and destroys her dress, forcing her to don a paper bag. The ungrateful prince rejects her, telling her to come back when she is "dressed like a real princess." She dumps him and skips off into the sunset, happily ever after, alone.

36   There you have it, "Thelma and Louise" all over again. Step out of line, and you end up solo or, worse, sailing crazily over a cliff to your doom. Alternatives like those might send you skittering right back to the castle. And I get that: the fact is, though I want my daughter to do and be whatever she wants as an adult, I still hope she'll find her Prince Charming and have babies, just as I have. I don't want her to be a fish without a bicycle; I want her to be a fish with another fish. Preferably, one who loves and respects her and also does the dishes and half the child care.

37   There had to be a middle ground between compliant and defiant, between petticoats and paper bags. I remembered a video on YouTube, an ad for a Nintendo game called Super Princess Peach. It showed a pack of girls in tiaras, gowns and elbow-length white gloves sliding down a zip line on parasols, navigating an obstacle course of tires in their stilettos, slithering on their bellies under barbed wire, then using their telekinetic powers to make a climbing wall burst into flames. "If you can stand up to really mean people," an announcer intoned, "maybe you have what it takes to be a princess."

38   Now here were some girls who had grit as well as grace. I loved Princess Peach even as I recognized that there was no way she could run in those heels, that her peachiness did nothing to upset the apple cart of expectation: she may have been athletic, smart and strong, but she was also adorable. Maybe she's what those once-unisex, postfeminist parents are shooting for: the melding of old and new standards. And perhaps that's a good thing, the ideal solution. But what to make, then, of the young women in the Girls Inc. survey? It doesn't seem to be "having it all" that's getting to them; it's the pressure to be it all. In telling our girls they can be anything, we have inadvertently demanded that they be everything. To everyone. All the time. No wonder the report was titled "The Supergirl Dilemma."

39   The princess as superhero is not irrelevant. Some scholars I spoke with say that given its post-9/11 timing, princess mania is a response to a newly dangerous world. "Historically, princess worship has emerged during periods of uncertainty and profound social change," observes Miriam Forman-Brunell, a historian at the University of Missouri–Kansas City. Francis Hodgson Burnett's original "Little Princess" was published at a time of rapid urbanization, immigration and poverty; Shirley Temple's film version was a hit during the Great Depression. "The original folk tales themselves," Forman-Brunell says, "spring from medieval and early modern European culture that faced all kinds of economic and demographic and social

upheaval—famine, war, disease, terror of wolves. Girls play savior during times of economic crisis and instability." That's a heavy burden for little shoulders. Perhaps that's why the magic wand has become an essential part of the princess get-up. In the original stories—even the Disney versions of them—it's not the girl herself who's magic; it's the fairy godmother. Now if Forman-Brunell is right, we adults have become the cursed creatures whom girls have the thaumaturgic power to transform.

40   In the 1990s, third-wave feminists rebelled against their dour big sisters, "reclaiming" sexual objectification as a woman's right—provided, of course, that it was on her own terms, that she was the one choosing to strip or wear a shirt that said "Porn Star" or make out with her best friend at a frat-house bash. They embraced words like "bitch" and "slut" as terms of affection and empowerment. That is, when used by the right people, with the right dash of playful irony. But how can you assure that? As Madonna gave way to Britney, whatever self-determination that message contained was watered down and commodified until all that was left was a gaggle of 6-year-old girls in belly-baring T-shirts (which I'm guessing they don't wear as cultural critique). It is no wonder that parents, faced with thongs for 8-year-olds and Bratz dolls' "passion for fashion," fill their daughters' closets with pink sateen; the innocence of Princess feels like a reprieve.

41   "But what does that mean?" asks Sharon Lamb, a psychology professor at Saint Michael's College. "There are other ways to express 'innocence'—girls could play ladybug or caterpillar. What you're really talking about is sexual purity. And there's a trap at the end of that rainbow, because the natural progression from pale, innocent pink is not to other colors. It's to hot, sexy pink—exactly the kind of sexualization parents are trying to avoid."

42   Lamb suggested that to see for myself how "Someday My Prince Will Come" morphs into "Oops! I Did It Again," I visit Club Libby Lu, the mall shop dedicated to the "Very Important Princess." Walking into one of the newest links in the store's chain, in Natick, Mass., last summer, I had to tip my tiara to the founder, Mary Drolet: Libby Lu's design was flawless. Unlike Disney, Drolet depended on focus groups to choose the logo (a crown-topped heart) and the colors (pink, pink, purple and more pink). The displays were scaled to the size of a 10-year-old, though most of the shoppers I saw were several years younger than that. The decals on the walls and dressing rooms—"I Love Your Hair," "Hip Chick," "Spoiled"—were written in "girlfriend language." The young sales clerks at this "special secret club for superfabulous girls" are called "club counselors" and come off like your coolest baby sitter, the one who used to let you brush her hair. The malls themselves are chosen based on a company formula called the G.P.I., or "Girl Power Index," which predicts potential sales revenues. Talk about newspeak: "Girl Power" has gone from a riot grrrl anthem to "I Am Woman, Watch Me Shop."

43   Inside, the store was divided into several glittery "shopping zones" called "experiences": Libby's Laboratory, now called Sparkle Spa, where girls concoct their own cosmetics and bath products; Libby's Room; Ear Piercing; Pooch Parlor (where divas in training can pamper stuffed poodles, pugs and Chihuahuas); and the Style Studio, offering "Libby Du" makeover choices, including 'Tween Idol, Rock Star, Pop Star and, of course, Priceless Princess. Each look includes hairstyle, makeup, nail polish and sparkly tattoos.

44   As I browsed, I noticed a mother standing in the center of the store holding a price list for makeover birthday parties—$22.50 to $35 per child. Her name was Anne McAuliffe; her daughters—Stephanie, 4, and 7-year-old twins Rory and Sarah—were dashing giddily up and down the aisles.

45   "They've been begging to come to this store for three weeks," McAuliffe said. "I'd never heard of it. So I said they could, but they'd have to spend their own money if they bought anything." She looked around. "Some of this stuff is innocuous," she observed, then leaned toward me, eyes wide and stage-whispered: "But . . . a lot of it is horrible. It makes them look like little prostitutes. It's crazy. They're babies!"

46   As we debated the line between frivolous fun and JonBenét, McAuliffe's daughter Rory came dashing up, pigtails haphazard, glasses askew. "They have the best pocketbooks here," she said breathlessly, brandishing a clutch with the words "Girlie Girl" stamped on it. "Please, can I have one? It has sequins!"

47   "You see that?" McAuliffe asked, gesturing at the bag. "What am I supposed to say?" On my way out of the mall, I popped into the 'tween mecca Hot Topic, where a display of Tinker Bell items caught my eye. Tinker Bell, whose image racks up an annual $400 million in retail sales with no particular effort on Disney's part, is poised to wreak vengeance on the Princess line that once expelled her. Last winter, the first chapter book designed to introduce girls to Tink and her Pixie Hollow pals spent 18 weeks on the *New York Times* children's best-seller list. In a direct-to-DVD now under production, she will speak for the first time, voiced by the actress Brittany Murphy. Next year, Disney Fairies will be rolled out in earnest. Aimed at 6- to 9-year-old girls, the line will catch them just as they outgrow Princess. Their colors will be lavender, green, turquoise—anything but the Princess's soon-to-be-babyish pink.

48   To appeal to that older child, Disney executives said, the Fairies will have more "attitude" and "sass" than the Princesses. What, I wondered, did that entail? I'd seen some of the Tinker Bell merchandise that Disney sells at its theme parks: T-shirts reading, "Spoiled to Perfection," "Mood Subject to Change Without Notice" and "Tinker Bell: Prettier Than a Princess." At Hot Topic, that edge was even sharper: magnets, clocks, light-switch plates and panties featured "Dark Tink," described as "the bad girl side of Miss Bell that Walt never saw."

49   Girl power, indeed.

50   A few days later, I picked my daughter up from preschool. She came tearing over in a full-skirted frock with a gold bodice, a beaded crown perched sideways on her head. "Look, Mommy, I'm Ariel!" she crowed. referring to Disney's Little Mermaid. Then she stopped and furrowed her brow. "Mommy, do you like Ariel?"

51   I considered her for a moment. Maybe Princess is the first salvo in what will become a lifelong struggle over her body image, a Hundred Years' War of dieting, plucking, painting and perpetual dissatisfaction with the results. Or maybe it isn't. I'll never really know. In the end, it's not the Princesses that really bother me anyway. They're just a trigger for the bigger question of how, over the years, I can help my daughter with the contradictions she will inevitably face as a girl, the dissonance that is as endemic as ever to growing up female. Maybe the best I can hope for is that her generation will get a little further with the solutions than we did.

52   For now, I kneeled down on the floor and gave my daughter a hug.

53   She smiled happily. "But, Mommy?" she added. "When I grow up, I'm still going to be a fireman." ◆

CRITICAL THINKING

1. Think about your consumer habits as a child. What did you want to buy, and how did you learn about the product? What made you want the product?

2. Why does the author object so strongly to the idea of princesses and princess toys? Explain.

3. How did Disney fill in the niche that little girls had created themselves? In your opinion, do you think the company went overboard? Why or why not?

4. Lyn Mikel Brown, co-author of *Packaging Girlhood: Rescuing Our Daughters from Marketers' Schemes*, notes "When one thing is so dominant, then it's no longer a choice: it's a mandate, cannibalizing all other forms of play." In what ways has the princess craze "cannibalized" other forms of play?

5. In addition to princesses, to what other toys and products does the author object and why?

6. How does the concept of princess conflict with the principles of feminism? Can a little girl understand both? Why or why not?

7. This article focuses on how young girls are the target of marketing gimmicks that channel them to desire certain toys and embrace certain types of play. Can the same argument be made for little boys? Explain.

8. What is the author's conclusion about the princess trend and her daughter? Does the author feel she is fighting a losing battle? What would you do in the same situation? Explain.

CRITICAL WRITING

1. *Research Writing:* Are popular toys—such as Princess gear, Bratz dolls, Lego sets, Matchbox cars—leading kids to unconsciously embrace prescribed gender roles? Visit the toy section of a department store such as Target, Walmart, or Kmart and take a look at the merchandise options. Write an essay discussing how the toys you saw could influence gender roles for children.

2. *Personal Narrative:* Write about how any toys you played with as a child did or did not influence the way you viewed yourself and the world around you.

GROUP PROJECTS

1. In small groups, research how popular culture, media, and marketing—including Internet and television—sell products to children. Locate Websites and identify television programs that target children. How do theme parks, such as Disneyland, and merchandise, such as DVDs and books, also

influence children? Report your findings to the class as part of a broader group discussion on this issue.

2. Research the Disney Princess phenomenon online and in stores—and even with children who play "princess." The author conjectures a few reasons for why princess play is popular with little girls. As a group, discuss the phenomenon and the popularity behind princess play. Why do you think it is so popular today? Do you think it can be harmful to young girls? Explain.

3. As a group, analyze several commercials airing during television programs for young children (girls as well as boys) and analyze them. How do the commercials use color, music, graphics, narration, other children, and celebrities to promote their product? What cultural assumptions do they make? How do they target little children? Do they lead children to embrace certain types of play? Explain.

Perspectives: Vital Signs

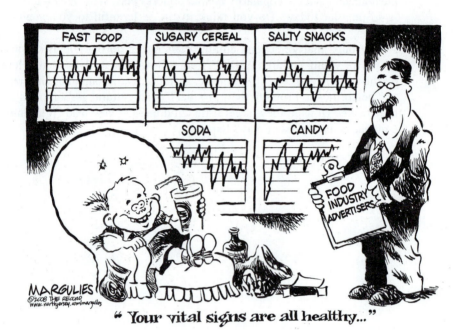

" Your vital signs are all healthy... "

THINKING CRITICALLY

1. What is your perception of how children are targeted by advertisers today? Have brand awareness and demand for branded products increased since you were a child? Explain your point of view.
2. What are the most troubling elements of children's consumer culture? What is the relationship between children's culture and consumer culture? Explain.
3. In your opinion, what limits, if any, should be imposed on advertising for the children's market? Explain.
4. What is this cartoon's claim about the trend toward marketing to children? What is the cartoonist trying to achieve?

CULTURE SHOCK

A Portfolio of Advertisements

The following section features 10 recently published magazine advertisements. Diverse in content and style, some ads use words to promote the product; others depend on emotion, name recognition, visual appeal, or association. They present a variety of sales pitches and marketing techniques. The ads are followed by questions to help you analyze how the ads work their appeal to promote their products. When studying them, consider how they target our social perception and basic desires for happiness, beauty, and success. Approach each as a consumer, an artist, a social scientist, and a critic with an eye for detail.

G A P

1. What is the expression of the woman in this ad? How does her expression contribute to the tone the ad wishes to set?
2. Do you know who the woman in the ad is? What sort of person do you imagine her to be? What is she wearing? Is what she is wearing important in promoting the product—a line of clothing? How does her role in pop culture promote the product?
3. What is this woman known for? Why do you think she is pictured without the equipment she uses as part of her profession?
4. Who would you say is the target audience for this ad? Why? Consider age, gender, lifestyle, and so on in your response.
5. Consider the different angles from which photographs included in this ad might have been taken. How would the ad's impact be different if the photo were shot from above? What if the woman in the photo were looking directly at the camera? Explain.

BOYS AND GIRLS CLUBS ——————————————

1. Do you find this ad particularly compelling? Why or why not? What kind of an impact does the universal statement made by the group have on the reader? Explain.
2. What is happening in this ad? Does the photographic element make the ad more effective? If so, why?
3. If you were leafing through a magazine and saw this ad, would you stop to look at it? Why or why not?
4. What message is this ad trying to convey? To whom is it addressed? What action does it want consumers to take?

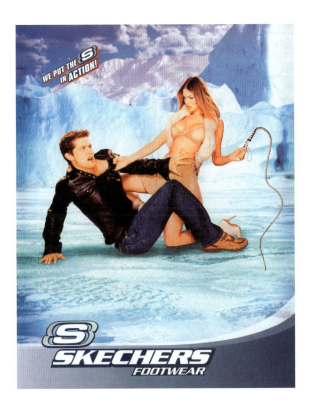

SKECHERS

1. Examine this advertisement carefully. What is happening in this ad? How does it sell footwear?
2. How do the artic setting, mountains, and ice contribute to the image? Do these elements tap into audience expectations about the product? Are they confusing? Entertaining? Explain.
3. Would you know what this ad was selling if there were no copy in the ad? Explain.
4. If you were leafing through a magazine and saw this ad, would you stop to read it? Why or why not?
5. Explain how this advertisement plays with language and our understanding of the conventions of expression.
6. In January 2007, Dolce and Gabbana pulled an ad that depicted an image that could have been interpreted as promoting violence against women (search Google under "controversial Dolce and Gabbana ad"). Could this ad be viewed similarly? Why or why not?

M & M'S

1. Evaluate this advertisement's use of color and texture. How does it promote the product? Would the effectiveness of this ad be the same if it were printed in black and white, such as in a newspaper? Explain.
2. What is this ad mimicking? Explain.
3. None of the text in this advertisement is "serious"; that is, the advertisers do not "speak" to the audience about the product. Evaluate the use of text in this ad. How does it complement the picture? Is anything lost by not telling the audience about the product? Why or why not?
4. Would you stop and look at this ad? Why or why not?
5. Evaluate the personification of the candy in this ad. Does this seem like an effective vehicle to promote the product? Explain.

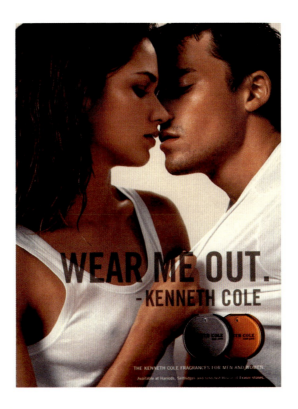

KENNETH COLE

1. What is this ad selling? How can you tell? If you had never heard of the company, Kenneth Cole, what might you guess this ad was selling? Explain.
2. How do the woman and man "sell" the fragrance?
3. Who is the target audience for this ad? How does the ad appeal to this target audience?
4. Would the impression of this ad, or its presumed effectiveness, be different if the subjects were smiling? Standing up straight? Who or why not?
5. Does this ad appeal to you? Why or why not?

1,000 songs. Impossibly small. iPod nano

A P P L E i P O D N A N O

1. If you did not know what an iPod was, could you determine anything about it from this ad? Explain.
2. How important is brand-name recognition to the success of this ad? Who would know what this brand was and what it was selling?
3. Who is the target audience for this brand? How does this ad appeal to that audience?
4. Would this ad be more effective or less effective if it did not feature a person holding the product? Explain.

HONDA

1. What makes you look at the ad? Why?
2. What does the image have to do with the product being sold? Do you find this ad confusing? Smart? Clever? Weird? Funny? Explain.
3. How does the written copy on the banana sell the product? How does the image of the banana reinforce the ad copy?
4. Who do you think is the target audience for this advertisement? How do you think a child would respond to it? A woman? A man? Explain.
5. Evaluate how symbolism serves as an unspoken form of language. How does symbolism work to sell the product in this advertisement?

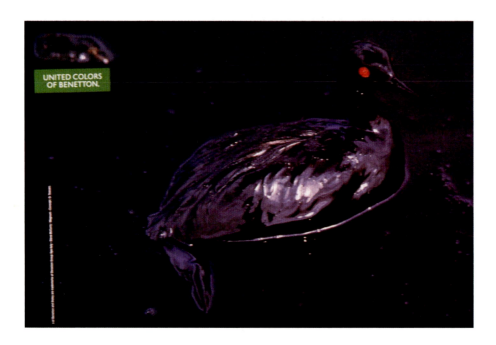

UNITED COLORS OF BENETTON ————————————————

1. What is the purpose of this ad? What is it selling?
2. How is this ad connected to the product it promotes?
3. What are your gut reactions to this ad? Do you find it disturbing? Offensive? Effective? Enlightening? Explain.
4. Evaluate the effectiveness of photographic decisions in this ad.

Which One of These Sneakers Is Me?
*Douglas Rushkoff**

Brand-name products target groups of consumers: sometimes large, diverse populations, such as Pepsi or Coke, or elite ones, such as Coach or Gucci. Brands depend on image—the image they promote and the image the consumer believes they will project by using the product. For teens, brands can announce membership in a particular group, value system, and personality type. Media analyst Douglas Rushkoff explains in this article that the younger generation is more consumer savvy, forcing retailers to rethink how they brand and market goods. Brands are still very important to them, but they like to think they are hip to the advertising game. But as Rushkoff explains, it is a game they cannot win.

1   I was in one of those sports "superstores" the other day, hoping to find a pair of trainers for myself. As I faced the giant wall of shoes, each model categorized by either sports affiliation, basketball star, economic class, racial heritage, or consumer niche, I noticed a young boy standing next to me, maybe 13 years old, in even greater awe of the towering selection of footwear.

2   His jaw was dropped and his eyes were glazed over—a psycho-physical response to the overwhelming sensory data in a self-contained consumer environment. It's a phenomenon known to retail architects as "Gruen Transfer," named for the gentleman who invented the shopping mall, where this mental paralysis is most commonly observed.

3   Having finished several years of research on this exact mind state, I knew to proceed with caution. I slowly made my way to the boy's side and gently asked him, "What is going through your mind right now?"

4   He responded without hesitation, "I don't know which of these trainers is 'me.'" The boy proceeded to explain his dilemma. He thought of Nike as the most utilitarian and scientifically advanced shoe, but had heard something about third-world laborers and was afraid that wearing this brand might label him as too anti-Green. He then considered a skateboard shoe, Airwalk, by an "indie" manufacturer (the trainer equivalent of a micro-brewery), but had recently learned that this company was almost as big as Nike. The truly hip brands of skate shoe were too esoteric for his current profile at school—he'd look like he was "trying." This left the "retro" brands, like Puma, Converse, and Adidas, none of which he felt any real affinity for, since he wasn't even alive in the 70s, when they were truly and nonironically popular.

5   With no clear choice and, more importantly, no other way to conceive of his own identity, the boy stood there, paralyzed in the modern youth equivalent of an existential crisis. Which brand am I, anyway?

6   Believe it or not, there are dozens, perhaps hundreds of youth culture marketers who have already begun clipping out this article. They work for hip, new advertising agencies and cultural research firms who trade in the psychology of our children

*Douglas Rushkoff, *The London Times*, April 30, 2000

and the anthropology of their culture. The object of their labors is to create precisely the state of confusion and vulnerability experienced by the young shopper at the shoe wall—and then turn this

Marketers spend millions developing strategies to identify children's predilections and then capitalize on their vulnerabilities.

state to their advantage. It is a science, though not a pretty one.

7   Yes, our children are the prey and their consumer loyalty is the prize in an escalating arms race. Marketers spend millions developing strategies to identify children's predilections and then capitalize on their vulnerabilities. Young people are fooled for a while, but then develop defense mechanisms, such as media-savvy attitudes or ironic dispositions. Then marketers research these defenses, develop new countermeasures, and on it goes. The revolutionary impact of a new musical genre is co-opted and packaged by a major label before it reaches the airwaves. The ability of young people to deconstruct and neutralize the effects of one advertising technique are thwarted when they are confounded by yet another. The liberation children experience when they discover the Internet is quickly counteracted by the lure of e-commerce Web sites, which are customized to each individual user's psychological profile in order to maximize their effectiveness.

8   The battle in which our children are engaged seems to pass beneath our radar screens, in a language we don't understand. But we see the confusion and despair that results—not to mention the ever-increasing desperation with which even 3-year-olds yearn for the next Pokemon trading card. How did we get in this predicament, and is there a way out? Is it your imagination, you wonder, or have things really gotten worse?

9   Alas, things seem to have gotten worse. Ironically, this is because things had gotten so much better.

10   In olden times—back when those of us who read the newspaper grew up—media was a one-way affair. Advertisers enjoyed a captive audience, and could quite authoritatively provoke our angst and stoke our aspirations. Interactivity changed all this. The remote control gave viewers the ability to break the captive spell of television programming whenever they wished, without having to get up and go all the way up to the set. Young people proved particularly adept at "channel surfing," both because they grew up using the new tool, and because they felt little compunction to endure the tension-provoking narratives of storytellers who did not have their best interests at heart. It was as if young people knew that the stuff on television was called "programming" for a reason and developed shortened attention spans for the purpose of keeping themselves from falling into the spell of advertisers. The remote control allowed young people to deconstruct TV.

11   The next weapon in the child's arsenal was the video game joystick. For the first time, viewers had control over the very pixels on their monitors. The television image was demystified.

12   Lastly, the computer mouse and keyboard transformed the TV receiver into a portal. Today's young people grew up in a world where a screen could as easily be used for expressing oneself as consuming the media of others. Now the media was up for grabs, and the ethic, from hackers to camcorder owners, was "do it yourself."

13   Of course, this revolution had to be undone. Television and Internet programmers, responding to the unpredictable viewing habits of the newly liberated, began to call our media space an "attention economy." No matter how many channels they had for their programming, the number of "eyeball hours" that human beings were willing to dedicate to that programming was fixed. Not coincidentally, the channel surfing habits of our children became known as "attention deficit disorder"—a real disease now used as an umbrella term for anyone who clicks away from programming before the marketer wants him to. We quite literally drug our children into compliance. Likewise, as computer interfaces were made more complex and opaque—think Windows—the do-it-yourself ethic of the Internet was undone. The original Internet was a place to share ideas and converse with others. Children actually had to use the keyboard! Now, the Internet encourages them to click numbly through packaged content. Web sites are designed to keep young people from using the keyboard, except to enter in their parents' credit card information.

14   But young people had been changed by their exposure to new media. They constituted a new "psychographic," as advertisers like to call it, so new kinds of messaging had to be developed that appealed to their new sensibility.

15   Anthropologists—the same breed of scientists that used to scope out enemy populations before military conquests—engaged in focus groups, conducted "trend-watching" on the streets, in order to study the emotional needs and subtle behaviors of young people. They came to understand, for example, how children had abandoned narrative structures for fear of the way stories were used to coerce them. Children tended to construct narratives for themselves by collecting things instead, like cards, bottlecaps called "pogs," or keychains and plush toys. They also came to understand how young people despised advertising—especially when it did not acknowledge their media-savvy intelligence.

16   Thus, Pokemon was born—a TV show, video game, and product line where the object is to collect as many trading cards as possible. The innovation here, among many, is the marketer's conflation of TV show and advertisement into one piece of media. The show and movies are essentially long advertisements. The storyline, such as it is, concerns a boy who must collect little monsters in order to develop his own character. Likewise, the Pokemon video game engages the player in a quest for those monsters. Finally, the card game itself (for the few children who actually play it) involves collecting better monsters—not by playing, but by buying more cards. The more cards you buy, the better you can play.

17   Kids feel the tug, but in a way they can't quite identify as advertising. Their compulsion to create a story for themselves—in a world where stories are dangerous—makes them vulnerable to this sort of attack. In marketers' terms, Pokemon is "leveraged" media, with "cross-promotion" on "complementary platforms." This is ad-speak for an assault on multiple fronts.

18   Moreover, the time a child spends in the Pokemon craze amounts to a remedial lesson in how to consume. Pokemon teaches them how to want things that they can't or won't actually play with. In fact, it teaches them how to buy things they don't even want. While a child might want one particular card, he needs to purchase them in packages whose contents are not revealed. He must buy blind and repeatedly until he gets the object of his desire.

19   Worse yet, the card itself has no value—certainly not as a plaything. It is a functionless purchase, slipped into a display case, whose value lies purely in its possession. It is analogous to those children who buy action figures from their favorite TV shows and movies with no intention of ever removing them from their packaging! They are purchased for their collectible value alone. Thus, the imagination game is reduced to some fictional moment in the future where they will, presumably, be resold to another collector. Children are no longer playing. They are investing.

20   Meanwhile, older kids have attempted to opt out of aspiration altogether. The "15–24" demographic, considered by marketers the most difficult to wrangle into submission, have adopted a series of postures they hoped would make them impervious to marketing techniques. They take pride in their ability to recognize when they are being pandered to and watch TV for the sole purpose of calling out when they are being manipulated. They are armchair media theorists, who take pleasure in deconstructing and defusing the messages of their enemies.

21   But now advertisers are making commercials just for them. Soft drink advertisements satirize one another before rewarding the cynical viewer: "image is nothing," they say. The technique might best be called "wink" advertising, for its ability to engender a young person's loyalty by pretending to disarm itself. "Get it?" the ad means to ask. If you're cool, you do.

22   New magazine advertisements for jeans, such as those created by Diesel, take this even one step further. The ads juxtapose imagery that actually makes no sense—ice cream billboards in North Korea, for example. The strategy is brilliant. For a media-savvy young person to feel good about himself, he needs to feel he "gets" the joke. But what does he do with an ad where there's obviously something to get that he can't figure out? He has no choice but to admit that the brand is even cooler than he is. An ad's ability to confound its audience is the new credential for a brand's authenticity.

23   Like the boy at the wall of shoes, kids today analyze each purchase they make, painstakingly aware of how much effort has gone into seducing them. As a result, they see their choices of what to watch and what to buy as exerting some influence over the world around them. After all, their buying patterns have become the center of so much attention!

24   But however media-savvy kids get, they will always lose this particular game. For they have accepted the language of brands as their cultural currency and the stakes in their purchasing decisions as something real. For no matter how much control kids get over the media they watch, they are still utterly powerless when it comes to the manufacturing of brands. Even a consumer revolt merely reinforces one's role as a consumer, not an autonomous or creative being.

25   The more they interact with brands, the more they brand themselves. ◆

CRITICAL THINKING

1. When you were a teenager, did you have particular brands to which you were most loyal? Did this loyalty change as you got older? Why did you prefer certain brands over others? What cultural and social influences contributed to your desire for that brand?

2. What can a brand tell you about the person who uses it? Explain.
3. Look up the phrase "Gruen Transfer" on the Internet. Were you aware of this angle of marketing practice? Does it change the way you think about how products are sold to you?
4. While the boy's dilemma in Rushkoff's introduction is humorous on the surface, it is a serious situation for the teen. Why is his choice of sneaker so important to him? What expectations does he seem to connect with his choice? What could happen if he picks the wrong shoe?
5. In order to stay in business, marketers have had to rethink how they sell products to the youth market. How is the youth market changing the way marketers do business? Explain.
6. How does Rushkoff support his essay? Evaluate his use of supporting sources. Are there any gaps in his article? If so, identify areas where his essay could be stronger. If not, highlight some of the essay's particular strengths.
7. In paragraph 9, Rushkoff notes that things have gotten worse because they have gotten better. What does he mean? What is the irony of the youth consumer market?
8. Rushkoff notes in paragraph 14 that the youth generation "constitutes a new psychographic." What makes this generation different from previous generations of consumers? If you are a part of this generation (ages 12 to 21), explain why you think you do or do not represent a "new psychographic."
9. In his conclusion, Rushkoff predicts that even media-savvy kids will still "lose" the game. Why will they fail? Explain.

CRITICAL WRITING

1. *Exploratory Writing:* Teens and young adults covet certain brand name clothing because they believe it promotes a particular image. What defines brand image? Is it something created by the company or by the people who use the product? How does advertising influence the social view we have of ourselves and of the brands we use? Write an essay on the connections between advertising and our cultural values of what is "in" and what is not.
2. *Interview:* Ask several people about the products they like and why they like them. Inquire about what they like about a brand and the reasons why they would not buy another brand. Ask your subjects to what degree brand factors into their decision to buy a particular product. Evaluate the results in a short essay on the purchasing habits of consumers and the importance of brands.

GROUP PROJECTS

1. In small groups, do some research on how the Internet is used as a marketing tool to sell to children. Locate Web sites for toys and games and evaluate how they market to children. What do these sites offer? How do they contribute to the desirability and sale of the product? Report your findings to the class.

2. In the past, toys modeled after a particular television program proved popular and marketable. As Rushkoff describes in the case of Pokemon, now toys are created first, and the television program and Internet Web site help market the product. Each member of your group should select a different popular cartoon to watch and research. After viewing each cartoon for a few days, research the products that are associated with the cartoon. In class, discuss how today's cartoons promote products.

3. Each member of your group should watch an hour of television aimed at children: Saturday morning programs, after-school features, Nickelodeon, or the Cartoon Network. Jot down the shows you watch and all the commercials that run during the programs. Include how much time is spent airing commercials. As a group, analyze the data. How many commercials ran during a 15-minute segment of programming? Was there a pattern to the commercials? Did any seem manipulative or compelling, and if so, how? (As an additional writing project, watch these programs with a child. Note his or her responses to the commercials. Did the child seem influenced by the ads? Explain.)

The Allure of Luxury
*James B. Twitchell**

While media and academic critics question the methods of advertising agencies and lament the sacrifice of values in the name of consumerism, professor James B. Twitchell openly embraces the media-driven world of advertising. In the next piece, Twitchell explores the joys of luxury and challenges the academic criticism that condemns our material instincts as shallow and self-centered. He realizes that his viewpoint may not be popular, but it is honest. Because the truth is, we love nice stuff. Is that so wrong?

At length I recollected the thoughtless saying of a great prince who, on being informed that the country had no bread, replied, "Let them eat cake."
—Jean-Jacques Rousseau, *Confessions*

1 Well, okay, so Marie Antoinette never said, "Let them eat cake." When Rousseau wrote those words, Marie was just 11 years old and living in Austria. But Americans used to like the story that, when the French queen was told by an official that the people were angry because they had no bread, she responded, *"Qu'ils mangent de la brioche."* We liked to imagine her saying it with a snarl and a curled lip. She was a luxury bimbo whose out-of-control spending grated on the poor and unfortunate French people. We fought a revolution to separate ourselves from exactly that kind of uppercrustiness. She got her just "desserts."

2 But that was 200 years ago. Now cake is one of *our* favorite foods, part of the fifth food group, totally unnecessary luxury consumption. We're not talking about a few crumbs, but the real stuff. Brioche by the loaf. Not for nothing has Marie become a favorite subject for current infotainment. Novelists, historians, biographers, and even hip young filmmaker Sofia Coppola are telling her story, not because we want her reviled but because we want to be like her.

3 And we're doing a pretty good job. Luxury spending in the United States has been growing more than four times as fast as overall spending, and the rest of the West is not far behind. You might think that modern wannabe Maries are grayhairs with poodles. Not so. This spending is being done by younger and younger consumers. Take a walk up Fifth Avenue, and then, at 58th, cross over and continue up Madison. You'll see who is swarming through the stores with names we all recognize: Louis Vuitton, Gucci, Prada, Dior, Coach.... Or cruise Worth Avenue or Rodeo Drive, and you'll see the same furious down-marketing and up-crusting. This is the Twinkiefication of deluxe.

4 You don't have to go to these streets of dreams to see who's on a sugar high. Take a tour of your local Costco or Sam's Club discount warehouse and you'll see the same stuff, only a day old and about to become stale, being consumed by a slightly older crowd. Observe the parking lot, where shiny new imported sedans and SUVs are parked beside aging subcompacts. Or spend an hour watching the Home

---

* James Twitchell, *The Wilson Quarterly*, Winter 2007

Shopping Network, a televised flea market for impulse buyers. Its call centers now have some 23,000 incoming phone lines capable of handling up to 20,000 calls a minute. The network no longer sells cubic zirconia rings. It sells Gucci handbags.

5   We've developed a powerful desire to associate with recognized objects of little intrinsic but high positional value, which is why Martha Stewart, our faux Marie, is down at Kmart introducing her Silver Label goods, why a courtier the likes of Michael Graves is designing toasters for Target (pronounced by wits, with an ironic French flair, tar-ZHAY), why the Duke of Polo, Ralph Lauren, is marketing house paint, and why suave Cole Porter–brand furniture is appearing on the floor at Ethan Allen stores.

6   Look around, and you will see that almost every category of consumables has cake at the top. This is true not just for expensive products such as town cars and McMansions, but for everyday objects. In bottled water, for instance, there is Evian, advertised as if it were a liqueur. In coffee, there's Starbucks; in ice cream, Häagen-Dazs; in sneakers, Nike; in wine, Chateau Mar-

> *[Now] the duchess's precious things are within your grimy reach. From her point of view, she might just as well take 'em to the dump.*

gaux; in cigars, Arturo Fuente Hemingway, and well, you know the rest. Having a few TVs around the house is fine, but what you really need is a home entertainment center worthy of Versailles, with a JBL Ultra Synthesis One audio system, a Vidikron Vision One front projector, a Stewart Ultramatte 150 screen, a Pioneer DV-09 DVD player, and an AMX ViewPoint remote control. Hungry for chow with your entertainment? Celebrity chef Wolfgang Puck has his own line of TV dinner entrées.

7   Ironically, what this poaching of deluxe by the middle class has done is make things impossible for the truly rich. Ponder this: A generation ago, the Duke and Duchess of Windsor surrounded themselves with the world's finest goods—from jewelry to bed linens to flatware. The duchess, the twice-divorced American Wallis Simpson, would never be queen, but that didn't prevent her from carrying off a passable imitation of Marie. In the Windsor household, the coasters were Cartier and the placemats were Porthault, and the pooches ate from silver-plated Tiffany bowls.

8   When Sotheby's auctioned more than 40,000 items from the Windsors' Paris home in 1997, the remnants of their royal life went out for bid. Most of the items listed in the Sotheby's catalog are still being made, either in the same form or in an updated version. In other words, the duchess's precious things are within your grimy reach. From her point of view, she might just as well take 'em to the dump.

9   • Chanel faux-pearl earrings given to the duchess by the duke can be picked up for about $360 at Chanel stores.

10   • The duchess's Cartier love bracelet in 18-karat gold with screw closure, which was presented by the president of Cartier to the Windsors and other "great lovers" in 1970 (among the other recipients: Elizabeth Taylor and Richard Burton, Sophia Loren and Carlo Ponti), is yours for $3,625 at Cartier boutiques.

11   • T. Anthony luggage, the Windsors' favorite (they owned 118 such trunks), is still being manufactured and can be bought in Manhattan.

12 • Hand-embroidered Porthault linens are stocked at your local mall.

13 • The Windsors' stationery from the Mrs. John L. Strong company, complete with hand-engraved monogrammed pieces on pure cotton paper, can be yours for $80 to $750, depending on the ornamentation.

14 • The duke's velvet slippers can be purchased for $188 at Brooks Brothers, which owns the London company that made them. Instead of an E for "Edward" below the embroidered crown, the slippers have a BB.

15 • Okay, okay, you'll never own as many scarves and gloves as the duchess did, but Hermes and Balenciaga sell exactly the same ones she wore for upward of $300 a pop.

16   Here's the takeaway: There is very little cake a rich person once gorged on that a middle-class person can't get on his plate. You name it; I can taste it. So I can't afford a casita on Bermuda, but I can get in on a time-share for a weekend. No, I can't own a stretch limo, but I can rent one by the hour. Maybe Venice is out this year, but I'll go to the Venetian in Vegas instead. I can't afford an Armani suit, but what about these eyeglasses with Giorgio's name plastered on them? Commodore Vanderbilt said that if you have to ask how much a yacht costs, you can't afford one, but check out my stateroom on my chartered Majestic Princess. True, I don't have my own Gulfstream V jet, but I can upgrade to first class on Delta with the miles I "earn" by using my American Express card. Is that my own Lexus out front? Or is it on lease from a used car dealer? You'll never know.

17   Lux populi may be the end of deluxe. "Real" luxury used to be for the "happy few," but in the world of the supra-12,000 Dow Jones industrial average, there are only the minted many. "Sudden Wealth Syndrome," as the *Los Angeles Times* has called it, is not just for dot.com innovators or contestants on *Who Wants to Be a Millionaire,* but for a generation that is inheriting its wealth through the steady attrition of the Generation Who Fought the War. The "wealth effect," as former Federal Reserve chairman Alan Greenspan termed it, drives more and more money to chase after goods whose production can hardly be called beneficial and cannot now even be called positional.

18   There's a story, perhaps apocryphal, that when Tom Ford, chief designer for Gucci in the 1990s, was passing through the Newark airport (what the hell was he doing there?!), he saw one of his swanky T-shirts on the tummy of a portly prole. He immediately canceled the clothing line. Too late. Perhaps the social construction of luxury as a material category has already been deconstructed into banality.

19   The very unreachableness of old luxe made it safe, like an old name, old blood, old land, an old coat of arms, or old service to the crown. Primogeniture, the cautious passage and consolidation of wealth to the firstborn male, made the anxiety of exclusion from luxe somehow bearable. After all, you knew your place from the moment of birth and had plenty of time to make your peace. If you drew the short straw, not to worry. A comfortable life as a vicar would await you. Or the officer corps.

20   The application of steam, then electricity, to the engines of production brought a new market to status objects, an industrial market made up of people who essentially bought their way into having a bloodline. These were the people who so

disturbed economist Thorstein Veblen, and from them this new generation of consumer has descended. First the industrial rich, then the inherited rich, and now the incidentally rich, the accidentally rich, the golden-parachute rich, the buyout rich, the lottery rich.

21   Call them yuppies, yippies, bobos, nobrows, or whatever, the consumers of the new luxury have a sense of entitlement that transcends social class, a conviction that the finest things are their birthright. Never mind that they may have been born into a family whose ancestral estate is a tract house in the suburbs, near the mall, not paid for, and whose family crest was downloaded from the Internet. Ditto the signet ring design. Language reflects this hijacking. Words such as *gourmet, premium, boutique, chic, accessory,* and *classic* have loosened from their elite moorings and now describe such top-of-category items as popcorn, hamburgers, discount brokers, shampoo, scarves, ice cream, and trailer parks. "Luxury for all" is an oxymoron, all right, the aspirational goal of modern culture, and the death knell of the real thing.

22   These new *customers* for luxury are younger than *clients* of the old luxe used to be, there are far more of them, they make their money much sooner, and they are far more flexible in financing and fickle in choice. They do not stay put. When Richie Rich starts buying tulips by the ton, Nouveau Riche is right there behind him picking them up by the pound.

23   In a sense, the filthy rich have only two genuine luxury items left: time and philanthropy. As the old paradox goes, the rich share the luxury of too much time on their hands with the very people on whom they often bestow their philanthropy. Who knows, maybe poverty will become the new luxury, as the philosophes predicted. Wonder Bread becomes the new cake. Once you've ripped out all the old patinaed hardware, once you've traded in the Bentley for a rusted-out Chevy, once you've carted all the polo pony shirts to Goodwill, once you've given the Pollock to the Met, once you've taken your last trip up Everest and into the Amazon, there's not much left to do to separate yourself but give the rest of the damned stuff away. Competitive philanthropy has its allure. Why do you think there are more than 20 universities with multibillion-dollar pledge campaigns? Those bobos sure as hell can't do it. Little wonder that Warren Buffett dumped his load rather casually on top of a pile amassed by another modern baron, almost as if to say, "Top that." Now that's a show stopper. Even The Donald can't trump that. ◆

CRITICAL THINKING

1. Why is materialism so criticized yet obviously so wholeheartedly embraced by American society? If we are basically lovers of luxury, why are we so quick to condemn advertising and consumerism?
2. What is luxury to you? Is there a point when it seems excessive? If so, what is your luxury threshold, and why?
3. Twitchell refers to Marie Antoinette in his opening paragraphs. Why does he choose her to demonstrate the American thirst for luxury? Explain.

4. Evaluate Twitchell's tone and style in this piece. What can you surmise from his tone and use of language? Does it make him more or less credible? Explain.

5. Twitchell lists a number of items belonging to the Windsors that were auctioned at Sotheby's. He observes that if the Duchess were alive today, she would probably "take 'em to the dump." Why would she do this? What happens when luxury is accessible to "the populi"?

6. How does Twitchell's opinion expressed in this essay differ from others in this section in his attitude toward advertising? Are they likely to be swayed by his argument? Why or why not?

7. According to Twitchell, why is luxury so important to Americans? What is the connection between desire and social status? In what ways is luxury "socially constructed"? Explain.

8. How well does Twitchell support his argument? Evaluate his use of supporting evidence. How well does he convince his readers that his position is reasonable and correct? Explain.

CRITICAL WRITING

1. *Exploratory Writing:* Twitchell wonders in his conclusion whether poverty will become the next luxury. Respond to his question with your own opinion.

2. *Personal Narrative:* Write a brief narrative about a time you experienced a decadent spending situation—either for yourself or with someone else. What motivated your spending? How did you feel after it?

GROUP PROJECTS

1. With your group, make a list of standard appliances, equipment, and possessions that people have in their homes—refrigerators, microwave ovens, pocketbooks, personal planners, fans, coffeemakers, DVD players, computers, VCRs, televisions, stereos (include components), iPods, blow-dryers, scooters, and so on. Make a list of at least 25 to 30 items. After the group has created a list, separately rank each item as a necessary, desirable, or luxury item. For example, you may decide a refrigerator is a necessary item but list an air conditioner as a luxury item. Do not look at how other members of your group rank the items until you are all finished. Compare your list with others in your group. Do the lists match, or are there some surprising discrepancies? Discuss the similarities and differences among your lists.

2. Examine the collection of ads on the preceding pages. Select one of the ads and identify the consumer group it targets. Develop a profile of a typical consumer of the product the ad promotes, the sort of people who are likely to purchase the product, and their motivations for owning it.

► **With These Words, I Can Sell You Anything**
*William Lutz**

► **The Language of Advertising**
Charles A. O'Neill

Words such as *help* and *virtually* and phrases such as *new and improved* and *acts fast* seem like innocuous weaponry in the arsenal of advertising. But not to William Lutz, who analyzes how such words are used in ads and how they misrepresent, mislead, and deceive consumers. In this essay, he alerts us to the special power of "weasel words," those familiar and sneaky little critters that "appear to say one thing when in fact they say the opposite, or nothing at all." The real danger, Lutz argues, is how such language debases reality and the values of the consumer. Marketing executive Charles A. O'Neill, however, disputes Lutz's criticism of advertising doublespeak. Although admitting to some of the craftiness of his profession, O'Neill defends the huckster's language—both verbal and visual—against claims that it distorts reality. Examining some familiar television commercials and magazine ads, he explains why the language may be charming and seductive but far from brainwashing.

With These Words, I Can Sell You Anything

William Lutz

1   One problem advertisers have when they try to convince you that the product they are pushing is really different from other, similar products is that their claims are subject to some laws. Not a lot of laws, but there are some designed to prevent fraudulent or untruthful claims in advertising. Even during the happy years of non-regulation under President Ronald Reagan, the FTC did crack down on the more blatant abuses in advertising claims. Generally speaking, advertisers have to be careful in what they say in their ads, in the claims they make for the products they advertise. Parity claims are safe because they are legal and supported by a number of court decisions. But beyond parity claims there are weasel words.

2   Advertisers use weasel words to appear to be making a claim for a product, when in fact they are making no claim at all. Weasel words get their name from the way weasels eat the eggs they find in the nests of other animals. A weasel will make a small hole in the egg, suck out the insides, then place the egg back in the nest. Only when the egg is examined closely is it found to be hollow. That's the way it is

---

* William Lutz, *Doublespeak* (excerpt), 1990; Charles A. O'Neill, original essay, updated 2008

with weasel words in advertising: Examine weasel words closely and you'll find that they're as hollow as any egg sucked by a weasel. Weasel words appear to say one thing when in fact they say the opposite, or nothing at all.

"Help"—The Number One Weasel Word

3 The biggest weasel word used in advertising doublespeak is "help." Now "help" only means to aid or assist, nothing more. It does not mean to conquer, stop, eliminate, end, solve, heal, cure, or anything else. But once the ad says "help," it can say just about anything after that because "help" qualifies everything coming after it. The trick is that the claim that comes after the weasel word is usually so strong and so dramatic that you forget the word "help" and concentrate only on the dramatic claim. You read into the ad a message that the ad does not contain. More importantly, the advertiser is not responsible for the claim that you read into the ad, even though the advertiser wrote the ad so you would read that claim into it.

4 The next time you see an ad for a cold medicine that promises that it "helps relieve cold symptoms fast," don't rush out to buy it. Ask yourself what this claim is really saying. Remember, "helps" means only that the medicine will aid or assist. What will it aid or assist in doing? Why, "relieve" your cold "symptoms." "Relieve" only means to ease, alleviate, or mitigate, not to stop, end, or cure. Nor does the claim say how much relieving this medicine will do. Nowhere does this ad claim it will cure anything. In fact, the ad doesn't even claim it will do anything at all. The ad only claims that it will aid in relieving (not curing) your cold symptoms, which are probably a runny nose, watery eyes, and a headache. In other words, this medicine probably contains a standard decongestant and some aspirin. By the way, what does "fast" mean? Ten minutes, one hour, one day? What is fast to one person can be very slow to another. "Fast" is another weasel word.

5 Ad claims using "help" are among the most popular ads. One says, "Helps keep you young looking," but then a lot of things will help keep you young looking, including exercise, rest, good nutrition, and a facelift. More importantly, this ad doesn't say the product will keep you young, only "young looking." Someone may look young to one person and old to another.

6 A toothpaste ad says, "Helps prevent cavities," but it doesn't say it will actually prevent cavities. Brushing your teeth regularly, avoiding sugars in foods, and flossing daily will also help prevent cavities. A liquid cleaner ad says, "Helps keep your home germ free," but it doesn't say it actually kills germs, nor does it even specify which germs it might kill.

7 "Help" is such a useful weasel word that it is often combined with other action-verb weasel words such as "fight" and "control." Consider the claim, "Helps control dandruff symptoms with regular use." What does it really say? It will assist in controlling (not eliminating, stopping, ending, or curing) the symptoms of dandruff, not the cause of dandruff nor the dandruff itself. What are the symptoms of dandruff? The ad deliberately leaves that undefined, but assume that the symptoms referred to in the ad are the flaking and itching commonly associated with dandruff. But just shampooing with any shampoo will temporarily eliminate these symptoms, so this shampoo isn't any different from any other. Finally, in order to benefit from this

product, you must use it regularly. What is "regular use"—daily, weekly, hourly? Using another shampoo "regularly" will have the same effect. Nowhere does this advertising claim say this particular shampoo stops, eliminates, or cures dandruff. In fact, this claim says nothing at all, thanks to all the weasel words.

8   Look at ads in magazines and newspapers, listen to ads on radio and television, and you'll find the word "help" in ads for all kinds of products. How often do you read or hear such phrases as "helps stop...," "helps overcome...," "helps eliminate...," "helps you feel...," or "helps you look..."? If you start looking for this weasel word in advertising, you'll be amazed at how often it occurs. Analyze the claims in the ads using "help," and you will discover that these ads are really saying nothing.

9   There are plenty of other weasel words used in advertising. In fact, there are so many that to list them all would fill the rest of this book. But, in order to identify the doublespeak of advertising and understand the real meaning of an ad, you have to be aware of the most popular weasel words in advertising today.

Virtually Spotless

10 One of the most powerful weasel words is "virtually," a word so innocent that most people don't pay any attention to it when it is used in an advertising claim. But watch out. "Virtually" is used in advertising claims that appear to make specific, definite promises when there is no promise. After all, what does "virtually" mean? It means "in essence of effect, although not in fact." Look at that definition again. "Virtually" means "not in fact." It does not mean "almost" or "just about the same as," or anything else. And before you dismiss all this concern over such a small word, remember that small words can have big consequences.

11   In 1971 a federal court rendered its decision on a case brought by a woman who became pregnant while taking birth control pills. She sued the manufacturer, Eli Lilly and Company, for breach of warranty. The woman lost her case. Basing its ruling on a statement in the pamphlet accompanying the pills, which stated that, "When taken as directed, the tablets offer virtually 100% protection," the court ruled that there was no warranty, expressed or implied, that the pills were absolutely effective. In its ruling, the court pointed out that, according to Webster's Third New International Dictionary, "virtually" means "almost entirely" and clearly does not mean "absolute" (Whittington v. Eli Lilly and Company, 333 F. Supp. 98). In other words, the Eli Lilly company was really saying that its birth control pill, even when taken as directed, did not in fact provide 100 percent protection against pregnancy. But Eli Lilly didn't want to put it that way, because then many women might not have bought Lilly's birth control pills.

12   The next time you see the ad that says that this dishwasher detergent "leaves dishes virtually spotless," just remember how advertisers twist the meaning of the weasel word "virtually." You can have lots of spots on your dishes after using this detergent, and the ad claim will still be true, because what this claim really means is that this detergent does not in fact leave your dishes spotless. Whenever you see or hear an ad claim that uses the word "virtually," just translate that claim into its real meaning. So the television set that is "virtually trouble free" becomes the television

set that is not in fact trouble free, the "virtually foolproof operation" of any appliance becomes an operation that is in fact not foolproof, and the product that "virtually never needs service" becomes the product that is not in fact service free.

New and Improved

13 If "new" is the most frequently used word on a product package, "improved" is the second most frequent. In fact, the two words are almost always used together. It seems just about everything sold these days is "new and improved." The next time you're in the supermarket, try counting the number of times you see these words on products. But you'd better do it while you're walking down just one aisle, otherwise you'll need a calculator to keep track of your counting.

14   Just what do these words mean? The use of the word "new" is restricted by regulations, so an advertiser can't just use the word on a product or in an ad without meeting certain requirements. For example, a product is considered new for about six months during a national advertising campaign. If the product is being advertised only in a limited test market area, the word can be used longer, and in some instances has been used for as long as two years.

15   What makes a product "new"? Some products have been around for a long time, yet every once in a while you discover that they are being advertised as "new." Well, an advertiser can call a product new if there has been "a material functional change" in the product. What is "a material functional change," you ask? Good question. In fact it's such a good question it's being asked all the time. It's up to the manufacturer to prove that the product has undergone such a change. And if the manufacturer isn't challenged on the claim, then there's no one to stop it. Moreover, the change does not have to be an improvement in the product. One manufacturer added an artificial lemon scent to a cleaning product and called it "new and improved," even though the product did not clean any better than without the lemon scent. The manufacturer defended the use of the word "new" on the grounds that the artificial scent changed the chemical formula of the product and therefore constituted "a material functional change."

16   Which brings up the word "improved." When used in advertising, "improved" does not mean "made better." It only means "changed" or "different from before." So, if the detergent maker puts a plastic pour spout on the box of detergent, the product has been "improved," and away we go with a whole new advertising campaign. Or, if the cereal maker adds more fruit or a different

> *Advertisers use weasel words to appear to be making a claim for a product when in fact they are making no claim at all.*

kind of fruit to the cereal, there's an improved product. Now you know why manufacturers are constantly making little changes in their products. Whole new advertising campaigns, designed to convince you that the product has been changed for the better, are based on small changes in superficial aspects of a product. The next time you see an ad for an "improved" product, ask yourself what was wrong with the old one. Ask yourself just how "improved" the product is. Finally, you might check to see whether the "improved" version costs more than the unimproved one. After all, someone has to pay for the millions of dollars spent advertising the improved product.

17   Of course, advertisers really like to run ads that claim a product is "new and improved." While what constitutes a "new" product may be subject to some regulation, "improved" is a subjective judgment. A manufacturer changes the shape of its stick deodorant, but the shape doesn't improve the function of the deodorant. That is, changing the shape doesn't affect the deodorizing ability of the deodorant, so the manufacturer calls it "improved." Another manufacturer adds ammonia to its liquid cleaner and calls it "new and improved." Since adding ammonia does affect the cleaning ability of the product, there has been a "material functional change" in the product, and the manufacturer can now call its cleaner "new," and "improved" as well. Now the weasel words "new and improved" are plastered all over the package and are the basis for a multimillion-dollar ad campaign. But after six months, the word "new" will have to go, until someone can dream up another change in the product. Perhaps it will be adding color to the liquid, or changing the shape of the package, or maybe adding a new, dripless pour spout, or perhaps a _____. The "improvements" are endless, and so are the new advertising claims and campaigns.

18   "New" is just too useful and powerful a word in advertising for advertisers to pass it up easily. So they use weasel words that say "new" without really saying it. One of their favorites is "introducing," as in, "Introducing improved Tide," or "Introducing the stain remover." The first is simply saying, here's our improved soap; the second, here's our new advertising campaign for our detergent. Another favorite is "now," as in, "Now there's Sinex," which simply means that Sinex is available. Then there are phrases like "Today's Chevrolet," "Presenting Dristan," and "A fresh way to start the day." The list is really endless because advertisers are always finding new ways to say "new" without really saying it. If there is a second edition of this book, I'll just call it the "new and improved" edition. Wouldn't you really rather have a "new and improved" edition of this book rather than a "second" edition?

Acts Fast

19   "Acts" and "works" are two popular weasel words in advertising, because they bring action to the product and to the advertising claim. When you see the ad for the cough syrup that "Acts on the cough control center," ask yourself what this cough syrup is claiming to do. Well, it's just claiming to "act," to do something, to perform an action. What is it that the cough syrup does? The ad doesn't say. It only claims to perform an action or do something on your "cough control center." By the way, what and where is your "cough control center"? I don't remember learning about that part of the body in human biology class.

20   Ads that use such phrases as "acts fast," "acts against," "acts to prevent," and the like are saying essentially nothing, because "act" is a word empty of any specific meaning. The ads are always careful not to specify exactly what "act" the product performs. Just because a brand of aspirin claims to "act fast" for headache relief doesn't mean this aspirin is any better than any other aspirin. What is the "act" that

this aspirin performs? You're never told. Maybe it just dissolves quickly. Since aspirin is a parity product, all aspirin is the same and therefore functions the same.

Works Like Anything Else

21 If you don't find the word "acts" in an ad, you will probably find the weasel word "works." In fact, the two words are almost interchangeable in advertising. Watch out for ads that say a product "works against," "works like," "works for," or "works longer." As with "acts," "works" is the same meaningless verb used to make you think that this product really does something, and maybe even something special or unique. But "works," like "acts," is basically a word empty of any specific meaning.

Like Magic

22 Whenever advertisers want you to stop thinking about the product and to start thinking about something bigger, better, or more attractive than the product, they use that very popular weasel word, "like." The word "like" is the advertiser's equivalent of a magician's use of misdirection. "Like" gets you to ignore the product and concentrate on the claim the advertiser is making about it. "For skin like peaches and cream" claims the ad for a skin cream. What is this ad really claiming? It doesn't say this cream will give you peaches-and-cream skin. There is no verb in this claim, so it doesn't even mention using the product. How is skin ever like "peaches and cream"? Remember, ads must be read literally and exactly, according to the dictionary definition of words. (Remember "virtually" in the Eli Lilly case.) The ad is making absolutely no promise or claim whatsoever for this skin cream. If you think this cream will give you soft, smooth, youthful-looking skin, you are the one who has read that meaning into the ad.

23   The wine that claims "It's like taking a trip to France" wants you to think about a romantic evening in Paris as you walk along the boulevard after a wonderful meal in an intimate little bistro. Of course, you don't really believe that a wine can take you to France, but the goal of the ad is to get you to think pleasant, romantic thoughts about France and not about how the wine tastes or how expensive it may be. That little word "like" has taken you away from crushed grapes into a world of your own imaginative making. Who knows, maybe the next time you buy wine, you'll think those pleasant thoughts when you see this brand of wine, and you'll buy it. Or, maybe you weren't even thinking about buying wine at all, but now you just might pick up a bottle the next time you're shopping. Ah, the power of "like" in advertising.

24   How about the most famous "like" claim of all, "Winston tastes good like a cigarette should"? Ignoring the grammatical error here, you might want to know what this claim is saying. Whether a cigarette tastes good or bad is a subjective judgment because what tastes good to one person may well taste horrible to another. Not everyone likes fried snails, even if they are called escargot. (*De gustibus non est disputandum*, which was probably the Roman rule for advertising as well as for defending the games in the Colosseum.) There are many people who say all cigarettes taste terrible, other people who say only some cigarettes taste all right, and still others

who say all cigarettes taste good. Who's right? Everyone, because taste is a matter of personal judgment. Moreover, note the use of the conditional, "should." The complete claim is, "Winston tastes good like a cigarette should taste." But should cigarettes taste good? Again, this is a matter of personal judgment and probably depends most on one's experiences with smoking. So, the Winston ad is simply saying that Winston cigarettes are just like any other cigarette: Some people like them and some people don't. On that statement, R. J. Reynolds conducted a very successful multimillion-dollar advertising campaign that helped keep Winston the number two–selling cigarette in the United States, close behind number one, Marlboro.

Can't It Be Up to the Claim?

25 Analyzing ads for doublespeak requires that you pay attention to every word in the ad and determine what each word really means. Advertisers try to wrap their claims in language that sounds concrete, specific, and objective, when in fact the language of advertising is anything but. Your job is to read carefully and listen critically so that when the announcer says that "Crest can be of significant value . . ." you know immediately that this claim says absolutely nothing. Where is the doublespeak in this ad? Start with the second word.

26 Once again, you have to look at what words really mean, not what you think they mean or what the advertiser wants you to think they mean. The ad for Crest only says that using Crest "can be" of "significant value." What really throws you off in this ad is the brilliant use of "significant." It draws your attention to the word "value" and makes you forget that the ad only claims that Crest "can be." The ad doesn't say that Crest is of value, only that it is "able" or "possible" to be of value, because that's all that "can" means.

27 It's so easy to miss the importance of those little words, "can be." Almost as easy as missing the importance of the words "up to" in an ad. These words are very popular in sale ads. You know, the ones that say, "Up to 50 percent off!" Now, what does that claim mean? Not much, because the store or manufacturer has to reduce the price of only a few items by 50 percent. Everything else can be reduced a lot less, or not even reduced. Moreover, don't you want to know 50 percent off of what? Is it 50 percent off the "manufacturer's suggested list price," which is the highest possible price? Was the price artificially inflated and then reduced? In other ads, "up to" expresses an ideal situation. The medicine that works "up to ten times faster," the battery that lasts "up to twice as long," and the soap that gets you "up to twice as clean"—all are based on ideal situations for using those products, situations in which you can be sure you will never find yourself.

Unfinished Words

28 Unfinished words are a kind of "up to" claim in advertising. The claim that a battery lasts "up to twice as long" usually doesn't finish the comparison—twice as long as what? A birthday candle? A tank of gas? A cheap battery made in a country not noted for its technological achievements? The implication is that the battery lasts twice as long as batteries made by other battery makers, or twice as long as earlier

model batteries made by the advertiser, but the ad doesn't really make these claims. You read these claims into the ad, aided by the visual images the advertiser so carefully provides.

29   Unfinished words depend on you to finish them, to provide the words the advertisers so thoughtfully left out of the ad. Pall Mall cigarettes were once advertised as "A longer, finer, and milder smoke." The question is, longer, finer, and milder than what? The aspirin that claims it contains "Twice as much of the pain reliever doctors recommend most" doesn't tell you what pain reliever it contains twice as much of. (By the way, it's aspirin. That's right; it just contains twice the amount of aspirin. And how much is twice the amount? Twice of what amount?) Panadol boasts that "nobody reduces fever faster," but, since Panadol is a parity product, this claim simply means that Panadol isn't any better than any other product in its parity class. "You can be sure if it's Westinghouse," you're told, but just exactly what it is you can be sure of is never mentioned. "Magnavox gives you more" doesn't tell you what you get more of. More value? More television? More than they gave you before? It sounds nice, but it means nothing, until you fill in the claim with your own words, the words the advertisers didn't use. Since each of us fills in the claim differently, the ad and the product can become all things to all people, and not promise a single thing.

30   Unfinished words abound in advertising, because they appear to promise so much. More importantly, they can be joined with powerful visual images on television to appear to be making significant promises about a product's effectiveness without really making any promises. In a television ad, the aspirin product that claims fast relief can show a person with a headache taking the product and then, in what appears to be a matter of minutes, claiming complete relief. This visual image is far more powerful than any claim made in unfinished words. Indeed, the visual image completes the unfinished words for you, filling in with pictures what the words leave out. And you thought that ads didn't affect you. What brand of aspirin do you use?

31   Some years ago, Ford's advertisements proclaimed "Ford LTD—700 percent quieter." Now, what do you think Ford was claiming with these unfinished words? What was the Ford LTD quieter than? A Cadillac? A Mercedes Benz? A BMW? Well, when the FTC asked Ford to substantiate this unfinished claim, Ford replied that it meant that the inside of the LTD was 700 percent quieter than the outside. How did you finish those unfinished words when you first read them? Did you even come close to Ford's meaning?

Combining Weasel Words

32   A lot of ads don't fall neatly into one category or another, because they use a variety of different devices and words. Different weasel words are often combined to make an ad claim. The claim, "Coffee-Mate gives coffee more body, more flavor," uses unfinished words ("more" than what?) and also uses words that have no specific meaning ("body" and "flavor"). Along with "taste" (remember the Winston ad and its claim to taste good), "body" and "flavor" mean nothing, because their meaning is entirely subjective. To you, "body" in coffee might mean thick, black, almost bitter

coffee, while I might take it to mean a light brown, delicate coffee. Now, if you think you understood that last sentence, read it again, because it said nothing of objective value; it was filled with weasel words of no specific meaning: "thick," "black," "bitter," "light brown," and "delicate." Each of those words has no specific, objective meaning, because each of us can interpret them differently.

33   Try this slogan: "Looks, smells, tastes like ground-roast coffee." So, are you now going to buy Taster's Choice instant coffee because of this ad? "Looks," "smells," and "tastes" are all words with no specific meaning and depend on your interpretation of them for any meaning. Then there's that great weasel word "like," which simply suggests a comparison but does not make the actual connection between the product and the quality. Besides, do you know what "ground-roast" coffee is? I don't, but it sure sounds good. So, out of seven words in this ad, four are definite weasel words, two are quite meaningless, and only one has any clear meaning.

34   Remember the Anacin ad—"Twice as much of the pain reliever doctors recommend most"? There's a whole lot of weaseling going on in this ad. First, what's the pain reliever they're talking about in this ad? Aspirin, of course. In fact, any time you see or hear an ad using those words "pain reliever," you can automatically substitute the word "aspirin" for them. (Makers of acetaminophen and ibuprofen pain relievers are careful in their advertising to identify their products as nonaspirin products.) So, now we know that Anacin has aspirin in it. Moreover, we know that Anacin has twice as much aspirin in it, but we don't know twice as much as what. Does it have twice as much aspirin as an ordinary aspirin tablet? If so, what is an ordinary aspirin tablet, and how much aspirin does it contain? Twice as much as Excedrin or Bufferin? Twice as much as a chocolate chip cookie? Remember those unfinished words and how they lead you on without saying anything.

35   Finally, what about those doctors who are doing all that recommending? Who are they? How many of them are there? What kind of doctors are they? What are their qualifications? Who asked them about recommending pain relievers? What other pain relievers did they recommend? And there are a whole lot more questions about this "poll" of doctors to which I'd like to know the answers, but you get the point. Sometimes, when I call my doctor, she tells me to take two aspirin and call her office in the morning. Is that where Anacin got this ad?

Read the Label, or the Brochure

36   Weasel words aren't just found on television, on the radio, or in newspaper and magazine ads. Just about any language associated with a product will contain the doublespeak of advertising. Remember the Eli Lilly case and the doublespeak on the information sheet that came with the birth control pills. Here's another example.

37   Estée Lauder cosmetics company announced a new product called "Night Repair." A small brochure distributed with the product stated that "Night Repair was scientifically formulated in Estée Lauder's U.S. laboratories as part of the Swiss Age-Controlling Skincare Program. Although only nature controls the aging process, this program helps control the signs of aging and encourages skin to look and feel younger." You might want to read these two sentences again, because they sound great but say nothing.

38   First, note that the product was "scientifically formulated" in the company's laboratories. What does that mean? What constitutes a scientific formulation? You wouldn't expect the company to say that the product was casually, mechanically, or carelessly formulated, or just thrown together one day when the people in the white coats didn't have anything better to do. But the word "scientifically" lends an air of precision and promise that just isn't there.

39   It is the second sentence, however, that's really weasely, both syntactically and semantically. The only factual part of this sentence is the introductory dependent clause—"only nature controls the aging process." Thus, the only fact in the ad is relegated to a dependent clause, a clause dependent on the main clause, which contains no factual or definite information at all and indeed purports to contradict the independent clause. The new "skin care program" (notice it's not a skin cream but a "program") does not claim to stop or even retard the aging process. What, then, does Advanced Night Repair, at a price of over $85 for a 1-ounce bottle, do? According to this brochure, nothing. It only "helps," and the brochure does not say how much it helps. Moreover, it only "helps control," and then it only helps control the "signs of aging," not the aging itself. Also, it "encourages" skin not to be younger but only to "look and feel" younger. The brochure does not say younger than what. Of the sixteen words in the main clause of this second sentence, nine are weasel words. So, before you spend all that money for Night Repair, or any other cosmetic product, read the words carefully and then decide if you're getting what you think you're paying for.

Other Tricks of the Trade

40   Advertisers' use of doublespeak is endless. The best way advertisers can make something out of nothing is through words. Although there are a lot of visual images used on television and in magazines and newspapers, every advertiser wants to create that memorable line that will stick in the public consciousness. I am sure pure joy reigned in one advertising agency when a study found that children who were asked to spell the word "relief" promptly and proudly responded "r-o-l-a-i-d-s."

41   The variations, combinations, and permutations of doublespeak used in advertising go on and on, running from the use of rhetorical questions ("Wouldn't you really rather have a Buick?" "If you can't trust Prestone, who can you trust?") to flattering you with compliments ("The lady has taste." "We think a cigar smoker is someone special." "You've come a long way, Baby."). You know, of course, how you're supposed to answer those questions, and you know that those compliments are just leading up to the sales pitches for the products. Before you dismiss such tricks of the trade as obvious, however, just remember that all of these statements and questions were part of very successful advertising campaigns.

42   A more subtle approach is the ad that proclaims a supposedly unique quality for a product, a quality that really isn't unique. "If it doesn't say Goodyear, it can't be polyglas." Sounds good, doesn't it? Polyglas is available only from Goodyear because Goodyear copyrighted that trade name. Any other tire manufacturer could make exactly the same tire but could not call it "polyglas," because that would be

copyright infringement. "Polyglas" is simply Goodyear's name for its fiberglass-reinforced tire.

43   Since we like to think of ourselves as living in a technologically advanced country, science and technology have a great appeal in selling products. Advertisers are quick to use scientific doublespeak to push their products. There are all kinds of elixirs, additives, scientific potions, and mysterious mixtures added to all kinds of products. Gasoline contains "HTA," "F-130," "Platformate," and other chemical-sounding additives, but nowhere does an advertisement give any real information about the additive. Shampoo, deodorant, mouthwash, cold medicine, sleeping pills, and any number of other products all seem to contain some special chemical ingredient that allows them to work wonders. "Certs contains a sparkling drop of Retsyn." So what? What's "Retsyn"? What's it do? What's so special about it? When they don't have a secret ingredient in their product, advertisers still find a way to claim scientific validity. There's "Sinarest. Created by a research scientist who actually gets sinus headaches." Sounds nice, but what kind of research does this scientist do? How do you know if she is any kind of expert on sinus medicine? Besides, this ad doesn't tell you a thing about the medicine itself and what it does.

Advertising Doublespeak Quick Quiz

The following is a list of statements from some recent ads. Test your awareness of advertising doublespeak by figuring out what each of these ads really says:

DOMINO'S PIZZA: "The pizza delivery experts."
TUMS: "Fast, effective heartburn relief."
SCOPE: "Get close with Scope"
CASCADE: "For virtually spotless dishes, nothing beats Cascade."
ADVIL: "The pain reliever for fast, strong pain relief."
DUNKIN DONUTS: "America runs on Dunkin."
SUDAFED: "Fast sinus relief that won't put you fast asleep."
TYLENOL: "Stop. Think. Tylenol."
MCDONALD'S: "I'm lovin' it."
MILLER LITE BEER: "Tastes great. Less filling."
PHILLIP'S MILK OF MAGNESIA: "Phillip's. The comfortable way."
KRAFT MACARONI AND CHEESE: "It's the cheesiest."
CRACKER BARREL: "Judged to be the best."
L'OREAL: "Because you're worth it."
BURGER KING: "Have it your way."
JC PENNEY: "It's all inside."
SARA LEE: "Nobody doesn't like Sara Lee."
TOYOTA: "Moving forward."
TACO BELL: "Think outside the bun."
MICROSOFT: "Where do you want to go today?"

The World of Advertising

44 In the world of advertising, people wear "dentures," not false teeth; they suffer from "occasional irregularity," not constipation; they need deodorants for their "nervous wetness," not for sweat; they use "bathroom tissue," not toilet paper; and they don't dye their hair, they "tint" or "rinse" it. Advertisements offer "real counterfeit diamonds" without the slightest hint of embarrassment, or boast of goods made out of "genuine imitation leather" or "virgin vinyl."

45 In the world of advertising, the girdle becomes a "body shaper," "form persuader," "control garment," "controller," "outerwear enhancer," "body garment," or "anti-gravity panties," and is sold with such trade names as "The Instead," "The Free Spirit," and "The Body Briefer."

46 A study some years ago found the following words to be among the most popular used in U.S. television advertisements: "new," "improved," "better," "extra," "fresh," "clean," "beautiful," "free," "good," "great," and "light." At the same time, the following words were found to be among the most frequent on British television: "new," "good-better-best," "free," "fresh," "delicious," "full," "sure," "clean," "wonderful," and "special." While these words may occur most frequently in ads, and while ads may be filled with weasel words, you have to watch out for all the words used in advertising, not just the words mentioned here.

47 Every word in an ad is there for a reason; no word is wasted. Your job is to figure out exactly what each word is doing in an ad—what each word really means, not what the advertiser wants you to think it means. Remember, the ad is trying to get you to buy a product, so it will put the product in the best possible light, using any device, trick, or means legally allowed. Your only defense against advertising (besides taking up permanent residence on the moon) is to develop and use a strong critical reading, listening, and looking ability. Always ask yourself what the ad is really saying. When you see ads on television, don't be misled by the pictures, the visual images. What does the ad say about the product? What does the ad not say? What information is missing from the ad? Only by becoming an active, critical consumer of the doublespeak of advertising will you ever be able to cut through the doublespeak and discover what the ad is really saying. ◆

 # The Language of Advertising
Charles A. O'Neill

1 In 1957, a short dozen years after World War II, many people had good reason to be concerned about Science. On the one hand, giant American corporations offered the promise of "Better Living Through Chemistry." Labs and factories in the U.S. and abroad turned out new "miracle" fabrics, vaccines, and building materials. Radar and other innovative technology developed during the War had found important applications in the fast-growing, surging crest of consumer-centric, late 1950s America.

2   But World War II American Science had also yielded The Bomb. Specialists working in secret laboratories had figured out how to translate the theoretical work of Dr. Einstein, and others, into weapons that did exactly what they were intended to do, incinerating hundreds of thousands of civilian Japanese men, women and children in the process. The USSR and the USA were locked in an arms race. Americans were told the Soviets held the advantage. Many families built bomb shelters in the yard, and millions of school children learned to "Duck and Cover."

3   So when Vance Packard wrote his seminal book, *The Hidden Persuaders*, (D. Mackay & Co) about a dark alliance of social scientists with product marketers and advertisers, he struck a resonant chord. The scientists who had brought us the weapons that helped win the war had now, apparently, turned their sights on the emerging consumer society, using market research and psychology to gain a better understanding of "people's subsurface desires, needs, and drives," to "find their points of vulnerability," By applying the principles of laboratory experimentation and scientific reasoning to learn about the fears, habits and aspirations of John and Mary Public, they would help businesses create products whose sales would be fueled by ever-more powerful advertising. Among many examples cited, Mr. Packard noted that what he called "depth probers" had learned that "fear of stern bankers was driving borrowers to more expensive loan companies. Banks began training their employees to be nice so as to attract more business." We were led to believe the banker's smile was a form of manipulation, a contrived courtesy. A New York Times best seller, the book sold more than 1 million copies.

4   The decade of the 1950s offered numerous examples of consumer excess. Cars from the era sported tail fins stretched to new extremes, for no aerodynamic or practical purpose. And it is impossible to miss the overtly sexual reference in the jutting chrome bumpers of the era's most flamboyant road machines. It was a time when Big was best, in starlets as well as the family car.

5   Consumer tastes change, but the advertising techniques described in the *Hidden Persuaders* are alive and well and appearing in newspapers, magazines, flat screen televisions, billboards, text messages and Web sites in your neighborhood.

6   Mr. Packard is certainly not alone as a critic of advertising. Every decade has brought a new generation of critics. We recognize the value of advertising, but on some level we can't quite fully embrace it as a "normal" part of our experience. At best, we view it as distracting. At worst, we view it as a pernicious threat to our health, wealth and social values.

7   How does advertising work? Why is it so powerful? Why does it raise such concern? What case can be made for and against the advertising business? In order to understand advertising, you must accept that it is not about truth, virtue, love, or positive social values. It is about selling a product. Ads play a role in moving customers through the sales process. This process begins with an effort to build awareness, typically achieved by tactics designed to break through the clutter of competitive messages. By presenting a description of product benefits, ads convince the customer to buy the product. Once prospects have become purchasers, advertising is used to sustain brand loyalty, reminding customers of all the good reasons for their original decision to buy.

8   But this does not sufficiently explain the ultimate, unique power of advertising. Whatever the product or creative strategy, advertisements derive their power from a

purposeful, directed combination of images. Images can take the form of words, sounds, or visuals, used individually or together. The combination of images is the language of advertising, a language unlike any other.

9 Everyone who grows up in the Western world soon learns that advertising language is different from other languages. We may have forgotten the sponsors, but we certainly know these popular slogans "sound like ads."

10 "Where's the beef?" (Wendy's restaurants)
"Please, don't squeeze the charmin." (Charmin bathroom tissue)
"M'm! M'm! Good!" (Campbell's Soup)
"I've fallen, and I can't get up!" (Lifecall)
"Can you hear me now?" (Verizon)
"Where do you want to go today? (Microsoft)
"The Real Thing" (Coca Cola)
"Reach out and touch someone" (AT&T)
"The Ultimate Driving Machine" (BMW)

Edited and Purposeful

11 These slogans may seem casual, but in fact they are carefully engineered. Slogans and all other types of advertising messages have a clear purpose; they are intended to trigger a specific response.

12 The response may be as utterly simple as "Say, I *am* hungry. Let's pull right on up to the drive-through window and order a big, juicy Wendy's burger, fast!" In the case of some advertising, our reactions may be more complex.

13 In 2008 McCain for President ran this ad:
"Who is Barack Obama? He says our troops in Afghanistan are [Obama's voice] "just air-raiding villages and killing civilians." How dishonorable. Congressional liberals voted repeatedly to cut off funding to our active troops, increasing the risk on their lives. How dangerous. Obama and congressional liberals. Too risky for America."

14 The message: "Obama isn't like the rest of us. He doesn't even support our troops. He is a dishonorable man! It would be dangerous and risky to vote for him."

Rich and Arresting

15 Advertisements cannot succeed unless they capture our attention. Of the hundreds of advertising messages in store for us each day, very few will actually command our conscious attention. The rest are screened out. The people who design and write ads know about this screening process; they anticipate and accept it as a premise of their business.

16 The classic, all-time favorite device used to breach the awareness barrier is sex. The desire to be sexually attractive to others is a basic instinct, and nothing is more powerful. Flip through any popular magazine, and you will find it packed with ads that are unabashedly, unapologetically sexual. Victoria's Secret, Calvin Klein and

every other clothing and fragrance marketer uses sex to sell. Popular media is a veritable playground of titillation, abounding with images of barely clothed men and women in poses suggesting that if only you would wear one of our little padded brassieres or spray our product behind your ears, a world of sexual adventure will reveal itself to you—even if, like many Americans these days, your Body Mass Index places you squarely in the rippling embrace of Obesity, a disease some attribute to mass market advertising for fat-laden, fast food.

17   If advertising created Obesity, it also offers the cure: Americans spend billions of dollars every year on "fat burning" nutritional supplements, and they are not marketed only by word of mouth. A full page ad in *People* magazine is typical, and contains all of the elements ads of this type seem to require.

18   1. A banner headline ("America's #1 Selling Weight-Loss Supplement)
      2. A promise ("I lost 55 lbs. fast with Hyrdroxycut!")
      3. Sex appeal, with a winsome, bikini-clad young woman in before (162 lbs.) and after (107 lbs.) photographs
      4. A testimonial ("When I was overweight, I felt ugly ... I was amazed and inspired by other women and their transformations with Hydroxycut ... I've lost 55 pounds and 13 inches off my waist ...)
      5. A payoff statement ("Now I'm confident and I feel sexy!")

19   Finally, for the benefit of skeptical readers who aren't quite sure they believe this product will work its magic for them, there is the customary scientific proof, in this case provided by Dr. Nick Evans, M.D.: "Based on the scientific studies ... and my personal experience using the product, I would recommend Hydroxycut to healthy adults wishing to lose weight."

20   Every successful advertisement uses a creative strategy based on an idea intended to attract and hold the attention of the targeted consumer audience. The strategy may include strong creative execution or a straightforward presentation of product features and customer benefits or even something as simple as mind-numbing repetition.

21   Soft drink and fast-food companies often take a distinctive approach. "Slice of life" ads (so-called because they purport to show people in "real-life" situations) created to sell Coke or Pepsi have often placed their characters in Fourth of July parades or other family events. The archetypical version of this ad is a photograph or TV spot filled-to-overflowing with babies frolicking with puppies in the sunlit foreground while their youthful parents play touch football. On the porch, Grandma and Pops are seen quietly smiling as they wait for all of this affection to transform itself in a climax of warmth, harmony, and joy. In part, these ads work through repetition: How-many-times-can-you-spot-the-logo-in-this-commercial?

22   These ads seduce us into feeling that if we drink the right combination of sugar, preservatives, caramel coloring, and secret ingredients, we'll join the crowd that—in the words of Coca-Cola's ad from 1971—will help "teach the world to sing ... in perfect harmony." A masterstroke of advertising cemented the impression that Coke was hip: not only an American brand, but a product and brand for all peace-loving peoples everywhere!

23   Ads do not often emerge like Botticelli's Venus from the sea, flawless and fully grown. Most often, the creative strategy is developed only after extensive research. "Who will be interested in our product? How old are they? Where do they live? How much money do they earn? What problem will our product solve?" Answers to these questions provide the foundation on which the creative strategy is built.

Involving

24   We have seen that the language of advertising is carefully engineered; we have discovered a few of the devices it uses to get our attention. Coke and Pepsi have caught our eye with visions of peace and love. An actress offers a winsome smile. Now

Symbols offer an important tool for involving consumers in advertisements, not so much because they carry meanings of their own, but because we bring meaning to them.

that they have our attention, advertisers present information intended to show us that their product fills a need and differs from the competition. It is the copywriter's responsibility to express, exploit, and intensify such product differences.

25   When product differences do not exist, the writer must glamorize the superficial differences—for example, differences in packaging. As long as the ad is trying to get our attention, the "action" is mostly in the ad itself, in the words and visual images. But as we read an ad or watch it on television, we become more deeply involved. The action starts to take place in us. Our imagination is set in motion, and our individual fears and aspirations, quirks, and insecurities come into play.

26   Consider, once again, the running battle among the low-calorie soft drinks. The cola wars have spawned many "look-alike" advertisements, because the product features and consumer benefits are generic, applying to all products in the category. Substitute one cola brand name for another, and the messages are often identical, right down to the way the cans are photographed in the closing sequence. This strategy relies on mass saturation and exposure for impact.

27   Some companies have set themselves apart from their competitors by making use of bold, even disturbing, themes and images. For example, it was not uncommon not long ago for advertisers in the fashion industry to make use of gaunt, languid models—models who, in the interpretation of some observers, displayed a certain form of "heroin chic." Something was most certainly unusual about the models appearing in ads for Prada and Calvin Klein products. A young woman in a Prada ad projects no emotion whatsoever; she is hunched forward, her posture suggesting that she is in a trance or drug-induced stupor. In a Calvin Klein ad, a young man is gaunt beyond reason. He is shirtless. As if to draw more attention to his peculiar posture and "zero body fat" status, he is shown pinching the skin next to his navel.

28   Do such advertisers as Prada and Calvin Klein bear moral responsibility for the rise of heroin use? Does "heroin chic" and its depiction of a decadent lifestyle exploit certain elements of our society—the young and clueless, for example? Or did these ads, and others of their ilk, simply reflect profound bad taste? In fact, on one level, all advertising is about exploitation: the systematic, deliberate identification

of our needs and wants, followed by the delivery of a carefully constructed promise that Brand X will satisfy them.

29   Symbols offer an important tool for involving consumers in advertisements, not so much because they carry meanings of their own, but because we bring meaning to them. One example is provided by the campaign begun in 1978 by Somerset Importers for Johnnie Walker Red Scotch. Sales of Johnnie Walker Red had been trailing sales of Johnnie Walker Black, and Somerset Importers needed to position Red as a fine product in its own right. Their agency produced ads that made heavy use of the color red. One magazine ad, often printed as a two-page spread, is dominated by a close-up photo of red autumn leaves. At lower right, the copy reads, "When their work is done, even the leaves turn to Red." Another ad—also suitably dominated by a photograph in the appropriate color—reads: "When it's time to quiet down at the end of the day, even a fire turns to Red." Red. Warm. Experienced. Seductive.

30   Advertisers use a variety of techniques and devices to engage us in the delivery of their messages. Some are subtle, making use of warm, entertaining, or comforting images or symbols. Others, like the McCain campaign ad, are direct, focused and intended to create a negative emotional reaction. Another common device used to engage our attention is old but still effective: the use of famous or notorious personalities as product spokespeople or models. Advertising writers did not invent the human tendency to admire or seek to identify with famous people. Once we have seen a famous person in an ad, we associate the product with the person: "Britney Spears drinks milk. She's a hottie. I want to be a hottie, too! 'Hey Mom, Got Milk?' " Nicole Richie pitches clothes by Jimmy Choo; Celine Dion pitches her own perfume; Sharon Stone sells Christal watches. The logic is faulty, but we fall under the spell just the same. Advertising works, not because Britney is a nutritionist, Celine is an expert perfumer-diva or because Sharon is a horologist, but because we participate in it. The ads bring the words, sounds and pictures. We bring the chemistry.

A Simple Language

31   Advertising language differs from other types of language in another important respect; it is a simple language. To determine how the text of a typical advertisement rates on a "simplicity index" in comparison with text in a magazine article, for example, try this exercise: Clip a typical story from the publication you read most frequently. Calculate the number of words in an average sentence. Count the number of words of three or more syllables in a typical 100-word passage, omitting words that are capitalized, combinations of two simple words, or verb forms made into three-syllable words by the addition of –ed or –es. Add the two figures (the average number of words per sentence and the number of three-syllable words per 100 words), then multiply the result by .4. According to Robert Gunning the result is the approximate grade level required to understand the content. He developed this formula, the "Fog Index," to determine the comparative ease with which any given piece of written communication can be read.

32   Let's apply the Fog Index to the complete text of pop star Britney Spears' 1999 ad for the National Fluid Milk Processing Board ("Got Milk?").

33   "Baby, one more time isn't enough. 9 out of 10 girls don't get enough calcium. It takes about 4 glasses of milk every day. So when I finish this glass, fill it up, baby. Three more times."

34   The average sentence in this ad is 7.4 words. There is only one three-syllable word, *calcium*. Counting *isn't* and *don't* as two words each, the ad is 40 words in length. The average number of three syllable words per hundred is 2.5.

> 7.4 words per sentence
> + 2.5 three syllable words/100
> 9.9
> 3.4
> 3.96

35   According to Gunning's scale, this ad is about as hard to read as a comic book, and you are just about to graduate from the fourth grade. But of course the text is only part of the message. The rest is the visual; in this case, a photo of Britney sprawled across a couch, legs in the air, while she talks on the phone. A plate holding cookies and a glass of milk is set next to her.

36   Why do advertisers generally favor simple language? The answer lies with the consumer: The average American adult is subject to an overwhelming number of commercial messages each day. As a practical matter, we would not notice many of these messages if length or eloquence were counted among their virtues. Today's consumer cannot take the time to focus on anything for long. Every aspect of modern life runs at an accelerated pace. Voice mail, pagers, mobile phones, text messages, e-mail, the Web—the world is always awake, always switched on, feeding our hunger for more information, now. Time generally, and TV-commercial time in particular, is experienced in increasingly smaller segments. Fifteen-second commercials are no longer unusual.

37   Advertising language is simple; in the engineering process, difficult words or images—which in other forms of communication may be used to lend color or fine shades of meaning—are edited out and replaced by simple words or images not open to misinterpretation. You don't need to be a college scholar to grasp the deliberate double entendre in "Baby, one more time isn't enough."

Who Is Responsible?

38 Some critics view the advertising business as a cranky, unwelcome child of the free enterprise system—a noisy, whining, brash kid who must somehow be kept in line, but can't just yet be thrown out of the house. In reality, advertising mirrors the fears, quirks, and aspirations of the society that creates it (and is, in turn, sold by it). This factor alone exposes advertising to parody and ridicule. The overall level of acceptance and respect for advertising is also influenced by the varied quality of the ads themselves. Some ads are deliberately designed to provoke controversy. But this is only one of the many charges frequently levied against advertising. Others include:

1. Advertising encourages unhealthy habits.
2. Advertising feeds on human weaknesses and exaggerates the importance of material things, encouraging "impure" emotions and vanities.

3. Advertising sells daydreams—distracting, purposeless visions of lifestyles beyond the reach of the majority of the people who are most exposed to advertising.
4. Advertising warps our vision of reality, implanting in us groundless fears and insecurities.
5. Advertising downgrades the intelligence of the public.
6. Advertising debases English.
7. Advertising perpetuates racial and sexual stereotypes.

39   What can be said in advertising's defense? Advertising is only a reflection of society. A case can be made for the concept that advertising language is an acceptable stimulus for the natural evolution of language. Is "proper English" the language most Americans actually speak and write, or is it the language we are told we should speak and write?

40   What about the charge that advertising debases the intelligence of the public? Those who support this particular criticism would do well to ask themselves another question: Exactly how intelligent is the public? Sadly, evidence abounds that "the public" at large is not particularly intelligent, after all. Johnny can't read. Susie can't write. And the entire family spends the night in front of the television, watching one mindless reality show after another. Ads are effective because they sell products. They would not succeed if they did not reflect the values and motivations of the real world. Advertising both reflects and shapes our perception of reality. Consider several brand names and the impressions they create: Ivory Snow is pure. Federal Express won't let you down. Absolut is cool. Mercedes represents quality. Our sense of what these brand names stand for has as much to do with advertising as with the objective "truth."

41   Advertising shapes our perception of the world as surely as architecture shapes our impression of a city. Good, responsible advertising can serve as a positive influence for change, while generating profits. Of course, the problem is that the obverse is also true: Advertising, like any form of mass communication, can be a force for both "good" and "bad." It can just as readily reinforce or encourage irresponsible behavior, ageism, sexism, ethnocentrism, racism, homophobia—you name it—as it can encourage support for diversity and social progress. People living in society create advertising. Society isn't perfect. In the end, advertising simply attempts to change behavior. Do advertisements sell distracting, purposeless visions? Occasionally. But maybe such visions are necessary components of the process through which our society changes and improves.

42   Perhaps, by learning how advertising works, we can become better equipped to sort out content from hype, product values from emotions, and salesmanship from propaganda. ◆

CRITICAL THINKING ————————————————

1. O'Neill's introduction describes the "alliance" between science and consumer marketing during the 1950s especially as it connected to the automotive industry. Evaluate the alliance he describes. Review some

automobile advertisements from the 1950s and 1960s to help you formulate your response. How would you assess this relationship between science and marketing today?

2. O'Neill says that advertisers create in consumers a sense of need for products. Do you think it is ethical for advertisers to create such a sense when their products are "generic" and do not differ from those of the competition? Consider ads for gasoline, beer, and instant coffee.

3. Toward the end of the essay, O'Neill anticipates potential objections to his defense of advertising. What are some of these objections? What does he say in defense of advertising? Which set of arguments do you find stronger?

4. O'Neill describes several ways in which the language of advertising differs from other kinds of language. Briefly list the ways he mentions. Can you think of any other characteristics of advertising language that set it apart?

5. Symbols are important elements in the language of advertising. Can you think of some specific symbols from the advertising world that you associate with your own life? Are they effective symbols for selling? Explain your answer.

6. Why do people buy products sold by famous people? What is the appeal of a product endorsed by a celebrity?

7. William Lutz teaches English and writes books about the misuse of language. Charles O'Neill is a professional advertiser. How do their views about advertising reflect their occupations? Which side of the argument do you agree with?

8. How effective do you think O'Neill's introductory paragraphs are? How well does he hook the reader? What particular audience might he be appealing to early on? What attitude toward advertising is established in the introduction?

9. A "weasel word" is a word so hollow it has no meaning. Consider your own reaction to weasel words when you hear them. Try to identify as many weasel words as you can. What are the words, and what do consumers think they mean?

10. Consider Lutz's argument that advertisers are trying to "trick" consumers with their false promises and claims. How much are our expectations of product performance influenced by the claims and slogans of advertising? How do you think O'Neill would respond to Lutz's accusation?

CRITICAL WRITING

1. *Exploratory Writing:* In his essay, O'Neill makes several generalizations that characterize the language of advertising. Think about ads that you have recently seen or read and make a list of your own generalizations about the language of advertising. Refer to some specific advertisements in your response.

2. *Persuasive Writing:* O'Neill believes that advertising language "mirrors the fears, quirks, and aspirations of the society that creates it." Do you agree or disagree with this statement? Explain your perspective in a brief essay, and support your response with examples.

3. *Analytical Writing:* Choose a brand-name product that you use regularly, or to which you have particular loyalty, and identify one or more of its competitors. Examine some advertisements for each brand. Write a short paper explaining what makes you prefer your brand to the others.

GROUP PROJECTS

1. Review Lutz's "Doublespeak Quick Quiz." Choose five items and analyze them, using dictionary meanings to explain what the ads are really saying.

2. With your group, think of some recent advertising campaigns that created controversy (Abercrombie and Fitch, Dove's 'Real Beauty,' PETA, Dolce and Gabbana, or Snickers). What made them controversial? How did this impact sales?

3. O'Neill notes that sometimes advertisers use symbols to engage their audience. With your group, create a list of brand symbols or logos, their corresponding products, and what lifestyle we associate with the logo or symbol. Are some logos more popular or prestigious? Explain.

4. Working in a group, develop a slogan and advertising campaign for one of the following products: sneakers, soda, a candy bar, or jeans. How would you apply the principles of advertising language to market your product? After completing your marketing plan, "sell" your product to the class. If time permits, explain the reasoning behind your selling technique.

CHAPTER
3

Generation Debt
The Financial Challenges We Face

Today's college graduates face challenges more difficult than the struggles faced by their parents at the same time in their lives. The first true economic depression since the 1920s may loom ahead. College tuition rates are at their highest, the job market is at a historic low, and a credit crisis threatens to bankrupt a nation. The group of young people who are heirs to this mess is most aptly named, in the words of *Village Voice* executive editor Laura Conway, "Generation Debt." The economic situation many "twixters" face is in itself controversial. On the one hand, today's twentysomethings point out that student loans, credit card debt, employment instability, lack of affordable healthcare, and financial irresponsibility have melded into a foreboding landscape that they have unwillingly inherited. On the other hand, some parents and elders argue that today's youth has come to expect too many handouts, does not know real struggle, and is unwilling to sacrifice.

It's a classic generational argument, but statistics seem to be pointing to a disturbing fact—that today's twentysomethings may be the first generation to be less successful than their parents. The trends are clear: More students face high debt than any other generation. More are returning home after college, unable to find a job or pay for an apartment, let alone buy a home or start a family—the hallmarks of adult life. Some tend to feel alienated and abandoned by government, which has effectively silenced them in political arenas. This chapter takes a look at the financial crisis many young Americans—indeed, all Americans—must deal with in the latter half of the first decade of the millennium.

The chapter begins with an excerpt from a book with the same title as this chapter— *Generation Debt*, by Anya Kamenetz. Writing as a member of the "post-millennials," Kamenetz describes a bleak economic scene in which today's twentysomethings are up to their ears in debt with little hope of digging their way out. An essay by Lev Grossman follows, "Grow Up? Not So Fast." It describes how "twixters"—young adults caught between adolescence and full adulthood—are dealing with a new social landscape. Economically unable to take on the responsibilities of adulthood, are young adults "creating" a new life phase?

The next two essays focus on the impact credit and debt have on young adults today. First, in "Maxed Out," James D. Scurlock describes how some college students, feeling overwhelmed by debt, made the ultimate choice—suicide—to escape their bills. Then, Tamara Draut describes how credit card companies target college students who have no way of paying off the debt they are so freely given in "Strapped."

A broader view of the social attitudes toward debt comes next. First, award-winning author Margaret Atwood explores the role debt has played in great novels and how literature reflects social attitudes of debt in "Debtor's Prism." Next, renowned documentary filmmaker Danny Schechter describes his research into the growing credit crisis and how it is affecting our entire nation in "Investigating the Nation's Exploding Credit Squeeze."

The chapter's Viewpoints takes a look at a growing trend—of college graduates returning to the parental nest. Known as "boomerang kids," they leave home only to return, unable to financially survive on their own. First, Ryan Healy, himself a twentysomething, urges his peers to go home and rely on parents for a bit longer in order to save money and pay down debt. Florinda Vasquez, writing from the perspective of a parent, wonders why parents aren't really being consulted in this decision. Should parents expect their kids to return home for awhile after college? Or is it time for young adults to spread their wings and make it on their own?

Generation Debt
Anya Kamenetz*

Many young Americans report that they are trapped by low-end jobs with low wages, few opportunities, high taxes, and huge student loans. Many fear that they are facing a lifetime of recycled debt. Sometime over the last 20 years, something happened: The cost of a college education skyrocketed. It became acceptable to carry large debt. People stopped expecting to work in one company for their entire career and started hopping around in search of a better deal. Unable to get on solid financial footing, college graduates started putting off marriage plans and moved back in with their parents. In this excerpt from the book with the same title, Anya Kamenetz explores some of the challenges her generation faces in an economic landscape vastly different from that of her parents' only a generation before.

1   The simplest definition of a "generation" is those people who pass through a specific stage of life at the same time. We tend to think of human life stages as natural demarcations of growth, like the rings on a tree. Yet social and economic structures also determine the divisions between infancy and old age. Since 1960, when historian Philippe Aries published the book *Centuries of Childhood*, scholars have been writing about how childhood was "discovered" for sentimental and moralistic reasons in eighteenth and nineteenth-century Europe. Before this historical turning point, infants were often farmed out to indifferent wet nurses, and seven-year-olds herded sheep.

2   Likewise, for most of human history, sexual maturity occurred just a year or two before marriage, and adolescence, as we know it, didn't exist. As Thomas Hine chronicles in *The Rise and Fall of the American Teenager*, when the United States was industrializing in the nineteenth century, people thirteen and up were the backbone of the semiskilled workforce. Teenagers came to America alone as immigrants. They ran weaving machines, dug mines, herded cattle, picked cotton, and fought wars. If they weren't slaves or indentured servants, they contributed their earnings to their families of origin until they got married and started families of their own.

3   American psychologist G. Stanley Hine popularized the term "adolescent" in 1904, as the rise of compulsory schooling and the move away from an agricultural economy began to lengthen the expected period of youthful preparation. It wasn't until the Great Depression, though, that teenagers' economic life assumed the limits it has today. Hine points out that Roosevelt's New Deal was explicitly designed to take jobs away from young people and give them to heads of households. Teenagers were thus compelled to enroll in high school in much larger numbers than ever before. Young people's secondary economic role has persisted ever since. The affluence and restiveness of postwar America gave new cultural prominence in the 1950s

* Anya Kamenetz, *Generation Debt*, 2007

to the modern version of teenhood, a distinct stage of life, a subculture, and a commercial market, funded ultimately by parents. The accepted age of independence for the middle class and above was pushed forward to twenty-one.

4   Now the postmillennial years are bringing in an entirely new life stage: "emerging adulthood," a term coined by developmental psychologist Jeffrey Jensen Arnett in a 2000 article. The Research Network on Transitions to Adulthood at the University of Pennsylvania is a group of dozen or so experts in various fields: sociologists, policy experts, developmental psychologists, and economists. Their 2005 book, *On the Frontier of Adulthood*, explores emerging adulthood in depth.

5   "More youth are extending education, living at home longer, and moving haltingly, or stopping altogether, along the stepping stones of adulthood," writes Frank F. Furstenberg, chair of the network. "A new period of life is emerging in which young people are no longer adolescents but not yet adults.... It is simply not possible for most young people to achieve economic and psychological autonomy as early as it was half a century ago." They underlying reason, once again, is an economic shift, this time to a labor market that rewards only the highly educated with livable and growing wages.

> *"A new period of life is emerging in which young people are no longer adolescents but not yet adults.... It is simply not possible for most young people to achieve economic and psychological autonomy as early as it was half a century ago."*

6   In 2002, there were 68 million people in the United States aged eighteen to thirty-four. The social and economic upheaval of the past three decades, not to mention that of the past five years, affects us in complex ways. We have all come of age as part of Generation Debt.

7   The Penn researchers use five milestones of maturity: leaving home, finishing school, becoming financially independent, getting married, and having a child. By this definition, only 46 percent of women and 31 percent of men were grown up by age thirty in 2000, compared to 77 percent of women and 65 percent of men of the same age in 1960.

8   "I went from being a child to being a mother," says Doris, now in her fifties. "I was married at twenty. By thirty I had four children and was divorced." Doris completed college and a master's degree while keeping house and raising her children, then supported her family as a medical physicist.

9   Doris' youngest daughter, Miriam, graduated from Southern Connecticut State University in 2000, after six years of work and school, with $20,000 in student loans and $5,000 in credit card debt. Now, at twenty-nine, she is living in Madison, Wisconsin, and training to be a commodities broker, a job she could have pursued with only a high school diploma. Her mother, who bought her first house with her husband in her early twenties, helped Miriam pay off her credit cards and gave her the down payment on the condo she lives in. Miriam earns $28,000 a year and just manages the minimum payments on her loans. She is single. She hasn't passed the five milestones of adulthood; she is barely out to the driveway.

10   Young people are falling behind first of all because of money. College tuition has grown faster than inflation for three decades, and faster than family income for the past fifteen years. Federal aid has lagged behind. An unprecedented explosion of

borrowing has made up the difference between what colleges charge and what families can afford. Between 1995 and 2005, the total volume of federal student loans rose 249 percent after inflation, to over $61 billion. Two-thirds of four-year students are graduating with loan debt, an average of up to $19,200 in 2004 and growing every year. Three out of four college students have credit cards, too, carrying an average unpaid balance of $2,169 in 2005. Nearly a quarter of all students, according to a 2004 survey, are actually putting their tuition directly on plastic.

11   Even as the price has risen, more young people than ever aspire to college. Over 90 percent of high school graduates of all backgrounds say in national surveys that they hope to go on to college. Yet the inadequacy of aid shoots down their hopes.

12   As a direct consequence of the decline in public investment in education at every level, young people today are actually less educated than their parents. The nationwide high school graduation level peaked in 1970 at 77 percent. It was around 67 percent in 2004. According to a recent study cited in the 2004 book *Double the Numbers*, by Richard Kazis, Joel Vargas, and Nancy Hoffman, of every 100 younger people who begin their freshman year of high school, just 38 eventually enroll in college, and only 18 graduate within 150 percent of the allotted time—six years for a bachelor's degree or three years for an associates' degree. Only 24.4 percent of the adult population has a B.A., according to the 2000 Census, and those 25 to 34 years old are a little less likely to have one than 45- to 54-year-olds. Sociologists call non-college youth "the forgotten majority."

13   Statistically, the typical college student is a striving young adult; nearly half are 24 or older. She (56 percent are women) is spending several years in chronic exhaustion splitting her days between a nearly full-time, low-wage job, and part-time classes at a community college or four-year public university. She uses her credit cards to make ends meet—for books, meals, and clothes—and barely manages the minimum payments. Overloaded and falling behind, she is likely to drop out for a semester or for good. Almost one in three Americans in his or her twenties is a college dropout, compared with one in five in the late 1960s.

14   What happens to the three out of four young people who don't get a four-year degree? They are much more likely to remain in the working class than previous generations. Youths eighteen to twenty-four are the most likely to hold minimum-wage jobs, giving them a poverty rate of 30 percent in 2000, according to the U.S. Census; that's the highest of any age group. For those aged twenty-five to thirty-four, the poverty rate is 15 percent, compared with 10 percent for older working adults.

15   As policy analyst Heather McGhee, formerly of the think tank Demos, points out, when the Boomers were entering the workforce in 1970, the nations' largest private employer was General Motors. They paid an average wage of $17.50 an hour in today's dollars. The largest employer in the post-industrial economy is Wal-Mart. Their average wage? Eight dollars an hour. The service-driven economy is also a youth-driven economy, burning young people's energy and potential over a deep-fat fryer. McDonalds is the nation's largest youth employer; workers under 24 make up nearly half of the food services, department store, and grocery store workforce nationwide. The working world has always been tough for those starting out, but today's economy relies on a new element—a "youth class." The entire labor market is downgrading toward what was once entry level.

16   For better-off, college-educated sons and daughters, it's the same song, different verse. An astonishing 44 percent of dependent students from families making over $100,000 a year borrowed money for school in 2002. Credit card debt is higher for the middle class than for the poor. Unable to find good jobs with a bachelor's degree, young people are swelling graduate school classes, only to join the ranks of the unemployed or underemployed, after all.

17   The middle class has been shrinking for two decades. On a family-by-family basis, this means that many people my age who grew up in comfort and security are experiencing a startling decline in their standard of living. Median annual earnings for male workers 25 to 34 sank nearly 20 percent in constant dollars between 1971 and 2002. We start out in the working world with large monthly debt payments but without health insurance, pension benefits, or dependable jobs. It is impossible to predict whether we will be able to make up these deficits with higher earnings later on, but the evidence suggests that most of us will not.

18   In the 1960s the phrase "midlife crisis" captured the malaise of educated middle-class man confronting his mortality and an unfulfilling job or family life. Today "quarter-life crisis" has entered the lexicon for a generation whose unbelievably expensive educations didn't guarantee them success, a sense of purpose, or even a livable income.

19   When we talk about economics, we are also talking about ambition, responsibility, trust, and family. The new economic realities are distorting the life paths and relationships of the young. We are spending more time moving in and out of school, finding and losing jobs. Some of us move back home, and we put off marriage, children, and home buying. The older generation's response to these changes has been a chorus of disapproval and dismay.

20   The scholars of the Research Network on Transitions to Adulthood, relying on hard data, make the point that economic factors far outweigh psychological ones in explaining what has happened to young adults. "The current changing timetable of adulthood has given rise to a host of questions about whether current generations of young people are more dependent on their parents, less interested in growing up, and more wary of making commitments," they write. Our generation's delay in entering adulthood is often interpreted as a reflection of the narrowed generation gap.

21   In the 1980s, President Ronald Reagan began to dismantle the welfare state and put to rest the liberal dream of ending poverty on a large scale in America. His rhetorical ace was the Cadillac driving, government-cheating "welfare queen." Creating this infamous bogeywoman blamed the poor for their own problems and made taking away their means of support into the morally right thing to do.

22   The lazy, irresponsible, possibly sociopathic "twixter" is this decade's welfare queen, an insidious image obscuring public perception of a real inequity. If you look at where public resources are directed—toward the already wealthy, toward building prisons and expanding the military, away from education and jobs programs—it is easy to see a prejudice against young people as a class.

23   This is not to say that the phenomenon of emerging adulthood in and of itself is exclusively bad. It's a fact of history, like the so-called discoveries of childhood and adolescence before it. This change in the way we experience the life cycle brings upsides and downsides that we may not realize for decades to come. My friends and I overwhelmingly relish the time that we have, as postmillennial young adults, to try

out prospective jobs, travel, volunteer, study, and form strong friendships before settling down into career and family responsibilities. Young women, especially, tend to appreciate the way their options have widened, and the chance that medical science gives us to possibly delay motherhood into our thirties and forties. The more money and education you start out with, the better this time of uncertainty starts to look. The problems arise because our society does not recognize this new state of life, and is instead withdrawing resources from young people. Therefore, the majority of us face obstacles that make it harder to see the bright side of emerging adulthood.

24   In the past few decades, the trend in the United States has been toward smaller families and looser kinship ties. The bonds of kinship in our national family are weakening too. It's not too dramatic to say that the nation is abandoning its children. In everything from national budget deficits to the rise of household debt to cuts in student aid and public funds for education, Americans are living in the present at the expense of the future. ◆

CRITICAL THINKING

1. What is the purpose of Kamenetz's recounting of the history of childhood and how childhood has been viewed over the centuries? What point is she trying to support by providing us with this background?
2. Kamenetz observes that the New Deal was largely responsible for our expectations of teenhood today. What factor does she identify as responsible for another shift that marks young adulthood?
3. What are the "five milestones of maturity"? Where are you on the timeline? Have you followed a linear timeline, or have you hopped around, reaching some milestones out of order? At what age would you expect to reach all five milestones? Explain.
4. What reasons does Kamenetz give for why young people are "falling behind"? Explain.
5. What is the "the forgotten majority?" Why are they forgotten? What does this segment of people represent now and in the future? Explain.
6. In paragraph 12, Kamenetz describes the typical college student. Summarize the characteristics she cites, and then describe how you and your friends compare.
7. What is the author's opinion of low-wage and/or service-driven employment? What does she imply happens to young workers who do not earn college degrees?
8. Do you think young people in their 20s are viewed as this decade's "welfare queens"? What comparison is Kamenetz making? Do you agree? Explain.

CRITICAL WRITING

1. *Persuasive Writing:* Sociologist Frank F. Furstenburg notes, "A new period of life is emerging in which young people are no longer adolescents but not yet adults.... It is simply not possible for most young people to achieve economic and psychological autonomy as early as it was half a century ago." Write an essay in which you either agree or disagree

with his assessment, using examples from the essay, personal experience, and outside research.

2. *Research Writing:* How might one of the Baby Boomers Kamenetz refers to in this essay respond to her arguments? Highlight key points in the essay, and interview at least three people over 50 about the differences between the lives/expectations of twentysomethings today and those of 30 years ago.

3. *Research Writing:* Kamenetz asserts that America is living in the present at the expense of the future. Research the history and future of Social Security and other forms of federal financial support, including student financial aid. Then respond to Kamenetz's argument with your own view, supported by your research.

GROUP PROJECTS

1. Kamentez observes that young adulthood is emerging as a "new" distinct phase of life, similar to the recognition of childhood and adolescence in centuries before. "This change in the way we experience the life cycle brings upsides and downsides that we may not realize for decades to come." As a group, discuss this phase of life. If you are beginning or are in the middle of it, what are your expectations from this phase of your life? What challenges do you face, and what benefits might you expect? If you are past young adulthood, compare your experience with the trend now emerging. Then, project what average young adulthood might look like in America 20 years from now.

2. Outline the financial reasons Kamenetz cites for why postmillennial youth is "generation debt." Discuss her reasoning and add more of your own. After discussing the topic with your group, share your views with the class as part of a broader discussion on the issue. Present solutions or strategies to mediate the challenges young adults face in an uncertain economy.

Grow Up? Not So Fast

*Lev Grossman**

When does adulthood begin? In terms of starting a family and being financially solvent, what was once a milestone reached in the 20s is more likely to be reached in the 30s. In this next article, author Lev Grossman looks at the new generation of twentysomethings, which he calls "twixters," because they are "betwixt and between" in that they are putting off becoming adults by living with their parents. Twixters tend to take 5 or more years to graduate college, put off marriage and children, and wander from city to city and from job to job. Rather than representing a passing trend, their numbers are growing. Is this a new life stage to look forward to after graduation?

---

* Lev Grossman, *Time Magazine*, January 16, 2005

1 Michele, Ellen, Nathan, Corinne, Marcus and Jennie are friends. All of them live in Chicago. They go out three nights a week, sometimes more. Each of them has had several jobs since college; Ellen is on her 17th, counting internships, since 1996. They don't own homes. They change apartments frequently. None of them are married, none have children. All of them are from 24 to 28 years old.

2 Thirty years ago, people like Michele, Ellen, Nathan, Corinne, Marcus and Jennie didn't exist, statistically speaking. Back then, the median age for an American woman to get married was 21. She had her first child at 22. Now it all takes longer. It's 25 for the wedding and 25 for baby. It appears to take young people longer to graduate from college, settle into careers and buy their first homes. What are they waiting for? Who are these permanent adolescents, these twentysomething Peter Pans? And why can't they grow up?

3 Everybody knows a few of them—full-grown men and women who still live with their parents, who dress and talk and party as they did in their teens, hopping from job to job and date to date, having fun but seemingly going nowhere. Ten years ago, we might have called them Generation X, or slackers, but those labels don't quite fit anymore. This isn't just a trend, a temporary fad or a generational hiccup. This is a much larger phenomenon, of a different kind and a different order.

4 Social scientists are starting to realize that a permanent shift has taken place in the way we live our lives. In the past, people moved from childhood to adolescence and from adolescence to adulthood, but today there is a new, intermediate phase along the way. The years from 18 until 25 and even beyond have become a distinct and separate life stage, a strange, transitional never-never land between adolescence and adulthood in which people stall for a few extra years, putting off the iron cage of adult responsibility that constantly threatens to crash down on them. They're betwixt and between. You could call them twixters.

5 Where did the twixters come from? And what's taking them so long to get where they're going? Some of the sociologists, psychologists and demographers who study this new life stage see it as a good thing. The twixters aren't lazy, the argument goes, they're reaping the fruit of decades of American affluence and social liberation. This new period is a chance for young people to savor the pleasures of irresponsibility, search their souls and choose their life paths. But more historically and economically minded scholars see it differently. They are worried that twixters aren't growing up because they can't. Those researchers fear that whatever cultural machinery used to turn kids into grownups has broken down, that society no longer provides young people with the moral backbone and the financial wherewithal to take their rightful places in the adult world. Could growing up be harder than it used to be?

6 The sociologists, psychologists, economists and others who study this age group have many names for this new phase of life—"youthhood," "adultescence"—and they call people in their 20s "kidults" and "boomerang kids," none of which

have quite stuck. Terri Apter, a psychologist at the University of Cambridge in England and the author of *The Myth of Maturity*, calls them "thresholders."

7   Apter became interested in the phenomenon in 1994, when she noticed her students struggling and flailing more than usual after college. Parents were baffled when their expensively educated, otherwise well-adjusted 23-year-old children wound up sobbing in their old bedrooms, paralyzed by indecision. "Legally, they're adults, but they're on the threshold, the doorway to adulthood, and they're not going through it," Apter says. The percentage of 26-year-olds living with their parents has nearly doubled since 1970, from 11% to 20%, according to Bob Schoeni, a professor of economics and public policy at the University of Michigan.

8   Jeffrey Arnett, a developmental psychologist at the University of Maryland, favors "emerging adulthood" to describe this new demographic group, and the term is the title of his new book on the subject. His theme is that the twixters are misunderstood. It's too easy to write them off as overgrown children, he argues. Rather, he suggests, they're doing important work to get themselves ready for adulthood. "This is the one time of their lives when they're not responsible for anyone else or to anyone else," Arnett says. "So they have this wonderful freedom to really focus on their own lives and work on becoming the kind of person they want to be." In his view, what looks like incessant, hedonistic play is the twixters' way of trying on jobs and partners and personalities and making sure that when they do settle down, they do it the right way, their way. It's not that they don't take adulthood seriously; they take it so seriously, they're spending years carefully choosing the right path into it.

9   But is that all there is to it? Take a giant step backward, look at the history and the context that led up to the rise of the twixters, and you start to wonder, Is it that they don't want to grow up, or is it that the rest of society won't let them?

School Daze

10 Matt Swann is 27. He took 6 1/2 years to graduate from the University of Georgia. When he finally finished, he had a brand-spanking-new degree in cognitive science, which he describes as a wide-ranging interdisciplinary field that covers cognition, problem solving, artificial intelligence, linguistics, psychology, philosophy and anthropology. All of which is pretty cool, but its value in today's job market is not clear. "Before the '90s maybe, it seemed like a smart guy could do a lot of things," Swann says. "Kids used to go to college to get educated. That's what I did, which I think now was a bit naïve. Being smart after college doesn't really mean anything. 'Oh, good, you're smart. Unfortunately your productivity's s___, so we're going to have to fire you.'"

11   College is the institution most of us entrust to watch over the transition to adulthood, but somewhere along the line that transition has slowed to a crawl. In a *Time* poll of people ages 18 to 29, only 32% of those who attended college left school by age 21. In fact, the average college student takes five years to finish. The era of the four-year college degree is all but over.

12   Swann graduated in 2002 as a newly minted cognitive scientist, but the job he finally got a few months later was as a waiter in Atlanta. He waited tables for the next year and a half. It proved to be a blessing in disguise. Swann says he learned more real-world skills working in restaurants than he ever did in school. "It taught me how to deal with people. What you learn as a waiter is how to treat people fairly,

especially when they're in a bad situation." That's especially valuable in his current job as an insurance-claims examiner.

13   There are several lessons about twixters to be learned from Swann's tale. One is that most colleges are seriously out of step with the real world in getting students ready to become workers in the postcollege world. Vocational schools like DeVry and Strayer, which focus on teaching practical skills, are seeing a mini-boom. Their enrollment grew 48% from 1996 to 2000. More traditional schools are scrambling to give their courses a practical spin. In the fall, Hendrix College in Conway, Ark., will introduce a program called the Odyssey project, which the school says will encourage students to "think outside the book" in areas like "professional and leadership development" and "service to the world." Dozens of other schools have set up similar initiatives.

14   As colleges struggle to get their students ready for real-world jobs, they are charging more for what they deliver. The resulting debt is a major factor in keeping twixters from moving on and growing up. Thirty years ago, most financial aid came in the form of grants, but now the emphasis is on lending, not on giving. Recent college graduates owe 85% more in student loans than their counterparts of a decade ago, according to the Center for Economic and Policy Research. In *Time*'s poll, 66% of those surveyed owed more than $10,000 when they graduated, and 5% owed more than $100,000. (And this says nothing about the credit-card companies that bombard freshmen with offers for cards that students then cheerfully abuse. Demos, a public-policy group, says credit-card debt for Americans 18 to 24 more than doubled from 1992 to 2001.) The longer it takes to pay off those loans, the longer it takes twixters to achieve the financial independence that's crucial to attaining an adult identity, not to mention the means to get out of their parents' house.

15   Meanwhile, those expensive, time-sucking college diplomas have become worth less than ever. So many more people go to college now—a 53% increase since 1970—that the value of a degree on the job market has been diluted. The advantage in wages for college-degree holders hasn't risen significantly since the late 1990s, according to the Bureau of Labor Statistics. To compensate, a lot of twixters go back to school for graduate and professional degrees. Swann, for example, is planning to head back to business school to better his chances in the insurance game. But piling on extra degrees costs precious time and money and pushes adulthood even further into the future.

Work in Progress

16   Kate Galantha, 29, spent seven years working her way through college, transferring three times. After she finally graduated from Columbia College in Chicago (major: undeclared) in 2001, she moved to Portland, Ore., and went to work as a nanny and as an assistant to a wedding photographer. A year later she jumped back to Chicago, where she got a job in a flower shop. It was a full-time position with real benefits, but she soon burned out and headed for the territories, a.k.a. Madison, Wis. "I was really busy but not accomplishing anything," she says. "I didn't want to stay just for a job."

17   She had no job offers in Madison, and the only person she knew there was her older sister, but she had nothing tying her to Chicago (her boyfriend had moved to Europe) and she needed a change. The risk paid off. She got a position as an assistant at a photo studio, and she loves it. "I decided it was more important to figure

out what to do and to be in a new environment," Galantha says. "It's exciting, and I'm in a place where I can accomplish everything. But starting over is the worst."

18   Galantha's frenetic hopping from school to school, job to job and city to city may look like aimless wandering. (She has moved six times since 1999. Her father calls her and her sister gypsies.) But *Emerging Adulthood*'s Arnett—and Galantha—see it differently. To them, the period from 18 to 25 is a kind of sandbox, a chance to build castles and knock them down, experiment with different careers, knowing that none of it really counts. After all, this is a world of overwhelming choice: there are 40 kinds of coffee beans at Whole Foods Market, 205 channels on DirecTV, 15 million personal ads on Match.com and 800,000 jobs on Monster.com. Can you blame Galantha for wanting to try them all? She doesn't want to play just the hand she has been dealt. She wants to look through the whole deck. "My problem is I'm really overstimulated by everything," Galantha says. "I feel there's too much information out there at all times. There are too many doors, too many people, too much competition."

19   Twixters expect to jump laterally from job to job and place to place until they find what they're looking for. The stable, quasi-parental bond between employer and employee is a thing of the past, and neither feels much obligation to make the relationship permanent. "They're well aware of the fact that they will not work for the same company for the rest of their life," says Bill Frey, a demographer with the Brookings Institution, a think tank based in Washington. "They don't think long-term about health care or Social Security. They're concerned about their careers and immediate gratification."

20   Twixters expect a lot more from a job than a paycheck. Maybe it's a reaction to the greed-is-good 1980s or to the whatever-is-whatever apathy of the early 1990s. More likely, it's the way they were raised, by parents who came of age in the 1960s as the first generation determined to follow its bliss, who want their children to change the world the way they did. Maybe it has to do with advances in medicine. Twixters can reasonably expect to live into their 80s and beyond, so their working lives will be extended accordingly, and when they choose a career, they know they'll be there for a while. But whatever the cause, twixters are looking for a sense of purpose and importance in their work, something that will add meaning to their lives, and many don't want to rest until they find it. "They're not just looking for a job," Arnett says. "They want something that's more like a calling, that's going to be an expression of their identity." Hedonistic nomads, the twixters may seem, but there's a serious core of idealism in them.

21   Still, self-actualization is a luxury not everybody can afford, and looking at middle- and upper-class twixters gives only part of the picture. Twixters change jobs often, but they don't all do it for the same reasons, and one twixter's playful experimentation is another's desperate hustling. James Côté is a sociologist at the University of Western Ontario and the author of several books about twixters, including *Generation on Hold* and *Arrested Adulthood*. He believes that the economic bedrock that used to support adolescents on their journey into adulthood has shifted alarmingly. "What we're looking at really began with the collapse of the youth labor market, dating back to the late '70s and early '80s, which made it more difficult for people to get a foothold in terms of financial independence," Côté says. "You need a college degree now just to be where blue-collar people the same age were 20 or 30 years ago, and if you don't have it, then you're way behind." In other words, it's not that twixters don't want to become adults. They just can't afford to.

22   One way society defines an adult is as a person who is financially independent, with a family and a home. But families and homes cost money, and people in their late teens and early 20s don't make as much as they used to. The current crop of twixters grew up in the 1990s, when the dotcom boom made Internet millions seem just a business proposal away, but in reality they're worse off than the generation that preceded them. Annual earnings among men 25 to 34 with full-time jobs dropped 17% from 1971 to 2002, according to the National Center for Education Statistics. Timothy Smeeding, a professor of economics at Syracuse University, found that only half of Americans in their mid 20s earn enough to support a family, and in *Time*'s poll only half of those ages 18 to 29 consider themselves financially independent. Michigan's Schoeni says Americans ages 25 and 26 get an average of $2,323 a year in financial support from their parents.

23   The transition to adulthood gets tougher the lower you go on the economic and educational ladder. Sheldon Danziger, a public-policy professor at the University of Michigan, found that for male workers ages 25 to 29 with only a high school diploma, the average wage declined 11% from 1975 to 2002. "When I graduated from high school, my classmates who didn't want to go to college could go to the Goodyear plant and buy a house and support a wife and family," says Steve Hamilton of Cornell University's Youth and Work Program. "That doesn't happen anymore." Instead, high school grads are more likely to end up in retail jobs with low pay and minimal benefits, if any. From this end of the social pyramid, Arnett's vision of emerging adulthood as a playground of self-discovery seems a little rosy. The rules have changed, and not in the twixters' favor.

Weddings Can Wait

24   With everything else that's going on—careers to be found, debts to be paid, bars to be hopped—love is somewhat secondary in the lives of the twixters. But that doesn't mean they're cynical about it. Au contraire: among our friends from Chicago—Michele, Ellen, Nathan, Corinne, Marcus and Jennie—all six say they are not ready for marriage yet but do want it someday, preferably with kids. Naturally, all that is comfortably situated in the eternally receding future. Thirty is no longer the looming deadline it once was. In fact, five of the Chicago six see marriage as a decidedly post-30 milestone.

25   "It's a long way down the road," says Marcus Jones, 28, a comedian who works at Banana Republic by day. "I'm too self-involved. I don't want to bring that into a relationship now." He expects to get married in his mid to late 30s. "My wife is currently a sophomore in high school," he jokes.

26   "I want to get married but not soon," says Jennie Jiang, 26, a sixth-grade teacher. "I'm enjoying myself. There's a lot I want to do by myself still."

27   "I have my career, and I'm too young," says Michele Steele, 26, a TV producer. "It's commitment and sacrifice, and I think it's a hindrance. Lo and behold, people have come to the conclusion that it's not much fun to get married and have kids right out of college."

28   That attitude is new, but it didn't come out of nowhere. Certainly, the spectacle of the previous generation's mass divorces has something to do with the healthy

skepticism shown by the twixters. They will spend a few years looking before they leap, thank you very much. "I fantasize more about sharing a place with someone than about my wedding day," says Galantha, whose parents split when she was 18. "I haven't seen a lot of good marriages."

29   But if twixters are getting married later, they are missing out on some of the social-support networks that come with having families of their own. To make up for it, they have a special gift for friendship, documented in books like Sasha Cagen's *Quirkyalone* and Ethan Watters' *Urban Tribes,* which asks the not entirely rhetorical question, Are friends the new family? They throw cocktail parties and dinner parties. They hold poker nights. They form book groups. They stay in touch constantly and in real time, through social-networking technologies like cell phones, instant messaging, text messaging and online communities like Friendster. They're also close to their parents. *Time'*s poll showed that almost half of Americans ages 18 to 29 talk to their parents every day.

30   Marrying late also means that twixters tend to have more sexual partners than previous generations. The situation is analogous to their promiscuous job-hopping behavior—like Goldilocks, they want to find the one that's just right—but it can give them a cynical, promiscuous vibe too. Arnett is worried that if anything, twixters are too romantic. In their universe, romance is totally detached from pragmatic concerns and societal pressures, so when twixters finally do marry, they're going to do it for Love with a capital L and no other reason. "Everybody wants to find their soul mate now," Arnett says, "whereas I think, for my parents' generation—I'm 47—they looked at it much more practically. I think a lot of people are going to end up being disappointed with the person that's snoring next to them by the time they've been married for a few years and they realize it doesn't work that way."

Twixter Culture

31 When it comes to social change, pop culture is the most sensitive of seismometers, and it was faster to pick up on the twixters than the cloistered social scientists. Look at the Broadway musical *Avenue Q,* in which puppets dramatize the vagaries of life after graduation. ("I wish I could go back to college," a character sings. "Life was so simple back then.") Look at that little TV show called *Friends,* about six people who put off marriage well into their 30s. Even twice-married Britney Spears fits the profile. For a succinct, albeit cheesy summation of the twixter predicament, you couldn't do much better than her 2001 hit "I'm Not a Girl, Not Yet a Woman."

32 The producing duo Edward Zwick and Marshall Herskovitz, who created the legendarily zeitgeisty TV series "Thirtysomething" and "My So-Called Life," now have a pilot with ABC called "1/4life," about a houseful of people in their mid-20s who can't seem to settle down. "When you talk about this period of transition being extended, it's not what people intended to do," Herskovitz says, "but it's a result of the world not being particularly welcoming when they come into it. Lots of people have a difficult time dealing with it, and they try to stay kids as long as they can because they don't know how to make sense of all this. We're interested in this process of finding courage and one's self."

33   As for movies, a lot of twixters cite *Garden State* as one that really nails their predicament. "I feel like my generation is waiting longer and longer to get married," says Zach Braff, 29, who wrote, directed and starred in the film about a twentysomething actor who comes home for the first time in nine years. "In the past, people got married and got a job and had kids, but now there's a new 10 years that people are using to try and find out what kind of life they want to lead. For a lot of people, the weight of all the possibility is overwhelming."

34   Pop culture may reflect the changes in our lives, but it also plays its part in shaping them. Marketers have picked up on the fact that twixters on their personal voyages of discovery tend to buy lots of stuff along the way. "They are the optimum market to be going after for consumer electronics, Game Boys, flat-screen TVs, iPods, couture fashion, exotic vacations and so forth," says David Morrison, president of Twentysomething, Inc., a marketing consultancy based in Philadelphia. "Most of their needs are taken care of by Mom and Dad, so their income is largely discretionary. [Many twentysomethings] are living at home, but if you look, you'll see flat-screen TVs in their bedrooms and brand-new cars in the driveway." Some twixters may want to grow up, but corporations and advertisers have a real stake in keeping them in a tractable, exploitable, pre-adult state—living at home, spending their money on toys.

Living with Peter Pan

35 Maybe the twixters are in denial about growing up, but the rest of society is equally in denial about the twixters. Nobody wants to admit they're here to stay, but that's where all the evidence points. Tom Smith, director of the General Social Survey, a large sociological data-gathering project run by the National Opinion Research Center, found that most people believe that the transition to adulthood should be completed by the age of 26, on average, and he thinks that number is only going up. "In another 10 or 20 years, we're not going to be talking about this as a delay. We're going to be talking about this as a normal trajectory," Smith says. "And we're going to think about those people getting married at 18 and forming families at 19 or 20 as an odd historical pattern."

36   There may even be a biological basis to all this. The human brain continues to grow and change into the early 20s, according to Abigail Baird, who runs the Laboratory for Adolescent Studies at Dartmouth. "We as a society deem an individual at the age of 18 ready for adult responsibility," Baird points out. "Yet recent evidence suggests that our neuropsychological development is many years from being complete. There's no reason to think 18 is a magic number." How can the twixters be expected to settle down when their gray matter hasn't?

37   A new life stage is a major change, and the rest of society will have to change to make room for it. One response to this very new phenomenon is extremely old-fashioned: medieval-style apprenticeship programs that give high school graduates a cheaper and more practical alternative to college. In 1996 Jack Smith, then CEO of General Motors, started Automotive Youth Educational Systems (AYES), a program

that puts high school kids in shops alongside seasoned car mechanics. More than 7,800 students have tried it, and 98% of them have ended up working at the business where they apprenticed. "I knew this was my best way to get into a dealership," says Chris Rolando, 20, an AYES graduate who works at one in Detroit. "My friends are still at pizza-place jobs and have no idea what to do for a living. I just bought my own house and have a career."

38   But success stories like Rolando's are rare. Child welfare, the juvenile-justice system, special-education and support programs for young mothers usually cut off at age 18, and most kids in foster care get kicked out at 18 with virtually no safety net. "Age limits are like the time limits for welfare recipients," says Frank Furstenberg, a sociologist who heads a research consortium called the MacArthur Network on Transitions to Adulthood. "They're pushing people off the rolls, but they're not necessarily able to transition into supportive services or connections to other systems." And programs for the poor aren't the only ones that need to grow up with the times. Only 54% of respondents in the *Time* poll were insured through their employers. That's a reality that affects all levels of society, and policymakers need to strengthen that safety net.

39   Most of the problems that twixters face are hard to see, and that makes it harder to help them. Twixters may look as if they have been overindulged, but they could use some judicious support. Apter's research at Cambridge suggests that the more parents sympathize with their twixter children, the more parents take time to discuss their twixters' life goals, the more aid and shelter they offer them, the easier the transition becomes. "Young people know that their material life will not be better than their parents'," Apter says. "They don't expect a safer life than their parents had. They don't expect more secure employment or finances. They have to put in a lot of work just to remain O.K." Tough love may look like the answer, but it's not what twixters need.

40   The real heavy lifting may ultimately have to happen on the level of the culture itself. There was a time when people looked forward to taking on the mantle of adulthood. That time is past. Now our culture trains young people to fear it. "I don't ever want a lawn," says Swann. "I don't ever want to drive two hours to get to work. I do not want to be a parent. I mean, hell, why would I? There's so much fun to be had while you're young." He does have a point. Twixters have all the privileges of grownups now but only some of the responsibilities. From the point of view of the twixters, upstairs in their childhood bedrooms, snuggled up under their Star Wars comforters, it can look all downhill.

41   If twixters are ever going to grow up, they need the means to do it—and they will have to want to. There are joys and satisfactions that come with assuming adult responsibility, though you won't see them on *The Real World*. To go to the movies or turn on the TV is to see a world where life ends at 30; these days, every movie is *Logan's Run*. There are few road maps in the popular culture— and to most twixters, this is the only culture—to get twixters where they need to go. If those who are 30 and older want the rest of the world to grow up, they'll have to show the twixters that it's worth their while. "I went to a Poster Children concert, and there were 40-year-olds still rocking," says Jennie Jiang. "It gave me hope." ◆

CRITICAL THINKING

1. Grossman asserts, "Everybody knows a few of them—full-grown men and women who still live with their parents, who dress and talk and party as they did in their teens, hopping from job to job and date to date, having fun but seemingly going nowhere." Do you know anyone who fits this description? Explain what you know about these people. If you don't know anyone like this, discuss why Grossman is incorrect in his assertion.
2. Grossman states that our current culture trains young people to fear becoming adults. Do you agree or disagree? Explain using concrete examples.
3. According to researcher Abigail Baird, 18 is not the magic number for adulthood, as the human brain continues to grow and change into the early 20s. With this in mind, should the official age of adulthood be changed from 18 to 21? Even older? Explain.
4. This article mentions many possible reasons for new "twixter" phenomenon. Skim through the article and find as many reasons as you can. Which ones seem the most plausible to you? Can you add any more of your own?
5. Grossman looks at how an undergraduate degree tends not to be practically useful for this new generation but is a necessity nonetheless. What specific points does Grossman make about the value of college? Do you agree or disagree with his view?
6. Do you like the term "twixter"? What other terms have been used for this new demographic group? Which do you prefer? Explain your preference.

CRITICAL WRITING

1. *Personal Narrative:* Try to predict where you will be in 10 years and the journey you will take to get there. Will you be a twixter? Think about what your goals are for the future and how you will accomplish them.
2. *Exploratory Writing:* What do you think has contributed to this so-called intermediate phase between adolescence and adulthood?

GROUP PROJECTS

1. As a group, create 10 survey questions to ask 50 or so 18- to 28-year-olds to find out if they fit the "twixter" model. Synthesize your data and share your results with the class.
2. In Grossman's article, the audience is told, "Corporations and advertisers have a real stake in keeping [twixters] in a tractable, exploitable, pre-adult state—living at home, spending their money on toys." Look through magazines, online advertisements, and television advertisements geared toward the 18- to 28-year-old set to find six examples to confirm Grossman's statement. Share these advertisements in a PowerPoint presentation to the entire class.

3. Watch Zach Braff's film *Garden State* with your group and discuss whether this movie is indeed one that really nails the predicament of being a twixter. Explore how the movie does or does not exemplify this new demographic.

CULTURE SHOCK

Boomerang Statistics

Young Adults Living At Home: 1960 to Present

Numbers in thousands. Data based on Current Population Survey (CPS) U.S. Census Bureau

	Total	
Age 25 to 34 years	Male	Female
2007	20,002	19,828
2006	19,824	19,653
2005	19,656	19,632
2004	19,553	19,587
2003	19,543	19,659
2002	19,220	19,428
2001	19,308	19,527
2000	18,563	19,222
1999	18,924	19,551
1998	19,526	19,828
1997	20,039	20,217
1996	20,390	20,528
1995	20,589	20,800
1994	20,873	21,073
1993	20,856	21,007
1992	21,125	21,368
1991	21,319	21,586
1990	21,462	21,779
1989	21,461	21,777
1988	21,320	21,649
1987	21,142	21,494
1986	20,956	21,097
1985	20,184	20,673
1984	19,876	20,297
1983	19,438	19,903
1982	19,090	19,614
1981	18,625	19,203
1980 Census	18,107	18,689
1970 Census	11,929	12,637
1960 Census	10,896	11,587

THINKING CRITICALLY

1. Several of the articles in this section make a point of noting the increasing numbers of young adults who return home to live with their parents after graduation. What can you determine about this trend based on the data in this graph?

2. There was a significant increase in the number of young adults living at home with their parents from 1960 to 1980. What happened over this 20-year period that might account for this jump?

3. In the previous article, Grossman observes that a new life stage is emerging. Based on the information in this graph, would you agree? Explain.

Maxed Out

James D. Scurlock*

Many of us know that feeling overwhelmed by debt is awful. This next piece, excerpted from James D. Scurlock's book, describes how some college students felt so helpless and hopeless because of their debt that they took their own lives. Scurlock interviewed their parents for his documentary, *Maxed Out*, and uncovered a predatory world in which credit card companies target students they *know* have no income, because they believe "Mommy and Daddy" will bail their kids out. But when parents have their own financial burdens, or when kids are too embarrassed to reveal their panic, the results can be deadly. Scurlock exposes how credit card issuers form multimillion-dollar partnerships with colleges, gain access to students and set them up for financial ruin—before they even have their first job.

1   Janne O'Donnell remembers when she took her took her son Sean to college. A National Merit Scholar from a small town in Oklahoma, Sean, she remembers, "was so excited to be in the big city, Dallas." As they carried Sean's belongings across the relatively small campus of the University of Texas at Dallas (UTD), she noticed a number of tables advertising credit cards. "But I didn't worry," she recalls. "Sean was 18, he didn't have a job. Who would give him a credit card?"

2   What she has learned since that day makes Janne's question seem impossibly naïve. Not only would they give him a credit card, they would practically shove it down his throat. And as soon as he maxed that one out, they'd reward him with another one, and another. In the industry's parlance, he was "building his credit history." "Sean was a smart kid," Janne says, "but he didn't know how he got in, or how to get out." Sean would drop out of UTD, move back home, and find himself working two minimum-wage jobs, paying down $12,000 in debt on ten credit cards and saving money—so he could declare bankruptcy. "I didn't understand," Janne says. "It was something that was never in my world." Back in Janne's day, you and your husband could both work full-time jobs and still not qualify for a credit card.

3   The Visa and Mastercard offers Sean received as he was digging himself deeper and deeper into desperation describe an extraordinarily responsible young man, who had "graduated into adulthood," whose "responsible use of credit" was to be rewarded by a coveted spot on a number of VIP lists—in short, a platinum young man who deserved a limitless supply of credit. What exactly he did to deserve this credit remains a mystery to his mother.

4   "If you're working or if you're in a trade school," Janne says, "they don't want you. Maybe they realize you know the value of a dollar. It's the college students who get the credit card offers. So we're setting up a two-tiered system, and I believe that they are manipulating the students. An easy market."

5   Several years ago, Janne met another mother, Trisha, from the Oklahoma City area, whose daughter had hanged herself in her dorm room after racking up credit card debt (the young woman, Mitzi, didn't leave a note but did spread out her credit card

---

* James D. Scurlock, *Maxed Out: Hard Times in the Age of Easy Credit*, 2007

bills on her bed by way of explanation). Trisha and Janne had separately written their children's schools demanding that credit card companies be kicked off campus, and both had been ignored. Then they took their stories to the newspapers, to *60 Minutes*, and finally, with the help of a local congressman, to the Oklahoma state legislature. A bill was introduced prohibiting credit card companies from marketing on college campuses, an idea which has since been made law in several other states. When it came time to testify, however, Trisha and Janne found themselves opposing the financial industry and its lobbyists, who were "discussing how much money they contributed to each congressman's campaign," recalls Janne. "That bill didn't have a chance. They didn't want to listen to these two mothers. They wanted to listen to the money." As it turns out, Janne was right: Congressmen have their own preferred customer lists.

6   In one of her last appearances before Congress, Julie Williams, at the time the comptroller of the currency and thus the nation's top banking regulator, assured the Senate Banking Committee that credit card companies have not only developed complex models that determine exactly how much credit to extend to a particular student at a particular school, but that these models have appropriate risk metrics built in. I would be curious to know the magic number these banks and credit card companies had assigned to Sean and Mitzi—in other words, their price. What that company expected to make over a lifetime from Janne's and Trisha's kids by selling them more credit—not just credit cards but home mortgages (and then equity lines of credit), auto loans, student loans, credit insurance, late fees, and so on. No one has ever asked the credit card companies for that particular number, but one thing is certain: It is much larger than people realize, and the competition for young customers is getting more and more intense.

7   Ten years ago, First USA (now owned by JP Morgan Chase) paid the University of Tennessee $19 million for access to its students and alumni—their telephone numbers, Social Security numbers, and addresses—setting off a bidding war for access to college students. In 2000, the company raised the stakes again by purchasing two high school students from New Jersey who'd offered to sell themselves as human billboards to any company willing to pay their college tuitions. If positioning the two friends—"Chris" and "Luke"—as a couple of hip surfer dudes who just happened to love First USA seemed a tad corny, the two students, who were working at a public relations firm, had already developed the perfect angle. Chris and Luke would position themselves as spokesmen for financial responsibility (wink, nod). Even for a credit card company, this was an act of extraordinary chutzpah, meaning the media ate it up. Chris and Luke appeared on *Fox News*, the *Today Show*, and *Good Morning America*, to name a few. Their Web site was featured on Yahoo! and received millions of hits. The financially responsible "celebrity surfers" from New Jersey, who were ferried to photo ops in limos, were a hit, at least for a few months.

8   In the end, the marriage of credit card behemoth and surfer-dude students turned sour. Chris dropped out of Pepperdine to start a career in the independent film business, and Luke tired of being manipulated by bossy PR people from First USA, though he

does admit that being flown in a private jet for lunch at the company's headquarters in Chicago was pretty cool. Plus, First USA was more about boring business mags like *Forbes* and *BusinessWeek* than about MTV and *Rolling Stone*. "We wanted to delve deeper into the aspect of financial responsibility, but we got the feeling that First USA was just a little more interested in getting credit card sign-ups," Chris relates in one of the less shocking revelations I'll hear in my lifetime. He estimates that, in exchange for the $50,000 First USA spent on the duo's freshman-year college tuition, the company has received roughly $20 million in free publicity and hundreds of thousands of new, college-age cardholders. Despite this appearing to be a fairly awesome deal for First USA, Luke says the company paid their tuition weeks late, nearly causing an early end to both his and Chris's college careers. "It was just weird," Luke says with a straight face.

9   Ultimately, there is one customer far more valuable to the corporations than the 18 to 24 demographic, and that customer is Wall Street, which supplies the funds that lenders like First USA resell in small chunks to people like Chris and Luke and Sean and Mitzi. At the time Chris and Luke were being hyped in the pages of the *Wall Street Journal* and *Fortune*, First USA had just been acquired by a larger bank, Bank One, for close to $8 billion (which itself would be later acquired by JP Morgan Chase). One of First USA's major selling points had been its access to the student markets. Perhaps Bank One recognized the perfect opportunity to justify its big purchase, to show analysts that its new brand was hip with the kids, that it would continue to aggressively pick the low-hanging fruit—"the easy market," as Janne put it.

10   Like Chris, Janne's son dropped out of college. Sean moved back home and tried to figure out a way to declare bankruptcy, finish school, and somehow get a law degree, his dream. Living at home and working more low-wage jobs must have been humiliating for a National Merit Scholar who'd left for the big city with so much potential, but it was harder on Janne and her husband, who were forced to choose between bailing out Sean or helping their younger son through college. In the end, Janne couldn't see denying her other son the same opportunity they'd given Sean. Sean accepted the decision, told his mother he felt like a failure, and two days later, hung himself. Thereafter, Sean's memory was commemorated by a constant stream of phone calls from bill collectors, threatening letters, and more offers for credit, one of which read, "We want you back!" One day a collector called up and suggested that Janne should pay up to honor Sean's memory.

11   "I gave you my son," she replied. "What more do you want?" ◆

CRITICAL THINKING

1. Sean's mother dismisses the credit card tables on campus, because she knows that her son doesn't have job, so she presumes he would not be given a credit card. Yet Sean does get a card. Why are credit card companies giving cards to students without jobs? How do they assume balances will be paid? Do you think it makes sense to give a credit card to an unemployed student? Is it a matter of self-management of one's finances? Explain.

2. Review the story of Chris and Luke, who sold themselves to First USA in exchange for college tuition. What accounted for their success? Why did they discontinue their relationship with the credit card company? Would you be more likely to sign up for a credit card promoted by another college student?

3. What does "low-hanging fruit" refer to? How are college students "low-hanging fruit" to credit card companies?
4. Janne mentions that the language used in letters offering Sean more credit made him seem like an outstanding credit card user worthy of obtaining even more credit. How do credit cards market themselves to students? If possible try to gather some offers on your own campus, such as near the campus bookstore, on tables, or even online. How does the language appeal to students and entice them to obtain a card?

WRITING ASSIGNMENTS

1. *Research and Evaluation:* Get the film *Maxed Out*. After watching the documentary, write a review of the movie.
2. *Research Writing:* Learn more about the history of credit cards at www.PBS.org—*The Secret History of the Credit Card*. Based on what you learn in the documentary, write an essay in which you explore the ethics of credit card marketing on college campuses.

GROUP PROJECTS

1. Most people never read the fine print on their credit card agreements. Go online and locate the user agreement for a credit card from a major credit card issuer such as Mastercard, Visa, or Discover. As a group, review the agreement and discuss whether the terms are clear. Identify any policies that seem particularly noteworthy.
2. In only a few years, Sean raked up over $12,000 in credit card debt. Many other college students accrue significant debt over the course of their time at school. Discuss the psychology of credit cards. What does it mean to own them? How does it make you feel? How does it influence your purchasing decisions? Allow each member of the group to share their point of view and recount a personal story connected to either getting a card or using one.

Strapped
*Tamara Draut**

Most graduates 20 years ago expected to leave college with some student-loan debt along with their newly earned diplomas. But many of today's graduates carry an additional burden— credit card debt. It used be "no job, no credit." The big credit card companies have erased this policy in favor of ensnaring young consumers by offering students sizable credit lines. The result is many students are up to their ears in credit card debt long before they have a job. This next excerpt from Tamara Draut's book *Strapped* explains why it is harder than ever for young adults to get ahead. Rather than preparing students to succeed, college campuses are promoting products that practically ensure that they never will.

---

* Tamara Draut, *Strapped: Why America's 20- and 30-Somethings Can't Get Ahead*, 2007

1   It starts with a free T-shirt. If you've strolled through a college campus lately, chances are you've witnessed the phenomenon known as *tabling*. It used to be tabling was the province solely of student campus groups, with table after table offering pamphlets and sign-up sheets for everything from the ultimate Frisbee team to the Young Democrats or Young Republicans. But in the last ten years, tabling has been co-opted by capitalism, particularly by the industry one young adult referred to as "those credit card pushers."

2   At colleges across America, especially at state universities, credit card companies have taken a page out of the student organizations' playbook and table alongside the best of them. But the card companies have a leg up on the student groups: swag, and lots of it. In exchange for filling out a credit card application, students can get free stuff ranging from T-shirts to mugs and pizzas. The tables are staffed not by marketing representatives from the company but by college students trying to earn an extra buck themselves. On college campuses, credit card companies not only find profitable customers, but cash-strapped minions to do their shilling for them.

3   But what about the colleges themselves? Where are they in this picture? Far too often, they're in on the profit mongering. This is especially true of big state universities. The University of Tennessee, for example, accepted $16 million from First USA (now Chase) in exchange for exclusive marketing rights on campus, and hundreds of other schools receive money for every new application filled out by students. According to Robert Manning, author of *Credit Card Nation*, these types of deals yield the 300 largest universities about $1 billion year.

4   The marketing onslaught has paid off: in 2002, the average college senior had six credit cards and an average balance of just over $3,200. Many college students are in deeper trouble. One in five students has credit card debt of $3,000 to $7,000. Not surprisingly, student credit card debt increases with each successive year and more than doubles from freshman to senior year.

5   Recently, some states have closed their open-door policies regarding on-campus credit card marketers. In 2003, West Virginia passed legislation requiring all the public colleges in the state to regulate credit card marketing on campus. Some schools in the state banned the practice outright, whereas West Virginia University simply put an end to swag—at least swag without permission granted by the university. According to a General Accounting Office report in 2001, at least twenty-four states had introduced legislation to restrict credit card marketing on campus, but so far only Arkansas, Louisiana, New York, and West Virginia have actually passed such legislation. Where state legislatures have failed to ban the practice, many individual schools have taken the initiative. In 1998, the University of Minnesota banned credit cards companies from campus. Smaller, private liberal arts colleges have been more effective at patrolling card marketing on campus. Enforcement is easier on small campuses, and there's less incentive for these elite schools to raise money through deals with the card companies, because they tend to have fat endowments and a steady stream of very high tuition monies filling their coffers.

6   But the card companies are nothing if not persistent. Even if they're forbidden to table on campus, they have other crafty methods to reach students. Some colleges make it really easy by selling the card companies their students' information. A report by the Maryland Public Interest Group found that Towson University sells its

student list to MBNA—although after the publication of the report, it told the authors they would stop this practice in mid 2004. If a college bans a company outright, the friendly campus bookstore will usually help out the card mongers by agreeing to stuff its bags with credit card offers.

7   About a quarter of students report using their credit cards to pay for tuition and books. What about the other three quarters? Certainly their credit card debt represents in part what we tend to think of as frivolous debt. Visa and Mastercard have no doubt funded a great many pizzas, kegs, and spring breaks.

8   The problem is that after graduation, the need for credit often morphs into a whole new category: survival debt. Making the transition from college grad to full-fledged working adult takes more than a good resume. For young twentysomethings who can't turn to Mom and Dad for start-up money, launching their adult lives often entails going further into credit card debt. And with substantial debt already built up from college, young adults can get caught off guard and tangled in a debt spiral they most likely never saw coming.

9   Of course, it's not only college grads who are using credit cards as a private safety net. In fact, the ubiquity of credit cards among under-34ers makes it hard to categorize young debtors. They're college-educated, non-college-educated, males, female, black, Hispanic, and white. They're receptionists, project managers, teachers, and health care workers. During the 1990s, credit card debt among those under age 34 grew by 47 percent. But that doesn't mean that young adults don't take debt seriously or that it isn't a major stress in their lives. This generation regards credit card debt as a necessary evil.

10   Every three years, the Federal Reserve collects information specifically on household credit card debt as part of its Survey of Consumer Finances, with 2004 being the latest data available. To compare credit card debt between Gen-Xers and the late Baby Boomers, we can use survey findings from 1989, when the 25- to 34-year-old population was made up of Baby Boomers, and 2004, when it was made up of Gen-Xers. My analysis of the data indeed confirms that Gen-Xers are more indebted than Baby Boomers were at the same age. In 2004, 25- to 34-year-olds averaged $4,358 in credit card debt—47 percent higher than it was for Baby Boomers in 1989.

11   Keep in mind that these numbers are based on self-reported amounts, not actual credit card statements. For many reasons, people tend to underreport their credit card debt. For example, in 2004, the average household credit card debt reported in the survey was just over $5,219. But aggregate data on outstanding credit card debt reported by the credit card industry puts the average household debt at $12,000. New survey research conducted by Demos of low- to middle-class households found that the average indebted under 34-er had just over $8,000 in credit card debt in 2005. According to these households, the most common reasons cited for their credit card debt were car repairs, loss of a job, and home repairs. Forty-five percent of under 34-ers reported using credit cards in the last year to pay for basic living expenses, such as rent, mortgage payments, groceries, and utilities. Not exactly the stuff of the young debtor stereotype.

12   The rise in credit card debt, coupled with the surge in student loan debt, is the main reason why today's young adults are spending much more on debt payments than the previous generation. On average those aged 25 to 34 years spent nearly 25 cents out of every dollar of income on debt payments in 2001, according to the Federal Reserve's data. That's more than double what Baby Boomers of the same

age spent on debt payments in 1989. The fact that young adults are already spending a quarter of their income on debt is particularly worrisome, because most in the 25-to-34 age group aren't homeowners. So that 25 cents is going to non-mortgage debt: primarily student loans, car loans, and credit cards.

13   The soaring debt among young adults is landing more of this generation in the throes of bankruptcy. By 2001, nearly 12 out of every 1,000 young adults aged 25 to 34 were filing for bankruptcy, a 19 percent increase since 1991. Young adults now have the second highest rate of bankruptcy, just after those aged 35 to 44.

14   As being young and single has become practically synonymous with being in debt, it's no surprise that when young people finally find love, they also find more debt. While the economic benefits of living together

> *As being young and single has become practically synonymous with being in debt, it's no surprise that when young people finally find love, they also find more debt.*

or getting married are still pretty good—especially in expensive cities—today's young couples aren't getting quite the economic benefits that previous generations enjoyed when they combined incomes. Why? Because in addition to joining together in matrimony, young couples today are joining together in debt servitude.

15   Despite being broke and in credit card debt, many of the young adults I spoke with actually managed to put some money into a savings account. Most young adults want to build up an emergency fund and save for retirement. Unfortunately, it isn't until they hit their thirties that they are able to do both.

16   Young adults aren't alone in struggling to save money. Over the last twenty years, our nation's personal saving rate has plummeted from about 8 percent through the 1980s and early 1990s to zero in 2005—its lowest point since the Great Depression. There is growing concern that Americans now live by the rule "If you have it, spend it." Most social critics hold up the Greatest Generation, those who came of age during the Great Depression, as the moral pinnacle of scrimping and saving. The Baby Boomers took a lot of flak during the 1980s for their spending habits. Remember yuppies? The Baby Boomers seemed to have invented conspicuous consumption. And now that the Baby Boomers have reached the age where they control the commentary on all things social, political and economic—they've taken to criticizing the younger generation for its spending habits.

17   If today's young adults can be accused of wanting it all too soon, the "it" isn't riches, gadgets, or luxury cars. The elusive "it" that today's twentysomethings are after is financial independence, and then, hopefully, financial security. All the buzz about young bucks making millions in stock options and entrepreneurial start-ups simply distracted attention from a bigger story. The 1990s ushered in the Era of Debt. While the popular media made it look as though riches had landed at our feet, the real new economy meant that obtaining a middle-class lifestyle now required a large credit line and five-figure student debt.

18   Without bold thinking and the courage to uphold our nation's most sacred values, a whole generation of young adults will come of age in an America that doesn't reward hard work, family values, or collective responsibilities. The grim economic reality and choked opportunity facing young adults didn't have to happen. And it doesn't have to continue. ◆

CRITICAL THINKING

1. In her introduction, Draut describes the practice of tabling and its role in connecting new students to their first credit card. What is your own experience with tabling? Were you approached on campus and offered a card? Did you get one, or do you know someone who did? Explain.
2. Some students are given credit cards by their parents "for emergencies." Do you think this is a good idea? If you have such an arrangement, have you ever used your card for something other than an emergency? What constituted an "emergency"?
3. Draut observes that "This generation regards credit card debt as a necessary evil." Do you agree? What is your personal view of credit card debt? Is it simply a way of life? Can you survive in this world without credit cards and the debt that comes with them? Explain.
4. What is Draut's argument in this essay? What is her objective? Evaluate her use of examples to support her view.
5. How did the spending habits of the Baby Boomers and Generation Xers contribute to our current consumption habits? Explain.

CRITICAL WRITING

1. *Expository Writing:* What, if anything, can the younger generation learn from the older generation about debt? Speak to a few people older than you about their views of debt, including student loans, credit card debt, and car loans. What is their view of debt? Does it differ from your view? Explain.
2. *Research Writing:* Draut notes that most social critics hold up the "Greatest Generation," those who came of age during the Great Depression. Research the social impact of the Great Depression. What are the merits of thrift? What role does it play in our social consciousness? Is it as important today as it was 50 years ago? As America once again faces the most challenging economic climate since the Great Depression, how might your generation measure up?
3. *Personal Narrative:* Write about a time when you had to make a personal choice that involved incurring debt. Describe the circumstances and your feelings about the incident.

GROUP PROJECTS

1. Draut's conclusion observes that "bold thinking" is needed to help the current generation reclaim its right to financial security and the American dream. As a group, outline the things you feel represent the American dream. After completing your list, discuss as a group or as a class the challenges you face in reaching that dream.
2. Several writers in this chapter cite government and corporate policies that have contributed to the current generation's debt crisis. As a group, discuss ways that students can turn the tide of the "Era of Debt." Include grassroots efforts, political policy, and campus initiatives in your discussion.

Debtor's Prism

Margaret Atwood*

Since ancient times, the notion of debt has been deeply interwoven into our culture, literature, and social structure. With the global markets in turmoil, Margaret Atwood looks at the history and meaning of being in hock. This next essay, adapted from acclaimed writer Margaret Atwood's novel *Payback*, describes the history and psychology of debt, its notable role in literature, and what we might learn from these as we face uncertain economic times.

1 Without memory, there is no debt. Put another way: Without story, there is no debt.

2 The story of debt reached a historic moment this week. An outsized bubble of interlocking debt burst, leading to the downfalls of prominent companies. Loans by and to the government, financial institutions, and consumers collided on an epic scale. Still, the idea of what we owe one another is an ancient theme, and this is just the latest chapter in a long cultural history.

3 A story is a string of actions occurring over time—one damn thing after another, as we glibly say in creative writing classes—and debt happens as a result of actions occurring over time. Therefore, any debt involves a plot line: how you got into debt, what you did, said, and thought while you were in there, and then—depending on whether the ending is to be happy or sad—how you got out of debt, or else how you got further and further into it until you became overwhelmed by it and sank from view.

4 The hidden metaphors are revealing: We get "into" debt, as if into a prison, swamp, or well, or possibly a bed; we get "out" of it, as if coming into the open air or climbing out of a hole. If we are "overwhelmed" by debt, the image is possibly that of a foundering ship, with the sea and the waves pouring inexorably in on top of us as we flail and choke. All of this sounds dramatic, with much physical activity: jumping in, leaping or clambering out, thrashing around, drowning. Metaphorically, the debt plot line is a far cry from the glum actuality, in which the debtor sits at a desk fiddling around with numbers on a screen, or shuffles past-due bills in the hope that they will go away, or paces the room wondering how he can possibly extricate himself from the fiscal molasses.

5 In our minds—as reflected in our language—debt is a mental or spiritual nonplace, like the Hell described by Christopher Marlowe's Mephistopheles when Faust asks him why he's not in Hell but right there in the same room as Faust. "Why, this is Hell, nor am I out of it," says Mephistopheles. He carries Hell around with him like a private climate: He's in it and it's in him. Substitute "debt" and you can see that, in the way we talk about it, debt is the same kind of placeless place. "Why, this is Debt, nor am I out of it," the beleaguered debtor might similarly declaim.

* Margaret Atwood, *The Wall Street Journal*, September 20, 2008

6   Which makes the whole idea of debt—especially massive and hopeless debt—sound brave and noble and interesting rather than merely squalid and gives it a larger-than-life tragic

Could it be that some people get into debt because, like speeding on a motorbike, it adds an adrenalin hit to their otherwise humdrum lives?

air. Could it be that some people get into debt because, like speeding on a motorbike, it adds an adrenalin hit to their otherwise humdrum lives? When the bailiffs are knocking at the door and the lights go off because you didn't pay the water bill and the bank's threatening to foreclose, at least you can't complain of ennui.

7   Debt can constitute one such story-of-my-life. Eric Berne's 1964 bestselling book on transactional analysis, *Games People Play,* lists five "life games"— patterns of behavior that can occupy an individual's entire lifespan, often destructively, but with hidden psychological benefits or payoffs that keep the games going. Needless to say, each game requires more than one player—some players being consciously complicit, others being unwitting dupes. "Alcoholic," "Now I've Got You, You Son of a Bitch," "Kick Me," and "See What You Made Me Do" are Berne's titles for four of these life games. The fifth one is called "Debtor."

8   Mr. Berne says, "'Debtor' is more than a game. In America it tends to become a script, a plan for a whole lifetime, just as it does in some of the jungles of Africa and New Guinea. There the relatives of a young man buy him a bride at an enormous price, putting him in their debt for years to come." In North America, says Mr. Berne, "the big expense is not a bride but a house, and the enormous debt is a mortgage; the role of the relatives is taken by the bank. Paying off the mortgage gives the individual a purpose in life." Indeed, I can remember a time from my own childhood—was it the 1940s?— when it was considered cute to have a framed petit-point embroidered motto hanging in the bathroom that said "God Bless Our Mortgaged Home." During this period, people would have mortgage-burning parties at which they would, in fact, burn the mortgage papers in the barbecue or fireplace once they'd paid the mortgage off.

9   I pause here to add that "mortgage" means "dead pledge"—"mort" from the French for "dead," "gage" for "pledge," like the part in medieval romances where the knight throws down his glove, thus challenging another knight to a duel—the glove or gage being the pledge that the guy will actually show up on time to get his head bashed in, and the accepting of the gage being a reciprocal pledge. Which should make you think twice about engagement rings, since they too are a gage or pledge— what actually are you pledging when you present such a ring to your one true love?

10   So "paying off the mortgage" is what happens when people play the life game of "Debtor" nicely. But what if they don't play nicely? Not-nice play involves cheating, as every child knows. But it's not always true that cheaters never prosper, and every child knows that, too: Sometimes they do prosper, in the playground and elsewhere.

11   Debt can have another kind of entertainment value when it becomes a motif, not in a real-life plot line, but in a fictional one. How this kind of debt plot unfolds and changes over time, as social conditions, class relations, financial climates, and literary fashions change; but debts themselves have been present in stories for a very long time.

12   I'd like to begin by interrogating a familiar character—a character so familiar that he's made it out of the fiction in which he stars into another kind of stardom: that of television and billboard advertising. That character is Ebenezer Scrooge, from Charles Dickens's *A Christmas Carol.* Even if you haven't read the book or seen the play or the several movies made about Scrooge, you'd probably recognize him if you met him on the street. "Give like Santa, save like Scrooge," as some ads have said, and we then have a lovable, twinkly old codger telling us about some great penny-pinching bargain or other.

13   But, wanting to have it both ways, the ads conflate two Scrooges: the reformed Scrooge, who signals the advent of grace and the salvation of his soul by going on a giant spend-o-rama, and the Scrooge we see at the beginning of the book—a miser so extreme that he doesn't even spend any of his money-hoard on himself—not on nice food, or heat, or warm outfits—not anything. Scrooge's abstemious gruel-eating lifestyle might have been applauded as a sign of godliness back in the days of the early bread-and-water saintly ascetic hermits, who lived in caves and said Bah! Humbug! to all comers. But this is not the case with mean old Ebenezer Scrooge, whose first name chimes with "squeezer" as well as with "geezer," whose last name is a combination of "screw" and "gouge," and whose author disapproves mightily of his ways:

14   Oh! But he was a tight-fisted hand at the grindstone, Scrooge! A squeezing, wrenching, grasping, scraping, clutching, covetous old sinner! Hard and sharp as flint, from which no steel had ever struck out generous fire; secret and self-contained and solitary as an oyster. The cold within him froze his old features, nipped his pointed nose, shrivelled his cheek, stiffened his gait; made his eyes red, his thin lips blue; and spoke out shrewdly in his grating voice.

15   That Scrooge has—consciously or not—made a pact with the Devil is signaled to us more than once. Not only is he credited with the evil eye, that traditional mark of sold-to-the-Devil witches, but he's also accused of worshipping a golden idol; and when, during his night of visions, he skips forward to his own future, the only comment he can overhear being made about himself in his former place of business is ". . . old Scratch has got his own at last, hey?" Old Scratch is of course the Devil, and if Scrooge himself isn't fully aware of the pact he's made, his author most certainly is.

16   But it's an odd pact. The Devil may get Scrooge, but Scrooge himself gets nothing except money, and he does nothing with it except sit on it. Scrooge has some interesting literary ancestors. Pact-makers with the Devil didn't start out as misers—quite the reverse. Christopher Marlowe's late–16th-century Doctor Faustus sells his body and soul to Mephistopheles with a loan document signed in blood, collection due in 24 years, but he doesn't do it cheaply. He has a magnificent wish list, which contains just about everything you can read about today in luxury magazines for gentlemen. Faust wants to travel; he wants to be very, very rich; he wants knowledge; he wants power; he wants to get back at his enemies; and he wants sex with a facsimile of Helen of Troy.

17   Marlowe's Doctor Faustus isn't mean and grasping and covetous. He doesn't want money just to have it—he wants to dispense it on his other wishes. He's got friends who enjoy his company, he's a big spender who shares his wealth around, he likes food and drink and fun parties and playing practical jokes, and he uses his

power to rescue at least one human being from death. In fact, he behaves like Scrooge, after Scrooge has been redeemed—the Scrooge who buys huge turkeys, giggles a lot, plays practical jokes on his poor clerk, Bob Cratchit, goes to his nephew's Christmas party and joins in the parlor games, and saves Bob's crippled offspring, Tiny Tim, leading us to wonder if Scrooge didn't inherit a latent gene for bon-vivantery from his distant ancestor Doctor Faustus—a gene that was just waiting to be epigenetically switched on.

18   The ghost of Scrooge's former business partner, Marley, displaying the principles of post-mortem-heart weighing worthy of the Ancient Egyptians and also of medieval Christianity, has to pay after death for Marley's sins during life. None of these sins involved a dalliance with Helen of Troy; all of them came from the relentless business practices typical both of Scrooge and of unbridled 19th-century capitalism. Marley totes a long chain made of "cash-boxes, keys, padlocks, ledgers, deeds, and heavy purses wrought in steel." He is fettered, he tells Scrooge, by the chain he forged in life—yet another example of the imagery of bondage and slavery so often associated with debt, except that now the chain is worn by the creditor. Indulging in grinding, usurious financial practices is a spiritual sin as well as a material one, for it requires a cold indifference to the needs and sufferings of others and imprisons the sinner within himself.

19   Scrooge is set free from his own heavy chain of cash boxes at the end of the book, when, instead of sitting on his pile of money, he begins to spend it. True, he spends it on others, thus displaying that most treasured of Dickensian body parts, an open heart; but the main point is that he does spend it. The saintly thing in earlier times would have been for him to have given the whole packet away, donned sackcloth, and taken up the begging bowl. But Dickens has nothing against Scrooge's being rich: in fact, there are quite a few delightful rich men in his work, beginning with Mr. Pickwick. It's not whether you have it; it's not even how you get it, exactly: the post-ghost Scrooge, for instance, doesn't give up his business, though whether it remained in part a moneylending business we aren't told. No, it's what you do with your riches that really counts.

20   Scrooge's big sin was to freeze his money; for money, as all students of it recognize, is of use only when it's moving, since it derives its value entirely from whatever it can translate itself into. Thus the Scrooges of this world who refuse to change their money into anything else are gumming up the works: currency is called "currency" because it must flow. Scrooge's happy ending is therefore entirely in keeping with the cherished core beliefs of capitalism. His life pattern is worthy of Andrew Carnegie—make a bundle by squeezing and grinding, then go in for philanthropy. We love him in part because, true to the laws of wish-fulfillment, which always involve a free lunch or a get-out-of-jail-free card, he embodies both sides of the equation—the greedy getting and the gleeful spending—and comes out of it just fine.

21   But we don't have enough cash. Or so we keep telling ourselves. And that's why you lied to the charity worker at your door and said, "I gave at the office." You want it both ways. Just like Scrooge.

22   I began by talking about debt as a story-of-my-life plot line, which is the approach Eric Berne takes in describing the variants of the life game of "Debtor."

23   But debt also exists as a real game—an old English parlor game. In fact, it's one of the games witnessed by the invisible Scrooge at his nephew's Christmas party. By no accident on the part of Dickens—for everything Scrooge is shown by the spirits must have an application to his own wicked life—this game is "Forfeits."

24   "Forfeits" has many variants, but here are the rules for perhaps the oldest and most complete form of it that we know about. The players sit in a circle, and one of them is selected to be the judge. Each player—including the judge—contributes a personal article. Behind the judge's back, one of these articles is selected and held up. The following verse is recited:

25   Heavy, heavy hangs over thy head.

26   What shall I do to redeem thee?

27   The judge—not knowing whose article it is—names some stunt or other that the owner of the article then has to perform. Much merriment is had at the absurdities that follow.

28   There's nothing we human beings can imagine, including debt, that can't be turned into a game—something done for entertainment. And, in reverse, there are no games, however frivolous, that cannot also be played very seriously and sometimes very unpleasantly. You'll know this yourself if you've ever played social bridge with a gang of white-haired, ruthless ace-trumpers or watched any news items about cheerleaders' mothers trying to assassinate their daughters' rivals. Halfway between tiddlywinks and the Battle of Waterloo—between kids' games and war games—fall hockey and football and their ilk, in which the fans shouting "Kill!" are only partly joking. But when the play turns nasty in dead earnest, the game becomes what Eric Berne calls a "hard game." In hard games the stakes are high, the play is dirty, and the outcome may well be a puddle of gore on the floor. ◆

CRITICAL THINKING

1. Is philanthropy an important part of life? Do you give to charity? Explain which charities you would give to if you had the funds.
2. Describe the organization of Atwood's essay. It has been referred to as a "meditation." Would you agree? Explain.
3. Try to calculate how much debt you will owe in 5 to 10 years. What plan of action would you need in order to pay down this debt?
4. Atwood asserts, "But it's not always true that cheaters never prosper, and every child knows that, too: Sometimes they do prosper, in the playground and elsewhere." From personal experience, have you known cheaters to prosper? Explain.
5. "Scrooge's happy ending is therefore entirely in keeping with the cherished core beliefs of capitalism." What are the core beliefs of capitalism?

CRITICAL WRITING

1. *Analytical Writing:* In this essay, Atwood analyzes how the concept of moneylending or debt plays out in *A Christmas Carol* by Dickens and in *Doctor Faustus* by Christopher Marlowe. For this writing assignment, find

a work of literature with debt, moneylending, or business dealings as one of its themes. After reading the novel, poem, or play, analyze how the work describes these concepts and how they alter the characters' lives. (Some works to consider: *The Merchant of Venice*, by William Shakespeare; *Middlemarch,* by George Eliot; *Robinson Crusoe*, by Daniel Defoe; Geoffrey Chaucer's *Shipman's Tale*, and "The Debt," by Paul Laurence Dunbar.)

2. *Exploratory Writing:* The title of this article is "Debtor's Prism," which is a play on "debtor's prison." Learn what the debtor's prison was used for throughout history, and then explore whether a modern form of the debtor's prison exists for yours and future generations.

GROUP PROJECTS

1. As a class or in large subgroups, play the game Forfeits. Review Atwood's article for instructions on how to play, or search online for a description of the game. Learn more about the game online, what it might have meant to Victorians, and what we might learn from it today.

2. Atwood suggests that her readers should "think twice about engagement rings, since they too are a gage or pledge—what actually are you pledging when you present such a ring to your one true love?" Review what Atwood means by "gage" or "pledge" when it comes to debt, and then as a group discuss whether marriage is also a form of debt, and if one should think twice about presenting an engagement ring to another based on Atwood's analogy.

Investigating the Nation's Exploding Credit Squeeze
*Danny Schechter**

The recent global financial crisis has brought our country and many parts of the world to their knees. It's easy for "armchair quarterbacks" to say what led to this, but many financial analysts actually made predictions and warned against the coming crisis. In this next article, written two years before the meltdown, Danny Schechter, the executive producer for Globalvision, Inc., asks his readers to notice what's going on and to do something to stop it. His words now bring on an eerie feeling, as what he wrote in 2006 came to a head in the January 21, 2008 global shares crash. Why did so many ignore the signs? Perhaps only true crisis can lead to change.

1 When I started out, my film was going to be about other people's economic woes. Soon I realized I was part of this story of how the credit industry targets poor and middle-class Americans. Not only was I a target, too, but all of us are.

---

* Danny Schechter, "Investigating the Nation's Exploding Credit Squeeze," *The Neiman Report*, Spring 2006

2   There is a credit divide in America that fuels our economic divide. Put another way, the globalization of our economy is about more than the outsourcing of jobs. There is a deeper shift underway from a society based around production, with the factory as the symbol of American economic prowess, to a culture driven by consumption, with the mall as its dominant icon.

3   My film, tentatively titled *In Debt We Trust*, combines storytelling, often in a voice laced with outrage, with investigative inquiry. It's about a nation where our credit score is the only score many people and institutions care about and where vast databases record our every purchase and consumer choice. Ours has become a nation in which the carrot of instant affluence is quickly menaced by the harsh stick of bill collectors, lawsuits, and foreclosures. And yet this bubble can burst: The slickest of our bankers and the savviest of our marketers have been able to undo the law of gravity, that what goes up must come down.

4   Viewers of our film will be transported behind the scenes to meet their biggest scammers, the engineers and operators of the billion dollar credit card industry who have researched the details and minutiae of consumer needs and our fantasies so that they can deploy the deceptive art of seductive marketing and modern usury. We will scrutinize a carefully conceived but stealth electronic Web designed to entrap, cajole and co-opt the most powerful consumer culture on earth. It teases us with a financial advance when we want it, then sucks it away from us with more force than we realize.

Reporting These Stories

5 In the old days the poor couldn't qualify for loans. Today they are considered among the better risks because, unlike the rich, many feel an obligation to pay back. Steve Barnett, who worked in the credit card industry and will appear in our film, explains: "These are the perfect customers. They need credit, so they're not all that concerned about interest. They'll take a higher interest if you will grant them credit. They'll pay off a small amount each month so they're in a sense 'on the hook.' And because of their own sense of values or because of their own background, their family background, they're not likely to declare bankruptcy again. Given the change of laws that's more difficult, anyway." And manufacturers now know they can spur sales by lending money to buyers up front and then get them to pay twice—first at the register, then with credit card payments, big interest rates, and compounded interest.

6   Given the ubiquitousness of these practices—and the reasons why they exist and persist that stretch from corporate America into the halls of government and revolve around issues of corporate greed and political favors—the expanding gaps between those who have (and then have more) and those who don't (but pay anyway) need to be explored and exposed by journalists. I am raising this issue and suggesting ways that it can be reported because I believe this is an essential story for us to tell.

7   Report more regularly on these credit issues; billions of dollars are involved, not to mention millions of lives.

8   Identify the key corporate institutions and contrast the compensation of their executives with the financial circumstances of their customers.

9   Shine a spotlight on how special interests and lobbyists for financial institutions contribute to members of Congress and other politicians, across party lines, to

ensure their desired policies and regulations. Investigate political influence affected by campaign contributions. Some reporting about this took place during the bankruptcy debate, but there has been little follow-up.

10   Examine the influence credit card companies have on media companies through their extensive advertising.

11   Take a hard look at the predatory practices in poor neighborhoods—and crimes committed against poor and working-class people, who are least able to defend themselves. Legal service lawyers tell me about how they are overwhelmed by the scale of mortgage scams involving homes whose values have been artificially inflated.

12   Focus attention on what consumers can do to fight back. Robert Manning, author of *Credit Card Nation*, explains: "If 10 percent of American credit cardholders withheld their monthly payments, it would bring the financial services industry to a standstill. At a larger issue, what we have to do is to get people involved at the state level, get their state attorneys general involved, aggressively filing class-action lawsuits and then putting pressure on key legislators to say, 'This is unacceptable that they're not representing and balancing the issues of commerce with consumers. The balance is tilted dramatically against the average American.'"

The Story's Key Ingredients

13   Class struggle is assuming a new form in the conflict between creditors and lenders that reaches into many Americans' homes, where each month bills are juggled and rejuggled with today's credit card bills paid by tomorrow's new card. Meanwhile, with interest compounding at usurious rates, indebtedness grows, and people sink even deeper into debts they cannot manage. In this conflict, companies function as well-organized machines while borrowers are forced to react as individuals. Many are browbeaten with lectures about "personal responsibility" by corporations that only pay lip service to any form of social responsibility.

> *Class struggle is assuming a new form in the conflict between creditors and lenders that reaches into many Americans' homes, where each month bills are juggled and rejuggled with today's credit card bills paid by tomorrow's new card.*

14   Centuries ago, we had debtor's prisons. Today, many homes become similar kinds of prisons, where debtors struggle with personal finance issues. The scale of indebtedness is staggering as consumers simply follow their government's lead. As of Christmas 2005 the national debt stood at $8,179,165,267,626.42. Break that down, and each American's share comes to $27,439.48, and our nation's debt increases $2.83 billion each day. Add to that two trillion more for consumer debt, including mortgages. That's a lot of money.

15   Who is really responsible for it? Few of us seem to know. And fewer appear to know what can be done about it. "They're never going to be repaid," says economic historian Michael Hudson, who for many years worked at Chase Bank. "Adam Smith said that no

government had ever repaid its debts, and the same can be said of the private sector. The U.S. government does not intend to repay its trillion-dollar debt to foreign central banks and, even if it did intend to, there's no way in which it could. Most of the corporations now are avoiding paying their pension fund debts and their health care debts."

16   The government and big companies might not have to pay, but regular people do, as our collective consumer debt has doubled in the past 10 years. With mortgage debt included, it's now reached seven trillion dollars. Hudson compares the plight of millions of debtors in the United States to serfs of an age gone by: "For many people, debts now absorb 40 percent of their income. So many people are paying all of their take-home wages over and above basic expenses for debt service. And that's rising. In effect, 90 percent of the American population is indebted to the top 10 percent of the population."

17   The coffers of creditors—funded by the most prestigious banks and financial institutions—are swelling with payments for arbitrarily imposed late fees and rising interest rates that seem to be largely unregulated. Borrowing is now a national habit. Fueling this shift globally has been our national debt—now in the trillions—as other countries finance our trade imbalances and keep our economy strong. Without that influx of money, the U.S. economy would be in crisis. Everyone in the know knows this, but they do little to deal with it, relying on the theory that if it ain't broke, don't fix it. Occasional warnings and lots of noise surface about cutting the government's annual deficit, including a devastating report by Comptroller General David Walker, who compares the United States today to Rome before its fall. He is dismissed as a prophet of gloom and barely covered while debt keeps growing. All of this borrowed money keeps people pacified and, for the most part, politically complacent for now.

18   So many of us live beyond our means. This is not news, but what isn't found in most news reporting is how this shift has been engineered through corporate decisions that are aided and abetted by government polices. Questions of by whom and for whom need more and better investigation, as well as a look at who are the losers and who are the winners.

19   Business reporting that focuses on the upticks and downticks of the market provides little room for explanation, analysis, or connecting-the-dots journalism. In part, that is a result of the fact that many of our major media companies don't operate in a world apart from these pressures. At least 10 credit-card solicitations have arrived recently in my mail, and the Disney (owner of ABC television network) card was in that pile. Many credit cards boast of partnerships and discounts from media companies and entertainment providers, from subscriptions to DVD's. Like car companies and airlines before them, the media industry has discovered that there's money to be made in the credit business and so credit card companies become big media advertisers. Why alienate them?

20   This credit squeeze is hitting the news business, too. Jobs are being cut and reporting trimmed. Joe Strupp of *Editor & Publisher* observed in his 2005 media wrap up, "Using the bizarre premise that newspapers can bring back lost circulation and ad revenue by making their products worse, top executives at major chains from The New York Times Company to Tribune took a butcher knife to staffing with buyouts and layoffs that appeared almost epidemic."

21   What happens to news business employees laid off in this environment? Like those in other industries where cost-cutting leads to unemployment, they enter what insiders in the credit business call "the turnstile," living on more and more credit from cards, soon to be followed by a dip into home equity. Nor have wages and benefits kept up with inflation, and many are being cut. Health care extensions after a job ends are over in 18 months and then what? What's the alternative? More debt is one of the few accessible options. The turnstile keeps turning as personal debt keeps growing. ◆

CRITICAL THINKING

1. In the introduction of this article, Schechter says he was a target of the credit industry. Find examples of how he was targeted, and explain whether his examples are effective in making his point.
2. Who is Schechter's audience? Cite examples from the article to support your answer. What does Schechter ask his audience to do?
3. How does Schechter describe poor and middle-class Americans? Why are they targeted by the credit industry? Do you agree with Schechter's representation?
4. Schechter implies that the government didn't take any action to fix the national debt due to the theory "If it ain't broke, don't fix it." Why wasn't it "broke"? When did it finally become "broke"?

CRITICAL WRITING

1. *Expository Writing:* Schechter asks his audience who is responsible for the scale of indebtedness in the United States. Based on the information in his article and others in this section, answer this question with your own viewpoint.
2. *Research Writing:* Comptroller General David Walker compared the United States today to Rome before its fall. Research the fall of Rome. While the ancient world is very different from our modern one, what cultural similarities exist? What might we learn from history?

GROUP PROJECTS

1. Watch Schechter's documentary *In Debt We Trust*. As a group, write a synopsis of the film and explain whether you agree or disagree with the following review and why: "Schechter's film is a compelling chronicle of how we got in over our heads . . . it should be required viewing for all high school and college students . . ."–Erica Freudenberger, *WoodStock Times*, July 27, 2006.
2. Locate a representative at a financial institution near you who would be willing to be interviewed. Create 10 questions on aspects of credit lending, and ask the financial representative your questions. Some sample questions might be, How are interest rates calculated for credit cards? How easy is it to lower the interest rate? Is credit given to individuals with little to no income? How are late fees imposed, and what is the rate? Are interest rates regulated?

Perspectives: Empty-nesters

© Mike Baldwin / Cornered

"Empty-nesters. They're hoping to sell before the flock tries to move back in."

CRITICAL THINKING

1. What issue does this cartoon raise? Explain.
2. What do the people selling the house hope to achieve?
3. Would this cartoon be understandable, or funny, if it appeared 20 years ago? Thirty years ago? Why or why not?

▶ **Twentysomething: Be Responsible, Go Back Home after College**
*Ryan Healy**

▶ **The Responsible Child?**
Florinda Vasquez

College grads are spreading their wings—only to fly right back home. "Failure to Launch" no longer carries the stigma it once did. In fact, according to the 2007 U.S. Census, 55 percent of men and 48 percent of women ages 18 to 24 live with their parents. The next two essays, which first appeared as blog entries, discuss different views of the "boomerang kid" phenomenon. On the one hand, moving back home makes good financial sense, if you can tolerate returning to the same place where curfews were once imposed and you have to mind your manners. On the other, parents may resent this intrusion on their newly gained freedom. Having an adult child at home is very different than housing a teenager, and some parents resent the presumption that their homes are hotels to crash in. As more and more kids return home, it is clear that some thoughtful discussion is needed on both sides.

Twentysomething: Be Responsible, Go Back Home After College
Ryan Healy

1 According to Monster.com, 60 percent of college graduates move home with mom and dad after graduation and the trend is on the rise. The statistic holds true with my friends from the class of 2006. More than half moved back to the suburbs to start adult life, much the same way they ended high school life—with their parents. A lot of people say generation Y needs to grow up and take some personal responsibility and that we have been coddled by our helicopter parents.

2 But when you look closely, it is glaringly apparent that moving back in with parents is one of the most responsible things a new college grad can do. By sucking it up at home for a year or two, young people give themselves the opportunity to take control of their career, take control

> *When you look closely, it is glaringly apparent that moving back in with parents is one of the most responsible things a new college grad can do. By sucking it up at home for a year or two, young people give themselves the opportunity to take control*

*Ryan Healy, Employee Evolution blog [www.employeerevolution.com], September 4, 2007. Florinda Vasquez, The 3 R's: Reading, 'Riting, and Randomness blog [www.3rsblog.com], September 6, 2007

of their finances and transition from the care-free college fantasy world to the real-world of work, marriage, kids, mortgages and car payments.

Take Control of Your Career

3 To live comfortably in a big city like New York, students are forced to take a high-paying, but less than satisfying job. Often, top graduates end up working for the best-paying investment bank or law firm. I'm sure you could find a small minority of conservative students who had dreams of becoming an I-banker since middle school, but for the most part, these jobs are going to the top tier students who are trying to make a quick buck before they retire at 30 (or so they say).

4 By moving home after graduation, you have little or no rent, which allows for more freedom when searching for a job. There is no need to sell out to an investment bank if your real goal is to work with underprivileged children. Depending on where your parents are located, you are probably missing out on the big city night life and social scene, but you have lots of opportunities to find the perfect job, regardless of pay. If ditching the social scene for career sake doesn't demonstrate responsibility and independence, I don't know what does.

Take Control of Your Finances

5 Real wages today are lower than they were for the past two generations of workers. Couple that fact with today's insane housing costs and an increase in contract workers not receiving benefits, just getting by on forty or fifty thousand a year in a major city is nearly impossible. Attempting to save any reasonable amount of money the first few years is a joke.

6 However, moving home with Mom and Dad will immediately save you about $700 a month in housing costs. At least there is some extra cash flow. In two years, you can save up enough to move out on your own without worrying about going into credit card debt for basic necessities, like fixing your car or buying groceries.

Take an Appropriate Adjustment Period between College and the Real World

7 People really do struggle adjusting from college to the real world. A good friend of mine just fulfilled her life-long dream of moving to New York. She still loves the city, but she is overwhelmed and doesn't exactly like her day job. Sure, many people go through this tough transition period, and chances are she will eventually enjoy it, but the transition from child to adult is different and oftentimes more difficult for today's youth.

8 "This period is not a transition, but an actual life stage," according to Jeffrey Arnett, associate professor at University of Missouri and author of *Emerging Adulthood: A Theory of Development from the Late Teens through Early Twenties*. Arnett describes the period between college and adulthood as "a self-focused stage where people have the freedom to focus on their own development." Notice he calls this period a stage in development and not just a transition between two stages.

9 So why do we still try to go from adolescent to adult in a matter of weeks or months? Moving home for awhile enables an appropriate and productive transition.

Rather than focus on rent, bills and kids, emerging adults living at home with their parents have the ability to focus on the most important aspects of emerging adult life: figuring out who they are and what career is right for them.

 ## The "Responsible" Child?

Florinda Vasquez

1 I know times have changed, and it's a lot harder for young adults to get started on their "real" lives these days. The late-night phone calls and long-distance online counseling of my son the insomniac—who actually does seem to be making a decent transition to the post-college, living-on-his-own, working-adult world—have reminded me of this lately. Even so, I have some major disagreements with this post blogger Ryan Healy, suggesting that it's a "responsible" decision to move back home after college.

2 I sent the link to my son for his take and to help gauge my own reaction. This is a snippet of our discussion via IM:

> **me:** Don't read this unless you have a few minutes, but speaking as a parent, I'm glad you're "irresponsible"
> **C:** only took a minute to read
> the points they make are kind of valid, but you could make the same argument for staying in the same city you went to school at
> **me:** or living at home while in college, and THEN moving out
> **C:** yeah
> but you need to have experience living on your own
> **me:** and once you have it, why move back home if you don't really have to?
> and where's "home" if your parents live in different places?
> **C:** there is a financial benefit
> but that's about it
> **me:** I can see that, but yeah. that's about it . . . especially if you've had that taste of being on your own already
> **C:** yeah
> **me:** it's hard on EVERYONE to go back
> **C:** yeah, I know
> in a vacuum it doesn't look bad

3 I guess it's hard to argue the benefits for a recent graduate, especially if everything reverts to pre-college status and parents are picking up the tab for everything. And if the grad takes advantage of that—in the "good" way—by working hard and saving up that money during this time period, he or she will be much better positioned financially for a more desirable lifestyle when the time to move out finally arrives. A friend of mine actually did this; she stayed in her parents' home until she'd been out of college about eight years, but when she did move out, it was into a house she bought on her own.

4   I actually think that being able to go away to college, living on or near campus, is a great opportunity. It's a taste of independence—being responsible for your own time management, for one thing, along with making lots of other choices—but it's also still sheltered, since most college kids aren't quite as "on their own" as they like to think they are. Directly and indirectly, most are still getting a substantial amount of support from parents during this time. But having had that taste of independence can mean giving it up when returning to the family home—and as a parent, I think to some extent that's entirely appropriate. Unless the recent grad is paying rent and other housing expenses to the parent, and doing his or her own laundry, errands, cleaning, etc.—that is, approximating living on one's own as closely as possible under the circumstances—I'm inclined to think "my house, my rules" applies, especially if there's also some amount of "my support" involved. And I'd suggest that rather than going away and coming back, one might ultimately arrive at the same place by attending a local university and living at home, preparing for a transition to independence after graduation. (I did this, and believe me, everyone was ready to move on after five years of it.)

5   For generations, it's been traditional for young adults to have to work their way up in the world; it's a formative experience intellectually, emotionally, and materially. Maybe I'm a traditionalist, but I see a lot of value to this. Depending on where you live and what you do, though, it can be harder to get on that footing and take longer to move forward—and I think that going back to the family home signals a reluctance to take on those challenges, as well as a sense of entitlement to a particular lifestyle that these young adults grew up with and don't want to sacrifice.

> *I think that going back to the family home signals a reluctance to take on those challenges, as well as a sense of entitlement to a particular lifestyle that these young adults grew up with and don't want to sacrifice.*

6   I gather that a lot of parents don't want them to have to sacrifice it, either. My take on the job of parenthood is that the goal is raising functional adults, and thereby ultimately working yourself out of a job—but I know that not all parents agree, and some have a hard time letting go appropriately. I'm not talking about kicking the baby birds out of the nest, mind you, and I don't think any parent wants to become truly unnecessary to his or her child, but I think we do more for them by helping them prepare to fly. (Teaching someone to fish vs. giving them a fish, you know...) I'm not sure letting them back into the nest really does help. I tend to think that moving back home after college has a lot more advantages for the child than the parents—but if the parents aren't ready to let go, I guess they get some benefit, too. If the parent is encouraging the child to return home, I wonder if that speaks more to the parent's needs than what's best for the young-adult child in the long run.

7   As I say, I'm probably a traditionalist, and my viewpoint is in line with my own experiences. I think those experiences were a good basis on which to raise my own child, though, and am glad to see him following that more traditional route; I hope that his upbringing has prepared him to make a good go of it. And considering that he was pretty anxious to get started on his own and not head back to stay with either of his parents after graduation, I guess he might be a bit of a traditionalist himself. ◆

CRITICAL THINKING

1. Florinda Vasquez observes of college graduates returning home, "it's hard on EVERYONE to go back." Describe the ways in which not only the college graduate is affected by moving back home but how others in the family are also affected.

2. Both Healy and Vasquez use the word "transition" to describe the time between graduating from college and becoming independent; however, Healy also tries to explain this as a "stage." What is Healy's purpose in calling the phenomenon "a stage"? In your opinion, is this phenomenon simply a transitional period, or a stage of life, or both? Explain.

3. Vasquez shares that a friend of hers stayed in her parents' home until she'd been out of college about 8 years. If adult children do move back home, what is the appropriate time span to live with one's parents? Eight years? Something else? How do you determine the appropriate length of time?

4. Healy reports, "A lot of people say Generation Y needs to grow up and take some personal responsibility and that we have been coddled by our helicopter parents." What are "helicopter parents" and how might they have contributed to the trend of kids coming home after graduation?

5. Vasquez asserts that the purpose of being a parent is "raising functional adults, and thereby ultimately working yourself out of a job." What else does she say about parenthood? Do you agree or disagree? What is the purpose of being a parent?

6. If an adult child does need to rely on his/her parents through the transition to full independence, which of the following paths, as Vasquez points out, is the best route to take: going away and coming back or attending a local university and living at home? In your opinion, which is the best solution and why?

CRITICAL WRITING

1. *Persuasive Writing:* Write your own blog entry. Convince other college students to either move back home after college or take off on their own. Provide concrete reasons to support your position.

2. *Technical Writing:* Write a contract agreement between a college graduate returning home to live with his or her parents. Consider in your contract issues such as rent, chores, grocery and telephone expenses, visitors, curfews, and other responsibilities in the home. In other words, what are the expectations of the child and what are the expectations of the parents?

3. *Analytical Writing:* Analyze the passage from Healy's article, "People really do struggle adjusting from college to the real world. A good friend of mine just fulfilled her life-long dream of moving to New York. She still loves the city, but she is overwhelmed and doesn't exactly like her day job. Sure, many people go through this tough transition period, and chances are she will eventually enjoy it, but the transition from child to adult is different and often times more difficult for today's youth." Is Healy's

example of his friend effective enough to get his point across? What exactly is the "struggle" his friend is going through? Analyze the specific words Healy uses to explain himself. Follow your analysis with your own opinion of whether "the transition from child to adult is different and often times more difficult for today's youth."

GROUP PROJECTS

1. With your group, make up a set of 10 survey questions asking other college students whether they plan on moving back home after school, and what that may entail, or if they plan on making it on their own, and what that may entail. Give your survey to 20 peers, and share your data with the rest of the class.
2. Crunch the numbers: As a group, agree on a city to live in after graduation. Research how much it will cost to live in that city on a monthly basis. To get you started, decide on a typical living establishment for twenty-somethings, then look up the average amount of rent paid; in addition, find out how much is needed for utilities, groceries, transportation, insurance, entertainment, and other necessities. If first and last month's rent and a security deposit are needed to rent an apartment, include that in your discussion.

Carbon Footprints

It's Not Easy Being Green

The issue of climate change is at the forefront of political and public policy debates. Natural disasters, human health, biodiversity, endangered species, water resources, international trade, financial services, transportation networks, agriculture—virtually any area of human experience is in some way affected by climate. Environmental models predict that the Earth's temperature is likely to rise from anywhere between 2 to 11 degrees Fahrenheit (1 to 6°C) by 2100. And while scientists and politicians now agree that the earth is indeed getting warmer, the challenge now is deciding what we can do about it. An increase in global temperatures may lead to other changes in our ecosystem—such as a rising sea level, altered weather patterns, and extinctions of species of animals. Agricultural yields and coastal communities are also at risk.

Many of us have heard the word "green" tossed around to describe everything from eco-friendly cars to buildings to marketing practices. Critics challenge that many companies that profess to be "green" are merely trying to cash in on the word and are doing little to decrease their carbon footprint. And because the label "green" isn't regulated, it can be tough to separate companies that really are implementing policies that are good for the environment from those who just like the label and the social approval it carries. This chapter takes a look at some of the issues connected to climate change and the new "green" movement that is sweeping our nation.

We begin with Al Gore's acceptance lecture upon receiving the Nobel Prize in 2007. Gore's speech describes the scope of the problem of climate change and the dire need to intervene now. His speech is followed by a comprehensive overview of the problem by *Atlantic Monthly* writer Gregg Easterbrook in "Global Warming: Who Loses—and Who Wins?" Easterbrook also raises an important question—could global warming have any benefits?

The next series of essays examines the concept of the "carbon footprint." First, Michael Specter describes the challenges we face in defining our carbon footprint, when there are no rules and little precedent to guide us, in "Big Foot." Next, Jeffrey Ball analyzes the carbon footprint of six common products in "Six Products, Six Carbon Footprints." What he reports may surprise you. Then, mother and scientist Jennifer Davidson fears what sort of world her daughter will inherit in "My Carbon Footprint: A Documentary, a Daughter, and All that Is Dear." Sure, she's trying, but her efforts pale in light of the challenges the planet now faces.

The chapter ends with two viewpoints that challenge us to rethink how we approach the problem of climate change. First, Ben Adler wonders "Are Cows Worse than Cars?" His piece is followed by a short essay by Witold Rybczynski who asks, "Can Cities Save the Planet?" The two essays, rather than presenting oppositional viewpoints, encourage us to think more expansively about solutions to the challenges of climate change.

Nobel Lecture on Global Warming
*Al Gore**

Former U.S. Vice President Al Gore has studied the environment and climatic change for over 30 years. His concern over the issue of global warming led to his participation in the 2006 Academy Award–winning film, "An Inconvenient Truth." Gore explains in the introduction to this film, "I very much hope that you will sense that my goal is to share with you both my passion for the Earth and my deep sense of concern for its fate. It is impossible to feel one without the other when you know all the facts. . . . The climate crisis is, indeed, extremely dangerous. In fact it is a true planetary emergency." For his efforts, Gore received the 2007 Nobel Peace Prize, which he shared with the Intergovernmental Panel on Climate Change. What follows is the lecture Gore delivered upon accepting the Nobel Prize on December 10, 2007.

1   Sometimes, without warning, the future knocks on our door with a precious and painful vision of what might be. One hundred and nineteen years ago, a wealthy inventor read his own obituary, mistakenly published years before his death. Wrongly believing the inventor had just died, a newspaper printed a harsh judgment of his life's work, unfairly labeling him "The Merchant of Death" because of his invention—dynamite. Shaken by this condemnation, the inventor made a fateful choice to serve the cause of peace.

2   Seven years later, Alfred Nobel created this prize and the others that bear his name.

3   Seven years ago tomorrow, I read my own political obituary in a judgment that seemed to me harsh and mistaken—if not premature. But that unwelcome verdict also brought a precious if painful gift: an opportunity to search for fresh new ways to serve my purpose.

4   Unexpectedly, that quest has brought me here. Even though I fear my words cannot match this moment, I pray what I am feeling in my heart will be communicated clearly enough that those who hear me will say, "We must act."

5   The distinguished scientists with whom it is the greatest honor of my life to share this award have laid before us a choice between two different futures—a choice that to my ears echoes the words of an ancient prophet: "Life or death, blessings or curses. Therefore, choose life, that both thou and thy seed may live."

6   We, the human species, are confronting a planetary emergency—a threat to the survival of our civilization that is gathering ominous and destructive potential even as we gather here. But there is hopeful news as well: we have the ability to solve this crisis and avoid the worst—though not all—of its consequences, if we act boldly, decisively and quickly.

7   However, despite a growing number of honorable exceptions, too many of the world's leaders are still best described in the words Winston Churchill applied to those who ignored Adolf Hitler's threat: "They go on in strange paradox, decided

* Al Gore, *Nobel Lecture on Global Warming*, December 10, 2007

only to be undecided, resolved to be irresolute, adamant for drift, solid for fluidity, all powerful to be impotent."

8 So today, we dumped another 70 million tons of global-warming pollution into the thin shell of atmosphere surrounding our planet, as if it were an open sewer. And tomorrow, we will dump a slightly larger amount, with the cumulative concentrations now trapping more and more heat from the sun.

9 As a result, the earth has a fever. And the fever is rising. The experts have told us it is not a passing affliction that will heal by itself. We asked for a second opinion. And a third. And a fourth. And the consistent conclusion, restated with increasing alarm, is that something basic is wrong.

> *The earth has a fever. And the fever is rising. The experts have told us it is not a passing affliction that will heal by itself.*

10 We are what is wrong, and we must make it right.

11 Last September 21, as the Northern Hemisphere tilted away from the sun, scientists reported with unprecedented distress that the North Polar ice cap is "falling off a cliff." One study estimated that it could be completely gone during summer in less than 22 years. Another new study, to be presented by U.S. Navy researchers later this week, warns it could happen in as little as 7 years.

12 Seven years from now.

13 In the last few months, it has been harder and harder to misinterpret the signs that our world is spinning out of kilter. Major cities in North and South America, Asia, and Australia are nearly out of water due to massive droughts and melting glaciers. Desperate farmers are losing their livelihoods. Peoples in the frozen Arctic and on low-lying Pacific islands are planning evacuations of places they have long called home. Unprecedented wildfires have forced a half million people from their homes in one country and caused a national emergency that almost brought down the government in another. Climate refugees have migrated into areas already inhabited by people with different cultures, religions, and traditions, increasing the potential for conflict. Stronger storms in the Pacific and Atlantic have threatened whole cities. Millions have been displaced by massive flooding in South Asia, Mexico, and 18 countries in Africa. As temperature extremes have increased, tens of thousands have lost their lives. We are recklessly burning and clearing our forests and driving more and more species into extinction. The very web of life on which we depend is being ripped and frayed.

14 We never intended to cause all this destruction, just as Alfred Nobel never intended that dynamite be used for waging war. He had hoped his invention would promote human progress. We shared that same worthy goal when we began burning massive quantities of coal, then oil and methane.

15 Even in Nobel's time, there were a few warnings of the likely consequences. One of the very first winners of the Prize in chemistry worried that "We are evaporating our coal mines into the air." After performing 10,000 equations by hand, Svante Arrhenius calculated that the earth's average temperature would increase by many degrees if we doubled the amount of CO_2 in the atmosphere.

16 Seventy years later, my teacher, Roger Revelle, and his colleague, Dave Keeling, began to precisely document the increasing CO_2 levels day by day.

17 But unlike most other forms of pollution, CO_2 is invisible, tasteless, and odorless—which has helped keep the truth about what it is doing to our climate out of sight and out of mind. Moreover, the catastrophe now threatening us is unprecedented—and we often confuse the unprecedented with the improbable.

18 We also find it hard to imagine making the massive changes that are now necessary to solve the crisis. And when large truths are genuinely inconvenient, whole societies can, at least for a time, ignore them. Yet as George Orwell reminds us: "Sooner or later a false belief bumps up against solid reality, usually on a battlefield."

19 In the years since this prize was first awarded, the entire relationship between humankind and the earth has been radically transformed. And still, we have remained largely oblivious to the impact of our cumulative actions.

20 Indeed, without realizing it, we have begun to wage war on the earth itself. Now, we and the earth's climate are locked in a relationship familiar to war planners: "Mutually assured destruction."

21 More than two decades ago, scientists calculated that nuclear war could throw so much debris and smoke into the air that it would block life-giving sunlight from our atmosphere, causing a "nuclear winter." Their eloquent warnings here in Oslo helped galvanize the world's resolve to halt the nuclear arms race.

22 Now science is warning us that if we do not quickly reduce the global warming pollution that is trapping so much of the heat our planet normally radiates back out of the atmosphere, we are in danger of creating a permanent "carbon summer."

23 As the American poet Robert Frost wrote, "Some say the world will end in fire; some say in ice." Either, he notes, "would suffice."

24 But neither need be our fate. It is time to make peace with the planet.

25 We must quickly mobilize our civilization with the urgency and resolve that has previously been seen only when nations mobilized for war. These prior struggles for survival were won when leaders found words at the 11th hour that released a mighty surge of courage, hope, and readiness to sacrifice for a protracted and mortal challenge.

26 These were not comforting and misleading assurances that the threat was not real or imminent; that it would affect others but not ourselves; that ordinary life might be lived even in the presence of extraordinary threat; that Providence could be trusted to do for us what we would not do for ourselves.

27 No, these were calls to come to the defense of the common future. They were calls upon the courage, generosity, and strength of entire peoples, citizens of every class and condition who were ready to stand against the threat once asked to do so. Our enemies in those times calculated that free people would not rise to the challenge; they were, of course, catastrophically wrong.

28 Now comes the threat of climate crisis—a threat that is real, rising, imminent, and universal. Once again, it is the 11th hour. The penalties for ignoring this challenge are immense and growing, and at some near point would be unsustainable and unrecoverable. For now we still have the power to choose our fate, and the remaining question is only this: Have we the will to act vigorously and in time, or will we remain imprisoned by a dangerous illusion?

29 Mahatma Gandhi awakened the largest democracy on earth and forged a shared resolve with what he called "Satyagraha"—or "truth force."

30 In every land, the truth—once known—has the power to set us free.

31 Truth also has the power to unite us and bridge the distance between "me" and "we," creating the basis for common effort and shared responsibility.

32 There is an African proverb that says, "If you want to go quickly, go alone. If you want to go far, go together." We need to go far, quickly.

33 We must abandon the conceit that individual, isolated, private actions are the answer. They can and do help. But they will not take us far enough without collective action. At the same time, we must ensure that in mobilizing globally, we do not invite the establishment of ideological conformity and a new lock-step "ism."

34 That means adopting principles, values, laws, and treaties that release creativity and initiative at every level of society in multifold responses originating concurrently and spontaneously.

35 This new consciousness requires expanding the possibilities inherent in all humanity. The innovators who will devise a new way to harness the sun's energy for pennies or invent an engine that's carbon negative may live in Lagos or Mumbai or Montevideo. We must ensure that entrepreneurs and inventors everywhere on the globe have the chance to change the world.

36 When we unite for a moral purpose that is manifestly good and true, the spiritual energy unleashed can transform us. The generation that defeated fascism throughout the world in the 1940s found, in rising to meet their awesome challenge, that they had gained the moral authority and long-term vision to launch the Marshall Plan, the United Nations, and a new level of global cooperation and foresight that unified Europe and facilitated the emergence of democracy and prosperity in Germany, Japan, Italy, and much of the world. One of their visionary leaders said, "It is time we steered by the stars and not by the lights of every passing ship."

37 In the last year of that war, you gave the Peace Prize to a man from my hometown of 2,000 people, Carthage, Tennessee. Cordell Hull was described by Franklin Roosevelt as the "Father of the United Nations." He was an inspiration and hero to my own father, who followed Hull in the Congress and the U.S. Senate and in his commitment to world peace and global cooperation.

38 My parents spoke often of Hull, always in tones of reverence and admiration. Eight weeks ago, when you announced this prize, the deepest emotion I felt was when I saw the headline in my hometown paper that simply noted I had won the same prize that Cordell Hull had won. In that moment, I knew what my father and mother would have felt were they alive.

39 Just as Hull's generation found moral authority in rising to solve the world crisis caused by fascism, so too can we find our greatest opportunity in rising to solve the climate crisis. In the Kanji characters used in both Chinese and Japanese, "crisis" is written with two symbols, the first meaning "danger," the second "opportunity." By facing and removing the danger of the climate crisis, we have the opportunity to gain the moral authority and vision to vastly increase our own capacity to solve other crises that have been too long ignored.

40 We must understand the connections between the climate crisis and the afflictions of poverty, hunger, HIV-Aids, and other pandemics. As these problems are linked, so too must be their solutions. We must begin by making the common rescue of the global environment the central organizing principle of the world community.

41   Fifteen years ago, I made that case at the "Earth Summit" in Rio de Janeiro. Ten years ago, I presented it in Kyoto. This week, I will urge the delegates in Bali to adopt a bold mandate for a treaty that establishes a universal global cap on emissions and uses the market in emissions trading to efficiently allocate resources to the most effective opportunities for speedy reductions.

42   This treaty should be ratified and brought into effect everywhere in the world by the beginning of 2010—two years sooner than presently contemplated. The pace of our response must be accelerated to match the accelerating pace of the crisis itself.

43   Heads of state should meet early next year to review what was accomplished in Bali and take personal responsibility for addressing this crisis. It is not unreasonable to ask, given the gravity of our circumstances, that these heads of state meet every three months until the treaty is completed.

44   We also need a moratorium on the construction of any new generating facility that burns coal without the capacity to safely trap and store carbon dioxide.

45   And most important of all, we need to put a *price* on carbon—with a CO_2 tax that is then rebated back to the people, progressively, according to the laws of each nation, in ways that shift the burden of taxation from employment to pollution. This is by far the most effective and simplest way to accelerate solutions to this crisis.

46   The world needs an alliance—especially of those nations that weigh heaviest in the scales where earth is in the balance. I salute Europe and Japan for the steps they've taken in recent years to meet the challenge, and the new government in Australia, which has made solving the climate crisis its first priority.

47   But the outcome will be decisively influenced by two nations that are now failing to do enough: the United States and China. While India is also growing fast in importance, it should be absolutely clear that it is the two largest CO_2 emitters—most of all, my own country—that will need to make the boldest moves or stand accountable before history for their failure to act.

48   Both countries should stop using the other's behavior as an excuse for stalemate and instead develop an agenda for mutual survival in a shared global environment.

49   These are the last few years of decision, but they can be the first years of a bright and hopeful future if we do what we must. No one should believe a solution will be found without effort, without cost, without change. Let us acknowledge that if we wish to redeem squandered time and speak again with moral authority, then these are the hard truths.

50   The way ahead is difficult. The outer boundary of what we currently believe is feasible is still far short of what we actually must do. Moreover, between here and there, across the unknown, falls the shadow.

51   That is just another way of saying that we have to expand the boundaries of what is possible. In the words of the Spanish poet, Antonio Machado, "Pathwalker, there is no path. You must make the path as you walk."

52   We are standing at the most fateful fork in that path. So I want to end as I began, with a vision of two futures—each a palpable possibility—and with a prayer that we will see with vivid clarity the necessity of choosing between those two futures and the urgency of making the right choice now.

53   The great Norwegian playwright, Henrik Ibsen, wrote, "One of these days, the younger generation will come knocking at my door."

186 ■ Chapter 4 / Carbon Footprints: It's Not Easy Being Green

54   The future is knocking at our door right now. Make no mistake, the next generation *will* ask us one of two questions. Either they will ask: "What were you thinking; why didn't you act?"

55   Or they will ask instead: "How did you find the moral courage to rise and successfully resolve a crisis that so many said was impossible to solve?"

56   We have everything we need to get started, save perhaps political will, but political will is a renewable resource.

57   So let us renew it, and say together: "We have a purpose. We are many. For this purpose we will rise, and we will act." ◆

CRITICAL THINKING

1. What words does Gore use to describe global warming? How does his description of the potential impact of global warming create a sense of urgency? Explain.

2. In what ways does this speech appeal to the emotions? To the intellect? In what ways does Gore leverage his political background in this speech? Explain.

3. Who is Gore's audience in this speech? What presumptions does he make about his audience?

4. How compelling is Gore's argument? Does the fact that he is a former vice president of the United States influence your reception of his speech? Does his reputation and background make him more or less credible? Explain.

5. Were there any points raised by Gore that came as a surprise to you? Or did he repeat information that is generally known? Explain.

CRITICAL WRITING

1. *Persuasive Writing:* Write a letter to your congressional representative in which you make an appeal for action on the issue of global warming. You may take any position on this issue you wish, but support your viewpoint with some data gathered from Gore's speech or from data you locate online.

2. *Exploratory Writing:* It is the year 2115, and you are writing your daily blog entry in your minicomputer diary about your day outdoors. Write about where you are, what you did, and what the climate was like in your "future blog." Use information from Gore's lecture to embellish your blog entry.

3. *Research and Analysis:* Conduct a poll on global warming to see how informed college students are on the issue. Craft a list of 5 to 10 questions designed to develop a profile on how informed the average college student is on the issue of global warming and its implications for the future. Each member of the group should give the survey to at least 20 students. Gather the responses and analyze the data to create a "profile." Share this profile with other groups in class. Are college students aware of the issues

surrounding global warming? If so, to what extent? And how do they feel about the issue? If they are not aware, is this cause for concern? Why or why not?

GROUP PROJECTS

1. What do college students think about the most pressing issues facing them today? Access the survey given by the Pew Research Center at http://people-press.org/reports/questionnaires/303.pdf. Each member of your group should poll at least 20 students. Compile the data and compare it to the results reported by the Pew Research Center. How are the concerns of college students similar to and different from those of the general public? Do you think age is a factor in how people respond to these concerns? Does political affiliation have any influence on the responses of college students? Does your survey reveal any strong disparities between groups? Explain.

2. As a group, research the Kyoto Protocol online. The United States is one of the few nations who did not ratify the treaty. After learning more about the Kyoto Protocol, write a one-page response expressing your view on why the United States should or should not ratify it. In addition to the treaty itself, you may reference the reasons other nations have cited for ratifying—or not ratifying, as in the case of Australia—the treaty. Share your response as part of an in-class debate on whether the United States should have ratified the Kyoto Protocol and what the responsibilities, if any, of a new Democratic Congress should be to the treaty today.

CULTURE SHOCK

Earth's Before and After Pics

Anne Casselman

Biologists Richard Primack and Abraham Miller-Rushing looked in an odd place to study the biological effects of global warming: old photographs. By comparing contemporary photos with shots from a century ago, "You can literally see that trees are leafing out and the plants are flowering earlier now," says Primack, of Boston University. He hopes their study, published this month in the *American Journal of Botany*, will spur citizens to dig up more climate change data from their old photo albums and journals.

The duo examined 286 dated photographs of the Arnold Arboretum in Boston and Concord, Massachusetts. They found that plants are flowering and trees are leafing 10 days earlier today than they were 100 years ago. Primack credits the 3 degree Fahrenheit temperature rise in eastern Massachusetts over the past century with jump-starting plant development in the spring.

"These kinds of changes are already being seen in Boston, and they will be seen in the rest of the United States in the next 100 years," he says. "We're going to see enormous changes in the distribution of plants and animals, agricultural patterns, and patterns of rainfall." Some plants may even begin flowering before pollinators are around to fertilize them. Hay fever could blossom, too, cautions Primack: "Plants may have a longer season of pollen production, which may extend the allergy season."

A Memorial Day observance for Civil War soldiers in Lowell, Massachusetts. May 30, 1868.
Courtesy of American Journal of Botany.

The same location in 2005 looks summer lush. May 30, 2005.
Courtesy of American Journal of Botany.

THINKING CRITICALLY

1. How much does knowing the context of this photo influence our interpretation of it?
2. If you were an environmental scientist and received these photos for research purposes, how would you interpret them? What factors would you consider? What conclusions would you infer, and how would you confirm your conclusions?
3. Read more about the research of Boston University professor Richard Primack at http://people.bu.edu/primack, and about his work in Concord, Massachusetts. After reviewing his work and articles, write a short essay summarizing his position on climate change and your personal reaction to his data.

Global Warming: Who Loses—and Who Wins?

Gregg Easterbrook*

We have heard the dire predictions. If global warming continues unchecked, the consequences could be devastating. Climate change in the next century and beyond could be enormously disruptive, warn some politicians and scientists, displacing populations, spreading,
disease, and even sparking wars. However, not everyone sees the future as impossibly bleak.
Could climate change also be a windfall for some people, businesses, and nations? In this
essay, environmental journalist Gregg Easterbrook describes some of the ways we might benefit from a warming world.

1 Coastal cities inundated, farming regions parched, ocean currents disrupted, tropical
diseases spreading, glaciers melting—an artificial greenhouse effect could generate
countless tribulations.

2 If the Earth's climate changes meaningfully—and the National Academy of Sciences, previously skeptical, said in 2005 that signs of climate change have become
significant—there could be broad-based disruption of the global economy unparal-
leled by any event other than World War II.

3 Economic change means winners as well as losers. Huge sums will be made and
lost if the global climate changes. Everyone wonders what warming might do to the
environment—but what might it do to the global distribution of money and power?

4 Whether mainly natural or mainly artificial, climate change could bring different
regions of the world tremendous benefits as well as drastic problems. The world had
been mostly warming for thousands of years before the industrial era began, and that
warming has been indisputably favorable to the spread of civilization. The trouble is
that the world's economic geography is today organized according to a climate that
has largely prevailed since the Middle Ages—runaway climate change would force
big changes in the physical ordering of society. In the past, small climate changes
have had substantial impact on agriculture, trade routes, and the types of products and
commodities that sell. Larger climate shifts have catalyzed the rise and fall of whole
societies. The Mayan Empire, for instance, did not disappear "mysteriously"; it likely
fell into decline owing to decades of drought that ruined its agricultural base and
deprived its cities of drinking water. On the other side of the coin, Europe's Medieval
Warm Period, which lasted from around 1000 to 1400, was essential to the rise of
Spain, France, and England: Those clement centuries allowed the expansion of farm
production, population, cities, and universities, which in turn set the stage for the
Industrial Revolution. Unless greenhouse-effect theory is completely wrong—and
science increasingly supports the idea that it is right—21st-century climate change
means that sweeping social and economic changes are in the works.

5 To date the greenhouse-effect debate has been largely carried out in abstractions—
arguments about the distant past (what do those 100,000-year-old ice cores in Greenland
really tell us about ancient temperatures, anyway?) coupled to computer-model

---

* Gregg Easterbrook, *The Atlantic Monthly,* April 2007

conjecture regarding the 22nd century, with the occasional Hollywood disaster movie thrown in. Soon, both abstraction and postapocalyptic fantasy could be pushed aside by the economic and political realities of a warming world. If the global climate continues changing, many people and nations will find themselves in possession of land and resources of rising value, while others will suffer dire losses—and these winners and losers could start appearing faster than you might imagine. Add artificially triggered climate change to the volatility already initiated by globalization, and the next few decades may see previously unthinkable levels of economic upheaval, in which fortunes are won and lost based as much on the physical climate as on the business climate.

6   It may sound odd to ask of global warming, What's in it for me? But the question is neither crass nor tongue-in-cheek. The ways in which climate change could skew the world's distribution of wealth should help us appreciate just how profoundly an artificial greenhouse effect might shake our lives. Moreover, some of the lasting effects of climate change are likely to come not so much from the warming itself but from how we react to it: If the world warms apprecia- bly, men and women will not

> *It may sound odd to ask of global warming, What's in it for me? . . . The ways in which climate change could skew the world's distribution of wealth should help us appreciate just how profoundly an artificial greenhouse effect might shake our lives.*

sit by idly, eating bonbons and reading weather reports; there will be instead what econ- omists call "adaptive response," most likely a great deal of it. Some aspects of this response may inflame tensions between those who are winning and those who are los- ing. How people, the global economy, and the international power structure adapt to climate change may influence how we live for generations. If the world warms, who will win? Who will lose? And what's in it for you?

Land

7 Real estate might be expected to appreciate steadily in value during the 21st century, given that both the global population and global prosperity are rising. The supply of land is fixed, and if there's a fixed supply of something but a growing demand, appre- ciation should be automatic. That's unless climate change increases the supply of land by warming currently frosty areas while throwing the amount of desirable land into tremendous flux. My hometown of Buffalo, New York, for example, is today so déclassé that some of its stately Beaux-Arts homes, built during the Gilded Age and overlooking a park designed by Frederick Law Olmsted, sell for about the price of one-bedroom condos in Boston or San Francisco. If a warming world makes the area less cold and snowy, Buffalo might become one of the country's desirable addresses.

8   At the same time, Arizona and Nevada, blazing growth markets today, might become unbearably hot and see their real-estate markets crash. If the oceans rise, Florida's rapid growth could be, well, swamped by an increase in its perilously high groundwater table. Houston could decline, made insufferable by worsened summer- time humidity, while the splendid, rustic Laurentide Mountains region north of Montreal, if warmed up a bit, might transmogrify into the new Poconos.

9   These are just a few of many possible examples. Climate change could upset the apple-carts of real-estate values all over the world, with low-latitude properties tanking while high latitudes become the Sun Belt of the mid-21st century.

10   Local changes in housing demand are only small beer. To consider the big picture, examine a Mercator projection of our planet, and observe how the Earth's landmasses spread from the equator to the poles. Assume global warming is reasonably uniform. (Some computer models suggest that warming will vary widely by region; for the purposes of this article, suffice it to say that all predictions regarding an artificial greenhouse effect are extremely uncertain.) The equatorial and low-latitude areas of the world presumably will become hotter and less desirable as places of habitation, plus less valuable in economic terms; with a few exceptions, these areas are home to developing nations where living standards are already low.

11   So where is the high-latitude landmass that might grow more valuable in a warming world? By accident of geography, except for Antarctica nearly all such land is in the Northern Hemisphere, whose continents are broad west-to-east. Only a relatively small portion of South America, which narrows as one travels south, is high latitude, and none of Africa or Australia is. (Cape Town is roughly the same distance from the equator as Cape Hatteras; Melbourne is about the same distance from the equator as Manhattan.) More specifically, nearly all the added land-value benefits of a warming world might accrue to Alaska, Canada, Greenland, Russia, and Scandinavia.

12   This raises the possibility that an artificial greenhouse effect could harm nations that are already hard pressed and benefit nations that are already affluent. If Alaska turned temperate, it would drive conservationists to distraction, but it would also open for development an area more than twice the size of Texas. Rising world temperatures might throw Indonesia, Mexico, Nigeria, and other low-latitude nations into generations of misery, while causing Canada, Greenland, and Scandinavia to experience a rip-roarin' economic boom. Many Greenlanders are already cheering the retreat of glaciers, since this melting stands to make their vast island far more valuable. Recently, *The Wall Street Journal* reported that the growing season in the portion of Greenland open to cultivation is already two weeks longer than it was in the 1970s.

13   And Russia! For generations poets have bemoaned this realm as cursed by enormous, foreboding, harsh Siberia. What if the region in question were instead enormous, temperate, inviting Siberia? Climate change could place Russia in possession of the largest new region of pristine, exploitable land since the sailing ships of Europe first spied the shores of what would be called North America. The snows of Siberia cover soils that have never been depleted by controlled agriculture. What's more, beneath Siberia's snow may lie geologic formations that hold vast deposits of fossil fuels, as well as mineral resources. When considering ratification of the Kyoto Protocol to regulate greenhouse gases, the Moscow government dragged its feet, though the treaty was worded to offer the Russians extensive favors. Why might this have happened? Perhaps because Russia might be much better off in a warming world: Warming's benefits to Russia could exceed those to all other nations combined.

14   Of course, it could be argued that politicians seldom give much thought—one way or the other—to actions whose value will become clear only after they leave

office, so perhaps Moscow does not have a grand strategy to warm the world for its own good. But a warmer world may be much to Russia's liking, whether it comes by strategy or accident. And how long until high-latitude nations realize global warming might be in their interests? In recent years, Canada has increased its greenhouse-gas output more rapidly than most other rich countries. Maybe this is a result of prosperity and oil-field development—or maybe those wily Canadians have a master plan for their huge expanse of currently uninhabitable land.

15   Global warming might do more for the North, however, than just opening up new land. Temperatures are rising on average, but when are they rising? Daytime? Nighttime? Winter? Summer? One fear about artificially triggered climate change has been that global warming would lead to scorching summer-afternoon highs, which would kill crops and brown out the electric power grid. Instead, so far a good share of the warming—especially in North America—has come in the form of night-time and winter lows that are less low. Higher lows reduce the harshness of winter in northern climes and moderate the demand for energy. And fewer freezes allow extended growing seasons, boosting farm production. In North America, spring comes ever earlier—in recent years, trees have flowered in Washington, D.C., almost a week earlier on average than a generation ago. People may find this creepy, but earlier springs and milder winters can have economic value to agriculture—and lest we forget, all modern societies, including the United States, are grounded in agriculture.

16   If a primary impact of an artificially warmed world is to make land in Canada, Greenland, Russia, Scandinavia, and the United States more valuable, this could have three powerful effects on the 21st-century global situation.

17   First, historically privileged northern societies might not decline geopolitically, as many commentators have predicted. Indeed, the great age of northern power may lie ahead, if Earth's very climate is on the verge of conferring boons to that part of the world. Should it turn out that headlong fossil-fuel combustion by northern nations has set in motion climate change that strengthens the relative world position of those same nations, future essayists will have a field day. But the prospect is seri-ous. By the middle of the 21st century, a new global balance of power may emerge in which Russia and America are once again the world's paired superpowers—only this time during a Warming War instead of a Cold War.

18   Second, if northern societies find that climate change makes them more wealthy, the quest for world equity could be dealt a huge setback. Despite the popu-lar misconception, globalized economics have been a positive force for increased equity. As the Indian economist Surjit Bhalla has shown, the developing world pro-duced 29 percent of the globe's income in 1950; by 2000 that share had risen to 42 percent, while the developing world's share of population rose at a slower rate. All other things being equal, we might expect continued economic globalization to distribute wealth more widely. But if climate change increases the value of northern land and resources, while leaving nations near the equator hotter and wracked by storms or droughts, all other things would not be equal.

19   That brings us to the third great concern: If climate change causes developing nations to falter, and social conditions within them deteriorate, many millions of jobless or hungry refugees may come to the borders of the favored North, demanding

to be let in. If the very Earth itself turns against poor nations, punishing them with heat and storms, how could the United States morally deny the refugees succor?

20   Shifts in the relative values of places and resources have often led to war, and it is all too imaginable that climate change will cause nations to envy each other's territory. This envy is likely to run both north–south and up–down. North–south? Suppose climate change made Brazil less habitable, while bringing an agreeable mild clime to the vast and fertile Argentinean pampas to Brazil's south. São Paulo is already one of the world's largest cities. Would a desperate, overheated Brazil of the year 2037—its population exploding—hesitate to attack Argentina for cool, inviting land? Now consider the up–down prospect: the desire to leave low-lying areas for altitude. Here's an example: Since its independence in 1947, Pakistan has kept a hand in the internal affairs of Afghanistan. Today Americans view this issue through the lens of the Taliban and al-Qaeda, but from Islamabad's perspective, the goal has always been to keep Afghanistan available as a place for retreat, should Pakistan lose a war with India. What if the climate warms, rendering much of Pakistan unbearable to its citizens? (Temperatures of 100-plus degrees are already common in the Punjab.) Afghanistan's high plateaus, dry and rocky as they are, might start looking pleasingly temperate as Pakistan warms, and the Afghans might see yet another army headed their way.

21   A warming climate could cause other land-grabs on a national scale. Today Greenland is a largely self-governing territory of Denmark that the world leaves in peace because no nation covets its shivering expanse. Should the Earth warm, Copenhagen might assert greater jurisdiction over Greenland, or stronger governments might scheme to seize this dwarf continent, which is roughly three times the size of Texas. Today Antarctica is under international administration, and this arrangement is generally accepted because the continent has no value beyond scientific research. If the world warmed for a long time—and it would likely take centuries for the Antarctic ice sheet to melt completely—international jockeying to seize or conquer Antarctica might become intense. Some geologists believe large oil deposits are under the Antarctic crust: In earlier epochs, the austral pole was densely vegetated and had conditions suitable for the formation of fossil fuels.

22   And though I've said to this point that Canada would stand to become more valuable in a warming world, actually, Canada and Nunavut would. For centuries, Europeans drove the indigenous peoples of what is now Canada farther and farther north. In 1993, Canada agreed to grant a degree of independence to the primarily Inuit population of Nunavut, and this large, cold region in the country's northeast has been mainly self-governing since 1999. The Inuit believe they are ensconced in the one place in this hemisphere that the descendants of Europe will never, ever want. This could turn out to be wrong.

23   For investors, finding attractive land to buy and hold for a warming world is fraught with difficulties, particularly when looking abroad. If considering plots on the pampas, for example, should one negotiate with the current Argentinian owners or the future Brazilian ones? Perhaps a safer route would be the contrarian one, focused on the likelihood of falling land values in places people may leave. If strict carbon-dioxide regulations are enacted, corporations will shop for "offsets," including projects that absorb carbon dioxide from the sky. Growing trees is a potential greenhouse-gas

offset, and can be done comparatively cheaply in parts of the developing world, even on land that people may stop wanting. If you jump into the greenhouse-offset business, what you might plant is leucaena, a rapidly growing tree species suited to the tropics that metabolizes carbon dioxide faster than most trees. But you'll want to own the land in order to control the sale of the credits. Consider a possible sequence of events: First, climate change makes parts of the developing world even less habitable than they are today; then, refugees flee these areas; finally, land can be snapped up at Filene's Basement prices—and used to grow leucaena trees.

Water

24 If Al Gore's movie, *An Inconvenient Truth,* is to be believed, you should start selling coastal real estate now. Gore's film maintains that an artificial greenhouse effect could raise sea levels 20 feet in the near future, flooding Manhattan, San Francisco, and dozens of other cities; Micronesia would simply disappear below the waves. Gore's is the doomsday number, but the scientific consensus is worrisome enough: In 2005, the National Academy of Sciences warned that oceans may rise between four inches and three feet by the year 2100. Four inches may not sound like a lot, but it would imperil parts of coastal Florida and the Carolinas, among other places. A three-foot sea-level rise would flood significant portions of Bangladesh, threaten the national survival of the Netherlands, and damage many coastal cities, while submerging pretty much all of the world's trendy beach destinations to boot. And the Asian Tigers? Shanghai and Hong Kong sit right on the water. Raise the deep a few feet, and these Tiger cities would be abandoned.

25 The global temperature increase of the last century—about one degree Fahrenheit—was modest and did not cause any dangerous sea-level rise. Sea-level worries turn on the possibility that there is some nonlinear aspect of the climate system, a "tipping point" that could cause the rate of global warming to accelerate markedly. One reason global warming has not happened as fast as expected appears to be that the oceans have absorbed much of the carbon dioxide emitted by human activity. Studies suggest, however, that the ability of the oceans to absorb carbon dioxide may be slowing; as the absorption rate declines, atmospheric buildup will happen faster, and climate change could speed up. At the first sign of an increase in the rate of global warming: Sell, sell, sell your coastal properties. Unload those London and Seattle waterfront holdings. Buy land and real property in Omaha or Ontario.

26 An artificial greenhouse effect may also alter ocean currents in unpredictable ways. Already there is some evidence that the arctic currents are changing, while the major North Atlantic current that moves warm water north from the equator may be losing energy. If the North Atlantic current falters, temperatures could fall in Europe even as the world overall warms. Most of Europe lies to the north of Maine yet is temperate because the North Atlantic current carries huge volumes of warm water to the seas off Scotland; that warm water is Europe's weathermaker. Geological studies show that the North Atlantic current has stopped in the past. If this current stops again because of artificial climate change, Europe might take on the climate of present-day Newfoundland. As a result, it might depopulate, while the economic value of everything within its icy expanse declines. The European Union makes approximately the same contribution to

the global economy as the United States makes: Significantly falling temperatures in Europe could trigger a worldwide recession.

27   While staying ready to sell your holdings in Europe, look for purchase opportunities near the waters of the Arctic Circle. In 2005, a Russian research ship became the first surface vessel ever to reach the North Pole without the aid of an icebreaker. If arctic sea ice melts, shipping traffic will begin transiting the North Pole. Andrew Revkin's 2006 book, *The North Pole Was Here,* profiles Pat Broe, who in 1997 bought the isolated far-north port of Churchill, Manitoba, from the Canadian government for $7. Assuming arctic ice continues to melt, the world's cargo vessels may begin sailing due north to shave thousands of miles off their trips, and the port of Churchill may be bustling. If arctic polar ice disappears and container vessels course the North Pole seas, shipping costs may decline—to the benefit of consumers. Asian manufacturers, especially, should see their costs of shipping to the United States and the European Union fall. At the same time, heavily trafficked southern shipping routes linking East Asia to Europe and to America's East Coast could see less traffic, and port cities along that route—such as Singapore—might decline. Concurrently, good relations with Nunavut could become of interest to the world's corporations.

28   Oh, and there may be oil under the arctic waters. Who would own that oil? The United States, Russia, Canada, Norway, and Denmark already assert legally complex claims to parts of the North Pole seas—including portions that other nations consider open waters not subject to sovereign control. Today it seems absurd to imagine the governments of the world fighting over the North Pole seas, but in the past many causes of battle have seemed absurd before the artillery fire began. Canada is already conducting naval exercises in the arctic waters, and making no secret of this.

29   Then again, perhaps ownership of these waters will go in an entirely different direction. The 21st century is likely to see a movement to create private-property rights in the ocean (ocean property rights are the most promising solution to overfishing of the open seas). Private-property rights in the North Pole seas, should they come into existence, might generate a rush to rival the Sooners' settlement of Oklahoma in the late 1800s.

30   Whatever happens to our oceans, climate change might also cause economic turmoil by affecting freshwater supplies. Today nearly all primary commodities, including petroleum, appear in ample supply. Freshwater is an exception: China is depleting aquifers at an alarming rate in order to produce enough rice to feed itself, while freshwater is scarce in much of the Middle East and parts of Africa. Freshwater depletion is especially worrisome in Egypt, Libya, and several Persian Gulf states. Greenhouse-effect science is so uncertain that researchers have little idea whether a warming world would experience more or less precipitation. If it turns out that rain and snow decline as the world warms, dwindling supplies of drinking water and freshwater for agriculture may be the next resource emergency. For investors this would suggest a cautious view of the booms in China and Dubai, as both places may soon face freshwater-supply problems. (Cost-effective desalinization continues to elude engineers.) On the other hand, where water rights are available in these areas, grab them.

31   Much of the effect that global warming will have on our water is speculative, so water-related climate change will be a high-risk/high-reward matter for investors and societies alike. The biggest fear is that artificially triggered climate change will shift rainfall away from today's productive breadbasket areas and toward what are now deserts or, worse, toward the oceans. (From the human perspective, all ocean rain represents wasted freshwater.) The reason Malthusian catastrophes have not occurred as humanity has grown is that for most of the last half century, farm yields have increased faster than population. But the global agricultural system is perilously poised on the assumption that growing conditions will continue to be good in the breadbasket areas of the United States, India, China, and South America. If rainfall shifts away from those areas, there could be significant human suffering for many, many years, even if, say, Siberian agriculture eventually replaces lost production elsewhere. By reducing farm yield, rainfall changes could also cause skyrocketing prices for commodity crops, something the global economy has rarely observed in the last 30 years.

32   Recent studies show that in the last few decades, precipitation in North America is increasingly the result of a few downpours rather than lots of showers. Downpours cause flooding and property damage, while being of less use to agriculture than frequent soft rains. Because the relationship between artificially triggered climate change and rainfall is conjectural, investors presently have no way to avoid buying land in places that someday might be hit with frequent downpours. But this concern surely raises a red flag about investments in India, Bangladesh, and Indonesia, where monsoon rains are already a leading social problem.

33   Water-related investments might be attractive in another way: for hydropower. Zero-emission hydropower might become a premium energy form if greenhouse gases are strictly regulated. Quebec is the Saudi Arabia of roaring water. Already the hydropower complex around James Bay is one of the world's leading sources of water-generated electricity. For 30 years, environmentalists and some Cree activists opposed plans to construct a grand hydropower complex that essentially would dam all large rivers flowing into the James and Hudson bays. But it's not hard to imagine Canada completing the reengineering of northern Quebec for hydropower, if demand from New England and the Midwest becomes strong enough. Similarly, there is hydropower potential in the Chilean portions of Patagonia. This is a wild and beautiful region little touched by human activity—and an intriguing place to snap up land for hydropower reservoirs.

Adaptation

34   Last October, the treasury office of the United Kingdom estimated that unless we adapt, global warming could eventually subtract as much as 20 percent of the gross domestic product from the world economy. Needless to say, if that happens, not even the cleverest portfolio will help you. This estimate is worst-case, however, and has many economists skeptical. Optimists think dangerous global warming might be averted at surprisingly low cost (see "Some Convenient Truths," September 2006). Once regulations create a profit incentive for the invention of greenhouse-gas–reducing technology, an outpouring of innovation is likely. Some of those who

formulate greenhouse-gas–control ideas will become rich; everyone will benefit from the environmental safeguards the ideas confer.

35   Enactment of some form of binding greenhouse-gas rules is now essential both to slow the rate of greenhouse-gas accumulation and to create an incentive for inventors, engineers, and businesspeople to devise the ideas that will push society beyond the fossil-fuel age. *The New York Times* recently groused that George W. Bush's fiscal 2007 budget includes only $4.2 billion for federal research that might cut greenhouse-gas emissions. This is the wrong concern: Progress would be faster if the federal government spent nothing at all on greenhouse-gas–reduction research—but enacted regulations that gave the private sector a significant profit motive to find solutions that work in actual use, as opposed to on paper in government studies. The market has caused the greenhouse-gas problem, and the market is the best hope of solving it. Offering market incentives for the development of greenhouse-gas controls—indeed, encouraging profit making in greenhouse-gas controls—is the most promising path to avoiding the harm that could befall the dispossessed of developing nations as the global climate changes.

36   Yet if global-warming theory is right, higher global temperatures are already inevitable. Even the most optimistic scenario for reform envisions decades of additional greenhouse-gas accumulation in the atmosphere, and that in turn means a warming world. The warming may be manageable, but it is probably unstoppable in the short term. This suggests that a major investment sector of the near future will be climate-change adaptation. Crops that grow in high temperatures, homes and buildings designed to stay cool during heat waves, vehicles that run on far less fuel, waterfront structures that can resist stronger storms—the list of needed adaptations will be long, and all involve producing, buying, and selling. Environmentalists don't like talk of adaptation, as it implies making our peace with a warmer world. That peace, though, must be made—and the sooner businesses, investors, and entrepreneurs get to work, the better.

37   Why, ultimately, should nations act to control greenhouse gases, rather than just letting climate turmoil happen and seeing who profits? One reason is that the cost of controls is likely to be much lower than the cost of rebuilding the world. Coastal cities could be abandoned and rebuilt inland, for instance, but improving energy efficiency and reducing greenhouse-gas emissions in order to stave off rising sea levels should be far more cost-effective. Reforms that prevent major economic and social disruption from climate change are likely to be less expensive, across the board, than reacting to the change. The history of antipollution programs shows that it is always cheaper to prevent emissions than to reverse any damage they cause.

38   For the United States, there's another argument that is particularly keen. The present ordering of the world favors the United States in nearly every respect—political, economic, even natural, considering America's excellent balance of land and resources. Maybe a warming world would favor the United States more; this is certainly possible. But when the global order already places America at No. 1, why would we want to run the risk of climate change that alters that order? Keeping the world economic system and the global balance of power the way they are seems very strongly in the U.S. national interest—and keeping things the way they are requires prevention of significant climate change. That, in the end, is what's in it for us. ◆

CRITICAL THINKING

1. What do you know about climate change? Is it a topic of concern or interest to you? Do you think it is an important issue? Explain.
2. Many arguments on climate change and the need to stop its progress have been couched in terms of disaster. How does Easterbrook approach the issue? How is his approach different?
3. How does Easterbrook use history to build his argument that climate change might not be as scary as we think?
4. What is Easterbrook's opinion of climate change?
5. Evaluate the tone and language in this essay. Is Easterbrook serious? Light? Foreboding? Humorous? How does his tone influence your view of his essay and his argument? Explain.
6. What role has Hollywood played in presenting the issue of climate change and its implications? Give some examples from your personal experience that have influenced your impression of the issue.
7. Easterbrook postulates that one reason why Russia "dragged its feet" in ratifying the Kyoto Protocol is because Russia is likely to benefit from climate change. How compelling is this argument? Could he have a point?
8. After reading Easterbrook's essay, has your position on global warming, or your view of the issue itself, changed in any way? Why or why not?
9. What is the problem, according to Easterbrook, with research on how to reduce greenhouse gases? What solution to this problem does he offer instead? Do you agree?

CRITICAL WRITING

1. *Research Writing:* Research the fall of the Mayan empire and the impact climate change had upon this ancient civilization. Write a report outlining how the Mayan empire may serve as an example of what might happen in modern civilizations faced with similar circumstances.
2. Easterbrook explains how some areas of the world could change radically due to climate change. If the world warmed 10 degrees in the next 100 years, and the ocean level rose as a result, what would that mean for the area of the world you come from? For example, if you grew up in Florida, would your hometown be underwater? Write a personal narrative describing the place where you grew up and how it might be different because of climate change.

GROUP PROJECTS

1. Conduct a poll on climate change to see how informed college students are on the issue. Craft a list of 5 to 10 questions designed to develop a profile on how informed the average college student is on the issue of climate change and its implications for the future. Each member of the group should give the survey to at least 20 students. Gather the responses and

analyze the data to create a "profile." Share this profile with other groups in class. Are college students aware of the issues surrounding climate change? If so, to what extent, and how do they feel about the issue? If not, is this cause for concern? Why or why not?

2. Easterbrook postulates that if some southern countries are made uninhabitable by climate change, millions of refugees may come to the boarders of northern countries. As a group, discuss this possibility and what it might mean for immigration policy in the next century. How might the world change in just a few generations?

CULTURE SHOCK

The House We All Build

The Ad Council reports that while many people are aware of environmental problems, they are not sure what they can do about them, or they feel that doing something would be too time-consuming or expensive. The Earth Share campaign aims to make people aware of how what we do now will shape our future and the future of our children. "With so many issues facing the world today, it's easy to become complacent when it comes to the environment," said Kurt Fries, executive group creative director at Foote Cone & Belding, Chicago, who collaborated on the ad above. "There is a general perception by many that it's not happening in my backyard so it doesn't affect me, therefore, I should probably use my resources in other ways. The fact is, we all face environmental issues every day that have a huge impact on the people closest to us. This work is designed to make people stop and realize that there are real, tangible consequences to doing nothing."

THINKING CRITICALLY

1. What is your first impression of this image? What is happening? What message does it seek to convey?
2. What is the meaning of the tag line, "We live in the house we all build"? Do you think this ad is likely to increase environmental awareness? Why or why not?
3. Evaluate the strengths and weaknesses of this ad.
4. Visit EarthShare.org and learn more about the ad campaign and its objective. After reviewing the information on the site, outline your own campaign to increase environmental awareness.

Big Foot
*Michael Specter**

In measuring carbon emissions, it's easy to confuse morality and science. "Green" awareness is sweeping the nation, and as we learn more about our individual impact on the environment, explains author Michael Spector, "An excessive carbon footprint has become the equivalent of wearing a scarlet letter." Companies are scrambling to promote green practices, because it is good for the environment but also because it is good for business.

1 A little more than a year ago, Sir Terry Leahy, who is the chief executive of the Tesco chain of supermarkets, Britain's largest retailer, delivered a speech to a group called the Forum for the Future, about the implications of climate change. Leahy had never before addressed the issue in public, but his remarks left little doubt that he recognized the magnitude of the problem. "I am not a scientist," he said. "But I listen when the scientists say that, if we fail to mitigate climate change, the environmental, social, and economic consequences will be stark and severe. . . . There comes a moment when it is clear what you must do. I am determined that Tesco should be a leader in helping to create a low-carbon economy. In saying this, I do not underestimate the task. It is to take an economy where human comfort, activity, and growth are inextricably linked with emitting carbon and to transform it into one which can only thrive without depending on carbon. This is a monumental challenge. It requires a revolution in technology and a revolution in thinking. We are going to have to rethink the way we live and work."

2 Tesco sells nearly a quarter of the groceries bought in the United Kingdom, it possesses a growing share of the markets in Asia and Europe, and late last year the chain opened its first stores in the United States. Few corporations could have a more visible—or forceful—impact on the lives of their customers. In his speech, Leahy, who is fifty-two, laid out a series of measures that he hoped would ignite "a revolution in green consumption." He announced that Tesco would cut its energy use in half by 2010, drastically limit the number of products it transports by air, and place airplane symbols on the packaging of those which it does. More important, in an effort to help consumers understand the environmental impact of the choices they make every day, he told the forum that Tesco would develop a system of carbon labels and put them on each of its seventy thousand products. "Customers want us to develop ways to take complicated carbon calculations and present them simply," he said. "We will therefore begin the search for a universally accepted and commonly understood measure of the carbon footprint of every product we sell—looking at its complete life cycle, from production through distribution to consumption. It will enable us to label all our products so that customers can compare their carbon footprint as easily as they can currently compare their price or their nutritional profile."

* Michael Specter, *New Yorker,* February 25, 2008

3   Leahy's sincerity was evident, but so was his need to placate his customers. Studies have consistently demonstrated that, given a choice, people prefer to buy products that are environmentally benign. That choice, however, is almost never easy. "A carbon label will put the power in the hands of consumers to choose how they want to be green," Tom Delay, the head of the British government's Carbon Trust, said. "It will empower us all to make informed choices and in turn drive a market for low-carbon products." Tesco was not alone in telling people what it would do to address the collective burden of our greenhouse-gas emissions. Compelled by economic necessity as much as by ecological awareness, many corporations now seem to compete as vigorously to display their environmental credentials as they do to sell their products.

4   In Britain, Marks & Spencer has set a goal of recycling all its waste and intends to become carbon-neutral by 2012—the equivalent, it claims, of taking a hundred thousand cars off the road every year. Kraft Foods recently began to power part of a New York plant with methane produced by adding bacteria to whey, a by-product of cream cheese. Not to be outdone, Sara Lee will deploy solar panels to run one of its bakeries in New Mexico. Many airlines now sell "offsets," which offer passengers a way to invest in projects that reduce CO_2 emissions. In theory, that would compensate for the greenhouse gas caused by their flights. This year's Super Bowl was fuelled by wind turbines. There are carbon-neutral investment banks, carbon-neutral real-estate brokerages, carbon-neutral taxi fleets, and carbon-neutral dental practices. Detroit, arguably America's most vivid symbol of environmental excess, has also staked its claim. ("Our designers know green is the new black," Ford declares on its home page. General Motors makes available hundreds of green pictures, green stories, and green videos to anyone who wants them.)

5   Possessing an excessive carbon footprint is rapidly becoming the modern equivalent of wearing a scarlet letter. Because neither the goals nor acceptable emissions limits are clear, however, morality is often mistaken for science. A recent article in *New Scientist* suggested that the biggest problem arising from the epidemic of obesity is the additional carbon burden that fat people—who tend to eat a lot of meat and travel mostly in cars—place on the environment. Australia briefly debated imposing a carbon tax on families with more than two children; the environmental benefits of abortion have been discussed widely (and simplistically). Bishops of the Church of England have just launched a "carbon fast," suggesting that during Lent parishioners, rather than giving up chocolate, forgo carbon. (Britons generate an average of a little less than ten tons of carbon per person each year; in the United States, the number is about twice that.)

6   Greenhouse-gas emissions have risen rapidly in the past two centuries, and levels today are higher than at any time in at least the past six hundred and fifty thousand years. In 1995, each of the six billion people on earth was responsible, on average, for one ton of carbon emissions. Oceans and forests can absorb about half that amount. Although specific estimates vary, scientists and policy officials increasingly agree that allowing emissions to continue at the current rate would induce dramatic changes in the global climate system. To avoid the most catastrophic effects of those changes, we will have to hold emissions steady in the next decade, then reduce them by at least sixty to eighty per cent by the middle of the century. (A delay of just

ten years in stopping the increase would require double the reductions.) Yet, even if all carbon emissions stopped today, the earth would continue to warm for at least another century. Facts like these have transformed carbon dioxide into a strange but powerful new currency, difficult to evaluate yet impossible to ignore.

> *Even if all carbon emissions stopped today, the earth would continue to warm for at least another century. Facts like these have transformed carbon dioxide into a strange but powerful new currency, difficult to evaluate yet impossible to ignore.*

7   A person's carbon footprint is simply a measure of his contribution to global warming. (CO_2 is the best known of the gases that trap heat in the atmosphere, but others—including water vapor, methane, and nitrous oxide—also play a role.) Virtually every human activity—from watching television to buying a quart of milk—has some carbon cost associated with it. We all consume electricity generated by burning fossil fuels; most people rely on petroleum for transportation and heat. Emissions from those activities are not hard to quantify. Watching a plasma television for three hours every day contributes two hundred and fifty kilograms of carbon to the atmosphere each year; an LCD television is responsible for less than half that number. Yet the calculations required to assess the full environmental impact of how we live can be dazzlingly complex. To sum them up on a label will not be easy. Should the carbon label on a jar of peanut butter include the emissions caused by the fertilizer, calcium, and potassium applied to the original crop of peanuts? What about the energy used to boil the peanuts once they have been harvested, or to mold the jar and print the labels? Seen this way, carbon costs multiply rapidly. A few months ago, scientists at the Stockholm Environment Institute reported that the carbon footprint of Christmas—including food, travel, lighting, and gifts—was six hundred and fifty kilograms per person.

8   As a source of global warming, the food we eat—and how we eat it—is no more significant than the way we make clothes or travel or heat our homes and offices. It certainly doesn't compare to the impact made by tens of thousands of factories scattered throughout the world. Yet food carries enormous symbolic power, so the concept of "food miles"—the distance a product travels from the farm to your home—is often used as a kind of shorthand to talk about climate change in general. "We have to remember our goal: reduce emissions of greenhouse gases," John Murlis told me not long ago when we met in London. "That should be the world's biggest priority." Murlis is the chief scientific adviser to the Carbon Neutral Company, which helps corporations adopt policies to reduce their carbon footprint as well as those of the products they sell. He has also served as the director of strategy and chief scientist for Britain's Environment Agency. Murlis worries that in our collective rush to make choices that display personal virtue, we may be losing sight of the larger problem. "Would a carbon label on every product help us?" he asked. "I wonder. You can feel very good about the organic potatoes you buy from a farm near your home, but half the emissions—and half the footprint—from those potatoes could come from the energy you use to cook them. If you leave the lid off, boil them at a high heat, and then mash your potatoes, from a carbon standpoint, you might as well drive to McDonald's and spend your money buying an order of French fries."

9   One particularly gray morning last December, I visited a Tesco store on Warwick Way, in the Pimlico section of London. Several food companies have promised

to label their products with the amount of carbon-dioxide emissions associated with making and transporting them. Last spring, Walkers crisps (potato chips) became the first of them to reach British stores, and they are still the only product on the shelves there with a carbon label. I walked over to the crisp aisle, where a young couple had just tossed three bags of Walkers Prawn Cocktail crisps into their shopping cart. The man was wearing fashionable jeans and sneakers without laces. His wife was toting a huge Armani Exchange bag on one arm and dragging their four-year-old daughter with the other. I asked if they paid attention to labels. "Of course," the man said, looking a bit insulted. He was aware that Walkers had placed a carbon label on the back of its crisp packages; he thought it was a good idea. He just wasn't sure what to make of the information.

10   Few people are. In order to develop the label for Walkers, researchers had to calculate the amount of energy required to plant seeds for the ingredients (sunflower oil and potatoes), as well as to make the fertilizers and pesticides used on those potatoes. Next, they factored in the energy required for diesel tractors to collect the potatoes, then the effects of chopping, cleaning, storing, and bagging them. The packaging and printing processes also emit carbon dioxide and other greenhouse gases, as does the petroleum used to deliver those crisps to stores. Finally, the research team assessed the impact of throwing the empty bags in the trash, collecting the garbage in a truck, driving to a landfill, and burying them. In the end, the researchers—from the Carbon Trust—found that seventy-five grams of greenhouse gases are expended in the production of every individual-size bag of potato chips.

11   "Crisps are easy," Murlis had told me. "They have only one important ingredient, and the potatoes are often harvested near the factory." We were sitting in a deserted hotel lounge in Central London, and Murlis stirred his tea slowly, then frowned. "Let's just assume every mother cares about the environment—what then?" he asked. "Should the carbon content matter more to her than the fat content or the calories in the products she buys?"

12   I put that question to the next shopper who walked by, Chantal Levi, a Frenchwoman who has lived in London for thirty-two years. I watched her grab a large bag of Doritos and then, shaking her head, return it to the shelf. "Too many carbohydrates," she said. "I try to watch that, but between the carbs and the fat and the protein, it can get to be a bit complicated. I try to buy locally grown, organic food," she continued. "It tastes better, and it's far less harmful to the environment." I asked if she was willing to pay more for products that carried carbon labels. "Of course," she said. "I care about that. I don't want my food flown across the world when I can get it close to home. What a waste."

13   It is a logical and widely held assumption that the ecological impacts of transporting food—particularly on airplanes over great distances—are far more significant than if that food were grown locally. There are countless books, articles, Web sites, and organizations that promote the idea. There is even a "100-Mile Diet," which encourages participants to think about "local eating for global change." Eating locally produced food has become such a phenomenon, in fact, that the word "locavore" was just named the 2007 word of the year by the New Oxford American Dictionary.

14   Paying attention to the emissions associated with what we eat makes obvious sense. It is certainly hard to justify importing bottled water from France, Finland, or Fiji to a place like New York, which has perhaps the cleanest tap water of any major

American city. Yet, according to one recent study, factories throughout the world are burning eighteen million barrels of oil and consuming forty-one billion gallons of fresh water every day, solely to make bottled water that most people in the U.S. don't need.

15   "Have a quick rifle through your cupboards and fridge and jot down a note of the countries of origin for each food product," Mark Lynas wrote in his popular handbook *Carbon Counter,* published last year by HarperCollins. "The further the distance it has traveled, the bigger the carbon penalty. Each glass of orange juice, for example, contains the equivalent of two glasses of petrol once the transport costs are included. Worse still are highly perishable fresh foods that have been flown in from far away—green beans from Kenya or lettuce from the U.S. They may be worth several times their weight in jet fuel once the transport costs are factored in."

16   Agricultural researchers at Iowa State University have reported that the food miles attached to items that one buys in a grocery store are twenty-seven times higher than those for goods bought from local sources. American produce travels an average of nearly fifteen hundred miles before we eat it. Roughly forty per cent of our fruit comes from overseas and, even though broccoli is a vigorous plant grown throughout the country, the broccoli we buy in a supermarket is likely to have been shipped eighteen hundred miles in a refrigerated truck. Although there are vast herds of cattle in the United States, we import ten per cent of our red meat, often from as far away as Australia or New Zealand.

17   In his speech last year, Sir Terry Leahy promised to limit to less than one per cent the products that Tesco imports by air. In the United States, many similar efforts are under way. Yet the relationship between food miles and their carbon footprint is not nearly as clear as it might seem. That is often true even when the environmental impact of shipping goods by air is taken into consideration. "People should stop talking about food miles," Adrian Williams told me. "It's a foolish concept: provincial, damaging, and simplistic." Williams is an agricultural researcher in the Natural Resources Department of Cranfield University, in England. He has been commissioned by the British government to analyze the relative environmental impacts of a number of foods. "The idea that a product travels a certain distance and is therefore worse than one you raised nearby—well, it's just idiotic," he said. "It doesn't take into consideration the land use, the type of transportation, the weather, or even the season. Potatoes you buy in winter, of course, have a far higher environmental ticket than if you were to buy them in August." Williams pointed out that when people talk about global warming, they usually speak only about carbon dioxide. Making milk or meat contributes less CO_2 to the atmosphere than building a house or making a washing machine. But the animals produce methane and nitrous oxide, and those are greenhouse gases, too. "This is not an equation like the number of calories or even the cost of a product," he said. "There is no one number that works."

18   Many factors influence the carbon footprint of a product: water use, cultivation and harvesting methods, quantity and type of fertilizer, even the type of fuel used to make the package. Sea-freight emissions are less than a sixtieth of those associated with airplanes, and you don't have to build highways to berth a ship. Last year, a study of the carbon cost of the global wine trade found that it is actually more

"green" for New Yorkers to drink wine from Bordeaux, which is shipped by sea, than wine from California, sent by truck. That is largely because shipping wine is mostly shipping glass. The study found that "the efficiencies of shipping drive a 'green line' all the way to Columbus, Ohio, the point where a wine from Bordeaux and Napa has the same carbon intensity."

19   Williams and his colleagues recently completed a study that examined the environmental costs of buying roses shipped to England from Holland and of those exported (and sent by air) from Kenya. In each case, the team made a complete life-cycle analysis of twelve thousand rose stems for sale in February—in which all the variables, from seeds to store, were taken into consideration. They even multiplied the CO_2 emissions for the air-freighted Kenyan roses by a factor of nearly three, to account for the increased effect of burning fuel at a high altitude. Nonetheless, the carbon footprint of the roses from Holland—which are almost always grown in a heated greenhouse—was six times the footprint of those shipped from Kenya. Even Williams was surprised by the magnitude of the difference. "Everyone always wants to make ethical choices about the food they eat and the things they buy," he told me. "And they should. It's just that what seems obvious often is not. And we need to make sure people understand that before they make decisions on how they ought to live."

20   How do we alter human behavior significantly enough to limit global warming? Personal choices, no matter how virtuous, cannot do enough. It will also take laws and money. For decades, American utilities built tall smokestacks, hoping to keep the pollutants they emitted away from people who lived nearby. As emissions are forced into the atmosphere, however, they react with water molecules and then are often blown great distances by prevailing winds, which in the United States tend to move from west to east. Those emissions—principally sulfur dioxide produced by coal-burning power plants—are the primary source of acid rain, and by the nineteen-seventies it had become clear that they were causing grave damage to the environment, and to the health of many Americans. Adirondack Park, in upstate New York, suffered more than anywhere else: hundreds of streams, ponds, and lakes there became so acidic that they could no longer support plant life or fish. Members of Congress tried repeatedly to introduce legislation to reduce sulfur-dioxide levels, but the Reagan Administration (as well as many elected officials, both Democratic and Republican, from regions where sulfur-rich coal is mined) opposed any controls, fearing that they would harm the economy. When the cost of polluting is negligible, so are the incentives to reducing emissions.

21   "We had a complete disaster on our hands," Richard Sandor told me recently, when I met with him at his office at the Chicago Climate Exchange. Sandor, a dapper sixty-six-year-old man in a tan cable-knit cardigan and round, horn-rimmed glasses, is the exchange's chairman and CEO. In most respects, the exchange operates like any other market. Instead of pork-belly futures or gold, however, CCX members buy and sell the right to pollute. Each makes a voluntary (but legally binding) commitment to reduce emissions of greenhouse gases—including carbon dioxide, methane, and nitrous oxide—and hydrofluorocarbons. Four hundred corporations now belong to the exchange, including a growing percentage of America's largest manufacturers. The members agree to reduce their emissions by a certain amount every year, a system commonly known as cap and trade. A baseline target,

or cap, is established, and companies whose emissions fall below that cap receive allowances, which they can sell (or save to use later). Companies whose emissions exceed the limit are essentially fined and forced to buy credits to compensate for their excess.

22   Sandor led me to the "trading floor," which, like most others these days, is a virtual market populated solely by computers. "John, can you get the carbon futures up on the big screen?" Sandor yelled to one of his colleagues. Suddenly, a string of blue numbers slid across the monitor. "There is our 2008 price," Sandor said. Somebody had just bid two dollars and fifteen cents per ton for carbon futures.

23   A former Berkeley economics professor and chief economist at the Chicago Board of Trade, Sandor is known as the "father of financial futures." In the nineteen-seventies, he devised a market in interest rates which, when they started to fluctuate, turned into an immense source of previously untapped wealth. His office is just north of the Board of Trade, where he served for two years as vice-chairman. The walls are filled with interest-rate arcana and mortgage memorabilia; his desk is surrounded by monitors that permit him to track everything from catastrophic-risk portfolios to the price of pollution.

24   Sandor invents markets to create value for investors where none existed before. He sees himself as "a guy from the sixties"—but one who believes that free markets can make inequality disappear. So, he wondered, why not offer people the right to buy and sell shares in the value of reduced emissions? "At first, people laughed when I suggested the whole futures idea," he said. "They didn't see the point of hedging on something like interest rates, and when it came to pollution rights, many people just thought it was wrong to take a business approach to environmental protection."

25   For Sandor, personal factors like food choices and driving habits are small facets of a far larger issue: making pollution so costly that our only rational choice is to stop. When he started, though, the idea behind a sulfur-dioxide–emissions market was radical. It also seemed distasteful; opponents argued that codifying the right to pollute would only remove the stigma from an unacceptable activity. You can't trade something unless you own it; to grant a company the right to trade in emissions is also to give it a property right over the atmosphere.

26   Sandor acknowledges the potential for abuse, but he remains convinced that emissions will never fall unless there is a price tag attached to them. "You are really faced with a couple of possibilities when you want to control something," he told me. "You can say, 'Hey, we will allow you to use only x amount of these pollutants.' That is the command approach. Or you can make a market."

27   In the late nineteen-eighties, Sandor was asked by an Ohio public-interest group if he thought it would be possible to turn air into a commodity. He wrote an essay advocating the creation of an exchange for sulfur-dioxide emissions. The idea attracted a surprising number of environmentalists, because it called for large and specific reductions; conservatives who usually oppose regulation approved of the market-driven solution.

28   When Congress passed the Clean Air Act in 1990, the law included a section that mandated annual acid-rain reductions of ten million tons below 1980 levels. Each large smokestack was fitted with a device to measure sulfur-dioxide emissions.

As a way to help meet the goals, the act enabled the creation of the market. "Industry lobbyists said it would cost ten billion dollars in electricity increases a year. It cost one billion," Sandor told me. It soon became less expensive to reduce emissions than it was to pollute. Consequently, companies throughout the country suddenly discovered the value of investing millions of dollars in scrubbers, which capture and sequester sulfur dioxide before it can reach the atmosphere.

29   Sandor still enjoys describing his first sulfur trade. Representatives of a small Midwestern town were seeking a loan to build a scrubber. "They were prepared to borrow millions of dollars and leverage the city to do it," he told me. "We said, 'We have a better idea.' " Sandor arranged to have the scrubber installed with no initial cost, and the apparatus helped the city fall rapidly below its required emissions cap. He then calculated the price of thirty years' worth of that municipality's SO_2 emissions and helped arrange a loan for the town. "We gave it to them at a significantly lower rate than any bank would have done," Sandor said. "It was a fifty-million-dollar deal and they saved seven hundred and fifty thousand dollars a year—and never had to pay a balloon mortgage at the end. I mention this because trading that way not only allows you to comply with the law, but it provides creative financing tools to help structure the way investments are made. It encourages people to comply at lower costs, because then they will make money."

30   The program has been an undisputed success. Medical and environmental savings associated with reduced levels of lung disease and other conditions have been enormous—more than a hundred billion dollars a year, according to the EPA. "When is the last time you heard somebody even talking about acid rain?" Sandor asked. "It was going to ravage the world. Now it is not even mentioned in the popular press. We have reduced emissions from eighteen million tons to nine million, and we are going to halve it again by 2010. That is as good a social policy as you are ever likely to see." No effort to control greenhouse-gas emissions or to lower the carbon footprint—of an individual, a nation, or even the planet—can succeed unless those emissions are priced properly. There are several ways to do that: they can be taxed heavily, like cigarettes, or regulated, which is the way many countries have established mileage-per-gallon standards for automobiles. Cap and trade is another major approach—although CO_2 emissions are a far more significant problem for the world than those which cause acid rain, and any genuine solution will have to be global.

31   Higher prices make conservation appealing—and help spark investment in clean technologies. When it costs money to use carbon, people begin to seek profits from selling fuel-efficient products like long-lasting light bulbs, appliances that save energy, hybrid cars, even factories powered by the sun. One need only look at the passage of the Clean Water Act, in 1972, to see that a strategy that combines legal limits with realistic pricing can succeed. Water had always essentially been free in America, and when something is free, people don't value it. The act established penalties that made it expensive for factories to continue to pollute water. Industry responded at once, and today the United States (and much of the developed world) manufactures more products with less water than it did fifty years ago. Still, whether you buy a plane ticket, an overcoat, a Happy Meal, a bottle of wine imported from Argentina, or a gallon of gasoline, the value of the carbon used to make those products is not reflected by their prices.

32   Trading schemes have many opponents, some of whom suggest that attaching an acceptable price to carbon will open the door to a new form of colonialism. After all, since 1850, North America and Europe have accounted for seventy per cent of all greenhouse-gas emissions, a trend that is not improving. Stephen Pacala, the director of Princeton University's Environmental Institute, recently estimated that half of the world's carbon-dioxide emissions come from just seven hundred million people, about ten per cent of the population.

33   If prices were the same for everyone, however, rich countries could adapt more easily than countries in the developing world. "This market driven mechanism subjects the planet's atmosphere to the *legal* emission of greenhouse gases," the anthropologist Heidi Bachram has written. "The arrangement parcels up the atmosphere and establishes the routinized buying and selling of 'permits to pollute' as though they were like any other international commodity." She and others have concluded that such an approach would be a recipe for social injustice.

34   No one I spoke to for this story believes that climate change can be successfully addressed solely by creating a market. Most agreed that many approaches—legal, technological, and financial—will be necessary to lower our carbon emissions by at least sixty per cent over the next fifty years. "We will have to do it all and more," Simon Thomas told me. He is the chief executive officer of Trucost, a consulting firm that helps gauge the full burden of greenhouse-gas emissions and advises clients on how to address them. Thomas takes a utilitarian approach to the problem, attempting to convince corporations, pension funds, and other investors that the price of continuing to ignore the impact of greenhouse-gas emissions will soon greatly exceed the cost of reducing them.

35   Thomas thinks that people finally are beginning to get the message. Apple computers certainly has. Two years ago, Greenpeace began a "Green my Apple" campaign, attacking the company for its "iWaste." Then, last spring, not long before Apple launched the iPhone, Greenpeace issued a guide to electronics which ranked major corporations on their tracking, reporting, and reduction of toxic chemicals and electronic waste. Apple came in last. The group's findings were widely reported, and stockholders took notice. (A company that sells itself as one of America's most innovative brands cannot afford to ignore the environmental consequences of its manufacturing processes.) Within a month, Steve Jobs, the company's CEO, posted a letter on the Apple Web site promising a "greener Apple." He committed the company to ending the use of arsenic and mercury in monitors and said that the company would shift rapidly to more environmentally friendly LCD displays.

36   "The success of approaches such as ours relies on the idea that even if polluters are not paying properly now, there is some reasonable prospect that they will have to pay in the future," Thomas told me. "If that is true, then we know the likely costs, and they are of significant value. If polluters never have to pay, then our approach will fail.

37   "You have to make it happen, though," he went on. "And that is the job of government. It has to set a level playing field so that a market economy can deliver what it's capable of delivering." Thomas, a former investment banker, started Trucost nearly a decade ago. He mentioned the free-market economist Friedrich von Hayek, who won the Nobel Prize in Economics in 1974. "There is a remarkable essay in

which he shows how an explosion, say, in a South American tin mine could work its way through the global supply chain to increase the price of canned goods in Europe," Thomas said. I wondered what the price of tin could have to do with the cost of global warming. "It is very much to the point," Thomas answered. "Tin became more expensive and the market responded. In London, people bought fewer canned goods. The information travelled all the way from that mine across the world without any person in that supply chain even knowing the reasons for the increase. But there was less tin available, and the market responded as you would have hoped it would." To Thomas, the message was simple: "If something is priced accurately, its value will soon be reflected in every area of the economy."

38   Without legislation, it is hard to imagine that a pricing plan could succeed. (The next Administration is far more likely to act than the Bush Administration has been. The best-known climate-change bill now before Congress, which would mandate capping carbon limits, was written by Senator Joseph Lieberman. Hillary Clinton, Barack Obama, and John McCain are co-sponsors. Most industrial leaders, whatever their ideological reservations, would prefer a national scheme to a system of rules that vary from state to state.) Even at today's anemic rates, however, the market has begun to function. "We have a price of carbon that ranges from two to five dollars a ton," Sandor told me. "And everyone says that is too cheap. Of course, they are right. But it's not too cheap for people to make money.

39   In 1977, Jimmy Carter told the American people that they would have to balance the nation's demand for energy with its "rapidly shrinking resources" or the result "may be a national catastrophe." It was a problem, the President said, "that we will not solve in the next few years, and it is likely to get progressively worse through the rest of this century. We must not be selfish or timid if we hope to have a decent world for our children and grandchildren." Carter referred to the difficult effort as the "moral equivalent of war," a phrase that was widely ridiculed (along with Carter himself, who wore a cardigan while delivering his speech, to underscore the need to turn down the thermostat).

40   Carter was prescient. We are going to have to reduce our carbon footprint rapidly, and we can do that only by limiting the amount of fossil fuels released into the atmosphere. But what is the most effective—and least painful—way to achieve that goal? Each time we drive a car, use electricity generated by a coal-fired plant, or heat our homes with gas or oil, carbon dioxide and other heat-trapping gases escape into the air. We can use longer-lasting light bulbs, lower the thermostat (and the air-conditioning), drive less, and buy more fuel-efficient cars. That will help, and so will switching to cleaner sources of energy. Flying has also emerged as a major carbon don't—with some reason, since airplanes at high altitudes release at least ten times as many greenhouse gases per mile as trains do. Yet neither transportation—which accounts for fifteen per cent of greenhouse gases—nor industrial activity (another fifteen per cent) presents the most efficient way to shrink the carbon footprint of the globe.

41   Just two countries—Indonesia and Brazil—account for about ten per cent of the greenhouse gases released into the atmosphere. Neither possesses the type of heavy industry that can be found in the West, or for that matter in Russia or India. Still, only the United States and China are responsible for greater levels of emissions.

That is because tropical forests in Indonesia and Brazil are disappearing with incredible speed. "It's really very simple," John O. Niles told me. Niles, the chief science and policy officer for the environmental group Carbon Conservation, argues that spending five billion dollars a year to prevent deforestation in countries like Indonesia would be one of the best investments the world could ever make. "The value of that land is seen as consisting only of the value of its lumber," he said. "A logging company comes along and offers to strip the forest to make some trivial wooden product, or a palm-oil plantation. The governments in these places have no cash. They are sitting on this resource that is doing nothing for their economy. So when a guy says, 'I will give you a few hundred dollars if you let me cut down these trees,' it's not easy to turn your nose up at that. Those are dollars people can spend on schools and hospitals."

42   The ecological impact of decisions like that are devastating. Decaying trees contribute greatly to increases in the levels of greenhouse gases. Plant life absorbs CO_2. But when forests disappear, the earth loses one of its two essential carbon sponges (the other is the ocean). The results are visible even from space. Satellite photographs taken over Indonesia and Brazil show thick plumes of smoke rising from the forest. According to the latest figures, deforestation pushes nearly six billion tons of CO_2 into the atmosphere every year. That amounts to thirty million acres— an area half the size of the United Kingdom—chopped down each year. Put another way, according to one recent calculation, during the next twenty-four hours, the effect of losing forests in Brazil and Indonesia will be the same as if eight million people boarded airplanes at Heathrow Airport and flew en masse to New York.

43   "This is the greatest remaining opportunity we have to help address global warming," Niles told me. "It's a no-brainer. People are paying money to go in and destroy those forests. We just have to pay more to prevent that from happening." Niles's group has proposed a trade: "If you save your forest, and we can independently audit and verify it, we will calculate the emissions you have saved and pay you for that." The easiest way to finance such a plan, he is convinced, would be to use carbon-trading allowances. Anything that prevents carbon dioxide from entering the atmosphere would have value that could be quantified and traded. Since undisturbed farmland has the same effect as not emitting carbon dioxide at all, people could create allowances by leaving their forests untouched or by planting new trees. (Rain forests are essential to planetary vitality in other ways, too, of course. More than a third of all terrestrial species live in forest canopies. Rising levels of CO_2 there alter the way that forests function, threatening to increase flooding and droughts and epidemics of plant disease. Elevated CO_2 in the forest atmosphere also reduces the quality of the wood in the trees, and that in turn has an impact on the reproduction of flowers, as well as that of birds, bees, and anything else that relies on that ecosystem.)

44   From both a political and an economic perspective, it would be easier and cheaper to reduce the rate of deforestation than to cut back significantly on air travel. It would also have a far greater impact on climate change and on social welfare in the developing world. Possessing rights to carbon would grant new power to farmers who, for the first time, would be paid to preserve their forests rather than destroy them. Unfortunately, such plans are seen by many people as morally

unattractive. "The whole issue is tied up with the misconceived notion of 'carbon colonialism,' " Niles told me. "Some activists do not want the Third World to have to alter their behavior, because the problem was largely caused by us in the West.

45   Environmental organizations like Carbon Trade Watch say that reducing our carbon footprint will require restructuring our lives, and that before we in the West start urging the developing world to do that, we ought to make some sacrifices; anything else would be the modern equivalent of the medieval practice of buying indulgences as a way of expiating one's sins. "You have to realize that, in the end, people are trying to buy their way out of bad behavior," Tony Juniper, the director of Friends of the Earth, told me. "Are we really a society that wants to pay rich people not to fly on private jets or countries not to cut down their trees? Is that what, ultimately, is morally right and equitable?"

46   Sandor dismisses the question. "Frankly, this debate just makes me want to scream," he told me. "The clock is moving. They are slashing and burning and cutting the forests of the world. It may be a quarter of global warming and we can get the rate to two per cent simply by inventing a preservation credit and making that forest have value in other ways. Who loses when we do that?

47   "People tell me, well, these are bad guys, and corporate guys who just want to buy the right to pollute are bad, too, and we should not be giving them incentives to stop. But we need to address the problems that exist, not drown in fear or lose ourselves in morality. Behavior changes when you offer incentives. If you want to punish people for being bad corporate citizens, you should go to your local church or synagogue and tell God to punish them. Because that is not our problem. Our problem is global warming, and my job is to reduce greenhouse gases at the lowest possible cost. I say solve the problem and deal with the bad guys somewhere else."

48   "We have to be careful not to rush from denial to despair," John Elkington told me, when I visited him not long ago at his offices at SustainAbility, the London-based environmental consulting firm he helped found more than two decades ago. He believes there is a danger that people will feel engulfed by the challenge, and ultimately helpless to address it.

49   "We are in an era of creative destruction," he said. Elkington has long been one of the most articulate of those who seek to marry economic prosperity with environmental protection. "What happens when you go into one of these periods is that before you get to the point of reconstruction, things have to fall apart. Detroit will fall apart. I think Ford"—a company that Elkington has advised for years—"will fall apart. They have just made too many bets on the wrong things. A bunch of the institutions that we rely on currently will, to some degree, decompose. I believe that much of what we count as democratic politics today will fall apart, because we are simply not going to be able to deal with the scale of change that we are about to face. It will profoundly disable much of the current political class."

50   He sat back and smiled softly. He didn't look worried. "I wrote my first report on climate change in 1978, for Herman Kahn, at the Hudson Institute," he explained. "He did not at all like what I was saying, and he told me, 'The trouble with you environmentalists is that you see a problem coming, and you slam your foot on the brakes and try and steer away from the chasm. The problem is that it often doesn't work. Maybe the thing to do is jam your foot on the pedal and see if you can just

jump across.' At the time, I thought he was crazy, but as I get older, I realize what he was talking about. The whole green movement in technology is in that space. It is an attempt to jump across the chasm." ◆

CRITICAL THINKING

1. Would you be persuaded to buy a product because it had a lower carbon footprint label than another product? Do you consider this when shopping for groceries or everyday items? Explain.
2. Define the term "locavore." Do you fit the profile of a locavore? Would you consider becoming one? Make a list of the things you buy that fall into this category and the things that do not, such as imported beer.
3. Some politicians have opposed any environmental restrictions or controls over corporations out of fear that new regulations "would harm the economy." In your opinion, when, if ever, should concerns for the environment take precedence over concerns for the economy?
4. Answer the question posed in this article: "Are we really a society that wants to pay rich people not to fly on private jets or countries not to cut down their trees? Is that what, ultimately, is morally right and equitable?"
5. The author notes that truly following a "green" ideology is "a monumental challenge." It requires a revolution in technology and a revolution in thinking. "We are going to have to rethink the way we live and work." Cite the ways, if any, you have gone green in your thinking and your daily life.

CRITICAL WRITING

1. *Persuasive Writing:* Agree or disagree with this statement: "Some activists do not want the Third World to have to alter their [environmental] behavior, because the problem was largely caused by us in the West."
2. *Expository Writing:* In this article, the agricultural researcher Adrian Williams disagrees with Sir Terry Leahy's notion of "food miles." Summarize the concept of food miles, and then analyze both Leahy's position and Williams's argument. Look carefully at the language both use when quoted by Specter. Whose argument is more effective, and why?
3. *Exploratory Writing:* Is it ethical for environmental agencies "to take a business approach to environmental protection"?

GROUP PROJECTS

1. With your group, skim the article to find all of the factors that could possibly influence the carbon footprint of a product. Then discuss which factors should be included when determining the carbon-footprint label for a product.
2. Arrange a tour of a local food-processing plant, factory, or manufacturing plant. Take notes on the tour to see if the tour guide mentions any environmentally friendly procedures that are in place, or in the works, for their company. Ask questions during and after the tour to find out more information on how this specific business is dealing with the climate crisis.

Six Products, Six Carbon Footprints

Jeffrey Ball*

Everybody's talking about it. But what exactly is a "carbon footprint"? And how is it calculated? In this next article, environmental editor Jeffrey Ball examines six common products with six very different carbon footprints. As you read about each product, think about others that may have similar origins and about how everything we use and do leaves its mark on the environment.

1 A new concept is entering the consumer lexicon: the carbon footprint.

2   First came organic. Then came fair trade. Now makers of everything from milk to jackets to cars are starting to tally up the carbon footprints of their products. That's the amount of carbon dioxide and other greenhouse gases that get coughed into the air when the goods are made, shipped and stored, and then used by consumers.

3   In the Gelsi household, reducing their carbon footprint is a family affair—they even wrote a musical about it. *MarketWatch* reporter Steve Gelsi offers tips for saving the environment and saving money while doing so.

4   So far, these efforts raise as many questions as they answer. Different companies are counting their products' carbon footprints differently, making it all but impossible for shoppers to compare goods. And even if consumers come to understand the numbers, they might not like what they find out. For instance, many products' global-warming impact depends less on how they're made than on how they're used. That means the easiest way to cut carbon emissions may be to buy less of a product or use it in a way that's less convenient.

5   So, what are the carbon footprints of some of the common products we use? How are they calculated? And what surprises do they hold? What follows is a look at six everyday items—cars, shoes, laundry detergent, clothing, milk, and beer—and the numbers that go with them.

6   But first, here's a number that will help you put all those carbon footprints in perspective. The U.S. emits the equivalent of about 118 pounds of carbon dioxide per resident every day, a figure that includes emissions from industry. Annually, that's nearly 20 metric tons per American—about five times the number per citizen of the world at large, according to the International Energy Agency.

7   Now, let's take a closer look at those six products.

Cars

8 The simplest statistic in the carbon-footprinting game may be this: For every mile it travels, the average car in the U.S. emits about one pound of carbon dioxide. Given typical driving distances and fuel-economy numbers, that translates into about five tons of carbon dioxide per car per year.

**Jeffrey Ball, The Wall Street Journal, October 6, 2008

9   A study by the University of Michigan's Center for Sustainable Systems found that, over its expected 120,000-mile life, an American-made midsize sedan emits the equivalent of about 63 tons of carbon dioxide. That number includes all emissions, from the making of the car's raw materials, such as steel and plastic, through the shredding of the car once it's junked.

10   The vast majority of those emissions—86%—came from the car's fuel use, the study found. Just 4% of emissions came from making and assembling the car. That means consumers can lower their footprint by buying a car with better fuel economy. Sometimes, the differences between models can be substantial. For one overview of how cars stack up, consider a new computer model paid for by Toyota Motor Corp. that computes the lifetime carbon footprints of about 400 auto models from multiple manufacturers.

11   To narrow things down, consider a handful of Toyota's own models. The Prius, a hybrid gasoline-and-electric car that averages 42 miles per gallon, has a lifetime carbon footprint of 44 metric tons, according to the updated computer model done for Toyota by Kreider & Associates, a consultant based in Boulder, Colo. The Corolla, a small sedan with a conventional gasoline engine rated at 29 miles per gallon, has a footprint of 64 tons. The Camry, a larger car rated at 23 miles per gallon, has a footprint of 95 tons. And the 4Runner, an SUV rated at 16 miles per gallon, has a footprint of 118 tons.

12   Gregory Keoleian, co-director of the Michigan center, says he used to advise people that the best way to minimize the carbon footprint of their driving was to keep their car as long as possible, since junking a car and manufacturing a new one produces pollution. But that was before hybrids hit the market and offered markedly better fuel economy. Now, he says, scrapping an old car in favor of a new model makes lots of sense. The introduction of the hybrid "changes the whole dynamic," Mr. Keoleian says. "Then, you replace."

Shoes

13   You may think you're at one with nature going for a walk in the woods in your sturdy hiking boots. But those boots pack a lot of carbon. The big reason: the leather.

14   Timberland Co., a Stratham, NH, shoe company with an outdoorsy image, has assessed the carbon footprint of about 40 of the shoe models it currently sells. The results range from about 22 pounds to 220 pounds per pair. Each of the shoes that has been carbon-footprinted comes with a label assessing its greenhouse-gas score on a scale of zero, which is best, to 10, which is worst.

15   Flip-flops tend to have footprints of 22 pounds to 44 pounds, says Pete Girard, senior analyst for environmental stewardship at Timberland. Shoes typically range from 66 pounds to 132 pounds. Hiking boots typically pack between 154 and 198 pounds, Mr. Girard says.

16   Though Timberland produces many of its shoes in Asia and sells them in the U.S., it has found that transportation typically accounts for less than 5% of the carbon footprint. By far the biggest contributor is the shoe's raw material. "For most Timberland shoes," says Betsy Blaisdell, Timberland's manager for environmental stewardship, "leather really drives the score."

17   The average dairy cow produces, every year, an amount of greenhouse gas equivalent to four tons of carbon dioxide, according to U.S. government figures. Most of that comes not from carbon dioxide, in fact, but from a more-potent greenhouse gas: methane. The cow's impact on the atmosphere is due largely to a process known scientifically as "enteric fermentation"—and colloquially as burping. A cow's multiple stomachs make it particularly efficient at transforming feed into bovine products: meat, milk and hide. But all that churning also produces lots of methane—a greenhouse gas that, pound for pound, is 25 times as damaging to the atmosphere as carbon dioxide, according to the United Nations. Converting those methane emissions into a carbon-dioxide–equivalent number is one step in calculating the cow's carbon footprint.

18   Take Timberland's Winter Park Slip On Boot. They're casual boots—not as heavy as hiking boots—but their uppers are all leather. Their footprint sits in the middle of the Timberland range, at 121 pounds per pair. Of that total, 8.5 pounds comes from the electricity used to make the boots at Timberland's factory in China's Guangdong Province. The remaining 112.5 pounds comes from the raw materials used to make the shoe: rubber for the outsole; ethyl vinyl acetate, or EVA, for the midsole; and, most of all, leather for the upper.

19   To come up with these numbers, Timberland first gets data from the factory on the amount of electricity the factory uses in a given period. Dividing that by the number of shoes the factory produces in that period yields a per-shoe energy-consumption figure. Timberland then checks those figures against tables that list average carbon-dioxide emissions per unit of energy produced. The tables are tailored to the specific power-plant fuel mix in the area where the factory sits. In China, which makes much of its power by burning coal, the carbon hit is greater than in, say, France, which makes most of its electricity with nuclear power.

Country Count

A sampling of various nations' carbon-dioxide emissions from fossil-fuel combustion, in annual tons per capita

Qatar 48.32
Australia 19.02
U.S. 19.0
Canada 16.52
Germany 10.0
Japan 9.49
United Kingdom 8.86
France 5.97
China 4.27
Mexico 3.97
India 1.13
World 4.28

Note: Includes carbon-dioxide emissions from fossil-fuel combustion throughout each economy, including industry. Figures are for 2006, the most recent year for which statistics are available.

Source: International Energy Agency

20   The harder part for Timberland is figuring out the emissions that come from the part of the process it doesn't control: the production of the raw materials before they get to the Timberland factory. Timberland gets that information from the databases of "life-cycle analysis" consultants, who put together tables showing the environmental impacts of producing given amounts of various materials, from rubber to polyester to leather.

21   Timberland's carbon-footprint calculations have prompted spats with some of Timberland's leather suppliers, Ms. Blaisdell says. They argue the carbon hit from a cow should fall not on their ledger, but on the ledger of beef producers. The leather producers reason that cows are grown mainly for meat, with leather as a by-product, so that growing leather doesn't yield any emissions beyond those that would have occurred anyway.

22   But Timberland has determined that 7% of the financial value of a cow lies in its leather. And life-cycle–analysis guidelines used by Timberland say the company should apply that percentage to compute the share of a cow's total emissions attributable to the leather. "We've had a lot of battles with our leather suppliers over this," Ms. Blaisdell says. Timberland officials, she says, "just follow the guidelines."

23   Timberland officials concede shortcomings with their method. By using an average energy-consumption number for all pairs of shoes, the calculations fail to recognize that some shoes require more electricity to assemble in the factory than do others. And Timberland's calculations omit the carbon impact of the leather and other materials that fall to the cutting-room floor. "No question, it's crude in some ways," Mr. Girard says. "But it's a step more information than our designers were making a decision on before."

Laundry Detergent

24 The recipe for a low-carbon load of laundry: Use liquid detergent instead of powder, wash your clothes in cool water and hang them out to dry. That's the message shoppers get when they walk down the detergent aisles at Tesco PLC stores in the U.K. Starting this spring, the retailer began slapping footprint-shaped carbon labels on Tesco-brand laundry detergent. Along with the carbon-footprint number, the label offers tips about lowering the score.

25   The carbon footprint of a load of laundry done with Tesco detergent varies from 1.3 pounds to 1.9 pounds, depending on what form of detergent is used, the labels report. According to Procter & Gamble Co., the average American family does about 300 loads of laundry per year, or about six loads per week. That suggests a per-family carbon footprint from doing laundry of about 480 pounds per year, or about 10 pounds per week. And that doesn't include running the dryer.

26   Solid capsules of detergent have the highest carbon footprint, according to Tesco. Powder has a slightly lower footprint; liquid has a lower one still; and concentrated liquid has the lowest of all. That's because making solid detergent uses more energy than making the liquid variety.

27   But consumers who care about their carbon emissions should do more than switch detergent forms, the labels advise. Doing the wash in cooler water— 86 degrees Fahrenheit instead of 104 degrees—will shave the carbon footprint of

each load by 0.3 pounds. That's as much of a reduction as you get from switching to liquid from powder.

28   The biggest way to cut the environmental impact of cleaning clothes, however, is to stop using a clothes dryer. Drying laundry outside on a line, Tesco says, will cut the carbon footprint of every load by a whopping 4.4 pounds.

29   Along with detergent, Tesco labels store-brand orange juice, light bulbs and potatoes. To trace the carbon footprints, Tesco uses data from its suppliers and information from life-cycle-analysis databases. The retailer is labeling products from its own brands first, because those were the ones it could most easily control. But Tesco is considering labeling other brands, as well as expanding the effort to its U.S. stores, which operate under the Fresh & Easy name.

30   The suppliers that make the labeled products "don't see a risk" in publicizing information about the environmental impacts of their products, says Katherine Symonds, Tesco's sustainability manager. For one thing, all forms of the detergent come from the same suppliers, so those suppliers wouldn't necessarily be hurt if consumers shifted from one form to another.

31   Ms. Symonds adds that Tesco carefully picked for its initial labels products whose carbon footprints likely wouldn't shock consumers. The retailer purposely avoided labeling the carbon footprint of beef, for instance, because beef's carbon footprint is significantly higher than that of many other foods. If Tesco had presented consumers "with a message that was so counterintuitive and difficult," Ms. Symonds says, "we might have found it difficult to take carbon labeling forward."

Jackets

32   Patagonia Inc.'s Talus jacket looks like a naturalist's dream. In fact, its carbon footprint is 66 pounds. That, Patagonia notes on its Web site, is 48 times the weight of the jacket itself. Over the past year, the Ventura, Calif., outdoor-equipment maker has computed and posted on its Web site the carbon footprints of 15 of its products. Because most of Patagonia's products are made in Asia or Latin America and sold in the U.S., the company expected that a big chunk of the carbon footprints came from transportation. It was wrong.

33   The fabric for the Talus is made in China, the zippers come from Japan, and the jacket is sewn in Vietnam. Yet all that transportation adds up to less than 1% of the product's total carbon footprint, Patagonia says. The majority of the footprint—71%, or about 47 pounds—comes in producing the polyester, which originates with oil.

34   "If we had listened to the rhetoric out there at the time, which was all around miles, we could have spent years rearranging our supply chain to reduce transportation, when really that's not the bulk of our concern," says Jill Dumain, Patagonia's director for environmental analysis. "There's a lot of reasons to have a tight supply chain, but environmentalism isn't one of them."

35   One way to slash the Talus jacket's carbon footprint would be to make it with recycled, rather than virgin, polyester. But when the jacket was being developed, the company that makes the fabric, Polartec LLC, of Lawrence, Massachusetts, couldn't find the right kind of recycled yarn in Asia, says Nate Simmons, director of marketing for the fabric maker. Polyester yarn with recycled content is more widely

available in the U.S. than in Asia, he says, and Polartec uses it to make some fabric for Patagonia. But the Talus is a particularly complicated jacket, because its material fuses together a weather-resistent outer layer with a warm, inner layer.

36   At the time the Talus was being developed, using recycled material would have required either making the fabric in the U.S. or shipping U.S.-made recycled-content yarn to Asia to be made into fabric. "It would have been extremely expensive," Mr. Simmons says. "Probably very few people would have bought it. And it wouldn't have had much of a positive impact because of that." The bottom line: In making the Talus, Patagonia decided that cost concerns outweighed environmental concerns. "Consumers are starting to put environmental values into their purchasing decisions, but it doesn't always translate into their being willing to pay a higher price," Patagonia's Ms. Dumain says.

37   Some Patagonia products—generally ones whose fabric isn't as complex as the Talus's—are made with recycled-content fabric. Among them is the Eco Rain Shell, which has a carbon footprint of just 15 pounds, Patagonia says. But the Eco Shell has a different environmental problem: A byproduct of manufacturing the material that makes the jacket water-repellent is perfluorooctanic acid, a substance that Patagonia says has been found accumulating in humans and animals and that scientists say could pose health risks. Patagonia lays out this conundrum on its Web site, saying it "reflects the complexities involved" in balancing concern for the environment with the need for performance.

Milk

38 Several studies of milk's carbon footprint are under way in the U.S. Each has come up with a different number, largely because each is counting things differently. A recent study by National Dairy Holdings, a Dallas-based dairy, found that the carbon footprint of a gallon of its milk in a plastic jug is either 6.19 pounds or 7.59 pounds. The difference rests in what kind of cases the jugs are placed in during transport from the milk-processing plant to the distribution center. Plastic cases, because they take more energy to produce, yield more carbon-dioxide emissions than do cardboard ones.

39   But National Dairy Holdings' study doesn't count all the emissions created by a gallon of milk. It includes those from the cows themselves (more than half of the total), from the processing of the milk and from the transport of the milk to a distribution center. It doesn't count the emissions earlier in the process: growing the cows' feed. Nor does it count the emissions later in the process: transporting the milk from the distribution center to the store and refrigerating it there.

40   That's because National Dairy Holdings did its study largely at the request of Wal-Mart Stores Inc., a big customer, which is trying to prod environmental improvements in its supply chain. So, National Dairy Holdings measured only its piece in the supply chain, explains Howard Depoy, the dairy's director of power, refrigeration and sustainability. That's "the CO_2 that we can control and manage," Mr. Depoy says.

41   Aurora Dairy Corp.'s Aurora Organic Dairy, a small organic-milk producer based in Boulder, Colo., is finishing a more complete study of the carbon footprint

of its milk. Its study, done by researchers at the University of Michigan's Center for Sustainable Systems, attempts to include emissions all the way from growing the cattle feed to refrigerating the processed milk in the store. The preliminary findings are that producing a half-gallon of Aurora's milk generates the equivalent of 7.2 pounds of carbon dioxide. That's essentially the same amount as the National Dairy Holdings study concluded is produced by an entire gallon of National Dairy Holdings' milk. But the National Dairy Holdings study left out much of the process that the Aurora study included.

42   Both studies found that the single biggest chunk of emissions from milk production comes from all that action in the cow's gut. Now, the U.S. dairy industry's main trade group, Dairy Management, Inc., is launching yet another study of milk's carbon footprint. It plans a complete measurement akin to Aurora Organic Dairy's.

43   The dairy industry doesn't plan to put carbon-footprint labels on milk cartons, says Rick Naczi, an executive vice president for Dairy Management. "It's something that would be very, very difficult to make understandable to consumers," he says.

Beer

44 When New Belgium Brewing Co. set out last year to compute the carbon footprint of a six-pack of its Fat Tire Amber Ale, it figured it would find transportation was the biggest problem. That's the emission source New Belgium thinks about most often. The microbrewer, based in Fort Collins, Colo., has been expanding into more states, necessitating more trucking of its beer.

45   When the numbers came in this summer, they showed that a six-pack's carbon footprint was about 7 pounds. The real surprise was where the bulk of that number came from: the refrigeration of the beer at stores. Transportation came in fourth, behind manufacturing the glass bottles and producing the barley and malt. "It seems that in every carbon-footprint study I've come across, people are surprised," says Jennifer Orgolini, New Belgium's sustainability director.

46   Now, New Belgium is considering switching to bottles with more recycled glass, because making them consumes less fuel. It's also considering buying barley and malt produced organically, rather than with chemical fertilizers, which are big emitters.

47   Refrigeration poses a tougher problem. Stores selling Fat Tire aren't owned by New Belgium, so even if the brewer wanted them to stop refrigerating the beer, they might not do so.

48   There are smaller potential fixes. Many stores could switch from less-efficient, open-front beer chillers to more-efficient models enclosed by clear doors. But that presents its own hurdle, Ms. Orgolini notes: "People don't want to have to open the door." ◆

CRITICAL THINKING

1. Why do efforts to track and reduce carbon footprints for various products "raise as many questions as they answer"? Explain.
2. Did the carbon footprint of any of the items described in this article surprise you? If so, what did you find illuminating, and why?

3. In a 2008 article on climate change, author Andrew Potter noted "It is the principles that underwrite modernity itself that are the problem." Based on the information in this article, describe some of the challenges modernity itself poses as we seek to reduce our carbon footprint.

4. At the end of this article, New Belgium Beer's sustainability director Jennifer Orgolini comments that "people don't want to have to open the door" of beer chillers. What is she saying about consumers? In your own opinion, at what point should the convenience of consumers be offset with the issues of the environment? Explain.

CRITICAL WRITING

1. *Analytical Writing:* Using the information provided in this article, prepare a short report on the likely carbon footprint of another household product, clothing item, or foodstuff.

2. *Persuasive Writing*: If you have not already done so, answer question 1 in the Group Projects section, and rank the issues on the list in order of most importance to you. After completing the exercise, write an explanation of why you ranked the issues in the order you did. Explain why the issue you chose as the most important is the most pressing issue facing Americans today and the one most worthy of both social and political attention.

3. *Creative Writing:* Write an essay in which you describe how life will be in the year 2150 due to global warming. As you craft your essay, consider climate scientist James E. Hansen's comment that our great grandchildren "will be living on a different planet." Include how people live, the products they use, and how they communicate and travel in your response.

GROUP PROJECTS

1. In January 2007, the Pew Research Center for the People and the Press surveyed Americans on the issue of climate change. They asked survey participants to rank the priorities listed below in order of greatest importance. As individuals, rank the issues below, and then compare your rankings with the group. Then compare your rankings with the Pew Survey results at the Pew Web site, http://people-press.org/report/303.

Budget deficit	Global warming	Minimum wage
Crime	Government ethics	Morality
Economy	Heath care	Poverty
Education	Heath insurance	Social Security
Employment	Illegal immigration	Stronger military
Energy	International trade	Taxes
Environment	Medicare	Terrorism

2. What do college students think about the most pressing issues facing them today? Access the survey given by the Pew Research Center at http://people-press.org/reports/questionnaires/303.pdf. Each member of your

group should poll at least 20 students, compile the data, and compare it to the results reported by the Pew Research Center. How are the concerns of college students similar and different from those of the general public? Do you think age is a factor in how people respond to these concerns? Does political affiliation have any influence on the responses of college students? Does your survey reveal any strong disparities between groups? Explain.

Perspectives: It's Not Easy Being Green!

Joe Heller, *Green Bay Press-Gazette*. Posted 04/21/2008

THINKING CRITICALLY

1. What is happening in this cartoon? Who is the creature in the middle of the footprint? What does he represent?
2. What does the footprint mean? What is a "carbon footprint"? Why does it matter to the creature in the drawing?
3. What do the words the creature is saying mean? How do they connect to who he is and what he represents?
4. Calculate your own carbon footprint. Visit the Nature Conservancy's Web site on climate change at http://www.nature.org/initiatives/climatechange/calculator. Report your score.

My Carbon Footprint: A Documentary, a Daughter, and All that Is Dear

Jennifer Davidson*

Columnist Jennifer Davidson thought of herself as a "moderate environmentalist" as she engaged in Earth-friendly practices to ensure a better environmental future for her daughter. After watching the 2006 movie, *An Inconvenient Truth*, however, Davidson finds herself in a fit of despair. The movie, which features Al Gore, "offers a passionate and inspirational look at [Gore's] fervent crusade to halt global warming's deadly progress in its tracks by exposing the myths and misconceptions that surround it." In this editorial, Davidson wonders what sort of world her daughter will live in if climate change continues unchecked.

1   I've always felt like a modest environmentalist. I use canvas grocery bags (OK, sometimes). I primarily buy cruelty free products, recycle at work and contribute a small stipend each month to purchase a portion of my energy from green sources. My daughter and I are protectors of snails in danger of being squashed on sidewalks, and we let no six-pack plastic ring go uncut. We care. Somehow I convinced myself that was enough.

2   Recently I had the opportunity to watch Al Gore's *An Inconvenient Truth*, documenting the state of Earth's global-warming condition due to greenhouse gases. Educated as a scientist, I appreciated the wealth of hard data Gore had compiled, but what brought me to weep, as if I had lost someone I loved, was the manner in which he gave meaning to the data. Under the layers of percentages, charts and graphs, the exposed bloody heart of his message beat as loud as Ichabod Crane's. Everything I love, everything that is dear to me, is at stake.

3   Everything I do is for my daughter. And for the first time I realized that none of it will matter if her ability to live on Earth is not sus-

Everything I do is for my daughter.

tained, or if I leave her a planet where the fresh water supply for millions is gone, where she'll face unbearably hot summers, an Arctic with no ice, and, in turn, warmer oceans, a teetering marine ecosystem and higher sea levels that will swallow coastal communities worldwide in one gulp. And will she walk upon a barren Earth, void of the rich species we have today? If these are the legacies I leave to my daughter, I will have realized my greatest failure as a parent.

4   Global warming is the result of a worldwide dependency on fossil fuels. However, America contributes slightly more than 30 percent of the problem. Here's what happens in bustling American homes much like my own. Unnecessary lights are left on, a few notches on the thermostat are chosen over a heavier sweater, the TV is alive, the radio hums, the dishwasher and dryer are rumbling at peak hours, and, "Shoot! I need to run to the store in my high-performance vehicle for the cat food I forgot earlier."

* Jennifer Davidson, *NewsReview,* March 8, 2007

5   In the simplest terms, Gore explains what the emissions from the energy and gasoline we gorge ourselves on each day do to our atmospheric layer—the thin, fragile shell that stabilizes the Earth's temperature. As we send more and more carbon emissions into our atmosphere, the very composition of this layer changes and thickens, trapping the sun's heat and unnaturally warming the planet.

6   Without perspective, a few degrees warmer doesn't really sound that bad. But as temperatures slowly continue to rise, the change in climate begins to unravel the fabric upon which the natural world is built, upon which human civilization depends. Gore took this fairly ambiguous concept and gave it life in tangible measures of potential destruction, suffering and extinction.

7   Our Arctic is melting. As the ice dwindles, more of the sun's rays are absorbed by the ocean rather than reflected by the ice that has disappeared. This warms Arctic waters and fuels destruction of the remaining ice.

8   Warmer temperatures have slurped-up ice shelves in Antarctica as well. Twenty to 25 miles of the Larsen B 700-foot tall ice shelf, the largest in the world, was expected to be stable for more than 100 years, explained Gore. But within 35 days it disappeared in March of 2002.

9   Reruns of what Gore referred to as "massive rushing torrents" in the middle of Greenland's ice sheet play over and over in my head. You see it and instinctively know something is very wrong. It was eerie and I felt vulnerable, as if the only thing protecting me from the rushing torrents was the thin layer of glass in my television. Freaky.

10   As silly as it sounds, it may not be far-fetched. Scientists from the National Center for Atmospheric Research, U.S. Geological Survey and several universities completed their research last year, funded by the National Science Foundation, on melting polar ice sheets due to temperature increases. The findings anticipate worldwide sea levels to rise more than 20 feet by the end of this century.

11   Gore paints a simpler picture. The San Francisco Bay? Underwater. Southern Florida? Gone. The World Trade Center Memorial in New York City? Swallowed. How about the Netherlands, Beijing, Shanghai, Calcutta? More than one-hundred-million people will be displaced. Where will they go? How will we handle a catastrophe of this magnitude with immeasurable social, economical and environmental consequences? I have so many questions.

12   Warmer oceans also threaten our ocean currents, weather patterns and the health of marine ecosystems. In the Arctic, polar bears are drowning from hypothermia and exhaustion as they attempt to swim increasing distances between fewer and fewer floating chunks of sea ice. Their diminishing habitat prompted the U.S. Fish and Wildlife Service to propose listing the bear as threatened under the Endangered Species Act in December of 2006.

13   Some species can respond to rising temperatures by rapidly migrating to an ecological niche with cooler temperatures. But this has significant consequences in the natural world. As new species invade, competition for resources, such as food, shelter and territory, can threaten or extinguish the weaker species. New strains of diseases can be introduced, which can wipe out a healthy population. Prey that was once controlled by predators can go unchecked and wreak havoc on the environment. In essence, we've triggered the Earth to wage war against itself. And we know what war looks like.

14   Gore wove a very personal side of his life into the documentary. He took us back in time when he was a small boy and he and his sister, Nancy, helped his father, a tobacco farmer, grow and harvest the plant. He talked about the death of his sister years later, when she succumbed to lung cancer from smoking since she was 14. "The idea that we were a part of this was so painful on so many levels. Whatever explanation that made sense in the past didn't cut it anymore. The day of reckoning comes, and you wish you had connected the dots more quickly."

15   I understand now. I've connected the dots, and it is my turn, as Gore says, to decide how I will react. ◆

CRITICAL THINKING

1. What do parents—indeed, all adults—owe, if anything, to the next generation? If you are a parent, describe how being a parent has made you more (or less) aware of the greater world you live in.
2. What strikes Davidson about the way Gore's movie describes climate change? How does Gore's description of the potential impact of global warming compare to Easterbrook's in the second essay? Explain.
3. In what ways does this essay appeal to the emotions? How does it appeal to the intellect?
4. How compelling is Davidson's argument? Does the fact that she has a science background influence your opinion of her points? Does her background as a parent make her more compelling or credible? Explain.
5. Davidson describes herself as a "moderate environmentalist." What does she mean by this? What do you think she will do as a result of watching Gore's movie?

CRITICAL WRITING

1. *Evaluation and Analysis:* Watch the movie *An Inconvenient Truth* and write a review of the film. What are the movie's strengths and weaknesses? What struck you as compelling? Questionable? Is the movie balanced? Biased? Slanted? Fair? Does it offer solutions? What is your personal reaction to the film?
2. *Personal Narrative:* Several of the writers in this chapter cite how radical changes in our environment will have an indelible impact on our lives. Write about a time when the weather or climate had a significant impact on your own life. It could be a memory of a blizzard when you were a child or a personal experience with a recent catastrophe, such as Hurricane Katrina.

GROUP PROJECT

1. Visit the Web site of the Woods Hole Oceanographic Institution (WHOI) at http://www.whoi.edu/institutes/occi, and read what it is saying about

climate change and the environment, especially its research on abrupt climate change. Each group should select a different, recent WHOI feature story (posted on the Web site under the "Related Topics" heading) and prepare a short report on the article for class discussion.

► **Are Cows Worse than Cars?**
Ben Adler*

► **Can Cities Save the Planet?**
Witold Rybczynski

While most people agree that climate change is a pressing problem, we seem to be at odds as to how to slow, and indeed reverse, the damage in time to prevent a global catastrophe. Obstacles to change include broad scale governmental fears of adversely affecting the economy and global market to personal concerns that our lives will be inconvenienced. The next two articles challenge our preconceived notions on what constitutes a real threat to the planet. The first piece posits that cows are worse than cars as the greater contributor of pollution and greenhouse gases. Everyone knows driving an SUV or leaving the lights on is bad for the earth. But when it comes to your environmental impact, what's on your plate may be just as important. The second essay makes us rethink green living which, the author argues, is more likely to be achieved by living in cites rather than on rural farms.

Are Cows Worse than Cars?
Ben Adler

1 These days almost any proposal to reduce global warming gets taken seriously, even by conservatives. Solar panels are proposed for powering everything except submarines. Oilman T. Boone Pickens wants to put windmills on every empty patch of land in Texas, and Republicans have finally found something to like about France: nuclear power.

2 But when Rajendra Pachauri, who runs the Intergovernmental Panel on Climate Change (IPCC), made a suggestion that could reduce global greenhouse gas emissions by as much as 18 percent, he was excoriated. Why was his proposal so unpalatable? Because he suggested eating less meat would be the easiest way people could reduce their carbon footprint, with one meat-free day per week as a first step. "How convenient for him: He's a vegetarian," sneered a *Pittsburgh Tribune*

* Ben Adler, *The American Prospect,* December 3, 2008; Witold Rybczynski, *Slate Magazine,* December 17, 2008

Review editorial. "Dr. Pachauri should be more concerned about his own diet. A new study shows that a deficiency of vitamin B-12, found primarily in meat, fish and milk, can lead to brain shrinkage." Boris Johnson, London's outspoken mayor, posted a long screed on his blog, declaring, "The whole proposition is so irritating that I am almost minded to eat more meat in response."

3   Johnson may not appreciate the environmental value of replacing his steak and kidney pie with a tofu scramble, but the benefits would be quite real. Animal agriculture is responsible for local pollution from animal waste and chemical use and for greenhouse gas emissions from the energy-intensive process of growing feed and raising livestock, plus the, ahem, byproducts of animal digestion. It would be much easier—and cheaper—to give up meat than to, say, convert an entire country's electrical grid to using solar, wind, or nuclear energy. A rural Montanan might have no choice but to drive to work, but he can certainly switch out his pork chop for pinto beans. While Pachauri was correct to note that one need not go vegan to help the environment—simply eating less meat would help—he could have also emphasized the more politically appealing point that one can be a carnivore and still reduce one's impact by choosing different meats. Even limiting one's meat consumption to chicken yields major environmental benefits—not to mention health and financial benefits.

4   What should be a surprise is not that Pachauri made the comments he did but that it took him so long to do so. In fact, the environmental movement has largely ignored meat consumption. The man with whom the IPCC shared its Nobel Prize for raising climate change awareness, Al Gore, has never mentioned the environmental impact of meat consumption. Green groups tell their conscientious constituents to trade in their SUV for a Prius and buy compact fluorescent light bulbs but haven't dared suggest that they give up steak.

5   Perhaps even more so than cars, meat is deeply embedded in American culture. Apple pie may be the quintessential American food, but McDonald's hamburgers aren't far behind. We carve turkey on Thanksgiving and host Fourth of July barbecues. Without meat, how do you know it's a meal? To most Americans, veggies and tofu are a laughable substitute. "It was a reaction to the '60s hippie cooking that gave this important idea of vegetarianism a bad name," says Alice Waters, the chef and author who is widely credited with creating the organic-food revolution. Environmentalists, who know they must change the stereotype that they are all either tree-hugging radicals or self-righteous scolds, may be reluctant to embrace vegetarianism because of those easily caricatured cultural connotations.

6   "Environmental groups don't want to come out too strongly on it," says Danielle Nierenberg, who researches the intersection of animal agriculture and climate change for both the Humane Society, an organization that promotes the compassionate treatment of animals, and the World Watch Institute, an environmental think tank. "People get very upset when they feel they are being told what to eat."

7   Now should be environmental vegetarianism's big moment. Global warming is the single biggest threat to the health of the planet, and meat consumption plays a bigger role in greenhouse gas emissions than even many environmentalists realize. The production and transportation of meat and dairy, particularly if you include the grains that are fed to livestock, is much more energy-intensive than it is for plants. Animals, especially cattle, also release gases like methane and nitrous oxide that,

pound for pound, are up to 30 times more damaging than carbon dioxide. Internationally there is an additional cost to animal agriculture: massive deforestation to make land available for grazing, which releases greenhouse gases as the trees are burned and removes valuable foliage that absorbs carbon dioxide. As a result, according to a 2006 United Nations report, internationally the livestock sector accounts for 18 percent of all greenhouse gas emissions—more than the transportation sector.

8   The numbers for the United States are more hotly contested. The Environmental Protection Agency (EPA) has estimated that meat is only half of the U.S. agriculture sector's share of domestic greenhouse gases and that the entire agriculture industry produces 7.56 percent of the U.S. contribution. This is considerably less than the transportation sector, which the EPA estimates accounts for roughly 29 percent of U.S. greenhouse gas emissions. The American Meat Institute, an industry trade association, cites the EPA numbers as credible. But they fail to take into account that 50 percent of grain is being fed to livestock and that its production and transportation costs should also be attributed to what you find in the meat or dairy aisle of the supermarket. Additionally, the EPA numbers do not include large categories such as the transportation of plants and animals.

9   In fact, some environmentalists allege that the Bush administration's EPA chose the lowest possible estimate, which the meat industry routinely cites, for political reasons. "With the EPA being in the pocket of the meat industry, it's not in their interest to come up with the best numbers," says Bruce Friedrich, who works on environmental issues for People for the Ethical Treatment of Animals.

10   The real U.S. figure is roughly halfway between the UN's and the EPA's numbers, according to independent experts. "There are many assumptions that one needs to make when quantifying emissions," explains Gidon Eshel, an environmental studies professor at Bard College at Simon's Rock. "It's not that any one assumption is correct. Almost all of them are defensible." Eshel estimates that if you used the UN's standards, animal agriculture would account for 10 percent or 11 percent of U.S. greenhouse gases.

11   Consumers may not have a say in whether or not another coal power plant will be built, but they do have control over how much meat they personally eat. A University of Chicago study co-authored by Eshel found that, for the average American, "the greenhouse gas emissions of various diets vary by as much as the difference between owning an average sedan versus a Sport Utility Vehicle." One meat eater going vegetarian results in putting the equivalent of 1.5 fewer tons of carbon dioxide into the atmosphere annually. Further, according to the study, if all Americans ate a vegan diet it would cut greenhouse gas emissions by at least 6 percent, probably more. Those savings would have a more immediate impact than would reducing the same amount of carbon through other means, because the average time scale for removing carbon dioxide from the atmosphere is about 10 times as slow as for methane. Most important, as Eshel notes, one can reduce personal greenhouse gas emissions through dietary change more easily and comfortably than, say, cutting back on electricity use by living in the dark or forgoing air conditioning all summer.

12   But meat eating has grown dramatically in developed countries in recent decades, with developing countries beginning to catch up. The average American

eats 200 pounds of meat, poultry, and fish per capita per year, 50 pounds more than Americans did in the 1950s. Between 1970 and 2002 the average person in a developing country went from consuming 24 pounds to 65 pounds of meat annually. In all, the world's total meat consumption in 2007 was estimated to be 284 million tons, compared to 71 million tons in 1961. It is expected to double by 2050. "You're seeing now India and China, with a growing middle class, are eating more meat," says Laura Shapiro, a culinary historian and author of *Something from the Oven*, about the cuisine of 1950s America.

13   Yet the environmental conversation remains solely about cars and power plants, not beef and pork.

14   Unlike the vitriol that Rajendra Pachauri encountered, Caryn Hartglass has been met with a different reaction when she suggests people eat less meat: deafening silence. Hartglass is the only paid staffer for Earth Save, the most prominent (using that term loosely, as it only has 3,000 members) organization dedicated solely to promoting an animal-free diet for environmental reasons. "I go to [environmental organizations'] Web sites and it's supposed to tell you what to do to reduce global warming and it doesn't say eat less meat," says Hartglass. "So I ask them why not. They say they're focusing on reducing carbon-dioxide emissions not methane-gas emissions."

15   Why are environmental groups and even politicians willing to tell Americans to drive smaller cars or take the bus to work but unwilling to tell them to eat less meat? If you live in a recently built suburb, you must drive most places whether you wish to or not. Walking or public transit simply isn't an option. But you could stop buying ground beef and start buying veggie burgers tomorrow, saving yourself some money and sparing yourself some cholesterol in the process. And yet no one, other than a small cadre of lonely fringe activists like Hartglass, devotes much energy to making the connection. Food experts and environmentalists generally worry that Americans might react with hostility similar to Boris Johnson's if asked to put down their hamburgers.

16   Their timidity is understandable. On the rare occasion that the federal government has tried to even suggest that Americans lower their meat consumption, it has failed. In 1977, the Senate Select Committee on Nutrition and Human Needs recommended eating less meat and dairy to combat heart disease. But the meat and dairy lobbies complained vociferously, and the committee rephrased the report to say that people should instead choose animal products that would "reduce saturated fat consumption." Just to be sure no one else got the foolish idea of suggesting Americans eat less meat, the beef industry spent heavily to successfully defeat Committee Chairman George McGovern in 1980.

17   But while politicians may have reason to fear the meat lobby, environmental groups are supposed to push the political envelope. They began calling for caps on carbon emissions in the late 1990s, before it was politically palatable, and both major party candidates for president endorsed cap-and-trade in 2008. Many people see their car or truck as a part of their identity, but that hasn't stopped the Sierra Club from ensuring that every American is aware of the environmental threat their vehicle poses. And yet, the major environmental groups have been unwilling to push the meat issue. "I don't know of anyone in the environmental community that has

taken a stance of 'we support no meat consumption because of global warming,'" says Tim Greef, deputy legislative director for the League of Conservation Voters. Adds Nierenberg, "It's the elephant in the room for environmentalists. They haven't found a good way to address it."

18   The Sierra Club's list of 29 programs—which includes such relatively small-bore issues as trash-transfer stations (they threaten "quality of life and property values")—does not include any on the impact of meat consumption. Their main list of things you can do to help prevent global warming mentions hanging your clothes out to dry instead of using a dryer but makes no mention of eating less meat. "The Sierra Club isn't opposed to eating meat, so that's sort of the long and short of it. [We are] not opposed to hunting, not opposed to ranching," says Josh Dorner, a spokesman for the Sierra Club, the nation's oldest and largest grass-roots environmental organization.

19   Of course, asking Americans to eat less meat is not the same thing as actively condemning ranching and hunting, but ranchers and hunters might consider it a threat to their livelihood and lifestyle all the same. And there's the rub. Though the Sierra Club does not have a position on meat consumption, it does ally with small ranchers and hunters on an array of issues, from opposing the development of giant feedlots to preserving land. "We believe that making connections with hunters and anglers is critical to ultimately getting a solution to global warming," says Dave Hamilton, director of the global warming and energy program at the Sierra Club. "They are often in places that are targets for what we're trying to do, and they are a key constituency for policy makers."

20   Calling for less meat consumption would almost certainly endanger that relationship. But the Sierra Club denies that is the reason for its lack of a stance on meat, saying that it focuses instead on issues where it can have a greater impact. "It does not necessarily pay to appear to be telling people how to live their lives," says Hamilton. "We want to give positive solutions. We've tried to focus on the things that we feel can make the greatest difference with the energy and resources that we have."

21   Other environmental groups, such as Natural Resources Defense Council, acknowledge that reducing meat consumption would be helpful in ameliorating emissions, but it simply is not a high priority. "We haven't taken a position [on meat]," says Elizabeth Martin Perera, a climate-policy specialist at the NRDC. "There's no reason not to; we just haven't gotten around to it." The League of Conservation Voters, which coordinates environmental political efforts, explains it as a process of fighting one battle at a time. "Once you deal with the largest emitters of carbon, complementary policies need to get passed," says Greef. "After they pass cap-and-trade, you will see work for a better transportation bill, work on deforestation and the logging industry. Meat falls into that bucket." When it comes to sorting out legislative priorities, Greef's position is sensible. The car-dependence of the American landscape and other energy-intensive consumption habits make attacking those larger emitters a higher priority domestically.

22   But environmental groups do more than just lobby Congress. First and foremost, they explain how our activities affect the environment. It is obvious that a car spews pollution, but to see your beef burrito first as a burping cow, and before that as oil being burned to grow corn to feed that cow, requires education. The movement also can advise the public on lifestyle choices and demonstrate how those choices can be

practical. A typical Sierra Club member cannot do much to pass cap-and-trade, but she can skip the bacon in her breakfast sandwich.

> It is obvious that a car spews pollution, but to see your beef burrito first as a burping cow, and before that as oil being burned to grow corn to feed that cow, requires education.

23   Remember those TV commercials that declared, "Beef, it's what's for dinner"? Only a few foods are so central to American cuisine and culture that they can assert their primacy simply by reminding you that you've always consumed them. Americans do indeed eat an extraordinary amount of meat, roughly twice their daily recommended dose of protein. But contrary to the commercial, this was not always the case—consumption has not just been driven by market demand. The other culprit is cheap corn.

24   Meat has become cheaper—and therefore more prevalent in American diets—in the last 30 years because it has been heavily subsidized, albeit indirectly. Ever since Secretary of Agriculture Earl Butz declared in 1973 that "what we want out of agriculture is plenty of food," American agricultural policy has encouraged overproduction and lower prices, primarily in the form of massive subsidies for corn. Livestock, in turn, consumes more than half the corn grown in the U.S., because it is cheaper to confine animals to a tight lot and funnel corn in than to allow them to graze freely on grass. With cheaper grain and denser, dirtier feedlots replacing free-range ranches, meat prices and meat quality have dropped, while meat's environmental impact has increased.

25   "The livestock doesn't get direct subsidies per se, but they have until recently done very well by getting subsidized corn," says Larry Mitchell, director of government affairs at the American Corn Growers Association (ACGA), a rival offshoot of the National Corn Growers Association (NCGA), which the ACGA contends represents agribusiness conglomerates rather than small farmers. "Most of the huge, confined animal-feeding operations, factory farms, wouldn't be viable if they had to pay the true cost of corn," Mitchell says.

26   Some environmental scientists contend that, in addition to filling local groundwater with animal waste and destroying the open spaces of the West with feedlots, grain-fed meat creates more emissions per pound than grass-fed meat. "Some work from the EPA suggests that you can reduce methane by half by not confining animals and not feeding them high-energy grains," says Nierenberg. But, she concedes, the evidence is mixed. Other studies, such as those promoted by conservatives, find the opposite: Eating grass gives cows gas. A spokesperson for the NCGA declined to comment for this article but referred me to Alex Avery, a researcher at the conservative Hudson Institute. Avery, who acknowledges that his research is underwritten by industry interests, cites studies suggesting that corn-fed livestock emits less methane.

27   Fundamentally, though, Avery and food-industry spokespeople don't acknowledge the role that cheap corn plays in the prevalence of meat in the American diet. "The world needs to eat," says Tamara McCann Thies, chief environmental counsel for the National Cattlemen's Beef Association, "and demand dictates how much beef is produced in the U.S. and elsewhere." Of course, demand is a product of price, and price is a product of production costs, and production costs are affected by subsidies. The world needs to eat, but it does not need to eat burgers.

28   Indeed, while a public-relations campaign would have some marginal impact, it has long been established that only government regulation can be certain to change America's consumption patterns. Despite all the publicity surrounding the ills of oil, average auto fuel efficiency has stagnated. And how many people do you know who hang-dry their clothes to keep the polar ice cap afloat?

29   So what would a political agenda to reduce the emissions from animal agriculture look like? The answer is surprisingly simple.

30   As with so many environmentally damaging habits, such as driving, our overconsumption of factory-farmed animals is the product of a set of indirect subsidies that make its cost artificially low. Much of the agriculture industry is exempt from compliance with the Clean Air and Clean Water Acts, thus reducing its business costs. Grain subsidies lower the cost of feed. And the Government Accountability Office recently found that the EPA has failed to hold factory farms accountable for massive violations, essentially another form of government subsidy by freeing them of the cost of compliance. Undoing any of these boondoggles would raise the cost of meat. Another option is to raise the standards of animal treatment, which would also make the production of meat more expensive. California recently passed a ballot proposal to ban cruelly overcrowded conditions in factory farms. By eliminating dense feedlots, which animal-rights activists and even many farmers regard as inhumane and which create local pollution, it should become more expensive to produce meat because it will require more land per animal. Although it is not clear how much meat consumption would fall as a result, it makes sense, as it does with driving, to at least remove the price advantage of such an environmentally destructive activity.

31   And, of course, the government could remove corn subsidies. Whatever the merits of grass-fed versus grain-fed meat, an increase in the price of corn would mean more expensive meat. But the institutional barriers to removing subsidies—the key committee positions of senators from farm states, the power of the Iowa caucuses, the political largesse of agriprocessor Archer Daniels Midland—make such a dramatic reversal in American agricultural policy an incredibly tall order. In any case, the environmental movement has not shown any desire to make this a top priority.

32   In the meantime, activists are taking small bites out of the problem. Food experts like Shapiro and Waters say that raising awareness about reducing portion size, which has grown over the years, is one first step. And a Web site called PB&J Campaign, launched in February 2007, encourages a plant-based diet for environmental reasons. Bernard Brown, the site's 31-year-old creator, says he is careful to advocate not outright vegetarianism but intermediate steps that are more realistic.

33   Yet they still have a long way to go. "I think it's amazing that even the greenest of green liberal environment activists, the vast majority of them tend to consume meat at the same rate as people who think global warming is a hoax," says Mike Tidwell, director of the Chesapeake Climate Action Network. "Meat consumption seems to be the last thing that progressive people address in their lifestyle. If I had a nickel for every global warming conference that had roast beef on the menu, I'd be rich."

Can Cities Save the Planet?
Witold Rybczynski

1 According to Timothy Beatley, an urban-planning professor at the University of Virginia and the author of *Green Urbanism*, the per-capita carbon dioxide emissions of American cities are almost twice as high as those of their European counterparts. Hardly surprising, since European cities are denser and more compact, homes are smaller, and people rely to a far greater extent on mass transit. So if Americans are to significantly reduce their carbon footprint, we will have to do a lot more than switch to reusable shopping bags and recycle our soda cans. But as a recent conference on "urban design after the age of oil" at the University of Pennsylvania (where I teach) demonstrated, there is something of a disconnect between the global-warming problem and the available solutions.

2 The problem is easily stated. In 1950, the global emission of carbon dioxide was 6 billion tons a year. Thanks to population growth, urbanization, the expansion of wealth, and massive industrialization around the world, by 2008 this has increased fivefold to 30 billion tons a year. Assuming that nothing is done to reduce emissions, by 2058, they will be 60 billion tons a year. Thus, to reduce global warming, whose effects are already beginning to be felt, it will be necessary to take drastic measures just to stay at the present level, nevermind actually making real progress. For example, to reduce the number of coal-fired generating plants, nuclear capacity in the United States will have to be doubled. To reduce car emissions, either Americans will have to drive half as many miles per year or cars will have to be twice as efficient. Buildings will have to use 25 percent less electricity.

3 The Penn conference featured many speakers proposing changes, large and small, as to how buildings and cities should be designed. The scientists were hard-nosed and slightly scary. Planning consultants were authoritative and self-assured—as planning consultants tend to be. They described new carbon-neutral cities, with wind farms and solar arrays, green roofs and urban farms, far-ranging mass transit, and large-scale water recycling. The Power Point images were mesmerizing. Most of the projects appear to be in the Gulf states. In the present economy, most are, I suspect, on hold.

4 A word that came up frequently was *holistic*, the implication being that we shouldn't change one thing until we know how it affects everything else. But that is not the way cities develop. The technologies that improved urban life in the past— gas lighting, pressurized water, electricity, streetcars, elevators—were developed separately, each according to its own technological schedule. This autonomy accounted, in large part, for the success of the industrial age. The other implication of *holistic* is that, by taking everything into account, we can control the future. But technologies have always had unintended consequences. Streetcars, for example, which replaced horse-drawn omnibuses and were not only faster but considerably cleaner, also encouraged suburban growth, enabled commercial strips to develop along rights of way, and created amusement parks (Coney Island in New York, Natatorium Park in Spokane, Washington) as end-of-line destinations. One would expect green technologies to similarly produce unforeseen side effects.

5   Another thing strikes me about green urbanism. Even assuming that anything at all gets built in the coming economic depression—during the Great Depression of the 1930s, building construction virtually halted—creating new cities and reconfiguring old ones will take many decades. We don't have that much time. On the other hand, Americans' rapid change in driving habits during the gas-price run-up of summer 2008 suggests that people can quickly alter the ways they behave: driving less, walking more, turning down the thermostat, turning off the lights. Yes, we should eventually change the way we build and plan cities, but it might be more effective in the short run to change the way we live in them.

6   Most of the planners at the Penn conference emphasized technological fixes, but if the point of no return has already been passed in global warming, as some of the scientists at the conference suggested, protective measures are at least as important, not least against the anticipated rise in sea levels. In that regard, I note an interesting news item from the Netherlands. The Dutch Parliament has asked a commission on coastal development to examine the idea of building a massive man-made island in the North Sea. The 31-mile-long island will provide 274,000 acres for housing and farming. Not coincidentally, the so-called Tulip Island (named because of its shape) will also act as a storm-surge barrier. The Dutch, who have managed water in their low-lying country for centuries, are the canaries in the coal mine as far as rising sea levels are concerned. Other coastal cities—and most large cities are on the water—should take note. ◆

CRITICAL THINKING

1. Ben Adler's essay was published by the *American Prospect*, a magazine that describes itself as providing "liberal intelligence." Can you find examples in the article that show a liberal slant? Does this slant affect the message of the article or what it seeks to challenge? Explain.

2. Witold Rybczynski states that green technologies may produce unforeseen side effects. Try to predict some unintended consequences to using green technology based on these articles and others in this chapter.

3. What impact does meat have on the environment? Answer the question posed by the title of the first essay: Are cows worse than cars?

4. What could account for the following statistics: "In all, the world's total meat consumption in 2007 was estimated to be 284 million tons, compared to 71 million tons in 1961. It is expected to double by 2050." Why is it expected to double? Does this figure surprise you? Why or why not?

5. According to Adler, "only government regulation can be certain to change America's consumption patterns." Do you think government should take part and regulate the amount of meat its citizens consume? Explain. According to this article, how could the government regulate the price of meat? (You may wish to research rationing practices during World War II for some background.)

6. Would you change your life, or your future life after graduation, based on the information provided in either of these articles? Explain.

CRITICAL WRITING

1. *Research Writing:* Research the man-made Dutch Tulip Island in the North Sea. Describe the protective measures taken by the Dutch in making this "storm-surge barrier." How will it function? How will it be made? What is its purpose? Are there any other countries looking into coastal development? Write a brief essay detailing your research, tying it to the broader issue of climate change and our impact on the environment.

2. *Exploratory Writing:* Explore the reasons why meat has become an integral part of the American diet. Give your own personal examples of mealtimes as well as exploring the concept of the American meal. If you do not eat meat, explain why someone who wishes to be environmentally conscious might want to follow your example.

GROUP PROJECTS

1. You are a group of urban planners who have been given the task of planning and designing a carbon-friendly city. Use the information given in the article "Can Cities Save the Planet?" along with your own creativity, imagination, and personal knowledge. As an extension of this project, rent the "2007 SimCity Societies," which encourages you to build eco-friendly cities. Try to implement some of your suggestions into the video game and review the results.

2. Keep a chart of which foods you eat for a week, trying to cut out as much meat as possible. After the week, analyze the data of your group. Was anyone in your group able to completely stop eating meat for the week? What obstacles did you have to overcome? How did you feel after completing the week?

Look at Me!

Celebrity and Our Fifteen Minutes of Fame

Just over 40 years ago, artist Andy Warhol commented, "In the future, everyone will be world-famous for fifteen minutes." With the advent of reality television, You Tube, MySpace, and Facebook, it would appear that the future is now. Warhol himself was deeply interested in fame and celebrity. He knew that any person could be famous if he or she leveraged the media and did something of interest, however fleeting, for the masses. But while Warhol may have implied that everyone may have a moment of glory, he recognized the disposable nature of celebrity.

Of course, there are legitimate celebrities, people famous for their talent in music, acting, sports, writing, politics—people whose notoriety is predicated on genuine accomplishment. There are also people who are famous for being famous—individuals of dubious talent who manage to gain notoriety because their behavior got media attention. Celebrities whose careers are dependent upon fame will vie for the spotlight and then do everything in their power to hold that spotlight. Unfortunately, some maintain their celebrity not for their achievements but for making poor judgments in their personal lives. And while celebrities have always been a part of pop culture, our obsession with celebrity has reached new heights. Celebrity antics even appear on the front pages of major metropolitan newspapers, rather than on the gossip pages in the entertainment section.

The attention and appeal of celebrity makes many of us long for notoriety in our own lives, even if it may be only within our own social circle. Warhol's famous quip was rephrased for the current decade by the Scottish artist Momus, who noted, "On the Web, everyone will be famous to fifteen people." Momus was referring to the current practice of social networking, blogging, and self-broadcasting on YouTube.

Why do we choose to laud some people over others? What are our expectations of celebrity, and what impact is our obsession with celebrity having on our culture? This chapter explores the rise of celebrity culture in our society—from how we construct celebrity to whom we chose to elevate and why to our deep-rooted desire to be famous.

The chapter opens with a topical overview by author Joseph Epstein, "The Culture of Celebrity." His essay is followed by an editorial, "Death to Film Critics! Hail to the CelebCult!" from acclaimed film critic Roger Ebert, who wonders what happens when we make icons out of people known only for their foolishness. The review of the construction of celebrity in our society continues with an essay by Rebecca Traister, "Return of the Brainless Hussies." Traister describes how pop culture seems to glorify women who make foolish choices, to the point that some young women may think that in order to be popular and liked, they may also need to play down their intelligence.

The next group of essays examines our own desire to achieve notoriety. While few of us will be as famous as Lindsay Lohan, many of us do enjoy the attention we may earn from posting something witty online. We all crave some recognition. But are we giving too much away voluntarily when we post information on blogs and social networking pages such as MySpace and Facebook? Are we making spectacles of ourselves, parading online the most intimate details of our lives? Lakshmi Chaudhry wonders what the current wave of online narcissism means to the culture as a whole in "Mirror, Mirror, on the Web." Christine Rosen continues this line of inquiry in "Virtual Friendship and the New Narcissism," in which she wonders whether social networking sites raise the bar on our level of self-absorption. Finally, Stuart Wolpert explores the nuances of constructing the self in his essay "Crafting Your Image for Your 1000 Friends on Facebook."

This chapter's Viewpoints section explores the role of reality TV in our culture. Why do we love reality TV? Is it a guilty pleasure? Are some voyeuristic programs preying on young people who just want to be famous? Do we build people up merely to make fun of them on the air? Are such programs ethical? On the one hand, there may be something sordid about watching people air their dirty laundry in public. On the other, reality program participants willingly exchange their privacy for time in front of the camera. And some people, as in the case of the final segment in this section, sell their rights to live and die on camera.

The Culture of Celebrity
Joseph Epstein*

What do Paris Hilton, Nicole Richie, and Tara Reid all have in common? In this next essay, author Joseph Epstein explores the distinctions between fame and celebrity, demonstrating that they are not mutually inclusive. The American pop-culture engine places the desire for celebrity at the forefront. We want to know every nuance of their lives, especially their embarrassments, mistakes, and failures. We wish we could be like them, while making fun of them. Many celebrities are known only for being known, rather than for their achievements. As Epstein explains, we now reserve our praise and attention for famous airheads.

1 Celebrity at this moment in America is epidemic, and it's spreading fast, sometimes seeming as if nearly everyone has got it. Television provides celebrity dance contests, celebrities take part in reality shows, perfumes carry the names not merely of designers but of actors and singers. Without celebrities, whole sections of the *New York Times* and the *Washington Post* would have to close down. So pervasive has celebrity become in contemporary American life that one now begins to hear a good deal about a phenomenon known as the Culture of Celebrity.

---

* Joseph Epstein, *The Weekly Standard,* October 17, 2005

2 The word "culture" no longer, I suspect, stands in most people's minds for whole congeries of institutions, relations, kinship patterns, linguistic forms, and the rest for which the early anthropologists meant it to stand. Words, unlike disciplined soldiers, refuse to remain in place and take orders. They insist on being unruly, and slither and slide around, picking up all sorts of slippery and even goofy meanings. An icon, as we shall see, doesn't stay a small picture of a religious personage but usually turns out nowadays to be someone with spectacular grosses. "The language," as Flaubert once protested in his attempt to tell his mistress Louise Colet how much he loved her, "is inept."

3 Today, when people glibly refer to "the corporate culture," "the culture of poverty," "the culture of journalism," "the culture of the intelligence community"—and "community" has, of course, itself become another of those hopelessly baggy-pants words, so that one hears talk even of "the homeless community"—what I think is meant by "culture" is the general emotional atmosphere and institutional character surrounding the word to which "culture" is attached. Thus, corporate culture is thought to breed selfishness practiced at the Machiavellian level; the culture of poverty, hopelessness and despair; the culture of journalism, a taste for the sensational combined with a short attention span; the culture of the intelligence community, covering-one's-own-behind viperishness; and so on. "*Culture*" used in this way is also brought in to explain unpleasant or at least dreary behavior. "The culture of NASA has to be changed," is a sample of its current usage. The comedian Flip Wilson, after saying something outrageous, would revert to the refrain line, "The debbil made me do it." So, today, when admitting to unethical or otherwise wretched behavior, people often say, "The culture made me do it."

4 As for "celebrity," the standard definition is no longer the dictionary one but rather closer to the one that Daniel Boorstin gave in his book *The Image: Or What Happened to the American Dream:* "The celebrity," Boorstin wrote, "is a person who is well-known for his well-knownness," which is improved in its frequently misquoted form as "a celebrity is someone famous for being famous." The other standard quotation on this subject is Andy Warhol's "In the future, everyone will be world-famous for fifteen minutes," which also frequently turns up in an improved misquotation as "everyone will have his fifteen minutes of fame."

5 But to say that a celebrity is someone well-known for being well-known, though clever enough, doesn't quite cover it. Not that there is a shortage of such people who seem to be known only for their well-knownness. What do a couple named Sid and Mercedes Bass do, except appear in bold-face in the *New York Times* "Sunday Styles" section and other such venues (as we now call them) of equally shimmering insignificance, often standing next to Ahmet and Mica Ertegun, also well-known for being well-known? Many moons ago, journalists used to refer to royalty as "face cards"; today celebrities are perhaps best thought of as bold faces, for as such do their names often appear in the press (and in a *New York Times* column with that very name, "Bold Face").

6 The distinction between celebrity and fame is one most dictionaries tend to fudge. I suspect everyone has, or prefers to make, his own. The one I like derives not from Aristotle, who didn't have to trouble with celebrities, but from the career of

Ted Williams. A sportswriter once said that he, Williams, wished to be famous but had no interest in being a celebrity. What Ted Williams wanted to be famous for was his hitting. He wanted everyone who cared about baseball to know that he was—as he believed and may well have been—the greatest pure hitter who ever lived. What he didn't want to do was to take on any of the effort off the baseball field involved in making this known. As an active player, Williams gave no interviews, signed no baseballs or photographs, chose not to be obliging in any way to journalists or fans. A rebarbative character, not to mention often a slightly menacing s.o.b., Williams, if you had asked him, would have said that it was enough that he was the last man to hit .400; he did it on the field, and therefore didn't have to sell himself off the field. As for his duty to his fans, he didn't see that he had any.

7   Whether Ted Williams was right or wrong to feel as he did is of less interest than the distinction his example provides, which suggests that fame is something one earns—through talent or achievement of one kind or another—while celebrity is something one cultivates or, possibly, has thrust upon one. The two are not, of course, entirely exclusive. One can be immensely talented and full of achievement and yet wish to broadcast one's fame further through the careful cultivation of celebrity; and one can have the thinnest of achievements and be talentless and yet be made to seem otherwise through the mechanics and dynamics of celebrity creation, in our day a whole mini (or maybe not so mini) industry of its own.

8   Or, another possibility, one can become a celebrity with scarcely any pretense to talent or achievement whatsoever. Much modern celebrity seems the result of careful promotion or great good luck or something besides talent and achievement: Mr. Donald Trump, Ms. Paris Hilton, Mr. Regis

> *One can become a celebrity with scarcely any pretense to talent or achievement whatsoever. Much modern celebrity seems the result of careful promotion or great good luck or something besides talent and achievement*

Philbin, take a bow. The ultimate celebrity of our time may have been John F. Kennedy Jr., notable only for being his parents' very handsome son—both his birth and good looks factors beyond his control—and, alas, known for nothing else whatsoever now, except for the sad, dying-young-Adonis end to his life.

9   Fame, then, at least as I prefer to think of it, is based on true achievement; celebrity on the broadcasting of that achievement, or the inventing of something that, if not scrutinized too closely, might pass for achievement. Celebrity suggests ephemerality, while fame has a chance of lasting, a shot at reaching the happy shores of posterity.

10   Oliver Goldsmith, in his poem "The Deserted Village," refers to "good fame," which implies that there is also a bad or false fame. Bad fame is sometimes thought to be fame in the present, or fame on earth, while good fame is that bestowed by posterity—those happy shores again. (Which doesn't eliminate the desire of most of us, at least nowadays, to have our fame here and hereafter, too.) Not false but wretched fame is covered by the word "infamy"—"Infamy, infamy, infamy," remarked the English wit Frank Muir, "they all have it in for me"—while the lower, or pejorative, order of celebrity is covered by the word "notoriety," also frequently misused to mean noteworthiness.

11   Leo Braudy's magnificent book on the history of fame, *The Frenzy of Renown*, illustrates how the means of broadcasting fame have changed over the centuries: from having one's head engraved on coins, to purchasing statuary of oneself, to (for the really high rollers—Alexander the Great, the Caesar boys) naming cities or even months after oneself, to commissioning painted portraits, to writing books or having books written about one, and so on into our day of the publicity or press agent, the media blitz, the public relations expert, and the egomaniacal blogger. One of the most successful of public-relations experts, Ben Sonnenberg Sr., used to say that he saw it as his job to construct very high pedestals for very small men.

12   Which leads one to a very proper suspicion of celebrity. As George Orwell said about saints, so it seems only sensible to say about celebrities: They should all be judged guilty until proven innocent. Guilty of what, precisely? I'd say of the fraudulence (however minor) of inflating their brilliance, accomplishments, worth, of passing themselves off as something they aren't, or at least are not quite. If fraudulence is the crime, publicity is the means by which the caper is brought off.

13   Is the current heightened interest in the celebrated sufficient to form a culture—a culture of a kind worthy of study? The anthropologist Alfred Kroeber defined culture, in part, as embodying "values which may be formulated (overtly as mores) or felt (implicitly as in folkways) by the society carrying the culture, and which it is part of the business of the anthropologist to characterize and define." What are the values of celebrity culture? They are the values, almost exclusively, of publicity. Did they spell one's name right? What was the size and composition of the audience? Did you check the receipts? Was the timing right? Publicity is concerned solely with effects and does not investigate causes or intrinsic value too closely. For example, a few years ago a book of mine called *Snobbery: The American Version* received what I thought was a too greatly mixed review in the *New York Times Book Review*. I remarked on my disappointment to the publicity man at my publisher's, who promptly told me not to worry: It was a full-page review, on page 11, right-hand side. That, he said, "is very good real estate," which was quite as important as, perhaps more important than, the reviewer's actual words and final judgment. Better to be tepidly considered on page 11 than extravagantly praised on page 27, left-hand side. Real estate, man, it's the name of the game.

14   We must have new names, Marcel Proust presciently noted—in fashion, in medicine, in art, there must always be new names. It's a very smart remark, and the fields Proust chose seem smart, too, at least for his time. (Now there must also be new names, at a minimum, among movie stars and athletes and politicians.) Implicit in Proust's remark is the notion that if the names don't really exist, if the quality isn't there to sustain them, it doesn't matter; new names we shall have in any case. And every sophisticated society somehow, more or less implicitly, contrives to supply them.

15   I happen to think that we haven't had a major poet writing in English since perhaps the death of W. H. Auden or, to lower the bar a little, Philip Larkin. But new names are put forth nevertheless—high among them in recent years has been that of Seamus Heaney—because, after all, what kind of a time could we be living in if we didn't have a major poet? And besides there are all those prizes that, year after year, must be given out, even if so many of the recipients don't seem quite worthy of them.

16   Considered as a culture, celebrity does have its institutions. We now have an elaborate celebrity-creating machinery well in place—all those short-attention-span television shows (*Entertainment Tonight, Access Hollywood, Lifestyles of the Rich and Famous*); all those magazines (beginning with *People* and far from ending with the *National Enquirer*). We have high-priced celebrity-mongers—Barbara Walters, Diane Sawyer, Jay Leno, David Letterman, Oprah—who not only live off others' celebrity but also, through their publicity-making power, confer it and have in time become very considerable celebrities each in his or her own right.

17   Without the taste for celebrity, they would have to close down the whole Style section of every newspaper in the country. Then there is the celebrity profile (in *Vanity Fair, Esquire, Gentlemen's Quarterly*; these are nowadays usually orchestrated by a press agent, with all touchy questions declared out-of-bounds), or the television talk-show interview with a star, which is beyond parody. Well, almost beyond: Martin Short in his parody of a talk-show host remarked to the actor Kiefer Sutherland, "You're Canadian, aren't you? What's that all about?"

18   Yet we still seem never to have enough celebrities, so we drag in so-called "It Girls" (Paris Hilton, Gisele Bündchen, other supermodels), tired television hacks (Regis Philbin, Ed McMahon), back-achingly boring but somehow sacrosanct news anchors (Walter Cronkite, Tom Brokaw). Toss in what I think of as the lower-class punditi, who await calls from various television news and chat shows to demonstrate their locked-in political views and meager expertise on major and cable stations alike: Pat Buchanan, Eleanor Clift, Mark Shields, Robert Novak, Michael Beschloss, and the rest. Ah, if only Lenny Bruce were alive today, he could do a scorchingly cruel bit about Dr. Joyce Brothers sitting by the phone wondering why Jerry Springer never calls.

19   Many of our current-day celebrities float upon "hype," which is really a publicist's gas used to pump up and set aloft something that doesn't really quite exist. Hype has also given us a new breakdown, or hierarchical categorization, of celebrities. Until twenty-five or so years ago great celebrities were called "stars," a term first used in the movies and entertainment and then taken up by sports, politics, and other fields. Stars proving a bit drab, "superstars" were called in to play, this term beginning in sports but fairly quickly branching outward. Apparently too many superstars were about, so the trope was switched from astronomy to religion, and we now have "icons." All this takes Proust's original observation a step further: the need for new names to call the new names.

20   This new ranking—stars, superstars, icons—helps us believe that we live in interesting times. One of the things celebrities do for us is suggest that in their lives they are fulfilling our fantasies. Modern celebrities, along with their fame, tend to be wealthy or, if not themselves beautiful, able to acquire beautiful lovers. Their celebrity makes them, in the view of many, worthy of worship. "So long as man remains free," Dostoyevsky writes in the Grand Inquisitor section of *The Brothers Karamazov,* "he strives for nothing so incessantly and painfully as to find someone to worship." If contemporary celebrities are the best thing on offer as living gods for us to worship, this is not good news.

21   But the worshipping of celebrities by the public tends to be thin, and not uncommonly it is nicely mixed with loathing. We also, after all, at least partially,

like to see our celebrities as frail, ready at all times to crash and burn. Cary Grant once warned the then-young director Peter Bogdanovich, who was at the time living with Cybill Sheppard, to stop telling people he was in love. "And above all," Grant warned, "stop telling them you're happy." When Bogdanovich asked why, Cary Grant answered, "Because they're not in love and they're not happy.... Just remember, Peter, people do not like beautiful people."

22   Grant's assertion is borne out by our grocery press, the *National Enquirer,* the *Star,* the *Globe,* and other variants of the English gutter press. All these tabloids could as easily travel under the generic title of the *National Schadenfreude,* for more than half the stories they contain come under the category of "See How the Mighty Have Fallen": Oh, my, I see where that bright young television sitcom star, on a drug binge again, had to be taken to a hospital in an ambulance! To think that the handsome movie star has been cheating on his wife all these years—snakes loose in the Garden of Eden, evidently! Did you note that the powerful senator's drinking has caused him to embarrass himself yet again in public? I see where that immensely successful Hollywood couple turn out to have had a child who died of anorexia! Who'd've thought?

23   How pleasing to learn that our own simpler, less moneyed, unglamorous lives are, in the end, much to be preferred to those of these beautiful, rich, and powerful people, whose vast publicity has diverted us for so long and whose fall proves even more diverting now. "As would become a lifelong habit for most of us," Thomas McGuane writes in a recent short story in the *New Yorker* called "Ice," "we longed to witness spectacular achievement and mortifying failure. Neither of these things, we were discreetly certain, would ever come to us; we would instead be granted the frictionless lives of the meek."

24   Along with trying to avoid falling victim to schadenfreude, celebrities, if they are clever, do well to regulate the amount of publicity they allow to cluster around them. And not celebrities alone. Edith Wharton, having published too many stories and essays in a great single rush in various magazines during a concentrated period, feared, as she put it, the danger of becoming "a magazine bore." Celebrities, in the same way, are in danger of becoming publicity bores, though few among them seem to sense it. Because of improperly rationed publicity, along with a substantial helping of self-importance, the comedian Bill Cosby will never again be funny. The actress Elizabeth McGovern said of Sean Penn that he "is brilliant, brilliant at being the kind of reluctant celebrity." At the level of high culture, Saul Bellow used to work this bit quite well on the literary front, making every interview (and there have been hundreds of them) feel as if given only with the greatest reluctance, if not under actual duress. Others are brilliant at regulating their publicity. Johnny Carson was very intelligent about carefully husbanding his celebrity, choosing not to come out of retirement, except at exactly the right time or when the perfect occasion presented itself. Apparently it never did. Given the universally generous obituary tributes he received, dying now looks, for him, to have been an excellent career move.

25   Careful readers will have noticed that I referred above to "the actress Elizabeth McGovern" and felt no need to write anything before or after the name Sean Penn. True celebrities need nothing said of them in apposition, fore or aft. The greatest celebrities are those who don't even require their full names mentioned: Marilyn, Johnny, Liz, Liza, Oprah, Michael (could be Jordan or Jackson—context usually clears this up fairly quickly), Kobe, Martha (Stewart, not Washington), Britney,

Shaq, J-Lo, Frank (Sinatra, not Perdue), O. J., and, with the quickest recognition and shortest name of all—trumpets here, please—W.

26   One has the impression that being a celebrity was easier at any earlier time than it is now, when celebrity-creating institutions, from paparazzi to gutter-press exposés to television talk-shows, weren't as intense, as full-court press, as they are today. In the *Times Literary Supplement,* a reviewer of a biography of Margot Fonteyn noted that Miss Fonteyn "was a star from a more respectful age of celebrity, when keeping one's distance was still possible." My own candidate for the perfect celebrity in the twentieth century would be Noël Coward, a man in whom talent combined with elegance to give off the glow of glamour—and also a man who would have known how to fend off anyone wishing to investigate his private life. Today, instead of elegant celebrities, we have celebrity criminal trials: Michael Jackson, Kobe Bryant, Martha Stewart, Robert Blake, Winona Ryder, and O. J. Simpson. Schadenfreude is in the saddle again.

27   American society in the twenty-first century, received opinion has it, values only two things: money and celebrity. Whether or not this is true, vast quantities of money, we know, will buy celebrity. The very rich—John D. Rockefeller and powerful people of his era—used to pay press agents to keep their names out of the papers. But today one of the things money buys is a place at the table beside the celebrated, with the celebrities generally delighted to accommodate, there to share some of the glaring light. An example is Mort Zuckerman, who made an early fortune in real estate, has bought magazines and newspapers, and is now himself among the punditi, offering his largely unexceptional political views on the McLaughlin Group and other television chat shows. Which is merely another way of saying that, whether or not celebrity in and of itself constitutes a culture, it has certainly penetrated and permeated much of American culture generally.

28   Such has been the reach of celebrity culture in our time that it has long ago entered into academic life. The celebrity professor has been on the scene for more than three decades. As long ago as 1962, in fact, I recall hearing that Oscar Cargill, in those days a name of some note in the English Department of NYU, had tried to lure the then-young Robert Brustein, a professor of theater and the drama critic for the New Republic, away from Columbia. Cargill had said to Brustein, "I'm not going to bulls—t you, Bob, we're looking for a star, and you're it." Brustein apparently wasn't looking to be placed in a new constellation, and remained at Columbia, at least for a while longer, before moving on to Yale and thence to Harvard.

29   The academic star, who is really the academic celebrity, is now a fairly common figure in what the world, that ignorant ninny, reckons the Great American Universities. Richard Rorty is such a star; so is Henry Louis Gates Jr. (who as "Skip" even has some celebrity nickname-recognition); and, at a slightly lower level, there are Marjorie Garber, Eve Sedgwick, Stanley Fish, and perhaps now Stephen Greenblatt. Stanley Fish doesn't even seem to mind that much of his celebrity is owed to his being portrayed in novels by David Lodge as an indefatigable, grubby little operator (though Lodge claims to admire Fish's happy vulgarity). Professors Garber and Sedgwick seem to have acquired their celebrity through the outrageousness of the topics they've chosen to write about.

30   By measure of pure celebrity, Cornel West is, at the moment, the star of all academic stars, a man called by *Newsweek* "an eloquent prophet with attitude." (A bit

difficult, I think, to imagine *Newsweek* or any other publication writing something similar of Lionel Trilling, Walter Jackson Bate, Marjorie Hope Nicolson, or John Hope Franklin.) He records rap CDs and appears at benefits with movie stars and famous athletes. When the president of Harvard spoke critically to West about his work not constituting serious scholarship (as if that had anything to do with anything), it made front-page news in the *New York Times*. When West left Harvard in indignation, he was instantly welcomed by Princeton. If West had been a few kilowatts more the celebrity than he is, he might have been able to arrange for the firing of the president of the university, the way certain superstars in the National Basketball Association—Magic Johnson, Isiah Thomas, Larry Bird, Michael Jordan—were able, if it pleased them, to have their coaches fired.

31   Genuine scholarship, power of ratiocination glowing brightly in the classroom, is distinctly not what makes an academic celebrity or, if you prefer, superstar. What makes an academic celebrity, for the most part, is exposure, which is ultimately publicity. Exposure can mean appearing in the right extra-academic magazines or journals: the *New York Review of Books*, the *London Review of Books,* the *Atlantic Monthly*; *Harper's* and the *New Republic* possibly qualify, as do occasional cameo performances on the op-ed pages of the *New York Times* or the *Washington Post*. Having one's face pop up on the right television and radio programs—PBS and NPR certainly, and enough of the right kinds of appearances on C-SPAN—does not hurt. A commercially successful, much-discussed book helps hugely.

32   So does strong public alignment with the correct political causes. Harvey Mansfield, the political philosopher at Harvard, is a secondary academic celebrity of sorts, but not much in demand, owing to his conservatism; Shelby Steele, a black professor of English who has been critical of various aspects of African-American politics, was always overlooked during the days when universities knocked themselves out to get black professors. Both men have been judged politically incorrect. The underlying and overarching point is, to become an academic celebrity you have to promote yourself outside the academy, but in careful and subtle ways.

33   One might have assumed that the culture of celebrity was chiefly about show business and the outer edges of the arts, occasionally touching on the academy (there cannot be more than twenty or so academic superstars). But it has also much altered intellectual life generally. The past ten years or so have seen the advent of the "public intellectual." There are good reasons to feel uncomfortable with that adjective "public," which drains away much of the traditional meaning of intellectual. An intellectual is someone who is excited by and lives off and in ideas. An intellectual has traditionally been a person unaffiliated, which is to say someone unbeholden to anything but the power of his or her ideas. Intellectuals used to be freelance, until fifty or so years ago, when jobs in the universities and in journalism began to open up to some among them.

34   Far from being devoted to ideas for their own sake, the intellectual equivalent of art for art's sake, the so-called public intellectual of our day is usually someone who comments on what is in the news, in the hope of affecting policy, or events, or opinion in line with his own political position or orientation. He isn't necessarily an intellectual at all, but merely someone who has read a few books, mastered a style, a jargon, and a maven's authoritative tone, and has a clearly demarcated political line.

35   But even when the public intellectual isn't purely tied to the news, or isn't thoroughly political, what he or she really is, or ought to be called, is a "publicity

intellectual." In Richard A. Posner's interesting book *Public Intellectuals,* intellectuals are in one place ranked by the number of media mentions they or their work have garnered, which, if I am correct about publicity being at the heart of the enterprise of the public intellectual, may be crude but is not foolish. Not knowledge, it turns out, but publicity is power.

36   The most celebrated intellectuals of our day have been those most skillful at gaining publicity for their writing and their pronouncements. Take, as a case very much in point, Susan Sontag. When Susan Sontag died at the end of last year, her obituary was front-page news in the *New York Times,* and on the inside of the paper, it ran to a full page with five photographs, most of them carefully posed—a variety, it does not seem unfair to call it, of intellectual cheesecake. Will the current prime ministers of England and France when they peg out receive equal space or pictorial coverage? Unlikely, I think. Why did Ms. Sontag, who was, let it be said, in many ways the pure type of the old intellectual—unattached to any institution, earning her living (apart from MacArthur Foundation and other grants) entirely from her ideas as she put them in writing—why did she attract the attention she did?

37   I don't believe Susan Sontag's celebrity finally had much to do with the power or cogency of her ideas. Her most noteworthy idea was not so much an idea at all but a description of a style, a kind of reverse or antistyle, that went by the name of Camp and that was gay in its impulse. Might it have been her politics? Yes, politics had a lot to do with it, even though when she expressed herself on political subjects, she frequently got things mightily askew: During the Vietnam war she said that "the white race is the cancer of human history." As late as the 1980s, much too late for anyone in the know, she called communism "fascism with a friendly face" (what do you suppose she found so friendly about it?). To cheer up the besieged people of Sarajevo, she brought them a production of Samuel Beckett's *Waiting for Godot.* She announced in the *New Yorker* that the killing of 3,000 innocent people on 9/11 was an act that America had brought on itself. As for the writing that originally brought her celebrity, she later came to apologize for *Against Interpretation,* her most influential single book. I do not know any people who claim to have derived keen pleasure from her fiction. If all this is roughly so, why, then, do you suppose that Susan Sontag was easily the single most celebrated—the greatest celebrity—intellectual of our time?

38   With the ordinary female professor's face and body, I don't think Ms. Sontag would quite have achieved the same celebrity. Her attractiveness as a young woman had a great deal to do with the extent of her celebrity; and she and her publisher took that (early) physical attractiveness all the way out. From reading Carl Rollyson and Lisa Paddock's biography *Susan Sontag: The Making of an Icon,* one gets a sense of how carefully and relentlessly she was promoted by her publisher, Roger Straus. I do not mean to say that Sontag was unintelligent, or talentless, but Straus, through having her always dramatically photographed, by sending angry letters to the editors of journals where she was ill-reviewed, by bringing out her books with the most careful accompanying orchestration, promoted this often difficult and unrewarding writer into something close to a household name with a face that was ready, so to say, to be Warholed. That Sontag spent her last years with Annie Leibovitz, herself the most successful magazine photographer of our day, seems somehow the most natural thing in the world. Even in the realm of the intellect, celebrities are not born but made, usually very carefully made—as was, indubitably, the celebrity of Susan Sontag.

39   One of the major themes in Leo Braudy's *The Frenzy of Renown* is the fame and celebrity of artists, and above all, writers. To sketch in a few bare strokes the richly complex story Braudy tells, writers went from serving power (in Rome) to serving God (in early Christendom) to serving patrons (in the eighteenth century) to serving themselves, with a careful eye cocked toward both the contemporary public and posterity (under Romanticism), to serving mammon, to a state of interesting confusion, which is where we are today, with celebrity affecting literature in more and more significant ways.

40   Writers are supposed to be aristocrats of the spirit, not promoters, hustlers, salesmen for their own work. Securing a larger audience for their work was not thought to be their problem. "Fit audience, though few," in John Milton's phrase, was all right, so long as the few were the most artistically alert, or aesthetically fittest. Picture Lord Byron, Count Tolstoy, or Charles Baudelaire at a lectern at Barnes & Noble, C-SPAN camera turned on, flogging (wonderful word!) his own most recent books. Not possible!

41   Some superior writers have been very careful caretakers of their careers. In a letter to one of his philosophy professors at Harvard, T. S. Eliot wrote that there were two ways to achieve literary celebrity in London: One was to appear often in a variety of publications; the other to appear seldom but always to make certain to dazzle when one did. Eliot, of course, chose the latter, and it worked smashingly. But he was still counting on gaining his reputation through his actual writing. Now good work alone doesn't quite seem to make it; the publicity catapults need to be hauled into place, the walls of indifference stormed. Some writers have decided to steer shy from publicity altogether: Thomas Pynchon for one, J. D. Salinger for another (if he is actually still writing or yet considers himself a writer). But actively seeking publicity was thought for a writer, somehow, vulgar—at least it was until the last few decades.

42   Edmund Wilson, the famous American literary critic, used to answer requests with a postcard that read:

43   Edmund Wilson regrets that it is impossible for him to: Read manuscripts, Write articles or books to order, Make statements for publicity purposes, Do any kind of editorial work, Judge literary contests, Give interviews, Conduct educational courses, Deliver lectures, Give talks or make speeches, Take part in writers congresses, Answer questionnaires, Contribute or take part in symposiums or "panels" of any kind, Contribute manuscripts for sale, Donate copies of his books to Libraries, Autograph books for strangers, Allow his name to be used on letterheads, Supply personal information about himself, Supply photographs of himself, Supply opinions on literary or other subjects.

44 A fairly impressive list, I'd say. When I was young, Edmund Wilson supplied for me the model of how a literary man ought to carry himself. One of the things I personally found most impressive about his list is that everything Edmund Wilson clearly states he will not do, Joseph Epstein has now done, and more than once, and, like the young woman in the Häagen-Dazs commercial sitting on her couch with an empty carton of ice cream, is likely to do again and again.

45   I tell myself that I do these various things in the effort to acquire more readers. After all, one of the reasons I write, apart from pleasure in working out the aesthetic problems and moral questions presented by my subjects and in my stories, is to find the best readers. I also want to sell books, to make a few shekels, to please my publisher, to continue to be published in the future in a proper way. Having a high threshold for praise, I also

don't in the least mind meeting strangers who tell me that they take some delight in my writing. But, more than all this, I have now come to think that writing away quietly, producing (the hope is) good work, isn't any longer quite sufficient in a culture dominated by the boisterous spirit of celebrity. In an increasingly noisy cultural scene, with many voices and media competing for attention, one feels—perhaps incorrectly but nonetheless insistently—the need to make one's own small stir, however pathetic. So, on occasion, I have gone about tooting my own little paper horn, doing book tours, submitting to the comically pompous self-importance of interviews, and doing so many of the other things that Edmund Wilson didn't think twice about refusing to do.

46   "You're slightly famous, aren't you, Grandpa?" my then eight-year-old granddaughter once said to me. "I am slightly famous, Annabelle," I replied, "except no one quite knows who I am." This hasn't changed much over the years. But of course seeking celebrity in our culture is a mug's game, one you cannot finally hope to win. The only large, lumpy kind of big-time celebrity available, outside movie celebrity, is to be had through appearing fairly regularly on television. I had the merest inkling of this fame when I was walking along one sunny morning in downtown Baltimore, and a red Mazda convertible screeched to a halt, the driver lowered his window, pointed a long index finger at me, hesitated, and finally, the shock of recognition lighting up his face, yelled, "C-SPAN!"

47   I was recently asked, through email, to write a short piece for a high price for a volume about the city of Chicago. When I agreed to do it, the editor of the volume, who is (I take it) young, told me how very pleased she was to have someone as distinguished as I among the volume's contributors. But she did have just one request. Before making things final, she wondered if she might see a sample of my writing. More than forty years in the business, I thought, echoing the character played by Zero Mostel in *The Producers,* and I'm still wearing the celebrity equivalent of a cardboard belt.

48   "Every time I think I'm famous," Virgil Thomson said, "I have only to go out into the world." So it is, and so ought it probably to remain for writers, musicians, and visual artists who prefer to consider themselves serious. The comedian Richard Pryor once said that he would deem himself famous when people recognized him, as they recognized Bob Hope and Muhammad Ali, by his captionless caricature. That is certainly one clear criterion for celebrity. But the best criterion I've yet come across holds that you are celebrated, indeed famous, only when a crazy person imagines he is you. It's especially pleasing that the penetrating and prolific author of this remark happens to go by the name of Anonymous. ◆

CRITICAL THINKING

1. Who are your favorite celebrities, and why are they your favorites? What are they known for?
2. What is the "culture of celebrity"? Is this term an oxymoron? In what ways has the American media engine created this culture, and how is it sustained?
3. If you could be famous, what would you want to be famous for? Would you also want to be a "celebrity"? Try to be as honest and thoughtful in your answer as possible.
4. According to Epstein, what is the distinction between being famous and being a celebrity? What example does he use to illustrate his point?

5. Should movie stars pay a price for their fame, such as enduring the paparazzi and fan adoration, or should they be seen as merely practicing a profession and be able to live in privacy? Explain your answer.

6. In *The Brothers Karamazov,* Dostoevsky writes, "So long as man remains free, he strives for nothing so incessantly and painfully as to find someone to worship." Do you agree with this statement? Do you think we worship celebrities? Explain.

CRITICAL WRITING

1. *Research and Persuasive Writing:* Choose three well-known celebrities, research their backgrounds, scrutinize their accomplishments, and make a case for or against their fame or celebrity by showing that they are "with scarcely any pretense to talent or achievement whatsoever," that their career seems to be "the result of careful promotion or great good luck," or that their fame has been earned through true talent or achievement.

2. *Speech Writing:* Twenty years from now, you will receive an award for a great accomplishment in your field of study. Write the acceptance speech to go along with receiving this award. Think about what type of award you would want to be presented with and what you did to receive it.

3. *Persuasive Writing:* Agree or disagree with this statement from the article: "American society in the twenty-first century, received opinion has it, values only two things: money and celebrity." Make sure to use concrete examples and details to illustrate your point.

GROUP PROJECTS

1. As a group, review a copy each of the *New York Times* and the *Washington Post,* and count how many times celebrities are mentioned in these "high-brow" newspapers. Which celebrities make the most news, and why?

2. Epstein's article mentions many celebrity names. As a group, write down why each person mentioned is famous. If there are some people mentioned in the article that you have not heard of before, look them up online to see who they are and why they are famous.

3. Decide on two authors whom you would characterize as having turned "celebrity" after becoming famous for their literature. Read articles on the authors and watch videotapes of interviews, book signings, lectures, and so on, and analyze how, why, and when they reached celebrity status.

Death to Film Critics! Hail to the CelebCult!
*Roger Ebert**

Years ago, to determine the methane and carbon-monoxide levels in underground mines, miners would use a canary to test the air. If the canary stopped singing, the miners knew to get out before they all died. Today, the expression "canary in a coal mine" is used to describe a harbinger of danger.

* Roger Ebert, *Chicago-Sun Times,* November 26, 2008

In this next editorial, Roger Ebert compares the firing of newspaper film critics to the canary in the coal mine. He laments the loss of true objective analysis in favor of giving the masses "mindless drivel" that sells newspapers and does little to advance our society as a whole. Film critics, he explains, are told to promote the celebrity engine instead of honestly evaluating the merits of the films they review. The result is that the cult of celebrity is ruining our culture overall.

1 A newspaper film critic is like a canary in a coal mine. When one croaks, get the hell out. The lengthening toll of former film critics acts as a poster child for the self-destruction of American newspapers, which once hoped to be more like the *New York Times* and now yearn to become more like the *National Enquirer*. We used to be the town crier. Now we are the neighborhood gossip.

2 The crowning blow came this week when the once-magisterial Associated Press imposed a 500-word limit on all of its entertainment writers. The 500-word limit applies to reviews, interviews, news stories, trend pieces and "thinkers." Oh, it can be done. But with "Synecdoche, New York?"

3 Worse, the AP wants its writers on the entertainment beat to focus more on the kind of brief celebrity items its clients apparently hunger for. The AP, long considered obligatory to the task of running a North American newspaper, has been hit with some cancellations lately, and no doubt has been informed what its customers want: affairs, divorces, addiction, disease, success, failure, death watches, tirades, arrests, hissy fits, scandals, who has been "seen with" somebody, who has been "spotted with" somebody, and "top ten" lists of the above. (Celebs "seen with" desire to be seen, celebs "spotted with" do not desire to be seen.)

4 The CelebCult virus is eating our culture alive, and newspapers voluntarily expose themselves to it. It teaches shabby values to young people, festers unwholesome curiosity, violates privacy, and is indifferent to meaningful achievement. One of the TV celeb shows has announced it will cover the Obama family as "a Hollywood story." I want to smash something against a wall.

> *The CelebCult virus is eating our culture alive, and newspapers voluntarily expose themselves to it. It teaches shabby values to young people, festers unwholesome curiosity, violates privacy, and is indifferent to meaningful achievement*

5 In *Toots,* a new documentary about the legendary Manhattan saloon keeper Toots Shor, there is a shot so startling I had to reverse the DVD to see it again. After dinner, Joe DiMaggio and Marilyn Monroe leave the restaurant, give their ticket to a valet, wait on the curb until their car arrives, tip the valet and then Joe opens the car door for Marilyn, walks around, gets in, and drives them away. This was in the 1950s. Brad Pitt and Angelina Jolie have not been able to do that once in their adult lifetimes. Celebrities do not use limousines because of vanity. They use them as a protection against cannibalism.

6 As the CelebCult triumphs, major newspapers have been firing experienced film critics. They want to devote less of their space to considered prose and more to ignorant gawking. What they require doesn't need to be paid for out of their payrolls. Why does the biggest story about *Twilight* involve its *fans?* Do we need interviews with 16-year-old girls about Robert Pattinson? When was the last time *they* read a paper? Isn't the movie obviously about sexual abstinence and the teen fascination with doomy, Goth death flirtation?

7   The age of film critics has come and gone. While the big papers on the coasts always had them (Bosley Crowther at the *New York Times,* Charles Champlin at the *Los Angeles Times*), many other major dailies had rotating bylines anybody might be writing under ("Kate Cameron" at the *New York Daily News,* "Mae Tinay" at the *Chicago Tribune*—get it?). Judith Crist changed everything at the *New York Herald-Tribune* when she panned *Cleopatra* (1963) and was banned from 20th Century-Fox screenings. There was a big fuss, and suddenly every paper hungered for a "real" movie critic. The Film Generation was upon us.

8   In the coverage of new directors and the rediscovery of classic films, no paper was more influential than the weekly *Village Voice,* with such critics as Andrew Sarris and Jonas Mekas. Earlier this year the *Voice* fired Dennis Lim and Nathan Lee, and recently fired all the local movie critics in its national chain, to be replaced, *Variety*'s Anne Thompson reported, by syndicating their critics on the two coasts, the *Voice*'s J. Hoberman and the *L.A. Weekly*'s Scott Foundas. Serious writers, yes, but....

9   Meanwhile, the *Detroit Free-Press* has decided it needs no film critic at all. Michael Wilmington is gone from the *Chicago Tribune,* Jack Mathews and Jami Bernard from the *New York Daily News,* Kevin Thomas from the *Los Angeles Times*—and the internationally-respected film critic of the *Chicago Reader,* Jonathan Rosenbaum, has retired, accepted a buy-out, will write for his blog, or something. I still see him at all the screenings. My shining hero remains Stanley Kauffmann of the *New Republic,* as incisive and penetrating as ever at 92. I don't give him points for his age, which anyone can attain simply by living long enough, but for his criticism. Study any review and try to find a wrong or unnecessary word. There is your man for an intelligent 500-word review.

10   Why do we need critics? A good friend of mine in a very big city was once told by his editor that the critic should "reflect the taste of the readers." My friend said, "Does that mean the food critic should love McDonald's?" The editor: "Absolutely." I don't believe readers buy a newspaper to read variations on the Ed McMahon line, "You are correct, sir!" A newspaper film critic should encourage critical thinking, introduce new developments, consider the local scene, look beyond the weekend fanboy specials, be a weatherman on social trends, bring in a larger context, teach, inform, amuse, inspire, be heartened, be outraged.

11   At one time all newspapers by definition did those things on every page. Now they are lascivious gossips, covering invented beats. On *one single day* recently, I was informed that Tom and Katie's daughter Suri "won't wear pants" and shares matching designer sunglasses with her mom. No, wait, they're not matching, they're only both wearing sunglasses. Eloping to Mexico: Heidi and Spencer. Britney is feeling old. Amy is in the hospital. George called Hugh in the middle of the night to accuse him of waging a campaign to take away the title of "sexiest man alive." Pete discussed naming his son Bronx Mowgli. Ann's jaw was wired shut. Karolina's belly button is missing. Madonna and A-Rod might, or might not, spend Thanksgiving together. Some of Valentino's makeup rubbed off on Sarah Jessica. Miley and Justin went out to lunch. Justin and Jessica took their dogs for a walk.

12   Perhaps fearing the challenge of reading a newspaper will prove daunting, papers are using increasing portions of their shrinking news holes in providing guides to reading themselves. Before the *Chicago Tribune*'s new design started

self-correcting (i.e., rolling itself back), I fully expected a box at the top of a page steering me to a story lower on the same page.

13   The celebrity culture is infantilizing us. We are being trained not to think. It is not about the disappearance of film critics. We are the canaries. It is about the death of an intelligent and curious readership, interested in significant things and able to think critically. It is about the failure of our educational system. It is not about dumbing-down. It is about snuffing out.

14   The news is still big. It's the newspapers that got small. ◆

CRITICAL THINKING

1. What does Ebert mean when he says that newspaper film critics "used to be the town crier," but now they are "the neighborhood gossip"? Explain.
2. What issue is Ebert raising in his editorial? What is his argument, and how persuasive is his case? What does he hope his readers will do as a result of reading his editorial?
3. According to Ebert, what do the newspapers believe its customers want to read about? Do you agree with the newspaper's assessment of its readership? What do you want to read about?
4. What is the "CelebCult" virus? How has it impacted newspapers and film critics and the general public? Who feeds the virus?
5. Who is Roger Ebert? What is he known for? What risks does he assume, if any, in speaking out this way against the culture of celebrity?

CRITICAL WRITING

1. *Expository Writing:* In this essay, Roger Ebert warns that celebrity culture is "infantilizing us" and training us "not to think." Write your own editorial exploring this claim.
2. *Analytical Writing:* What claims does Ebert make in this editorial? Make a list of his claims, and evaluate how he supports each. Write a response to his editorial directly addressing his claims, commenting on the strengths and weaknesses of his argument.

GROUP PROJECTS

1. Test Ebert's claims about the vacuous nature of celebrity gossip. Get several copies of your local newspaper, and review the headlines and sections. Which sections are larger? Which stories lead? What information does the newspaper feel its readers care about most, based on the headlines and bylines it prints? Discuss your analysis as a group.
2. Research the work of some of the film critics Ebert cites, including Stanley Kauffmann. Then, read some film reviews in your local paper. Based on what you read, discuss the similarities and differences between how career film critics write and the reviews published in many papers today. Select a recent film and watch it as a group. Discuss the film's merits, and prepare your own review of it, employing either the style of past film critics or the 500-word gossipy review style promoted by today's papers.

Perspectives: Public Library

Cartoonstock.com cgon137

THINKING CRITICALLY

1. What is happening in this cartoon? What contemporary social issue does it highlight?
2. What stereotypes does the cartoon use to convey its point? What do the people look like? Who is getting what book?
3. Review the words in the cartoon and what they mean. What is the cartoonist saying about people who read celebrity biographies?

Return of the Brainless Hussies

*Rebecca Traister**

It appears that many of America's most famous young women are known not only for their beauty but for their lack of intelligence. From *American Idol* Kelly Pickler to Paris Hilton to an army of jiggly video stars, vapid females seem to be everywhere these days. Are young women playing to the stereotype that they are more attractive and likable when they play dumb? Why are we glorifying female stupidity by honoring this trait in our most publicized celebrities? In this next essay, Rebecca Traister wonders, have we really gone this far backward, Baby?

1 During the last week of April 2006, Ellen DeGeneres welcomed Paris Hilton and her four Chihuahuas to her daytime talk show, ostensibly for a special episode about dogs. Once the host had the hotel heiress sitting down, however, she pressed her on a non-canine issue, asking whether she was hurt by Pink's video for "Stupid Girls," which mocks Hilton and her shopping-zombie peers for their essentially somnambulant behavior, and which two weeks earlier, DeGeneres had praised on her show. "I haven't even seen it yet," said the hotel heiress, in her flat monotone. "But I think . . . it's just a form of flattery."

2 Any thinking person who has seen Pink's video, in which she sends up Jessica Simpson's "These Boots Were Made for Walking" video by humping a soapy car, imitates an Olsen twin in Montana-size sunglasses and Wyoming-size handbag walking straight into the plate-glass door of a boutique, and savagely mocks Hilton's appearance in a dingy night-vision sex tape, would not confuse the clip with any known form of flattery. Especially if that thinking person heard the "Stupid Girls" lyrics, which go, in part: "They travel in packs of two or three/ With their itsy-bitsy doggies and their teeny-weeny tees/ Where, oh where, have the smart people gone?"

3 But Hilton is not a thinking person. Or, if she is, she hasn't let on. For the purposes of the American public, she is chief Stupid Girl, unembarrassed to admit that she doesn't know what Wal-Mart is, to testify that she isn't aware that London is in the United Kingdom, or to get the name of her own video game wrong; Hilton is so vacant that her behavior recently inspired a new Page Six epithet: "celebutard." When DeGeneres pressed her on whether she felt any responsibility as a role model to young girls, Hilton averred: "I think I definitely am a role model. I work very hard. I came from a name, but I've done my own thing." DeGeneres neglected to point out that doing one's own thing in the face of terrible privilege is not the same as being a role model, especially when one's own thing involves trademarking the phrase "That's hot."

4 Listening to Hilton try to have a conversation, the wind whistling between her eardrums, makes it hard to ignore claims of cultural critics who have noticed an alarming new vogue for feminine vapidity. In addition to Pink's sharp-toothed

* Rebecca Traister, *Salon*, May 19, 2006

treatise, the recent *American Idol* ascension of blond malapropism-spewing Kellie Pickler prompted a spate of stories about how playing dumb seems a sure way to get embraced by the American public. And Oprah recently summoned Pink, Naomi Wolf, *Female Chauvinist Pigs* author Ariel Levy and others for an episode called "Stupid Girls," which she kicked off by ominously announcing that culture is "devaluing an entire generation of young girls" by celebrating women as jiggly video stars, boobie-flashing twits, half-clad clotheshorses, and label-whoring anorexics. To hear media watchdogs tell it, dumbness—authentic or put on—is rampant in pop-culture products being consumed by kids; it gets transmitted through their downy skin and into their bloodstreams through the books and magazines they read, the television they watch, the trends they analyze like stock reports, and the celebrities they aspire to be.

5 In an effort to find out exactly what signals teens could be picking up, I spent a couple of weeks as immersed in girl pop culture as an old-fogy 30-year-old can get—reading sudsy high school novels and teen magazines, surfing MySpace, and watching MTV reality shows—waiting to see if I'd be overtaken with the urge to don giant sunglasses and pretend not to understand math. I found myself pleasantly surprised at some of the teen media I encountered—surprised enough to consider that the criticism we've been hearing may be vastly overblown by grown-ups who've forgotten the air-popped diversions of their own youth. But I was dismayed enough by the rest of it to acknowledge that the adults crying "fire" have a troubling point. Some of the images currently being retailed to teens illuminate both how far young women have come, and how easy it still is to cling to, recycle, and sell outmoded yet comfortable images of unthreatening femininity.

6 More problematic than teen literature is the craze for celebrity. Of all the evidence out there about the propagation of stupid-girl culture, it's most convincing to hear Pink talk about it. To begin with, she's 25. And her lyrics on the subject raise good questions: "Whatever happened to the dreams of a girl president?/ She's dancing in the video next to 50 Cent." In *Entertainment Weekly*, Pink pointed out that she doesn't actually think the women she goes after are truly stupid. "They've dumbed themselves down to be cute," she said. "I just feel like one image is being force-fed down people's throats. There's a lot of smart women. There's a lot of smart girls. Who is representing them?"

7 It's an excellent question. We have never been more soaked in celebrity culture. And yet, which celebrities hold teens in their thrall? There are women like skeletal Nicole Richie, who even venerable columnist Liz Smith recently took time to bemoan, "became a 'star' as soon as her weight dropped to scary skinny, [and who is] famous for being thin." There's Lohan, who may or may not be a good actress, but whose craft has come second to carousing and the development of her handbag collection. Even the Olsen twins, kajillionaires whose business acumen was widely touted when they were preteens, seemed to shrivel when they hit their 18th birthday. Now, their reputations as precocious entrepreneurs are shadowed by their profiles as consumptive, shabby-chic munchkins: little, dim, and more famous than ever.

8 The video clips that played behind Winfrey's dirge for the emancipated female at the start of her show amplified concerns about the dearth of female role models: There were Lohan, Richie and Jessica Simpson, "Video Vixen" Karrine Steffans, a "rose ceremony" from desperate-mate-foraging spectacle *The Bachelor*, along with anachronistic shots of senescent stars like Madonna and J. Lo showing off their

attenuated limbs and bubblicious booty, respectively. In a taped interview for *Oprah*, a worked-up Wolf said, "What's beaming at young teenage girls is unfortunately an image of celebrity perfection which is pretty mindless."

9   Pink told Oprah that she and her friends could name only three celebrity women her age and under who were known for being bright; they were Natalie Portman, Reese Witherspoon, and Angelina Jolie, though both Witherspoon and Jolie are over 30. There are a few other young favorites who could have quali-

> **Pink told Oprah that she and her friends could name only three celebrity women her age and under who were known for being bright; they were Natalie Portman, Reese Witherspoon, and Angelina Jolie, though both Witherspoon and Jolie are over 30.**

fied for the list: Maggie Gyllenhaal, Alicia Keys, and Pink herself, who was recently reported to be reading Maya Angelou's I Know Why the Caged Bird Sings and Levy's Female Chauvinist Pigs, and whose bristling ditty "Dear Mr. President" is smart enough to be getting banned in high schools across the country. But basically, the pickings are slim.

10   And while vacuous pink-fleshed icons of privilege would seem to hold sway mostly on white-girl culture, the picture isn't much brighter on African-American radar, where celebrity and material aspiration is embodied by mute, bling-laden, gyrating "video girls," the most famous of whom is Karrine Steffans. Steffans' recent tell-all, *Confessions of a Video Vixen,* earned her a place on Oprah's couch, where she cried about the way she had been objectified by the rappers she danced for and slept with. But her book isn't being read as a cautionary tale; it's become a cult hit with young readers who refer to it as "Superhead," the nickname Steffans earned in her years as a dancer, presumably by administering super head to a variety of famous men. Days after she appeared on *Oprah*, it was reported in the *New York Post* that Steffans would be moving on to porn.

11   If there were anywhere I would have expected to find an airhead ethos come alive, it would have been in the crop of teen magazines I'd always considered beauty-obsessed gateway drugs to full-blown fashion addiction. A stack of these volumes, with their citrus typeface and cotton-candy cover lines, seemed to promise unthreatening vapidity inside, right down to Pink herself on the cover of *Seventeen*, next to the thunder-stealing headline: "I'm a stupid girl every other day." Inside, the magazines confirmed some of my suspicions with expensive fashion spreads, headlines that read, "So You Want to Be Sienna Miller," and the occasional, lame deployment of teenage patois, like "for realz." But to my surprise, the same issue of (recently defunct) *ElleGirl* that printed those words also featured book reviews under the headline "Word: Reading Comprehension Is Sexy." *CosmoGirl* interviewed *Napoleon Dynamite* star Jon Heder, who advised, "Guys love smart girls, so don't act dumber than you are," and published love advice from *Saturday Night Live* eggheads Tina Fey and Amy Poehler.

12   Most startling were the "Real Life" pages over at *Seventeen*, one of which explained threats to American privacy." After 9/11, Congress passed the USA Patriot Act, which lets the Feds look at your private medical and financial records," read the text. "Plus, it just came out that the National Security Agency has been eavesdropping on people's phone calls since 2002—without warrants!" A later section on

"anti-American feelings" explained that "The US is very wealthy compared with other nations and has a lot more resources and weapons. Many people . . . feel we use this power to help our own interests—like they believe we invaded Iraq to get cheaper oil—and that we don't respect or care about their way of life."

13   So it's not Susan Sontag. But it's a hell of a lot closer than the "plaids are in for fall" pap I remember reading as a 12- or 13-year-old (17-year-olds do not read *Seventeen*). Yes, teen magazines are riddled with images of richly swaddled urchins who look a couple of PowerBars short of a healthy Body Mass Index. But the editorial content presented a serious progression. The reason that the late magazine *Sassy* is so revered by women my age is because it treated its readers like human beings with interests: in their own health, in music, books, movies, politics. Now, it seems, *Sassy*'s mainstream sisters have begun treating young women with a similar regard.

14   My attempt at honest immersion in teenage-girl land necessarily stalled online, specifically on MySpace. I spent hours in the maze of profiles and messages; I saw dishabille Lolitas beckoning to Web-savvy Humbert Humberts, suggestively Sapphic images on the home pages of girls who claimed to be 15 and 16, several teens who listed *The South Beach Diet* as their favorite book. But I also visited pages of 17- and 18-year-olds decorated with teddy bears and pictures of horses. Teen women use MySpace to post enunciations of their devotion to field hockey, feminism, God, and Kanye West. MySpace is a country unto itself. Finding the evidence for any argument you'd like to make about American teens is possible: A search mechanism will dredge up any predilection or bad habit or nickname. Reading public expressions that would only recently have been private—cringey blogs chronicling breakups and bad grades, extensive online exchanges about girls cashing in their "v-cards" and plotting to get wine coolers for sleepovers—will confuse anyone who ever thought of a diary as something that had a lock and key, or who threaded a phone cord up the stairs and down the hall and under a door so that they could trade whispered secrets with friends, far out of earshot.

15   But my perplexity at the "Hiya! LOL! XO!" genre of communication was based in a lack of context for what I was watching, context I didn't lack when I turned on my television and found *My Super Sweet Sixteen*. A reality show on MTV, the program chronicles the celebratory excesses of 15-year-old girls (and boys) who persuade their parents to shower them with adulation and automobiles as they make the profound passage between teenager and incrementally older teenager. Watching this orgy of consumption on a couple of occasions, before beginning this story, is the closest I have come to fearing that the end of the world is near. These kids get carried into their parties on litters; they get dropped from helicopters; invitations are handed out by manservants.

16   *Super Sweet's* new sister show is *Tiara Girls,* which follows beauty pageant contestants. The pageant circuit, on the opposite side of the culture war divide from some of the lavish, celebrity-studded events featured on *My Super Sweet Sixteen,* is no less materialistic. Contestants discuss the amount of money they spend on dresses; they hire pageant coaches; and whatever the current line on pageantry is, there is no focus on the female intellect. In one episode, an aspiring Miss Louisiana Queen of Hope prepared for the interview segment with a little quizzing from her coach. What, asked the coach, is the vice president's name? "Wait," the contestant said, stalling. "His name's Kennedy, right?" It's a knee-slapper that apparently never

gets old; the *Tiara Girls* season finale has been advertised by a clip of another pageant entrant flubbing the name of the commander in chief himself, then grumping to the camera: "It's a beauty pageant; what does it matter who the president is?" In one episode, a contestant's father ordered her to stop doing her homework to prepare for competition. "But I want to do my homework," the young woman said hopelessly to the camera.

17   *Sweet Sixteen* and *Tiara Girls* are transmitting aggressively mixed signals to their viewers. On one hand, they're car wrecks that mock their subjects in strict accordance with the basest class and cultural assumptions out there. The hyper-affluent party throwers on *Sweet Sixteen* come across as empty-headed, entitled brats, while the mostly lower-class beauty contestants appear simultaneously thick and shallow. But the degradation of the subjects is the backbeat to the melody being broadcast to kids: This is what you are supposed to look like; this is what you do look like; these are our expectations of you; if you fulfill them, you too can be on television.

18   Both shows demonstrate the complicity of parents in their kids' exploitation. If it long ago ceased to astound me that any kid could survive seeing their own avarice and vapidity broadcast on national television, the question remains: Why on earth would their parents participate? But on *Super Sweet Sixteen* and *Tiara Girls,* parents seem to be seeking the same cable-television spotlight that must motivate their children to self-exposure, without any concern that a nation (let alone their neighbors) will get to see them pushing their daughters to get collagen lip injections, or enabling their offspring's insatiable greed by never setting limits and getting them two cars.

19   When describing what's problematic in trashy teen fiction, Wolf wrote of the good old days, when the fictional younger generation's role was to poke holes in their parents' social artifice and find their own paths. Today, Wolf complained, teenage heroines "try on adult values and customs as though they were going to wear them forever. The narrative offer the perks of the adult world not as escapist fantasy but in a creepily photorealistic way."

20   The tension between adolescent and adult has always been a tricky mix of imitation and rejection. Vexing her elders, adopting ill-advised role models, and cleaving to habits that will most aggravate her parents is basically the job description of a teenager. But we're in a period when adult and teenage worlds seem to be meshing, making Wolf's implied wish—that teenagers would crumple up and jettison parental mores—a complicated proposition. Adults push children to learn and socialize earlier than ever; we rush them with Baby Einstein videos, obsess over their achievements, and wail over their failures. We treat them as mini-me's at the same time that we infantilize them, fretting over just about every message that's been transmitted to them from the moment they are expelled from the womb, except for the ones we set for them by example.

21   Adults have made careless consumption the crowning American pursuit. We have invented and happily consume magalogs full of luxury items. Teenagers didn't create Paris Hilton. In fact, they wouldn't have any idea who she was if adults hadn't elevated her from a dull table-dancing heiress by circulating a porn tape and giving her a reality show. Teenage girls don't write the *Gossip Girl* books; 35-year-old Cecily von Ziegesar does. And consider the cabal of studio heads, publicists, club owners, photographers, designers, and magazine publishers who have colluded to

make Lindsay Lohan famous, drunk, and ubiquitous so that she can sell their magazines, movies, and handbags to teens who might rightly get the impression that they should live like her. Eliot Spitzer, of all people, recently accused the grown-ups over at Lohan's record company of goosing her popularity by bribing radio stations and MTV to play her music. It's all in the name of legitimate American enterprise, sure. But how can we be surprised when the kids we are hustling take our cues and mimic even our most corrupt behaviors?

22   And how about the fact that it's not just teens photo realistically aping the adults, but adults who are aping their own teens? The Alcotts and Austens and Brontës that Wolf recalls with deserved reverence would have blanched had they encountered the slice of the maternal population currently striving to look and dress like their daughters. Which is more alarming—reading about Lohan drinking too much and collapsing from "exhaustion," or reading about her mother, Dina, sponging off her daughter's success and cavorting with her beyond every velvet rope? It's fair to ask, as Pink does, how many girls long to mimic Lohan. But it's also reasonable to wonder whether any of their mothers long to live like Dina?

23   The current wave of flaky-chic is no more potent than other historical iterations of American worship of the dumb blonde, which has venerable roots with Marilyn Monroe and Judy Holliday. Teens (and adults, for that matter) have never fallen for celebrity heroes based on their great calculus grades. But that particular mold of femininity was one of the constructs from which women's liberation was supposed to deliver us. What does it mean that in 2004, Jessica Simpson got famous for being flummoxed by a can of Chicken of the Sea tuna on *Newlyweds,* and that in 2006, Kellie Pickler became a star by asking, "What's a ballsy?" For one thing, it means that the same young women who had hung on Simpson's every word about staying a virgin till marriage and who were calling in their votes for Pickler were also getting the message that it's funny and attractive to be an idiot.

24   *MTV News* producer Jim Fraenkel told the *New York Post*'s Farrah Weinstein in a piece about Pickler that he "wouldn't necessarily say that she's so savvy she's tapped into the idea that America loves a stupid girl, so much as that she may think of herself as Jessica Simpson was." But aren't both realizations pretty much the same thing? And aren't they both an embarrassing sign that we haven't come very far at all, baby?

25   Yes, they are. But modern women, like generations of men before them, now have many areas in which to hunt for role models. They receive instructions that directly contradict the Pickler-Simpson Principle of Sexy Vacancy every day: achieve, go to school, work, make money, compete. Retro visions of stupid appeal are answered by fresh acknowledgment of energetic female sexuality that is far more open—if dangerously commodified in its own way, critics argue— than ever before. None of it is in perfect balance; women are punished for their progress all the time, in media and politics and in classrooms. Adolescent girls still have no female president to look up to, and too few artists and tycoons and athletes and activists. But there is no denying the past half-century's earth-shaking and positive shifts in the gender terrain. As has been widely reported (with varying degrees of rancor) women now make up more than half the country's collegiate student body.

26   But these new, varied, and wildly threatening options help to explain and under-gird a rejuvenated craze for dumb chic. Perhaps, as social progress propels women slowly but undeniably forward into public spheres of influence, baser human impulses—erotic desire, capitalist greed—dig in, summoning and then clinging to a dusty daydream of the fast-fading ideal woman of yesteryear.

27   Working on this story, I received an e-mail from a Harvard graduate student who told me that while he'd dated only smart girls, he "liked the 'idea' of dating a dumb girl." The fantasy, the student explained, "is almost certainly formed for us by the media representations of . . . celebrities [like Hilton, Lohan, and Simpson]. Blonde dumb girls are sexy. And won't talk back. Add in various shades of male ego/guaranteed superiority notions, and you've pretty much got it." In a world in which male superiority is no longer guaranteed, it becomes a lascivious desire that can be gratified, performatively if need be, by willing women. As Pink trills, mock-ingly, "Maybe if I act like that/ that guy will call me back."

28   But it's time to put that transactional model for romance out of its misery, and make room in the pop firmament for examples that sound more like Pink's self-assessment: "I'm so glad that I'll never fit in/ That will never be me/ Outcasts and girls with ambition/ That's what I wanna see." ◆

CRITICAL THINKING

1. Who were the female celebrities from your childhood? Who were they in your teen years? Ask your parents or older adults this same question. How do female celebrities from the past compare to the young women we focus our cameras on today? Are they different or fundamentally the same?

2. According to Traister, why do the women she mentions—such as Jessica Simpson, the Olsen twins, and Paris Hilton—get so much attention from the press and the general public? How have they made female stupidity desirable? Have you noticed this phenomenon yourself? Does it represent an aberration or a trend? Explain.

3. Traister observes that programs such as *My Super Sweet Sixteen* not only glorify the worst of human behavior but also encourage youth to covet the very things the show seems to mock. Do you agree?

4. Why are people so willing to allow themselves to be exploited on reality television? According to Traister, what motivates youth and their parents to broadcast the most intimate details of their lives?

5. What mixed signals are teens getting from media today? What messages are conveyed to young women? What messages are conveyed to young men? Is media constructing reality or merely reflecting it? Explain.

6. What culpability do adults have in the creation of the "cult of celebrity?" Explain.

CRITICAL WRITING

1. *Research and Analysis:* What issue does the singer Pink raise in her song "Stupid Girls"? Review the lyrics in the song and write a short essay responding to her points with your own perspective.

2. *Expository Writing:* Traister quotes an e-mail she received from a Harvard graduate student who expresses a personal yearning to date "a dumb girl." What reasons does he give? What qualities do you look for in a significant other, and how many of these qualities are driven by social norms and media-constructed ideals? Explain.

3. *Personal Narrative:* Have you ever aspired to be on a reality program? If so, why? What program would you want to be on? What would your expectations be during the program and after it? Would you expect to be a celebrity. Why or why not?

GROUP PROJECTS

1. As a group, discuss this statement: "America loves a stupid girl." In what ways is this statement true or untrue? Identify women in popular culture who represent both intelligent and unintelligent females. What are each known for? Why are they famous?

2. Watch Pink's video "Stupid Girls" online. Identify the women she holds up for ridicule and the personalities to which she objects. As a group, answer her question: "Where have all the smart girls gone?"

3. Plan a follow-up program for Ellen DeGeneres on the issue of the glorification of "stupid women" in the media. Who would you have on her show and why? What issues would you address? Share your program with the class.

Mirror, Mirror, on the Web
Lakshmi Chaudry*

Mirror, mirror, on the wall, who's the fairest of them all? Maybe the over 100 million MySpace users or the 132 million registrants on Facebook. The Web has become a place where we are all beautiful, witty, talented, and popular, especially if we are describing ourselves. But why do we need to be the center of attention and admired by so many? Lakshmi Chaudry explores this new generation of fame seekers who are recreating Narcissus' pool and shows that we haven't learned anything from his cautionary tale.

1 "Everyone, in the back of his mind, wants to be a star," says YouTube co-founder Chad Hurley, explaining the dizzying success of the online mecca of amateur video in *Wired* magazine. And thanks to MySpace, YouTube, Facebook, LiveJournal and other bastions of the retooled Web 2.0, every Jane, Joe or Jamila can indeed be a star, be it as wannabe comics, citizen journalists, lip-syncing geeks, military bloggers, aspiring porn stars or even rodent-eating freaks.

* Lakshmi Chaudry, *The Nation,* January 11, 2007

2   We now live in the era of micro-celebrity, which offers endless opportunities to celebrate that most special person in your life, i.e., you—who not coincidentally is also *Time* magazine's widely derided Person of the Year for 2006. An honor once reserved for world leaders, pop icons and high-profile CEOs now belongs to "you," the ordinary netizen with the time, energy and passion to "make a movie starring my pet iguana...mash up 50 Cent's vocals with Queen's instrumentals...blog about my state of mind or the state of the nation or the steak-frites at the new bistro down the street."

3   The editors at *Time* tout this "revolution" in the headiest prose: "It's a story about community and collaboration on a scale never seen before. It's about the cosmic compendium of knowledge on Wikipedia and the million-channel people's network YouTube and the online metropolis MySpace. It's about the many wresting power from the few and helping one another for nothing and how that will not only change the world, but also change the way the world changes."

4   This is the stuff of progressive fantasy: change, community, collaboration. And it echoes our cherished hope that a medium by, of and for the people will create a more democratic world. So it's easy to miss the editorial sleight of hand that slips from the "I" to the "we," substitutes individual self-expression for collective action and conflates popular attention with social consciousness.

5   For all the talk about coming together, Web 2.0's greatest successes have capitalized on our need to feel significant and admired and, above all, to be seen. The latest iteration of digital democracy has indeed brought with it a new democracy of fame, but in doing so it has left us ever more in the thrall of celebrity, except now we have a better shot at being worshiped ourselves. As MySpace luminary Christine Dolce told the *New York Post*, "My favorite comment is when people say that I'm their idol. That girls look up to me."

6   So we upload our wackiest videos to YouTube, blog every sordid detail of our personal lives so as to insure at least fifty inbound links, add 200 new "friends" a day to our MySpace page with the help of FriendFlood.com, all the time hoping that one day all our efforts at self-promotion will merit—at the very least—our very own Wikipedia entry.

7   In *The Frenzy of Renown*, written in 1986, Leo Braudy documented the long and intimate relationship between mass media and fame. The more plentiful, accessible and immediate the ways of gathering and distributing information have become, he wrote, the more ways there are to be known: "In the past that medium was usually literature, theater, or public monuments. With the Renaissance came painting and engraved portraits, and the modern age has added photography, radio, movies, and television. As each new medium of fame appears, the human image it conveys is intensified and the number of individuals celebrated expands." It's no surprise then that the Internet, which offers vastly greater immediacy and accessibility than its top-down predecessors, should further flatten the landscape of celebrity.

8   The democratization of fame, however, comes at a significant price. "Through the technology of image reproduction and information reproduction, our relation to the increasing number of faces we see every day becomes more and more transitory, and 'famous' seems as devalued a term as 'tragic,'" Braudy wrote. And the easier it is to become known, the less we have to do to earn that honor. In ancient Greece, when

fame was inextricably linked to posterity, an Alexander had to make his mark on history to insure that his praises would be sung by generations to come. The invention of the camera in the nineteenth century introduced the modern notion of fame linked inextricably to a new type of professional: the journalist. Aspiring celebrities turned increasingly to achievements that would bring them immediate acclaim, preferably in the next day's newspaper, and with the rise of television, on the evening news.

9   The broadcast media's voracious appetite for spectacle insured that notoriety and fame soon became subsumed by an all-encompassing notion of celebrity, where simply being on TV became the ultimate stamp of recognition. At the same time, advertisers sought to redefine fame in terms of buying rather than doing, fusing the American Dream of material success with the public's hunger for stars in programs such as *Lifestyles of the Rich and Famous.*

10   But the advent of cyber-fame is remarkable in that it is divorced from any significant achievement—farting to the tune of "Jingle Bells," for example, can get you on VH1. While a number of online celebrities are rightly known for doing something (a blogger like Markos Moulitsas, say), and still others have leveraged their virtual success to build lucrative careers (as with the punk-rock group Fall Out Boy), it is no longer necessary to do either in order to be "famous."

11   Fame is now reduced to its most basic ingredient: pblic attention And the attention doesn't have to be positive either, as in the case of the man in Belfast who bit the head off a mouse for a YouTube video. "In our own time merely being looked at carries all the necessary ennoblement," Braudy wrote twenty years ago, words that ring truer than ever today.

12   Celebrity has become a commodity in itself, detached from and more valuable than wealth or achievement. Even rich New York socialites feel the need for their own blog, SocialiteRank.com, to get in on the action. The advice for aspiring celebutantes may be tongue-in-cheek—"To become a relevant socialite, you are virtually required to have your name in the press"—but no less true in this age of Paris Hilton wannabes.

13   Fame is no longer a perk of success but a necessary ingredient, whether as a socialite, chef, scholar or skateboarder. "For a great many people it is no longer enough to be very good at what you do. One also has to be a public figure, noticed and celebrated, and preferably televised," writes Hal Niedzviecki in his book *Hello, I'm Special.* When it is more important to be seen than to be talented, it is hardly surprising that the less gifted among us are willing to fart our way into the spotlight.

> *Fame is now reduced to its most basic ingredient: public attention. . . . Fame is no longer a perk of success but a necessary ingredient, whether as a socialite, chef, scholar or skateboarder.*

14   The fantasy of fame is not new, but what is unprecedented is the primacy of the desire, especially among young people. "I wanna be famous because I would love it more than anything. . . . Sometimes I'll cry at night wishing and praying for a better life to be famous . . . To be like the others someday too! Because i know that I can do it!" declares Britney Jo, writing on iWannaBeFamous.com.

15   She is hardly unusual. A 2000 Interprise poll revealed that 50 percent of kids under 12 believe that becoming famous is part of the American Dream. It's a dream increasingly shared by the rest of the world, as revealed in a recent survey of British

children between 5 and 10, who most frequently picked being famous as the "very best thing in the world." The views of these young children are no different from American college freshmen, who, according to a 2004 survey, most want to be an "actor or entertainer." Our preoccupation with fame is at least partly explained by our immersion in a media-saturated world that constantly tells us, as Braudy described it, "we should [be famous] if we possibly can, because it is the best, perhaps the only, way to be." Less obvious, however, is how our celebrity culture has fueled, and been fueled by, a significant generational shift in levels of narcissism in the United States.

16   In the 1950s, only 12 percent of teenagers between 12 and 14 agreed with the statement, "I am an important person." By the late 1980s, the number had reached an astounding 80 percent, an upward trajectory that shows no sign of reversing. Preliminary findings from a joint study conducted by Jean Twenge, Keith Campbell and three other researchers revealed that an average college student in 2006 scored higher than 65 percent of the students in 1987 on the standard Narcissism Personality Inventory test, which includes statements such as "I am a special person," "I find it easy to manipulate people" and "If I were on the Titanic, I would deserve to be on the first lifeboat." In her recent book *Generation Me*, Twenge applies that overarching label to everyone born between 1970 and 2000.

17   According to Twenge and her colleagues, the spike in narcissism is linked to an over-all increase in individualism, which has been fostered by a number of factors, including greater geographical mobility, breakdown of traditional communities and, more impor-tant, "the self-focus that blossomed in the 1970s [and] became mundane and common-place over the next two decades." In schools, at home and in popular culture, children over the past thirty-odd years have been inculcated with the same set of messages: You're spe-cial; love yourself; follow your dreams; you can be anything you want to be.

18   These mantras, in turn, have been woven into an all-pervasive commercial nar-rative used to hawk everything from movie tickets to sneakers. Just do it, baby, but make sure you buy that pair of Nikes first. The idea that every self is important has been redefined to suit the needs of a cultural marketplace that devalues genuine community and selfhood in favor of "success." In this context, "feeling good about myself" becomes the best possible reason to staple one's stomach, buy that shiny new car, or strip for a Girls Gone Wild video. The corollary of individualism becomes narcissism, an inflated evaluation of self-worth devoid of any real sense of "self" or "worth."

19   Since a key component of narcissism is the need to be admired and to be the center of attention, Generation Me's attraction to fame is inevitable. "You teach kids they're special. And then they watch TV, the impression they get is that everyone should be rich and famous. Then they hear, 'You can be anything you want.' So they're like, 'Well, I want to be rich and famous,'" says Twenge. Or if not rich and famous, at least to be "seen"—something the rest of us plebeians can now aspire to in the brave new media world. "To be noticed, to be wanted, to be loved, to walk into a place and have others care about what you're doing, even what you had for lunch that day: that's what people want, in my opinion," *Big Brother* contestant Kaysar Ridha told the *New York Times*, thus affirming a recent finding by Drew Pinsky and Mark Young that reality TV stars are far more narcissistic than actors, comedians or musicians—perhaps because they reflect more closely the reason the rest of us are obsessed more than ever with "making it."

20   Not only do Americans increasingly want to be famous, but they also believe they will be famous, more so than any previous generation. A Harris poll conducted in 2000 found that 44 percent of those between the ages of 18 and 24 believed it was at least somewhat likely that they would be famous for a short period. Those in their late twenties were even more optimistic: Six in ten expected that they would be well-known, if only briefly, sometime in their lives. The rosy predictions of our destiny, however, contain within them the darker conviction that a life led outside the spotlight would be without value. "People want the kind of attention that celebrities receive more than anything else," says Niedzviecki. "People want the recognition, the validation, the sense of having a place in the culture [because] we no longer know where we belong, what we're about or what we should be about."

21   Without any meaningful standard by which to measure our worth, we turn to the public eye for affirmation. "It's really the sense that Hey, I exist in this world, and that is important. That I matter," Niedzviecki says. Our "normal" lives therefore seem impoverished and less significant compared with the media world, which increasingly represents all that is grand and worthwhile, and therefore more "real."

22   No wonder then that 16-year-old Rachel, Britney Jo's fellow aspirant to fame on iWannaBeFamous.com, rambles in desperation, "I figured out that I am tired of just dreaming about doing something, I am sick of looking for a "regular" job... I feel life slipping by, and that 'something is missing' feeling begins to dominate me all day and night, I can't even watch the Academy Awards ceremony without crying...that is how I know...that is me....I have to be...in the movies!!!"

23   The evolution of the Internet has both mirrored and shaped the intense focus on self that is the hallmark of the post-boomer generation. "If you aren't posting, you don't exist. People say, 'I post, therefore I am,'" Rishad Tobaccowala, CEO of Denuo, a new media consultancy, told *Wired*, inadvertently capturing the essence of Web 2.0, which is driven by our hunger for self-expression. Blogs, amateur videos, personal profiles, even interactive features such as Amazon.com's reviews offer ways to satisfy our need to be in the public eye.

24   But the virtual persona we project online is a carefully edited version of ourselves, as "authentic" as a character on reality TV. People on reality TV "are ultra–self-aware versions of the ordinary, über-facsimiles of themselves in the same way that online personals are recreations of self constantly tweaked for maximum response and effect," writes Niedzviecki in his book.

25   Self-expression glides effortlessly into self-promotion as we shape our online selves—be it on a MySpace profile, LiveJournal blog or a YouTube video—to insure the greatest attention. Nothing beats good old-fashioned publicity even in the brave new world of digital media. So it should come as no shock that the oh-so-authentic LonelyGirl15 should turn out to be a PR stunt or that the most popular person on MySpace is the mostly naked Tila Tequila, the proud purveyor of "skank pop" who can boast of 1,626,097 friends, a clothing line, a record deal and making the cover of *Maxim UK* and *Stuff* magazines. YouTube has become the virtual equivalent of Los Angeles, the destination de rigueur for millions of celebrity aspirants, all hoping they will be the next Amanda Congdon, the videoblogger now with a gig on ABCNews.com, or the Spiridellis brothers, who landed venture capital funding because of their wildly popular video "This Land."

26   Beginning with the dot-com boom in the 1990s through to its present iteration as Web 2.0, the cultural power of the Internet has been fueled by the modern-day Cinderella fantasy of "making it." With their obsessive focus on A-list bloggers, upstart twentysomething CEOs and an assortment of weirdos and creeps, the media continually reframe the Internet as yet another shot at the glittering prize of celebrity. "We see the same slow channeling of the idea that your main goal in life is to reach as many people as possible all over the world with your product. And your product is you," says Niedzviecki. "As long as that's true, it's very hard to see how the Internet is going to change that." As long as more democratic media merely signify a greater democracy of fame—e.g., look how that indie musician landed a contract with that major label—we will remain enslaved by the same narrative of success that sustains corporate America.

27   In our eagerness to embrace the Web as a panacea for various political ills, progressives often forget that the Internet is merely a medium like any other, and the social impact of its various features—interactivity, real-time publishing, easy access, cheap mass distribution—will be determined by the people who use them. There is no doubt that these technologies have facilitated greater activism, and new forms of it, both on- and offline. But we confuse the Web's promise of increased visibility with real change. Political actions often enter the ether of the media world only to be incorporated into narratives of individual achievement. And the more successful among us end up as bold-faced names, leached dry of the ideas and values they represent—yet another face in the cluttered landscape of celebrity, with fortunes that follow the usual trajectory of media attention: First you're hot, and then you're not.

28   "It's all about you. Me. And all the various forms of the First Person Singular," writes cranky media veteran Brian Williams in his contribution to *Time*'s year-end package. "Americans have decided the most important person in their lives is . . . them, and our culture is now built upon that idea." So, have we turned into a nation of egoists, uninterested in anything that falls outside our narrow frame of self-reference?

29   As Jean Twenge points out, individualism doesn't necessarily preclude a social conscience or desire to do good. "But [Generation Me] articulates it as 'I want to make a difference,'" she says. "The outcome is still good, but it does put the self in the center." Stephen Duncombe, on the other hand, author of the new book *Dream: Re-imagining Progressive Politics in an Age of Fantasy*, argues that rather than dismiss our yearning for individual recognition, progressives need to create real-world alternatives that offer such validation. For example, in place of vast anonymous rallies that aim to declare strength in numbers, he suggests that liberal activism should be built around small groups. "The size of these groups is critical. They are intimate affairs, small enough for each participant to have an active role in shaping the group's direction and voice," he writes. "In these 'affinity groups,' as they are called, every person is recognized: in short, they exist."

30   Such efforts, however, would have to contend with GenMe's aversion to collective action. "The baby boomers were self-focused in a different way. Whether it was self-examination like EST or social protest, they did everything in groups. This new generation is allergic to groups," Twenge says. And as Duncombe admits, activism is a tough sell for a nation weaned on the I-driven fantasy of celebrity that serves as "an escape from democracy with its attendant demands for responsibility and participation."

31   There is a happier alternative. If these corporate technologies of self-promotion work as well as promised, they may finally render fame meaningless. If everyone is onstage, there will be no one left in the audience. And maybe then we rock stars can finally turn our attention to life down here on earth. Or it may be life on earth that finally jolts us out of our admiring reverie in the mirrored hall of fame. We forget that this growing self-involvement is a luxury afforded to a generation that has not experienced a wide-scale war or economic depression. If and when the good times come to an end, so may our obsession with fame. "There are a lot of things on the horizon that could shake us out of the way we are now. And some of them are pretty ugly," Niedzviecki says. "You won't be able to say that my MySpace page is more important than my real life. ... When you're a corpse, it doesn't matter how many virtual friends you have." Think global war, widespread unemployment, climate change. But then again, how cool would it be to vlog your life in the new Ice Age—kind of like starring in your very own *Day After Tomorrow*. LOL. ◆

CRITICAL THINKING ─────────────────────

1. Who is Narcissus? How does his story connect to the points Chaudry makes in her essay? Explain.
2. Think of some examples of when "it is more important to be seen than to be talented."
3. What is your personal definition of the American Dream? Does it include becoming famous? Explain.
4. As a child, were you told "You're special; love yourself; follow your dreams; you can be anything you want to be"? Explain the outcome of being given (or not being given) this message.
5. Do you agree or disagree with this statement: "Life led outside the spotlight would be without value"? Explain your answer.
6. What is Chaudry's tone in this essay? How does she feel about social networking sites and the people who use them?
7. How does Chaudry define "Generation Me?" Are you a member of this generation? What is she saying about social trends for this generation? Explain.

CRITICAL WRITING

1. *Personal Narrative:* Do you want to be rich and famous? Discuss where you see yourself 5 years, 10 years, and 20 years from now.
2. *Research Writing:* In the distant past, the medium to becoming well-known "was usually literature, theater, or public monuments." Research a famous person from history (before 1900) and show how his or her popularity grew and which media were used to expand this popularity.
3. *Personal Narrative:* Take a standard Narcissism Personality Inventory test which can be located online at various sites, such as www.4degreez.com. Evaluate your score. Are you narcissistic? What does it mean to be narcissistic? How does your score compare to your online social activities? What are the advantages and disadvantages of being narcissistic?

GROUP PROJECTS

1. In this article, Chaudry states, "So we upload our wackiest videos to YouTube, blog every sordid detail of our personal lives so as to insure at least fifty inbound links, add 200 new 'friends' a day to our MySpace page with the help of FriendFlood.com, all the time hoping that one day all our efforts at self-promotion will merit—at the very least—our very own Wikipedia entry." Have each member of your group discuss how many videos you have collectively placed on YouTube, how many times you have blogged personal details, how many online friends you have, if you have a Wikipedia entry, and your other online exploits.

2. As a group, discuss some of the challenges and benefits a "me first" mentality can have on a generation. If social networking, reality television, blogging, and vlogging are defining elements of your generation, how might these trends be viewed historically in the future? What will social critics identify as unique and transformational about this phenomenon? After discussing the issue as a group, write a short essay exploring the impact the media Chaudry describes in this essay will have on society and history.

Virtual Friendship and the New Narcissism
*Christine Rosen**

How is a Facebook page like a self-portrait? What do they reveal about subjects and how they view themselves? More than simply connecting us with each other, social networking sites allow us to present a persona to the world—publicly sharing who we know, what we think, what we do, and even what we own. In this slightly abridged essay, sociologist and writer Christine Rosen wonders whether social networking sites raise the bar on our level of self-absorption and desire to be famous.

1 For centuries, the rich and the powerful documented their existence and their status through painted portraits. A marker of wealth and a bid for immortality, portraits offer intriguing hints about the daily life of their subjects—professions, ambitions, attitudes, and, most importantly, social standing. Such portraits, as German art historian Hans Belting has argued, can be understood as "painted anthropology," with much to teach us, both intentionally and unintentionally, about the culture in which they were created.

2 Self-portraits can be especially instructive. By showing the artist both as he sees his true self and as he wishes to be seen, self-portraits can at once expose and obscure, clarify and distort. They offer opportunities for both self-expression and self-seeking. They can display egotism and modesty, self-aggrandizement and self-mockery.

* Christine Rosen, *The New Altantis,* Summer 2007

3   Today, our self-portraits are democratic and digital; they are crafted from pixels rather than paints. On social networking websites like MySpace and Facebook, our modern self-portraits feature background music, carefully manipulated photographs, stream-of-consciousness musings, and lists of our hobbies and friends. They are interactive, inviting viewers not merely to look at, but also to respond to, the life portrayed online. We create them to find friendship, love, and that ambiguous modern thing called *connection*. Like painters constantly retouching their work, we alter, update, and tweak our online self-portraits; but as digital objects they are far more ephemeral than oil on canvas. Vital statistics, glimpses of bare flesh, lists of favorite bands and favorite poems all clamor for our attention—and it is the timeless human desire for attention that emerges as the dominant theme of these vast virtual galleries.

> *Today, our self-portraits are democratic and digital; they are crafted from pixels rather than paints. . . . Like painters constantly retouching their work, we alter, update, and tweak our online self-portraits; but as digital objects they are far more ephemeral than oil on canvas.*

4   Although social networking sites are in their infancy, we are seeing their impact culturally: in language (where *to friend* is now a verb), in politics (where it is de rigueur for presidential aspirants to catalogue their virtues on MySpace), and on college campuses (where not using Facebook can be a social handicap). But we are only beginning to come to grips with the consequences of our use of these sites: for friendship, and for our notions of privacy, authenticity, community, and identity.

Making Connections

5   The earliest online social networks were arguably the Bulletin Board Systems of the 1980s that let users post public messages, send and receive private messages, play games, and exchange software. Some of those BBS's, like The WELL (Whole Earth 'Lectronic Link) that technologist Larry Brilliant and futurist Stewart Brand started in 1985, made the transition to the World Wide Web in the mid-1990s. (Now owned by Salon.com, The WELL boasts that it was "the primordial ooze where the online community movement was born.") Other websites for community and connection emerged in the 1990s, including Classmates.com (1995), where users register by high school and year of graduation; Company of Friends, a business-oriented site founded in 1997; and Epinions, founded in 1999 to allow users to give their opinions about various consumer products.

6   A new generation of social networking websites appeared in 2002 with the launch of Friendster, whose founder, Jonathan Abrams, admitted that his main motivation for creating the site was to meet attractive women. Unlike previous online communities, which brought together anonymous strangers with shared interests, Friendster uses a model of social networking known as the "Circle of Friends" (developed by British computer scientist Jonathan Bishop), in which users invite friends and acquaintances—that is, people they already know and like—to join their network.

7   Friendster was an immediate success, with millions of registered users by mid-2003. But technological glitches and poor management at the company allowed a new social networking site, MySpace, launched in 2003, quickly to surpass it.

Originally started by musicians, MySpace has become a major venue for sharing music as well as videos and photos. It is now the behemoth of online social networking, with over 100 million registered users. Connection has become big business: In 2005, Rupert Murdoch's News Corporation bought MySpace for $580 million.

8 Besides MySpace and Friendster, the best-known social networking site is Facebook, launched in 2004. Originally restricted to college students, Facebook—which takes its name from the small photo albums that colleges once gave to incoming freshmen and faculty to help them cope with meeting so many new people—soon extended membership to high schoolers and is now open to anyone. Still, it is most popular among college students and recent college graduates, many of whom use the site as their primary method of communicating with one another. Millions of college students check their Facebook pages several times every day and spend hours sending and receiving messages, making appointments, getting updates on their friends' activities, and learning about people they might recently have met or heard about.

9 There are dozens of other social networking sites, including Orkut, Bebo, and Yahoo 360°. Microsoft recently announced its own plans for a social networking site called Wallop; the company boasts that the site will offer "an entirely new way for consumers to express their individuality online." (It is noteworthy that Microsoft refers to social networkers as "consumers" rather than merely "users" or, say, "people.") Niche social networking sites are also flourishing: there are sites offering forums and fellowship for photographers, music lovers, and sports fans. There are professional networking sites, such as LinkedIn, that keep people connected with present and former colleagues and other business acquaintants.

10 Despite the increasingly diverse range of social networking sites, the most popular sites share certain features. On MySpace and Facebook, for example, the process of setting up one's online identity is relatively simple: Provide your name, address, e-mail address, and a few other pieces of information, and you're up and running and ready to create your online persona. MySpace includes a section, "About Me," where you can post your name, age, where you live, and other personal details such as your zodiac sign, religion, sexual orientation, and relationship status. There is also a "Who I'd Like to Meet" section, which on most MySpace profiles is filled with images of celebrities. Users can also list their favorite music, movies, and television shows, as well as their personal heroes; MySpace users can also blog on their pages. A user "friends" people—that is, invites them by e-mail to appear on the user's "Friend Space," where they are listed, linked, and ranked. Below the Friends space is a Comments section where friends can post notes. MySpace allows users to personalize their pages by uploading images and music and videos; indeed, one of the defining features of most MySpace pages is the ubiquity of visual and audio clutter. With silly, hyper flashing graphics in neon colors and clip-art style images of kittens and cartoons, MySpace pages often resemble an overdecorated high school yearbook.

11 By contrast, Facebook limits what its users can do to their profiles. Besides general personal information, Facebook users have a "Wall" where people can leave them brief notes, as well as a Messages feature that functions like an in-house Facebook e-mail account. You list your friends on Facebook as well, but in general, unlike MySpace friends, which are often complete strangers (or spammers), Facebook friends tend to be part of one's offline social circle. (This might change, however, now that Facebook has opened its site to anyone rather than

restricting it to college and high school students.) Facebook (and MySpace) allow users to form groups based on mutual interests. Facebook users can also send "pokes" to friends; these little digital nudges are meant to let someone know you are thinking about him or her. But they can also be interpreted as not-so-subtle come-ons; one Facebook group with over 200,000 members is called "Enough with the Poking, Let's Just Have Sex."

Won't You Be My Digital Neighbor?

12 According to a survey recently conducted by the Pew Internet and American Life Project, more than half of all Americans between the ages of twelve and seventeen use some online social networking site. Indeed, media coverage of social networking sites usually describes them as vast teenage playgrounds—or wastelands, depending on one's perspective. Central to this narrative is a nearly unbridgeable generational divide, with tech-savvy youngsters redefining friendship while their doddering elders look on with bafflement and increasing anxiety. This seems anecdotally correct; I can't count how many times I have mentioned social networking websites to someone over the age of forty and received the reply, "Oh yes, I've heard about that MyFace! All the kids are doing that these days. Very interesting!"

13 Numerous articles have chronicled adults' attempts to navigate the world of social networking, such as the recent *New York Times* essay in which columnist Michelle Slatalla described the incredible embarrassment she caused her teenage daughter when she joined Facebook: "everyone in the whole world thinks its super creepy when adults have facebooks," her daughter instant-messaged her. "unfriend paige right now. im serious. . . . i will be soo mad if you dont unfriend paige right now actually." In fact, social networking sites are not only for the young. More than half of the visitors to MySpace claim to be over the age of 35. And now that the first generation of college Facebook users have graduated, and the site is open to all, more than half of Facebook users are no longer students. What's more, the proliferation of niche social networking sites, including those aimed at adults, suggests that it is not only teenagers who will nurture relationships in virtual space for the foreseeable future.

The New Taxonomy of Friendship

14 There is a Spanish proverb that warns, "Life without a friend is death without a witness." In the world of online social networking, the warning might be simpler: "Life without hundreds of online 'friends' is virtual death." On these sites, friendship is the stated raison d'être. "A place for friends," is the slogan of MySpace. Facebook is a "social utility that connects people with friends." Orkut describes itself as "an online community that connects people through a network of trusted friends." Friendster's name speaks for itself.

15 But "friendship" in these virtual spaces is thoroughly different from real-world friendship. In its traditional sense, friendship is a relationship which, broadly speaking, involves the sharing of mutual interests, reciprocity, trust, and the revelation of intimate details over time and within specific social (and cultural) contexts. Because friendship depends on mutual revelations that are concealed from the rest of the

world, it can only flourish within the boundaries of privacy; the idea of public friendship is an oxymoron.

16   The hypertext link called "friendship" on social networking sites is very different: public, fluid, and promiscuous, yet oddly bureaucratized. Friendship on these sites focuses a great deal on collecting, managing, and ranking the people you know. Everything about MySpace, for example, is designed to encourage users to gather as many friends as possible, as though friendship were philately. If you are so unfortunate as to have but one MySpace friend, for example, your page reads: "You have 1 friends," along with a stretch of sad empty space where dozens of thumbnail photos of your acquaintances should appear.

17   The structure of social networking sites also encourages the bureaucratization of friendship. Each site has its own terminology, but among the words that users employ most often is "managing." The Pew survey mentioned earlier found that "teens say social networking sites help them manage their friendships." There is something Orwellian about the management-speak on social networking sites: "Change My Top Friends," "View All of My Friends" and, for those times when our inner Stalins sense the need for a virtual purge, "Edit Friends." With a few mouse clicks one can elevate or downgrade (or entirely eliminate) a relationship.

18   To be sure, we all rank our friends, albeit in unspoken and intuitive ways. One friend might be a good companion for outings to movies or concerts; another might be someone with whom you socialize in professional settings; another might be the kind of person for whom you would drop everything if he needed help. But social networking sites allow us to rank our friends publicly. And not only can we publicize our own preferences in people, but we can also peruse the favorites among our other acquaintances. We can learn all about the friends of our friends—often without having ever met them in person.

Status-Seekers

19   Of course, it would be foolish to suggest that people are incapable of making distinctions between social networking "friends" and friends they see in the flesh. The use of the word "friend" on social networking sites is a dilution and a debasement, and surely no one with hundreds of MySpace or Facebook "friends" is so confused as to believe those are all real friendships. The impulse to collect as many "friends" as possible on a MySpace page is not an expression of the human need for companionship, but of a different need no less profound and pressing: the need for status. Unlike the painted portraits that members of the middle class in a bygone era would commission to signal their elite status once they rose in society, social networking websites allow us to create status—not merely to commemorate the achievement of it. There is a reason that most of the MySpace profiles of famous people are fakes, often created by fans: Celebrities don't need legions of MySpace friends to prove their importance. It's the rest of the population, seeking a form of parochial celebrity, that does.

20   But status-seeking has an ever-present partner: anxiety. Unlike a portrait, which, once finished and framed, hung tamely on the wall signaling one's status, maintaining status on MySpace or Facebook requires constant vigilance. As one 24-year-old

wrote in a *New York Times* essay, "I am obsessed with testimonials and solicit them incessantly. They are the ultimate social currency, public declarations of the intimacy status of a relationship. . . . Every profile is a carefully planned media campaign."

21   The sites themselves were designed to encourage this. Describing the work of B. J. Fogg of Stanford University, who studies "persuasion strategies" used by social networking sites to increase participation, *The New Scientist* noted, "The secret is to tie the acquisition of friends, compliments and status—spoils that humans will work hard for—to activities that enhance the site." As Fogg told the magazine, "You offer someone a context for gaining status, and they are going to work for that status." Network theorist Albert-László Barabási notes that online connection follows the rule of "preferential attachment"—that is, "when choosing between two pages, one with twice as many links as the other, about twice as many people link to the more connected page." As a result, "while our individual choices are highly unpredictable, as a group we follow strict patterns." Our lemming-like pursuit of online status via the collection of hundreds of "friends" clearly follows this rule.

22   What, in the end, does this pursuit of virtual status mean for community and friendship? Writing in the 1980s in *Habits of the Heart*, sociologist Robert Bellah and his colleagues documented the movement away from close-knit, traditional communities to "lifestyle enclaves," which were defined largely by "leisure and consumption." Perhaps today we have moved beyond lifestyle enclaves and into "personality enclaves" or "identity enclaves"—discrete virtual places in which we can be different (and sometimes contradictory) people, with different groups of like-minded, though ever-shifting, friends.

Beyond Networking

23   This past spring, Len Harmon, the director of the Fischer Policy and Cultural Institute at Nichols College in Dudley, Massachusetts, offered a new course about social networking. Nichols is a small school whose students come largely from Connecticut and Massachusetts; many of them are the first members of their families to attend college. "I noticed a lot of issues involved with social networking sites," Harmon told me when I asked him why he created the class. How have these sites been useful to Nichols students? "It has relieved some of the stress of transitions for them," he said. "When abrupt departures occur—their family moves or they have to leave friends behind—they can cope by keeping in touch more easily."

24   So perhaps we should praise social networking websites for streamlining friendship the way e-mail streamlined correspondence. In the nineteenth century, Emerson observed that "friendship requires more time than poor busy men can usually command." Now, technology has given us the freedom to tap into our network of friends when it is convenient for us. "It's a way of maintaining a friendship without having to make any effort whatsoever," as a recent graduate of Harvard explained to the *New Yorker*. And that ease admittedly makes it possible to stay in contact with a wider circle of offline acquaintances than might have been possible in the era before Facebook. Friends you haven't heard from in years, old buddies from elementary school, people you might have (should have?) fallen out of touch with—it is now easier than ever to reconnect to those people.

25   But what kind of connections are these? In his excellent book *Friendship: An Exposé*, Joseph Epstein praises the telephone and e-mail as technologies that have greatly facilitated friendship. He writes, "Proust once said he didn't much care for the analogy of a book to a friend. He thought a book was better than a friend, because you could shut it—and be shut of it—when you wished, which one can't always do with a friend." With e-mail and caller ID, Epstein enthuses, you can. But social networking sites (which Epstein says "speak to the vast loneliness in the world") have a different effect: they discourage "being shut of" people. On the contrary, they encourage users to check in frequently, "poke" friends, and post comments on others' pages. They favor interaction of greater quantity but less quality.

26   This constant connectivity concerns Len Harmon. "There is a sense of, 'if I'm not online or constantly texting or posting, then I'm missing something,'" he said of his students. "This is where I find the generational impact the greatest—not the use of the technology, but the overuse of the technology." It is unclear how the regular use of these sites will affect behavior over the long run—especially the behavior of children and young adults who are growing up with these tools. Almost no research has explored how virtual socializing affects children's development. What does a child weaned on Club Penguin learn about social interaction? How is an adolescent who spends her evenings managing her MySpace page different from a teenager who spends her night gossiping on the telephone to friends? Given that "people want to live their lives online," as the founder of one social networking site recently told *Fast Company* magazine, and they are beginning to do so at ever-younger ages, these questions are worth exploring.

27   The few studies that have emerged do not inspire confidence. Researcher Rob Nyland at Brigham Young University recently surveyed 184 users of social networking sites and found that heavy users "feel less socially involved with the community around them." He also found that "as individuals use social networking more for entertainment, their level of social involvement decreases." Another recent study conducted by communications professor Qingwen Dong and colleagues at the University of the Pacific found that "those who engaged in romantic communication over MySpace tend to have low levels of both emotional intelligence and self-esteem."

28   The implications of the narcissistic and exhibitionistic tendencies of social networkers also cry out for further consideration. There are opportunity costs when we spend so much time carefully grooming ourselves online. Given how much time we already devote to entertaining ourselves with technology, it is at least worth asking if the time we spend on social networking sites is well spent. In investing so much energy into improving how we present ourselves online, are we missing chances to genuinely improve ourselves?

29   We should also take note of the trend toward giving up face-to-face for virtual contact—and, in some cases, a preference for the latter. Today, many of our cultural, social, and political interactions take place through eminently convenient technological surrogates—Why go to the bank if you can use the ATM? Why browse in a bookstore when you can simply peruse the personalized selections Amazon.com has made for you? In the same vein, social networking sites are often

convenient surrogates for offline friendship and community. In this context it is worth considering an observation that Stanley Milgram made in 1974, regarding his experiments with obedience: "The social psychology of this century reveals a major lesson," he wrote. "Often it is not so much the kind of person a man is as the kind of situation in which he finds himself that determines how he will act." To an increasing degree, we find and form our friendships and communities in the virtual world as well as the real world. These virtual networks greatly expand our opportunities to meet others, but they might also result in our valuing less the capacity for genuine connection. As the young woman writing in the *Times* admitted, "I consistently trade actual human contact for the more reliable high of smiles on MySpace, winks on Match.com, and pokes on Facebook." That she finds these online relationships more reliable is telling: it shows a desire to avoid the vulnerability and uncertainty that true friendship entails. Real intimacy requires risk—the risk of disapproval, of heartache, of being thought a fool. Social networking websites may make relationships more reliable, but whether those relationships can be humanly satisfying remains to be seen. ◆

CRITICAL THINKING

1. This essay makes the bold statement: "Public friendship is an oxymoron." From your point of view, discuss what the meaning of friendship is and if social networking sites are using the term "friend" properly.
2. Rosen compares online networking pages to "self-portraits." Explore this concept in more depth. In what ways is this true? If you have a personal page, discuss what that page says about you and in what ways is it indeed a "self-portrait." How are painted portraits and Web sites similar? How are they different?
3. What does Rosen mean when she uses the term "Orwellian" and the phrase "our inner Stalins" when referring to social networking sites? To what or whom is she referring, and how do these references connect to her point?
4. What does Rosen think of online networking sites? Identify areas in her essay in which she reveals her viewpoint.
5. The author comments, "Tech-savvy youngsters [are] redefining friendship while their doddering elders look on with bafflement and increasing anxiety." Do you find this to be true? How do your older family members view social networking sites? Do any of them have MySpace or Facebook sites? Why or why not?

CRITICAL WRITING

1. *Expository Writing:* Write an essay exploring the consequences of social networking sites on the future of friendship and community.
2. *Analytical Writing:* This article gives the evolution of social networking sites. Outline this evolution, showing how these sites have evolved from "the primordial ooze" of the 1980s to the newest site being planned by Microsoft.

GROUP PROJECTS

1. Each member of your group should track all of their online correspondence—received and sent—for a period of one week. This should include e-mail, IM, text messaging, and posting on social networking sites. Keep track of how much time you spend online. Discuss your personal results with the group. Discuss as a group how the Internet both enhances and complicates life, and whether it is indeed changing our personal relationships with each other and our personal view of ourselves, for better or for worse.

2. Rosen notes that social networking sites promote self-centeredness, thereby reducing our ability to cope with emotions, and that they cheapen what it means to be a friend. Interview at least 10 people of different age groups regarding how they use social networking sites. Create simple questions, but make them broad enough to allow for the expression of detailed viewpoints and options. Discuss the interviews as a group, and write a short essay evaluating the role of social networking on the lives of people today. Based on your surveys, can you predict the role social networking will have in our lives in the next decade?

Crafting Your Image for Your 1,000 Friends on Facebook

*Stuart Wolpert**

Identities can be changed, and are being changed, at a rapid rate on the Internet. Users of Facebook and MySpace can become anyone they want to be at the click of a mouse. But are there downfalls to showing the cyberworld a "you" that isn't necessarily "you"? Or can people finally become who they really want to be and fulfill their own destinies? In this article, author Stuart Wolpert reports on the growing trend of image adjusting and the rise of the public profile.

1 Students are creating idealized versions of themselves on social networking websites—Facebook and MySpace are the most popular—and using these sites to explore their emerging identities, UCLA psychologists report. Parents often understand very little about this phenomenon, they say.

2 "People can use these sites to explore who they are by posting particular images, pictures or text," said UCLA psychology graduate student Adriana Manago, a researcher with the Children's Digital Media Center, Los Angeles (CDMCLA), and lead author of a study that appears in a special November–December issue of the *Journal of Applied Developmental Psychology* devoted to the developmental implications of online social networking. "You can manifest your ideal self. You can manifest who you want to be and then try to grow into that.

* Stuart Wolpert, *UCLA Newsroom*, November 18, 2008

3   "We're always engaging in self-presentation; we're always trying to put our best foot forward," Manago added. "Social networking sites take this to a whole new level. You can change what you look like, you

These websites intensify the ability to present yourself in a positive light and explore different aspects of your personality and how you present yourself.

can Photoshop your face, you can select only the pictures that show you in a perfect lighting. These websites intensify the ability to present yourself in a positive light and explore different aspects of your personality and how you present yourself. You can try on different things, possible identities, and explore in a way that is common for emerging adulthood. It becomes psychologically real. People put up something that they would like to become—not completely different from who they are but maybe a little different—and the more it gets reflected off of others, the more it may be integrated into their sense of self as they share words and photos with so many people."

4   "People are living life online," said Manago's co-author Patricia Greenfield, a UCLA distinguished professor of psychology, director of the CDMCLA and co-editor of the journal's special issue. "Social networking sites are a tool for self-development."

5   The websites allow users to open free accounts and to communicate with other users, who number in the tens of millions on Facebook and MySpace. Participants can select "friends" and share photos, videos and information about themselves—such as whether they are currently in a relationship—with these friends. Many college students have 1,000 or more friends on Facebook or MySpace. Identity, romantic relations and sexuality all get played out on these social networking sites, the researchers said.

6   "All of these things are what teenagers always do," Greenfield said, "but the social networking sites give them much more power to do it in a more extreme way. In the arena of identity formation, this makes people more individualistic and more narcissistic; people sculpt themselves with their profiles. In the arena of peer relations, I worry that the meaning of 'friends' has been so altered that real friends are not going to be recognized as such. How many of your 1,000 'friends' do you see in person? How many are just distant acquaintances? How many have you never met?"

7   "Instead of connecting with friends with whom you have close ties for the sake of the exchange itself, people interact with their 'friends' as a performance, as if on a stage before an audience of people on the network," Manago said.

8   "These social networking sites have a virtual audience, and people perform in front of their audience," said Michael Graham, a former UCLA undergraduate psychology student who worked on this study with Greenfield and Manago for his honors thesis. "You're a little detached from them. It's an opportunity to try different things out and see what kind of comments you get.

9   "Sometimes people put forth things they want to become, and sometimes people put forth things that they're not sure about how other people will respond," he added. "They feel comfortable doing that. If they put something forward that gets rave reviews from people, it can alter the way they view their own identity. Through this experimentation, people can get surprised by how the molding goes."

10   Is this exploration of identity through these websites psychologically healthy?

11 "Every medium has its strengths and weaknesses, its psychological costs and benefits," said Greenfield, an expert in developmental psychology and media effects. "Costs may be the devaluing of real friendships and the reduction of face-to-face interaction. There are more relationships, but also more superficial relationships. Empathy and other human qualities may get reduced because of less face-to-face contact. On the other hand, new college students can make contact with their future roommates and easily stay in touch with high school friends, easing the social transition to college, or from one setting to another."

12 "I hate to be an older person decrying the relationships that young people form and their communication tools, but I do wonder about them," said Kaveri Subrahmanyam, associate director of the CDMCLA, professor of psychology at California State University, Los Angeles, and senior editor of the special journal issue. "Having 1,000 friends seems to be like collecting accessories."

13 Middle school is too young to be using Facebook or MySpace, Subrahmanyam believes, but by ninth grade, she considers the websites to be appropriate. She recommends that parents speak with their children, starting at about age 10, concerning what they do online and with whom they are interacting. Subrahmanyam notes that some of parents' greatest online fears—that their children will be harassed by predators or receive other unwanted or inappropriate Internet contact—have been decreasing, although parents may not know this.

14 In her own study in the journal, Subrahmanyam and colleagues Stephanie Reich of the University of California, Irvine, Natalia Waechter of the Austrian Institute for Youth Research and Guadalupe Espinoza, a UCLA psychology graduate student, report that, for the most part, college students are interacting with "people they see in their offline, or physical, lives."

15 "Young people are not going online to interact with strangers or for purposes removed from their offline lives," she said. "Mostly they seem to be using these social networking sites to extend and strengthen their offline concerns and relationships."

16 Research shows that adolescents who have discussed online safety with their parents and teachers are less likely to have a meeting with anyone they met online, Subrahmanyam noted.

17 "The best thing that parents can do is to have a rough idea of what their teens do online and have discussions with them about being safe online," she said.

18 What does having 1,000 friends do to your relationships with your true friends?

19 "Relationships now may be more fleeting and more distant," Manago said. "People are relating to others trying to promote themselves and seeing how you compare with them. We found a lot of social comparisons, and people are comparing themselves against these idealized self-presentations.

20 "Women feel pressure to look beautiful and sexy, yet innocent, which can hurt their self-esteem" she said. "Now you are part of the media; your MySpace profile page is coming up next to Victoria's Secret models. It can be discouraging to feel like you cannot live up to the flawless images you see."

21 "You're relating to people you don't really have a relationship with," Greenfield said. "People have a lot of diffuse, weak ties that are used for informational purposes; it's not friendship. You may never see them. For a large number of people, these are relationships with strangers. When you have this many people in your

network, it becomes a performance for an audience. You are promoting yourself. The line between the commercial and the self is blurring.

22   "The personal becomes public, which devalues close relationships when you display so much for everyone to see," Greenfield added.

23   "Who we are is reflected by the people we associate with," Manago said. "If I can show that all these people like me, it may promote the idea that I am popular or that I associate with certain desirable cliques."

24   Not much remains private.

25   "You can be at a party or any public place, and someone can take a picture of you that appears on Facebook the next day," Manago said.

26   However, Graham said, the social networking sites can also strengthen relationships. He also said many people have "second-tier friends that they may have met once but would not have stayed in touch with if not for the MySpace or Facebook networks."

27   The study by Manago, Greenfield and Graham, along with co-author Goldie Salimkhan, a former UCLA psychology undergraduate major, was based on small focus groups with a total of 11 women and 12 men, all UCLA students who use MySpace frequently.

28   One male student in the study said of MySpace, "It's just a way to promote yourself to society and show everyone, 'I'm moving up in the world, I've grown. I've changed a lot since high school.'"

29   How honestly do people present themselves on these sites?

30   Another male student in a focus group said, "One of my friends from high school, I saw her profile and I was like, 'Whoa, she's changed so much from high school,' and I see her this summer and I'm like, 'No, she's exactly the same!' Her MySpace is just a whole other level."

31   "Just at the age where peers are so important, that's where social networking—which is all about peers—is very attractive," Greenfield said. "Just at the age where you're exploring identity and developing an identity, that's where this powerful tool for exploring identity is very appealing. These sites are perfectly suited for the expanded identity exploration characteristic of emerging adults."

32   Another study in the special issue of the journal, conducted by Larry Rosen of California State University, Dominguez Hills, and colleagues Nancy Cheever and Mark Carrier, shows that parents have high estimates of the dangers of social networking but very low rates of monitoring and of setting limits on their children.

33   Rosen and his colleagues found that a parenting style that is marked by rational discussion, monitoring of children, setting limits and giving reasons for the limits is associated with less risky online behavior by children.

34   Greenfield advises parents of adolescents not to give their child a computer with Internet access in his or her bedroom.

35   "But even with a computer in a family room, complete monitoring is impossible," she said. "Children have so much independence that parents have to instill a compass inside them. Seeing what they are doing on the computer and discussing it with them is a good way to instill that compass."

36   In an additional study in the journal that highlights the beneficial nature of Facebook "friends," Charles Steinfield, Nicole B. Ellison and Cliff Lampe of Michigan State University examine the relationship between Facebook use and

social capital, a concept that describes the benefits one receives from one's social relationships. They focus on "bridging social capital," which refers to the benefits of a large, heterogeneous network—precisely the kind of network these sites can support.

37   Their article argues that there is a direct connection between students' social capital and their use of Facebook, and using data over a two-year period, they found that Facebook use appears to precede students' gains in bridging social capital.

38   They also found that Facebook use appears to be particularly beneficial for students with lower self-esteem, as it helps them overcome the barriers they would otherwise face in building a large network that can provide access to information and opportunity.

39   "Young people do seem to be aware of the differences between their close friends and casual acquaintances on Facebook," Steinfield said. "Our data suggest that students are not substituting their online friends for their offline friends via Facebook; they appear to be using the service to extend and keep up with their network." ◆

CRITICAL THINKING

1. Is your own online identity an "idealized version" of yourself? Explain. If you do not have an online identity, explain why not.
2. According to Wolpert, when putting an image online of what someone hopes to become, that person may achieve a self-fulfilling prophecy. Explain how this could happen.
3. Do you agree that people who have an online identity are performing, "as if on a stage before an audience of people on the network"? Give examples of how someone could be "performing" instead of just relaying information.
4. Are online profiles this generation's answer to voyeurism and exhibitionism?

CRITICAL WRITING

1. *Expository Writing:* Define "friend." Are online and offline friends the same entities, or do you view them separately? Some questions to consider: if you met one of your online friends offline, and you discovered that their "identity" was quite skewed from what you had been led to believe, would you still view this person as a friend? If an online friend suddenly disappeared, would you grieve? In other words, write an essay defining what makes someone a "friend." Use examples of online and offline friends.
2. *Persuasive Writing:* Take a side. Are online identities beneficial or detrimental to overall psychological health? Write an essay in which you persuade someone to have an online identity or else try to persuade someone to give up the process.

GROUP PROJECTS

1. With your group, create a fictional identity, either on MySpace or Facebook. Be as creative as you want. Throughout the semester, check on your "character" and see how many people ask to become friends with you.

Carry on these friendships. Report back at the end of the semester with why you think your person was popular or ignored.

2. As a group, find three Facebook or MySpace users whom everyone in the group knows personally or has had offline contact with. Compare the offline persona of each person to his or her online identity. Is there a discrepancy in image? Explain the differences if any and explain how their online identities exemplify their offline identities.

VIEWPOINTS

▶ **The Case for Reality TV**
Michael Hirschorn*

▶ **Reality TV: Should We Really Watch?**
Elizabeth Larkin

▶ **The Strange Life and Impending Death of Jade Goody**
Meredith Blake

While reality television programs are fodder for critics, there is no denying their popularity. Far from a passing fad, there are more reality television programs than ever before. Several programs have emerged as constant hits, including *Survivor, Project Runway, Big Brother*, and *American Idol*. Others track the daily lives of people known only for having money, as in the case of *The Real Housewives* series on Bravo. First, Michael Hirschorn notes that the critics can tut-tut all they want, but reality shows rule television for a simple reason: The best of them are far more compelling than the worn-out sitcoms and crime dramas the networks keep churning out. Elizabeth Larkin challenges that watching reality programming, especially the kind that holds up people for ridicule, is morally suspect. Just because something is entertaining, she counters, doesn't mean we should watch it. The section ends with a look at the publicized death of Jade Goody, a contestant from the British version of *Big Brother*, who sold the rights to film her death from cervical cancer. Noted Goody, "I lived my life on camera, and now maybe I will die on camera." Goody died on March 22, 2009.

 # The Case for Reality TV
Michael Hirschorn

1   This past January, I had the pleasure of serving as official spear-catcher for a *CBS Evening News* report on the increasing levels of humiliation on *American Idol* and other reality-TV shows, including some on my channel, VH1. The segment featured

---

* Michael Hirschorn, *The Atlantic,* May 2007; Elizabeth Larkin, *About.com,* 2004; Meredith Blake, *Salon.com;* February 19, 2009

snippets of our shows *I Love New York* (a dating competition with an urban vibe) and *Celebrity Fit Club* (which tracks the efforts of overweight singers and actors to get back in shape, and, by extension, reignite their careers). "VH1, among other things, showcases faded celebrities who are fat," said the CBS correspondent Richard Schlesinger.

2   In between shots of me fake-working at my computer and fake-chatting with the amiable Schlesinger while fake-strolling down our corporate-looking hallway, I took my best shot at defending the alleged horrors of *AI* and *Celebrity Fit Club*. But it was clear that *CBS News* was set on bemoaning what it saw as yet another outrage against the culture. The central complaint, per Katie Couric's intro to the report, was that more people had watched *American Idol* the previous week than watched the State of the Union address on all the broadcast networks combined. When the segment ended, Couric signed off with an extravagant eye roll. "We're doing our part here at *CBS News*," she seemed to be saying, "but the barbarians are massing at the gates, people." A line had been drawn in the sand, as if the news were now akin to an evening at the Met.

3   Is there an easier position to take in polite society than to patronize reality TV? Even television programmers see the genre as a kind of visual Hamburger Helper: cheap filler that saves

Is there an easier position to take in polite society than to patronize reality TV?

them money they can use elsewhere for more worthy programming. Reality shows cost anywhere from a quarter to half as much to produce as scripted shows. The money saved on *Extreme Makeover: Home Edition*, the logic goes, allows ABC to pay for additional gruesome medical emergencies and exploding ferries on *Grey's Anatomy*. NBC's crappy *Fear Factor* pays for the classy *Heroes*.

4   As befits a form driven largely by speed and cost considerations, reality TV is not often formally daring. Fifteen years after MTV's *The Real World* set the template for contemporary reality TV by placing seven strangers in a downtown Manhattan loft, reality television has developed its own visual shorthand: short doses of documentary footage interspersed with testimonials (often called OTF's, for "on-the-fly" interviews) in which the participants describe, ex post facto, what they were thinking during the action you are watching.

5   The current boom may be a product of the changing economics of the television business, but reality TV is also the liveliest genre on the set right now. It has engaged hot-button cultural issues—class, sex, race—that respectable television, including the august *CBS Evening News*, rarely touches. And it has addressed a visceral need for a different kind of television at a time when the Web has made more tradition-ally produced video seem as stagey as Molière.

6   Reality TV may be an awkward admixture of documentary (with its connota-tions of thousands of hours of footage patiently gathered, redacted by monk-like figures into the purest expression of truth possible in 90 to 120 minutes) and scripted (with its auteurs and Emmys and noble overtones of craft). But this kludge also happens to have allowed reality shows to skim the best elements of scripted TV and documentaries while eschewing the problems of each. Reality shows steal the story structure and pacing of scripted television but leave behind the canned plots and characters. They have the visceral impact of documentary reportage without the

self-importance and general lugubriousness. Where documentaries must construct their narratives from found matter, reality TV can place real people in artificial surroundings designed for maximum emotional impact.

7   Scripted television is supposedly showing new ambition these days, particularly in the hour-long drama form. *Studio 60 on the Sunset Strip* was going to bring the chatty intelligence of *The West Wing* back to prime time. *Lost* was going to challenge network audiences like never before, with complex plots, dozens of recurring characters, and movie-level production values. Shows are bigger now: On *24* this season, a nuclear bomb exploded. But network prime-time television remains dominated by variants on the police procedural (*Law & Order, CSI, Criminal Minds*), in which a stock group of characters (ethnically, sexually, and generationally diverse) grapples with endless versions of the same dilemma. The episodes have all the ritual predictability of Japanese Noh theater: Crimes are solved, lessons are learned, order is restored.

8   Reality shows have leaped into this imaginative void. Discovery's *Deadliest Catch*, which began its third season in April, is an oddly transfixing series about . . . crab fishermen in the Bering Sea. As a straightforward documentary, *Catch* would have been worthy fodder, but the producers have made it riveting by formatting the whole season as a sporting event, with crab tallies for each of the half dozen or so boats and a race-against-the-clock urgency that, for all its contrivance, gives structure and meaning to the fishermen's efforts.

9   Narrative vibrancy is not the only thing that electrifies these shows. Reality TV presents some of the most vital political debate in America, particularly about class and race. Fox's *Nanny 911* and ABC's *Supernanny* each offer object lessons on the hazards of parenting in an age of instant gratification and endless digital diversion. ABC's *Extreme Makeover: Home Edition* features intensely emotional tales of people who have fallen through the cracks of Bush-era America—often blue-collar families ravaged by disease, health-care costs, insurance loopholes, layoffs, and so forth. My channel's *The (White) Rapper Show* turned into a running debate among the aspiring white MC's over cultural authenticity—whether it is more properly bestowed by class or race.

10   Class realities are plumbed to remarkable effect on *The Real Housewives of Orange County*, a "docu soap" that completed its second season on Bravo this spring. The show is inspired by a trio of suburban dramas: The O. C., *Desperate Housewives*, and the 1999 movie *American Beauty*. Lacking the visual panache, or the budgets, of its scripted forebears, *Real Housewives* nonetheless goes deeper, charting the spiritual decay of life in gated communities, where financial anxieties, fraying families, and fear of aging leave inhabitants grasping for meaning and happiness as they steer their Escalades across Southern California's perfectly buffed, featureless landscape. *Crash*, the 2006 Oscar winner, trafficked in similar white California dread, but with all the nuance of a two-by-four to the face.

11   In *Real Housewives*, businessman Lou Knickerbocker stages a photo shoot to promote his new "highly oxygenated" water, variously called "Aqua Air" and "O. C. Energy Drink" ("We have patented technology that produces water from air"). The models are attractive-ish teen and twenty something girls: Lou's daughter Lindsey, by ex-wife Tammy; a few other daughters of O. C. housewives; and a newcomer whom Lou apparently found waitressing at a local restaurant.

12   Lou and Tammy made piles of money—it's not clear how—but their finances seem to have fractured along with their marriage. The photo shoot, therefore, is throwing off more than the normal amount of flop sweat. Lou apparently has personally selected the girls, which means he has declined to showcase his other daughter, Megan, because of her tattoos and lack of physical fitness. Lou believes the "Aqua Air Angels" should embody the Aqua Air ideal, which is why they can't drink or smoke and must have grade-point averages higher than 3.5. "This is a photo shoot," he barks after a fight breaks out between one of the girls and the waitress, "not a gang bang, for chrissakes."

13   The detail is what puts the scene over: Lou's lip-smacking focus on the girls, the girls' bland acquiescence. "That's it, baby, smile," Lou urges his daughter. "Show those teeth," says Tammy. A similar scenario on *Desperate Housewives* could never have been quite this preposterous, quite this blandly amoral. The characters would have been scripted with softening, redeeming qualities, or been rendered comically evil. Lou would've gotten his comeuppance, like Wallace Shawn's money-siphoning literary agent in that series. Here, the apparent willingness of the young women and at least some of the parents to indulge Lou's bottom-of-the-barrel scheming outlines, in a few short brushstrokes, a community's shared value system.

14   Value systems are smashed into each other, like atoms in an accelerator, on ABC's *Wife Swap*, where the producers find the most extreme pairings possible: lesbian mommies with bigots, godless cosmopolites with Bible thumpers. On one February show, a Pentecostal family, the Hoovers, was paired with the family of a former pastor, Tony Meeks, who has turned from God to follow his rock-and-roll dreams (mom Tish rocks out as well). "I feel by being there," Kristin Hoover said, "I was able to remind Tony that God still loves him and is not finished with him." The episode took seriously the Hoovers' commitment to homeschooling and their rejection of contemporary culture (a rejection not taken to the extreme of declining an invitation to appear on reality TV). Compare this with the tokenism of "born-again Christian" Harriet Hayes on NBC's dramedy *Studio 60 on the Sunset Strip*. Harriet's but a cipher, a rhetorical backboard against which ex-boyfriend Matt Albie can thwack his heathen wisecracks.

15   The competitions and elimination shows are latter-day Milgram experiments that place real people in artificial situations to see what happens. *The Apprentice* is Darwinism set loose inside an entrepreneurial Habitrail. Post-9/11, *Survivor* became less a fantasy and more a metaphor for an imagined post-apocalyptic future. What happens on these shows might be a Technicolor version of how we behave in real life, but so is most fiction. Creative endeavors—written, scripted, or produced—should be measured not by how literally they replicate actual life but by how effectively they render emotional truths. The best moments found on reality TV are unscriptable, or beyond the grasp of most scriptwriters. It's no coincidence that 2006's best scripted dramas—*The Wire*, HBO's multi season epic of inner-city Baltimore; and *Children of Men*, Alfonso Cuarón's futuristic thriller—were studies in meticulously crafted "realness," deploying naturalistic dialogue, decentered and chaotic action, stutter-step pacing, and a reporter's eye for the telling detail. *The Wire*'s season and Cuarón's movie both ended on semi resolved novelistic notes, scorning the tendency in current television and cinema toward easy narrative

closure. Watching them only threw into higher relief the inability of so much other scripted product to get beyond stock characterizations and pat narrative.

16   For all the snobbism in the doc community, reality TV has actually contributed to the recent boom in documentary filmmaking. The most successful docs of recent vintage have broken through in part by drawing heavily from reality television's bag of tricks, dropping the form's canonical insistence on pure observation. In *Fahrenheit 9/11*, Michael Moore brings an Army recruiter with him to confront legislators and urge them to enlist their children in the Iraq War effort. In *Bowling for Columbine*, Moore takes children who were shot at Columbine to a Kmart, where they ask for a refund on the bullets that are still lodged in their bodies. Of course, Moore's never been a doc purist. *TV Nation*, his short-lived 1994 television series, prefigured a long line of gonzo reality, from *Joe Millionaire* to *Punk'd*. Having the Serbian ambassador sing along to the *Barney* theme song ("I love you, you love me") while statistics about the number of Bosnians killed during the breakup of Yugoslavia appeared on the screen was not only ur-reality; it was ur-Borat. And speaking of talking animals, *March of the Penguins* turned stunning footage of mating and migrating penguins into an utterly contrived Antarctic version of *Love Story*.

17   The resistance to reality TV ultimately comes down to snobbery, usually of the generational variety. People under 30, in my experience, tend to embrace this programming; they're happy to be entertained, never mind the purity of conception. As an unapologetic producer of reality shows, I'm obviously biased, but I also know that any genre that provokes such howls of protest is doing something interesting. Try the crab. ◆

 ## Reality TV: Should We Really Watch?
Elizabeth Larkin

1 Media both in America and around the world seem to have "discovered" that so-called reality shows are very profitable, resulting in a growing string of such shows in recent years. Although not all are successful, many do achieve significant popularity and cultural prominence. That does not mean, however, that they are good for society or that they should be aired.

2   The first thing to keep in mind is that "reality TV" is nothing new—one of the most popular examples of this sort of entertainment is also one of the oldest, *Candid Camera*. Originally created by Allen Funt, it showcased hidden video of people in all manner of unusual and strange situations and was popular for many years. Even game shows, long a standard on television, are a sort of reality TV.

3   Today's programming, including a new version of *Candid Camera* produced by Funt's son, goes quite a bit further. The primary basis for many of these shows (but not all) seems to be to put people in painful, embarrassing, and humiliating situations for the rest of us to watch—and, presumably, laugh at and be entertained by.

4   These reality TV shows wouldn't be made if we didn't watch them, so why do we watch them? Either we find them entertaining or we find them so shocking that

we are simply unable to turn away. I'm not sure that the latter is an entirely defensible reason for supporting such programming; turning away is as easy as hitting a button on the remote control. The former, however, is a bit more interesting.

Humiliation as Entertainment

5 What we are looking at here is, I think, an extension of *Schadenfreude*, a German word used to describes people's delight and entertainment at the failings and problems of others. If you laugh at someone slipping on the ice, that's Schadenfreude. If you take pleasure in the downfall of a company you dislike, that is also Schadenfreude. The latter example is certainly understandable, but I don't think that's what we're seeing here. After all, we don't know the people on reality shows.

6   So what causes us to derive entertainment from the suffering of others? Certainly there may be catharsis involved, but that is also achieved through fiction— we don't need to see a real person suffer in order to have a cathartic experience. Perhaps we are simply happy that these things aren't happening to us, but that seems more reasonable when we see something accidental and spontaneous rather than something deliberately staged for our amusement.

7   That people do suffer on some reality TV shows is beyond question—the very existence of reality programming may be threatened by the increase in lawsuits by people who have been injured and/or traumatized by the stunts these shows have staged. One of the reasons such programming is attractive is that it can be much cheaper than traditional shows, but that may change as insurance premiums for reality TV begin to reflect higher to insurers.

8   There is never any attempt to justify these shows as enriching or worthwhile in any way, though certainly not every program needs to be educational or highbrow. Nevertheless, it **does** raise the question as to why they are made. Perhaps a clue about what is going on lies in the aforementioned lawsuits. According to Barry B. Langberg, a Los Angeles lawyer who represents one couple:

9   Something like this is done for no other reason than to embarrass people or humiliate them or scare them. The producers don't care about human feelings. They don't care about being decent. They only care about money.

10   Comments from various reality TV producers often fail to demonstrate much sympathy or concern with what their subjects experience—what we are seeing is a great callousness towards other human beings who are treated as means towards achieving financial and commercial success, regardless of the consequences for them. Injuries, humiliation, suffering, and higher insurance rates are all just the "cost of doing business" and a requirement for being edgier.

Where's the Reality?

11 One of the attractions of reality television is the supposed "reality" of it—unscripted and unplanned situations and reactions. One of the ethical problems of reality television is the fact that it isn't nearly as "real" as it pretends to be. At least in dramatic

shows one can expect the audience to understand that what they see on the screen doesn't necessarily reflect the reality of the actors' lives; the same, however, cannot be said for heavily edited and contrived scenes on sees on reality shows.

> *One of the attractions of reality television is the supposed "reality" of it—unscripted and unplanned situations and reactions. One of the ethical problems of reality television is the fact that it isn't nearly as "real" as it pretends to be.*

12   There is now a growing concern about how reality television shows can help perpetuate racial stereotypes. In many shows a similar black female character has been featured—all different women, but very similar character traits. It's gone so far that Africana.com has trademarked the expression The Evil Black Woman to describe this sort of individual: brazen, aggressive, pointing fingers, and always lecturing others on how to behave.

13   MSNBC has reported on the matter, noting that after so many "reality" programs, we can discern a pattern of "characters" that isn't very far different from the stock characters found in fictional programming. There's the sweet and naive person from a small town looking to make it big while still retaining small-town values. There's the party girl/guy who's always looking for a good time and who shocks those around them. There's the aforementioned Evil Black Woman with an Attitude, or sometimes Black Man with an Attitude—and the list goes on.

14   MSNBC quotes Todd Boyd, critical-studies professor at the University of Southern California's School of Cinema-Television as saying "We know all these shows are edited and manipulated to create images that look real and sort of exist in real time. But really what we have is a construction.... The whole enterprise of reality television relies on stereotypes. It relies on common stock, easily identifiable images."

15   Why do these stock characters exist, even in so-called "reality" television that it supposed to be unscripted and unplanned? Because that's the nature of entertainment. Drama is more readily propelled by the use of stock characters, because the less you have to think about who a person really is, the more quickly the show can get to things like the plot (such as it may be). Sex and race are especially useful for stock characterizations, because they can pull from a long and rich history of social stereotypes.

16   This is especially problematic when so few minorities appear in programming, whether reality or dramatic, because those few individuals end up being representatives of their entire group. A single angry white man is just an angry white man, while an angry black man is an indication of how all black men "really" are. MSNBC explains:

17   "Indeed, the [Sista with an Attitude] feeds off preconceived notions of African American women. After all, she's an archetype as old as D. W. Griffith, first found in the earliest of movies where slave women were depicted as ornery and cantankerous, uppity Negresses who couldn't be trusted to remember their place. Think Hattie McDaniel in *Gone With the Wind*, bossing and fussing as she yanked and tugged on Miss Scarlett's corset strings. Or Sapphire Stevens on the much-pilloried *Amos N' Andy,* serving up confrontation on a platter, extra-spicy, don't hold the sass. Or Florence, the mouthy maid on *The Jeffersons.*

18   How do stock characters appear in "unscripted" reality shows? First, the people themselves contribute to the creation of these characters because they know, even if unconsciously, that certain behavior is more likely to get them air time. Second, the shows editors contribute mightily to the creation of these characters, because they completely validate just that motivation. A black woman sitting around smiling isn't perceived to be as entertaining as a black woman pointing her finger at a white man and angrily telling him what to do.

19   An especially good (or egregious) example of this can be found in Manigault-Stallworth, a star of Donald Trump's *The Apprentice*. She has been called "the most hated woman on television" because of the behavior and attitude people see her with. But how much of her on-screen persona is real and how much is a creation of the shows editors? Quite a lot of the latter, according to Manigault-Stallworth in an e-mail quoted by MSNBC:

20   What you see on the show is a gross misrepresentation of who I am. For instance they never show me smiling, it's just not consistent with the negative portrayal of me that they want to present. Last week they portrayed me as lazy and pretending to be hurt to get out of working, when in fact I had a concussion due to my serious injury on the set and spent nearly... 10 hours in the emergency room. It's all in the editing!

21   Reality television shows are not documentaries. People are not put into situations simply to see how they react—the situations are heavily contrived, they are altered in order to make things interesting, and large amounts of footage are heavily edited into what the show's producers think will result in the best entertainment value for viewers. Entertainment, of course, often comes from conflict—so conflict will be created where none exists. If the show cannot incite conflict during the filming, it can be created in how pieces of footage are stitched together. It's all in what they choose to reveal to you—or not reveal, as the case may be.

Moral Responsibility

22   If a production company creates a show with the explicit intention of trying to make money from the humiliation and suffering which they themselves create for unsuspecting people, then that seems to me to be immoral and unconscionable. I simply cannot think of any excuse for such actions—pointing out that others are willing to watch such events does not relieve them of the responsibility for having orchestrated the events and willed the reactions in the first place. The mere fact that they **want** others to experience humiliation, embarrassment, and/or suffering (and simply in order to increase earnings) is itself unethical; actually going forward with it is even worse.

23   What of the responsibility of the reality TV advertisers? Their funding makes such programming possible, and therefore they must shoulder part of the blame as well. An ethical position would be to refuse to underwrite any programming, no matter how popular, if it is designed to deliberately cause others humiliation, embarrassment, or suffering. It's immoral to do such things for fun (especially on a regular basis), so it's certainly immoral to do it for money or to pay to have it done.

24   What of the responsibility of contestants? In shows which accost unsuspecting people on the street, there isn't really any. Many, however, have contestants who volunteer and sign releases—so aren't they getting what they deserve? Not necessarily. Releases don't necessarily explain everything that will happen, and some are pressured to sign new releases part way through a show in order to have a chance at winning—if they don't, all they have endured up to that point will have been for nothing. Regardless, the producers' desire to cause humiliation and suffering in others for profit remains immoral, even if someone volunteers to be the object of humiliation in exchange for money.

25   Finally, what about the reality TV viewers? If you watch such shows, **why**? If you find that you are entertained by the suffering and humiliation of others, that's a problem. Perhaps an occasional instance wouldn't merit comment, but a weekly schedule of such pleasure is another matter entirely.

26   I suspect that people's ability and willingness to take pleasure in such things may stem from the increasing separation we experience from others around us. The more distant we are from each other as individuals, the more readily we can objectify each other and fail to experience sympathy and empathy when others around us suffer. The fact that we are witnessing events not in front of us but rather on television, where everything has an unreal and fictional air about it, probably aids in this process as well.

27   I'm not saying that you shouldn't watch reality TV programming, but the motivations behind being a viewer are ethically suspect. Instead of passively accepting whatever media companies try to feed you, it would be better to take some time to reflect on **why** such programming is made and **why** you feel attracted to it. Perhaps you will find that your motivations themselves are not so attractive. ◆

 ## The Strange Life and Impending Death of Jade Goody
Meredith Blacke

1   It's something of a cliche that reality TV has little in common with actual reality, but the ongoing saga of terminally ill UK reality star Jade Goody proves the opposite can occasionally be true.

2   For those who don't follow British pseudo-celebrity, Goody rose to infamy in 2002 as a contestant on *Big Brother.* During her stint on the wildly popular show, Goody referred to her vagina as a "kebab," hooked up with a housemate, and displayed stunning ignorance about everything from asparagus to Saddam Hussein. An early favorite for eviction, she instead finished in fourth place and became a national sensation, parlaying her 15 minutes into a small fortune. Along with fellow "chav" Katie Price, Goody became a love-her or hate-her working-class hero, combining the brashness of Roseanne Barr, the intellect of Jessica Simpson, and the shameless

self-promotion of Paris Hilton, all in the body of a female wrestler. Needless to say, Goody's cultural ubiquity (including numerous reality spin-offs and a series of workout DVDs) has lead to much hand-wringing in the fiercely judgmental British press, all the more so because of her unapologetically "common" roots.

3   In 2007, Goody's appearance on *Celebrity Big Brother* erupted in an international incident. After calling Bollywood actress Shilpa Shetty "Shilpa Poppadom," Goody was branded a racist and evicted from the house. The drama incited the opprobrium of everyone from Gordon Brown to the Archbishop of York. (In America, the President weighs in on Alex Rodriguez; in the UK, it's Jade Goody.)

4   Despite tearful apologies, Goody's moment in the sun finally seemed to be over, at least until last August. While filming the Indian version of *Big Brother* as a public act of contrition, Goody learned that she had cervical cancer. She left the show immediately, and in the intervening months has been staging a very public battle with the disease in—what else?—a series of reality specials on UK television. Not surprisingly, Goody herself has suggested that she might even allow cameras to record her dying moments. "I've lived in front of the cameras. And maybe I'll die in front of them," she told the *Daily Mail*.

5   The ongoing saga came to head last weekend, when Goody was told that she had only weeks to live. The next day, Goody's younger, ex-con boyfriend proposed to her, and they will wed this weekend in a hastily planned ceremony. Naturally, the ceremony will be televised, and *OK! Magazine* has bought the rights to the photos for a reported $1 million (GBP 700,000), all of which is to go into a trust for her two young sons. Goody has not been bashful about her goal: making as much money for her children as possible before she dies. Her outspokenness has also led to a surge in screening for cervical cancer, and once again Gordon Brown has weighed in—this time, approvingly.

6   However it ends, Goody's story is undeniably sad, disturbing and poignant. While it's fair to dismiss most reality show antics as depraved and desperate, there is something admirable in Goody's consistency and commitment to living publicly.

> *While it's fair to dismiss most reality show antics as depraved and desperate, there is something admirable in Goody's consistency and commitment to living publicly.*

Unlike many hypocritical celebrities (see: Madonna, Angelina, Britney) who bemoan their lack of privacy while ruthlessly exploiting the free publicity that comes with it, Goody realizes that her fame and fortune entirely depends on her willingness to be on camera. Her impending death merely represents the ultimate dramatic twist in her already tumultuous life, and she is savvy enough to recognize the monetary worth of this most unfortunate of events. It also brings a sobering dose of actual reality to reality television. Sensationalizing death is one thing, but it's hard to sanitize the image of a grown woman sobbing like a baby or powdering her head before visiting her boyfriend in prison.

7   As Libby Brooks argues in the *Guardian*, most reality TV operates on the assumption that the viewer is looking down on the subject. This has certainly been the case with Goody, whose looks, weight and accent have all provided endless fodder for mockery. But in a final twist, hardly anyone seems to be making fun of

her these days; the formerly merciless press has all but canonized Goody, praising her bravery in glowing editorials while providing endless, occasionally sordid coverage of her every move. In effect, she has become the new "People's Princess." Whatever you might think about Goody and her notoriety, there's something perversely heroic about an undereducated woman from an impoverished background pulling such a dramatic, albeit tragic, switcharoo. ◆

CRITICAL THINKING

1. Do you watch reality TV programs? If so, which ones? What inspires you to watch these programs? What is their appeal?
2. If you could be a contestant on a reality television program, which one would you go on, and why?
3. Why does Larkin believe watching reality programs is unethical, or at the very least, morally questionable? Do all reality television programs exploit their participants in one way or another? Does the fact that people on reality programs agree to be followed on camera make this acceptable? Why or why not?
4. Hirschorn notes that most respectable television critics automatically debunk the role of reality TV in our culture and the quality and appeal of subject matter. In your opinion, what accounts for this disparity between the critics and the viewing public?
5. According to Hirschorn, in what ways does reality TV fill the void left by traditional programming? Do you agree or disagree with his assessment?
6. While Jade Goody made the decision to broadcast her final days willingly, and for profit, many critics still felt that such a thing had no business on television. Express your own opinion on this issue. Was Goody exploited? Was her decision in poor taste? Should her offer have been refused? Why or why not?

CRITICAL WRITING

1. *Expository Writing:* Write a short essay addressing the ways that reality television programs do or do not represent actual reality. Refer to current programs in your essay to support your points.
2. *Research Writing:* Visit the *NewsHour* Web site, at www.pbs.org/newshour/forum/july00/reality.html, on the popularity of reality programming, featuring Robert Thompson, head of the Center for the Study of Popular Television at Syracuse University, and Frank Farley, a past president of the American Psychological Association and professor at Temple University. Read the questions and responses posted at the Web site, and respond to them with your own viewpoint. Note that the Web site was first posted in 2000. How has reality television changed since then?

GROUP PROJECTS

1. With your group, compile a list of reality programs and their contestant profiles. (You may have to look up these programs online to see the most recent contestant roster.) What programs were the most successful? Did they appeal to a broad, multicultural audience? Discuss your list and observations in class as part of a wider discussion on diversity and reality TV programs.

2. Develop your own reality TV program plot. Include the show's premise, its object and goal, why people would want to watch it, and who would be a typical contestant. Outline the program and present it to the class. The class should vote on which program it finds the most engaging.

Perspectives on Gender

Bridging the Gap

We have witnessed enormous changes in the social and professional lives of men and women over the past century. Traditional ways of defining others and ourselves along gender lines have been irrevocably altered. Only 100 years ago, the full financial responsibility of a family was squarely on the shoulders of men. Women could not vote and had limited legal resources at their disposal. Sex was something that happened within the confines of marriage. Women were expected to remain at home, relegated to housework and childrearing. Men were expected to be the disciplinarians of family life, with limited involvement in the daily lives of their children. Now, women may pursue many different career options and lifestyles. Men are not expected to be the sole breadwinner, and men and women together often share financial responsibilities. Sexual mores have relaxed, and both men and women enjoy greater freedoms socially, professionally, and intellectually than they ever have before.

Most college-age men and women were born after the Sexual Revolution of the 1960s and the feminist movement of the 1970s, but these movements have largely shaped the way men and women interact, view each other, evaluate opportunity, and envision the future. However, while much has changed, and we have moved toward greater gender equality, vestiges of gender bias and sexism remain. The essays in this section examine how society has changed its expectations of gender and how these changes have affected men and women as they continue to define themselves and their relationships with each other and society as a whole.

In "My Most Attractive Adversary," Madeleine Begun Kane, a former lawyer, describes how expressions of subtle sexism, such as physical compliments paid by men to women in professional settings, belittle women and reinforce dated notions about women in the workforce. Jake Brennan questions the way men are portrayed by the popular media in "Has Male Bashing Gone Too Far?" Why is it acceptable, he wonders, to make men look stupid on television?

The next two essays explore how our gender identity is influenced by the world and people around us. First, in "The New Girl Order," Kay Hymowitz observes the "Carrie Bradshaw effect" whereby many young women seek independence, careers, and freedom before starting families. And because *Sex in the City* is rerun all over the globe, aspiring "Carries" are popping up in some unexpected places. Then, Scott Russell Sanders challenges some widely held assumptions that men enjoy power and privilege in "The Men We Carry in Our Minds," as he describes the role of men in his childhood and how these men shaped his view of what it means to be male. Balancing these two perspectives, linguist and social scientist Steven Pinker discusses the differences between men and women and how biological variations may influence career choice and career advancement in "The Science of Difference."

The next essay examines the trend of hypermasculinity in hip-hop music. In "Hip-Hop: Beyond Beats and Rhymes," the author observes that a great deal of hip-hop music glorifies violence, denigrates women, and promotes "bad boy" attitudes that are ultimately hurting young black males and damaging society in general. The fear is that the hypermasculine thug image is becoming the mainstream stereotype of the young black male and that this image *promotes* an attitude in which intelligence and reason are subjugated in favor of brute force and violence.

The chapter's Viewpoints section takes a closer look at men and women in sports. It has been over 35 years since Title IX became law, ensuring equal opportunity for women in education and in sports. Since then, we have witnessed a fourfold increase in women's participation in intercollegiate athletics. Yet women are still judged more on how pretty they look on the field or on the court than by how well they play. And while Title IX paved the way for many women to become professional female athletes, critics argue that revisions to the act are unfair to men. Jennifer L. Knight and Traci A. Giuliano describe disparities in athletic expectations in their essay "He's a Laker; She's a 'Looker,' " followed by a humorous explanation from Graham Hays, about "Why Men Don't Watch Women's Sports." The section ends with an editorial by *Sports Illustrated* columnist E. M. Swift, who argues that the need for Title IX has passed in his essay "Gender Inequality."

My Most Attractive Adversary
Madeleine Begun Kane*

Women may seem to have made tremendous progress professionally and academically, but they are held back by indirect sexist comments and attitudes. They are caught in a catch-22. If they react against these seemingly small slights, they appear to be overreacting or too sensitive. But to let them pass may signal that such comments are somehow acceptable. In the next essay, humorist and self-described "recovering lawyer" Madeleine Begun Kane holds that subtle sexism maintains gender differences.

1 "Our Portia has come up with an excellent solution." A trial judge said this about me several years ago in open court, when I was still a full-time litigator. I've never forgotten it. Not because it was a compliment to be compared to so formidable a lawyer as Shakespeare's Portia, although I think he meant it as a compliment. But what I really remember is my discomfort at being singled out as a woman in what, even today, remains a predominantly male world.

2 Despite our progress in the battle against workplace discrimination, the fact of being a female is almost always an issue. It may not be blatant, but it usually lurks just below the surface. We are not lawyers, executives, and managers. We are female lawyers, female executives, and female managers. Just when we are lulled into believing otherwise, something happens to remind us, and those around us, of our gender in subtle yet unsettling ways.

> *Men often use physical compliments to call attention to the fact that we are different. . . . It's a clever technique, because any response other than a gracious "thank you" seems like a petty overreaction.*

---

* Madeleine Begun Kane, *Women's Village*, 2002

3   Men often use physical compliments to call attention to the fact that we are different. References to "my lovely opponent" or "my most attractive adversary" remain remarkably common. It's a clever technique, because any response other than a gracious "thank you" seems like a petty overreaction.

4   Consequently, unless the remark is obviously offensive, as in references to certain unmentionable body parts, a simple nod or "thank you" is usually the prudent response. Of course if you're feeling less cautious, you may want to return the compliment. Done with a slight note of irony, this can be an effective way to get your point across. But saying, "You look very handsome yourself, Your Honor," is probably not a good idea.

5   Concern for the tender female sensibility rivals compliments in the subtle sexism department. I've experienced this most often during business meetings—high-powered meetings where a lone female is surrounded by her peers and superiors. At some point during the meeting the inevitable will happen. One of the men will use an expletive—a minor one in all likelihood. The expedient course is to ignore it. She is a woman of the world. She has heard and possibly used such language—and even worse.

6   But is she allowed to ignore it? Of course not! That would be too easy. The curser inevitably turns to the lone female (who until this moment has somehow managed not to blush) and apologizes. This singles her out as a delicate female who doesn't quite belong and needs to be protected. This also reminds everyone that the rest of the group would be ever so much more comfortable, at ease, and free to be themselves, if only a woman hadn't invaded their turf.

7   This has happened to me more times than I care to recall. And I still don't know the proper response. Should I ignore both the profanity and the apology? Is it best to graciously accept the apology, as if one were appropriate? Or should I say what I'm always tempted to say: "That's all right, I swear like a sailor, too."

8   Most women, myself included, overlook these subtle forms of sexism. I'm troubled by this, and I worry that by being silent, I'm giving up an opportunity to educate. For while some men use these tactics deliberately, others don't even know they're being offensive. Nevertheless, I usually smile discreetly and give a gracious nod. And wonder if I'm doing the right thing, or if I'm mistaking cowardice for discretion. ◆

CRITICAL THINKING

1. Do we have certain ingrained gender expectations when it comes to occupations? For example, do we expect men to be mechanics or lawyers or firefighters and women to be teachers or nurses or secretaries? Are these expectations changing, or are they still common assumptions?

2. Kane opens her essay with a story about how she was called "Portia" by a judge. Who is Portia? Why is Kane uncomfortable with what she believes to be a compliment by the judge? Explain.

3. Kane objected to compliments, such as "my lovely opponent" and "my most attractive adversary," made by male professionals. How do such compliments undermine her role as a lawyer and a professional? Do you think the men intended to slight her? Why or why not?

4. What profession do you hope to pursue? Is your profession a male- or female-dominated one, or is it balanced with both sexes? Do you think that gender will ever be an issue in your chosen profession?

5. In paragraphs 5 and 6, Kane describes a business meeting in which a man apologizes to a woman for his offensive language. Why does she object to such apologies? What assumptions do men make in offering such an apology?

6. Kane observes that it is difficult for women to openly object to sexist compliments, because to do so could backfire on them. How could their objections work against them? Explain.

7. Why does Kane worry about remaining silent against subtle sexism? What could happen if she doesn't remain silent? What would you do?

CRITICAL WRITING

1. *Research and Analysis:* In paragraph 2, Kane states that women are not "lawyers, executives, and managers." Instead, they are "female lawyers, female executives, and female managers." Interview a woman who holds a professional position in law, medicine, or business and ask her about this observation and whether she feels that the word "female" floats in front of her professional title, unspoken but still "lurking beneath the surface." Summarize your interview and analyze the discussion.

2. *Personal Narrative:* Write about a time when you felt awkward because of your gender. Describe the situation, the experience, and why you felt uncomfortable. With a critical eye, analyze the situation and think about how social expectations of gender may have contributed to your feelings of discomfort.

GROUP PROJECTS

1. Kane argues that gender bias "lurks beneath the surface," reminding women that they are women in what traditionally have been male professions. When does referencing gender cross a line into sexism? Is it sexist to refer to a woman as a "lady doctor" or a man as a "male nurse"? Are such references as common as Kane maintains? As a group, make a list of professions and their titles. Include old titles and their newer ones (for example, "mailman" and "postal carrier"). Has renaming the titles of these professions decreased sexism in the workplace?

2. In paragraph 7, Kane laments that she has experienced the apology-for-swearing scenario at many business meetings. As a group, consider her situation and develop a few comebacks she could use if she faced the situation again. Share your comebacks with the class.

Perspectives: What She Wore

Mike Luckovich, *Atlanta Journal Constitution,* March 23, 2007

THINKING CRITICALLY

1. Who is the woman in the left-hand panel? What is she doing and what point is she trying to make?
2. Who is the man in the right-hand panel? Where is he? What is he saying and what is the meaning of his words?
3. What point is this cartoon trying to make? What issue does it raise? Explain.

Has Male Bashing Gone Too Far?
Jake Brennan*

> The first essay in this section addressed the ways sexism can be subtly disguised in the professional world. This next essay addresses how television can promote equally damaging sexism, in this case, against men. Because television reaches a broad and diverse audience, it can influence culture and social opinion. Over the years, television has served as a positive instrument for change. But as a conduit for social persuasion, could television harm one group of people as much as it may help another? In the next editorial, Jake Brennan questions the depiction of men as lazy, incompetent, insensitive, or simply stupid on television programs and in commercials. While such depictions may seem funny, stereotypical "male bashing," he argues, hurts men and society as a whole.

1 Is it just me, or are men in general (i.e., not just me) being depicted as fools, oafs and incompetent boobs in the media these days? As Jerry Seinfeld, the genius behind a sitcom with two classic buffoons—"hipster doofus" Kramer and "stocky, bald" George—would say, "What's the deal with dolts showing up everywhere as today's average male?" Are we really so incompetent?

2 And furthermore, isn't this a bit of a double standard? Women have fought the stereotype of being weak, submissive or incompetent and empowered themselves quite well, just as overweight people have countered a lazy image. And rightly so.

3 Well, it's high time we men stood up for ourselves as well! I mean, what are we, a bunch of weenies? What's stopping us? Male guilt? Puh-lease! Or worse, do we just sit idly by and take this thrashing because somewhere deep inside we have an inkling that, God forbid, the stereotype contains a grain of truth?

4 The backlash against male domination in our society has reached the point where we expect a father in a sitcom or TV commercial to be an oafish, grunting Neanderthal, as in Tim Allen's famous caricature of the "typical" male. Take the male leads in *Everybody Loves Raymond* or *The King of Queens*, for example: blundering nitwits, most of the time.

A Few Examples

5 Current TV commercials for Cottonelle bathroom tissue and the Honda Pilot depict men as so unrefined that, in one case, they use bar napkins as toilet paper, and in the other, the guy acts like he was raised by wolves—literally!

6 On *Queer Eye for the Straight Guy*, homosexuals are telling men how to be men and how to treat their women, because the straight men are too incompetent to tune in to women's tastes. Gay men are straightening out straight guys, for crying out loud!

---

* Jake Brennan, *AskMen.com*, August 13, 2007

7   *Friends'* Joey became softer over the years. He became less of a macho player than he was and was distilled down to his knucklehead essence. He's more like the prototype for all such fatheads, Homer Simpson.

Why Men Are Made Fun Of

8   The most obvious reason men are being ridiculed this way is because we're easy targets. Like any other group of people, we have our flaws.

9   Let's take it from a woman's perspective for a minute here. What is it, exactly, that's so interesting about a leather ball going through an iron hoop or between steel uprights? Why does fizzy liquid in aluminum cans necessarily go with these activities? And—this is crucial—why does releasing the intestinal gas caused by this canned liquid by asking someone to pull our finger never get old?

10   But these things are important, dammit! I mean, aren't they? That's what magazines like *Maxim* and programs like *The Man Show*, which often target young, single men as if they're simply beer-swilling, thong-snapping meatheads, would have us believe. And this guy-oriented entertainment is popular, which means guys are identifying with the point of view that is presented. So it's no use saying that stereotypes of men as lunkheads are simply untrue.

Men vs. Guys

11   Such guys fit the bill laid out by Jerry Seinfeld in his stand-up special, *I'm Telling You for the Last Time:* "Women always want to know what men are thinking. You really want to know what we're thinking about? Okay, I'll tell you. . . . Nothin'. Guys are just walking around, looking around."

12   That's right, guys are. The stereotype isn't really so much about all men, but rather about guys of the male gender.

13   If you don't see the difference, here's an example. Given two plastic cups stacked together too tightly to separate:

14   • A **woman** will hand it to a male, to give him a problem to solve (and thereby pad his ego, which she knows he needs to survive), while simultaneously testing whether he's a man or a guy (women love to test us).

15   • A **man** might put ice in the top cup and run the bottom cup under hot water; the bottom expands while the top contracts, and the two are easily separated.

16   • A **guy** will twist and grimace until a) veins pop out of his forehead, then b) the cups break in his hands. Cue cursing, followed by despondent silence, during which he just wants to be left alone.

17   In short, a guy is a caricature composed of the particularly unfemale male traits: stubbornness, inability to listen or plan ahead, a desire to show off, a fascination with basic human functions, etc.

18   Think men being cast as guys is new? Recall, if you will, the male lead on one of the earliest television sitcoms. No, not *Leave It to Beaver*. Are you paying attention? I'm talking about the unforgettable role of Ralph Kramden, brought alive by Jackie Gleason on *The Honeymooners* (or, if that was too highbrow for you, Fred

Flintstone was his cartoon version). Also recall *All in the Family*'s addle-minded anchor, Archie Bunker. And, lest we forget, there's also George Jefferson.

19 All these fellas were strong-willed (read: stubborn), generally buffoonish husbands with one key that kept men and (especially) women watching: their kind, lovable hearts. That's also true of Kevin James's character on *The King of Queens*; Joey Tribbiani, despite his laughable shortcomings, is still a *Friend*; and likewise, in case you missed it, the notion was built right into the title of Ray Romano's show, *Everybody Loves Raymond*.

Free-Market Satire

20 The distinction between men and guys is a major reason, I'd say, why males don't rise up and fight the female powers who increasingly have a say in the media. In our society, the consumer is the final decision maker, and the broad reach of the guy stereotype means it has found a market.

21 Men—not just women— find many of these lampoons funny because there's obviously more than a little truth to all this; satire only works if the exaggerations and distortions made stem

Remember: a stereotype is a portrait of what is perceived, rightly or wrongly, to be an average. And averages are affected by extremes.

from the truth. Remember: a stereotype is a portrait of what is perceived, rightly or wrongly, to be an average. And averages are affected by extremes. Sure, some males are guys, but hey, some blondes are ditzy. You know, it takes all kinds, variety is the spice of life, a bird in the hand is worth two in the bush, or something like that.

22 So, males either know they're not like that (like you, of course, cultured man reader) and can therefore laugh at the stereotype, or the guys among us identify and laugh at themselves and the fact that they're getting away with it all.

23 The beauty in all this is that laughing at yourself makes you look like a good sport. I mean, what's the alternative? Complain and you'll look like a weak whiner, which is definitely unmanly, or a woman hater, which will only get you in deeper sheep dip. No, women have cultivated the perfect climate for this ridicule to perpetuate itself.

24 Once you've come to accept your lot as a male, bear this in mind: despite the considerable advances of Western women over the past two generations, in 2004 it's safe to say that, for better or worse, men are still wearing the pants in this society (changes in fashion during this period notwithstanding).

25 When you consider the weight of influence in the spheres of politics, business and the arts, yup, the scales still tip toward male. And if men want to continue to have their cake a little while longer, they're going to have to accept that, from time to time, some of that cake will be rammed down their throat. ◆

CRITICAL THINKING

1. Think about the ways men and women are portrayed on television and television commercials. Are there certain gender-based stereotypes that seem common? What makes a male character interesting and engaging?

What makes a female character noteworthy and interesting? Are the criteria different?

2. Evaluate how the author supports the thesis of his essay. First, identify Brennan's thesis. Then, analyze each supporting element he uses to prove his point. Does the author allow for alternative points of view? Does he try to see multiple sides of the issue? Explain.

3. What is the difference between a "man" and a "guy"? Explain.

4. Consider the contrast between male sitcom characters and men in real life. Do male characters on television mirror men in the real world? Do the characters on television influence your perception of men in general?

5. This editorial identifies Joey's character on *Friends* and Raymond's character on *Everybody Loves Raymond* as two that particularly portray men as inept. Watch either program and evaluate the character for yourself. How are other male characters depicted in TV programs, such as Chandler and Ross in *Friends* or Robbie or Frank in *Everybody Loves Raymond*?

6. Some social critics have observed that the portrayal of men as generally unintelligent would never be acceptable if directed at women. Respond to this view in your own words. Support your response with examples from the essay and your television viewing experience.

CRITICAL WRITING

1. *Research and Analysis:* Brennan notes that presenting men as basically dumb "guys" is nothing new. Research a few programs from each decade, starting in the 1950s, and describe how men and women are portrayed in these programs. Describe how television gender roles have, or have not, changed.

2. *Exploratory Writing:* Write about a male or female television character that you particularly enjoy watching. Explain why you chose this character and what made him or her so appealing to you. Do you see this character as a role model or simply entertaining? Explain.

3. *Exploratory Writing:* Consider the ways Hollywood influences our cultural perspectives of gender and identity. Write an essay exploring the influence, however slight, film and television have had on your own perceptions of gender. If you wish, interview other students for their opinions on this issue, and address some of their points in your essay.

GROUP PROJECTS

1. Visit the network Web sites of CBS, NBC, ABC, FOX, or CW. Working as a group, identify the male lead characters in five prime-time programs; exclude dramas, as Brennan has done, and try to categorize each character. Provide a brief explanation next to each, supporting your categorization of the character. Do any characters not fall into any category? If so, which ones, and why? Share your list with the class. Did other groups categorize characters differently? Discuss this.

2. Consider Brennan's ideas in the context of our broader culture. Do you agree that television programs and commercials present men as inept or stupid because that is what our society thinks is funny? Working as a group, prove or disprove this idea using movies, television, popular music, and print media such as advertisements as examples.

The New Girl Order
Kay S. Hymowitz*

Young women today are marrying later, having children later, and, as many pursue meaningful careers, they have more disposable income than ever before. Across the globe, women are changing the cultural landscape and challenging long-held traditional gender roles. Do such changes represent a positive shift, or could they have negative implications in the long run? As Kay S. Hymowitz discusses in the next essay, the Carrie Bradshaw lifestyle is showing up in unexpected places with unintended consequences.

1　After my LOT Airlines flight from New York touched down at Warsaw's Frédéric Chopin Airport a few months back, I watched a middle-aged passenger rush to embrace a waiting younger woman—clearly her daughter. Like many people on the plane, the older woman wore drab clothing and had the short, square physique of someone familiar with too many potatoes and too much manual labor. Her Poland-based daughter, by contrast, was tall and smartly outfitted in pointy-toed pumps, slim-cut jeans, a cropped jacket revealing a toned midriff (Yoga? Pilates? Or just a low-carb diet?), and a large, brass-studded leather bag, into which she dropped a silver cell phone.

2　Yes: Carrie Bradshaw is alive and well and living in Warsaw. Well, not just Warsaw. Conceived and raised in the United States, Carrie may still see New York as a spiritual home. But today you can find her in cities across Europe, Asia, and North America. Seek out the trendy shoe stores in Shanghai, Berlin, Singapore, Seoul, and Dublin, and you'll see crowds of single young females (SYFs) in their twenties and thirties, who spend their hours working their abs and their careers, sipping cocktails, dancing at clubs, and (yawn) talking about relationships. *Sex and the City* has gone global; the SYF world is now flat.

> *Carrie Bradshaw is alive and well and living in Warsaw. Well, not just Warsaw. Today you can find her in cities across Europe, Asia, and North America.*

3　Is this just the latest example of American cultural imperialism? Or is it the triumph of planetary feminism? Neither. The globalization of the SYF reflects a series of stunning demographic and economic shifts that are pointing much of the world—with important exceptions, including Africa and most of the Middle

* Kays S. Hymowitz, *City Journal*, Summer 2002

East—toward a New Girl Order. It's a man's world, James Brown always reminded us. But if these trends continue, not so much.

4   Three demographic facts are at the core of the New Girl Order. First, women—especially, but not only, in the developed world—are getting married and having kids considerably later than ever before. According to the UN's World Fertility Report, the worldwide median age of marriage for women is up two years, from 21.2 in the 1970s to 23.2 today. In the developed countries, the rise has been considerably steeper—from 22.0 to 26.1.

5   Demographers get really excited about shifts like these, but in case you don't get what the big deal is, consider: in 1960, 70 percent of American 25-year-old women were married with children; in 2000, only 25 percent of them were. In 1970, just 7.4 percent of all American 30- to 34-year-olds were unmarried; today, the number is 22 percent. That change took about a generation to unfold, but in Asia and Eastern Europe the transformation has been much more abrupt. In today's Hungary, for instance, 30 percent of women in their early thirties are single, compared with 6 percent of their mothers' generation at the same age. In South Korea, 40 percent of 30-year-olds are single, compared with 14 percent only 20 years ago.

6   Nothing-new-under-the-sun skeptics point out, correctly, that marrying at 27 or 28 was once commonplace for women, at least in the United States and parts of northern Europe. The cultural anomaly was the 1950s and '60s, when the average age of marriage for women dipped to 20—probably because of post-Depression and postwar cocooning. But today's single 27-year-old has gone global—and even in the West, she differs from her late-marrying great-grandma in fundamental ways that bring us to the second piece of the demographic story. Today's aspiring middle-class women are gearing up to be part of the paid labor market for most of their adult lives; unlike their ancestral singles, they're looking for careers, not jobs. And that means they need lots of schooling.

7   In the newly global economy, good jobs go to those with degrees, and all over the world, young people, particularly women, are enrolling in colleges and universities at unprecedented rates. Between 1960 and 2000, the percentages of 20-, 25-, and 30-year-olds enrolled in school more than doubled in the U.S., and enrollment in higher education doubled throughout Europe. And the fairer sex makes up an increasing part of the total. The majority of college students are female in the U.S., the U.K., France, Germany, Norway, and Australia, to name only a few of many places, and the gender gap is quickly narrowing in more traditional countries like China, Japan, and South Korea. In a number of European countries, including Denmark, Finland, and France, over half of all women between 20 and 24 are in school. The number of countries where women constitute the majority of graduate students is also growing rapidly.

8   That educated women are staying single is unsurprising; degreed women have always been more likely to marry late, if they marry at all. But what has demographers taking notice is the sheer transnational numbers of women postponing marriage while they get diplomas and start careers. In the U.K., close to a third of 30-year-old college-educated women are unmarried; some demographers predict that 30 percent of women with university degrees there will remain forever childless. In Spain—not so long ago a culturally Catholic country where a girl's family would jealously chaperone her until handing her over to a husband at 21 or so—women now constitute

54 percent of college students, up from 26 percent in 1970, and the average age of first birth has risen to nearly 30, which appears to be a world record.

9   Adding to the contemporary SYF's novelty is the third demographic shift: urbanization. American and northern European women in the nineteenth and early twentieth centuries might have married at 26, but after a long day in the dairy barn or cotton mill, they didn't hang out at Studio 54 while looking for Mr. Right (or, as the joke has it, Mr. Right for Now). In the past, women who delayed marriage generally lived with their parents; they also remained part of the family economy, laboring in their parents' shops or farms, or at the very least, contributing to the family kitty. A lot of today's bachelorettes, on the other hand, move from their native village or town to Boston or Berlin or Seoul because that's where the jobs, boys, and bars are—and they spend their earnings on themselves.

10   By the mid-1990s, in countries as diverse as Canada, France, Hungary, Ireland, Portugal, and Russia, women were out-urbanizing men, who still tended to hang around the home village. When they can afford to, these women live alone or with roommates. The Netherlands, for instance, is flush with public housing, some of it reserved for young students and workers, including lots of women. In the United States, the proportion of unmarried twentysomethings living with their parents has declined steadily over the last 100 years, despite skyhigh rents and apartment prices. Even in countries where SYFs can't afford to move out of their parents' homes, the anonymity and diversity of city life tend to heighten their autonomy. Belgians, notes University of Maryland professor Jeffrey Jensen Arnett, have coined a term—"hotel families"—to describe the arrangement.

11   Combine these trends—delayed marriage, expanded higher education and labor force participation, urbanization—add a global media and some disposable income, and voilà: an international lifestyle is born. One of its defining characteristics is long hours of office work, often in quasi-creative fields like media, fashion, communications, and design—areas in which the number of careers has exploded in the global economy over the past few decades. The lifestyle also means whole new realms of leisure and consumption, often enjoyed with a group of close girlfriends: trendy cafés and bars serving sweetish coffee concoctions and cocktails; fancy boutiques, malls, and emporiums hawking cosmetics, handbags, shoes, and $100-plus buttock-hugging jeans; gyms for toning and male watching; ski resorts and beach hotels; and, everywhere, the frustrating hunt for a boyfriend and, though it's an ever more vexing subject, a husband.

12   The SYF lifestyle first appeared in primitive form in the U.S. during the seventies, after young women started moving into higher education, looking for meaningful work, and delaying marriage. Think of ur-SYF Mary Richards, the pre-Jordache career girl played by Mary Tyler Moore, whose dates dropped her off—that same evening, of course—at her apartment door. By the mid-1990s, such propriety was completely passé. Mary had become the vocationally and sexually assertive Carrie Bradshaw, and cities like New York had magically transformed into the young person's pleasure palace evoked by the hugely popular TV show *Sex and the City*. At around the same time, women in Asia and in post-Communist Europe began to join the SYF demographic, too. Not surprisingly, they also loved watching themselves, or at least Hollywood versions of themselves, on television. *Friends, Ally McBeal,*

and *Sex and the City* became global favorites. In repressive places like Singapore and China, which banned *SATC*, women passed around pirated DVDs.

13   By the late 1990s, the SYF lifestyle was fully globalized. Indeed, you might think of SYFs as a sociological Starbucks: no matter how exotic the location, there they are, looking and behaving just like the American prototype. They shop for shoes in Kyoto, purses in Shanghai, jeans in Prague, and lip gloss in Singapore; they sip lattes in Dublin, drink cocktails in Chicago, and read lifestyle magazines in Kraków; they go to wine tastings in Boston, speed-dating events in Amsterdam, yoga classes in Paris, and ski resorts outside Tokyo. "At the fashionable Da Capo Café on bustling Kolonaki Square in downtown Athens, Greek professionals in their 30s and early 40s luxuriate over their iced cappuccinos," a *Newsweek International* article began last year. "Their favorite topic of conversation is, of course, relationships: men's reluctance to commit, women's independence, and when to have children." Thirty-seven-year-old Eirini Perpovlov, an administrative assistant at Associated Press, "loves her work and gets her social sustenance from her parea, or close-knit group of like-minded friends."

14   Sure sounds similar to this July's *Time* story about Vicky, "a purposeful, 29-year-old actuary who . . . loves nothing better than a party. She and her friends meet so regularly for dinner and at bars that she says she never eats at home anymore. As the pictures on her blog attest, they also throw regular theme parties to mark holidays like Halloween and Christmas and last year took a holiday to Egypt." At the restaurant where the reporter interviews them, Vicky's friends gab about snowboarding, iPods, credit-card rates, and a popular resort off the coast of Thailand. Vicky, whose motto is "work hard, play harder," is not from New York, London, or even Athens; she's from the SYF delegation in Beijing, China, a country that appears to be racing from rice paddies to sushi bars in less than a generation—at least for a privileged minority.

15   With no children or parents to support, and with serious financial hardship a bedtime story told by aging grandparents, SYFs have ignited what *The Economist* calls the "Bridget Jones economy"—named, of course, after the book and movie heroine who is perhaps the most famous SYF of all. Bridget Jonesers, the magazine says, spend their disposable income "on whatever is fashionable, frivolous, and fun," manufactured by a bevy of new companies that cater to young women. In 2000, Marian Salzman—then the president of the London-based Intelligence Factory, an arm of Young & Rubicam—said that by the 1990s, "women living alone had come to comprise the strongest consumer bloc in much the same way that yuppies did in the 1980s."

16   SYFs drive the growth of apparel stores devoted to stylish career wear, like Ann Taylor, which now has more than 800 shops in the United States, and the international Zara, with more than 1,000 in 54 countries. They also spend paychecks at the Paris-based Sephora, Europe's largest retailer of perfumes and cosmetics, which targets younger women in 14 countries, including such formerly sober redoubts as Poland and the Czech Republic. The chain plans to expand to China soon. According to *Forbes*, the Chinese cosmetics market, largely an urban phenomenon, was up 17 percent in 2006, and experts predict a growth rate of between 15 and 20 percent in upcoming years. Zara already has three stores there.

17   The power of the SYF's designer purse is also at work in the entertainment industry. By the mid-1990s, "chick lit," a contemporary urban version of the Harlequin romance with the SYF as heroine, was topping bestseller lists in England and the United States. Now chick lit has spread all over the world. The books of the Irish writer Marian Keyes, one of the first and most successful chick-litterateurs, appear in 29 languages. *The Devil Wears Prada* was an international hit as both a book (by Lauren Weisberger) and a movie (starring Meryl Streep). Meantime, the television industry is seeking to satisfy the SYF's appetite for single heroines with *Sex and the City* clones like *The Marrying Type* in South Korea and *The Balzac Age* in Russia.

18   Bridget Jonesers are also remaking the travel industry, especially in Asia. A 2005 report from MasterCard finds that women take four out of every ten trips in the Asia-Pacific region—up from one in ten back in the mid-1970s. While American women think about nature, adventure, or culture when choosing their travel destinations, says MasterCard, Asian women look for shopping, resorts, and, most of all, spas. Female travelers have led to what the report calls the "spa-ification of the Asian hotel industry." That industry is growing at a spectacular rate—200 percent annually.

19   And now the maturing Bridget Jones economy has begun to feature big-ticket items. In 2003, the Diamond Trading Company introduced the "right-hand ring," a diamond for women with no marital prospects but longing for a rock. ("Your left hand is your heart; your right hand is your voice," one ad explains.) In some SYF capitals, women are moving into the real-estate market. Canadian single women are buying homes at twice the rate of single men. The National Association of Realtors reports that in the U.S. last year, single women made up 22 percent of the real-estate market, compared with a paltry 9 percent for single men. The median age for first-time female buyers: 32. The real-estate firm Coldwell Banker is making eyes at these young buyers with a new motto, "Your perfect partner since 1906," while Lowe's, the home-renovation giant, is offering classes especially for them. SYFs are also looking for wheels, and manufacturers are designing autos and accessories with them in mind. In Japan, Nissan has introduced the Pino, which has seat covers festooned with stars and a red CD player shaped like a pair of lips. It comes in one of two colors: "milk tea beige" and pink.

20   Japan presents a striking example of the sudden rise of the New Girl Order outside the U.S. and Western Europe. As recently as the nation's boom years in the 1980s, the dominant image of the Japanese woman was of the housewife, or *sengyoshufu*, who doted on her young children, intently prepared older ones for the world economy, and waited on the man of the house after his 16-hour day at the office. She still exists, of course, but about a decade ago, she met her nemesis: the Japanese SYF. Between 1994 and 2004, the number of Japanese women between 25 and 29 who were unmarried soared from 40 to 54 percent; even more remarkable was the number of 30- to 34-year-old females who were unmarried, which rocketed from 14 to 27 percent. Because of Tokyo's expensive real-estate market, a good many of these young single women have shacked up with their parents, leading a prominent sociologist to brand them "parasite singles." The derogatory term took off, but the girls weren't disturbed; according to *USA Today*, many proudly printed up business cards bearing their new title.

21   The New Girl Order may represent a disruptive transformation for a deeply traditional society, but Japanese women sure seem to be enjoying the single life.

Older singles who can afford it have even been buying their own apartments. One of them, 37-year-old Junko Sakai, wrote a best-selling plaint called *The Howl of the Loser Dogs*, a title that co-opts the term *makeinu*—"loser"—once commonly used to describe husbandless 30-year-olds. "Society may call us dogs," she writes, "but we are happy and independent." Today's Japanese SYFs are world-class shoppers, and though they must still fight workplace discrimination and have limited career tracks—particularly if they aren't working for Westernized companies—they're somehow managing to earn enough yen to keep the country's many Vuitton, Burberry, and Issey Miyake boutiques buzzing. Not so long ago, Japanese hotels wouldn't serve women traveling alone, in part because they suspected that the guests might be spinsters intent on hurling themselves off balconies to end their desperate solitude. Today, the losers are happily checking in at Japanese mountain lodges, not to mention Australian spas, Vietnamese hotels, and Hawaiian beach resorts.

22   And unlike their foreign counterparts in the New Girl Order, Japanese singles don't seem to be worrying much about finding Mr. Right. A majority of Japanese single women between 25 and 54 say that they'd be just as happy never to marry. Peggy Orenstein, writing in the *New York Times Magazine* in 2001, noted that Japanese women find American-style sentimentality about marriage puzzling. Yoko Harruka, a television personality and author of a book called *I Won't Get Married*—written after she realized that her then-fiancé expected her to quit her career and serve him tea—says that her countrymen propose with lines like, "I want you to cook miso soup for me for the rest of my life." Japanese SYFs complain that men don't show affection and expect women to cook dinner obediently while they sit on their duffs reading the paper. Is it any wonder that the women prefer Burberry?

23   Post-Communist Europe is also going through the shock of the New Girl Order. Under Communist rule, women tended to marry and have kids early. In the late eighties, the mean age of first birth in East Germany, for instance, was 24.7, far lower than the West German average of 28.3. According to Tomáš Sobotka of the Vienna Institute of Demography, young people had plenty of reasons to schedule an early wedding day. Tying the knot was the only way to gain independence from parents, since married couples could get an apartment, while singles could not. Furthermore, access to modern contraception, which the state proved either unable or unwilling to produce at affordable prices, was limited. Marriages frequently began as the result of unplanned pregnancies.

24   And then the Wall came down. The free market launched shiny new job opportunities, making higher education more valuable than under Communist regimes, which had apportioned jobs and degrees. Suddenly, a young Polish or Hungarian woman might imagine having a career and some fun at the same time. In cities like Warsaw and Budapest, young adults can find pleasures completely unknown to previous generations of singles. In one respect, Eastern European and Russian SYFs were better equipped than Japanese ones for the new order. The strong single woman, an invisible figure in Japan, has long been a prominent character in the social landscape of Eastern Europe and Russia, a legacy, doubtless, of the Communist-era emphasis on egalitarianism (however inconsistently applied) and the massive male casualties of World War II.

25   Not that the post-Communist SYF is any happier with the husband material than her Japanese counterpart is. Eastern European gals complain about men overindulged by widowed mothers and unable to adapt to the new economy. According to *The Economist*, many towns in what used to be East Germany now face *Frauenmangel*—a lack of women—as SYFs who excelled in school have moved west for jobs, leaving the poorly performing men behind. In some towns, the ratio is just 40 women to 100 men. Women constitute the majority of both high school and college graduates in Poland. Though Russian women haven't joined the new order to the same extent, they're also grumbling about the men. In Russian TV's *The Balzac Age*, which chronicles the adventures of four single thirty-something women, Alla, a high-achieving yuppie attorney, calls a handyman for help in her apartment. The two—to their mutual horror—recognize each other as former high school sweethearts, now moving in utterly different social universes.

26   There's much to admire in the New Girl Order—and not just the previously hidden cleavage. Consider the lives most likely led by the mothers, grandmothers, great-grandmothers, and so on of the fashionista at the Warsaw airport or of the hard-partying Beijing actuary. Those women reached adulthood, which usually meant 18 or even younger; married guys from their village, or, if they were particularly daring, from the village across the river; and then had kids—end of story, except for maybe some goat milking, rice planting, or, in urban areas, shop tending. The New Girl Order means good-bye to such limitations. It means the possibility of more varied lives, of more expansively nourished aspirations. It also means a richer world. SYFs bring ambition, energy, and innovation to the economy, both local and global; they simultaneously promote and enjoy what author Brink Lindsey calls "the age of abundance." The SYF, in sum, represents a dramatic advance in personal freedom and wealth.

27   But as with any momentous social change, the New Girl Order comes with costs—in this case, profound ones. The globalized SYF upends centuries of cultural traditions. However limiting, those traditions shaped how families formed and the next generation grew up. So it makes sense that the SYF is partly to blame for a worldwide drop in fertility rates. To keep a population stable, or at its "replacement level," women must have an average of at least 2.1 children. Under the New Girl Order, though, women delay marriage and childbearing, which itself tends to reduce the number of kids, and sometimes—because the opportunity costs of children are much higher for educated women—they forgo them altogether. Save Albania, no European country stood at or above replacement levels in 2000. Three-quarters of Europeans now live in countries with fertility rates below 1.5, and even that number is inflated by a disproportionately high fertility rate among Muslim immigrants. Oddly, the most Catholic European countries—Italy, Spain, and Poland—have the lowest fertility rates, under 1.3. Much of Asia looks similar. In Japan, fertility rates are about 1.3. Hong Kong, according to the CIA's World Factbook, at 0.98 has broken the barrier of one child per woman.

28   For many, fertility decline seems to be one more reason to celebrate the New Girl Order. Fewer people means fewer carbon footprints, after all, and thus potential environmental relief. But while we're waiting for the temperature to drop a bit, economies will plunge in ways that will be extremely difficult to manage—and that,

ironically, will likely spell the SYF lifestyle's demise. As Philip Longman explains in his important book *The Empty Cradle*, dramatic declines in fertility rates equal aging and eventually shriveling populations. Japan now has one of the oldest populations in the world—one-third of its population, demographers predict, will be over 60 within a decade. True, fertility decline often spurs a temporary economic boost, as more women enter the workforce and increase income and spending, as was the case in 1980s Japan. In time, though, those women—and their male peers—will get old and need pensions and more health care.

29   And who will pay for that? With fewer children, the labor force shrinks, and so do tax receipts. Europe today has 35 pensioners for every 100 workers, Longman points out. By 2050, those 100 will be responsible for 75 pensioners; in Spain and Italy, the ratio of workers to pensioners will be a disastrous one-to-one. Adding to the economic threat, seniors with few or no children are more likely to look to the state for support than are elderly people with more children. The final irony is that the ambitious, hardworking SYF will have created a world where her children, should she have them, will need to work even harder in order to support her in her golden years.

30   Aging populations present other problems. For one thing, innovation and technological breakthroughs tend to be a young person's game—think of the young Turks of the information technology revolution. Fewer young workers and higher tax burdens don't make a good recipe for innovation and growth. Also, having fewer people leads to declining markets, and thus less business investment and formation. Where would you want to expand your cosmetics business: Ireland, where the population continues to renew itself, or Japan, where it is imploding?

31   And finally, the New Girl Order has given birth to a worrying ambivalence toward domestic life and the men who would help create it. Many analysts argue that today's women of childbearing age would have more kids if only their countries provided generous benefits for working mothers, as they do in Sweden and France. And it's true that those two countries have seen fertility rates inch up toward replacement levels in recent years. But in countries newly entering the New Girl Order, what SYFs complain about isn't so much a gap between work and family life as a chasm between their own aspirations and those of the men who'd be their husbands (remember those Japanese women skeptical of a future cooking miso soup). Adding to the SYF's alienation from domesticity is another glaring fact usually ignored by demographers: the New Girl Order is fun. Why get married when you can party on?

32   That raises an interesting question: Why are SYFs in the United States—the Rome of the New Girl Order—still so interested in marriage? By large margins, surveys suggest, American women want to marry and have kids. Indeed, our fertility rates, though lower than replacement level among college-educated women, are still healthier than those in most SYF countries (including Sweden and France). The answer may be that the family has always been essential ballast to the individualism, diversity, mobility, and sheer giddiness of American life. It helps that the U.S., like northwestern Europe, has a long tradition of "companionate marriage"—that is, marriage based not on strict roles but on common interests and mutual affection. Companionate marriage always rested on the assumption of female equality. Yet countries like Japan are joining the new order with no history of companionate

relations, and when it comes to adapting to the new order, the cultural cupboard is bare. A number of analysts, including demographer Nicholas Eberstadt, have also argued that it is America's religiousness that explains our relatively robust fertility, though the Polish fertility decline raises questions about that explanation.

33   It's by no means certain that Americans will remain exceptional in this regard. The most recent census data show a "sharp increase," over just the past six years, in the percentage of Americans in their 20s who have never married. Every year sees more books celebrating the SYF life, boasting titles like *Singular Existence* and *Living Alone and Loving It*. And SYFs will increasingly find themselves in a disappointing marriage pool. The *New York Times* excited considerable discussion this summer with a front-page article announcing that young women working full-time in several cities were now outearning their male counterparts. A historically unprecedented trend like this is bound to have a further impact on relations between the sexes and on marriage and childbearing rates.

34   Still, for now, women don't seem too worried about the New Girl Order's downside. On the contrary. The order marches on, as one domino after another falls to its pleasures and aspirations. Now, the *Singapore Times* tells us, young women in Vietnam are suddenly putting off marriage because they "want to have some fun"— and fertility rates have plummeted from 3.8 children in 1998 to 2.1 in 2006.

35   And then there's India. "The Gen Now bachelorette brigade is in no hurry to tie the knot," reports the *India Tribune*. "They're single, independent, and happy." Young urbanites are pushing up sales of branded apparel; Indian chick lit, along with *Cosmopolitan* and *Vogue*, flies out of shops in Delhi and Mumbai. Amazingly enough, fertility rates have dropped below replacement level in several of India's major cities, thanks in part to aspirant fashionistas. If in India—India!—the New Girl Order can reduce population growth, then perhaps nothing is beyond its powers. At the very least, the Indian experiment gives new meaning to the phrase "shop till you drop." ◆

CRITICAL THINKING

1. According to Hymowitz, why are young adults, especially young women, waiting longer than ever to get married and have children? How does the information she reports in this essay compare to your own plans for marriage and family?
2. Is Hymowitz supportive or critical of "the New Girl Order" she describes? Identify areas in her essay that reveal her point of view on this topic.
3. How does Hymowitz describe the New Girl Order? What cultural icons does she refer to in her description?
4. What warning does Hymowitz give if the New Girl Order continues unchecked? Is this warning valid? How should we respond?
5. According to Hymowitz, what is a "hotel family" or a "parasite single"? Do you see versions of these in the United States? Explain.
6. Hymowitz asks, "Why are SYFs [Single Young Females] in the United States . . . still so interested in marriage?" Answer this question from your

own perspective. How does the marriage culture in the United States differ from the marriage culture in other countries, such as Japan?

7. How have young, single women created a "Bridget Jones economy"? Explain.

CRITICAL WRITING

1. *Compare and Contrast:* How do the points Hymowitz raises in her essay connect to points made by essays in Chapter 9 on the decline of marriage? Analyze and discuss the possible cause/effect connections between this essay and an essay from Chapter 9.

2. *Expository Writing:* Write an essay in which you consider your own sense of cultural conditioning. Do you feel your behavior has been conditioned by sex-role expectations? In what ways? Is there a difference between the "real" you and the person you present to the world? If there is a difference, is it the result of cultural pressure? Explain.

GROUP PROJECTS

1. As a group, develop a list of questions designed to elicit student opinion on perceptions of feminism and gender roles in the first decade of the twenty-first century. What does feminism mean to the people you interview? How do men and women feel about it? Would they define themselves as supporting feminism? What about perceptions of gender and our expectations of men and women. How do the definitions they provide compare to a dictionary definition of feminism? Discuss your results with the class as part of a broader discussion on perceptions of contemporary gender roles.

2. Consider the connection Hymowitz draws between *Sex and the City* and how young women view themselves. Discuss the effects of the media's influence on gender roles—on how young men and young women define themselves. Some of the areas of your discussion might draw from television, film, art, advertising, newspapers, music, and other popular media. How do media representations of women and men reinforce or refute the common stereotypes?

The Men We Carry in Our Minds
*Scott Russell Sanders**

Satistically, men tend to hold more positions of power and wealth than women do. Many women feel that simply being born male automatically confers status and power or, at the very least, makes life easier. This cultural assumption, however, may only apply to a very small

---

* Scott Russell Sanders, *The Paradise of Bombs*, 1984

segment of the male population. Is it fair to stereotype men this way? Writer Scott Russell Sanders grew up in rural Tennessee and Ohio, where men aged early from lives of punishing physical labor or died young in military service. When he got to college, Sanders was baffled when the daughters of lawyers, bankers, and physicians accused him and his sex of "having cornered the world's pleasures." In this essay, Sanders explores the differences between the men and women in his life and how male power is often dependent on class and social influence.

1   "This must be a hard time for women," I say to my friend Anneke. "They have so many paths to choose from, and so many voices calling them."

2   "I think it's a lot harder for men," she replies.

3   "How do you figure that?"

4   "The women I know feel excited, innocent, like crusaders in a just cause. The men I know are eaten up with guilt."

5   "Women feel such pressure to be everything, do everything," I say. "Career, kids, art, politics. Have their babies and get back to the office a week later. It's as if they're trying to overcome a million years' worth of evolution in one lifetime."

6   "But we help one another. And we have this deep-down sense that we're in the right—we've been held back, passed over, used—while men feel they're in the wrong. Men are the ones who've been discredited, who have to search their souls."

7   I search my soul. I discover guilty feelings aplenty—toward the poor, Native Americans, the whales, an endless list of debts. But toward women I feel something more confused, a snarl of shame, envy, wary, tenderness, and amazement. This muddle troubles me. To hide my unease I say, "You're right, it's tough being a man these days."

8   "Don't laugh," Anneke frowns at me. "I wouldn't be a man for anything. It's much easier being the victim. All the victim has to do is break free. The persecutor has to live with his past."

9   How deep is that past? I find myself wondering. How much of an inheritance do I have to throw off?

10   When I was a boy growing up on the back roads of Tennessee and Ohio, the men I knew labored with their bodies. They were marginal farmers, just scraping by, or welders, steelworkers, carpenters; they swept floors, dug ditches, mined coal, or drove trucks, their forearms ropy with muscle; they trained horses, stoked furnaces, made tires, stood on assembly lines wrestling parts onto cars and refrigerators. They got up before light, worked all day long, whatever the weather, and when they came home at night, they looked as though somebody had been whipping them. In the evenings and on weekends, they worked on their own places, tilling gardens that were lumpy with clay, fixing broken-down cars, hammering on houses that were always too drafty, too leaky, too small. The bodies of the men I knew were twisted and maimed in ways visible and invisible. The nails of their hands were black and split, the hands tattooed with scars. Some had lost fingers. Heavy lifting had given many of them finicky backs and guts weak from hernias. Racing against conveyor belts had given them ulcers. Their ankles and knees ached from years of standing on concrete. Anyone who had worked for long around machines was hard of hearing. They squinted, and the skin of their faces was creased like the leather of old work gloves. There were times, studying them, when I dreaded growing up. Most of them

coughed, from dust or cigarettes, and most of them drank
cheap wine or whiskey, so their
eyes looked bloodshot and
bruised. The fathers of my
friends always seemed older
than the mothers. Men wore out sooner. Only women lived into old age.

> *The fathers of my friends always seemed older than the mothers. Men wore out sooner. Only women lived into old age.*

11   As a boy I also knew another sort of man, who did not sweat and break down like mules. They were soldiers, and so far as I could tell, they scarcely worked at all. But when the shooting started, many of them would die. This was what soldiers were for, just like a hammer was for driving nails. Warriors and toilers: those seemed, in my boyhood vision, to be the chief destinies for men. They weren't the only destinies, as I learned from having a few male teachers, from reading books, and from watching television. But the men on television—the politicians, the astronauts, the generals, the savvy lawyers, the philosophical doctors, the bosses who gave orders to both soldiers and laborers—seemed as remote and unreal to me as the figures in Renaissance tapestries. I could no more imagine growing up to become one of these cool, potent creatures than I could imagine becoming a prince.

12   A nearer and more hopeful example was that of my father, who had escaped from a red dirt farm to a tire factory, and from the assembly line to the front office. Eventually, he dressed in a white shirt and tie. He carried himself as if he had been born to work with his mind. But his body, remembering the earlier years of slogging work, began to give out on him in his fifties, and it quit on him entirely before he turned 65.

13   A scholarship enabled me not only to attend college, a rare enough feat in my circle, but even to study in a university meant for the children of the rich. Here I met for the first time young men who had assumed from birth that they would lead lives of comfort and power. And for the first time, I met women who told me that men were guilty of having kept all the joys and privileges of the earth for themselves. I was baffled. What privileges? What joys? I thought about the maimed, dismal lives of most of the men back home. What had they stolen from their wives and daughters? The right to go five days a week, 12 months a year, for 30 or 40 years to a steel mill or a coal mine? The right to drop bombs and die in war? The right to feel every leak in the roof, every gap in the fence, every cough in the engine as a wound they must mend? The right to feel, when the layoff comes or the plant shuts down, not only afraid but ashamed?

14   I was slow to understand the deep grievances of women. This was because, as a boy, I had envied them. Before college, the only people I had ever known who were interested in art or music or literature, the only ones who read books, the only ones who ever seemed to enjoy a sense of ease and grace were the mothers and daughters. Like the menfolk, they fretted about money, they scrimped and made do. But when the pay stopped coming in, they were not the ones who had failed. Nor did they have to go to war, and that seemed to me a blessed fact. By comparison with the narrow, ironclad days of fathers, there was an expansiveness, I thought, in the days of mothers. They went to see neighbors, to shop in town, to run errands at school, at the library, at church. No doubt, had I looked harder at their lives, I would have envied them less. It was not my fate to become a woman, so it was easier for

me to see the graces. I didn't see then what a prison a house could be, since houses seemed to be brighter, handsomer places than any factory. I did not realize—because such things were never spoken of—how often women suffered from men's bullying. Even then I could see how exhausting it was for a mother to cater all day to the needs of young children. But if I had been asked, as a boy, to choose between tending a baby and tending a machine, I think I would have chosen the baby. (Having now tended both, I know I would choose the baby.)

15   So I was baffled when the women at college accused me and my sex of having cornered the world's pleasures. I think something like my bafflement has been felt by other boys (and by girls as well) who grew up in dirt-poor farm country, in mining country, in black ghettoes, in Hispanic barrios, in the shadows of factories, in Third World nations—any place where the fate of men is just as grim and bleak as the fate of women.

16   When the women I met at college thought about the joys and privileges of men, they did not carry in their minds the sort of men I had known in my childhood. They thought of their fathers, who were bankers, physicians, architects, stockholders, the big wheels of the big cities. They were never laid off, never short of cash at month's end, never lined up for welfare. These fathers made decisions that mattered. They ran the world.

17   The daughters of such men wanted to share in this power, this glory. So did I. They yearned for a say over their future, for jobs worthy of their abilities, for the right to live at peace, unmolested, whole. Yes, I thought, yes, yes. The difference between me and these daughters was that they saw me, because of my sex, as destined from birth to become like their fathers and, therefore, as an enemy to their desires. But I knew better. I wasn't an enemy, in fact or in feeling. I was an ally. If I had known then how to tell them so, would they have believed me? Would they now? ◆

CRITICAL THINKING

1. Consider the stereotypical view that being male automatically grants one power, status, and privilege. Then think about three men you know well, such as a father, brother, or friend. Do their everyday life experiences bear out this generalization?

2. In paragraph 7, Sanders states he has feelings of guilt toward a number of minority groups or social causes, but his feelings toward women are more complicated. What do you think might be the reasons for his feelings? Can you identify with this perspective?

3. Do you think Sanders feels women, not men, are the privileged class? Explain.

4. How do you think women from the different socioeconomic groups Sanders mentions in his essay would respond to his ideas? For example, how would the educated daughters of the lawyers and bankers respond? How about the women from Sanders's hometown?

5. What are the occupations and obligations of the men mentioned in the article? What socioeconomic segment of society is Sanders describing? What does this suggest about the relationship between gender and class?

6. Sanders relates his argument entirely in the first person, using personal anecdotes to illustrate his point. How does this approach influence the reader? Would this essay be different if he told it from a third-person point of view? Explain.
7. In paragraph eight, Sanders's friend Anneke says she "wouldn't be a man for anything. It is much easier being the victim." What does Anneke mean by this statement? Do you agree with her view? Why or why not?
8. What effect do Anneke's comments have on Sanders's audience? Why do you think he quotes her? How do her comments support his argument?

CRITICAL WRITING

1. *Exploratory Writing:* Write an essay in which you consider your own sense of cultural conditioning. Do you think your behavior has been conditioned by sex-role expectations? In what ways? Is there a difference between the "real" you and the person you present to the world? If there is a difference, is it the result of cultural conditioning?
2. *Analytical Writing:* What does it mean to be a man today? Write an essay explaining what you think it means to be male in today's society. How do men factor into current social, intellectual, political, economic, and religious equations? What opportunities are available—or not available—to men? Do you think it is easier or better to be male in American culture?

GROUP PROJECT

1. With your group, try to define the terms "masculine" and "feminine." You might include library research on the origins of the words or research their changing implications over the years. Develop your own definition for each word, and then discuss with the rest of the class how you arrived at your definitions.

The Science of Difference
*Steven Pinker**

During a speech he made in January 2005, at a National Bureau of Economics Research Conference on diversifying the science and engineering workforce Harvard University President Lawrence H. Summers commented that biological factors could be the reason why there were more men than women in high-end science and engineering positions. His comments sparked a great deal of controversy, especially among female academics, who challenged his viewpoint as sexist. Several months later, Summers resigned from his

---

* Steven Pinker, *The New Republic Online*, February 7, 2005

position as president of Harvard. In this next essay, Harvard professor and Summers's supporter Steven Pinker explores the idea that men and women are biologically different and that we should admit this fact.

1   When I was an undergraduate in the early 1970s, I was assigned a classic paper, published in *Scientific American*, that began: "There is an experiment in psychology that you can perform easily in your home. . . . Buy two presents for your wife, choosing thing . . . she will find equally attractive." Just ten years after those words were written, the author's blithe assumption that his readers were male struck me as comically archaic. By the early '70s, women in science were no longer an oddity or a joke but a given. Today, in my own field, the study of language development in children, a majority of the scientists are women. Even in scientific fields with a higher proportion of men, the contributions of women are so indispensable that any talk of turning back the clock would be morally heinous and scientifically ruinous.

2   Yet to hear the reaction to [former] Harvard President Lawrence Summers's remarks at a conference on gender imbalances in science, in which he raised the possibility of innate sex differences, one might guess that he had proposed exactly that. Nancy Hopkins, the eminent MIT biologist and advocate for women in science, stormed out of the room to avoid, she said, passing out from shock. An engineering dean called his remarks "an intellectual tsunami," and, with equal tastelessness, a *Boston Globe* columnist compared him to people who utter racial epithets or wear swastikas. Alumnae threatened to withhold donations, and the National Organization of Women called for his resignation. Summers was raked in a letter signed by more than 100 Harvard faculty members and shamed into issuing serial apologies.

3   Summers did not, of course, say that women are "natively inferior," that "they just can't cut it," that they suffer "an inherent cognitive deficit in the sciences," or that men have "a monopoly on basic math ability," as many academics and journalists assumed. Only a madman could believe such things. Summers's analysis of why there might be fewer women in mathematics and science is commonplace among economists who study gender disparities in employment, though it is rarely mentioned in the press or in academia when it comes to discussions of the gender gap in science and engineering. The fact that women make up only 20 percent of the workforce in science, engineering, and technology development has at least three possible (and not mutually exclusive) explanations. One is the persistence of discrimination, discouragement, and other barriers. In popular discussions of gender imbalances in the workforce, this is the explanation most mentioned. Although no one can deny that women in science still face these injustices, there are reasons to doubt they are the only explanation. A second possibility is that gender disparities can arise in the absence of discrimination as long as men and women differ, on average, in their mixture of talents, temperaments, and interests—whether this difference is the result of biology, socialization, or an interaction of the two. A third explanation is that child rearing, still disproportionately shouldered by women, does not easily coexist with professions that demand Herculean commitments of time. These considerations speak against the reflex of attributing every gender disparity to gender discrimination and call for research aimed at evaluating the explanations.

4   The analysis should have been unexceptionable. Anyone who has fled a cluster of men at a party debating the fine points of flat-screen televisions can appreciate that fewer women than men might choose engineering, even in the absence of arbitrary barriers. (As one female social scientist noted in *Science Magazine*, "Reinventing the curriculum will not make me more interested in learning how my dishwasher works.") To what degree these and other differences originate in biology must be determined by research, not fatwa. History tells us that how much we want to believe a proposition is not a reliable guide as to whether it is true.

5   Nor is a better understanding of the causes of gender disparities inconsequential. Overestimating the extent of sex discrimination is not without costs. Unprejudiced people of both sexes who are responsible for hiring and promotion decisions may be falsely charged with sexism. Young women may be pressured into choosing lines of work they don't enjoy. Some proposed cures may do more harm than good; for example, gender quotas for grants could put deserving grantees under a cloud of suspicion, and forcing women onto all university committees would drag them from their labs into endless meetings. An exclusive focus on overt discrimination also diverts attention from policies that penalize women inadvertently because of the fact that, as the legal theorist Susan Estrich has put it, "Waiting for the connection between gender and parenting to be broken is waiting for Godot." A tenure clock that conflicts with women's biological clocks, and family-unfriendly demands like evening seminars and weekend retreats, are obvious examples. The regrettably low proportion of women who received tenured job offers from Harvard during Summers's presidency may be an unintended consequence of his policy of granting tenure to scholars early in their careers, when women are more likely to be bearing the full burdens of parenthood.

6   Conservative columnists had a field day pointing to the Harvard hullabaloo as a sign of runaway political correctness at elite universities. Indeed, the quality of discussion among the nation's leading scholars and pundits is not a pretty sight. Summers's critics repeatedly mangled his suggestion that innate differences might be one cause of gender disparities (a suggestion that he drew partly from a literature review in my book, *The Blank Slate*) into the claim that they must be the only cause. And they converted his

> *The belief, still popular among some academics (particularly outside the biological sciences), that children are born unisex and are molded into male and female roles by their parents and society is becoming less credible.*

suggestion that the statistical distributions of men's and women's abilities are not identical to the claim that all men are talented and all women are not—as if someone heard that women typically live longer than men and concluded that every woman lives longer than every man. Just as depressing is an apparent unfamiliarity with the rationale behind political equality, as when Hopkins sarcastically remarked that, if Summers were right, Harvard should amend its admissions policy, presumably to accept fewer women. This is a classic confusion between the factual claim that men and women are not indistinguishable and the moral claim that we ought to judge people by their individual merits rather than the statistics of their group.

7   Many of Summers's critics believe that talk of innate gender differences is a relic of Victorian pseudoscience, such as the old theory that cogitation harms women by diverting blood from their ovaries to their brains. In fact, much of the scientific literature has reported numerous statistical differences between men and women. As I noted in *The Blank Slate*, for instance, men are, on average, better at mental rotation and mathematical word problems; women are better at remembering locations and at mathematical calculation. Women match shapes more quickly, are better at reading faces, are better spellers, retrieve words more fluently, and have a better memory for verbal material. Men take greater risks and place a higher premium on status; women are more solicitous to their children.

8   Of course, just because men and women are different does not mean that the differences are triggered by genes. People develop their talents and personalities in response to their social milieu, which can change rapidly. So some of today's sex differences in cognition could be as culturally determined as sex differences in hair and clothing. But the belief, still popular among some academics (particularly outside the biological sciences), that children are born unisex and are molded into male and female roles by their parents and society is becoming less credible. Many sex differences are universal across cultures (the twentieth-century belief in sex-reversed tribes is as specious as the nineteenth-century belief in blood-deprived ovaries), and some are found in other primates. Men's and women's brains vary in numerous ways, including the receptors for sex hormones.

9   Variations in these hormones, especially before birth, can exaggerate or minimize the typical male and female patterns in cognition and personality. Boys with defective genitals who are surgically feminized and raised as girls have been known to report feeling like they are trapped in the wrong body and to show characteristically male attitudes and interests. And a meta-analysis of 172 studies by psychologists Hugh Lytton and David Romney in 1991 found virtually no consistent difference in the way contemporary Americans socialize their sons and daughters. Regardless of whether it explains the gender disparity in science, the idea that some sex differences have biological roots cannot be dismissed as Neanderthal ignorance.

10   Since most sex differences are small and many favor women, they don't necessarily give an advantage to men in school or on the job. But Summers invoked yet another difference that may be more consequential. In many traits, men show greater variance than women and are disproportionately found at both the low and high ends of the distribution. Boys are more likely to be learning disabled or retarded but also more likely to reach the top percentiles in assessments of mathematical ability, even though boys and girls are similar in the bulk of the bell curve. The pattern is readily explained by evolutionary biology. Since a male can have more offspring than a female—but also has a greater chance of being childless (the victims of other males who impregnate the available females)—natural selection favors a slightly more conservative and reliable baby-building process for females and a slightly more ambitious and error-prone process for males. That is because the advantage of an exceptional daughter (who still can have only as many children as a female can bear and nurse in a lifetime) would be canceled out by her unexceptional sisters, whereas an exceptional son, who might sire several dozen grandchildren, can more than make up for his dull, childless brothers. One doesn't have to accept the evolutionary

explanation to appreciate how greater male variability could explain, in part, why more men end up with extreme levels of achievement.

11   What are we to make of the breakdown of standards of intellectual discourse in this affair—the statistical innumeracy, the confusion of fairness with sameness, the refusal to glance at the scientific literature? It is not a disease of tenured radicals; comparable lapses can be found among the political right (just look at its treatment of evolution). Instead, we may be seeing the operation of a fascinating bit of human psychology.

12   The psychologist Philip Tetlock has argued that the mentality of taboo—the belief that certain ideas are so dangerous that it is sinful even to think them—is not a quirk of Polynesian culture or religious superstition but is ingrained into our moral sense. In 2000, he reported asking university students their opinions of unpopular but defensible proposals, such as allowing people to buy and sell organs or auctioning adoption licenses to the highest-bidding parents. He found that most of his respondents did not even try to refute the proposals but expressed shock and outrage at having been asked to entertain them. They refused to consider positive arguments for the proposals and sought to cleanse themselves by volunteering for campaigns to oppose them. Sound familiar?

13   The psychology of taboo is not completely irrational. In maintaining our most precious relationships, it is not enough to say and do the right thing. We have to show that our heart is in the right place and that we don't weigh the costs and benefits of selling out those who trust us. If someone offers to buy your child or your spouse or your vote, the appropriate response is not to think it over or to ask how much. The appropriate response is to refuse even to consider the possibility. Anything less emphatic would betray the awful truth that you don't understand what it means to be a genuine parent or spouse or citizen. (The logic of taboo underlies the horrific fascination of plots whose protagonists are agonized by unthinkable thoughts, such as *Indecent Proposal* and *Sophie's Choice*.) Sacred and tabooed beliefs also work as membership badges in coalitions. To believe something with a perfect faith, to be incapable of apostasy, is a sign of fidelity to the group and loyalty to the cause. Unfortunately, the psychology of taboo is incompatible with the ideal of scholarship, which is that any idea is worth thinking about, if only to determine whether it is wrong.

14   At some point in the history of the modern women's movement, the belief that men and women are psychologically indistinguishable became sacred. The reasons are understandable: Women really had been held back by bogus claims of essential differences. Now anyone who so much as raises the question of innate sex differences is seen as "not getting it" when it comes to equality between the sexes. The tragedy is that this mentality of taboo needlessly puts a laudable cause on a collision course with the findings of science and the spirit of free inquiry. ◆

CRITICAL THINKING ───────────────

1. How does Pinker's introduction frame the rest of his essay? Does his example reinforce the points he makes about women in science? How does it help position Pinker and his viewpoint on the issue? Explain.

2. What reasons does Pinker offer for why women are underrepresented in science, engineering, and technology fields?

3. As a college student, do you feel that your gender, and the expectations placed upon it, influence your future career choices? Will this impact how far you go in your career? Explain.

4. What does Pinker say about sex differences? Do you agree or disagree with his viewpoint?

5. What is the "psychology of taboo"? How does it apply to Summers's remarks? Given this underlying dynamic, what are we able to say about our beliefs and our ability to pursue meaningful debate? Explain.

6. Summarize Pinker's position in this essay. Does he think Summers was right?

CRITICAL WRITING

1. *Research and Persuasive Writing:* Research the controversy that stemmed from Lawrence Summers's comments at the NBER Conference (Wikipedia has a good list of resources on the Lawrence Summers article) and write an essay about your perspective on the issue. Be sure to read the transcript of his actual speech, as well as his personal response to the controversy, at http://www.president.harvard.edu/speeches/2005/nber.html. Were his comments taken out of context? Were they inappropriate, especially in light of where he was speaking? Explain.

2. *Exploratory Writing:* Pinker comments, "The belief, still popular among some academics, that children are born unisex and are molded into male and female roles by their parents and society is becoming less credible." Write an essay in which you consider your own sense of cultural conditioning. Do you feel your behavior has been conditioned by sex-role expectations? If so, in what ways? Is there a difference between the "real" you and the person you present to the world? If there is a difference, is it the result of cultural pressure related to gender-based expectations of behavior? Explain.

GROUP PROJECTS

1. What role, if any, does biology play in our lives as men and women? Make a list of commonly assumed sex-differences (eg., boys like to play with trucks, girls like to play with dolls). After you have compiled your list, weigh in on whether these conventions hold scientific merit or are socially constructed perceptions.

2. Is it harder to grow up male or female in America today? As a group, discuss which gender faces the greatest and most daunting challenges and why. Will this situation get worse? Offer suggestions to help ease the gender-related challenges college-age men and women face in today's culture. Discuss your group's points as part of a larger class dialogue on men and women in today's society.

Hip-Hop: Beyond Beats and Rhymes?

*Byron Hurt**

Filmmaker Byron Hurt, a life-long hip-hop fan, was watching rap music videos on BET when he realized that each video was nearly identical. Guys in fancy cars threw money at the camera while scantily clad women danced in the background. As he discovered how stereotypical rap videos had become, Hurt, a former Northeastern University quarterback, decided to make a film about the gender politics of hip-hop, the music and the culture that he grew up with. "The more I grew and the more I learned about sexism and violence and homophobia, the more those lyrics became unacceptable to me," he says. "And I began to become more conflicted about the music that I loved." The result was the PBS documentary *Hip-Hop: Beyond Beats and Rhymes*, a film that tackles issues of masculinity, sexism, violence and homophobia in today's hip-hop culture. This article about the film notes the connection between violence and masculinity that increasingly is putting young men and boys in front of—and behind—the trigger. And hip-hop music, with its glorification of violence, meaningless sex, and drugs isn't helping matters.

1   In *Hip-Hop: Beyond Beats and Rhymes*, author Kevin Powell says, "We live in a society where manhood is all about conquering and violence. . . . And what we don't realize is that kind of manhood ultimately kills you." But this preoccupation with violence is not unique to hip-hop culture. As author, teacher and radio host Michael Dyson says, "When you think about American society, the notion of violent masculinity is at the heart of American identity." From the outlaw cowboy in American history to the hypermasculine thug of gangster rap, violent masculinity is an enduring symbol of American manhood itself.

2   Such violence has become so pervasive—not just in popular culture forms such as music, movies and video games, but also in military culture and sports—that many Americans have become desensitized to it, supporting violent culture through consumerism, even unwittingly. "America is a very hypermasculine, hyperaggressive nation," filmmaker Byron Hurt says. "So it stands to reason that a rapper like 50 Cent can be commercially palatable in a nation that supports a culture of violence."

3   Hip-hop culture itself was born out of the devastated South Bronx ghettoes, where thousands of residents, mostly poor and black or Latino, were all but abandoned by the city. Music, dance and rapping became not only a way to respond to violence in the community, but also to reflect what was happening within it. As many poor neighborhoods of color became further devastated in the 1980s and 1990s, gangster rap lyrics proliferated, echoing the proliferation of guns, gangs and prison culture—mentalities stemming from what Kevin Powell refers to as a "forced environment."

4   For many young men and boys, hypermasculinity is inextricable from race and class. Anti-violence educator Jackson

For many young men and boys, hypermasculinity is inextricable from race and class.

---

* Excerpt from *Hip-Hop: Beyond Beats and Rhymes,* directed by Byron Hurt, posted March 20, 2007; Independent Television Service (ITVS), http://www.pbs.org/independentlens/hiphop/film.htm

Katz explains it: "If you're a young man growing up in this culture, and the culture is telling you that being a man means being powerful . . . but you don't have a lot of real power, one thing that you do have access to is your body and your ability to present yourself physically as somebody who's worthy of respect. And I think that's one of the things that accounts for a lot of the hypermasculine posturing by a lot of young men of color and a lot of working-class white guys as well. Men who have more power, men who have financial power and workplace authority and forms of abstract power like that don't have to be as physically powerful because they can exert their power in other ways."

5   The images of hypermasculine men of color, in hip-hop culture and elsewhere, play into both myths and realities. Professor and writer James Peterson uses the example of the Public Enemy logo—a black male figure within the target of a gun— as one way in which black men navigate the inner city. Hypermasculine posturing can also serve as a defense mechanism. As history professor Jelani Cobb explains, "The reason why braggadocio and boast is so central to the history of hip-hop is because you're dealing with the history of black men in America. And there's a whole lineage of black men wanting to deny their own frailty. In some ways you have to do that . . . like a psychic armor."

6   One method of countering limited modes of masculinity is to create more diverse ways in which young men and boys can communicate—ways that might include, but also go beyond, traditional notions of what it means to "be a man."

7   Author William Pollack blames these stereotypical expectations of what it means to be male for punishing boys who do not conform while demanding "stoicism and silence at an enormous emotional cost." This either/or scenario leaves few options for young men and boys to act beyond stereotypes of hypermasculinity and violence.

8   What's the solution? *Hip-Hop: Beyond Beats and Rhymes* filmmaker Byron Hurt mentions that getting "men to take a hard look at [them]selves" might be one way to reach beyond the limits of stereotypical masculinity. "We're in this box," he says, "and in order to be in that box, you have to be strong, you have to be tough, you have to have a lot of girls, you gotta have money, you have to be a player or a pimp, know you gotta be in control, you have to dominate other men, other people, you know if you are not any of those things, then you know people call you soft or weak or a chump, and nobody wants to be any of those things. So everybody stays inside the box." Through introspection and an opportunity to engage in dialogue around what masculinity means, young men and boys could find ways to move outside of the box. ◆

CRITICAL THINKING

1. What do you need to know about hip-hop to understand the point of the article and the film that it examines? Explain.
2. Define "hypermasculinity." How is it different from masculinity? What does the word *hypermasculinity* imply? Explain.
3. Jackson Katz explains, "If you're a young man growing up in this culture, and the culture is telling you that being a man means being powerful . . . but you don't have a lot of real power, one thing that you do have access

to is your body and your ability to present yourself physically as somebody who's worthy of respect." In your own words, describe the images of masculinity in America today. Do you agree or disagree with Katz's assessment? Why or why not?

4. Why does Hurt feel that hip-hop artists who cash in on hypermasculinity are setting back racial equality? Explain.

5. In what ways is the hypermasculinity promoted in hip-hop music, and embraced by young males, limiting and harmful? In what ways can it be viewed as ironic?

6. What is the "box" that Byron Hurt says holds men, especially young black men, back? How does culture and society contribute to the creation of this box?

CRITICAL WRITING

1. *Personal Narrative:* Do you think that music can influence behavior? Write about a time when music—or another medium, such as drama in a film or an image in a piece of art—influenced the way you behaved. Describe the incident and your behavior and why the medium influenced you the way it did.

2. *Persuasive Writing:* In an essay on the problems with hip-hop—"In Search of Notorious PhDs"—social critic Lindsay Johns expresses his concern for the way some hip-hop artists glorify music that conveys the message that "to be black means to be physical, violent, homophobic, and über macho." Find his article online and write an essay expressing your own viewpoint on this issue. Can lyrics and images be harmful? Are they just in fun or maybe to shock but not to be taken seriously? Explain.

3. *Expository Writing:* Compare the images of females on hip-hop music covers and videos to real women. What images of women are they promoting? Assume you are a foreign visitor to the United States who has never seen a music video or listened to hip-hop music. What might you assume about the cultural attitude toward American women based on what you see and hear? Explain.

GROUP PROJECTS

1. How do some hip-hop lyrics create a culture of self-loathing? Look up the lyrics of some popular hip-hop songs [Warning: Some are sexually explicit and violent] and, as a group, analyze them for their social and cultural messages.

2. With your group, view the clips and read about the independent movie *Hip-Hop: Beyond Beats and Rhymes.* After visiting all parts of the movie's Web site (http://www.pbs.org/independentlens/hiphop) and after watching the clips, prepare a presentation to the class on this issue, drawing from lyrics, online research, and your own experience.

CULTURE SHOCK

50 Cent

The preceding article discussed the violence, sexism, and hypermasculinity promoted by some very popular hip-hop artists. The lyrics in this type of music, and its glorification of hypermasculinity, send a message to youth that such traits are not only permissible, they are cool. Do we take such images seriously, or are they just a marketing ploy? Do they hurt anyone? Consider this billboard of 50 Cent. As you analyze the image, consider the points in the preceding essay as well as your own personal perspective.

THINKING CRITICALLY

1. Who are your favorite music artists? How are men and women portrayed in videos and music jackets by these artists? How do the artists portray themselves?
2. What is happening in the photo featured here? If you were shopping in a music store and were unfamiliar with 50 Cent, would you stop and take a closer look at the picture? Why or why not?
3. What audience do you think 50 Cent is trying to attract? How does the image appeal to this audience?
4. Do you think men would have a different reaction to this image than women? Why or why not?
5. In what ways does this image support some of the points made in the previous essay? Explain.

► **He's a Laker; She's a "Looker"**
*Jennifer L. Knight and Traci A. Giuliano**

► **Why Men Don't Watch Women's Sports**
Graham Hays

► **Gender Inequality**
E. M. Swift

Are female athletes taken less seriously than male athletes? Are they judged more on their looks than on their abilities? Is their competition devalued by the media? It is important to remember that less than 40 years ago, many women were barred from playing sports in college. In fact, many women were barred from attending college. In 1971, only 18 percent of women completed 4-year degrees. Now, women represent the majority of college graduates, largely because Title IX ensured that they were presented with equal opportunity, including equal opportunity in sports. The result was a boom in women's athletics. Today, young women can set their sights on a college basketball scholarship just as much as young men can. The question at hand, now that the playing field has been leveled, is, Do we still need Title IX?

This section's Viewpoints takes a look at women and men in sports, both in college and in the professional arena. First, Jennifer L. Knight and Traci A. Giuliano explain how the media perpetuates stereotypes that serve to trivialize women's sports. The time has come, they explain, for the media to present balanced coverage of female athletes and to stop promoting outdated stereotypes. Only then, they argue, will the public begin to see female athletes as great competitors first and as women second. Then Graham Hays, commentator for ESPN's Out of the Box, explains that men just don't like to watch women's sports. It isn't media imbalance, he asserts, it's *athletic* imbalance—men are just more interesting to watch. Finally, *Sports Illustrated* columnist E. M. Swift explains why he thinks the time for Title IX has passed.

He's a Laker; She's a "Looker"

Jennifer L. Knight and Traci A. Giuliano

1   In an era in which men's professional sports is becoming characterized by multimillion dollar contracts, player's union lockouts, illegal steroid use, and an individualistic mentality, disgruntled sports fans are increasingly turning to women's professional

---

* Jennifer L. Knight and Traci A. Giuliano, abridged from *Sex Roles*, August 2001, entire article online at http://www.southwestern.edu/academic/bwp/pdf/2002bwp-knight_giuliano.pdf; Graham Hays, *ESPN.com*, August 22, 2003; E. M. Swift, *SI.com* (*Sports Illustrated*), October 10, 2006

sports for entertainment. Indeed, leagues such as the Women's National Basketball Association (WNBA), the Ladies' Professional Golf Association (LPGA), the Women's Pro Softball League (WPSL), the Women's Pro Tennis Tour (WTA), and the Women's United Soccer Association (WUSA) are a welcome sign for fans searching for team-oriented play, affordable seats, and accessible sports stars (Wulf, 1997). In addition to the burgeoning field of women's professional sport, the Olympic Games have also been a showcase for successful female athletes. In the 1996 Atlanta Games, U.S. women's teams earned gold medals in gymnastics, soccer, softball, and basketball (with the softball and basketball teams reclaiming their titles at the 2000 Sydney Games). Their winter counterparts in the 1998 Nagano Games also fared well, with the first-place women's hockey team and with individual stars Picabo Street, Tara Lipinski, and Christine Witty securing victories.

2   Female athletes competing at the interscholastic and intercollegiate levels have also made great strides. The Title IX court decision of 1972 requires all federally funded programs, including athletics, to provide equal treatment and opportunity for participation for men and women. The implication for sports programs was that high schools and public universities subsequently were required to spend equivalent amounts of time and money for male and female athletes' scholarships, recruitment, facilities, supplies, travel, and services (Curtis & Grant, 2001). In part because of these improved opportunities, girls and women's involvement in sport has reached an all-time high. Whereas in 1971, only 1 in 27 girls participated in high school athletics, over 1 in 3 participated in 1997 (Women's Sports Foundation, 1998).

3   Although women's participation in professional, Olympic, intercollegiate, and interscholastic sport has reached unprecedented highs, research shows that media coverage of female athletes still lags behind that of men's (Tuggle & Owen, 1999). For example, women were featured on the cover of *Sports Illustrated* a scant four times out of 53 issues in 1996 (Women's Sports Foundation, 1997). A longitudinal study of *Sports Illustrated* feature articles from the mid-1950s to the late 1980s also revealed that the popular sport magazine allots far fewer column inches and photographs per article for women's sport as compared to men's (Salwen & Wood, 1994). A similar pattern was exhibited in television coverage of the Olympics, both in 1992 (Higgs & Weiller, 1994) and in 1996, purportedly "the year of women's sports" (Eastman & Billings, 1999). Even coverage of collegiate and high school sport is gender biased—boys receive more

4   and longer articles than do girls (Sagas, Cunningham, Wigley, & Ashley, 2000). In effect, this "symbolic annihilation" (Gerbner, 1972) of women's sport by the media conveys the inaccurate idea that women's sport is inferior to and not as noteworthy as men's sport.

> *Coverage of women's sport is inferior to that of men's not only in quantity but in quality as well. Sport commentators and writers often allude or explicitly refer to a female athlete's attractiveness, emotionality, femininity, and heterosexuality, yet male athletes are depicted as powerful, independent, dominating, and valued.*

Coverage of women's sport is inferior to that of men's not only in quantity but in quality as well (Duncan & Messner, 2000). Sport commentators and writers often allude or explicitly refer to a female athlete's attractiveness, emotionality, femininity, and heterosexuality (all of which effectively convey to the audience that her stereotypical gender role is more salient than her athletic role), yet male athletes are depicted as powerful, independent, dominating, and valued (Sabo & Jansen, 1992).

5   Because competitively participating in sports is inconsistent with society's prescribed female role, the media coverage of female athletes seems to be trying to protect female athletes from rejection (or, more cynically, giving the public what they think it "wants") by emphasizing other aspects of their "femaleness," such as their attractiveness (Kane, 1996). For instance, although Gabrielle Reese, Anna Kournikova, Katarina Witt, and Jan Stephenson are all exceptional athletes, the media often focus on their attractiveness, a problem that is much less common for male athletes. In effect, the media tend to represent female athletes as women first (i.e., through focusing on their hair, nails, clothing, and attractiveness) and as athletes second; however, male athletes for the most part are portrayed solely in terms of their athleticism (Boutilier & San Giovanni, 1983).

6   This trivialization of women athletes is consistent with schema theory, which proposes that people have implicit cognitive structures that provide them with expectancies when processing information (Fiske & Taylor, 1991). One of the most socially constructed and dichotomous stereotypes is that of gender (Burn, O'Neal, & Nederend, 1996). Gender schema theory argues that people are socialized (e.g., through parents, teachers, peers, toys, and the popular media) into believing that gender differences are significant and worth maintaining (Bem, 1981). Although there is actually more variability within than between the sexes, the concept of distinct and exclusive gender differences persists nonetheless (Martin, 1987).

7   When people do violate our well-ingrained schemas (as would a female truck driver or a male secretary), they are consequently perceived more negatively than are people who are schema-consistent (Knight, Giuliano, & Sanchez-Ross, 2001). It may be, then, that men are readily portrayed by the media as athletes first because being an athlete is consistent with the traditional male role (Coakley & White, 1992). However, for women, being an athlete contradicts the conventional female role, and thus media coverage emphasizes other aspects of their "femaleness" (such as their attractiveness). Consequently, the narratives of male athletes are free to focus on their athletic accomplishments, whereas the portrayals of female athletes focus on aspects of their femininity, possibly to make these female athletes appear more gender-role consistent.

8   The trivialization of women's sports by the media is well established, but researchers have yet to empirically investigate how differential portrayals of male and female athletes affect the public's view of the athletes. Although researchers have speculated as to how people's beliefs might be influenced by biased coverage (Fasting, 1999), there is a dearth of research on the actual consequences of these differential portrayals as well as on the extent to which the media can truly influence people's perceptions of athletes. In addition, members of the media argue that they simply provide coverage that "the public wants," yet this also remains to be substantiated by empirical research. In other words, to what end the media merely reflects or actively refracts public opinion is still unknown. As such, the purpose of the present investigation was to address these previously unanswered questions in the sport literature.

9   To explore how gender-consistent and inconsistent portrayals of athletes affect people's perceptions, [we designed] a hypothetical Olympic profile in which the

focal point of the article was either a male or female athlete's physical attractiveness (a typically female portrayal) or athleticism (a typically male portrayal).

10   In general, we predicted that female athletes described as attractive would be perceived more positively (e.g., as more likable, more dedicated to sports, and more heroic) than female athletes who were not described in such a manner, because being attractive "softens" the perceived gender-role inconsistency of a female athlete. Conversely, [we expected] male athletes described as attractive to be perceived more negatively than would males not described as such, because the gender schema for male athletes leads people to expect that a man's athleticism, rather than his physical attractiveness, should be the focus of a magazine article.

11   Furthermore, [we expected] the results to be qualified by the gender of the participant. Because women typically are more accepting of schema-inconsistency (Greendorfer, 1993) and of female athletes in general (Nixon, Maresca, & Silverman, 1979), three-way interactions were expected such that male participants would perceive gender-typical behavior (i.e., articles about attractive female athletes and athletic male athletes) positively, whereas female participants would be more likely to value atypical, out-of-role behavior (i.e., articles about athletic female athletes or attractive male athletes).

Method

Participants

12   Data were collected from 92 predominantly white undergraduate students (40 men, 52 women) at a small liberal arts university in the Southwest. Participants were recruited primarily from introductory psychology and economics classes and were given extra credit in their courses for completing the study. Additional participants were recruited from the men and women's Division III soccer teams at the university, and they were given small prizes as incentives.

Design and Materials

13   [. . .] Because newspaper and magazine articles rarely just describe physical attributes, a picture of the hypothetical athlete was included in the article. [. . .] In the article emphasizing the athlete's physical attractiveness, the athlete was described as "becoming known as much for his [her] incredible body as for his [her] powerful strokes," as being one of *People Magazine*'s "Fifty Most Beautiful People in the World," and as having recently signed a modeling contract to make a "Wet and Wild" calendar for Speedo swimwear after the Olympics. By contrast, in the article that focused on the athlete's athleticism, he or she was described as "becoming known both for his [her] incredible speed and his [her] powerful strokes," as being one of *Sports Illustrated*'s "Fifty Up-and-Coming Athletes," and as having recently signed a contract to model for a Speedo promotional calendar. [. . .]

Procedure

14   Potential participants were approached and told that the current study was "an investigation of people's perceptions of Olympic athletes." After agreeing to complete the questionnaire, participants read a hypothetical newspaper account about an athlete (who ostensibly had competed in the 1996 Summer Olympic Games) and then made

judgments in response to the coverage and the athlete involved. All participants saw identical profiles, except that the first names (i.e., the gender) and type of coverage (i.e., attractive- or athletic-focused) varied according to each of the four specific experimental conditions.

15   After reading four profiles (three additional hypothetical profiles were included as part of a separate investigation) and completing the corresponding response sheets, participants recorded their answers to demographic questions (e.g., age, gender, athletic status, and the amount of time they spend following sports through the media) and other personality measures, including the Bem Sex-Role Inventory (Bem, 1974) and the Sex-Role Egalitarian Scale (Beere, King, Beere, & King, 1984). Upon completion of the questionnaire, participants were told that the article was hypothetical, thanked for their participation, and dismissed.

Results

16   [. . .] As expected, female athletes depicted in terms of their attractiveness were seen as more attractive than those depicted in terms of their athleticism only; by contrast, there was no difference in the perceived attractiveness of male athletes described as attractive or as athletic.

17   Additionally, there were several main effects of the focus of the article. Athletes whose coverage focused on their attractiveness were viewed as less talented than were athletes who were described in an athletic manner. Athletes described as attractive were also seen as less aggressive than athletes described as athletic. Furthermore, athletes portrayed as attractive were viewed as less heroic than were athletes portrayed as athletic. Finally, when attractiveness was the focus of the article, people liked the article less than when the coverage focused on the athlete's athletic ability.

Discussion

18 The results of the present study confirm that people's perceptions of athletes are influenced by the gender of the athlete and by the type of media coverage provided in the article. Interestingly, although the same picture was used in each condition, a female athlete whose attractiveness was the main focus of an article was perceived to be more physically attractive than was a female athlete whose athletic accomplishments were the focus of an article. However, the same pattern was not found with male athletes. Previous research has demonstrated that people have weaker schemas for ideal athletes than for ideal persons because the general public has fewer experiences (and thus, fewer cognitive associations) with the very specific category of "an ideal athlete" as opposed to the broader category of "an ideal person" (Martin & Martin, 1995). It follows that perhaps the schema for a female athlete is not as strong as that for a male athlete (because of less "mere exposure" through their "symbolic annihilation" by the media; Gerbner, 1972), and thus people's perceptions (especially of attractiveness it seems) of a female athlete are more malleable and open to alteration. As such, this study implies that people are more apt to rely on peripheral information (such as the angle provided by the type of coverage) to form impressions of a female athlete.

19   Regardless of athlete gender, however, focusing on attractiveness to the exclusion of athletic ability had striking consequences on how athletes were perceived. Interestingly, our results indicate that male athletes are also affected by trivializing coverage; however, since men are rarely portrayed by the media in terms of their attractiveness (as female athletes often are), this marginalizing coverage seems to predominantly affect female athletes. Because of this negative effect on impressions of female and male athletes, the media need to be cognizant of (a) the damage that focusing on athletes' attractiveness can have on people's perceptions, (b) the fact that people might prefer articles that focus on an athlete's athleticism more than ones that focus on attractiveness, and (c) the reality that they do not merely reflect public opinion; they, in fact, can actively shape it.

20   Interestingly, participant gender was not a significant factor in ratings of the athlete or the article—a finding contrary to some previous research (Fisher, Genovese, Morris, & Morris, 1977), but consistent with other research (Michael, Gilroy, & Sherman, 1984). Perhaps this heralds a change in men's attitudes toward female athletes. Although women have traditionally been more accepting than men of female athletes (Nixon, Maresca, & Silverman, 1979), with the accomplishments of female athletes at the professional, Olympic, college, and high school levels, men might now be more aware and, hence, more accepting of women's sport.

21   An examination of the open-ended responses further confirmed what the quantitative data revealed. For example, one female participant shrewdly noted about the female athlete whose coverage centered on her attractiveness, "If I were her, I would be offended that this article talked more about my physical appearance than my talent—a typical attitude towards women. They can't resist talking about your appearance." A male participant similarly remarked, "If this was done in an edition of *Cosmopolitan* I might have liked it, but it told me nothing about her as an athlete." Yet another male participant said, "I wonder what her priorities are . . . is she using the 'swimming thing' to parlay a sweet modeling career?" Open-ended responses about male athletes portrayed as attractive revealed that they, too, were perceived in a negative light. A female participant wrote that this athlete was "a snobby rich kid who is a good swimmer and is used to everyone telling him how great he is." Another female participant remarked, "The article gave no mention of sports or athletic profile, only appearance. When speaking of an athlete in an Olympic sport, that is disconcerting."

22   There were several limitations of the present study, most notably that the kind of methodology used (i.e., "effects" research) cannot truly simulate the long-term consequences of the media as a tool of socialization (Lewis, 1991). Although this kind of research does have certain limitations, other researchers have recognized its potential theoretical and practical value. For instance, in their research involving "face-ism," Archer and his colleagues took a qualitative finding (i.e., that pictures of women in the media often feature their entire body, whereas photographs of men usually only feature their heads) and experimentally determined through a quantitative methodology that this pattern results in men appearing smarter and in women appearing objectified (Archer, Iritani, Kimes, & Barrios, 1983). In a similar vein, the current research has shown the negative impressions and effects that can occur from articles which focus exclusively on an athlete's attractiveness. It is through this process of triangulation and examining the same phenomenon from different

paradigms and disciplinary perspectives that we will begin to be able to truly understand social patterns and their potential effect on society.

23   Another potential limitation was that some of the conditions within the study lacked external validity (i.e., male athletes are seldom depicted in terms of their attractiveness). Although articles such as these are rarely found in the print media, it was important to include them in the present study so that it could be empirically determined how gender-atypical portrayals of male and female athletes affect people's perceptions. That is, a conscious decision was made to trade internal for external validity in the present case. Finally, participants were not asked to report their race, and thus, the race of the participant was not taken into account in analyses. Although the majority of participants were white, previous research shows that white and black participants weigh certain characteristics differently when evaluating the attractiveness of white and black individuals (Hebl & Heatherton, 1998). Diverse audiences (in terms of age, socioeconomic status, education level, sexual orientation, and political orientation) might also differ with regards both to how much they like articles that focus on male and female athletes' attractiveness and athleticism and to their subsequent impressions of the athletes.

24   Opportunities are rife for future quantitative research in the area of gendered portrayals in the sport media. For example, the photographs selected for inclusion in the present study were both of white targets. Because people have different expectations and schemas for black female athletes, the results from the present study might not generalize to athletes of other races. For instance, it traditionally is more acceptable for minority and working-class female athletes to participate in gender-inappropriate sports (e.g., basketball, soccer, hockey) than for white and middle-class female athletes because of the former group's more dynamic perceptions of femininity (Cahn, 1994). As such, further research is necessary to investigate the potential interactions among participant race, participant gender, athlete race, and athlete gender (Gissendaner, 1994).

25   In a broader scope, more experimental quantitative research should be conducted to empirically verify what descriptive qualitative studies have been reporting all along—that female athletes receive trivializing coverage from the media. For instance, "gender marking" (i.e., qualifying athletic contests and teams for women as though men's contests are the norm or standard) is very prevalent in television coverage of female athletes (Kane, 1996). Sports writers and commentators often use gendered labels to describe games in which female athletes participate (e.g., the "Women's Final Four"), yet male athletic contests are not referred to in these gendered terms (e.g., the "Final Four" rather than the "Men's Final Four"). Although researchers have speculated that this type of coverage marginalizes female athletes by making them appear to be "the other" rather than the norm, research has yet to empirically demonstrate the consequences of gender marking. Exploring how these and other types of gender-stereotypical portrayals affect both male and female athletes is an important next step in the sport literature.

26   In the meantime, the present study provides an empirical perspective to the burgeoning psychological and sociological fields that study the media, sport, and gender. At no other time in history have women had as much personal encouragement (Weiss & Barber, 1995) or as many opportunities to participate in sport (Women's Sport Foundation, 1998) as they do now, yet coverage of women's

sport still lags behind men's coverage in both quantity and quality. The media need to be cognizant of the effects of their trivializing and marginalizing coverage and of the fact that this type of coverage may not be "what the public wants" after all. Hopefully, with a sustained and diligent commitment from the media, sport will be viewed as an unconditionally acceptable and beneficial activity for women.

Why Men Don't Watch Women's Sports
Graham Hays

1 It's not like they were competing against the Super Bowl—or even *Who Wants to Marry My Dad.* It was the biggest weekend of the year in professional women's sports, but most men weren't watching.

2 The WUSA's third championship was decided when Washington beat Atlanta in overtime in the Founders Cup III in San Diego, while the WNBA's frenzied playoff race concluded with a frantic finish.

3 The two most prominent women's professional leagues showcased their best and brightest on an August weekend begging for events between the end of the PGA Championship and the start of the U.S. Open, the NFL regular season and baseball's stretch run. So why won't most men watch women's sports? Count me among the viewers, but I've got some theories about the rest of my brothers.

Male fantasies no longer require women.

4 Ask the typical male sports fan about his fantasy life, and he's more likely to tell you about Tom Brady's knee than his significant other's bedroom attire. We've become a culture obsessed with statistics. From NASDAQ to Zogby, numbers rule our lives. This isn't a bad thing when handled in moderation, but put 12 men in a room together, hand them some yards-per-carry printouts, and you've got the makings of a cult.

5 And until someone finds a way to effectively market women's fantasy leagues to a market saturated with everything from fantasy NASCAR to fantasy bass fishing—that's not a joke—women's sports won't capture the

And until someone finds a way to effectively market women's fantasy leagues to a market saturated with everything from fantasy NASCAR to fantasy bass fishing—that's not a joke—women's sports won't capture the hearts of male sports fans.

hearts of male sports fans. After all, what does a Lisa Leslie blocked shot really mean, if it doesn't give you bragging rights for being a more successful fantasy manager?

What's the over-under on the Sparks and Comets?

6 If sports fans were interested solely in the purity of athletic competition, bookies would be out of business and horse racing would be a quaint hobby for animal lovers. You can bet on the WNBA—over/unders, point spreads, the whole bailiwick—but

women's sports aren't big gambling business. And since men will turn daily chores, foodstuff and even bodily functions into wagers the way MacGyver turned sewing implements into complex machinery, it's only worth watching if it can be gambled on.

You have to know someone to enjoy the sport.

7 Men don't know Abby Wambach from Abby Conklin—for the record, Wambach is a star in the WUSA while Conklin played for the University of Tennessee women's basketball team. Men say they don't know the players and thus don't have any connection to the game. Which makes it tough to explain preseason football. Honestly, do you really feel a bond to Jody Gerut of the Padres or Jordan Babineaux of the Seattle Seahawks? You may know your local team's back-up shortstop, but you don't give a hoot about Cesar Izturis.

And your mother dresses you funny.

8 Established leagues can get away with the occasional Atlanta Thrashers or Minnesota Wild, but don't give those already inclined to laugh for all the wrong reasons a legitimate reason to chuckle. Atlanta Beat? Boston Breakers? Detroit Shock? At least the grammatical nightmare that was the Utah Starzz pulled out their Strunk and White before moving to San Antonio. Silver Stars won't sell a ton of merchandise, but at least it won't break a spell-check. And please, there's no reason for a league that plays indoor games in the summer to have a team named the Sun, no matter what the name of their parent casino. You're trying to get people to forget it's summer, remember?

I'll give you my opinion as soon as I find out what it is.

9 It's tough to stay up to speed on all the issues when cable has upwards of 200 chan-nels. Heck, just keeping up with all the developments on reality television is a full-time job. That's why men love having talking heads keep them up to speed. Not sure about this whole Arab–Israeli crisis and couldn't find Tikrit on a map if there were $300 on the line? Tune in Chris Matthews or Bill O'Reilly—oops, don't want to get sued—and you'll be castigating State Department policy inside of 20 minutes.

10   And then consider these two words: sports radio. Sure, Bill from Yonkers didn't actually watch the Mets game—are you kidding? *Body Shots* was on Showtime 7—but he knows Jeromy Burnitz was a bum and a traitor because Mad Mark told him so, and Mad Mark has a radio show, a brand of hot sauce and mil-lions of loyal listeners. So maybe men don't watch women's sports precisely because they have to watch women's sports. Without the reassuring screams—volume suggests authority—of a talking head, watching sports requires thought. And who has time for that these days?

Serena Williams isn't in charge of uniforms.

11 Because of course, men do watch women's tennis, the sport where the women play in short skirts and tight-fitting tops. Viewers tuned in to watch the 1999 Women's World Cup—even before Brandi Chastain made herself famous—because the U.S. team played skilled, compelling soccer and represented the country with honor. But it didn't hurt that the squad was full of attractive women. So perhaps men don't

watch women's sports because they hold it to such exacting standards. Imagine if watching men's sports depended on the athlete's being both talented and attractive. Randy Johnson? Thanks for playing. Dirk Nowitzki? Next. Jason Sehorn? Close, but there's that talent issue.

What do I care if the maxi pad is super-absorbent?

12 Men aren't especially comfortable with the mysteries of their own bodies, so commercials geared towards the gender more in touch with the physical form are as unsettling as the thought that Michael Jackson has children that contain his genetic material. It's hard to stay focused on a game when every commercial break finds men scrambling for the nearest soundproof room. There's a reason Preparation H had to settle for Don Zimmer, and it's not because the old guy has tremendous stage presence. Nobody wants to see Alex Rodriguez talking about that itching, burning sensation.

13 Furthermore, consider how much men value beer, shoes and sports drinks. The athletes who sell them on television earn points by association. And since the only women you're likely to see in Miller Lite ads couldn't run 100 yards without toppling over, equality in commercials is a long way off.

The feminine mystique

14 It's really all Betty Friedan's fault. Here's the typical man, just trying to quietly go through life replacing his divots and changing his oil every 3,000 miles, only to find himself blamed for generations of inequality. It's not as if he had anything to do with glass ceilings or salary differences in the workplace. Heck, last year's three-percent bump was barely enough to pay for that new Big Bertha ERC II Forged Titanium Driver. So maybe men think it's time to take a stand. To leap to the rampart and stand shoulder to shoulder with Vijay Singh and Andy Rooney. Women can join men's clubs and the old-boys network, but they'll never take sports.

They aren't good enough.

15 The holy grail of complaints about women's sports, and an excuse that sounds especially curious when ABC is broadcasting 12-year-old boys playing baseball in prime time. Women aren't as fast, don't jump as high and don't kick as hard as their male counterparts.

16 After all, who would want to watch UConn–Duke women battle for No. 1 when the Bulls and Warriors are about to tip off?

 ## Gender Inequality
E. M. Swift

1 *No person in the United States shall, on the basis of sex, be excluded from participation in, be denied the benefits of, or be subject to discrimination under any educational programs or activity receiving federal financial assistance.*

—From the preamble to Title IX of the Education Amendments of 1972

2 Thus is it clearly stated: You can't be excluded from participating in a sport because of your sex. Yet this important law is flaunted every year, every season. Only today, the victims are men, not the women that Title IX was originally enacted to protect.

3 The most recent, egregious example of male sex discrimination in intercollegiate sports occurred at James Madison University in Harrisonburg, Virginia where the visitor's board voted to eliminate 10 of the university's 28 sports teams: seven men's teams (archery, cross-country, gymnastics, indoor track, outdoor track, swimming and wrestling) and three women's teams (archery, fencing, gymnastics).

4 If you are a member of the James Madison men's cross-country team, next year you will be "excluded from participation in" your sport on the basis of your sex. It's as simple as that. You have no team. I recommend that you file a lawsuit. Because the James Madison women's cross-country team will continue to compete.

5 Why? In this instance, it isn't about money. The James Madison Board enacted the cuts to comply with Title IX, at least as it is interpreted by the Department of Education, which hews to the misguided concept of "proportionality": that if 61 percent of a student population is female, then 61 percent of the student athletes must be female, too. Never mind if a majority of those women have no interest in competing in intercollegiate sports, do not feel discriminated against, are not discriminated against and stand to gain absolutely nothing from the elimination of men's sports teams. Numbers are numbers.

6 "With so many teams, we faced an insurmountable challenge coming into compliance with Title IX," said Joseph Damico, rector of the JMU Board of Visitors. "Fundamentally, that is why the Board voted today for this plan." That is the evil of quotas—and "proportionality" is a quota by another name. JMU fielded 15 women's sports and 13 men's sports before the vote to eliminate the 10 sports—not exactly the ratio one would expect of an institution out of compliance with Title IX. A majority of its student athletes (50.7 percent) were women.

7 Problem was, the overall enrollment of the school is 61 percent female. By the standard of "proportionality"—a word that isn't used in the original Title IX amendment—the James Madison sports program was out of whack. Next year it'll be in whack: 61 percent of the athletes will be female, 39 percent male.

8 That's whacked out and it needs to be stopped. Why not racial proportionality in sports, too? Isn't that what civil rights is all about? Sixty-seven percent white, 14 percent African American, 13 percent Hispanic, 6 percent Asian American—let's count noses, colors and genders, take to the field and fight, team, fight!

9 Look, Title IX was needed in 1972. And it worked brilliantly. But the world has changed. I was a junior in college when it was passed. Now my son is a senior in college. A generation has elapsed, and women's sports are here to stay. Thank God and Title IX. But because of Title IX's unintended consequences, in 2006 the law is causing more harm than good.

Title IX was needed in 1972. And it worked brilliantly. But the world has changed.

Women's sports are no longer on life support. They are vibrant, popular, well-funded and growing. They can be taken off the endangered-species list.

10   Meanwhile, the percentage of women attending college relative to men continues to increase—enrollment nationally is approximately 57 percent women to 43 percent men today. If "proportionality" continues to be adhered to by school administrators, the number of men's collegiate sports programs will continue to shrink.

11   That wasn't the idea behind Title IX. It was designed to create, not eliminate, opportunity. But since its enactment, more than 170 men's wrestling teams have disappeared. Eighty men's tennis teams, 45 track teams and 106 men's gymnastics teams have been axed.

12   UCLA's men's swimming team, which boasted 22 Olympic medals, is gone, along with some 30 other men's swimming and diving programs. Forty schools have dropped football. Walk-on male athletes in all sports are routinely turned away to keep rosters at a minimum so the male/female ratios in college sports programs don't get thrown off.

13   It's social engineering, and it's wrong. If you believe that being on a team, practicing, and learning discipline through sports is beneficial to the development of the individual, as I do, then as a society, we are poorer every time a school eliminates any athletic program—male or female. School administrators don't enforce gender proportionality for chemistry, economics or English-lit classes. Why should they try to engineer gender ratios in sports?

14   There is a wealth of data that show that young males, as a whole, are more inclined toward athletic competition than young females. That doesn't mean the female athletes are any less committed or driven than men. It means that—surprise!—men and women are different, creatures of Mars and Venus, and that a higher percentage of men like, and perhaps need, to compete. They crave being on teams, even if they don't start. It adds to their self-esteem and channels their energy in a constructive fashion. While many women's collegiate teams must actively recruit participants in order to fill their rosters, men's teams turn away walk-ons in droves.

15   Over a 15-year period between 1980 and 1994, the National Center for Educational Statistics polled high school seniors and found that 20 percent of males were more interested in participating in sports than females, and more than twice as many exercised vigorously on a daily basis.

16   In collegiate intramural sports, whose numbers are largely determined on the basis of interest, 78 percent of participants are male, 22 percent female. Put another way, most guys have a more difficult time adapting to life without sports than most girls do.

17   Yet there are some 580 more women's teams at NCAA schools today than men's teams, a disparity that is likely to continue to grow. Faced with budgetary cuts last summer, the board at Rutgers University elected to eliminate six teams, five of which were men's: lightweight and heavyweight crew, tennis, swimming and diving, and fencing. "The minute you start cuts, you have to meet the proportionality test," said Athletic Director Robert E. Mulcahy III.

18   Shame on the proportionality test. Shame on the budgetary cuts. And shame on administrators at Rutgers and James Madison for allowing Title IX to become a dirty word to advocates of men's sports such as wrestling, cross-country and track. The law was never intended to be a zero-sum game, the right hand welcoming a female athlete as the left hand shoves a male out the door.

19   After word reached members of the James Madison cross-country team that the men's team would be eliminated in '07 while the women's team would continue, runners on both squads shared a tearful four-hour bus ride home from a meet in Pennsylvania. "Fourteen guys and 19 girls, all crying together," Jennifer Chapman, a senior on the women's team, told the *New York Times*. "How is that supposed to have been Title IX's intent?" ◆

CRITICAL THINKING

1. Do we hold female athletes to different standards than male athletes? Is it important for a female athlete to "look good" in addition to playing well?
2. Knight and Giuliano note that female sports figures are judged more on their attractiveness than on their athletic prowess. Do you think the media indeed gives more "face time" to a female athlete judged to be beautiful— say, Anna Kournikova—than to one who is known for her abilities alone, such as Martina Navratilova? Does the media do the same thing to male athletes? Explain.
3. According to Knight and Giuliano, what role does the media play in conveying the idea that women's sports are inferior to men's sports? Explain.
4. What is "schema theory"? How does it connect to the trivialization of women athletes and women's sports?
5. In his editorial, Hays argues that, overall, men's sports are simply more exciting to watch than women's. Evaluate how well Hays supports his view. What is your view?
6. How do Knight and Giuliano support their argument that coverage of female athletes is not only unequal but also actually reinforces stereotypes that in turn serve to further trivialize women's sports in general? Evaluate their research and methods. How convincing is their argument? Explain.
7. What is Hays's tone in his essay? How does he use humor and sarcasm to convey his point? Does his technique work? What do you need to know in order to understand his tone? Explain.
8. What is "proportionality?" Do you think that athletic programs should be based on proportionality? Why or why not?
9. Swift argues that Title IX is no longer needed. Do you agree? Is it necessary today? What might happen if it were repealed?

CRITICAL WRITING

1. *Research and Analysis:* Visit a sports-themed Web-site, such as ESPN.com, or pick up a copy of a sports-themed publication, such as *Sports Illustrated* or *Sporting News*, and critically evaluate the content for gender bias. What is the ratio of male to female sports coverage? Are articles the same length? Are female athletes described differently than male athletes? In addition to analyzing the text, examine the photographs accompanying the stories for any differences in the photographic portrayal of male and female athletes.

2. *Research Writing:* Research the history of Title IX. Why was it passed and what does it protect or guarantee? Arrange an interview with a coach or coaches in your athletic department to discuss the impact of Title IX—both positive and negative—on the history of athletic activity at your school over the past 30 years.

3. *Expository Writing:* Write an essay exploring how the world would be different if Title IX had *not* passed in 1972. If you think your life is different because of this act, write about what impact it had on you.

4. *Persuasive Writing:*Write a response to Hays's argument that men just don't like women's sports in which you either agree or disagree with his view. Use humor as the stylistic means to get your point across.

GROUP PROJECTS

1. Each member of your group should visit several sports-related Web sites, such as ESPN.com and SI.com, and locate some current articles on women in sports. Are the stories about female athletes parallel to the reporting on male athletes? Are men and women judged on similar or different criteria? If photographs accompany the articles, are the photos similar in style and content (action shots, etc.). Discuss your findings as a group, connecting your research to points made by the writers in this section.

2. Swift argues that Title IX is no longer needed. Each member of your group should interview 5 to 10 students on the issue. Ask students what they know about Title IX and whether they think it is a necessary law and why. Review the responses as a group. Discuss current opinion on this act and whether the time has come for reform.

CULTURE SHOCK

The *Onion* is a parody newspaper published weekly in print and online, featuring satirical "news" articles on national and international topics. The *Onion*'s articles "comment on current events, both real and imagined." The publication also parodies a traditional newspaper in appearance, editorial voice, and features that include letters, editorials, man-on-the-street interviews, and stock quotes.

Annika Sorenstam Has Another Remarkable Year For A Lady

December 1, 2005 | Issue 41 • 48

WEST PALM BEACH, FL—Annika Sorenstam, the absolutely adorable doll of golf's lighter, gentler side and a true lady who has absolutely charmed ladies' golf fans since joining the always-heartwarming Ladies' Professional Golf Association Tour in 1994, capped off another sensational ten-victory year and became the first lady in history to win two straight ADT Championships For Ladies.

Miss Sorenstam, hitting from the ladies' tee throughout the tournament, finished with a 6-under 282 for a two-stroke ladies' victory, just barely holding off little ladies Soo-Yun Kang, Michele Redman, and Lisolette Neumann. "I thought I had a chance to catch up to her, but there was no stopping that lady today," Neumann said. "All you can do is lower your eyes demurely, curtsy, and say 'Congratulations, ma'am,' in a meek tone of voice befitting a lady."

Sweeping all the major lady-awards for a fifth year and moving within 22 ladies' wins of the all-time ladies' record, Miss Sorenstam is carving out her place in ladies' history alongside legendary golfers such as Nancy Lopez and Kathy Whitworth, both also ladies.

Miss Sorenstam, who took up the sport of ladies' golf when she was just a little lady at 12 years old, has been a feminine golfing inspiration to a whole new generation of ladies, including young lady Michelle Wie and ladies' tour rookie, Paula Creamer, whose play proves her a lady despite her brief, unladylike tiff with Miss Sorenstam over an eighteenth-hole drop in the ladies' first round of the ADT Championship.

As the lady champion, Miss Sorenstam is expected to reap her proportional rewards. In addition to her career earnings of over $2.5 million—a fraction of Tiger Woods' $40 million-plus once thought unimaginable—male golf insiders expect Miss Sorenstam to receive attention from sponsors, such as ladies-wear companies, ladies' hygiene product manufacturers, and other markets of which regular golfers are ignorant or only dimly aware.

"She has proven that the ladies can play golf just like men, if not, of course, actually with men," Professional Golf Association Tour Executive Vice President Edward L. Moorhouse said of Miss Sorenstam, who in 2003 became the first lady to play on the real PGA Tour since true ladies' lady Babe Didrikson Zaharias, the grande dame [big lady] of golf, did so in 1945. "This lady golfer truly deserves our admiration in the form of the highest honor men can grant her: the honorary title First Lady of Golf."

Of course, Sorenstam's honors will include a polite and proper phone call from Laura Bush, the first lady of the United States, who will offer not only her congratulations but those of her husband George, the leader of the free world.

"You're welcome to drop by the big tour and play a round or two with the men any time you like, little lady," Moorhouse added. "As long as it's not a big event or someplace like Augusta, that bastion of golf tradition where ladies are not allowed."

THINKING CRITICALLY

1. How does this article use satire to make a point? What point is the article making?
2. What words are repeated in this article? What titles are used for men and women? Note that the names of men and women are not referred to in the same way in the article. How does this difference connect back to the point the article is making?
3. If you saw this article and did not know that the *Onion* is a satire, would you take the contents of the article seriously? Why or why not?

CHAPTER
7

Race and Racism
Can We Be Color-Blind?

As a nation of immigrants, the United States comprises many races, ethnic traditions, religions, and languages. Under a common political and legal system, we agree that we have the right to life, liberty, and the pursuit of happiness. Many of us take pride in our cultural differences. And, in theory, we Americans embrace the principles of the Declaration of Independence: that we are all created equal, in spite of our differences. But the social reality demonstrates that differences can pose challenges to the very fabric of American culture. Racism is one of these challenges.

Racism is the conviction that people of a particular race or ethnicity possess traits that distinguish them as superior or inferior to another racial or ethnic group. The roots of racism are disturbingly deep in American history, extending all the way back to the early seventeenth century and the Puritan settlers' blatant mistreatment of Native Americans. Considered uncivilized savages, and wrongfully named "Indians," indigenous tribes were stripped of their land, their power, and their way of life by white European immigrants. Over the following centuries, every new immigrant group to arrive on American soil—Irish, Italian, Polish, German, Mexican, Chinese— experienced some form of racism and racial profiling, usually at the hands of the groups that came before them. But as America became more ethnically blended, prejudice against some groups decreased and even disappeared.

The candidacy of Barack Obama for the highest office in the land raised new questions about racism in America. His campaign itself raised many questions— foremost, could people vote color-blind? The answer, of course, is "yes." So now what does it mean for the United States to have a black president? Some people view Obama's election as proof that Americans have finally overcome institutionalized racism. Others view it as the end of a long struggle for equality and access to power. Still others say we have a long way to go. In this chapter, we will look at a few of the issues that remain regarding racial inequality, including what Barack Obama's election to the presidency might mean to the dynamics of race in America.

Alan Jenkins begins the discussion with an examination of the connections of race to inequality, stereotypes, and poverty. His essay, "Inequality, Race, and Remedy," briefly reviews the history of racism and describes current challenges for removing racial barriers. Jenkins charges that until Americans can honestly admit that racism still runs rampant in this country, we cannot begin to remedy it. In "Leaving Race Behind," Amitai Etzioni discusses how racial identification holds us back as a nation. The expanding Hispanic population, he explains, represents an opportunity for us to dismantle institutionalized racism in America. David Brooks, however, wonders if racism can ever really be erased. In "People Like Us," he hazards to state that no matter how much lip service we publicly pay to diversity, we still tend to gather with people who look, act, and believe "basically like ourselves."

The next essay addresses the issue of racial profiling of Arab Americans. More than ever, people who appear to be of Middle Eastern descent find themselves eyed with suspicion. Laura Fokkena wonders how much Hollywood's depiction of Middle Easterners as terrorists perpetuates such stereotypes. In "Are You a Terrorist, or Do You Play One on TV?" Fokkena concedes that September 11 put many Americans on edge. She wonders why Hollywood thinks it is acceptable to promote images of Muslims as terrorist threats.

The next two essays take a more personal look at race and ethnicity. In his essay, "Why I'm Black, Not African American," John H. McWhorter explains why he feels the title "African American" poorly serves blacks in the United States. Gary Kamiya explores our desire to pigeonhole ourselves along racial lines in "Black vs. 'Black.'" He argues that as long as quotation marks are connected to definitions of ethnicity, we will remain a racist society.

On November 4, 2008, history was made when a 47-year-old senator from Illinois broke the color barrier to become the first black president of the United States. "If there is anyone out there who doubts that America is a place where anything is possible, who still wonders if the dream of our founders is alive in our time, who still questions the power of our democracy, tonight is your answer," declared president-elect Barack Obama the night of his election. This chapter's Viewpoints section takes a close look at the election of Barack Obama and what it means to our concepts of race and the construction of the "black American narrative." Does Obama's election signal that racism is over? Does his presidency represent a rebalancing of power? Is it time for us to rethink race entirely?

Inequality, Race, and Remedy

Alan Jenkins*

It would be hopeful to believe that race is no longer a factor in poverty and that we can be a color-blind society. But America still has a legacy to overcome—and to achieve. In this next essay, Alan Jenkins, executive director of the Opportunity Agenda, an organization dedicated to expanding opportunity in America, explains why we cannot ignore the past if we are to create a more hopeful future. The truth is, he explains, racial barriers still exist, and to overcome them, we must admit that. Can we ever become a color-blind society?

1 Our nation, at its best, pursues the ideal that what we look like and where we come from should not determine the benefits, burdens, or responsibilities that we bear in our society. Because we believe that all people are created equal in terms of rights, dignity, and the potential to achieve great things, we see inequality based on race, gender, and other social characteristics as not only unfortunate but unjust. The value of equality, democratic voice, physical and economic security, social mobility, a shared sense of responsibility for one another, and a chance to start over after misfortune or missteps—what many Americans call *redemption*—are the moral pillars of the American ideal of opportunity.

2 Many Americans of goodwill who want to reduce poverty believe that race is no longer relevant to understanding the problem or to fashioning solutions for it. This view often reflects compassion as well as pragmatism. But we cannot solve the

* Alan Jenkins, *The American Prospect*, April 22, 2007

problem of poverty—or, indeed, be the country that we aspire to be—unless we honestly unravel the complex and continuing connection between poverty and race.

3   Since our country's inception, race-based barriers have hindered the fulfillment of our shared values, and many of these barriers persist today. Experience shows, moreover, that reductions in poverty do not reliably reduce racial inequality, nor do they inevitably reach low-income people of color. Rising economic tides do not reliably lift all boats.

4   In 2000, after a decade of remarkable economic prosperity, the poverty rate among African Americans and Latinos taken together was still 2.6 times greater than that for white Americans. This disparity was stunning, yet it was the smallest difference in poverty rates between whites and others in more than three decades. And from 2001 to 2003, as the economy slowed, poverty rates for most communities of color increased more dramatically than they did for whites, widening the racial poverty gap. From 2004 to 2005, while the overall number of poor Americans declined by almost one million, to 37 million, poverty rates for most communities of color actually increased. Reductions in poverty do not inevitably close racial poverty gaps, nor do they reach all ethnic communities equally.

5   Poor people of color are also increasingly more likely than whites to find themselves living in high-poverty neighborhoods with limited resources and limited options. An analysis by the Opportunity Agenda and the Poverty and Race Research Action Council found that while the percentage of Americans of all races living in high-poverty neighborhoods (those with 30 percent or more residents living in poverty) declined between 1960 and 2000, the racial gap grew considerably. Low-income Latino families were three times as likely as low-income white families to live in these neighborhoods in 1960, but 5.7 times as likely in 2000. Low-income blacks were 3.8 times more likely than poor whites to live in high-poverty neighborhoods in 1960, but 7.3 times more likely in 2000.

6   These numbers are troubling, not because living among poor people is somehow harmful in itself, but because concentrated high-poverty communities are far more likely to be cut off from quality schools, housing, health care, affordable consumer credit, and other pathways out of poverty. And African Americans and Latinos are increasingly more likely than whites to live in those communities. Today, low-income blacks are more than three times as likely as poor whites to be in "deep poverty"—meaning below half the poverty line—while poor Latinos are more than twice as likely.

The Persistence of Discrimination

7   Modern and historical forces combine to keep many communities of color disconnected from networks of economic opportunity and upward mobility. Among those forces is persistent racial discrimination that, while subtler than in past decades, continues to deny opportunity to millions of Americans. Decent employment and housing are milestones on the road out of poverty. Yet these are areas in which racial discrimination stubbornly persists. While the open hostility and "Whites Only" signs of the Jim Crow era have largely disappeared, research shows that identically qualified candidates for jobs and housing enjoy significantly different opportunities depending on their race.

8   In one study, researchers submitted identical résumés by mail for more than 1,300 job openings in Boston and Chicago, giving each "applicant" either a distinctively "white-sounding" or "black-sounding" name—for instance, "Brendan Baker" versus "Jamal Jones." Résumés with white-sounding names were 50 percent more likely than those with black-sounding names to receive callbacks from employers. Similar research in California found that Asian American and, especially, Arab American résumés received the least-favorable treatment compared to other groups. In recent studies in Milwaukee and New York City, meanwhile, live "tester pairs" with comparable qualifications but of differing races tested not only the effect of race on job prospects but also the impact of an apparent criminal record. In Milwaukee, whites reporting a criminal record were more likely to receive a callback from employers than were blacks without a criminal record. In New York, Latinos and African Americans without criminal records received fewer callbacks than did similarly situated whites and at rates comparable to whites with a criminal record.

9   Similar patterns hamper the access of people of color to quality housing near good schools and jobs. Research by the U.S. Department of Housing and Urban Development (HUD) shows that people of color receive less information from real estate agents, are shown fewer units, and are frequently steered away from predominantly white neighborhoods. In addition to identifying barriers facing African Americans and Latinos, this research found significant levels of discrimination against Asian Americans and that Native American renters may face the highest discrimination rates (up to 29 percent) of all.

10   This kind of discrimination is largely invisible to its victims, who do not know that they have received inaccurate information or been steered away from desirable neighborhoods and jobs. But its influence on the perpetuation of poverty is nonetheless powerful.

The Present Legacy of Past Discrimination

11 These modern discriminatory practices often combine with historical patterns. In New Orleans, for example, as in many other cities, low-income African Americans were intentionally concentrated in segregated, low-lying neighborhoods and public-housing developments at least into the 1960s. In 2005, when Hurricane Katrina struck and the levees broke, black neighborhoods were most at risk of devastation. And when HUD announced that it would close habitable public-housing developments in New Orleans rather than clean and reopen them, it was African Americans who were primarily prevented from returning home and rebuilding. This and other failures to rebuild and invest have exacerbated poverty—already at high levels—among these New Orleanians.

Since our country's inception, race-based barriers have hindered the fulfillment of our shared values, and many of these barriers persist today.

12   In the case of Native Americans, a quarter of whom are poor, our government continues to play a more flagrant role in thwarting pathways out of poverty. Unlike other racial and ethnic groups, most Native Americans are members of sovereign

tribal nations with a recognized status under our Constitution. High levels of Native American poverty derive not only from a history of wars, forced relocations, and broken treaties by the United States, but also from ongoing breaches of trust—like our government's failure to account for tens of billions of dollars that it was obligated to hold in trust for Native American individuals and families. After more than a decade of litigation, and multiple findings of governmental wrongdoing, the United States is trying to settle these cases for a tiny fraction of what it owes.

13   The trust-fund cases, of course, are just the latest in a string of broken promises by our government. But focusing as they do on dollars and cents, they offer an important window into the economic status that Native American communities and tribes might enjoy today if the U.S. government lived up to its legal and moral obligations.

14   Meanwhile, the growing diversity spurred by new immigrant communities adds to the complexity of contemporary poverty. Asian American communities, for example, are culturally, linguistically, and geographically diverse, and they span a particularly broad socioeconomic spectrum.

15   Census figures from 2000 show that while one third of Asian American families have annual incomes of $75,000 or more, one fifth have incomes of less than $25,000. While the Asian American poverty rate mirrored that of the country as a whole, Southeast Asian communities reflected far higher levels. Hmong men experienced the highest poverty level (40.3 percent) of any racial group in the nation.

Race and Public Attitudes

16 Americans' complex attitudes and emotions about race are crucial to understanding the public discourse about poverty and the public's will to address it. Researchers such as Martin Gilens and Herman Gray have repeatedly found that the mainstream media depict poor people as people of color—primarily African Americans—at rates far higher than their actual representation in the population. And that depiction, the research finds, interacts with societal biases to erode support for antipoverty programs that could reach all poor people.

17   Gilens found, for instance, that while blacks represented only 29 percent of poor Americans at the time he did his research, 65 percent of poor Americans shown on television news were black. In a more detailed analysis of TV newsmagazines in particular, Gilens found a generally unflattering framing of the poor, but the presentation of poor African Americans was more negative still. The most "sympathetic" subgroups of the poor—such as the working poor and the elderly—were underrepresented on these shows, while unemployed working-age adults were overrepresented. And those disparities were greater for African Americans than for others, creating an even more unflattering (and inaccurate) picture of the black poor.

18   Gray similarly found that poor African Americans were depicted as especially dysfunctional and undeserving of assistance, with an emphasis on violence, poor choices, and dependency. As Gray notes, "The black underclass appears as a menace and a source of social disorganization in news accounts of black urban crime, gang violence, drug use, teenage pregnancy, riots, homelessness, and general aimlessness. In news accounts, poor blacks (and Hispanics) signify a social menace that must be contained."

19   Research also shows that Americans are more likely to blame the plight of poverty on poor people themselves, and less likely to support antipoverty efforts, when they perceive that the people needing help are black. These racial effects are especially pronounced when the poor person in the story is a black single mother. In one study, more than twice the number of respondents supported individual solutions (like the one that says poor people "should get a job") over societal solutions (such as increased education or social services) when the single mother was black.

20   This research should not be surprising. Ronald Reagan, among others, effectively used the "racialized" mental image of the African American "welfare queen" to undermine support for antipoverty efforts. And the media face of welfare recipients has long been a black one, despite the fact that African Americans have represented a minority of the welfare population. But this research also makes clear that unpacking and disputing racial stereotypes is important to rebuilding a shared sense of responsibility for reducing poverty in all of our communities.

Removing Racial Barriers

21   We cannot hope to address poverty in a meaningful or lasting way without addressing race-based barriers to opportunity. The most effective solutions will take on these challenges together.

22   That means, for example, job-training programs that prepare low-income workers for a globalized economy, combined with antidiscrimination enforcement that ensures equal access to those programs and the jobs to which they lead. Similarly, strengthening the right to organize is important in helping low-wage workers to move out of poverty, but it must be combined with civil-rights efforts that root out the racial exclusion that has sometimes infected union locals. And it means combining comprehensive immigration reform that offers newcomers a pathway to citizenship with living wages and labor protections that root out exploitation and discourage racial hierarchy.

23   Another crucial step is reducing financial barriers to college by increasing the share of need-based grants over student loans and better coordinating private-sector scholarship aid—for example, funds for federal Pell Grants should be at least double current levels. But colleges should also retain the flexibility to consider racial and socioeconomic background as two factors among many, in order to promote a diverse student body (as well as diverse workers and leaders once these students graduate). And Congress should pass the DREAM Act, which would clear the path to a college degree and legal immigration status for many undocumented students who've shown academic promise and the desire to contribute to our country.

24   Lack of access to affordable, quality health care is a major stress on low-income families, contributing to half of the nation's personal bankruptcies. Guaranteed health care for all is critical, and it must be combined with protections against poor quality and unequal access that, research shows, affect people of color irrespective of their insurance status.

25   Finally, we must begin planning for opportunity in the way we design metropolitan regions, transportation systems, housing, hospitals, and schools. That means, for example, creating incentives for mixed-income neighborhoods that are well publicized and truly open to people of all races and backgrounds.

26   A particularly promising approach involves requiring an "opportunity impact statement" when public funds are to be used for development projects. The statement would explain, for example, whether a new highway will connect low-income communities to good jobs and schools or serve only affluent communities. It would detail where and how job opportunities would flow from the project, and whether different communities would share the burden of environmental and other effects (rather than having the project reinforce traditional patterns of inequality). It would measure not only a project's expected effect on poverty but on opportunity for all.

27   When we think about race and poverty in terms of the shared values and linked fate of our people, our approach to politics as well as policy begins to change. Instead of balancing a list of constituencies and identity groups, our task becomes one of moving forward together as a diverse but cohesive society, addressing through unity the forces that have historically divided us. ◆

CRITICAL THINKING

1. Jenkins opens his essay with the comment, "Our nation, at its best, pursues the ideal that what we look like and where we come from should not determine the benefits, burdens, or responsibilities that we bear in our society." What are the ideals of America? Do we believe in equality for all, at least in theory? If so, how well do we, as a society, promote the values of equality? Explain.

2. What are the connections between race and poverty in the United States? Why does Jenkins feel it is important to address these connections in order to promote a more color-blind society? Explain.

3. Jenkins observes that while "Jim Crow" signs barring African Americans from employment have disappeared, employment racism still persists. In what ways does employment racism perpetuate the cycle of poverty?

4. In addition to employment inequalities, what other forms of racism are rampant in America? Can you think of any other examples in addition to the ones Jenkins cites?

5. What external forces can influence race and perceptions of race? How can perceptions drive racism in the United States?

6. What steps does Jenkins offer to help remedy racial inequalities and remove racial barriers?

CRITICAL WRITING

1. *Research and Writing:* Jenkins describes how "attitudes and emotions about race" are often media-driven. Write an essay exploring how race is presented in the media. In your response, cite several examples of how various races are presented and how these representations can influence public opinions in general.

2. *Research and Persuasive Writing:* Visit the ACLU's Web site on racial inequality at http://www.aclu.org and review its information about race and race relations. What are the most pressing issues concerning race and

racial inequality today? Select an issue on the Web site and research it in greater depth. Write a short essay summarizing the issue, your position, and your thoughts about it.

3. *Expository Writing:* What is your own perception of race? Do you think you enjoy certain benefits or encounter certain obstacles because of your race? Explain.

GROUP PROJECTS

1. In this essay, Jenkins offers some suggestions for working toward a more color-blind society. With your group acting as a "think tank," evaluate each of his suggestions for plausibility, implementation strategies, and outcome.
2. Jenkins charges that the media, especially television, contributes to racism by presenting groups of people differently. With the help of *TV Guide* or another television guide, make a list of programs on prime-time—from 8:00 to 11:00 PM—network television, and describe the characters in terms of race and ethnicity. For example, are African Americans more likely to be portrayed as dysfunctional or poor? Based on your review of the prime-time lineup, discuss how television may contribute to racial stereotypes. Alternatively, if your data reveal little or no racism, make a note of that as well. Share the results of your group discussion with the class.

Leaving Race Behind
*Amitai Etzioni**

Caucasian, Black, Asian, Hispanic, Native American—official forms ask us to indicate our race. In this next essay, author and sociology professor Amitai Etzioni explains why he hesitates to mark any specific race. Why is this information important at all? He then explains why the growing Hispanic population raises troubling questions about why race matters to the government, and why the time has come to stop asking this question on forms. The U.S. Census Bureau estimates that the next U.S. census will cite almost 50 million citizens claiming Hispanic origins living in the United States, comprising 15 percent of the total population. It projects that within the next 40 years, Hispanics will represent one quarter of the total population in the United States. Etzioni explains why this trend creates a golden opportunity to address the ills of racism in America.

1 Some years ago the United States government asked me what my race was. I was reluctant to respond because my 50 years of practicing sociology—and some powerful personal experiences—have underscored for me what we all know to one degree or another, that racial divisions bedevil America, just as they do many other societies across the world. Not wanting to encourage these divisions, I refused to

---

* Amitai Etzioni, *The American Scholar*, September 1, 2006

check off one of the specific racial options on the U.S. Census form and instead marked a box labeled "Other." I later found out that the federal government did not accept such an attempt to deemphasize race, by me or by some 6.75 million other Americans who tried it. Instead the government assigned me to a racial category, one it chose for me. Learning this made me conjure up what I admit is a far-fetched association. I was in this place once before.

2   When I was a Jewish child in Nazi Germany in the early 1930s, many Jews who saw themselves as good Germans wanted to "pass" as Aryans. But the Nazi regime would have none of it. Never mind, they told these Jews, we determine who is Jewish and who is not. A similar practice prevailed in the Old South, where if you had one drop of African blood you were a Negro, disregarding all other facts and considerations, including how you saw yourself.

3   You might suppose that in the years since my little Census-form protest the growing enlightenment about race in our society would have been accompanied by a loosening of racial categories by our government. But in recent years the United States government has acted in a deliberate way to make it even more difficult for individuals to move beyond racial boxes and for American society as a whole to move beyond race.

4   Why the government perpetuates racialization and what might be done to diminish the role of race in our lives are topics that have become especially timely as Hispanics begin to take a more important role demographically, having displaced African-Americans as the largest American minority. How Hispanics view themselves and how they are viewed by others are among the most important factors affecting whether or not we can end race as a major social divide in America.

5   Treating people differently according to their race is as un-American as a hereditary aristocracy and as American as slavery. The American ethos was formed by people who left the social stratification of the Old World to live in a freer, more fluid society. They sought to be defined by what they accomplished, not by what they were born with. As Arthur M. Schlesinger Jr. puts it in his book *The Disuniting of America*, one of the great virtues of America is that it defines individuals by where they are going rather than by where they have been. Achievement matters, not origin. The national ideal says that all Americans should be able to compete as equals, whatever their background. American society has been divided along racial lines since its earliest days.

> *Treating people differently according to their race is as un-American as a hereditary aristocracy and as American as slavery. The national ideal says that all Americans should be able to compete as equals, whatever their background.*

6   Racial characterizations have trumped the achievement ideal; people born into a non-white race, whatever their accomplishments, have been unable to change their racial status. Worse, race has often been their most defining characteristic, affecting most, if not all, aspects of their being.

7   As a result, we have been caught, at least since the onset of the civil rights movement, in ambivalence. On the one hand, we continue to dream of the day when all Americans will be treated equally, whatever their race; we rail against—and sometimes punish—those who discriminate according to race in hiring, housing, and social life. At the same time, we have ensconced in law many claims based on

race: requirements that a given proportion of public subsidies, loans, job training, educational assistance, and admission slots at choice colleges be set aside for people of color. Many Americans, including African-Americans, are uneasy about what some people consider reverse discrimination. Courts have limited its scope; politicians have made hay by opposing it; and some of its beneficiaries feel that their successes are hollow, because they are unsure whether their gains reflect hard-won achievements or special favors. There must be a better way to deal with past and current injustice. And the rapid changes in American demographics call for a reexamination of the place of race in America.

Enter the Hispanic

8   We have grown accustomed to thinking about America in black and white and might well have continued to do so for decades to come except that Hispanics complicate this simplistic scheme: they do not fit into the old racial categories. Some Hispanics appear to many Americans to be black (for example, quite a few Cuban-Americans), others as white (especially immigrants from Argentina and Chile), and the appearance of still others is hard for many people to pigeonhole. Anyone seeing the lineup of baseball players honored as Major League Baseball's "Latino Legends Team" would find that the players vary from those who are as fair-skinned as Roger Clemens to those who are as dark-skinned as Jackie Robinson. More important by far, survey after survey shows that most Hispanics object to being classified as either black or white. A national survey conducted in 2002 indicated that 76 percent of Hispanics say the standard racial categories used by the U.S. Census do not address their preferences. The last thing most of those surveyed desire is to be treated as yet another race—as "brown" Americans.

9   Hispanics would have forced the question of how we define one another even if they were just another group of immigrants among the many that have made America what it is. But Hispanics are not just one more group of immigrants. Not only have Hispanic numbers surpassed those of black Americans, who until 2003 made up America's largest minority group, Hispanics have been reliably projected to grow much faster than African-Americans or any other American group. Thus, according to the Census, in 1990 blacks constituted 12 percent of the population and Hispanics 9 percent. By 2000, Hispanics caught up with blacks, amounting to 12.5 percent of the population compared to 12.3 percent for blacks. By 2050, Hispanics are projected to be 24.3 percent of the American population, compared to 14.7 percent for blacks. In many cities, from Miami to Los Angeles, in which African-Americans have been the largest minority group, Hispanics' numbers are increasingly felt. While once Hispanics were concentrated in the areas bordering Mexico, their numbers are now growing in places like Denver, St. Paul, and even New England.

10   Immigration fuels the growth of Hispanics relative to the growth of African-Americans, because Latin-American immigration, legal and illegal, continues at an explosive pace, while immigration from Africa is minuscule. Hispanics also have more children than African-Americans. During the most recent year for which data are available, 2003 to 2004, one of every two people added to America's population was Hispanic. And while black Americans have long been politically mobilized and active, Hispanics are just beginning to make their weight felt in American politics.

11   The rapid growth in the number, visibility, and power of Hispanics will largely determine the future of race in America, a point highlighted by Clara E. Rodriguez in her book *Changing Race: Latinos, the Census, and the History of Ethnicity in the U.S.* If Hispanics are to be viewed as brown or black (and some on the left aspire to color them), and above all if Hispanics develop the sense of disenfranchisement and alienation that many African-Americans have acquired (often for very good reasons), then America's immutable racial categories will only deepen.

12   If, on the other hand, most Hispanics continue to see themselves as members of one or more ethnic groups, then race in America might be pushed to the margins. Racial categories have historically set us apart; ethnic categories are part of the mosaic that makes up America. It has been much easier for an individual to assimilate from an ethnic perspective than from a racial one. Race is considered a biological attribute, a part of your being that cannot be dropped or modified. Ethnic origin, in contrast, is where you came from. All Americans have one hyphen or another attached to their ethnic status: we're Polish-, or German-, or Anglo-, or Italian-Americans. Adding Cuban-Americans or Mexican-Americans to this collage would create more comfortable categories of a comparable sort.

The Race Trap

13   Many people take it for granted that genes determine race, just as genes determine gender. And we also tend to believe that racial categories are easy to discern (though we all know of exceptions).

14   One way to show how contrived racial divisions actually are is to recall that practically all of the DNA in all human beings is the same. Our differences are truly skin deep. Moreover, the notion that most of us are of one race or another has little basis in science. The Human Genome Project informs us not only that 99.9 percent of genetic material is shared by all humans, but also that variation in the remaining 0.1 percent is greater within racial groups than across them. That is, not only are 99.9 percent of the genes of a black person the same as those of a white person, but the genes of a particular black person may be more similar to the genes of a white person than they are to another black person.

15   This point was driven home to college students in a sociology class at Penn State in April 2005. Following their professor's suggestion, the students took DNA tests that had surprising results. A student who identified himself as "a proud black man" found that only 52 percent of his ancestry traced back to Africa, while the other 48 percent was European. Another student who said she takes flak from black friends for having a white boyfriend found that her ancestry was 58 percent European and only 42 percent African. These two students are not alone: an estimated one-third of the African-American population has European ancestry.

16   Which people make up a distinct race and which are considered dark-skinned constantly changes as social prejudices change. Jewish-, Slavic-, Irish-, and Polish-Americans were considered distinct races in the mid-19th and early 20th centuries—and dark races at that, as chronicled in great detail in Matthew Frye Jacobson's book *Whiteness of a Different Color: European Immigrants and the Alchemy of Race* and in a well-documented book by Noel Ignatiev, *How the Irish Became White*. Ignatiev

found that in the 1850s, Irish people were considered non-white in America and were frequently referred to as "niggers turned inside out." (Blacks were sometimes called "smoked Irish.")

17   The capriciousness of racial classifications is further highlighted by the way the U.S. Census, the most authoritative and widely used source of social classifications, divides Americans into races. When I ask my students how many races they think there are in America, they typically count four: white, black, Asian, and Native American. The Census says there are 15 racial categories: white, African-American, American Indian/Alaska Native, Asian Indian, Chinese, Filipino, Japanese, Korean, Vietnamese, "other Asian," Native Hawaiian, Guamanian/Chamorro, Samoan, and "other Pacific Islander," and as of 2000, one more for those who feel they are of some other race. (Hispanic is not on this list because the Census treats Hispanic as an ethnicity and asks about it on a separate question, but immediately following that question, the Census asks, "So what is your race, anyhow?")

18   The arbitrary nature of these classifications is demonstrated by the Census Bureau itself, which can change the race of millions of Americans by the stroke of a pen. The Census changed the race of Indian- and Pakistani-Americans from white in 1970 to Asian in 1980. In 1930 the Census made Mexicans into a different race but then withdrew this category. Similarly, Hindu made a brief appearance as a race in the 1930 and 1940 Censuses but was subsequently withdrawn.

19   Anthropologists have found that some tribes do not see colors the way many of us do; for instance, they do not "see" a difference between brown and yellow. Members of these tribes are not color-blind, but some differences found in nature (in the color spectrum) simply don't register with them, just as young American children are unaware of racial differences until someone introduces them to these distinctions. We draw a line between white and black, but people's skin colors have many shades. It is our social prejudices that lead us to make sharp racial categories.

20   I am not one of those postmodernists who, influenced by Nietzsche and Foucault, claim that there are no epistemological truths, that all facts are a matter of social construction. I disagree with Nietzsche's description of truth as "a mobile army of metaphors, metonyms, and anthropomorphisms—in short a sum of human relations, which have been enhanced, transposed, and embellished poetically and rhetorically and which after long use seem firm, canonical, and obligatory to a people." However, there is no doubt that social construction plays a significant role in the way we "see" racial differences, although our views may in turn be affected by other factors that are less subject to construction; for example, historical differences.

21   Most important is the significance we attribute to race and the interpretations we impose on it. When we are told only that a person is, say, Asian-American, we often jump to a whole list of conclusions regarding that person's looks, intelligence, work ethic, and character; we make the same sort of jumps for Native Americans, blacks, and other races. Many things follow from these knee-jerk characterizations: whether we will fear or like this person, whether we will wish to have him or her as a neighbor or as a spouse for one of our children—all on the basis of race. In short, we load on to race a great deal of social importance that is not a reflection of the "objective" biological differences that exist. To paraphrase the UNESCO Constitution, racial divisions are made in the minds of men and women, and that is where they will have to be ended.

Defining the Hispanic

22 If racial categories have long been settled, the social characterization of the Hispanic is up for grabs. We still don't know whether Hispanics will be defined as a brown race—and align themselves with those in the United States who are, or who see themselves, as marginalized or victimized—or if they will be viewed as a conglomerate of ethnic groups, of Mexican-Americans, Cuban-Americans, Dominican-Americans, and so forth, who will fit snugly into the social mosaic.

23 The term "Hispanic" was first used in the Census in 1980. Before that, Mexican-Americans and Cuban-Americans were classified as white (except when a Census interviewer identified an individual as a member of a different racial group). Until 1980, Hispanics were part of the great American panorama of ethnic groups. Then the Census combined these groups into a distinct category unlike any other. It was as if the federal government were to one day lump together Spanish-, Italian-, and Greek-Americans into a group called "Southern European" and begin issuing statistics on how their income, educational achievements, number of offspring, and so on compare to those of Northern Europeans.

24 And as we've seen, those who define themselves as Hispanic are asked to declare a race. In the 1980 Census, the options included, aside from the usual menu of races, that ambiguous category "Other." There were 6.75 million Americans, including me, who chose this option in 1980. Most revealing: 40 percent of Hispanics chose this option. (Note that they—and I—chose this category despite the nature of the word "Other," which suggests the idea of "not being one of us." Had the category been accorded a less loaded label, say "wish not to be identified with any one group," it seems likely that many millions more would have chosen this box.)

25 To have millions of Americans choose to identify themselves as "Other" created a political backlash, because Census statistics are used both to allocate public funds to benefit minority groups and to assess their political strength. Some African-American groups, especially, feared that if African-Americans chose "Other" instead of marking the "African-American" box, they would lose public allotments and political heft.

26 But never underestimate our government. The Census Bureau has used a statistical procedure to assign racial categories to those millions of us who sought to butt out of this divisive classification scheme. Federal regulations outlined by the Office of Management and Budget, a White House agency, ruled that the Census must "impute" a specific race to those who do not choose one. For several key public-policy purposes, a good deal of social and economic data must be aggregated into five racial groups: white, black, Asian, American Indian or Alaska Native, and native Hawaiian or other Pacific Islander. How does the government pick a race for a person who checked the "Other" box? They turn to the answers for other Census questions: for example, income, neighborhood, education level, or last name. The resulting profiles of the U.S. population (referred to as the "age-race modified profile") are then used by government agencies in allotting public funds and for other official and public purposes.

27 But the Census isn't alone in oversimplifying the data. Increasingly, other entities, including the media, have treated Hispanics as a race rather than an ethnic

group. This occurs implicitly when those who generate social data—such as government agencies or social scientists—break down the data into four categories: white, black, Asian, and Hispanic, which is comparable to listing apples, oranges, bananas, and yams. In their profile of jail inmates, the Bureau of Justice Statistics lists inmates' origins as "white, black, Hispanic, American Indian/Alaska Native, Asian/Pacific Islander, and more than one race." The *New York Times* ran a front-page story in September 2005 in which it compared the first names used by whites, blacks, Asians, and Hispanics. Replace the word *Hispanics* with the name of another ethnic group, say Jews, and the unwitting racial implication of this classification will stand out.

28   Still other studies include Hispanics when they explicitly refer to racial groups. For example, a 2001 paper by Sean Reardon and John T. Yun examines what they call "racial balkanization among suburban schools," where there is increased segregation among black, Hispanic, and Asian students. A 2005 *Seattle Times* story uses racial terminology when it reports "Latinos have the fewest numbers among racial groups in master's-of-business programs nationwide, with about 5,000 enrolling annually." Similarly, the *San Diego Union Tribune* states: "A brawl between Latino and black students resulted in a lockdown of the school and revealed tensions between the two largest racial groups on campus."

29   A handful of others go a step further and refer to Hispanics as a "brown race." For example, following the recent Los Angeles mayoral election, the *Houston Chronicle* informed us that "Villaraigosa's broad-based support has analysts wondering whether it is evidence of an emerging black–brown coalition." And National Public Radio reported: "There is no black and brown alliance at a South Central Los Angeles high school."

30   One way or another, all of these references push us in the wrong direction—toward racializing Hispanics and deepening social divisions. America would be best served if we moved in the opposite direction.

A New Taxonomy

31 Thus far, workers at the U.S. Census Bureau, following the White House's instructions, seem determined to prevent any deemphasis of race. They are testing iterations of the wording for the relevant questions in the 2010 Census—but all of these possibilities continue to require people to identify themselves by race. Moreover, Census bureaucrats will continue to impute race to those who refuse to do so themselves, ignoring the ever-growing number of people, especially Hispanics, who do not fit into this scheme.

32   Imagine if instead the federal government classified people by their country (or countries) of origin. For some governmental purposes, it might suffice to use large categories, such as Africa (which would exclude other so-called black groups, such as Haitians and West Indians that are now included in references to "black" Americans), Asia, Europe, Central America, and South America (the last two categories would not, of course, include Spain). For other purposes, a more detailed breakdown might work better—using regions such as the Middle East and Southeast Asia, for example—and if still more detail was desired, specific countries could be used, as we do for

identifying ethnic groups (Irish, Polish, Cuban, Mexican, Japanese, Ethiopian, and so on). Kenneth Prewitt, a former director of the U.S. Census Bureau, has suggested the use of ethnic categories. As we have seen, ethnic origins carry some implications for who we are, but these implications decline in importance over time. Above all, they do not define us in some immutable way, as racial categories do. A category called something like "wish not to be identified with any particular group" should be included for those who do not want to be characterized, even by ethnicity, or for others who view themselves as having a varied and combined heritage.

33   The classification of Americans who are second-generation and beyond highlights the importance of the no-particular-group category. Although a fourth-generation Italian-American might still wish to be identified as Italian, he might not, particularly if he has grandparents or parents who are, say, Greek, Korean, and Native American. Forcing such a person to classify himself as a member of one ethnic group conceals the significance of the most important American development in social matters: out-marriage. Out-marriage rates for all groups other than African-Americans are so high that most of us will soon be tied to Americans of a large variety of backgrounds by the closest possible social tie, the familial one. Approximately 30 percent of third-generation Hispanics and 40 percent of third-generation Asians marry people of a different racial or ethnic origin. Altogether, the proportion of marriages among people of different racial or ethnic origins has increased by 72 percent since 1970. The trend suggests more of this in the future. Even if your spouse is of the same background, chances are high that the spouse of a sibling or cousin will represent a different part of the American collage. At holidays and other family events, from birthdays to funerals, we will increasingly be in close connection with "Others." Before too long most Americans will be "Tiger Woods" Americans, whose parental heritage is black, Native American, Chinese, Caucasian, and Thai. Now is the time for our social categories to reflect this trend—and its capacity for building a sense of one community—rather than conceal it.

Where Do We Go from Here?

34 Changing the way we divide up society will not magically resolve our differences or abolish racial prejudices. Nor does a movement toward a color-blind nation mean that we should stop working for a more just America. A combination of three major approaches that deal with economic and legal change could allow us to greatly downgrade the importance of race as a social criterion and still advance social justice. These approaches include reparations, class-based social programs, and fighting discrimination on an individual basis.

35   To make amends for the grave injustice that has been done to African-Americans by slavery and racial prejudice, as well as to bring to a close claims based on past injustices—and the sense of victimhood and entitlement that often accompanies these claims—major reparations are called for. One possible plan might allot a trillion dollars in education, training, and housing vouchers to African-Americans over a period of 20 years. (The same sort of plan might be devised for Native Americans.)

36   Such reparations cannot make full compensation for the sins of slavery, of course. But nothing can. Even so, if Jews could accept restitution from Germany and

move on (Germany and Israel now have normal international relations, and the Jewish community in Germany is rapidly growing), could not a similar reconciliation between black and white Americans follow reparations? A precedent in our own history is the payment of reparations to Japanese-Americans because of their internment in World War II. In 1988, the U.S. government issued a formal apology in the Civil Liberties Act and awarded $20,000 to each living person who had been interned. About 80,000 claims were awarded, totaling $1.6 billion.

37   Part of the deal should be that once reparations are made for the sins against African-Americans in the past, black people could no longer claim special entitlements or privileges on the basis of their race. Reparations thus would end affirmative action and minority set-asides as we have known them.

38   At the same time, Americans who are disadvantaged for any reason not of their own doing—the handicapped; those who grew up in parts of the country, such as Appalachia, in which the economy has long been lagging; those whose jobs were sent overseas who are too old to be retrained—would be given extra aid in applying for college admissions and scholarships, housing allowances, small-business loans, and other social benefits. The basis for such aid would be socioeconomic status, not race. The child of a black billionaire would no longer be entitled to special consideration in college admissions, for instance, but the child of a poor white worker who lost his job to outsourcing and could not find new employment would be.

39   Social scientists differ in their estimates of the extent to which differences in opportunity and upward mobility between blacks and whites are due to racial prejudice and the extent to which they are due to economic class differences. But most scholars who have studied the matter agree that economic factors are stronger than racial ones, possibly accounting for as much as 80 percent of the differences we observe. A vivid example: In recent years, Wake County in North Carolina made sure that its public school classes were composed of students of different economic backgrounds, disregarding racial and ethnic differences. The results of this economic integration overshadowed previous attempts to improve achievement via racial integration. While a decade ago, only 40 percent of blacks in grades three through eight scored at grade level, in the spring of 2005, 80 percent did so.

40   Class differences affect not only educational achievement, health, and job selection but also how people are regarded or stereotyped. Fifty years ago, a study conducted at Howard University showed that although adjectives used to describe whites and blacks were quite different, that variance was greatly reduced when class was held constant. People described upper-class whites and upper-class blacks in a remarkably similar fashion, as intelligent and ambitious. People also described lower-class whites and lower-class blacks in a similar way, as dirty and ignorant. The author concluded that "stereotypes vary more as a function of class than of race."

41   If race-based discrimination were a thing of the past, and black Americans were no longer subjected to it, then my argument that reparations can lead to closure would be easier to sustain. Strong evidence shows, however, that discrimination remains very much with us. A 1990 Urban Institute study found that when two

people of different races applied for the same job, one in eight times the white was offered the job and an equally qualified African-American was not. Another Urban Institute study, released in 1999, found that racial minorities received less time and information from loan officers and were quoted higher interest rates than whites in most of the cities where tests were conducted.

42   The victims of current racial discrimination should be fully entitled to remedies in court and through such federal agencies as the Equal Employment Opportunity Commission. These cases should be dealt with on an individual basis or in a class-action suit where evidence exists to support one. Those who sense discrimination should be required to prove it. It shouldn't be assumed that because a given work-place has more people of race *x* than race *y*, discrimination must exist.

A Vision of the Future

43 In the end, it comes down to what Americans envision for our future together: either an open society, in which everyone is equally respected (an elusive goal but perhaps closer at hand than we realize), or an even more racialized nation, in which "people of color" are arrayed in perpetual conflict with white people. The first possibility is a vision of America as a community in which people work out their differences and make up for past injustices in a peaceful and fair manner; the other is one in which charges of prejudice and discrimination are mixed with real injustices, and in which a frustrated sense of victimhood and entitlement on the one hand is met with guilt and rejection on the other.

44   A good part of what is at stake is all too real: the distribution of assets, income, and power, which reparations, class-based reforms, and the courts should be able to sort out. But don't overlook the importance of symbols, attitudes, and feelings, which can't be changed legislatively. One place to start is with a debate over the official ways in which we classify ourselves and the ways we gather social data, because these classifications and data are used as a mirror in which we see ourselves reflected.

45   Let us begin with a fairly modest request of the powers that be: Give us a chance. Don't make me define my children and myself in racial terms; don't "impute" a race to me or to any of the millions of Americans who feel as I do. Allow us to describe ourselves simply as Americans. I bet my 50 years as a sociologist that we will all be better for it. ◆

CRITICAL THINKING

1. Why does Etzioni decline to indicate his race? What point does he make by recounting his personal experiences?
2. Is it possible to be considered one race by the U.S. government but to see yourself as a different race? Explain.
3. Do you think the government and other institutions should change the "race" category to "ethnicity"? Should there be no section on race or ethnicity at all? Would this make the process of gathering information easier or more confusing?

4. Have you ever felt discriminated against because of your race? Have you ever found yourself making stereotypical assumptions of others based on their ethnicity, even inadvertently? Explain.
5. Is Hispanic a "race"? Why would the government want to know racial information? What issues connected to race are unique to this population?
6. What is the "race trap"? Why is it harmful? Explain.
7. The author suggests that government aid be distributed according to socioeconomic status not race: "The child of a black billionaire would no longer be entitled to special consideration in college admissions, for instance, but the child of a poor white worker who lost his job to outsourcing and could not find new employment would be." Do you agree with basing aid on socioeconomic status instead of race? How might this change the racial divide in the United States?
8. According to Etzioni, what unique opportunity do we now have to think "beyond race"? How are Hispanics connected to this opportunity? Explain.

CRITICAL WRITING

1. *Persuasive Writing:* Write a letter to the U.S. government suggesting how race should be considered, or not, on documents, censuses, and other forms. Give concrete examples and detailed support for your point of view.
2. *Personal Narrative:* Etzioni recounts a personal experience in which race made him acutely aware of how disclosing this information can be abused. Describe how important or unimportant race has been in your life thus far. Write about a defining moment that changed or influenced your view of yourself, or someone in your family, connected to your ethnicity.
3. *Exploratory Writing:* Explain this paradox from the article: "Treating people differently according to their race is as un-American as a hereditary aristocracy, and as American as slavery."

GROUP PROJECTS

1. With your group, list as many forms as you can think of that require people to denote race—come up with at least 10 different occurrences. Then explain why these forms need to contain this information.
2. As a group, research DNA testing for race and ethnicity. How much does it cost, what steps are involved, and what types of results are given? How accurate are the results? Would you consider doing genetic testing? Explain your reasoning.
3. Etzioni notes that racial information has a history of causing more harm than good. Discuss as a group the ways that racial information on government forms could be abused and whether the time has come to eliminate this question from forms, no matter what good intentions, such as affirmative action, may be behind it.

People Like Us
David Brooks*

> From the hallowed halls of academia to the boardrooms of Fortune 500 companies, the con-
> cept of racial and social diversity is an important factor in efforts to create a balanced, equal
> society. But despite efforts to promote diversity, all too often we witness "self-segregation."
> As David Brooks explains in this next essay, while we tend to pay lip service to ideals of diver-
> sity, we really prefer to associate with "people like us." Is the melting pot merely a myth?

1   Maybe it's time to admit the obvious. We don't really care about diversity all that
much in America, even though we talk about it a great deal. Maybe somewhere in
this country there is a truly diverse neighborhood in which a black Pentecostal
minister lives next to a white antiglobalization activist, who lives next to an
Asian short-order cook, who lives next to a professional golfer, who lives next
to a postmodern-literature professor and a cardiovascular surgeon. But I have never
been to or heard of that neighborhood. Instead, what I have seen all around the country
is people making strenuous efforts to group themselves with people who are basically
like themselves.

2   Human beings are capable of drawing amazingly subtle social distinctions and
then shaping their lives around them. In the Washington, D.C., area, Democratic
lawyers tend to live in suburban Maryland, and Republican lawyers tend to live in
suburban Virginia. If you asked a Democratic lawyer to move from her $750,000
house in Bethesda, Maryland, to a $750,000 house in Great Falls, Virginia, she'd
look at you as if you had just asked her to buy a pickup truck with a gun rack and to
shove chewing tobacco in her kid's mouth. In Manhattan the owner of a $3 million
SoHo loft would feel out of place moving into a $3 million Fifth Avenue apartment.
A West Hollywood interior decorator would feel dislocated if you asked him to
move to Orange County. In Georgia a barista from Athens would probably not fit in
serving coffee in Americus.

3   It is a common complaint that every place is starting to look the same. But
in the information age, the late writer James Chapin once told me, every place
becomes more like itself. People are less often tied down to factories and mills,
and they can search for places to live on the basis of cultural affinity. Once they
find a town in which people share their values, they flock there and reinforce
whatever was distinctive about the town in the first place. Once Boulder, Colorado, became known as congenial to politically progressive mountain bikers,
half the politically progressive mountain bikers in the country (it seems) moved
there; they made the place so culturally pure that it has become practically a parody of itself.

4   But people love it. Make no mistake—we are increasing our happiness by seg-
menting off so rigorously. We are finding places where we are comfortable and

---

* David Brooks, *The Atlantic*, September 2003

where we feel we can flourish. But the choices we make toward that end lead to the very opposite of diversity. The United States might be a diverse nation when considered as a whole, but block by block and institution by institution, it is a relatively homogeneous nation.

5   When we use the word "diversity" today, we usually mean racial integration. But even here our good intentions seem to have run into the brick wall of human nature. Over the past generation, reformers have tried heroically, and in many cases successfully, to end housing discrimination. But recent patterns aren't encouraging: according to an analysis of the 2000 census data, the 1990s saw only a slight increase in the racial integration of neighborhoods in the United States. The number of middle-class and upper–middle-class African-American families is rising, but for whatever reasons—racism, psychological comfort—these families tend to congregate in predominantly black neighborhoods.

6   In fact, evidence suggests that some neighborhoods become more segregated over time. New suburbs in Arizona and Nevada, for example, start out reasonably well integrated. These neighborhoods don't yet have reputations, so people choose their houses for other, mostly economic reasons. But as neighborhoods age, they develop personalities (that's where the Asians live, and that's where the Hispanics live), and segmentation occurs. It could be that in a few years, the new suburbs in the Southwest will be nearly as segregated as the established ones in the Northeast and the Midwest.

7   Even though race and ethnicity run deep in American society, we should in theory be able to find areas that are at least culturally diverse. But here, too, people show few signs of being truly interested in building diverse communities. If you run a retail company and you're thinking of opening new stores, you can choose among dozens of consulting firms that are quite effective at locating your potential customers. They can do this because people with similar tastes and preferences tend to congregate by ZIP code.

8   The most famous of these precision marketing firms is Claritas, which breaks down the U.S. population into 62 psycho-demographic clusters, based on such factors as how much money people make, what they like to read and watch, and what products they have bought in the past. For example, the "suburban sprawl" cluster is composed of young families making about $41,000 a year and living in fast-growing places such as Burnsville, Minnesota, and Bensalem, Pennsylvania. These people are almost twice as likely as other Americans to have three-way calling. They are two and a half times as likely to buy Light n' Lively Kid Yogurt. Members of the "towns and gowns" cluster are recent college graduates in places such as Berkeley, California, and Gainesville, Florida. They are big consumers of Dove Bars and Saturday Night Live. They tend to drive small foreign cars and to read *Rolling Stone* and *Scientific American.*

9   Looking through the market research, one can sometimes be amazed by how efficiently people cluster—and by how predictable we all are. If you wanted to sell imported wine, obviously you would have to find places where rich people live. But did you know that the 16 counties with the greatest proportion of imported-wine drinkers are all in the same three metropolitan areas (New York, San Francisco, and Washington, D.C.)? If you tried to open a motor-home dealership in Montgomery

County, Pennsylvania, you'd probably go broke, because people in this ring of the Philadelphia suburbs think RVs are kind of uncool. But if you traveled just a short way north, to Monroe County, Pennsylvania, you would find

> *Even though race and ethnicity run deep in American society, we should in theory be able to find areas that are at least culturally diverse. But here, too, people show few signs of being truly interested in building diverse communities.*

yourself in the fifth motor-home-friendliest county in America.

10   Geography is not the only way we find ourselves divided from people unlike us. Some of us watch *Fox News*, while others listen to NPR. Some like David Letterman, and others—typically in less urban neighborhoods—like Jay Leno. Some go to charismatic churches; some go to mainstream churches. Americans tend more and more often to marry people with education levels similar to their own and to befriend people with backgrounds similar to their own.

11   My favorite illustration of this latter pattern comes from the first, noncontroversial chapter of *The Bell Curve*. Think of your 12 closest friends, Richard J. Herrnstein and Charles Murray write. If you had chosen them randomly from the American population, the odds that half of your 12 closest friends would be college graduates would be six in a thousand. The odds that half of the 12 would have advanced degrees would be less than one in a million. Have any of your 12 closest friends graduated from Harvard, Stanford, Yale, Princeton, CalTech, MIT, Duke, Dartmouth, Cornell, Columbia, Chicago, or Brown? If you chose your friends randomly from the American population, the odds against your having four or more friends from those schools would be more than a billion to one.

12   Many of us live in absurdly unlikely groupings, because we have organized our lives that way.

13   It's striking that the institutions that talk the most about diversity often practice it the least. For example, no group of people sings the diversity anthem more frequently and fervently than administrators at just such elite universities. But elite universities are amazingly undiverse in their values, politics, and mores. Professors in particular are drawn from a rather narrow segment of the population. If faculties reflected the general population, 32 percent of professors would be registered Democrats and 31 percent would be registered Republicans. Forty percent would be evangelical Christians. But a recent study of several universities by the conservative Center for the Study of Popular Culture and the American Enterprise Institute found that roughly 90 percent of those professors in the arts and sciences who had registered with a political party had registered Democratic. Fifty-seven professors at Brown were found on the voter-registration rolls. Of those, 54 were Democrats. Of the 42 professors in the English, history, sociology, and political science departments, all were Democrats. The results at Harvard, Penn State, Maryland, and the University of California at Santa Barbara were similar to the results at Brown.

14   What we are looking at here is human nature. People want to be around others who are roughly like themselves. That's called *community*. It probably would

be psychologically difficult for most Brown professors to share an office with someone who was pro-life, a member of the National Rifle Association, or an evangelical Christian. It's likely that hiring committees would subtly—even unconsciously—screen out any such people they encountered. Republicans and evangelical Christians have sensed that they are not welcome at places like Brown, so they don't even consider working there. In fact, any registered Republican who contemplates a career in academia these days is both a hero and a fool. So, in a semi–self-selective pattern, brainy people with generally liberal social mores flow to academia, and brainy people with generally conservative mores flow elsewhere.

15   The dream of diversity is like the dream of equality. Both are based on ideals we celebrate, even as we undermine them daily. (How many times have you seen someone renounce a high-paying job or pull his child from an elite college on the grounds that these things are bad for equality?) On the one hand, the situation is appalling. It is appalling that Americans know so little about one another. It is appalling that many of us are so narrow-minded that we can't tolerate a few people with ideas significantly different from our own. It's appalling that evangelical Christians are practically absent from entire professions, such as academia, the media, and filmmaking. It's appalling that people should be content to cut themselves off from everyone unlike themselves.

16   The segmentation of society means that often we don't even have arguments across the political divide. Within their little validating communities, liberals and conservatives circulate half-truths about the supposed awfulness of the other side. These distortions are believed because it feels good to believe them.

17   On the other hand, there are limits to how diverse any community can or should be. I've come to think that it is not useful to try to hammer diversity into every neighborhood and institution in the United States. Sure, Augusta National should probably admit women, and university sociology departments should probably hire a conservative or two. It would be nice if all neighborhoods had a good mixture of ethnicities. But human nature being what it is, most places and institutions are going to remain culturally homogeneous.

18   It's probably better to think about diverse lives, not diverse institutions. Human beings, if they are to live well, will have to move through a series of institutions and environments, which may be individually homogeneous but, taken together, will offer diverse experiences. It might also be a good idea to make national service a rite of passage for young people in this country: it would take them out of their narrow neighborhood segment and thrust them in with people unlike themselves. Finally, it's probably important for adults to get out of their own familiar circles. If you live in a coastal, socially liberal neighborhood, maybe you should take out a subscription to *The Door*, the evangelical humor magazine; or maybe you should visit Branson, Missouri. Maybe you should stop in at a megachurch. Sure, it would be superficial familiarity, but it beats the iron curtains that now separate the nation's various cultural zones.

19   Look around at your daily life. Are you really in touch with the broad diversity of American life? Do you care? ◆

CRITICAL THINKING

1. When you were growing up, with whom did your parents socialize? Where did they live and what social functions were they likely to attend? Now that you are an adult, with whom do you chose to socialize? What is the demographic anatomy of your social group? Is it influenced by race and ethnicity? Is it influenced by common interests? Explain.

2. What does Brooks mean when he says "Human beings are capable of drawing amazingly subtle social distinctions and then shaping their lives around them" (paragraph 2)? What examples does he give of such distinctions? Can you think of any "subtle distinctions" in your own life that influence where you live and with whom you choose to associate? Explain.

3. What is "cultural affinity"? How does it influence the social and cultural values of a particular area? How is it reinforced, and how can it break down? Explain.

4. When we refer to the word "diversity," what do we usually mean? What types of diversity are identified by the author? What factors tend to influence people to find others like them?

5. What is ironic about the institutions that stress diversity (paragraph 13)? Why do they emphasize the need for diversity, and how do they fall short of actually practicing it? Explain.

6. Brooks states that he believes when we live with "people like us" we tend to be happier. Do you agree? If this is true, why do we tend to pay so much lip service to the idea of diversity but actually fail to achieve it?

7. Brooks begins his essay with the statement, "We don't really care about diversity all that much in America, even though we talk about it a great deal." Do you agree? Why or why not?

CRITICAL WRITING

1. *Personal Narrative:* Describe the neighborhood in which you currently live. How does it connect to the points Brooks makes in his essay? (A dormitory can be considered a "neighborhood.") Consider also in your narrative the reasons why you chose the college you now attend and the social groups with which you associate. Draw connections between your own "cultural cluster" and Brooks's observations on diversity in practice.

2. *Exploratory Writing:* In paragraph 11, Brooks discusses how the first chapter of *The Bell Curve* describes our tendency to connect with "people like us." Apply Herrnstein and Murray's hypothesis to your own life. Write down the names of your 12 closest friends and think about their socioeconomic backgrounds, race and ethnicity, religion, political leanings, and intellectual pursuits. Then consider them as a group. Write a short essay about what you discover about your own group and how it compares to the observations made in *The Bell Curve*. What do your results reveal about the multicultural face of the nation, especially as it applies to race?

3. *Persuasive Writing:* Write an essay in which you explain why you believe diversity is or is not important to the success of society. Is diversity more critical in certain situations but less important in others? Explain your point of view while also making references to the text.

GROUP PROJECTS

1. In paragraph 5, Brooks observes that many neighborhoods have failed to be truly racially integrated "for whatever reasons." With your group, interview a diverse group of students on where they grew up. Name the region, state, city, or town—even the neighborhood—and ask them to describe their hometown's demographic profile, including social, intellectual, professional, and economic dimensions. Ask the people you interview for their impressions about why their family lived where they did and the cultural influences they experienced. Prepare a report on your findings. What did you discover about demographic clustering? What might it mean for diversity efforts in the next 20 years?

2. As a group, discuss how ethnic and racial differences divide and unite us as a nation. According to the report *Changing America by the President's Initiative on Race,* the gaps among races and ethnic groups in the areas of education, jobs, economic status, health, housing, and criminal justice are substantial. Access this report at http://www.access.gpo.gov/eop/ca/pdfs/toc.pdf. Choose one subject area from its table of contents, and read through that chapter and charts. Then, summarize what you have learned about the differences among racial and ethnic groups, and discuss how you think these disparities affect our chances of creating a society in which all Americans can participate equally.

Perspectives:
History Marches On

THINKING CRITICALLY

1. What issue is this cartoon raising? What connections exist between immigration and racism?
2. What is "nativism"?
3. What is the history behind each of the first three panels (1780, 1850, and 1920)? What happened after these immigrant groups entered the United States? What might one infer will happen following the "Now" panel, based on the history highlighted by the previous three panels?

Are You a Terrorist, or Do You Play One on TV?
Laura Fokkena *

Sometimes racial stereotypes can be more than simply insulting; they can interfere with the daily lives of the people victimized by them. As journalist Laura Fokkena observes in the next essay, Hollywood has long cast people from the Middle East as terrorists. This stereotype wasn't helped by the tragic events of September 11. The perpetuation of the Arab-as-terrorist stereotype has caused Fokkena, who is American, and her husband, who is Egyptian, to face the scrutiny of air-port security, to be kept off of flights, and to be eyed with suspicion merely because he resem-bles the same ethnicity as the Muslim extremists who committed acts of terrorism. As Fokkena explains, racial profiling, on the street or on the screen, is nothing new for some people.

1   Several years ago I came home from work one night to find my Egyptian husband and his Jordanian friend up past midnight watching *Aladdin*. Our daughter—then a toddler and the rightful owner of the video—had gone to bed hours earlier and left the two of them to enjoy their own, private cultural-studies seminar in our living room.

2   "Oh, God, now the sultan's marrying her off!" cried Jordanian Friend. "It's bar-baric, but hey, it's home," quipped my husband, repeating lyrics from the film while rolling his r's in a baritone imitation of an accent he's never had.

3   I admit it: I purchased Disney crap. In my own defense, I try to avoid all strains of happily-ever-after princess stories. But, other than a few grainy videos that you can order from, say, Syria, *Aladdin* is one of the rare movies with an Arab heroine available for the 2-to-6-year-old set. And so I had taken my chances with it.

4   My husband preferred to tell my daughter bedtime stories taken straight out of *1,001 Nights*, before they'd been contorted at the hands of Hollywood. (Tales of Ali Baba's clever servant, Morghana, are far more feminist than the big screen version of *Aladdin* ever was.) For my daughter's sake, I think this is wonderful. But it's also disappointing to see yet another example of unadulterated Middle Eastern literature trapped in Middle Eastern communities, told in whispers to children at bedtime, while the world at large is bombarded with a mammoth, distorted, Hollywood ver-sion replete with hook-nosed villains, limping camels, a manic genie, and Jasmine's sultan dad, who is (of course) a sexist.

5   While Native Americans, Asian Americans, and numerous other ethnic groups have had significant success in battling racist and inaccurate media images of their communities, Muslims and Middle Easterners are just beginning to decry stereotyp-ical portrayals of Arabs and Islam. In April, following another crisis in the West Bank, Edward Said wrote a short piece, published in both the American and Arab press, stressing the importance of media savvy. "We have simply never learned the importance of systematically organizing our political work in this country on a mass level, so that, for instance, the average American will not immediately think of 'terrorism' when the word 'Palestinian' is pronounced."

* Laura Fokkena, *PopPolitics*, November 2002

6   After September 11, an astonishing number of films and television programs were cancelled, delayed, or taken out of production due to unfortunate coincidences between their violent plotlines and, well, reality. It went without saying that all this mad scrambling was for the benefit of a nation momentarily unwilling to see the fun in shoot-em-up action adventures, and that it was not—at least in the case of movies with Middle Eastern characters—indicative of a sudden dose of sensitivity towards anti-Arab stereotyping.

7   But apparently Hollywood has either declared the grieving period over or has decided that what we need most right now are *more* escapist fantasies of Americans kicking the asses of aliens and foreigners. A number of films initially pushed back have since been released (some, like *Black Hawk Down* and *Behind Enemy Lines,* were actually moved up), and television series that were hastily rewritten to eradicate any terrorist references have now been rewritten again, this time to highlight them.

8   This first became obvious back in March, when CBS was bold enough to broadcast *Executive Decision* (albeit opposite the Oscars). *Executive Decision,* originally released in 1996, is a mediocre thriller that depicts Muslim terrorists hijacking a 747 en route to Washington, D.C. Like most films in its genre, wild-eyed Arabs are foiled by the technological, intellectual, and ultimately moral superiority of Americans.

9   *Executive Decision* has since appeared repeatedly on various cable networks, along with *True Lies* (1994), *The Siege* (1998), and *Not Without My Daughter* (1991). NBC's *The West Wing* has written a fictional Arab country into its plotline (and assassinated its defense minister); *Law and Order* opened this year's season with the story of an American convert to Islam who murders a women's rights activist. Islam is treated with varying degrees of nuance in each of these works, but it is always approached as a dilemma to be overcome—one always needs to *do* something about these troublesome Muslims—rather than folded unproblematically into the background, the way Josh and Toby's Judaism is presented on *The West Wing*, or the way Betty Mahmoody's Christianity is portrayed in *Not Without My Daughter*.

10   According to a report from Human Rights Watch, the federal government received reports of 481 anti-Muslim hate crimes in 2001, 17 times the number it received the year before. It also noted that more than 2,000 cases of harassment were reported to Arab and Muslim organizations. The Bush Administration and the Department of Justice have responded on the one hand by condemning hate crimes against the Muslim and Middle Eastern communities, and on the other by rounding up Muslims and Middle Easterners for questioning. Most notoriously, the FBI and Justice Department announced last fall their intent to schedule "interviews" with 5,000 men of Arab descent between the ages of 18 and 33. More than 1,000 men were detained indefinitely and incommunicado in the aftermath of September 11, most of them on minor visa charges.

11   Yet racial profiling and ethnic stereotyping are nothing new to Americans of Middle Eastern descent. Hollywood has long used images of bumbling, accented Arabs and Iranians as shorthand for "vile enemy," depicting them as stupid (witness the terrorist lackey in *True Lies* who forgets to put batteries in his camera when making a video to release to the press), yet nevertheless deeply threatening to all that is good and right with America. So ingrained is the image of Arab-as-terrorist that Ray Hanania, an Arab-American satirist, titled his autobiography *I'm Glad I Look Like a Terrorist* ("Almost every TV or Hollywood Arab terrorist looks like some uncle or

aunt or cousin of mine. The scene where Fred Dryer [of TV's *Hunter*] pounces on a gaggle of terrorists in the movie *Death Before Dishonor* [1987] looks like an assault on a Hanania family reunion").

> *Racial profiling and ethnic stereotyping are nothing new to Americans of Middle Eastern descent. Hollywood has long used images of bumbling, accented Arabs and Iranians as shorthand for "vile enemy," depicting them as stupid . . . yet nevertheless deeply threatening to all that is good and right with America.*

12   Within hours of the Oklahoma City bombing in 1995, there were rumors of Arab or Muslim involvement and real fear within the Middle Eastern community about being falsely associated with the atrocity. Despite the regular drum of tension in Northern Ireland and the civil wars that burn throughout Africa and the Americas, only those who look Middle Eastern—even Sikhs, young women, and members of the Secret Service—have been the targets of this particular brand of racial profiling.

13   Nowhere is this game of Pin-The-Bomb-Threat-On-The-Muslim more obvious than at the airport. A few years ago, I flew out of Cairo with my husband and discovered that F.W.A. (Flying While Arab) is no joke. We landed in Paris with a crying baby and were ushered to the back of the line while the airline attendants processed every other passenger. My husband was unconcerned; he was used to the routine. But I was acutely aware of two things: 1) that the baby was on her last diaper; and 2) that diaper was feeling heavy.

14   Our turn finally came a good three hours later, whereupon we spent another 45 minutes having our carry-on luggage examined and reexamined, answering the same questions again and again, and waiting while security checked and rechecked their computer database. All this over a graduate student from Egypt, married to an American citizen, during a time when world politics were calm enough that Bill Clinton's main preoccupation was rubbing lipstick smudges off his fly.

15   As it happened, most of the French airline workers were on strike that week (imagine that!) so we were sent to an airport hotel for the night and told we could take our connecting flight to D.C. the next day. While the other Americans and Europeans on our flight took the opportunity to spend a free night in Paris, my husband was instructed not to leave the hotel. I suppose the baby and I could have taken our crisp blue passports and gone into the city without him, but the thought of taking advantage of my American citizenship—something I'd just been born into by chance, mind you—while he stayed behind watching bad French television in the hotel lounge was too much to take.

16   Of course, it would be a mistake to assume that the most egregious offenses of racial profiling take place at the airport. The Council on American-Islamic Relations reports that half of the discrimination complaints it received in 2001 were work-related, and there has been a leap in the number of outright hate crimes, including at least three murders, since September 11.

17   The *Atlantic Monthly* featured an essay by Randall Kennedy, Harvard law professor and author of *Nigger: The Strange Career of a Troublesome Word*, comparing racial profiling to its "alter ego," affirmative action. "Supporters of profiling, who are willing to impose what amounts to a racial tax on profiled groups, denounce as betrayals of 'color blindness' programs that require racial diversity," he wrote.

"A similar turnabout can be seen on the part of many of those who support affirmative action. Impatient with talk of communal needs in assessing racial profiling, they very often have no difficulty with subordinating the interests of individual white candidates to the purported good of the whole."

18   Kennedy's piece reaches no conclusions—other than to affirm the need for the debate in the first place—but I see no contradiction here. When workers are paid unequally for doing equivalent work, union organizers naturally argue that all workers should be paid what the highest-earning worker is paid, a process called "leveling up." Both the opposition to racial profiling and the support of affirmative action are about leveling up.

19   In both cases, marginalized groups who have suffered from stereotyping and injustice are asking to be considered full-fledged participants in our culture, to be given the same benefit of the doubt that white people have been given for centuries. Membership has its privileges, including job promotions, tenure, the ability to speed in a school zone and get off with a warning, and impromptu nights in Paris cafés. Whether one considers these things rights or luxuries, they are the aspects of citizenship that make one feel both accepted in and loyal to one's community and culture.

20   Some, like Ann Coulter—a columnist so out of touch even the *National Review* fired her—call those who complain about such matters "crazy," "paranoid," "immature nuts," and (my favorite) "ticking time bombs." Though most people would find her language over-the-top, there are many people who agree with the sentiment: that an increase in security, even if it means engaging in racial profiling, is a necessary evil in these dark times.

21   Lori Hope, in a *My Turn* column published in *Newsweek* last spring, worried that in alerting a flight attendant of a suspicious-looking traveler ("He was olive-skinned, black-haired, and clean-shaven, with a blanket covering his legs and feet"), she might have "ruined an innocent man's day" when the man was removed from the flight. Nevertheless, she said, "I'm not sure I regret it . . . it's not the same world it was half a lifetime ago."

22   And for her, it probably isn't. But for the thousands of people who have been falsely associated with a handful of extremists for no reason other than their ancestry or their religion, for those who have been targeted not for their crimes but for the color of their skin, not a whole lot has changed.

23   The assumption in all these discussions is that getting kicked off a plane is merely a *hassle*. Granted, no one should be hassled because of their race or ethnicity, but c'mon, be reasonable. This is just a little annoyance we're talking about, the way watching the mad professor getting chased around by psychotic Libyans in *Back to the Future* is "fun," "just a joke," you know, like someone in blackface. National security is the real issue. Anyone who can't see that must have something to hide.

24   But those who argue that it's an inevitable necessity should look to countries like Egypt, where racial and religious profiling as a manner of combating Islamic extremism is obviously unworkable. Ethnic stereotyping, whether by Hollywood or by the FBI, solidifies the wedge between what we call "mainstream" culture and those who are perceived to be on the outside of it. "Ruining an innocent man's day" isn't the point, just as the *hassle* of moving to a different seat on the bus wasn't the point for Rosa Parks. Didn't we hammer all this out 40 years ago? ◆

CRITICAL THINKING

1. Consider the way Hollywood traditionally presents terrorists in the movies. How can Hollywood's stereotyping hurt people of Middle Eastern descent living in America? Or is it just harmless Hollywood entertainment?

2. In what ways has Hollywood promoted the stereotype of Arabs as terrorists? What do you think of this stereotype? Is it art imitating life? Is it unfair? Explain.

3. How has racial profiling directly affected Fokkena's life and that of her family? Explain.

4. Evaluate Fokkena's connection between racial profiling and affirmative action. In what ways are they similar, and how are they different?

5. In paragraph 21, Fokkena refers to an essay written by Lori Hope that appeared in *Newsweek*. Read about the Lawyers Committee for Civil Rights suit against the airline that ejected a passenger from the flight on the recommendation of another passenger at http://www.lccr.com/khan .doc. Do you think Hope was correct in voicing her concerns? What about the airline? Explain.

6. What event does Fokkena allude to in her final sentence? Why does she end her essay with this reference?

CRITICAL WRITING

1. *Expository Writing:* Fokkena opens her essay with a reference to Disney's *Aladdin*, a movie she purchases because it featured an Arab heroine. Consider the ways Hollywood influences our cultural perspectives of race and ethnicity. Write an essay exploring the influence, however slight, film and television have had on your own perception of race. If you wish, interview other students for their opinions on this issue, and address some of their observations in your essay.

2. *Personal Narrative:* Write an essay discussing your own family's sense of ethic or racial identity. What are the *ethnic* origins of some of your family's values, traditions, and customs? Have these customs ever been questioned by people who did not understand them? What assumptions do you think other people may have about your family?

GROUP PROJECTS

1. The Patriot Act was designed to "deter and punish terrorist acts in the United States and around the world, to enhance law enforcement investigatory tools, and for other purposes." Research the Patriot Act online. What does the Patriot Act allow the government to do? How does it connect to racial profiling and issues of freedom? Discuss the Patriot Act as a group.

2. As a group, identify as many movies as you can involving highjackings, espionage, and terrorist activity over the last 15 years (you may try the Internet Movie Database at http://www.imdb.com to assist your research.) Who are the villains? Prepare a demographic pie chart depicting the data you collect. Is the stereotyping as bad as Fokkena indicates? Explain.

CULTURE SHOCK

Which Man Looks Guilty?

Since its inception in 1920, the nonprofit, nonpartisan American Civil Liberties Union (ACLU) has grown from a small group of activists to an organization of nearly 400,000 members with offices in almost every state. The ACLU's mission is to fight civil liberties violations wherever and whenever they occur. It is also active in national and state government arenas and is dedicated to upholding the Bill of Rights. This ad addressing racial profiling appeared as part of the ACLU of Florida's Racial Profiling campaign in 2002.

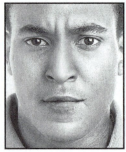 

Which man looks guilty? If you picked the man on the right, you're wrong. Wrong for judging a person based upon the color of their skin. Because if you look closely, you'll see that they're the same man. Unfortunately, racial stereotyping like this happens everyday. On America's highways, police stop drivers based on their skin color rather than for the way they are driving. For example, in Florida 80% of those stopped and searched were black and Hispanic, while they constituted only 5% of all drivers. These humiliating and illegal searches are violations of the Constitution and must be fought. Help us defend your rights. Support the ACLU. www.aclu.org **american civil liberties union**

THINKING CRITICALLY

1. At first glance, did you think the photos were of two different people? At what point did you realize they were the same man?
2. Did you seriously consider the question posed by the ad? If so, which man did you chose? Was race a factor? Why or why not?
3. What point is this ad trying to make? How effective is this ad at getting its message across?
4. How important is the audience to the effectiveness of this ad? Where would you expect to see it? Where would it work, and where would it carry less impact? Explain.

American Civil Liberties Union, Florida Chapter

Why I'm Black, Not African American
*John H. McWhorter**

> Many of the essays in this chapter explore race and ethnicity and how we identify ourselves through definitions of race. In this next essay, John H. McWhorter, senior fellow at the Manhattan Institute think tank, explains why he feels "African American" is inaccurate. In fact, McWhorter asserts, the term is misleading and confusing. There is a great difference between the immigrant from Nigeria and the seventh-generation descendent of slaves in rural Georgia or urban Detroit. The time has come, he explains, to go back to "Black—with a capital B."

1 It's time we descendants of slaves brought to the United States let go of the term "African American" and go back to calling ourselves Black—with a capital B.

2   Modern America is home now to millions of immigrants who were born in Africa. Their cultures and identities are split between Africa and the United States. They have last names like Onwughalu and Senkofa. They speak languages like Wolof, Twi, Yoruba, and Hausa, and speak English with an accent. They were raised on African cuisine, music, dance and dress styles, customs and family dynamics. Their children often speak or at least understand their parents' native language.

3   Living descendants of slaves in America neither knew their African ancestors nor even have elder relatives who knew them. Most of us worship in Christian churches. Our cuisine is more southern U.S. than Senegalese. Starting with ragtime and jazz, we gave America intoxicating musical beats based on African conceptions of rhythm but with melody and harmony based on Western traditions.

4   Also, we speak English. Black Americans' home speech is largely based on local dialects of England and Ireland. Africa echoes in the dialect only as a whisper, in certain aspects of sound and melody. A working-class black man in Cincinnati has more in common with a working-class white man in Providence than with a Ghanaian.

5   With the number of African immigrants in the United States nearly tripling since 1990, the use of "African American" is becoming increasingly strained. For example, Alan Keyes, the Republican Senate candidate in Illinois, has claimed that as a descendant of slaves, he is the "real" African American, compared with his Democratic rival, Barack Obama, who has an African father and a white mother. And the reason Keyes and others are making arguments such as this is rather small, the idea being that "African American" should refer only to people with a history of subordination in this country—as if African immigrants, such as Amadou Diallo, who was killed by police while reaching for his wallet, or Caribbean ones, such as torture victim Abner Louima, have found the United States to be the Land of Oz.

6   We are not African to any meaningful extent, but we are not white either—and that is much of why Jesse Jackson's presentation of the term "African American" caught on so fast. It sets us apart from the mainstream. It carries an air of standing protest, a

---

* John H. McWhorter, *Los Angeles Times*, September 8, 2004

reminder that our ancestors were brought here against their will, that their descendants were treated like animals for centuries, and that we have come a long way since then.

7   But we need a way of sounding those notes with a term that, first, makes some sense and, second, does not insult the actual African Americans taking their place in our country. And our name must also celebrate our history here, in the only place that will ever be our home. To term ourselves as part "African" reinforces a sad implication: that our history is basically slave ships, plantations, lynching, fire hoses in Birmingham, and then South Central, and that we need to look back to Mother Africa to feel good about ourselves.

8   But what about the black business districts that thrived across the country after slavery was abolished? What about Frederick Douglass, Ida B. Wells, W. E. B. DuBois, Gwendolyn Brooks, Richard Wright, and Thurgood Marshall, none born in Africa and all deeply American people? And while we're on Marshall, what about the civil rights revolution, a moral awakening that we gave to ourselves and the nation? My roots trace back to working-class Black people—Americans, not foreigners—and I'm proud of it. I am John Hamilton McWhorter the Fifth. Four men with my name and appearance, doing their best in a segregated

> *We need a way of sounding those notes with a term that, first, makes some sense and, second, does not insult the actual African Americans taking their place in our country.*

America, came before me. They and their dearest are the heritage that I can feel in my heart, and they knew the sidewalks of Philadelphia and Atlanta, not Sierra Leone.

9   So, we will have a name for ourselves—and it should be Black. "Colored" and "Negro" had their good points but carry a whiff of *Plessy vs. Ferguson* and Bull Connor about them, so we will let them lie. "Black" isn't perfect, but no term is.

10   Meanwhile, the special value of "Black" is that it carries the same potent combination of pride, remembrance, and regret that "African American" was designed for. Think of what James Brown meant with "Say it loud, I'm Black and I'm proud." And then imagine: "Say it loud, I'm African American and I'm proud."

11   Since the late 1980s, I have gone along with using "African American" for the same reason that we throw rice at a bride—because everybody else was doing it. But no more. From now on, in my writings on race I will be returning to the word I grew up with, which reminds me of my true self and my ancestors who worked here to help make my life possible: Black. ◆

CRITICAL THINKING

1. Why does McWhorter think that "Black" is a better name than "African American"? Explain.
2. McWhorter feels that the African American designation "reinforces a sad implication: that our history is basically slave ships, plantations, lynching, fire hoses in Birmingham, and then South Central, and that we need to look back to Mother Africa to feel good about ourselves." Do you agree? How can this term both celebrate and mourn a cultural history?

3. According to McWhorter, in what ways can the title "African American" be confusing for immigrants, such as those from the Caribbean? Explain.
4. McWhorter comments that "the special value of 'Black' is that it carries the same potent combination of pride, remembrance, and regret that 'African American' was designed for." Do you agree? Why or why not?

CRITICAL WRITING

1. *Expository Writing:* In this essay, McWhorter explains why he has chosen to label himself as "Black" rather than "African American." Write a similarly themed essay in which you explain what title you would chose for yourself. This title may be based on race or ethnicity (e.g., "Why I am Irish") or other criteria you determine.
2. *Expository Writing:* Write an essay discussing your own family's sense of ethnic or racial identity. What are the origins of some of your family's values, practices, and customs? Have these customs met with prejudice by people who did not understand them? Explain.

GROUP PROJECT

1. Access the *Salon* RoundTable discussion "Hanging Separately" at http://salon1999.com/12nov1995/feature/race.html, regarding race relations between whites and blacks. Read the various commentaries about establishing a dialogue between races by well-known cultural critics, including Shelby Steele and Stanley Crouch. As a group, evaluate their responses and answer the critics directly with your own opinions.

Black vs. "Black"
*Gary Kamiya**

On February 10, 2007, Barack Obama announced his candidacy for President of the United States in front of the Old State Capitol Building in Springfield, Illinois—the same steps on which Abraham Lincoln stood in 1858 to deliver his famous house-divided-cannot-stand speech. In June of 2008, the Democratic National Committee nominated Obama the democratic candidate for the U.S. Presidency. Some controversy has surrounded his ethnicity. The son of a white mother and a Kenyan father, is he really white? Is he really black? Not descended from slaves, can he claim the African-American narrative as his own? In this next essay, Gary Kamiya, an executive editor at *Salon* magazine, explores the nuances between "black" and black. Barack Obama is black—he just isn't "black," he explains. And if his candidacy helps take those quotation marks off race in America, it's a good thing.

---

* Gary Kamiya, *Salon.com*, January 23, 2007

1   Barack Obama's candidacy has brought the issue of race back to center stage in America. A provocative shot was fired by Debra Dickerson, who in the January 22, 2007, issue of *Salon* argued that because Barack Obama is not a descendant of African slaves, he is not black. Dickerson's piece raises a number of important issues. But I think she has it wrong about Obama's blackness, or lack thereof. Obama is black—he just isn't "black."

2   To explain what I mean, let me delve a little into my own racial background. I started a part-time teaching gig last week at the University of California at Berkeley, and part of the paperwork (which included a form on which you had to pledge allegiance to the state of California, an entity I had not thought needed my vassalage) was a form that asked what my ethnicity was. You had to identify yourself as white, black, Asian or Latino. I think there were a few others, though I can't remember. I'm half-Japanese, so I looked for a mixed-race box, but there wasn't one. I asked the woman who was doing the paperwork if I could put down that I was half-white and half-Asian, but she said, "No, you just have to choose one." Even though I knew I was probably bumming out some U.C. diversity honcho, I put an X in the box marked "white."

3   Why did I choose "white"? It was a matter of intellectual honesty. This takes a bit of explaining.

4   The truth is, I don't think of myself as either white or Asian. In fact, I don't think of myself in racial terms at all. If asked, I of course identify myself as what I am—mixed-race, or Eurasian, or half-Japanese. I try to work the Scottish part of the mix in as well, because I like trumpeting my weird mongrel gene pool. But although I know I am a person of mixed race, that fact plays only the most minor role in my sense of myself. I am a mixed-race person, not a "mixed-race person."

5   What's the difference? People whose race or ethnicity defines their identity, or at least makes up a major part of it, are what I think of as quotation-mark people. They are not only mixed-race, they are "mixed-race." Those whose race or ethnicity has little or nothing to do with their identity, with their sense of themselves, are non–quotation-mark people. They may recognize themselves as black or Latino or Asian, be whatever race or ethnicity they are to the core, and proudly affirm they are such, but they aren't "black" or "Latino" or "Asian."

6   For me, my racial background has never meant anything one way or the other. There are no doubt many specific reasons for this, including my parents' unconcern about race, not having had any kind of a Japanese upbringing (whatever that means), growing up in Berkeley in the '60s, and so on. The bottom line is that no one ever really paid any attention to my race, so I didn't either. If I do think about it, it's with a smug, slightly juvenile sense of satisfaction that I'm different from just about everybody else and in a "cool" way. Beyond that, though, my racial background is meaningless. It plays no role in my sense of myself.

Whiteness is the marker of racial invisibility in America. White, in other words, means no race, not the master race.

7   What this adds up to for me is that when I am forced against my will to make a reductive choice, as I was at U.C., the most honest thing is to choose white. I do that not because I see whiteness as a positive identification,

or as my identity, but for precisely the opposite reason: because whiteness is the marker of racial invisibility in America. White, in other words, means no race, not the master race. I don't "feel" either Japanese or white. To feel either would involve some bad-faith reduction of my identity. But if forced to choose, I choose white, because that category, inaccurate as it is, reflects the fact that my racial background does not form my identity.

8   This is, in fact, how most white people in America—unless they subscribe to some virulent form of identity politics, whether on the Ku Klux Klan right or the I-am-a-member-of-the-oppressors left—see themselves. White people don't go around feeling "white" unless they are either racists or have just come out of a corporate diversity consciousness-raising session.

9   Of course, the fact that white people are the majority in America makes it easy for them not to feel "white." A majority group's racial identity, since it encounters no external obstacles, singling out, or bigotry, is always invisible to itself. But—and now we come to the interesting racial questions posed by Barack Obama—I would argue that not all members of minority ethnic or racial groups, even ones that have historically been subject to racism, necessarily see themselves as "Asian" or "Latino" or "black." They may just see themselves as Asian or Latino or black. This doesn't mean they necessarily reject any cultural traditions or community ties: It simply means they see themselves first and foremost as human beings who happen to be a certain race or ethnicity.

10   Let me be clear. I am not talking about disavowing one's culture or background, acting "white," or any other external actions. I am simply talking about an inner freedom from a superficial definition imposed by others. This freedom can—and in the case of blacks, probably usually does—coexist with a stronger consciousness of one's racial identity than exists for white Americans, whose racial status is invisible to themselves. For many minorities—even though their minority status makes their ethnicity more visible to others, and thus to themselves, and even though they may have suffered from racial or ethnic prejudice—visibility and prejudice alone do not necessarily create a race or ethnicity-based identity.

11   And if that's the case, they're lucky. Because who wants to go around carrying the burden of being "Asian" or "black" all the time? It's a burden because it's a phantom, an abstract concept that nonetheless weighs you down. To feel "Asian," for me, would be to embrace an entirely political definition of myself, one simultaneously empty and all-encompassing. I would become a caricature of myself, a spokesman for a "myself" entirely constructed by others. Having no racial self-identification is a utopian state because it allows you to escape this malignant mirror. In America, the white majority is fortunate to enjoy this. But so are many minorities.

12   Of course, I know perfectly well that not everyone is dealt this lucky hand. It's all well and good to preach color-blindness, to celebrate a society without quotation marks, but as long as racism exists, it puts pressure on those who are subject to it to define their identity in terms laid down by others. The quotation marks appear as a reaction to the deforming gaze of the dominant group. This is true to some degree for all minority groups, and far more so for black people. Blacks were stigmatized in a way different from that of any other racial group.

Blackness was so demonized that blacks alone were—and still to a large degree are—defined by the notorious "one drop" rule: One drop of black blood, and you were considered black. For years, the concept of being mixed race did not apply to black people. Today, whites are in a state of confused transition about this concept; most see the one-drop rule as perpetuating an outmoded binary, oppositional state of race relations and are waiting for a signal from the black community that would allow them to abandon it. But no clear signal is forthcoming. The one-drop rule, ironically, is now defended not so much by whites as by many blacks, who regard refusing to identify as "black" as a betrayal of racial solidarity, and correctly see the advent of a mixed-race category that is not trumped by "blackness," à la Tiger Woods' "Cablinasian," as threatening the very cornerstone of their own identities.

13   This, too, is understandable. Blacks, who were enslaved, treated as inferiors, and discriminated against in every aspect of life, got dealt by far the worst racial hand, and it's accordingly the hardest for them to move beyond a race-based identity. Any person who isn't black who tries to gloss over this fact, and blandly demands that blacks simply stop seeing themselves as "black," is insensitive to the power of history and the identity-distorting effects of dominance.

14   And yet, removing the quotation marks from around one's racial identity is ultimately liberating. It is, I believe, what every human being on earth wants to do. I disagree with Colin Powell about many things, but I find his racial credo, one he learned from his parents, admirable. Powell's parents taught him a simple mantra: "My race is somebody else's problem. It's not my problem." The greatest of all American novels, Mark Twain's story of Huck Finn and the runaway slave Jim, floating down the Mississippi on a voyage to find the American soul, is a tale of how the love between a black man and a white boy washes away Huck's quotation marks, leaving them both free—Huck figuratively, Jim literally.

15   Barack Obama simply happens to represent a very public manifestation of this non–quotation-mark approach to race. There are many, many other African-American blacks who exemplify the same approach. Dickerson argues that Obama is not black because he is not the descendant of African slaves. But I would argue that blackness—or, more accurately, "blackness"—is determined not by whether one is descended from slaves, but the degree to which one sees one's identity as determined by one's race. Clearly, the fact that Obama's father was African, not American, plays a role in his well-known lack of "blackness," as does the fact that his mother is white. And yet, I believe that none of this is determinative. Someone of Obama's background could be "black"—and a Ronald Washington from Detroit might not be "black" at all. It depends on how they see themselves; if others see them differently, that's their problem.

16   White Americans are obviously drawn to blacks (and yes, they do see Obama as black) who are not "black." Everyone is comfortable with Colin Powell and Condoleezza Rice—and that goes triple for Barack Obama, who is not only racially unthreatening but charismatic and attractive. This is hardly surprising. No one is drawn to someone who threatens them, or whose persona creates a sense of racial guilt. But I can understand why this sudden, rapturous embrace of a black man who

is not "black" might be exasperating to many blacks. It gives rise to suspicions that white America just wants to happily declare "racism is over" and move on, not confronting the degree to which its weariness with "blackness" is really a sophisticated form of racism. The heart of Dickerson's equivocal uneasiness with Obama is her fear that embracing him is just too damn easy for white people, who haven't really settled their accounts with black folks yet.

17   There is no doubt something to this suspicion. A pathology as vast and deep as racism is not expunged in a decade. And "blackness" is not so easy to separate from blackness as my somewhat facile use of quotation marks suggests. What happens when the mask becomes the face? For many whites, it may be easier to just turn away from what can be the troubling, intertwined complexities of black and "black" identities, and embrace a black man who presents no such problems.

18   But having said that, I believe that white America's embrace of Obama is a virtually unalloyed good. It's good because Obama is a dynamic and exciting candidate who is offering not only a racial truce but also a fresh and progressive take on many issues. But it's also good because that embrace demonstrates that we're moving toward racial invisibility. It is in everyone's interests—blacks and whites and Latinos and Asians and the growing number of mongrels like me—for racial quotation marks to disappear. And the best way to get rid of them is to establish greater trust and communication between blacks and whites. The more black people come to trust white people, the more they believe—to quote Dr. King—that they are "judged by the content of their character, not the color of their skin," the less they will be compelled to define themselves as "black," and the more liberated they will be to explore a purely human destiny, not one bound by something as meaningless and stupid as race. The fact that so many whites have embraced the black senator from Illinois, even if he does not share the experiences or worldview of some African Americans, will, I hope, help build that trust. After all, the guy is still black.

19   We are caught in a time of churn and change, when the old racial rules no longer apply. We have tried the old, formal, accuse-and-apologize model. It was needed in its day, but we are past that now. Now we need something lighter, something more fragile, more intimate, to wash away the last of this terrible, false duality that has poisoned America for too long. We need friendship. We need trust. We need love. And love surrounded by quotation marks isn't love at all. ◆

CRITICAL THINKING

1. According to Kamiya, why are many Americans comfortable with Obama's blackness? Explain.
2. What is the difference between "black" and black? Why does Debra Dickerson, who is African American, assert that Obama is not "black"? Do you agree?
3. Why does Kamiya decide to check "white" on his information form? Why does he think it will "[bum] out some U.C. diversity honcho"?

4. How do we categorize people based on "what" they are? Is it important? Does including a section on race on information forms and applications perpetuate racism by emphasizing differences and forcing people to categorize themselves? Why or why not?
5. How does Kamiya's personal account in the beginning of his essay support his overall point? Explain.
6. What does Kamiya hope Obama's election will do to the quotation marks around the word *black*? Explain.

CRITICAL WRITING

1. *Exploratory Writing:* Kamiya provides a personal perspective on the ways forms force people to identify themselves by race and the ways we mentally do, or do not, think of race. Write an essay about what is important to your own sense of identity. Is race an important factor? What about other factors, such as gender, age, religion, or education? In your opinion, on what criteria do the people you meet judge you? What do you want them to judge you by? By what criteria do you identify yourself?
2. *Exploratory Writing:* Why is it so important to Americans to know "what" people are? Write an exploratory essay on this subject. If you wish, interview a few people for their perspective and comment in your essay on their response to this question.
3. *Persuasive Writing:* Read Debra Dickerson's essay, "Colorblind," that appeared in the January 22, 2007 issue of *Salon* magazine. How could this essay be considered "race baiting?" What issues does it raise? Write an essay in which you either agree, in whole or in part, with her argument that Obama and his subsequent election do not represent a victory for "blacks" America.

GROUP PROJECTS

1. In his essay, Kamiya explains his confusion over the checkboxes on the information form he is asked to fill out for the University of California at Berkley. With your group, consider the stereotypes we associate with race, class, and cultural experience. Consider how the following factors influence our perceptions of race: economics, income, education, politics, religion, traditions, taste or lifestyle, profession, and self-image.
2. As a nation of people from many countries and cultures, the question of race seems to be one that many Americans want to ask. Have each member of your group answer the question, What is your ethnic background? In their own words, have group members introduce themselves to the rest of the group. Then, as a group, discuss what we "do" with this information. How does the answer define us to others? What presumptions do we make? What are others likely to think, and why?

Our Biracial President

James Hannaham *

On January 20, 2009, America swore in its 44th President of the United States. Elected by the people, Barack Obama represented a striking departure—he is a democrat, one of his parents is not American, and he is black. His election has been hailed as a victory against institutionalized racism, and it is symbolic of new beginnings. Now any native-born child— black, white, or brown—can aspire to the highest office in the land regardless of race. But while Obama's election has been hailed as a victory by many, some critics warn that we must not mistakenly believe that racism is "over" in the United States. In this next editorial, James Hannaham, a creative writing teacher at the Pratt Institute in Brooklyn, explains why, when the starry glow around his election fades, Obama will allow us to see ourselves in black and white.

1 Voters across the United States and citizens around the world are calling the election of Barack Obama a historic moment, and it is indeed groundbreaking in many important ways. We have elected a man unashamed of his African blood into the nation's highest office. In historical terms, this is a milestone of race relations in the United States, a quantum leap unimaginable until this moment. For some cynics and paranoid supporters, it was impossible until the moment John McCain, in the most gracious and touching moment of his campaign, conceded.

2 Obama's presidency carries a huge burden of symbolic proof. As the president-elect's acceptance speech emphasized, his victory caresses America's image of itself as a place where equal opportunity exists for anyone who works hard enough. It helps erase a stigma against people of African descent that has lasted more than 500 years and included some of the lowest moments in our supposedly modern and enlightened age—Jim Crow, apartheid, slavery. It allows people of all colors around the globe to point to Obama and feel as if their struggle may not be a dead end after all, and that someone who shares at least some of their experiences and perspectives can offer genuine respect and perhaps even empathy to millions who have so frequently been overlooked and despised. It is a sign to humanity that the United States can walk democracy like we talk it. This is no small thing.

3 But this big-picture vision of the Global Village as the Kingdom of Obamaland is too starry-eyed to hold sway for long—maybe not even until he's sworn in. An Obama presidency by no means represents the end of racism, just a hopeful sign of the beginning of the end. To see it as proof that anyone can be president, no matter their origins, is ludicrous. It isn't as if Obama became president because the Electoral College has an affirmative action policy operating on a quota system. He is a man whose impeccable résumé, spotless personal history, elite education, leadership abilities, attractiveness, seriousness, sexual orientation, marriage to a woman of his own perceived race, whose gender, maybe even complexion and definitely choice of running mate, have made him what some employers have a tendency to call "overqualified."

* James Hannaham, *Salon*, November 6, 2008

4   During his race for the presidency, many people had misgivings about Obama's supposed lack of experience, but few had anything to say about whether he had the appropriate qualifications to hold office, other than to wonder if America was ready for a president so suave he could play the first black James Bond. Perhaps if Obama were as inept as the man whose broken pretzels and hanging chads he will need to sweep up from the Oval Office carpet, yet still a contender for commander in chief, we could finally lay racial prejudice into its chilly crypt and be done with it. Because among other things, white supremacy has meant that unqualified but well-connected and rich white people's dreams have fallen into their laps, while overqualified people of color have striven their whole lives to get nowhere. Obama has cleared a path for fairness.

5   Still, privilege is no Death Star, and one Luke Skywalker can't obliterate it with a couple of lasers, no matter how well-placed. It did not vaporize last night, so in the Obama presidency, we can look forward to some amusing and possibly infuriating contretemps that will arise from an African-American family leading the country. (Why was this never the premise for a sitcom?) The same battles will rage over affirmative action—will we cheat ourselves out of the next Obama by cutting it back?—and issues of discrimination in representation, education, housing, etc. For me, racism won't be over until a bunch of black people can move into a neighborhood and watch the property values rise.

6   Nevertheless, there are plenty of immediate, serious sighs of relief that we can now legitimately heave. The pendulum has swung the other way. Obama's long coat-tails have given Democrats a majority in the Senate and the House. Sarah Palin will have to return her expensive wardrobe and go study the Republican foreign policy playbook for at least four years. We will have the most intriguing first lady since, well, Hillary Clinton. Perhaps most important, Republicans will not choose the next couple of Supreme Court justices. The likelihood of a conservative majority overturning *Roe v. Wade* or other pieces of legislation important to the left has been severely reduced.

7   We have an intelligent man in the White House, a literate guy who not only reads books but has written two himself. "That one" doesn't try to hide his background and attempt to broaden his appeal with a veneer of folksiness; instead he approaches others without pretense. He has a beautiful voice: calm, reassuring, persuasive, sexy. With just these superficial qualities, he has already done a great deal for America's image around the world. A McCain presidency, a Canadian warned me last night, would have made America "superfluous," the debt slaves of China. Already we've seen Obama's image on countless bootlegged T-shirts, chiseled into an FDR-like, constructivist symbol of progressive politics, creativity, and open-mindedness. His election alone has rescued the world's opinion of America's ability to adapt and move forward.

Both radical leftists and radical right-wingers need to understand the same thing: Obama is not Malcolm X. He's not even Kanye West. His motorcade will not consist of souped-up cars with wheels that spin and bump up and down outside the White House; he will not sport a diamond grill that reads "PREZ."

8   But both radical leftists and radical right-wingers need to understand the same thing: Obama is not Malcolm X. He's not even Kanye West. His motorcade will not consist of souped-up cars with wheels that spin and bump up and down outside the White House; he will not sport a

diamond grill that reads "PREZ." He's a moderate. The right has changed the definition of the liberalism over the last 40 years by hectoring Democratic candidates,
saying that they will overtax and -spend, even as the current administration chucks
billions of dollars into the furnaces of Iraq and Afghanistan. It's hard to now imagine a president getting elected without claiming to be a fiscal conservative, certainly
not as we climb out of the current financial disaster. As someone elected largely
because of our failing economy, Obama will have to toe the line of fiscal policy
pretty carefully and make a lot of practical and shrewd decisions fast.

9   On social issues, however, there's no comparison. John McCain's "health of the
woman" air quotes could easily have lost him the support of even pro-life women.
While there's no guarantee that Obama's brilliantly run, tech-savvy campaign will
lead to a well-run White House, the decisions that we've watched Obama make have
suggested reconciliation, sharpness, flexibility, ability to delegate responsibility to
capable experts—in short, a solid footing in the reality-based community. But one
of Obama's great strengths can also melt into his most frustrating quality—he tries
to hear all voices without prejudice. His desire to listen to the Rev. Jeremiah
Wright's claptrap surely cost him the trust of many Americans. There is a point at
which a leader should be able to make a judgment about whether he's listening to a
real viewpoint or just plain crazy-talk, and Obama's high tolerance for nut-job
rhetoric may return to haunt him in the coming years. He may not want to waste too
much time listening to lunatics, even if they happen to run foreign countries.

10   Obama's acceptance of his Caucasian genes is another quality that sets him closer to
the center than to Malcolm X. I've said it before and I'll keep saying it: Obama's biracial.
He's an African American, certainly—in strictly genetic terms, he's more literally African
American than other American black folks, whose veins are awash in various percentages
of African, Native American, and European blood. This is not to say that he hasn't received
some of the same treatment as black Americans, or that he is not welcome among them, or
that people should denigrate his need to make his background understandable to people
who think that "biracial" means a type of airplane. It suggests something far less divisive.
It means that black and white people (not to mention other ethnicities chained to the binary
idiocy of American race relations) can share his victory equally.

11   As Obama gave his acceptance speech in Chicago, the media seemed to enjoy
focusing on the elation of black communities in Harlem, in Kenya, and at More-
house College, or on the tear-stained faces of Oprah and Jesse Jackson, as if black
people had always been primarily invested in Obama's triumph. But we can't forget
that the black political establishment, and a big chunk of their constituency, was initially very slow to warm to the candidate. (Well, except the Kenyans.) Here, he was
the white man's black candidate, carefully vetted before winning the trust everyone
seemed to think black people would lavish upon him based solely on his race.

12   Obama's Caucasian heritage has not evaporated just because he's the first
American president to be unashamed to have a shot of espresso in his vanilla latte.
By voting for him, whites have shown their acceptance on a major level, but if
everyone continues to interpret his presidency primarily in terms of race, we're simply perpetuating the same old values. The Obama presidency gives us the opportunity to see more clearly into a future when the pain and injustice of the past, though
it will not be forgotten, can be transformed into a shared purpose, and we can help
the grand family squabble of American race relations to settle down. Like most

American families, we'll have our differences, but we will be able to sit down at the same table and show each other some respect. ◆

CRITICAL THINKING

1. What does the expression "to see in black and white" mean? Why is this expression ironic when used in reference to race relations?
2. Hannaham observes that electing a "black" man to the U.S. presidency is "a quantum leap unimaginable until this moment." What makes this election particularly significant? Could it have happened sooner? For example, do you think Colin Powell could have won the 2000 election? Why or why not?
3. What does Hannaham mean when he says our new president has "a shot of espresso in his vanilla latte"? Do you think this is an apt metaphor?
4. Hannaham uses a reference to the film *Star Wars* in his article. Why do you think he uses this reference, and what analogy is he trying to make?
5. In paragraph 11, the author makes reference to former president George W. Bush. Which moments in Bush's presidency is the author directly referring to? Why does he highlight this aspect of the former president's tenure in office? Explain.
6. How does Hannaham define "white supremacy"? What does "white supremacy" mean to you, and how does it compare to the author's version?

CRITICAL WRITING

1. *Research Writing:* Hannaham makes the comment that black people were not always "primarily invested in Obama's triumph." Research articles written by black political activists in the two years leading up to the election, and report on the sentiment felt about Obama by these leaders of the black community. What was the initial criticism of Obama? Was there a turning point, when black leaders and the black public began to support Obama? What caused the turning point?
2. *Exploratory Writing:* The author of this article states, "Racism won't be over until a bunch of black people can move into a neighborhood and watch the property values rise." Write an essay in which you explore what racism means to you and how you would know when it is finally over.

GROUP PROJECTS

1. Hannaham jokes that there should have been a sitcom written about an African-American family leading the country. Could such a sitcom have existed before Barack Obama was elected? With your group, write a humorous episode of what life might be like for the Obamas.
2. Hannaham states, "Obama is not Malcolm X. He's not even Kanye West." As a group, discuss who Malcolm X and Kanye West are and what Hannaham means. What do they represent culturally, socially, and politically? Compare and contrast Barack Obama to Malcolm X and Kanye West, and share your observations with the class as part of a broader discussion on race and society.

VIEWPOINTS

▶ **The End of White America?**
Hua Hsu*

▶ **The End of the Black American Narrative**
Charles Johnson

It is significant that the titles of both readings in this chapter's Viewpoints section have the word "end" in them. The election of Barack Obama has been hailed as a "new beginning" for America: for blacks and whites, our society, and our history. With every new beginning, there is an end of something that came before. The two readings in this section explore what it means to be "white" or "black" or "multiethnic" in the United States today. What does the election of Barack Obama mean to our concepts of race and how we think of ourselves within our ethnic and political groups and in the greater context of our society and culture? Has the time come to stop checking off little boxes identifying our ethnic background? Should racial information matter?

First, music critic and writer Hua Hsu conjectures that the election of Barack Obama symbolizes the beginning of a "postracial" society in "The End of White America?". The fact that the majority of Americans voted for him represents a gradual erosion of "whiteness" as the touchstone of what it means to be American. If the end of white America is a cultural and demographic inevitability, what will the new mainstream look like—and how will white Americans fit into it? What will it mean to be white when whiteness is no longer the norm? And will a more ethnically diverse America be less racially divided—or more so?

Just as whites are considering how they fit into a postracial society in which they represent an ethnic minority, blacks now must think about the impact of the election of our first black president. In "The End of the Black American Narrative," African American author Charles Johnson discusses why blacks must now move beyond the traditional black American narrative of oppression. This narrative, he admits, served African Americans well—both as a history and as a bonding story that helped many overcome the injustices of institutionalized racism. But the time has come, he asserts, to write the next chapter in the story.

The End of White America?
Hua Hsu

1   "Civilization's going to pieces," he remarks. He is in polite company, gathered with friends around a bottle of wine in the late-afternoon sun, chatting and gossiping. "I've gotten to be a terrible pessimist about things. Have you read *The Rise of the Colored Empires* by this man Goddard?" They hadn't. "Well, it's a fine book, and everybody ought to read it. The idea is if we don't look out the white race will be—will be utterly submerged. It's all scientific stuff; it's been proved."

---

* Hua Hsu, *The Atlantic*, February/March 2009; Charles Johnson, *The American Scholar*, 2008 (*Both essays have been slightly abridged for space and may be read online in their entirety.*)

2   He is Tom Buchanan, a character in F. Scott Fitzgerald's *The Great Gatsby*, a book that nearly everyone who passes through the American education system is compelled to read at least once. Although Gatsby doesn't gloss as a book on racial anxiety—it's too busy exploring a different set of anxieties entirely—Buchanan was hardly alone in feeling besieged. The book by "this man Goddard" had a real-world analogue: Lothrop Stoddard's *The Rising Tide of Color Against White World-Supremacy*, published in 1920, five years before *Gatsby*. Nine decades later, Stoddard's polemic remains oddly engrossing. He refers to World War I as the "White Civil War" and laments the "cycle of ruin" that may result if the "white world" continues its infighting. The book features a series of foldout maps depicting the distribution of "color" throughout the world and warns, "Colored migration is a universal peril, menacing every part of the white world."

3   As briefs for racial supremacy go, *The Rising Tide of Color* is eerily serene. Its tone is scholarly and gentlemanly, its hatred rationalized and, in Buchanan's term, "scientific." And the book was hardly a fringe phenomenon. It was published by Scribner, also Fitzgerald's publisher, and Stoddard, who received a doctorate in history from Harvard, was a member of many professional academic associations. It was precisely the kind of book that a 1920s man of Buchanan's profile—wealthy, Ivy League–educated, at once pretentious and intellectually insecure—might have been expected to bring up in casual conversation.

4   As white men of comfort and privilege living in an age of limited social mobility, of course, Stoddard and the Buchanans in his audience had nothing literal to fear. Their sense of dread hovered somewhere above the concerns of everyday life. It was linked less to any immediate danger to their class's political and cultural power than to the perceived fraying of the fixed, monolithic identity of whiteness that sewed together the fortunes of the fair-skinned.

5   From the hysteria over Eastern European immigration to the vibrant cultural miscegenation of the Harlem Renaissance, it is easy to see how this imagined worldwide white kinship might have seemed imperiled in the 1920s. There's no better example of the era's insecurities than the 1923 Supreme Court case *United States v. Bhagat Singh Thind*, in which an Indian-American veteran of World War I sought to become a naturalized citizen by proving that he was Caucasian. The Court considered new anthropological studies that expanded the definition of the Caucasian race to include Indians, and the justices even agreed that traces of "Aryan blood" coursed through Thind's body. But these technicalities availed him little. The Court determined that Thind was not white "in accordance with the understanding of the common man" and therefore could be excluded from the "statutory category" of whiteness. Put another way: Thind was white, in that he was Caucasian and even Aryan. But he was not white in the way Stoddard or Buchanan were white.

6   The '20s debate over the definition of whiteness—a legal category? a common-sense understanding? a worldwide civilization?—took place in a society gripped by an acute sense of racial paranoia, and it is easy to regard these episodes as evidence of how far we have come. But consider that these anxieties surfaced when whiteness was synonymous with the American mainstream, when threats to its status were largely imaginary. What happens once this is no longer the case—when the fears of

Lothrop Stoddard and Tom Buchanan are realized, and white people actually become an American minority?

7   Whether you describe it as the dawning of a post-racial age or just the end of white America, we're approaching a profound demographic tipping point. According to an August 2008 report by the U.S. Census Bureau, those groups currently categorized as racial minorities—blacks and Hispanics, East Asians and South Asians—will account for a majority of the U.S. population by the year 2042. Among Americans under the age of 18, this shift is projected to take place in 2023, which means that every child born in the United States from here on out will belong to the first post-white generation.

8   Obviously, steadily ascending rates of interracial marriage complicate this picture, pointing toward what Michael Lind has described as the "beiging" of America. And it's possible that "beige Americans" will self-identify as "white" in sufficient numbers to push the tipping point further into the future than the Census Bureau projects. But even if they do, whiteness will be a label adopted out of convenience and even indifference, rather than aspiration and necessity. For an earlier generation of minorities and immigrants, to be recognized as a "white American," whether you were an Italian or a Pole or a Hungarian, was to enter the mainstream of American life; to be recognized as something else, as the Thind case suggests, was to be permanently excluded. As Bill Imada, head of the IW Group, a prominent Asian American communications and marketing company, puts it: "I think in the 1920s, 1930s, and 1940s, [for] anyone who immigrated, the aspiration was to blend in and be as American as possible so that white America wouldn't be intimidated by them. They wanted to imitate white America as much as possible: learn English, go to church, go to the same schools."

9   Today, the picture is far more complex. To take the most obvious example, whiteness is no longer a precondition for entry into the highest levels of public office. The son of Indian immigrants doesn't have to become "white" in order to be elected governor of Louisiana. A half-Kenyan, half-Kansan politician can self-identify as black and be elected president of the United States.

10   As a purely demographic matter, then, the "white America" that Lothrop Stoddard believed in so fervently may cease to exist in 2040, 2050, or 2060, or later still. But where the culture is concerned, it's already all but finished. Instead of the long-standing model of assimilation toward a common center, the culture is being remade in the image of white America's multiethnic, multicolored heirs.

11   For some, the disappearance of this centrifugal core heralds a future rich with promise. In 1998, President Bill Clinton, in a now-famous address to students at Portland State University, remarked:

12   Today, largely because of immigration, there is no majority race in Hawaii or Houston or New York City. Within five years, there will be no majority race in our largest state, California. In a little more than 50 years, there will be no majority race in the United States. No other nation in history has gone through demographic change of this magnitude in so short a time ... [These immigrants] are energizing our culture and broadening our vision of the world. They are renewing our most basic values and reminding us all of what it truly means to be American.

13   Not everyone was so enthused. Clinton's remarks caught the attention of another anxious Buchanan—Pat Buchanan, the conservative thinker. Revisiting the president's speech in his 2001 book, *The Death of the West*, Buchanan wrote: "Mr. Clinton assured us that it will be a better America when we are all minorities and realize true 'diversity.' Well, those students [at Portland State] are going to find out, for they will spend their golden years in a Third World America."

14   Today, the arrival of what Buchanan derided as "Third World America" is all but inevitable. What will the new mainstream of America look like, and what ideas or values might it rally around? What will it mean to be white after "whiteness" no longer defines the mainstream? Will anyone mourn the end of white America? Will anyone try to preserve it?

15   Another moment from *The Great Gatsby:* as Fitzgerald's narrator and Gatsby drive across the Queensboro Bridge into Manhattan, a car passes them, and Nick Carraway notices that it is a limousine "driven by a white chauffeur, in which sat three modish negroes, two bucks and a girl." The novelty of this topsy-turvy arrangement inspires Carraway to laugh aloud and think to himself, "Anything can happen now that we've slid over this bridge, anything at all...."

16   For a contemporary embodiment of the upheaval that this scene portended, consider Sean Combs, a hip-hop mogul and one of the most famous African Americans on the planet. Combs grew up during hip-hop's late-1970s rise, and he belongs to the first generation that could safely make a living working in the industry—as a plucky young promoter and record-label intern in the late 1980s and early 1990s, and as a fashion designer, artist, and music executive worth hundreds of millions of dollars a brief decade later.

17   In the late 1990s, Combs made a fascinating gesture toward New York's high society. He announced his arrival into the circles of the rich and powerful not by crashing their parties, but by inviting them into his own spectacularly over-the-top world. Combs began to stage elaborate annual parties in the Hamptons, not far from where Fitzgerald's novel takes place. These "white parties"—attendees are required to wear white—quickly became legendary for their opulence (in 2004, Combs showcased a 1776 copy of the Declaration of Independence) as well as for the cultures-colliding quality of Hamptons elites paying their respects to someone so comfortably nouveau riche. Prospective business partners angled to get close to him and praised him as a guru of the lucrative "urban" market, while grateful partygoers hailed him as a modern-day Gatsby.

18   "Have I read *The Great Gatsby*?" Combs said to a London newspaper in 2001. "I am the Great Gatsby."

19   Yet whereas Gatsby felt pressure to hide his status as an arriviste, Combs celebrated his position as an outsider–insider—someone who appropriates elements of the culture he seeks to join without attempting to assimilate outright. In a sense, Combs was imitating the old WASP establishment; in another sense, he was subtly provoking it, by over-enunciating its formality and never letting his guests forget that there was something slightly off about his presence. There's a silent power to throwing parties where the best-dressed man in the room is also the one whose public profile once consisted primarily of dancing in the background of Biggie Smalls videos. ("No one would ever expect a young black man to be coming to a party with

the Declaration of Independence, but I got it, and it's coming with me," Combs joked at his 2004 party, as he made the rounds with the document, promising not to spill champagne on it.)

20   In this regard, Combs is both a product and a hero of the new cultural mainstream, which prizes diversity above all else, and whose ultimate goal is some vague notion of racial transcendence, rather than subversion or assimilation. Although Combs's vision is far from representative—not many hip-hop stars vacation in St. Tropez with a parasol-toting manservant shading their every step—his industry lies at the heart of this new mainstream. Over the past 30 years, few changes in American culture have been as significant as the rise of hip-hop. The genre has radically reshaped the way we listen to and consume music, first by opposing the pop mainstream and then by becoming it. From its constant sampling of past styles and eras—old records, fashions, slang, anything—to its mythologization of the self-made black antihero, hip-hop is more than a musical genre: it's a philosophy, a political statement, a way of approaching and remaking culture. It's a lingua franca not just among kids in America, but also among young people worldwide. And its economic impact extends beyond the music industry, to fashion, advertising, and film. (Consider the producer Russell Simmons—the ur-Combs and a music, fashion, and television mogul—or the rapper 50 Cent, who has parlayed his rags-to-riches story line into extracurricular successes that include a clothing line; book, video game, and film deals; and a startlingly lucrative partnership with the makers of Vitamin Water.)

21   But hip-hop's deepest impact is symbolic. During popular music's rise in the 20th century, white artists and producers consistently "mainstreamed" African American innovations. Hip-hop's ascension has been different. Eminem notwithstanding, hip-hop never suffered through anything like an Elvis Presley moment, in which a white artist made a musical form safe for white America. This is no dig at Elvis—the constrictive racial logic of the 1950s demanded the erasure of rock and roll's black roots, and if it hadn't been him, it would have been someone else. But hip-hop—the sound of the post–civil-rights, post-soul generation—found a global audience on its own terms.

22   Today, hip-hop's colonization of the global imagination, from fashion runways in Europe to dance competitions in Asia, is Disneyesque. This transformation has bred an unprecedented cultural confidence in its black originators. Whiteness is no longer a threat or an ideal: it's kitsch to be appropriated, whether with gestures like Combs's "white parties" or the trickle-down epidemic of collared shirts and cuff links currently afflicting rappers. And an expansive multiculturalism is replacing the us-against-the-world bunker mentality that lent a thrilling edge to hip-hop's mid-1990s rise.

23   Peter Rosenberg, a self-proclaimed "nerdy Jewish kid" and radio personality on New York's Hot 97 FM—and a living example of how hip-hop has created new identities for its listeners that don't fall neatly along lines of black and white—shares another example: "I interviewed [the St. Louis rapper] Nelly this morning, and he said it's now very cool and in to have multicultural friends. Like you're not really considered hip or 'you've made it' if you're rolling with all the same people."

24   Just as Tiger Woods forever changed the country-club culture of golf, and Will Smith confounded stereotypes about the ideal Hollywood leading man, hip-hop's

rise is helping redefine the American mainstream, which no longer aspires toward a single iconic image of style or class. Successful network-television shows like *Lost, Heroes*, and *Grey's Anatomy* feature wildly diverse casts, and an entire genre of half-hour comedy, from *The Colbert Report* to *The Office*, seems dedicated to having fun with the persona of the clueless white male. The youth market is following the same pattern: consider the Cheetah Girls, a multicultural, multiplatinum, multiplatform trio of teenyboppers who recently starred in their third movie, or Dora the Explorer, the precocious, bilingual 7-year-old Latina adventurer who is arguably the most successful animated character on children's television today. In a recent address to the Association of Hispanic Advertising Agencies, Brown Johnson, the Nickelodeon executive who has overseen Dora's rise, explained the importance of creating a character who does not conform to "the white, middle-class mold." When Johnson pointed out that Dora's wares were outselling Barbie's in France, the crowd hooted in delight.

25   Pop culture today rallies around an ethic of multicultural inclusion that seems to value every identity—except whiteness. "It's become harder for the blond-haired, blue-eyed commercial actor," remarks Rochelle Newman-Carrasco, of the Hispanic marketing firm Enlace. "You read casting notices, and they like to cast people with brown hair because they could be Hispanic. The language of casting notices is pretty shocking because it's so specific: 'Brown hair, brown eyes, could look Hispanic.' Or, as one notice put it: 'Ethnically ambiguous.'"

26   "I think white people feel like they're under siege right now—like it's not okay to be white right now, especially if you're a white male," laughs Bill Imada, of the IW Group. Imada and Newman-Carrasco are part of a movement within advertising, marketing, and communications firms to reimagine the profile of the typical American consumer. (Tellingly, every person I spoke with from these industries knew the Census Bureau's projections by heart.)

27   "There's a lot of fear and a lot of resentment," Newman-Carrasco observes, describing the flak she caught after writing an article for a trade publication on the need for more-diverse hiring practices. "I got a response from a friend—he's, like, a 60-something white male, and he's been involved with multicultural recruiting," she recalls. "And he said, 'I really feel like the hunted. It's a hard time to be a white man in America right now, because I feel like I'm being lumped in with all white males in America, and I've tried to do stuff, but it's a tough time.'"

28   "I always tell the white men in the room, 'We need you,'" Imada says. "We cannot talk about diversity and inclusion and engagement without you at the table. It's okay to be white!

29   "But people are stressed out about it. 'We used to be in control! We're losing control!'"

30   If they're right—if white America is indeed "losing control," and if the future will belong to people who can successfully navigate a postracial, multicultural landscape—then it's no surprise that many white Americans are eager to divest themselves of their whiteness entirely.

31   "I get it: as a straight white male, I'm the worst thing on Earth," Christian Lander says. Lander is a Canadian-born, Los Angeles–based satirist who in January 2008 started a blog called "Stuff White People Like" (stuffwhitepeoplelike.com), which

pokes fun at the manners and mores of a specific species of young, hip, upwardly mobile whites. (He has written more than 100 entries about whites' passion for things like bottled water, "the idea of soccer," and "being the only white person around.") At its best, Lander's site—which formed the basis for a recently published book of the same name (reviewed in the October 2008 *Atlantic*)—is a cunningly precise distillation of the identity crisis plaguing well-meaning, well-off white kids in a post-white world.

32   Lander's "white people" are products of a very specific historical moment, raised by well-meaning Baby Boomers to reject the old ideal of white American gentility and to embrace diversity and fluidity instead. ("It's strange that we are the kids of Baby Boomers, right? How the hell do you rebel against that? Like, your parents will march against the World Trade Organization next to you. They'll have bigger white dreadlocks than you. What do you do?") But his lighthearted anthropology suggests that the multicultural harmony they were raised to worship has bred a kind of self-denial.

33   Matt Wray, a sociologist at Temple University who is a fan of Lander's humor, has observed that many of his white students are plagued by a racial-identity crisis: "They don't care about socioeconomics; they care about culture. And to be white is to be culturally broke. The classic thing white students say when you ask them to talk about who they are is, 'I don't have a culture.' They might be privileged, they might be loaded socioeconomically, but they feel bankrupt when it comes to culture . . . They feel disadvantaged, and they feel marginalized. They don't have a culture that's cool or oppositional." Wray says that this feeling of being culturally bereft often prevents students from recognizing what it means to be a child of privilege—a strange irony that the first wave of whiteness-studies scholars, in the 1990s, failed to anticipate.

34   "The best defense is to be constantly pulling the rug out from underneath yourself," Wray remarks, describing the way self-aware whites contend with their complicated identity. "Beat people to the punch. You're forced as a white person into a sense of ironic detachment. Irony is what fuels a lot of white subcultures. You also see things like Burning Man, when a lot of white people are going into the desert and trying to invent something that is entirely new and not a form of racial mimicry. That's its own kind of flight from whiteness. We're going through a period where whites are really trying to figure out: Who are we?"

35   The "flight from whiteness" of urban, college-educated, liberal whites isn't the only attempt to answer this question. You can flee into whiteness as well. This can mean pursuing the authenticity of an imagined past: think of the deliberately white-bread world of Mormon America, where the '50s never ended, or the anachronistic WASP entitlement flaunted in books like last year's *A Privileged Life: Celebrating WASP Style,* a handsome coffee-table book compiled by Susanna Salk, depicting a world of seersucker blazers, whale pants, and deck shoes. (What the book celebrates is the "inability to be outdone," and the "self-confidence and security that comes with it," Salk tells me. "That's why I call it 'privilege.' It's this privilege of time, of heritage, of being in a place longer than anybody else.") But these enclaves of preserved-in-amber whiteness are likely to be less important to the American future than the construction of whiteness as a somewhat pissed-off minority culture.

36   As with the unexpected success of the apocalyptic *Left Behind* novels, or the Jeff Foxworthy–organized Blue Collar Comedy Tour, the rise of country music and auto racing took place well off the American elite's radar screen. (None of Christian Lander's white people would be caught dead at a NASCAR race.) These phenomena reflected a growing sense of cultural solidarity among lower-middle-class whites—a solidarity defined by a yearning for American "authenticity," a folksy realness that rejects the global, the urban, and the effete in favor of nostalgia for "the way things used to be."

37   Like other forms of identity politics, white solidarity comes complete with its own folk heroes, conspiracy theories (Barack Obama is a secret Muslim! The U.S. is going to merge with Canada and Mexico!), and laundry lists of injustices. The targets and scapegoats vary—from multiculturalism and affirmative action to a loss of moral values, from immigration to an economy that no longer guarantees the American worker a fair chance—and so do the political programs they inspire. But the core grievance, in each case, has to do with cultural and socioeconomic dislocation—the sense that the system that used to guarantee the white working class some stability has gone off-kilter.

38   Wray is one of the founders of what has been called "white-trash studies," a field conceived as a response to the perceived elite-liberal marginalization of the white working class. He argues that the economic downturn of the 1970s was the precondition for the formation of an "oppositional" and "defiant" white-working-class sensibility—think of the rugged, anti-everything individualism of 1977's *Smokey and the Bandit*. But those anxieties took their shape from the aftershocks of the identity-based movements of the 1960s. "I think that the political space that the civil-rights movement opens up in the mid-1950s and '60s is the transformative thing," Wray observes. "Following the black-power movement, all of the other minority groups that followed took up various forms of activism, including brown power and yellow power and red power. Of course the problem is, if you try and have a 'white power' movement, it doesn't sound good."

39   The result is a racial pride that dares not speak its name, and that defines itself through cultural cues instead—a suspicion of intellectual elites and city dwellers, a preference for folksiness and plainness of speech (whether real or feigned), and the association of a working-class white minority with "the real America." (In the Scots-Irish belt that runs from Arkansas up through West Virginia, the most common ethnic label offered to census takers is "American.") Arguably, this white identity politics helped swing the 2000 and 2004 elections, serving as the powerful counterpunch to urban white liberals, and the McCain–Palin campaign relied on it almost to the point of absurdity (as when a McCain surrogate dismissed Northern Virginia as somehow not part of "the real Virginia") as a bulwark against the threatening multiculturalism of Barack Obama. Their strategy failed, of course, but it's possible to imagine white identity politics growing more potent and more forthright in its racial identifications in the future, as "the real America" becomes an ever-smaller portion of, well, the real America, and as the soon-to-be white minority's sense of being besieged and disdained by a multicultural majority grows apace.

40   At the moment, we can call this the triumph of multiculturalism, or postracialism. But just as whiteness has no inherent meaning—it is a vessel we fill with our hopes and anxieties—these terms may prove equally empty in the long run. Does being postracial mean that we are past race completely, or merely that race is no longer essential to how we identify ourselves? Karl Carter, of Atlanta's

youth-oriented GTM, Inc. (Guerrilla Tactics Media), suggests that marketers and advertisers would be better off focusing on matrices like "lifestyle" or "culture" rather than race or ethnicity. "You'll have crazy in-depth studies of the white consumer or the Latino con-

> *But just as whiteness has no inherent meaning—it is a vessel we fill with our hopes and anxieties—these terms may prove equally empty in the long run.*

sumer," he complains. "But how do skaters feel? How do hip-hoppers feel?"

41   The logic of online social networking points in a similar direction. The New York University sociologist Dalton Conley has written of a "network nation," in which applications like Facebook and MySpace create "crosscutting social groups" and new, flexible identities that only vaguely overlap with racial identities. Perhaps this is where the future of identity after whiteness lies—in a dramatic departure from the racial logic that has defined American culture from the very beginning. What Conley, Carter, and others are describing isn't merely the displacement of whiteness from our cultural center; they're describing a social structure that treats race as just one of a seemingly infinite number of possible self-identifications.

42   The problem of the 20th century, W. E. B. Du Bois famously predicted, would be the problem of the color line. Will this continue to be the case in the 21st century, when a black president will govern a country whose social networks increasingly cut across every conceivable line of identification? The ruling of *United States v. Bhagat Singh Thind* no longer holds weight, but its echoes have been inescapable: we aspire to be postracial, but we still live within the structures of privilege, injustice, and racial categorization that we inherited from an older order. We can talk about defining ourselves by lifestyle rather than skin color, but our lifestyle choices are still racially coded. We know, more or less, that race is a fiction that often does more harm than good, and yet it is something we cling to without fully understanding why—as a social and legal fact, a vague sense of belonging and place that we make solid through culture and speech.

43   But maybe this is merely how it used to be—maybe this is already an outdated way of looking at things. "You have a lot of young adults going into a more diverse world," Carter remarks. For the young Americans born in the 1980s and 1990s, culture is something to be taken apart and remade in their own image. "We came along in a generation that didn't have to follow that path of race," he goes on. "We saw something different." This moment was not the end of white America; it was not the end of anything. It was a bridge, and we crossed it. ◆

The End of the Black American Narrative

Charles Johnson

1   As a writer, philosopher, artist, and black American, I've devoted more than 40 years of my life to trying to understand and express intellectually and artistically different aspects of the black American narrative. At times during my life, especially when I was young, it was a story that engaged me emotionally and consumed my imagination. I've produced novels, short stories, essays, critical articles, drawings,

and PBS dramas based on what we call the black American story. To a certain degree, teaching the literature of black America has been my bread and butter as a college professor. It is a very old narrative, one we all know quite well, and it is a tool we use, consciously or unconsciously, to interpret or to make sense of everything that has happened to black people in this country since the arrival of the first 20 Africans at the Jamestown colony in 1619. A good story always has a meaning (and sometimes layers of meaning); it also has an epistemological mission: namely, to show us something. It is an effort to make the best sense we can of the human experience, and I believe that we base our lives, actions, and judgments as often on the stories we tell ourselves about ourselves (even when they are less than empirically sound or verifiable) as we do on the severe rigor of reason. This unique black American narrative, which emphasizes the experience of victimization, is quietly in the background of every conversation we have about black people, even when it is not fully articulated or expressed. It is our starting point, our agreed-upon premise, our most important presupposition for dialogues about black America. We teach it in our classes, and it is the foundation for both our scholarship and our popular entertainment as they relate to black Americans. Frequently it is the way we approach each other as individuals.

2　　As a writer and a teacher of writing, I have to ask myself over and over again, just what is a story. How do we shape one? How many different forms can it take? What do stories tell us about our world? What details are necessary, and which ones are unimportant for telling it well? I constantly ask my creative writing students two questions: Does the story work technically? And, if so, then, what does it say? I tell them that, like a work of philosophy (which is the sister discipline to storytelling among the interpretive arts), a narrative vision must have the qualities of coherence, consistency, and completeness. The plot of a modern story must be streamlined and efficient if it is to be easily understood. And, like Edgar Allan Poe in his 1842 essay "On the Aim and the Technique of the Short Story," I argue that a dramatic narrative should leave the listener with "a certain unique or single effect" that has emotional power. For the last 32 years, I've stressed to my students that a story must have a conflict that is clearly presented, one that we care about, a dilemma or disequilibrium for the protagonist that we, as readers, emotionally identify with. The black American story, as we tell it to ourselves, beautifully embodies all these narrative virtues.

3　　The story begins with violence in the 17th-century slave forts sprinkled along the west coast of Africa, where debtors, thieves, war prisoners, and those who would not convert to Islam were separated from their families, branded, and sold to Europeans who packed them into the pestilential ships that cargoed 20 million human beings (a conservative estimate) to the New World.

4　　As has been documented time and again, the life of a slave—our not-so-distant ancestors—was one of thinghood. Former languages, religions, and cultures were erased, replaced by the Peculiar Institution, in which the person of African descent was property, and systematically—legally, physically, and culturally—denied all sense of self-worth. A slave owns nothing, least of all himself. He desires and dreams at the risk of his life, which is best described as relative to (white) others, a reaction to their deeds, judgments, and definitions of the world. And these definitions, applied to blacks, were not kind. For 244 years (from 1619 to 1863), America was a slave state with a guilty conscience: two and a half centuries scarred by slave revolts, heroic black (and abolitionist) resistance to oppression, and, more than anything else, physical, spiritual, and psychological suffering so staggering it silences the mind when we study the classic slave narratives of Equiano or Frederick Douglass. Legal bondage, the peculiar antebellum world, ended during the Civil War, but the Emancipation Proclamation did not bring liberation.

5   Legal freedom instead gradually brought segregation, America's version of apartheid. But "separate" clearly was not "equal." Black Americans were not simply segregated; they were methodically disenfranchised, stripped of their rights as citizens. From the 1890s through the 1950s, the law of black life was experienced as second-class citizenship. In the century after the Emancipation Proclamation, members of each generation of black Americans saw their lives disrupted by race riots, lynchings, and the destruction of towns and communities, such as the Greenwood district of black homes, businesses, and churches in Tulsa, Oklahoma, on May 31, 1921. The challenge for black America and the conflict for its story, then, was how to force a nation that excluded black people from its promise of "life, liberty, and the pursuit of happiness" after the Revolutionary War, and failed to redress this grievance after Reconstruction, to honor these principles enshrined in its most sacred documents.

6   What I have described defines the general shape of the black American group narrative before the beginning of the civil rights movement, the most important and transformative domestic event in American history after the War Between the States. The conflict of this story is first slavery, then segregation and legal disenfranchisement. The meaning of the story is group victimization, and every black person is the story's protagonist. This specific story was not about ending racism, which would be a wonderful thing; but ending racism entirely is probably as impossible for human beings as ending crime, or as quixotic as President Bush's "war on terror." No, the black American story was not as vague as that. It had a clearly defined conflict. And our ancestors fought daily for generations, with courage and dignity, to change this narrative. That was the point of their lives, their sacrifices, each and every day they were on this earth. We cannot praise enough the miracle they achieved, the lifelong efforts of our leaders and the anonymous men and women who kept the faith, demonstrated, went to jail, registered black people to vote in the Deep South, changed unjust laws, and died in order that Americans of all backgrounds might be free. I have always seen their fight for us as noble.

7   Among those I pay special tribute to is W. E. B. Du Bois, one of the founders of the NAACP, who deeply understood the logic and structure of this narrative as it unfolded from Reconstruction through the 1950s. It was a sign of his prescience that he also could see beyond this ancient story while still in the midst of it and fighting mightily to change it.

8   In 1926, Du Bois delivered an address titled, "Criteria of Negro Art" at the Chicago Conference for the NAACP. His lecture, which was later published in *The Crisis*, the official publication of the NAACP, which Du Bois himself edited, took place during the most entrenched period of segregation, when the opportunities for black people were so painfully circumscribed. "What do we want?" he asked his audience. "What is the thing we are after?" Listen to Du Bois 82 years ago:

9   What do we want? What is the thing we are after? As it was phrased last night it had a certain truth: We want to be Americans, full-fledged Americans, with all the rights of American citizens. But is that all? Do we want simply to be

Americans? Once in a while through all of us there flashes some clairvoyance, some clear idea, of what America really is. We who are dark can see America in a way that white Americans cannot. And seeing our country thus, are we satisfied with its present goals and ideals? ...

10   If you tonight suddenly should become full-fledged Americans; if your color faded, or the color line here in Chicago was miraculously forgotten; suppose, too, you became at the same time rich and powerful; what is it that you would want? What would you immediately seek? Would you buy the most powerful of motor cars and outrace Cook County? Would you buy the most elaborate estate on the North Shore? Would you be a Rotarian or a Lion or a What-not of the very last degree? Would you wear the most striking clothes, give the richest dinners, and buy the longest press notices?

11   Even as you visualize such ideals you know in your heart that these are not the things you really want. You realize this sooner than the average white American because, pushed aside as we have been in America, there has come to us not only a certain distaste for the tawdry and flamboyant but a vision of what the world could be if it were really a beautiful world; if we had the true spirit; if we had the Seeing Eye, the Cunning Hand, the Feeling Heart; if we had, to be sure, not perfect happiness, but plenty of good hard work, the inevitable suffering that comes with life; sacrifice and waiting, all that—but, nevertheless, lived in a world where men know, where men create, where they realize themselves and where they enjoy life. It is that sort of world we want to create for ourselves and for all America.

12   This provocative passage is, in part, the foundation for my questioning the truth and usefulness of the traditional black American narrative of victimization. When compared with black lives at the dawn of the 21st century, and 40 years after the watershed events of the civil rights movement, many of Du Bois' remarks now sound ironic, for all the impossible things he spoke of in 1926 are realities today. We are "full-fledged Americans, with the rights of American citizens." We do have "plenty of good hard work" and live in a society where "men create, where they realize themselves and where they enjoy life." Even more ironic is the fact that some of our famous rappers and athletes who like "living large," as they say, seem obsessed with what Du Bois derisively called "the tawdry and flamboyant" (they call it "bling"). Furthermore, some of us do use the freedom paid for with the blood of our ancestors to pursue conspicuous consumption in the form of "powerful motor cars," "elaborate estates," "striking clothes," and "the richest dinners."

13   To put this another way, we can say that 40 years after the epic battles for specific civil rights in Montgomery, Birmingham, and Selma, after two monumental and historic legislative triumphs—the Civil Rights Act of 1964 and the Voting Rights Act of 1965—and after three decades of affirmative action that led to the creation of a true black middle class (and not the false one E. Franklin Frazier described in his classic 1957 study, *Black Bourgeoisie*), a people oppressed for so long have finally become, as writer Reginald McKnight once put it, "as polymorphous as the dance of Shiva." Black Americans have been CEOs at AOL

Time Warner, American Express, and Merrill Lynch; we have served as secretary of state and White House national security adviser. Well over 10,000 black Americans have been elected to offices around the country, and at this moment Senator Barack Obama holds us in suspense with the possibility that he may be selected as the Democratic Party's first biracial, black American candidate for president. We have been mayors, police chiefs, best-selling authors, MacArthur fellows, Nobel laureates, Ivy League professors, billionaires, scientists, stockbrokers, engineers, theoretical physicists, toy makers, inventors, astronauts, chess grandmasters, dot-com millionaires, actors, Hollywood film directors, and talk show hosts (the most prominent among them being Oprah Winfrey, who recently signed a deal to acquire her own network); we are Protestants, Catholics, Muslims, Jews, and Buddhists (as I am). And we are not culturally homogeneous. When I last looked, West Indians constituted 48 percent of the "black" population in Miami. In America's major cities, 15 percent of the black American population is foreign born—Haitian, Jamaican, Senegalese, Nigerian, Cape Verdean, Ethiopian, Eritrean, and Somalian—a rich tapestry of brown-skinned people as culturally complex in their differences, backgrounds, and outlooks as those people lumped together under the all too convenient labels of "Asian" or "European." Many of them are doing better—in school and business—than native-born black Americans. I think often of something said by Mary Andom, an Eritrean student at Western Washington University, and quoted in an article published in 2003 in the *Seattle Times*: "I don't know about 'chitlings' or 'grits.' I don't listen to soul music artists such as Marvin Gaye or Aretha Franklin.... I grew up eating *injera* and listening to *Tigrinya* music.... After school, I cook the traditional coffee, called *boun*, by hand for my mother. It is a tradition shared amongst mother and daughter."

14   No matter which angle we use to view black people in America today, we find them to be a complex and multifaceted people who defy easy categorization. We challenge, culturally and politically, an old group narrative that fails at the beginning of this new century to capture even a fraction of our rich diversity and heterogeneity. My point is not that black Americans don't have social and cultural problems in 2008. We have several nagging problems, among them poor schools and far too many black men in prison and too few in college. But these are problems based more on the inequities of class, and they appear in other groups as well. It simply is no longer the case that the essence of black American life is racial victimization and disenfranchisement, a curse and a condemnation, a destiny based on color in which the meaning of one's life is thinghood, created even before one is born. This is not something we can assume. The specific conflict of this narrative reached its dramatic climax in 1963 in Birmingham, Alabama, and at the breathtaking March on Washington; its resolution arrived in 1965, the year before I graduated from high

> *It simply is no longer the case that the essence of black American life is racial victimization and disenfranchisement, a curse and a condemnation, a destiny based on color in which the meaning of one's life is thinghood, created even before one is born. This is not something we can assume.*

school, with the Voting Rights Act. Everything since then has been a coda for almost half a century. We call this long-extended and still ongoing anticlimax the post–civil-rights period. If the NAACP is struggling these days to recruit members of the younger generation and to redefine its mission in the 21st century—and it is struggling to do that—I think it is a good sign that the organization Du Bois led for so long is now a casualty of its own successes in the 1960s.

15   Yet, despite being an antique, the old black American narrative of pervasive victimization persists, denying the overwhelming evidence of change since the time of my parents and grandparents, refusing to die as doggedly as the Ptolemaic vision before Copernicus or the notion of phlogiston in the 19th century, or the deductive reasoning of the medieval schoolmen. It has become ahistorical. For a time it served us well and powerfully, yes, reminding each generation of black Americans of the historic obligations and duties and dangers they inherited and faced, but the problem with any story or idea or interpretation is that it can soon fail to fit the facts and becomes an ideology, even kitsch.

16   This point is expressed eloquently by Susan Griffin in her 1982 essay "The Way of All Ideology," where she says, "When a theory is transformed into an ideology, it begins to destroy the self and self-knowledge.... No one can tell it anything new. It is annoyed by any detail which does not fit its worldview.... Begun as a way to restore one's sense of reality, now it attempts to discipline real people, to remake natural beings after its own image."

17   In his superb book *In My Father's House*, philosopher Kwame Anthony Appiah writes, "There is nothing in the world that can do all we ask race to do for us." We can easily amend or revise this insight and apply it to the pre–21st-century black American narrative, which can do very little of the things we need for it to do today.

18   But this is an enduring human problem, isn't it? As phenomenologist Edmund Husserl revealed a hundred years ago, we almost always perceive and understand the new in terms of the old—or, more precisely, we experience events through our ideas, and frequently those are ideas that bring us comfort, ideas received from our parents, teachers, the schools we attend, and the enveloping culture, rather than original ones of our own. While a story or model may disclose a particular meaning for an experience, it also forces into the background or conceals other possible meanings. Think of this in light of novelist Ralph Ellison's brilliant notion of "invisibility," where—in his classic *Invisible Man*—the characters encountered by his nameless protagonist all impose their ideologies (explanations and ideas) on the chaos of experience, on the mysterious, untamed life that forever churns beneath widely accepted interpretations and explanations of "history" and "culture," which in our social world, for Ellison, are the seen. I know, personally, there is value in this Ellisonian idea, because in the historical fictions I've been privileged to publish, like "Martha's Dilemma" in my second collection, *Soulcatcher and Other Stories*, I discovered that the most intriguing, ambiguous, and revealing material for stories can often be found in the margins of the codified and often repeated narrative about slavery. In this case, I dramatized a delicious anecdote about what happened to Martha and her slaves right after the death of George.

19   What I am saying is that "official" stories and explanations and endlessly repeated interpretations of black American life over decades can short-circuit direct

perception of the specific phenomenon before us. The idea of something—an intellectual construct—is often more appealing and perfect (in a Platonic sense) than the thing itself, which always remains mysterious and ambiguous and messy, by which I mean that its sense is open-ended, never fixed. It is always wise, I believe, to see all our propositions (and stories) as provisional, partial, incomplete, and subject to revision on the basis of new evidence, which we can be sure is just around the corner.

20   Nevertheless, we have heavily and often uncritically invested for most of our lives in the pre–21st-century black American narrative. In fact, some of us depend upon it for our livelihood, so it is not easy to let go, or to revise this story. Last October, Nation of Islam minister Louis Farrakhan spoke for two and a half hours at the Atlanta Civic Center. He and his mentor, black separatist Elijah Muhammad, provided black Americans with what is probably the most extreme, Manichean, and mythological version of the black American narrative, one that was anti-integrationist. In this incomplete and misleading rendition of the black American story, the races are locked in eternal struggle. As a story, this narrative fails because it is conceived as melodrama, a form of storytelling in which the characters are flat, lack complexity, are either all good or all bad, and the plot involves malicious villains and violent actions. Back in the 1930s when Elijah Muhammad shaped his myth of Yacub, which explained the origins of the white race as "devils," he sacrificed the credibility of both character and plot for the most simplistic kind of dramatic narrative. Farrakhan covered many subjects that day last October, but what I found most interesting is that he said successful black people like Oprah Winfrey, Senator Obama, Colin Powell, and Condoleezza Rice give black Americans a false impression of progress. In other words, their highly visible successes do not change the old narrative of group victimization. Minister Farrakhan seems unwilling to accept their success as evidence that the lives of black Americans have improved. He seems unwilling to accept the inevitability of change. He was quoted in the press as saying, "A life of ease sometimes makes you forget the struggle." And despite the battles for affirmative action that created a new middle class, he added, "It's becoming a plantation again, but you can't fight that because you want to keep your little job."

21   I beg to differ with Farrakhan, with his misuse of language, his loose, imprecise diction, because we obviously do not live on plantations. And wasn't job opportunity one of the explicit goals of the black American narrative? Farrakhan's entire life has been an investment in a story that changed as he was chasing it. So we can understand his fierce, personal, and even tragic attachment to dusty, antebellum concepts when looking at the uncharted phenomena in the early 21st century that outstrip his concepts and language.

22   However, it is precisely because Farrakhan cannot progress beyond an oversimplified caricature of a story line for racial phenomena that the suddenly notorious Rev. Jeremiah Wright praises him, saying "His depth of analysis . . . when it comes to the racial ills of this nation is astounding and eye-opening," and, "He brings a perspective that is helpful and honest." Recently Wright called the Nation of Islam leader, "one of the most important voices in the 20th and 21st centur[ies]." I do not doubt that Wright and Farrakhan are men who have experienced the evil of racism and want to see the conditions of our people improve, or that both have records of community service. But it is the emotional attachment to a dated narrative, one leavened with the 1960s-era liberation theology of James Cone, that predictably leads Wright to proclaim that the

U.S. government created the AIDS virus to destroy blacks (he invokes the old and proven, the ghastly Tuskegee syphilis experiment, in an effort to understand a new affliction devastating black people, and thus commits the logical fallacy known as *misuse of analogy*); that Jesus was "a black man"; and that the brains of blacks and whites operate differently. The former pastor of Trinity United Church of Christ in Chicago has made these paranoid and irresponsible statements publicly again and again without offering the slightest shred of evidence for these claims. "A bunch of rants that aren't grounded in truth" was how Barack Obama described his former minister's incendiary oratory, which is clearly antithetical not only to the postracial spirit of the Illinois senator's own speeches but also to his very racially and geographically mixed background. For in the realm of ideological thinking, especially from the pulpit, feeling and faith trump fact, and passion (as well as beliefs based on scripture) replaces fidelity to the empirical and painstaking logical demonstration.

23 But if the old, black American narrative has outlived its usefulness as a tool of interpretation, then what should we do? The answer, I think, is obvious. In the 21st century, we need new and better stories, new concepts, and new vocabularies and grammar based not on the past but on the dangerous, exciting, and unexplored present, with the understanding that each is, at best, a provisional reading of reality, a single phenomenological profile that one day is likely to be revised, if not completely overturned. These will be narratives that do not claim to be absolute truth, but instead more humbly present themselves as a very tentative thesis that must be tested every day in the depths of our own experience and by all the reliable evidence we have available, as limited as that might be. For as Bertrand Russell told us, what we know is always "vanishingly small." These will be narratives of individuals, not groups. And is this not exactly what Martin Luther King Jr. dreamed of when he hoped a day would come when men and women were judged not by the color of their skin, but instead by their individual deeds and actions, and the content of their character?

24 I believe this was what King dreamed and, whether we like it or not, that moment is now. ◆

CRITICAL THINKING ———————————————

1. Why does Hua reference *The Great Gatsby* in his introduction to his essay? How does he tie this theme into the rest of the essay? What connections exist between the story and the points he raises about race and racism?
2. Hua conjectures that we are entering a "post-racial age." What does this term mean, and what does it say about the society we lived in before this "new" age? Explain.
3. Review Bill Clinton's comment (paragraph 12 of Hua's essay) on the end of "majority race" and why this is a good thing for America. Connect his comment to points Johnson makes in his essay about the black American narrative.
4. Hua notes that Pat Buchanan warned that the arrival of "Third World America" is all but inevitable. What does this term imply? How does it incite fear and promote racism? What response would be appropriate to such a claim?

5. Hua notes that Sean Combs has identified himself as the Great Gatsby. What does he mean? How does his lifestyle compare to Jake Gatsby? What visible connections has he made between himself and the character in Fitzgerald's novel? What happens to Gatsby?

6. What impact has hip-hop music had on America's push toward a postracial age?

7. Why do some whites feel disenfranchised by the multi-ethnic movement in music, education, Hollywood, and popular culture? How do they "pull the rug out from under themselves," and why should they? What backlash in American subculture has resulted?

8. Johnson mentions some specific key figures whom he feels are repeating the black American narrative to our social detriment. Whom does he identify, and why does he feel these individuals are unable move beyond the narrative to write the next chapter? What is the social cost of repeating the same story to the next generation?

9. How does Johnson's recounting of the framework of the black American narrative support his points? How did this narrative hold people together? Why does he feel it is time to move on? Explain.

10. Both authors mention W. E. B. Du Bois. Who was Du Bois? What is his connection to the points the authors seek to make in these essays?

CRITICAL WRITING

1. *Research Writing:* Read *The Great Gatsby* and research the book by Stoddard Lothrop, *The Rising Tide of Color Against White World-Supremacy*, published in 1920. What did "white race" mean? What did it mean to Stoddard in 1920, and how has this definition changed (or not changed) today?

2. *Expository Writing:* Both of these essays explore the "end" of something—the end of "white America" and the end of the "black American narrative"—both are about the culture, society, politics, and stories that connect people and help them identify how they fit in a larger social context. Select one of the "ends" and write an essay exploring what the next 100 years might be like as a new beginning.

3. *Expository Writing:* Answer the question Hua poses at the end of his essay: "The problem of the 20th century, W. E. B. Du Bois famously predicted, would be the problem of the color line. Will this continue to be the case in the 21st century, when a black president will govern a country whose social networks increasingly cut across every conceivable line of identification?"

4. *Exploratory Writing:* Do you think we will be more ethnically and racially melded as a nation in the next century? Write an essay postulating what race might mean 100 years from now. What about 200 years from now?

5. *Personal Narrative:* Examine your own racial and/or ethnic background. Write about whether this background has contributed to your perception of yourself and how you relate to others.

GROUP PROJECTS

1. With your group, construct a demographic picture of the future, say, in 100 years. Try to conjecture what the face of the nation will look like. Are there still checkboxes asking for one's race on job applications? What will the typical family look like? Will people still wonder what a person's ethnic background is? Share your vision, and the reasoning behind it, with the rest of the class.

2. As a group, discuss what "traditional American" and "American mainstream society" mean. How would you define these terms for a foreign visitor? Discuss this question as a group, and develop a definition. Share your group's definition with the rest of the class.

3. Hua identifies several famous people, namely Tiger Woods and Sean Combs, in his essay for their contributions to a post-racial society. As a group, identify the people he cites, and any other well-known figures who have contributed to a postracial culture, and discuss how these individuals have contributed to our cultural identity and how we think—or don't think—about race.

The American University System

Still Making the Grade?

By the time you enter the halls of your college or university as a first-year student, you will have spent over 20,000 hours in school—not including the time used to complete homework or participate in extracurricular activities. You would probably agree that a good education is the key to success later in life, no matter what field you chose, and that a college education is becoming an increasingly important qualification for many career paths.

The most obvious benefits of a college education are economic ones—college graduates tend to earn more than high school graduates. According to a U.S. Census Bureau report, the average adult holding a bachelor's degree will, over a lifetime, earn a million dollars more than an adult holding only a high school diploma. So while the cost of a college education may seem steep at the time you enroll, the benefits are likely to last a lifetime.

There are other benefits, too. Compared to non–college graduates, college grads and their children tend to enjoy better health and form stronger, more enduring social networks. They enjoy more professional opportunities and a higher quality of life overall. According to a 2002 report published by the Carnegie Foundation, college graduates tend to be "more open-minded, more cultured, more rational, more consistent and less authoritarian [than non–college graduates]; and these benefits are also passed along to succeeding generations."

However, despite its many benefits, college life and a university education are often the subject of controversy. From the moment a high school junior takes the PSAT exam, questions abound: Does today's college curriculum prepare students for the real world? Do the liberal arts matter in today's world? Are college campuses truly a haven for the exchange of ideas and free expression, or are some ideas more acceptable than others? And what happens if you express an unpopular point of view? This chapter examines issues that university faculty and students grapple with today.

We begin with a look at how college curricula have changed over the last generation. In "How to Get a College Education," Jeffrey Hart, a college professor at Dartmouth, discovers to his dismay that today's college freshmen are not arriving on campus with a solid foundation in history, philosophy, politics, and literature. He wonders what this means for college students as they graduate and become citizens of the world. This viewpoint from a seasoned professor is followed by that of a recently appointed professor, Alicia Shepard, who wonders why so many students think a B is a bad grade. In "A's for Everyone," Shepard describes how underperforming students often believe that hard work and good intentions should be enough to earn an A. If everyone gets an A, she wonders, why give grades at all?

In spite of the emphasis on good grades, most college students hope to get a good education as well. Many aspire to attend the prestigious Ivy League schools, recognized as some of the best institutions in the country. But according to William Deresiewicz, an Ivy League education may not be all that it's touted to be. In "The Disadvantages of an Elite Education," he explains how Ivy League schools can perpetuate class divisions, discourage creativity and innovation, and prevent graduates from truly connecting with the world around them. According to the author, the education and socialization that these elite institutions afford their grads feeds the bottom line: Ivy League schools are in the business of turning out Ivy League donors—graduates who will financially support the institution they attended.

Business is also the theme of James Twitchell's essay that follows. In "Higher Ed, Inc.," he says that instead of serving altruistic and noble purposes, colleges and universities behave more like big corporations. An authority on consumerism, and a college professor himself, Twitchell argues that colleges and universities are increasingly concerned with branding. That is, like big business, they promote mascots and team colors to promote brand appeal, and students are the consumers of the "product"— a university diploma.

The next essay, by Joe Queenan, takes a humorous look at the phenomenon of "helicopter parents"—that is, those who hover over their college-age children and are unable to let go. Himself the parent of college-age children, Queenan compares his own college experience to that of his kids.

While college offers students the opportunity to exercise the personal freedoms and responsibilities of adulthood, a college campus is not, in fact, the "real world." Campus policies often aim to control student behavior. Some administrators have even acted *in loco parentis*—in place of a parent—in an effort to control students. This chapter's Viewpoints section examines the balance between students' rights as fledgling adults and the responsibilities of campus administration to ensure that students are safe and thriving. If college students are truly adults, do they need college administrators playing Mom and Dad, controlling what they decide to do outside the classroom? And what expectations do parents have of both students and administrators?

How to Get a College Education
Jeffrey Hart*

Most students arrive at college ready to learn. But what happens if they arrive completely unequipped to handle the coursework assigned because they lack a foundation in literature and history? As senior professor Jeffrey Hart describes, many of today's freshmen cannot connect on many issues because they don't understand the basics. In this essay, the Dartmouth professor explains how such students can still get an outstanding college education if they keep their eye on the goal.

1 It was in the fall term of 1988 that the truth burst in upon me, like something had gone terribly wrong in higher education. It was like the anecdote in Auden, where the guest at a garden party, sensing something amiss, suddenly realizes that there is a corpse on the tennis court.

2 As a professor at Dartmouth, my hours had been taken up with my own writing and with teaching a variety of courses—a yearly seminar, a yearly freshman

* Jeffrey Hart, *The National Review Online*, September 29, 2006

composition course (which—some good news—all senior professors in the Dartmouth English Department are required to teach), and courses in my eighteenth-century specialty. Oh, I knew that the larger curriculum lacked shape and purpose, that something was amiss; but I deferred thinking about it.

3   Yet there does come that moment.

4   It came for me in the freshman composition course. The students were required to write essays based upon assigned reading—in this case, some Frost poems, Hemingway's *In Our Time, Hamlet*. Then, almost on a whim, I assigned the first half of Allan Bloom's surprise best seller, *The Closing of the American Mind*. When the time came to discuss the Bloom book, I asked them what they thought of it.

5   They hated it.

6   Oh, yes, they understood perfectly well what Bloom was saying: that they were ignorant, that they believed in clichés, that their education so far had been dangerous piffle, and that what they were about to receive was not likely to be any better.

7   No wonder they hated it. After all, they were the best and the brightest, Ivy Leaguers with stratospheric SAT scores, the Masters of the Universe. Who is Bloom? What is the University of Chicago, anyway?

8   So I launched into an impromptu oral quiz.

9   Could anyone (in that class of 25 students) say anything about the Mayflower Compact?

10   Complete silence.

11   John Locke?

12   Nope.

13   James Madison?

14   Silentia.

15   Magna Carta? The Spanish Armada? The Battle of Yorktown? The Bull Moose party? Don Giovanni? William James? The Tenth Amendment?

16   Zero. Zilch. Forget it.

17   The embarrassment was acute, but some good came of it. The better students, ashamed that their first 12 years of schooling had mostly been wasted (even if they had gone to Choate or Exeter), asked me to recom-

> *What these [course] fads have done to the liberal arts and social sciences curricula since around 1968 is to clutter it with all sorts of nonsense, nescience, and distraction.*

mend some books. I offered such solid things as Samuel Eliot Morison's *Oxford History of the United States*, Max Farrand's *The Framing of the Constitution*, Jacob Burckhardt's *The Civilization of the Renaissance in Italy*. Several students asked for an informal discussion group, and so we started reading a couple of Dante's *Cantos* per week, Dante being an especially useful author, because he casts his net so widely—the ancient world, the (his) modern world, theology, history, ethics.

18   I quickly became aware of the utter bewilderment of entering freshmen. They emerge from the near-nullity of K–12 and stroll into the chaos of the Dartmouth curriculum, which is embodied in a course catalogue about as large as a telephone directory.

19   Sir, what courses should I take? A college like Dartmouth—or Harvard, Princeton, et cetera—has requirements so broadly defined that almost anything goes for

degree credit. Of course, freshmen are assigned faculty "advisors," but most of them would rather return to the library or the Bunsen burner.

20   Thus it developed that I began giving an annual lecture to incoming freshmen on the subject, "What Is a College Education? And How to Get One, Even at Dartmouth."

21   One long-term reason why the undergraduate curriculum at Dartmouth and all comparable institutions is in chaos is specialization. Since World War II, success as a professor has depended increasingly on specialized publication. The ambitious and talented professor is not eager to give introductory or general courses. Indeed, his work has little or nothing to do with undergraduate teaching. Neither Socrates nor Jesus, who published nothing, could possibly receive tenure at a first-line university today.

22   But in addition to specialization, recent intellectual fads have done extraordinary damage, viz:

- So-called postmodernist thought ("deconstruction," etc.) asserts that one "text" is as much worth analyzing as any other, whether it be a movie, a comic book, or Homer. The lack of a "canon" of important works leads to course offerings in, literally, anything.
- "Affirmative Action" is not just a matter of skewed admissions and hiring but also a mentality or ethos. That is, if diversity is more important than quality in admissions and hiring, why should it not be so in the curriculum? Hence the courses in things like Nicaraguan Lesbian Poetry.
- Concomitantly, ideology has been imposed on the curriculum to a startling degree. In part this represents a sentimental attempt to resuscitate Marxism, with assorted victim groups standing in for the old proletariat; in part it is a new Identity Politics in which being black, lesbian, Latino, homosexual, radical feminist, and so forth takes precedence over any scholarly pursuit. These victimologies are usually presented as "studies" programs outside the regular departments, so as to avoid the usual academic standards. Yet their course offerings carry degree credit.

23   On an optimistic note, I think that most or all of postmodernism, the Affirmative Action/multicultural ethos, and the victimologies will soon pass from the scene. The great institutions have a certain sense of self-preservation. Harvard almost lost its law school to a Marxist faculty faction but then cleaned house. Tenure will keep the dead men walking for another 20 years or so, but then we will have done with them.

24   But for the time being, what these fads have done to the liberal arts and social sciences curricula since around 1968 is to clutter it with all sorts of nonsense, nescience, and distraction. The entering student needs to be wary lest he waste his time and his parents' money and come to consider all higher education an outrageous fraud. The good news is that the wise student can still get a college education today, even at Dartmouth, Harvard, Yale, and Princeton.

25   Of course the central question is one of *telos*, or goal. What is the liberal arts education supposed to produce? Once you have the answer to this question, course selection becomes easy.

26   I mean to answer that question here. But first, I find that undergraduates and their third-mortgaged parents appreciate some practical tips, such as:

27   Select the "ordinary" courses. I use *ordinary* here in a paradoxical and challenging way. An ordinary course is one that has always been taken and obviously should be taken—even if the student is not yet equipped with a sophisticated rationale for so doing. The student should be discouraged from putting his money on the cutting edge of interdisciplinary cross-textuality.

28   Thus, do take American and European history, an introduction to philosophy, American and European literature, the Old and New Testaments, and at least one modern language. It would be absurd not to take a course in Shakespeare, the best poet in our language. There is art and music history. The list can be expanded, but these areas every educated person should have a decent knowledge of—with specialization coming later on.

29   I hasten to add that I applaud the student who devotes his life to the history of China or Islam, but that, too, should come later. America is part of the narrative of European history.

30   If the student should seek out those "ordinary" courses, then it follows that he should avoid the flashy come-ons. Avoid things like Nicaraguan Lesbian Poets. Yes, and anything listed under "Studies," any course whose description uses the words "interdisciplinary," "hegemonic," "phallocratic," or "empowerment," anything that mentions "keeping a diary," any course with a title like "Adventures in Film."

31   Also, any male professor who comes to class without a jacket and tie should be regarded with extreme prejudice, unless he has won a Nobel Prize.

32   All these are useful rules of thumb. A theoretical rationale for a liberal arts education, however, derives from that telos mentioned above. What is such an education supposed to produce?

33   A philosophy professor I studied with as an undergraduate had two phrases he repeated so often that they stay in the mind, a technique made famous by Matthew Arnold.

34   He would say, "History must be told."

35   History, he explained, is to a civilization what memory is to an individual, an irreducible part of identity.

36   He also said, "The goal of education is to produce the citizen." He defined the citizen as the person who, if need be, could re-create his civilization.

37   Now, it is said that Goethe was the last man who knew all the aspects of his civilization (I doubt that he did), but that after him things became too complicated. My professor had something different in mind. He meant that the citizen should know the great themes of his civilization, its important areas of thought, its philosophical and religious controversies, the outline of its history and its major works. The citizen need not know quantum physics, but he should know that it is there and what it means. Once the citizen knows the shape, the narrative, of his civilization, he is able to locate new things—and other civilizations—in relation to it.

38   The narrative of Western civilization can be told in different ways, but a useful paradigm has often been called "Athens and Jerusalem." Broadly construed, "Athens" means a philosophical and scientific view of actuality and "Jerusalem" a spiritual and scriptural one. The working out of Western civilization represents an interaction—tension, fusion, conflict—between the two.

39   Both Athens and Jerusalem have a heroic, or epic, phase. For Athens, the Homeric poems are a kind of scripture, the subject of prolonged ethical meditation. In time the old heroic ideals are internalized as heroic philosophy in Socrates, Plato, and Aristotle.

40   For Jerusalem, the heroic phase consists of the Hebrew narratives. Here again, a process of internalization occurs, Jesus internalizing the Mosaic Law. Socrates is the heroic philosopher, Jesus the ideal of heroic holiness, both new ideals in their striking intensity.

41   During the first century of the Christian Era, Athens and Jerusalem converge under the auspices of Hellenistic thought, most notably in Paul and in John, whose gospel defined Jesus by using the Greek term for order, *logos*.

42   Athens and Jerusalem were able to converge, despite great differences, because in some ways they overlap. The ultimate terms of Socrates and Plato, for example, cannot be entirely derived from reason. The god of Plato and Aristotle is monotheistic, though still the god of the philosophers. Yet Socrates considers that his rational universe dictates personal immortality.

43   In the Hebrew epic, there are hints of a law prior to the law of revelation and derived from reason. Thus, when Abraham argues with God over the fate of Sodom and Gomorrah, Abraham appeals to a known principle of justice, which God also assumes.

44   Thus Athens is not pure reason, and Jerusalem is not pure revelation. Both address the perennial question of why there is something rather than nothing.

45   From the prehistoric figures in Homer and in Genesis—Achilles, Abraham— the great conversation commences. Thucydides and Virgil seek order in history. St. Augustine tries to synthesize Paul and Platonism. Montaigne's skepticism would never have been articulated without a prior assertion of cosmic order. Erasmus believed Christianity would prevail if only it could be put in the purest Latin. Shakespeare made a world and transcended Lear's storm with that final, calmed and sacramental Tempest. Rousseau would not have proclaimed the goodness of man if Calvin had not said the opposite. Dante held all the contradictions together in a total structure—for a glorious moment. Kafka could not see beyond the edges of his nightmare, but Dostoyevsky found love just beyond the lowest point of sin. The eighteenth-century men of reason knew the worst and settled for the luminous stability of a bourgeois republic.

46   By any intelligible standard, the other great civilization was China, yet it lacked the Athens–Jerusalem tension and dynamism. Much more static, its symbols were the Great Wall and the Forbidden City, not Odysseus/Columbus, Chartres, the Empire State Building, the love that moves the sun and the other stars.

47   When undergraduates encounter the material of our civilization—that is, the liberal arts—then they know that they are going somewhere. They are becoming citizens. ◆

CRITICAL THINKING

1. What does Hart's use of language and his style of writing reveal about his own education? What expectations does he have of his audience?
2. Does Hart's background as a professor at Dartmouth make him an expert on this issue? Why or why not? How much does his argument rely on the reader's acceptance of his authority on this issue?

3. Take the impromptu quiz Hart poses to his students. How many of the things he cites did you know at least something about? Do not look up any of the items on the list before answering the question.

The Mayflower Compact	The Bull Moose Party
John Locke	Don Giovanni
The Magna Carta	William James
The Spanish Armada	The Tenth Amendment
The Battle of Yorktown	

4. Based on your responses to question three, and after learning their subsequent answers (your instructor will provide answers, but you can look them up in advance), how relevant do you think the issues on the list are to your ability to get a good college education? Explain.
5. Based on Hart's essay, how well prepared do you feel you are to tackle a college curriculum? Are there any college courses you will take or avoid taking based on his argument?
6. According to the author, how has specialization harmed the undergraduate curriculum? Explain.
7. What are the "victimologies"? In Hart's opinion, how are such courses harming students' college educations?

CRITICAL WRITING

1. *Personal Narrative:* Hart mentions the bewilderment of college freshmen upon embarking on a college curriculum. What courses should I take? Describe your own experience as a new freshman. What guidance did you receive? How confident were you on your course selection? How happy are you with your current course load? Do you feel comfortable or confused, as Hart describes in his essay?
2. *Exploratory Writing:* Write an essay on what a college education means to you. Include what skills, knowledge, and abilities you feel a college education should confer after four years of study.
3. *Exploratory Writing:* Write an essay in which you address the importance of a foundation in the liberal arts—specifically in history, literature, and philosophy—on a college education. Alternatively, you could write about why such subjects are not important to a good college education.

GROUP PROJECT

1. With your group, craft a college core curriculum that every student must take before graduation, regardless of his or her major. Select 12 courses to be taken over the four-year time span of the average bachelor's degree. You may be general in your selection ("Western Civilization I and II") or very specific ("Gender and Power in Modern America"). After compiling your curriculum, share your list with the class to see which courses the groups chose in common and which ones were different. Together as a

class, narrow the list down to 12. If your college or university has a core curriculum, compare your final list to the one outlined in your student handbook.

A's for Everyone!
*Alicia C. Shepard**

In an era of rampant grade inflation, some college students find it shocking to discover there are five letters in the grading system. It used to be that earning a B in a course was cause for celebration. But across college campuses nationwide, many students argue that an A is the only acceptable grade. Increasingly, students are arguing with their professors to have their low grades raised, urging them to consider hard work rather than skill, talent, and performance as meriting an A grade. Today's parents are also putting pressure on their children to achieve high grades, adding to student anxieties. In this next essay, professor Alicia C. Shepard describes the trend from the perspective of a teacher and as a parent.

1 It was the end of my first semester teaching journalism at American University. The students had left for winter break. As a rookie professor, I sat with trepidation in my office on a December day to electronically post my final grades.

2 My concern was more about completing the process correctly than anything else. It took an hour to compute and type in the grades for three classes, and then I hit "enter." That's when the trouble started.

3 In less than an hour, two students challenged me. Mind you, there had been no preset posting time. They had just been religiously checking the electronic bulletin board that many colleges now use.

4 "Why was I given a B as my final grade?" demanded a reporting student via e-mail. "Please respond ASAP, as I have never received a B during my career here at AU and it will surely lower my GPA."

5 I must say I was floored. Where did this kid get the audacity to so boldly challenge a professor? And why did he care so much? Did he really think a prospective employer was going to ask for his GPA?

6 I checked the grades I'd meticulously kept on the electronic blackboard. He'd missed three quizzes and gotten an 85 on two of the three main writing assignments. There was no way he was A material. I let the grade mar his GPA because he hadn't done the required work.

7 I wasn't so firm with my other challenger. She tracked me down by phone while I was still in my office. She wanted to know why she'd received a B-plus. Basically, it was because she'd barely said a word in class, so the B-plus was subjective. She harangued me until, I'm ashamed to admit, I agreed to change her grade to an

* Alicia C. Shepard, *The Washington Post*, June 5, 2005

A-minus. At the time, I thought, "Geez, if it means that much to you, I'll change it." She thanked me profusely, encouraging me to have a happy holiday.

> *Many students believe that simply working hard—though not necessarily doing excellent work—entitles them to an A. "I can't tell you how many times I've heard a student dispute a grade, not on the basis of in-class performance, but on the basis of how hard they tried."*

8   Little did I know the pressure was just beginning.

9   The students were relentless. During the spring semester, they showed up at my office to insist I reread their papers and boost their grades. They asked to retake tests they hadn't done well on. They bombarded me with e-mails questioning grades. More harassed me to change their final grade. I began to wonder if I was doing something wrong, sending out some sort of newbie signal that I could be pushed around. Then I talked to other professors in the School of Communication. They all had stories.

10   My colleague, Wendy Swallow, told me about one student who had managed to sour her Christmas break one year. Despite gaining entry into AU's honors program, the student missed assignments in Swallow's newswriting class and slept through her midterm. Slept through her midterm! Then she begged for lenience.

11   "I let her take it again for a reduced grade," Swallow says, "but with the warning that if she skipped more classes or missed more deadlines, the midterm grade would revert to the F she earned by missing it. She then skipped the last three classes of the semester and turned in all her remaining assignments late. She even showed up late for her final."

12   Swallow gave the student a C-minus, which meant she was booted out of the honors program. The student was shocked. She called Swallow at home hysterical about being dropped from the program. To Swallow, the C-minus was a gift. To the student, an undeserved lump of Christmas coal.

13   "She pestered me for several days by phone," says Swallow, who did not relent and suggested the student file a formal grievance. She didn't. "The whole exchange, though, made for a very unpleasant break. Now I wait to post my grades until the last minute before leaving for the semester, as by then most of the students are gone, and I'm less likely to get those instantaneous complaints."

14   Another colleague told me about a student she had failed. "He came back after the summer trying to convince me to pass him because other professors just gave him a C," says Leena Jayaswal, who teaches photography. Never mind that he didn't do her required work.

15   John Watson, who teaches journalism ethics and communications law at American, has noticed another phenomenon: Many students, he says, believe that simply working hard—though not necessarily doing excellent work—entitles them to an A. "I can't tell you how many times I've heard a student dispute a grade, not on the basis of in-class performance," says Watson, "but on the basis of how hard they tried. I appreciate the effort, and it always produces positive results, but not always the exact results the student wants. We all have different levels of talent."

16   It's a concept that many students (and their parents) have a hard time grasping. Working hard, especially the night before a test or a paper due date, does not necessarily produce good grades.

17   "At the age of 50, if I work extremely hard, I can run a mile in eight minutes," says Watson. "I have students who can jog through a mile in seven minutes and barely sweat. They will always finish before me, and that's not fair. Or is it?"

18   Last September, AU's Center for Teaching Excellence hosted a lunchtime forum to provide faculty members tips on how to reduce stressful grade confrontations. I eagerly attended.

19   The advice we were given was solid: Be clear up front about how you grade and what is expected, and, when possible, use a numerical grading system rather than letter grades. If the grade is an 89, write that on the paper rather than a B-plus.

20   "The key," said AU academic counselor Jack Ramsay, "is to have a system of grading that is as transparent as possible."

21   Yet even the most transparent grading system won't eliminate our students' desperate pursuit of A's. Of the 20 teachers who came to the session, most could offer some tale of grade harassment.

22   "Most of the complaints that colleagues tell me about come from B students," said James Mooney, special assistant to the dean for academic affairs in the College of Arts and Sciences. "They all want to know why they didn't get an A. Is there something wrong with a B?"

23   Apparently there is. "Certainly there are students who are victims of grade inflation in secondary school," said Mooney. "They come to college, and the grading system is much more rigorous. That's one of the most difficult things to convey to the students. If you're getting a B, you're doing well in a course."

24   But his interpretation is rarely accepted by students or their parents. And the pressure on professors to keep the A's coming isn't unique to AU. It's endemic to college life, according to Stuart Rojstaczer, a Duke University professor who runs a Web site called Gradeinflation.com. At Duke and many other colleges, A's outnumber B's, and C's have all but disappeared from student transcripts, his research shows.

25   Last spring, professors at Princeton University declared war on grade inflation, voting to slash the number of A's they award to 25 percent of all grades. At Harvard, where half of the grades awarded are A's, the university announced that it would cut the number of seniors graduating with honors from 91 percent to about 50 percent.

26   Despite those moves, Rojstaczer doesn't think it will be easy to reverse the rising tide of A's. He points out that in 1969, a quarter of the grades handed out at Duke were C's. By 2002, the number of C's had dropped to less than ten percent.

27   Rojstaczer, who teaches environmental science, acknowledged in an op-ed piece he wrote for the *Post* two years ago that he rarely hands out C's, "and neither do most of my colleagues. And I can easily imagine a time when I'll say the same thing about B's."

28   Arthur Levine, president of Columbia University Teacher's College and an authority on grading, traces what's going on to the Vietnam War. "Men who got low grades could be drafted," Levine says. "The next piece was the spread of graduate schools where only A's and B's were passing grades. That soon got passed on to undergraduates and set the standard."

29   And then there's consumerism, he says. Pure and simple, tuition at a private college runs, on average, nearly $28,000 a year. If parents pay that much, they expect nothing less than A's in return. "Therefore, if the teacher gives you a B, that's not acceptable," says Levine, "because the teacher works for you. I expect A's, and if I'm getting B's, I'm not getting my money's worth."

30   Rojstaczer agrees: "We've made a transition where attending college is no longer a privilege and an honor; instead college is a consumer product. One of the negative aspects of this transition is that the role of a college-level teacher has been transformed into that of a service employee."

31   Levine argues that we "service employees" are doing students a disservice if we cave in to the demand for top grades. "One of the things an education should do is let you know what you do well in and what you don't," he says. "If everybody gets high grades, you don't learn that."

32   But, as I'd already seen, many students aren't interested in learning that lesson— and neither are their parents. When AU administrator James Mooney polled professors about grade complaints, he was appalled to learn that some overwrought parents call professors directly to complain. "One colleague told me he got a call from the mother of his student and she introduced herself by saying that she and her husband were both attorneys," said Mooney. "He thought it was meant to intimidate him."

33   Though I haven't received any menacing phone calls from parents, Mom and Dad are clearly fueling my students' relentless demand for A's. It's a learned behavior. I know, because I'm guilty of inflicting on my son the same grade pressure that now plays out before me as a university professor.

34   Last fall, when my Arlington High School senior finally got the nerve to tell me that he'd gotten a C in the first quarter of his AP English class, I did what any self-respecting, grade-obsessed parent whose son is applying to college would do. I cried. Then I e-mailed his teacher and made an appointment for the three of us to meet. My son's teacher was accommodating. She agreed that if my son did A work for the second quarter, colleges would see a B average for the two quarters, not that ruinous C.

35   There's a term for the legions of parents like me. The parents who make sure to get the teacher's e-mail and home phone number on Back to School Night. The kind who e-mail teachers when their child fails a quiz. The kind who apply the same determination to making sure their child excels academically that they apply to the professional world.

36   We are called "helicopter parents" because we hover over everything our kids do, like Secret Service agents guarding the president. (My son refers to me as an Apache attack helicopter, and he's Fallujah under siege.) Only we aren't worried about our kids getting taken out by wild-eyed assassins. We just want them to get into a "good" (whatever that means) college.

37   "Parents today have this intense investment in seeing their kids do well in school," says Peter Stearns, provost at George Mason University and author of *Anxious Parenting: A History of Modern Child Rearing in America.* "This translates into teachers feeling direct and indirect pressure to keep parents off their backs by handing out reasonably favorable grades and making other modifications, like having up to 18 valedictorians."

38   High school administrators who haven't made those modifications sometimes find themselves defending their grading policies in court. Two years ago, a senior at New Jersey's Moorestown High School filed a $2.7 million lawsuit after she was told she'd have to share being valedictorian with another high-achieving student. A similar episode occurred in Michigan, where a Memphis High School senior who'd just missed being valedictorian claimed in a lawsuit that one of his A's should have been an A-plus.

39   That hyperconcern about grades and class rankings doesn't disappear when kids finally pack for college. Along with their laptops and cell phones, these students bring along the parental anxiety and pressure they've lived with for 18 years.

40   One of my students, Rachael Scorca, says that her parents have always used good grades as an incentive. And they've continued to do so during college. "In high school, my social life and curfew revolved around A's," explains Scorca, a broadcast journalism major. "I needed over a 90 average in order to go out during the week and keep my curfew as late as it was. Once college came and my parents couldn't control my hours or effort, they started controlling my bank account. If I wasn't getting good grades, they wouldn't put money in my account, and, therefore, I wouldn't have a social life."

41   But most of my students tell me the pressure to get top grades doesn't come from their parents any longer. They've internalized it. "I'd say most of the pressure just comes from my personal standards," says Molly Doyle. "It's also something I take pride in. When people ask me how my grades are, I like being able to tell them that I've got all A's and B's."

42   During my second semester of teaching, I received this e-mail from a student who'd taken my fall class on "How the News Media Shape History" and wasn't satisfied with his grade. He (unsuccessfully) tried bribery.

43   "Professor. I checked my grade once I got here and it is a B," he wrote. "I have to score a grade better than a B+ to keep my scholarship, and I have no idea how I ended up with a B. In addition, to that I have brought you something from the GREAT INDIAN CONTINENT."

44   I invited him to come to my office, so I could explain why he'd gotten a B, but after several broken appointments, he faded away.

45   Other students were more persistent, particularly a bright young man who'd been in the same class as the briber. He'd gotten an A-minus and made it clear in an e-mail he wasn't happy with it: "I have seen a number of the students from the class, and we inevitably got to talking about it. I had assumed that you are a tough grader and that earning an A-minus from you was a difficult task, but upon talking to other students, it appears that that grade was handed out more readily than I had thought. Not that other students did not deserve a mark of that caliber, but I do feel as though I added a great deal to the class. I feel that my work, class participation, and consistency should have qualified me for a solid A."

46   When I ignored the e-mail, he pestered me a second time: "I know it's a great pain in the ass to have an A-minus student complain, but I'm starting to wonder about the way grades are given. I would be very curious to know who the A students were. While other students may have outdone me with quiz grades, I made up for it with participation and enthusiasm. I really feel that I deserved an A in your class. If

I was an A-minus student, I assume that you must have handed out a lot of C's and D's. I don't mean to be a pain—I have never contested anything before. I feel strongly about this, though."

47   I shouldn't have done it, but I offered to change the grade. My student was thrilled. He wrote, "With grade inflation being what it is and the levels of competition being so high, students just can't afford to be hurt by small things. I thought that you did a great job with the course."

48   But when I completed the required paperwork, the grade change was rejected by a university official. Though no one questioned me the first time I did it, grades can be changed only if they are computed incorrectly. "How fair is it to change his grade?" an assistant dean asked me. "What about other kids who might be unhappy but didn't complain?"

49   I e-mailed my student to let him know that he would have to live with an A-minus. "The gods who make these decisions tell me that they rejected it because it's not considered fair to all the other students in the class," I wrote. "The grade you got was based on a numerical formula, and you can only change a grade if you made a mathematical error. I'm sorry."

50   "That seems illogical to me," he e-mailed back. "If a student feels that a grade was inappropriate and wishes to contest that grade, that student obviously must contact the person who gave it to them. Who was I supposed to contact? What was the process that I was to follow? The lack of logic in all this never fails to amaze me!"

51   I told him whom to contact. I'm not sure if he ever followed through, but I saw him recently and he smiled and stopped to talk. Nothing was mentioned about the grade.

52   The day before this spring semester's grades were due, I bumped into another professor racing out of the building. "What's the hurry?" I asked.

53   She told me she had just posted her grades and wanted to get off campus fast. But she wasn't quick enough. Within eight minutes, a B-minus student had called to complain.

54   A few hours after I entered my final grades, I got an e-mail from a student, at 1:44 a.m. She was unhappy with her B. She worked so hard, she told me. This time, though, I was prepared. I had the numbers to back me up, and I wouldn't budge on her grade. No more Professor Softie. ◆

CRITICAL THINKING

1. Professor Shepard is shocked that a student would challenge the grade she assigned. Have you ever felt that a grade you received was unfair? If so, did you ask your professor for clarification? Did you challenge the professor to change it? Explain.
2. The author changes one grade after the student challenges the subjective nature of class participation. In your opinion, should class participation be a factor in grade determination? Why or why not?
3. How has electronic grade posting influenced the issue of grade challenging and grade inflation?

4. What are "helicopter parents"? Does it make Shepard's argument more credible when she admits that she is one?
5. In your opinion, what is a "good grade" and why?

CRITICAL WRITING

1. *Persuasive Writing:* Professor Watson notes that many students believe that "working hard" should carry weight when factoring grades. What do you think? Is this a fair system? What is the line between talent and product and effort and earnestness? For example, if writing comes easily to you, and you excel in it, do you deserve a lower grade than someone who works twice as hard but writes half as well?
2. *Personal Narrative:* Write about an experience you had as a student connected to a grade you received in class. It could be about a poor grade you felt you did not deserve or the pressure to earn a grade because of parental influence or looming college admissions.
3. *Persuasive Writing:* How important are grades? Write an essay in which you argue either for or against grading systems in higher education.

GROUP PROJECTS

1. Visit the grade inflation Web site at http://www.gradeinflation.com and review the data on its site. Discuss the issue of grade inflation with your group and what it might mean to the value of grades in general. If your school appears on the Web site, discuss its ranking specifically.
2. Conduct a poll on the issue of grade challenging among your peer group. Create a list of five to seven questions addressing grading (e.g., *Do you think the grading system is fair? What is a good grade? Have you ever challenged a grade and, if so, what grade did you challenge and what was the result?*) After conducting your surveys, gather as a group to discuss the results. Compare your results to the points made by Shepard in her essay.

CULTURE SHOCK

The College Track: Onward and Upward
*Karlyn Bowman**

The average college student of the 1960s was very different from the average college student today. For example, in 1966, almost half of all college-enrolled women said their highest degree would be a bachelor's. In 2007, almost half indicated they intended to go on for their master's. Students expect to do well in school, with 62 percent expecting to carry at least a B average. The charts below describe the plans, proclivities, and politics of college students 40 years ago and today. The current data come from students enrolled in 4-year colleges and is provided by the Institute of Politics at Harvard University.

Academic Advances

Forty years ago, when the data series analyzed here began, just three in ten college freshmen had fathers who had a college education. Now, a majority do. Young college students today have higher education goals than their predecessors did a generation ago. The changes have been particularly dramatic for young women, with a fivefold increase in the number who plan to become doctors and a threefold increase in the number who plan to get a Ph.D.

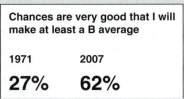

Chances are very good that I will make at least a B average

1971	2007
27%	**62%**

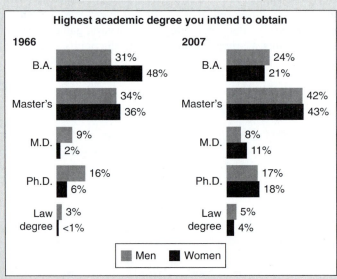

Highest academic degree you intend to obtain

	1966		2007	
	Men	Women	Men	Women
B.A.	31%	48%	24%	21%
Master's	34%	36%	42%	43%
M.D.	9%	2%	8%	11%
Ph.D.	16%	6%	17%	18%
Law degree	3%	<1%	5%	4%

■ Men ■ Women

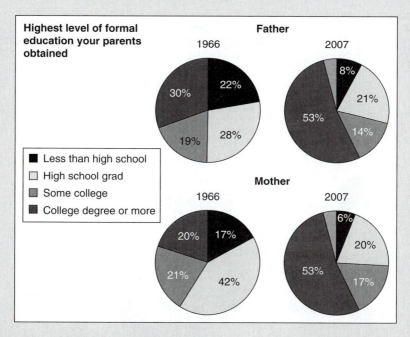

Objectives and Ideology

Over the past 40 years, college freshmen have changed their views about some objectives that will be essential or very important to them. Their ideological views have changed, too. In recent years, the number who consider themselves far left or liberal has risen slightly, as has the smaller number on the conservative or far right. Pluralities describe themselves as middle-of the road.

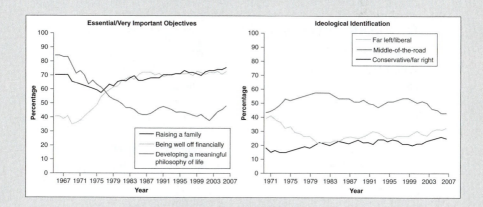

Views and Values

College students' views are unformed on many topics, but on some, such as special preferences in hiring and education, they are strongly defined—in opposition. Also, college students favored Barack Obama over John McCain by significant margins.

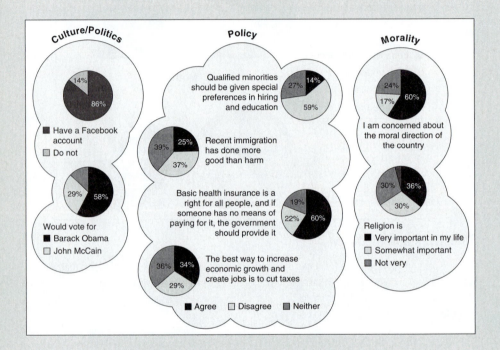

THINKING CRITICALLY

1. Did any of the information on the charts and graphs regarding students' goals, objectives, views, or values surprise you?
2. Based on the information in the charts and graphs here, what social trends can you determine from the data? Can you project what the numbers might look like in another 40 years?
3. In small groups, discuss the results in the "Policy" graph under the "Views and Values" section. Where would you fall on these graphs?
4. Conduct your own survey to see how students compare to the data on the graphs here. What social, political, and economic factors influence the data you collected on your particular campus?

The Disadvantages of an Elite Education
William Deresiewicz*

It used to be that the Ivy League schools represented the best education money could buy. Graduation from such prestigious universities would prepare students to take on leadership roles in business, medicine, education, politics, and law. It may surprise you to read what former English professor and literary critic William Deresiewicz has to say about the quality of an elite education. Deresiewicz points out that these schools isolate students from the wider world, promote class inequality, and fail to encourage students to think for themselves. In short, elite schools fail to do the very thing they profess to do—create visionary leaders.

1   It didn't dawn on me that there might be a few holes in my education until I was about 35. I'd just bought a house, the pipes needed fixing, and the plumber was standing in my kitchen. There he was, a short, beefy guy with a goatee and a Red Sox cap and a thick Boston accent, and I suddenly learned that I didn't have the slightest idea what to say to someone like him. So alien was his experience to me, so unguessable his values, so mysterious his very language, that I couldn't succeed in engaging him in a few minutes of small talk before he got down to work. Fourteen years of higher education and a handful of Ivy League degrees, and there I was, stiff and stupid, struck dumb by my own dumbness. "Ivy retardation," a friend of mine calls this. I could carry on conversations with people from other countries, in other languages, but I couldn't talk to the man who was standing in my own house.

2   It's not surprising that it took me so long to discover the extent of my miseducation, because the last thing an elite education will teach you is its own inadequacy. As two dozen years at Yale and Columbia have shown me, elite colleges relentlessly encourage their students to flatter themselves for being there, and for what being there can do for them. The advantages of an elite education are indeed undeniable. You learn to think, at least in certain ways, and you make the contacts needed to launch yourself into a life rich in all of society's most cherished rewards. To consider that while some opportunities are being created, others are being cancelled and that while some abilities are being developed, others are being crippled is, within this context, not only outrageous but inconceivable.

3   I'm not talking about curricula or the culture wars, the closing or opening of the American mind, political correctness, canon formation, or what have you. I'm talking about the whole system in which these skirmishes play out. Not just the Ivy League and its peer institutions, but also the mechanisms that get you there in the first place: the private and affluent public "feeder" schools, the ever-growing parastructure of tutors and test-prep courses and enrichment programs, the whole admissions frenzy and everything that leads up to and away from it. The message, as always, is the medium. Before, after, and around the elite college classroom, a constellation of values is ceaselessly inculcated.

* William Deresiewicz, *American Scholar*, Summer 2008

4   As globalization sharpens economic insecurity, we are increasingly committing ourselves—as students, as parents, as a society—to a vast apparatus of educational advantage. With so many resources devoted to the business of elite academics and so many people scrambling for the limited space at the top of the ladder, it is worth asking what exactly it is you get in the end—what it is we all get, because the elite students of today, as their institutions never tire of reminding them, are the leaders of tomorrow.

5   The first disadvantage of an elite education, as I learned in my kitchen that day, is that it makes you incapable of talking to people who aren't like you. Elite schools pride themselves on their diversity, but that diversity is almost entirely a matter of ethnicity and race. With respect to class, these schools are largely—indeed increasingly—homogeneous. Visit any elite campus in our great nation and you can thrill to the heartwarming spectacle of the children of white businesspeople and professionals studying and playing alongside the children of black, Asian, and Latino businesspeople and professionals. At the same time, because these schools tend to cultivate liberal attitudes, they leave their students in the paradoxical position of wanting to advocate on behalf of the working class while being unable to hold a simple conversation with anyone in it. Witness the last two Democratic presidential nominees, Al Gore and John Kerry: one each from Harvard and Yale, both earnest, decent, intelligent men, both utterly incapable of communicating with the larger electorate.

6   But it isn't just a matter of class. My education taught me to believe that people who didn't go to an Ivy League or equivalent school weren't worth talking to, regardless of their class. I was given the unmistakable message that such people were beneath me. We were "the best and the brightest," as these places love to say, and everyone else was, well, something else: less good, less bright. I learned to give that little nod of understanding, that slightly sympathetic "Oh," when people told me they went to a less prestigious college. (If I'd gone to Harvard, I would have learned to say "in Boston" when I was asked where I went to school—the Cambridge version of noblesse oblige.) I never learned that there are smart people who don't go to elite colleges, often precisely for reasons of class. I never learned that there are smart people who don't go to college at all. I also never learned that there are smart people who aren't "smart." The existence of multiple forms of intelligence has become commonplace, but however much elite universities like to sprinkle their incoming classes with a few actors or violinists, they select for and develop one form of intelligence: the analytic. While this is broadly true of all universities, elite schools, precisely because their students (and faculty and administrators) possess this one form of intelligence to such a high degree, are more apt to ignore the value of others. One naturally prizes what one most possesses and what most makes for one's advantages. But social intelligence and emotional intelligence and creative ability, to name just three other forms, are not distributed preferentially among the educational elite. The "best" are the brightest only in one narrow sense. One needs to wander away from the educational elite to begin to discover this.

7   What about people who aren't bright in any sense? I have a friend who went to an Ivy League college after graduating from a typically mediocre public high school. One of the values of going to such a school, she once said, is that it teaches

you to relate to all people. Some people are smart in the elite-college way, some are smart in other ways, and some aren't smart at all. It should be embarrassing not to know how to talk to any of them, if only because talking to people is the only real way of knowing them. Elite institutions are supposed to provide a humanistic education, but the first principle of humanism is Terence's: "nothing human is alien to me." The first disadvantage of an elite education is how very much of the human it alienates you from.

8   The second disadvantage, implicit in what I've been saying, is that an elite education inculcates a false sense of self-worth. Getting to an elite college, being at an elite college, and going on from an elite college—all involve numerical rankings: SAT, GPA, GRE. You learn to think of yourself in terms of those numbers. They come to signify not only your fate but your identity; not only your identity but your value. It's been said that what those tests really measure is your ability to take tests, but even if they measure something real, it is only a small slice of the real. The problem begins when students are encouraged to forget this truth, when academic excellence becomes excellence in some absolute sense, when "better at X" becomes simply "better."

9   There is nothing wrong with taking pride in one's intellect or knowledge. There is something wrong with the smugness and self-congratulation that elite schools connive at from the moment the fat envelopes come in the mail. From orientation to graduation, the message is implicit in every tone of voice and tilt of the head, every old-school tradition, every article in the student paper, every speech from the dean. The message is: You have arrived. Welcome to the club. And the corollary is equally clear: You deserve everything your presence here is going to enable you to get. When people say that students at elite schools have a strong sense of entitlement, they mean that those students think they deserve more than other people because their SAT scores are higher.

10   At Yale, and no doubt at other places, the message is reinforced in embarrassingly literal terms. The physical form of the university—its quads and residential colleges, with their Gothic stone façades and wrought-iron portals—is constituted by the locked gate set into the encircling wall. Everyone carries around an ID card that determines which gates they can enter. The gate, in other words, is a kind of governing metaphor—because the social form of the university, as is true of every elite school, is constituted the same way. Elite colleges are walled domains guarded by locked gates, with admission granted only to the elect. The aptitude with which students absorb this lesson is demonstrated by the avidity with which they erect still more gates within those gates, special realms of ever-greater exclusivity—at Yale, the famous secret societies, or as they should probably be called, the open-secret societies, since true secrecy would defeat their purpose. There's no point in excluding people unless they know they've been excluded.

11   One of the great errors of an elite education, then, is that it teaches you to think that measures of intelligence and academic achievement are measures of value in some moral or metaphysical sense. But they're not. Graduates of elite schools are not more valuable than stupid people, or talentless people, or even lazy people. Their pain does not hurt more. Their souls do not weigh more. If I were religious, I would say, God does not love them more. The political implications should be clear. As John Ruskin told an older elite, grabbing what you can get isn't any less wicked when you grab it with the

power of your brains than with the power of your fists. "Work must always be," Ruskin says, "and captains of work must always be. . . . [But] there is a wide difference between being captains . . . of work, and taking the profits of it."

One of the great errors of an elite education, then, is that it teaches you to think that measures of intelligence and academic achievement are measures of value in some moral or metaphysical sense. But they're not.

12   The political implications don't stop there. An elite education not only ushers you into the upper classes; it trains you for the life you will lead once you get there. I didn't understand this until I began comparing my experience, and even more, my students' experience, with the experience of a friend of mine who went to Cleveland State. There are due dates and attendance requirements at places like Yale, but no one takes them very seriously. Extensions are available for the asking; threats to deduct credit for missed classes are rarely, if ever, carried out. In other words, students at places like Yale get an endless string of second chances. Not so at places like Cleveland State. My friend once got a D in a class in which she'd been running an A because she was coming off a waitressing shift and had to hand in her term paper an hour late.

13   That may be an extreme example, but it is unthinkable at an elite school. Just as unthinkably, she had no one to appeal to. Students at places like Cleveland State, unlike those at places like Yale, don't have a platoon of advisers and tutors and deans to write out excuses for late work, give them extra help when they need it, pick them up when they fall down. They get their education wholesale, from an indifferent bureaucracy; it's not handed to them in individually wrapped packages by smiling clerks. There are few, if any, opportunities for the kind of contacts I saw my students get routinely—classes with visiting power brokers, dinners with foreign dignitaries. There are also few, if any, of the kind of special funds that, at places like Yale, are available in profusion: travel stipends, research fellowships, performance grants. Each year, my department at Yale awards dozens of cash prizes for everything from freshman essays to senior projects. This year, those awards came to more than $90,000—in just one department.

14   Students at places like Cleveland State also don't get A−'s just for doing the work. There's been a lot of handwringing lately over grade inflation, and it is a scandal, but the most scandalous thing about it is how uneven it's been. Forty years ago, the average GPA at both public and private universities was about 2.6, still close to the traditional B−/C+ curve. Since then, it's gone up everywhere, but not by anything like the same amount. The average GPA at public universities is now about 3.0, a B; at private universities, it's about 3.3, just short of a B+. And at most Ivy League schools, it is closer to 3.4. But there are always students who don't do the work, or who are taking a class far outside their field (for fun or to fulfill a requirement), or who aren't up to standard to begin with (athletes, legacies). At a school like Yale, students who come to class and work hard expect nothing less than an A−. And most of the time, they get it.

15   In short, the way students are treated in college trains them for the social position they will occupy once they get out. At schools like Cleveland State, they're being trained for positions somewhere in the middle of the class system, in the depths of one bureaucracy or another. They're being conditioned for lives with few second chances,

no extensions, little support, narrow opportunity—lives of subordination, supervision, and control, lives of deadlines, not guidelines. At places like Yale, of course, it's the reverse. The elite like to think of themselves as belonging to a meritocracy, but that's true only up to a point. Getting through the gate is very difficult, but once you're in, there's almost nothing you can do to get kicked out. Not the most abject academic failure, not the most heinous act of plagiarism, not even threatening a fellow student with bodily harm—I've heard of all three—will get you expelled. The feeling is that, by gosh, it just wouldn't be fair—in other words, the self-protectiveness of the old-boy network, even if it now includes girls. Elite schools nurture excellence, but they also nurture what a former Yale graduate student I know calls "entitled mediocrity." A is the mark of excellence; A− is the mark of entitled mediocrity. It's another one of those metaphors, not so much a grade as a promise. It means, don't worry, we'll take care of you. You may not be all that good, but you're good enough.

16   Here, too, college reflects the way things work in the adult world (unless it's the other way around). For the elite, there's always another extension—a bailout, a pardon, a stint in rehab—always plenty of contacts and special stipends—the country club, the conference, the year-end bonus, the dividend. If Al Gore and John Kerry represent one of the characteristic products of an elite education, George W. Bush represents another. It's no coincidence that our current president, the apotheosis of entitled mediocrity, went to Yale. Entitled mediocrity is indeed the operating principle of his administration, but as Enron and WorldCom and the other scandals of the dot-com meltdown demonstrated, it's also the operating principle of corporate America. The fat salaries paid to underperforming CEOs are an adult version of the A−. Anyone who remembers the injured sanctimony with which Kenneth Lay greeted the notion that he should be held accountable for his actions will understand the mentality in question—the belief that once you're in the club, you've got a God-given right to stay in the club. But you don't need to remember Ken Lay, because the whole dynamic played out again last year in the case of Scooter Libby, another Yale man.

17   If one of the disadvantages of an elite education is the temptation it offers to mediocrity, another is the temptation it offers to security. When parents explain why they work so hard to give their children the best possible education, they invariably say it is because of the opportunities it opens up. But what of the opportunities it shuts down? An elite education gives you the chance to be rich—which is, after all, what we're talking about—but it takes away the chance not to be. Yet the opportunity not to be rich is one of the greatest opportunities with which young Americans have been blessed. We live in a society that is itself so wealthy that it can afford to provide a decent living to whole classes of people who in other countries exist (or in earlier times existed) on the brink of poverty or, at least, of indignity. You can live comfortably in the United States as a schoolteacher, or a community organizer, or a civil rights lawyer, or an artist—that is, by any reasonable definition of comfort. You have to live in an ordinary house instead of an apartment in Manhattan or a mansion in L.A.; you have to drive a Honda instead of a BMW or a Hummer; you have to vacation in Florida instead of Barbados or Paris, but what are such losses when set against the opportunity to do work you believe in, work you're suited for, work you love, every day of your life?

18   Yet it is precisely that opportunity that an elite education takes away. How can I be a schoolteacher—wouldn't that be a waste of my expensive education? Wouldn't

I be squandering the opportunities my parents worked so hard to provide? What will my friends think? How will I face my classmates at our 20th reunion, when they're all rich lawyers or important people in New York? And the question that lies behind all these: Isn't it beneath me? So a whole universe of possibility closes, and you miss your true calling.

19   This is not to say that students from elite colleges never pursue a riskier or less lucrative course after graduation, but even when they do, they tend to give up more quickly than others. (Let's not even talk about the possibility of kids from privileged backgrounds not going to college at all, or delaying matriculation for several years, because however appropriate such choices might sometimes be, our rigid educational mentality places them outside the universe of possibility—the reason so many kids go sleepwalking off to college with no idea what they're doing there.) This doesn't seem to make sense, especially since students from elite schools tend to graduate with less debt and are more likely to be able to float by on family money for a while. I wasn't aware of the phenomenon myself until I heard about it from a couple of graduate students in my department, one from Yale, one from Harvard. They were talking about trying to write poetry, how friends of theirs from college called it quits within a year or two while people they know from less prestigious schools are still at it. Why should this be? Because students from elite schools expect success and expect it now. They have, by definition, never experienced anything else, and their sense of self has been built around their ability to succeed. The idea of not being successful terrifies them, disorients them, defeats them. They've been driven their whole lives by a fear of failure—often, in the first instance, by their parents' fear of failure. The first time I blew a test, I walked out of the room feeling like I no longer knew who I was. The second time, it was easier; I had started to learn that failure isn't the end of the world.

20   But if you're afraid to fail, you're afraid to take risks, which begins to explain the final and most damning disadvantage of an elite education: that it is profoundly anti-intellectual. This will seem counterintuitive. Aren't kids at elite schools the smartest ones around, at least in the narrow academic sense? Don't they work harder than anyone else—indeed, harder than any previous generation? They are. They do. But being an intellectual is not the same as being smart. Being an intellectual means more than doing your homework.

21   If so few kids come to college understanding this, it is no wonder. They are products of a system that rarely asked them to think about something bigger than the next assignment. The system forgot to teach them, along the way to the prestige admissions and the lucrative jobs, that the most important achievements can't be measured by a letter or a number or a name. It forgot that the true purpose of education is to make minds, not careers.

22   Being an intellectual means, first of all, being passionate about ideas—and not just for the duration of a semester, for the sake of pleasing the teacher, or for getting a good grade. A friend who teaches at the University of Connecticut once complained to me that his students don't think for themselves. Well, I said, Yale students think for themselves, but only because they know we want them to. I've had many wonderful students at Yale and Columbia, bright, thoughtful, creative kids whom it's been a pleasure to talk with and learn from. But most of them have

seemed content to color within the lines that their education had marked out for them. Only a small minority have seen their education as part of a larger intellectual journey, have approached the work of the mind with a pilgrim soul. These few have tended to feel like freaks, not least because they get so little support from the university itself. Places like Yale, as one of them put it to me, are not conducive to searchers.

23   Places like Yale are simply not set up to help students ask the big questions. I don't think there ever was a golden age of intellectualism in the American university, but in the 19th century, students might at least have had a chance to hear such questions raised in chapel or in the literary societies and debating clubs that flourished on campus. Throughout much of the 20th century, with the growth of the humanistic ideal in American colleges, students might have encountered the big questions in the classrooms of professors possessed of a strong sense of pedagogic mission. Teachers like that still exist in this country, but the increasingly dire exigencies of academic professionalization have made them all but extinct at elite universities. Professors at top research institutions are valued exclusively for the quality of their scholarly work; time spent on teaching is time lost. If students want a conversion experience, they're better off at a liberal arts college.

24   When elite universities boast that they teach their students how to think, they mean that they teach them the analytic and rhetorical skills necessary for success in law or medicine or science or business. But a humanistic education is supposed to mean something more than that, as universities still dimly feel. So when students get to college, they hear a couple of speeches telling them to ask the big questions, and when they graduate, they hear a couple more speeches telling them to ask the big questions. And in between, they spend four years taking courses that train them to ask the little questions—specialized courses, taught by specialized professors, aimed at specialized students. Although the notion of breadth is implicit in the very idea of a liberal arts education, the admissions process increasingly selects for kids who have already begun to think of themselves in specialized terms—the junior journalist, the budding astronomer, the language prodigy. We are slouching, even at elite schools, toward a glorified form of vocational training.

25   Indeed, that seems to be exactly what those schools want. There's a reason elite schools speak of training leaders, not thinkers—holders of power, not its critics. An independent mind is independent of all allegiances, and elite schools, which get a large percentage of their budget from alumni giving, are strongly invested in fostering institutional loyalty. As another friend, a third-generation Yalie, says, the purpose of Yale College is to manufacture Yale alumni. Of course, for the system to work, those alumni need money. At Yale, the long-term drift of students away from majors in the humanities and basic sciences toward more practical ones like computer science and economics has been abetted by administrative indifference. The college career office has little to say to students not interested in law, medicine, or business, and elite universities are not going to do anything to discourage the large percentage of their graduates who take their degrees to Wall Street. In fact, they're showing them the way. The liberal arts university is becoming the corporate university, its center of gravity shifting to technical fields where scholarly expertise can be parlayed into lucrative business opportunities.

26   It's no wonder that the few students who are passionate about ideas find themselves feeling isolated and confused. I was talking with one of them last year about
his interest in the German Romantic idea of *bildung*, the upbuilding of the soul. But,
he said—he was a senior at the time—it's hard to build your soul when everyone
around you is trying to sell theirs.

27   Yet there is a dimension of the intellectual life that lies above the passion for
ideas, though so thoroughly has our culture been sanitized of it that it is hardly surprising if it was beyond the reach of even my most alert students. Since the idea of
the intellectual emerged in the 18th century, it has had, at its core, a commitment to
social transformation. Being an intellectual means thinking your way toward a vision
of the good society and then trying to realize that vision by speaking truth to power.
It means going into spiritual exile. It means foreswearing your allegiance, in lonely
freedom, to God, to country, and to Yale. It takes more than just intellect; it takes
imagination and courage. "I am not afraid to make a mistake," Stephen Dedalus says,
"even a great mistake, a lifelong mistake, and perhaps as long as eternity, too."

28   Being an intellectual begins with thinking your way outside of your assumptions and the system that enforces them. But students who get into elite schools are
precisely the ones who have best learned to work within the system, so it's almost
impossible for them to see outside it, to see that it's even there. Long before they got
to college, they turned themselves into world-class hoop-jumpers and teacher-
pleasers, getting A's in every class no matter how boring they found the teacher or
how pointless the subject, racking up eight or 10 extracurricular activities no matter
what else they wanted to do with their time. Paradoxically, the situation may be better at second-tier schools and, in particular, again, at liberal arts colleges than at the
most prestigious universities. Some students end up at second-tier schools because
they're exactly like students at Harvard or Yale, only less gifted or driven. But others
end up there because they have a more independent spirit. They didn't get straight
A's because they couldn't be bothered to give everything in every class. They concentrated on the ones that meant the most to them or on a single strong extracurricular passion or on projects that had nothing to do with school or even with looking
good on a college application. Maybe they just sat in their room, reading a lot and
writing in their journal. These are the kinds of kids who are likely, once they get to
college, to be more interested in the human spirit than in school spirit, and to think
about leaving college bearing questions, not resumés.

29   I've been struck, during my time at Yale, by how similar everyone looks. You
hardly see any hippies or punks or art-school types, and at a college that was known
in the '80s as the Gay Ivy, few out lesbians and no gender queers. The geeks don't
look all that geeky; the fashionable kids go in for understated elegance. Thirty-two
flavors, all of them vanilla. The most elite schools have become places of a narrow and
suffocating normalcy. Everyone feels pressure to maintain the kind of appearance—
and affect—that go with achievement. (Dress for success, medicate for success.)
I know from long experience as an adviser that not every Yale student is appropriate
and well-adjusted, which is exactly why it worries me that so many of them act that
way. The tyranny of the normal must be very heavy in their lives. One consequence
is that those who can't get with the program (and they tend to be students from poorer

backgrounds) often polarize in the opposite direction, flying off into extremes of disaffection and self-destruction. But another consequence has to do with the large majority who can get with the program. I taught a class several years ago on the literature of friendship. One day we were discussing Virginia Woolf's novel *The Waves*, which follows a group of friends from childhood to middle age. In high school, one of them falls in love with another boy. He thinks, "To whom can I expose the urgency of my own passion? . . . There is nobody—here among these grey arches, and moaning pigeons, and cheerful games and tradition and emulation, all so skillfully organized to prevent feeling alone." A pretty good description of an elite college campus, including the part about never being allowed to feel alone. What did my students think of this, I wanted to know. What does it mean to go to school at a place where you're never alone? Well, one of them said, I do feel uncomfortable sitting in my room by myself. Even when I have to write a paper, I do it at a friend's. That same day, as it happened, another student gave a presentation on Emerson's essay on friendship. Emerson says, he reported, that one of the purposes of friendship is to equip you for solitude. As I was asking my students what they thought that meant, one of them interrupted to say, wait a second, why do you need solitude in the first place? What can you do by yourself that you can't do with a friend?

30 So there they were: one young person who had lost the capacity for solitude and another who couldn't see the point of it. There's been much talk of late about the loss of privacy, but equally calamitous is its corollary, the loss of solitude. It used to be that you couldn't always get together with your friends even when you wanted to. Now that students are in constant electronic contact, they never have trouble finding each other. But it's not as if their compulsive sociability is enabling them to develop deep friendships. "To whom can I expose the urgency of my own passion?": my student was in her friend's room writing a paper, not having a heart-to-heart. She probably didn't have the time; indeed, other students told me they found their peers too busy for intimacy.

31 What happens when busyness and sociability leave no room for solitude? The ability to engage in introspection, I put it to my students that day, is the essential precondition for living an intellectual life, and the essential precondition for introspection is solitude. They took this in for a second, and then one of them said, with a dawning sense of self-awareness, "So are you saying that we're all just, like, really excellent sheep?" Well, I don't know. But I do know that the life of the mind is lived one mind at a time: one solitary, skeptical, resistant mind at a time. The best place to cultivate it is not within an educational system whose real purpose is to reproduce the class system.

32 The world that produced John Kerry and George Bush is indeed giving us our next generation of leaders. The kid who's loading up on AP courses junior year or editing three campus publications while double-majoring, the kid whom everyone wants at their college or law school but no one wants in their classroom, the kid who doesn't have a minute to breathe, let alone think, will soon be running a corporation or an institution or a government. She will have many achievements but little experience, great success but no vision. The disadvantage of an elite education is that it's given us the elite we have and the elite we're going to have. ◆

CRITICAL THINKING

1. In his introduction, William Deresiewicz tells an anecdote about how he was unable to talk with his plumber. Why does Deresiewicz blame his education for why he cannot have a conversation with his plumber?

2. Deresiewicz points out that students at elite schools are taught that not only are they the most intelligent—the "best and brightest"—but that students at other schools are simply not as smart. Respond to this observation with your own view.

3. Are you following an educational path that will give you "the opportunity to do work you believe in, work you're suited for, work you love, every day of your life?" Explain.

4. The author notes that his students have either "lost the capacity for solitude" or can't "see the point of it." Why does he feel it is important to be alone? What is the importance of solitude? Do you agree? Explain.

5. Deresiewicz, himself a former Yale professor, states that "places like Yale are simply not set up to help students ask the big questions." Why does he feel this way about his alma mater? Do you think your school will help you ask "the big questions"? Why or why not?

6. The author is himself a graduate of an elite school. Despite the drawbacks he cites, do you think he would have wanted to go to a less prestigious school? If given the choice, what decision do you think most students would make about which school to attend and why?

CRITICAL WRITING

1. *Reader's Response:* Respond to one or more points in this essay that struck you as noteworthy. Some questions to ponder: Does Deresiewicz adequately reflect your experience in high school and college? Does he understand your generation? Is he justified in being alarmed at what elite colleges are producing? Do elite colleges produce elite snobs? Respond with your point of view.

2. *Exploratory Writing:* Deresiewicz states that "the true purpose of education is to make minds, not careers." Write an essay in which you explore what the true purpose of education is. Is it to develop the mind? To provide the tools for a meaningful career? Both?

3. *Research Writing:* Interview two people, one who graduated from an Ivy League or equivalent elite school and one who graduated from a state school. Create some questions to probe their feelings about the quality of their educations, their school's ability to prepare them to be thinkers, and how their education did or did not help them connect to the world. How did their educational experiences differ? Connecting to points Deresiewicz makes in this essay, write an analysis of your interviews.

GROUP PROJECTS

1. Deresiewicz points out, "For the elite, there's always another extension—a bailout, a pardon, a stint in rehab—always plenty of contacts and special

stipends—the country club, the conference, the year-end bonus, the dividend." The problem, he implies, is that many people entrusted with leadership positions have such a sense of entitlement that they fail to truly understand that actions have consequences. Who else does he identify by name as falling into this trap? With your group, research the careers and scandals of some of the men he names. Did their educations contribute to their failings? To their successes? Why or why not?

2. Make a chart reflecting what should be accomplished or demonstrated in a college class in order to receive an A, B, C, D, or F grade. Does everyone in your group agree with each other? Have you ever received a grade, either higher or lower, that surprised you? How do you think Alicia Shepard, author of "A's for Everyone!" would respond to Deresiewicz's points about grades?

Higher Ed, Inc.
*James Twitchell**

Have the hallowed halls of academia become just one more thing to be bought and sold? Has consumer culture taken over the "ivory tower"? In the next essay, James Twitchell, professor of English and advertising at the University of Florida, explains why he thinks colleges and universities are more interested in brand development than in brain development. In a market in which students are customers and mascots are licensed, has higher education become just one more consumer product?

1   In the early afternoon of December 2, 1964, Mario Savio took off his shoes and climbed onto the hood of a car. Savio was a junior majoring in philosophy at the University of California, Berkeley, and he was upset that the administration of the university had arrested a handful of students and forbidden student groups to set up tables promoting various political and social causes. So he put himself "upon the gears" of the machine:

> If this is a firm, and if the Board of Regents are the board of directors, and if President Kerr in fact is the manager, then I'll tell you something: The faculty are a bunch of employees, and we're the raw material! But we're a bunch of raw material[s] that don't mean to have any process upon us, don't mean to be made into any product, don't mean to end up being bought by some clients of the university, be they the government, be they industry, be they organized labor, be they anyone! We're human beings!

* James Twitchell, *The Wilson Quarterly*, Summer 2004; excerpted from *Branded Nation*, 2004

2   In the four decades since Savio's expression of defiance, Higher Ed, Inc., has become a huge business indeed. And as is typical of absorbent capitalism, it does not deny its struggles so much as market them. Mario Savio died in 1996. To honor his activism and insight, the academic senate at Berkeley agreed to name a set of steps in Sproul Plaza, the site of many political speeches, the Savio Steps. In an interesting bit of corporate assimilation, Savio became a lasting part of his own observations: He himself got branded.

3   Although Mario Savio didn't mention it, the success story of Higher Ed, Inc., is based foursquare on the very transformation that allowed him access to Berkeley. For each generation since World War II, the doors to higher education have opened wider. Unquestionably, university education is the key component in a meritocracy, the *sine qua non* of an open market. A university degree is the stamp that says— whether it's true or not—this kid is educated, qualified, smart. The more prestigious the university, in theory, the smarter the kid. And increased access to university life has succeeded beyond anyone's wildest expectation. In fact, the current dilemma is the price of success. There are too many seats, too much supply, and not enough Marios. The boom is over. Now the marketing begins.

4   Counting everything but its huge endowment holdings, Higher Ed, Inc., is a $250 to $270 billion business—bigger than religion, much bigger than art. And though no one in the business will openly admit it, getting into college is a cinch. The problem, of course, is that too many students want to get into the same handful of nameplate colleges, making it seem that the entire market is tight. It most certainly is not. Here's the crucial statistic: There are about 2,500 four-year colleges in this country, and only about 100 of them refuse more applicants than they accept. Most schools accept 80 percent or more of those who apply. It's the rare student who can't get in somewhere.

5   The explosive growth of Higher Ed, Inc., is evident in increasing enrollments, new construction, expanding statewide university systems, more federal monies, and changes in the professoriate. In the 1950 census, for example, there were 190,000 faculty members. A decade later, shortly before Savio took to the hood of the car, there were 281,000. In 1970, when I entered the ranks, there were 532,000, and in 1998, the latest year for which figures are available from the U.S. Department of Education, some 1,074,000. And remember, what distinguishes the academic world is a lifetime hold on employment. About 70 percent of today's faculty have tenured or tenure-track jobs. Even ministers get furloughed. Museum directors get canned. But make it through the tenure process, and you're set forever.

6   At the turn of the twentieth century, one percent of high school graduates attended college; that figure is now close to 70 percent. This is an industry that produces a yearly revenue flow more than six times the revenue generated by the steel industry. Woe to the state without a special funding program (with the word *merit* in it) that assures middle-class kids who graduate in the upper half of their high school class a pass to State U. College has become what high school used to be, and thanks to grade inflation, it's almost impossible to flunk out.

7   If real estate's motto is "location, location, location," higher education's is "enrollment, enrollment, enrollment." College enrollment hit a record level of 14.5 million in fall 1998, fell off slightly, and then reached a new high of 15.3 million

in 2000. How did this happen, when the qualified applicant pool remained relatively stable? Despite decreases in the traditional college-age population during the 1980s and early 1990s, total enrollment increased because of the high enrollment rate of students who previously had been excluded. What has really helped Higher Ed, Inc., is its ability to open up new markets. Although affirmative action was certainly part of court-mandated fair play, it was also a godsend. It insulated higher education from the market shocks suffered by other cultural institutions. In addition, universities have been able to extend their product line upward, into graduate and professional schools. Another growth market? Foreign students. No one talks about it much, but this market has been profoundly affected by 9/11. Foreign students have stopped coming. There are enough rabbits still in the python that universities haven't been affected yet. But they will be.

8   What makes this enrollment explosion interesting from a marketing point of view is that Savio's observations ("the faculty are a bunch of employees, and we're the raw material") have been confirmed. What he didn't appreciate is that instead of eating up raw material and spitting it out, Higher Ed, Inc., has done something far more interesting. As it has grown, its content has been profoundly changed—dumbed down, some would say. There's a reason for that. At the undergraduate level, it's now in the business of delivering consumer satisfaction.

9   I teach at a large public university, the University of Florida. As I leave the campus to go home, I bike past massive new construction. Here's what's being built: On my distant left, the student union is doubling in size—food court, ballrooms, cineplex, bowling alley, three-story hotel, student legal services and bicycle repair (both free), career counseling, and all manner of stuff that used to belong in the mall, including a store half the size of a football field with a floor devoted to selling what is called spiritware (everything you can imagine with the school logo and mascot), an art gallery, video games, an optical store, a travel agency, a frame store, an outdoor outfitter, and a huge aquarium filled with only orange and blue (the school colors) fish. On a normal day some 20,000 patrons pass through the building. The student union is looking eerily like a department store. So is the university.

10   On my immediate left, I pass the football stadium. One side of it is being torn apart to add a cluster of skyboxes. Skyboxes are a valuable resource, as they are almost pure profit. The state is not paying for them. The athletic department is. They will be rented mainly to corporations to allow their VIPs air-conditioned splendor high above the hoi polloi. The skyboxes have granite countertops, curved ceilings, and express elevators. In a skybox, you watch the football game on television. Better yet, the skyboxes allow what's forbidden to the groundlings: alcohol. How expensive are these splendid aeries? There are 347 padded, 21-inch seats in the Bull Gator Deck. They'll run you $14,000 a person, and you get only four games in the box. For the other four, you're in the stands. Don't worry about doing the math. The boxes are already sold out. I teach in a huge building that looks like the starship Enterprise. It houses classrooms and faculty offices and cost $10 million when it was built a few years ago. These skyboxes and some club seats are coming in at $50 million. Everyone agrees, the skyboxes are a good idea. They'll make money. Better yet, they'll build the brand.

11   Across from the football stadium, at the edge of the campus on my right, is the future of my institution. I pass an enormous new building with a vast atrium of aggressively wasted space. This building houses the headquarters of the University of Florida Foundation. The foundation funnels millions of dollars of private money the state will never know about into and through various parts of the university. I don't complain. No one does. Two decades ago, the foundation gave nothing to the English department; now, about a hundred grand a year comes our way. In front of the foundation, where a statue of some illustrious donor or beloved professor would stand at an elite school, is a bronze statue of the athletic department's trademarked mascots, Albert and Alberta Alligator.

12   On this side of campus, enrollment, enrollment, enrollment is becoming endowment, endowment, endowment. Americans donate more money to higher education than to any other cause except religion. And Florida, with its millions of retirees looking for "memorial opportunities," is a cash cow just waiting for the farmer's gentle hands. The residents of Florida have almost no interest in funding education, especially not K–12 education, which really is in dire shape. But there are wads of money to fund bits and pieces of the campus in exchange for good feelings and occasional naming rights.

13   American colleges and universities raise about $25 billion a year from private sources. Public universities are new to this game, but they've learned that it's where the action is. Private dollars now account for about 30 percent of the University of Illinois' annual budget, about 20 percent of Berkeley's, and about 10 percent of Florida's. In a sense, tuition-paying undergrads are now the loss leaders in the enterprise. What used to be the knowledge business has become the business of selling an experience, an affiliation, a commodity that can be manufactured, packaged, bought, and sold. Don't misunderstand. The intellectual work of universities is still going on and has never been stronger. Great creative acts still occur, and discoveries are made. But the experience of higher education, all the accessories, the amenities, the aura, has been commercialized, outsourced, franchised, branded. The professional manager has replaced the professor as the central figure in delivering the goods.

Elite schools are no longer in the traditional education business. What they offer is just one more thing that you shop for, one more thing you consume, one more story you tell and are told. It's no accident that you hear students talking about how much the degree costs and how much it's worth.

14   From a branding point of view, what happens in the classroom is beside the point. I mean that literally. The old image of the classroom as fulfillment of the Socratic ideal is no longer even invoked. Higher Ed, Inc., is more like a sawmill. A few years ago, Harvard University started a small department called the Instructional Computing Group, which employs several people to videotape about 30 courses a semester. Although it was intended for students who unavoidably missed class, it soon became a way not to attend class. Any enrolled student could attend on the Web, fast-forwarding through all the dull parts. This is "distance education" from a dorm room, at an advertised $37,928 a year.

15   Elite schools are no longer in the traditional education business. They are in the sponsored research and edutainment business. What they offer is just one more thing that you shop for, one more thing you consume, one more story you tell and are told. It's no accident that you hear students talking about how much the degree costs and how much it's worth. That's very much how the schools themselves talk as they look for new sources of research or developmental funding. In many schools there's even a period called "shopping around," in which the student attends as many classes as possible looking for a "fit," almost like channel surfing.

16   So we do college as we do lunch or do shopping or do church. That's because for most students in the upper-tier schools, the real activity is getting in and then continuing on into the professional schools. No one cares what's taught in grades 13–16. How many times have I heard my nonacademic friends complain that there's no coherence in the courses their kids are exposed to? Back in the 1950s, introductory courses used the same textbooks, not just intramurally but extramurally. So Introduction to Writing (freshman English) used the same half-dozen handbooks all across the country. No longer. The writing courses are a free-for-all. Ditto the upper-level courses. Here are some subjects my department covers in what used to be English 101, the vanilla composition course: attitudes toward marriage, business, best sellers, carnivals, computer games, fashion, horror films, The Simpsons, homophobia, living arrangements, rap music, soap operas, Elvis, sports, theme parks, AIDS, play, and the ever-popular marginalization of this or that group.

17   But cries that the classroom is being dumbed down or politicized miss the point. Hardly anyone in Higher Ed, Inc., cares about what is taught, because that is not our charge. We are not in the business of transmitting what E. D. Hirsch would call cultural literacy; nor are we in the business of teaching the difference between the right word and the almost right word, as Mark Twain might have thought important. We're in the business of creating a total environment, delivering an experience, gaining satisfied customers, and applying the "smart" stamp when they head for the exits. The classroom reflects this. Our real business is being transacted elsewhere on campus.

18   The most far-reaching changes in postsecondary education are not seen on the playing fields or in the classroom or even in the admissions office. They're inside the administration, in an area murkily called "development." If you don't believe it, enter the administration building of any school that enrolls more than 10,000 students (10 percent of campuses of that size or larger now account for a shade less than 50 percent of all students) and ask for the university development office. You'll notice how, on this part of the campus, the carpets are thick, the wainscoting is polished, and the lights are dimmed. Often, the development office has a new name picked up from the corporate model. Sometimes it's hidden inside Public Affairs, or, more commonly, Public Relations. My favorite: University Advancement. The driving force at my university is now the University of Florida Foundation.

19   Development is both PR and fundraising, the intersection of getting the brand out and the contributions in, and daily it becomes more crucial. That's because schools like mine have four basic revenue streams: student tuition, research funding, public (state) support, and private giving. The least important is tuition; the most prestigious is external research dollars; the most fickle is state support; and the most remunerative is what passes through the development office. Leaf through the

Chronicle of Higher Education, the weekly journal of the industry, and you'll see how much newsprint is devoted to the comings and goings of development. Consider where the development office is housed on most campuses, often right beside the president's office, and note how many people it employs.

20   At many schools, there's also a buried pipeline that connects the development office with the admissions office. Most academic administrators prefer that it be buried deep, but from time to time someone digs it up. In the *Wall Street Journal* for February 3, 2003, Daniel Golden reported on how the formal practice of giving preference to students whose parents are wealthy—called "development admits"—has profound implications not just for affirmative action but for the vaunted academic ideal of fair play.

21   Remember the scene in the third season of *The Sopranos*, when Carmella has a lunch meeting with the dean of Columbia University's undergraduate school? She thinks the lunch is about her daughter, Meadow, but the dean wants a little development money. Carmella listens to his charming patter before being hit with the magic number of $50,000. She goes to Tony, who protests that the Ivy League is extorting them and says he won't give more than five G's. But the dean eventually gets his 50 G's; Tony, the consummate shakedown artist, has met his match.

22   When enrollments began to escalate in the 1960s, what used to be a pyramid system—with rich, selective schools at the top (read Ivy League and a handful of other elites) and then a gradation downward through increasing supply and decreasing rigor to junior and community college systems at the base—became an hourglass lying on its side. There's now a small bubble of excellent small schools on one side (Ivy League schools qualify as small) that are really indistinguishable, and, on the other, a big bubble of huge schools of varying quality. The most interesting branding is occurring on the small-bubble side, as premier schools vie for dominance, but the process is almost exactly the same, although less intense, for the big suppliers.

23   Good schools have little interest in the bachelor's degree. In fact, the better the school, the less important the terminal undergraduate degree. The job of the student is to get in, and the job of the elite school is to get the student out into graduate school. The schools certify students as worthy of further education, in law, medicine, the arts, or business.

24   Premier schools have to separate their students from the rest of the pack by generating a story about how special they are. We have the smart ones, they say. That's why they care little about such hot-button issues as grade inflation, teaching quality, student recommendations, or even the curriculum. It's not in their interest to tarnish the brand by drawing distinctions among their students. These schools essentially let the various tests—LSAT, MCAT, GRE—make the distinctions for them. And, if you notice, they never divulge how well their students do on those tests to the outside world. They have this information, but they keep it to themselves. They're not stupid; they have to protect the brand for incoming consumers, because that's where they really compete.

25   In one of the few candid assessments of the branding of Higher Ed, Inc., Robert L. Woodbury, former chancellor of the University of Maine system, noted the folly of the current institutional *U.S. News and World Report* rankings:

> When Consumer Reports rates and compares cars, it measures them on the basis of categories such as performance, safety, reliability, and value. It tries to measure "outputs"—in short, what the car does. U.S. News mostly looks at

"inputs" (money spent, class size, test scores of students, degrees held by faculty), rather than assessing what the college or university actually accomplishes for students over the lives of their enrollment. If Consumer Reports functioned like U.S. News, it would rank cars on the amount of steel and plastic used in their construction, the opinions of competing car dealers, the driving skills of customers, the percentage of managers and sales people with MBAs, and the sticker price on the vehicle (the higher, the better).

26   The emphasis on "inputs" explains why the elite schools aren't threatened by what others fear: the much-ballyhooed "click" universities, such as the University of Phoenix and Sylvan Learning Systems, because those schools generate no peer effects. So, too, there's no threat from corporate universities, such as those put together by Microsoft, Motorola, and Ford, or even from the Open University of England and the Learning Annex. The industrial schools have not yet made their presence felt, though they will. The upper tier on the small side of the hourglass is not threatened by "learning at a distance" or "drive-through schools," because the elites are not as concerned with learning as they are with maintaining selectivity at the front door and safe passage to still-higher education at the back door.

27   So what's it like at the upper end among the deluxe brand-name schools, where Harry Winston competes with Tiffany, where Louis Vuitton elbows Prada, where Lexus dukes it out with Mercedes? In a word, it's brutal, an academic arms race.

28   How did the competition become so intense? Until 1991, the Ivy League schools and the Massachusetts Institute of Technology met around a conference table each April to fix financial aid packages for students who had been admitted to more than one school. That year, after the Justice Department sued the schools, accusing them of antitrust violations, the universities agreed to stop the practice. As happened with Major League Baseball after television contracts made the teams rich, bidding pandemonium broke out. Finite number of players + almost infinite cash = market bubble. Here's the staggering result: Over the past three decades, tuition at the most select schools has increased fivefold, nearly double the rate of inflation. Yet precious few students pay the full fare. The war is fought over who gets in and how much they're going to have to be paid to attend.

29   The fact of the matter is that the cost of tuition has become unimportant in the Ivy League. Like grade inflation, it's uncontrollable—and hardly anyone in Higher Ed, Inc., really cares. As with other luxury providers, the higher the advertised price, the longer the line. The other nifty irony is that, among elite schools, the more the consumer pays for formal education (or at least is charged), the less of it he or she gets. The mandated class time necessary to qualify for a degree is often less at Stanford than at State U. As a general rule, the better the school, the shorter the week. At many good schools, the weekend starts on Thursday.

30   Ask almost anyone in the education industry what's the most overrated brand and they'll tell you "Harvard." It's one of the most timid and derivative schools in the country, yet it has been able to maintain a reputation as the über-brand. Think of any important change in higher education, and you can bet (1) that it didn't originate at Harvard, and (2) that if it's central to popular recognition, Harvard now owns it. Why is Harvard synonymous with the *ne plus ultra*? Not because of what comes out of the place but because of what goes in: namely, the best students, the most

contributed money, and, especially, the deepest faith in the brand. Everyone knows that Harvard is the most selective university, with a refusal rate of almost 90 percent. But more important, the school is obscenely rich, with an endowment of almost $20 billion. Remember that number. It's key to the brand. The endowment is greater than the assets of the Dell computer company, the gross domestic product of Libya, the net worth of all but five of the Forbes 400, or the holdings of every nonprofit in the world except the Roman Catholic Church.

31   In a marketing sense, the value of the endowment is not monetary but psychological: Any place with that many zeros after the dollar sign has got to be good. The huge endowments of the nameplate schools force other schools, the second-tier schools, to spend themselves into penury. So your gift to Harvard does more harm than good to the general weal of Higher Ed, Inc. It does, however, maintain the Harvard brand.

32   With the possible exception of Harvard, the best schools are about as interchangeable as the second-tier ones. All premier schools have essentially the same teaching staff, the same student amenities, the same library books, the same wondrous athletic facilities, the same carefully trimmed lawns, the same broadband connection lines in the dorms. Look at the Web sites for the most selective schools, and you'll see almost exactly the same images irrespective of place, supposed mission, et cetera. True, they may attempt to slide in some attention-getting fact ("If you use our library, you may notice our Gutenberg Bible," or "The nuclear accelerator is buried beneath the butterfly collection"), but by and large, the Web sites are like the soap aisle at Safeway.

33   If you really want evidence of the indistinguishability of the elites, consider the so-called viewbook, the newest marketing tool sent to prospective applicants. The viewbook is a glossy come-on, bigger than a prospectus and smaller than a catalog, that sets the brand. As with the Web sites, what you see in almost every view is a never-ending loop of smiling faces of diverse backgrounds, classrooms filled with eager beavers, endless falling leaves in a blue-sky autumn, lush pictures of lacrosse, squash, and rugby (because football, basketball, and baseball are part of the mass-supplier brands), and a collection of students whose interests are just like yours. From a branding point of view, the viewbook is additionally interesting because it illustrates how repeating a claim is the hallmark of undifferentiated producers. Here's what Nicolaus Mills, an American studies professor at Sarah Lawrence College, found a decade ago, just as the viewbook was starting to become standardized. Every school had the same sort of glossy photographs proving the same claim of diversity:

34   "Diversity is the hallmark of the Harvard/Radcliffe experience," the first sentence in the Harvard University register declares. "Diversity is the virtual core of University life," the University of Michigan bulletin announces. "Diversity is rooted deeply in the liberal arts tradition and is key to our educational philosophy," Connecticut College insists. "Duke's 5,800 undergraduates come from regions which are truly diverse," the Duke University bulletin declares. "Stanford values a class that is both ethnically and economically diverse," the Stanford University bulletin notes.

35   Brown University says, "When asked to describe the undergraduate life at the college—and particularly their first strongest impression of Brown as freshmen—students consistently bring up the same topic: the diversity of the student body."

36   In this kind of marketing, Higher Ed, Inc., is like the crowd in Monty Python's *Life of Brian*. Graham Chapman as Brian, the man mistaken for the Messiah, exhorts a crowd of devotees: "Don't follow me! Don't follow anyone! Think for yourselves! You are all individuals!" To which the crowd replies in perfect unison, "Yes, Master, we are all individuals. We are all individuals. We are all individuals."

37   The elite schools have to produce an entering class that's not just the best and brightest they can gather, but one that will demonstrate an unbridgeable quality gap between themselves and other schools. They need this entering class because it's precisely what they will sell to the next crop of consumers. It's the annuity that gives them financial security. In other words, what makes Higher Ed, Inc., unlike other American industries is that its consumer value is based almost entirely on who is consuming the product. At the point of admissions, the goal is not money. The goal is to publicize who's getting in. That's the product. Who sits next to you in class generates value.

38   So it's to the advantage of a good school to exploit the appearance of customer merit, not customer need. But how to pay for this competitive largesse if tuition is not the income spigot? At four-year private colleges and universities, fully three-quarters of all undergraduates get aid of some sort. In fact, 44 percent of all "dependent" students, a technical term that refers to young, single undergraduates with annual family incomes of $100,000 or less, get aid. What elite schools lose on tuition they recover elsewhere. Take Williams College, for example. The average school spends about $11,000 a student and takes in $3,500 in tuition and fees; Williams, a superbrand, spends about $75,000 per student and charges, after accounting for scholarships and other items, a net of $22,000. Why? Because Williams figures that to maintain its brand value, to protect its franchise, it can superdiscount fees and make up the difference with the cash that's to come in the future. In theory, if an elite school could get the right student body, it would be in its best interest to give the product away: no tuition in exchange for the very best students. (That's a policy not without risk, as Williams found last year when Moody's lowered its credit rating, because the college had dipped too deeply into endowment to fund its extraordinary incoming class.)

39   How does the brand sensitivity of the elite institutions affect the quality of the educational experience for the rest of us? How dangerous is it that schools follow the corporate model of marketing? The prestige school has other money pots than tuition. Every two weeks, for example, Harvard's endowment throws off enough cash to cover all undergraduate tuition. But what happens to schools below the privileged top tier? They, too, have to discount their sticker prices to maintain perceived value. So competition at the top essentially raises costs everywhere, though only some schools have pockets deep enough to afford the increase. The escalation in competitive amenities is especially acute in venues where a wannabe school is next to an elite one.

40   Things get worse the further you move from the top. To get the students it needs to achieve a higher ranking in annual surveys—and thereby draw better students, who boost external giving, which finances new projects, raises salaries, and increases the endowment needed for getting better students, who'll win the institution a higher national ranking, which . . . et cetera—the second-tier school must perpetually treat students as transient consumers.

41   Really good schools have all those so-called competitive amenities, all those things that attract students but have nothing to do with their oft-stated lofty mission and often get little use—Olympic-quality gyms, Broadway-style theaters, personal trainers, glitzy student unions with movie theaters, and endless playing fields, mostly covered with grass, not athletes. This marketing madness is now occurring among the mass superinstitutions. So the University of Houston has a $53 million wellness center with a five-story climbing wall; Washington State University has the largest Jacuzzi on the West Coast (it holds 53 students); Ohio State University is building a $140 million complex featuring batting cages, ropes courses, and the now-essential climbing wall; and the University of Southern Mississippi is planning a full-fledged water park. These schools, according to Moody's, are selling billions of dollars of bonds for construction that has nothing whatsoever to do with education. It's all about branding.

42   The commercialization of higher education has had many salutary effects: wider access, the dismantling of discriminatory practices, increased breadth and sophistication in many fields of research, and an intense, often refreshing, concern about customer relations. But consider other consequences for a place such as the University of Florida, which is a typical mass-provider campus. To get the student body we need for a respectable spot in the national rankings, we essentially give the product away. We have no choice. Other states will take our best students if we don't. Ivy League monies come from endowment and have the promise of being replenished if the school retains its reputation. But state universities are heavily dependent on the largesse of state legislatures, and to keep the money coming, they need to be able to boast about their ability to attract the state's best and brightest. So about half of them have been sucked into simple-minded plans that are essentially a subvention of education for middle-class kids. Everyone admits that most of these kids would go to college anyway. But would they go to the state system? Who wants to find out the hard way?

43   Mario Savio was right. Before all else, the modern university is a business selling a branded product. "The Age of Money has reshaped the terrain of higher education," writes David Kirp, of the Goldman School of Public Policy at the University of California, Berkeley. "Gone, except in the rosy reminiscences of retired university presidents, is any commitment to maintaining a community of scholars, an intellectual city on a hill, free to engage critically with the conventional wisdom of the day. The hoary call for a 'marketplace of ideas' has turned into a double-entendre."

44   Administrators and the professoriate have not just allowed this transformation of the academy, they've willingly, often gleefully, collaborated in it. The results have not been all bad. But the fact is that we've gone from artisanal guild to department store, from gatekeeper to ticket taker, from page turner to video clicker. This commodification, selling out, commercialization, corporatization—whatever you want to call it—is what happens when marketing becomes an end, not a means.

45   Universities are making money by lending their names to credit card companies, selling their alumni lists, offering their buildings for "naming rights," and extending their campuses to include retirement communities and graveyards. It's past time for the participants in Higher Ed, Inc., to recall what Savio said years ago: The university is being industrialized not by outside forces but by internal ones. Rather like the child who, after murdering his parents, asks for leniency because he's an orphan, universities grown plump feeding at the commercial trough now

complain that they've been victimized by the market. This contention of victimization is, of course, a central part of the modern Higher Ed, Inc., brand. The next words you'll hear will be "Please give. We desperately need your support!" ◆

CRITICAL THINKING

1. How does the story of Mario Savio help set up Twitchell's argument? Does it draw in his audience? Explain.
2. Twitchell describes his campus at the University of Florida. Based on his description, do you think he approves of the recent changes and the new additions? How might students view the renovations? How does your own campus compare to his description?
3. What does Twitchell mean when he says, "At the undergraduate level, [colleges are] in the business of delivering customer satisfaction." Who are the customers? How do colleges aim to satisfy them? Does this aim run counter to the purpose of a college education? Why or why not?
4. What role does "development" play in higher education? Do you think Twitchell approves of it? Explain.
5. In your opinion, do you think your own college has become too commercialized? Can you think of any examples that demonstrate the commercialization of your institution?
6. Twitchell asserts that "hardly anyone in Higher Ed., Inc., cares about what is taught." Do you think other professors would agree? Administrators? Students? Explain.
7. What is the meaning of the title of Twitchell's essay? How does it apply to his primary points?
8. According to Robert Woodbury, what is wrong with the way *U.S. News and World Report* ranks colleges?
9. Why has the cost of an undergraduate education become "unimportant" to Ivy League schools and many top ranking universities? Explain.
10. How are students in today's colleges both the consumer and the product?

CRITICAL WRITING

1. *Descriptive and Analytical Writing:* Twitchell observes that Harvard is the "über-brand" and that it devotes a great deal of effort into promoting its brand. Describe the "brand" of your own college or university. Include colors, mascots, taglines, and messages given to students and alumni. What does your brand say about your school? About its students? What message does it project to encourage new students to apply and attend?
2. *Expository Writing:* In your opinion, do you think college has become too commercialized? Why or why not?
3. *Expository Writing:* Twitchell notes that the goal of many elite colleges is to get their undergraduates into graduate school. Is an undergraduate education merely a pit stop along the way to graduate school? What plans do you have after graduation? Do you plan to earn an advanced degree? Why or why not?

4. *Personal Narrative:* What attracted you to the college you now attend? Was it its history? Because your relatives went there? Location? Great sports teams? An attractive financial package? Academic reputation? Describe your personal reasons for choosing your particular school.

GROUP PROJECTS

1. With your group, research at least six peer institutions by visiting their Web sites and reading the "about" pages that outline the school's mission. How are they similar and different? Are they, as Twitchell implies, pretty much the same across the board? How do the mission statements and viewbook points compare to those of your own institution? Discuss.
2. As a group, review the college "brands" below for several colleges and universities. What do you know about these schools? How much of what you know hinges on the school's PR efforts and its branding? In what ways are these logos unique, and in what ways are they similar? Do they convey any meaning to nonalumni? Do they resonate with alumni and students? What elements are important to a good college logo?
3. After discussing these logos—as well as the logo of your own school, if it does not appear below—create a new logo for your school. If you like your current logo, explain why you would not change it.

Northeastern University

Notre Dame University

University of Florida

University of Arkansas

Duke University

University of Connecticut

Just Let Go Already

Joe Queenan*

The departure for college stirs many pangs of fear in the hearts of parents. They worry whether their children will fit in and be happy, safe, and supported. They hope their children study, enjoy their chosen majors, and achieve academic success. But are today's parents too involved in the lives of their college-bound children? In the next essay, author Joe Queenan takes a humorous look at helicopter parenting.

1   On January 1, 1971, as Notre Dame was hijacking the Texas Longhorns' undefeated season in the Cotton Bowl, I telephoned my father to discuss this sublime development. At the time I was a senior at St. Joseph's College, on a tiny Philadelphia campus with no football program. My father, for his part, was a high school dropout who worked as a security guard.

2   About the only thing we had in common was Notre Dame football: he, because of what the team symbolized to despised Irish-Americans during his youth; me, because Notre Dame usually won its games. Waxing poetic, we agreed that the Fighting Irish were the very finest of fellows, that the peculiarly symbiotic relationship between the pigskin and the Holy Grail had again produced a rapturous triumph of good over evil, North over South, Notre Dame over Texas, Us over Them.

3   In short, God was in his heaven and all was right with the world.

4   If memory serves me correctly, that was the only time I had a telephone conversation with my father during my four years of college. Chitchat was never part of his repertory. Moreover, I didn't even have a phone on which he could reach me. But also, college was a place you went to with the specific intention of getting away from your parents.

5   There were other reasons we rarely talked on the phone.

6   Only recently has America become a nation in which college-educated parents raise college-educated children; back in my era, parents and children were often separated by a vast cultural divide. My father had no frame of reference for my collegiate experience. He had no real interest in it, and he certainly wasn't going to call me out of the blue to inquire about the moldy smell emanating from the heating unit in my dorm, or the quality of the school infirmary, much less the nautical imagery in "Hamlet." The entire time I was at St. Joseph's, roughly 10 miles across Philadelphia from our home, he never came to visit.

> *Thanks to an inexpensive cell phone program that encourages the entire family to stay in touch in countless situations where communication is neither necessary nor desirable, I talk to my children all the time.*

7   This was not a helicoptering parent. How different my experience is with my own children. Thanks to an inexpensive cell phone program that encourages the entire family to stay in touch in countless situations where communication is

* Joe Queenan, *New York Times*, January 8, 2006

neither necessary nor desirable, I talk to my children all the time. I talk to them about cell death, the reign of Vespasian, the faded splendors of Babylon, the oxymoron "Ivy League football."

8   I talk to them about surrealism, Boston's deceptively unpleasant climate, the gradual but inexorable ravishing of the Amish countryside. I talk to them about their grandmother's health, their aunt's persistent orthodontic problems, the McMansions being built by the McParvenus down the street. And in the desperately anachronistic way that baby boomers try to keep on top of things that have long since passed them by, I talk to them about Nine Inch Nails, Garbage, Weezer, Fifty Cent and, yes, even the fabulously insignificant Fountains of Wayne.

9   None of these conversations are even vaguely necessary. Especially the one about Weezer. One night I called my 21-year-old daughter, a senior majoring in biochemistry at Harvard, to ask her why bananas turn brown. Another night I asked her to explain Coldplay. Reciprocating, she phoned at 9 o'clock one Friday morning to express her disappointment at the way "Tender Is the Night" simply peters out at the end.

10   This discussion immediately assumed its place in the category "Conversations I never had at 9 a.m. with my father."

11   This got me to thinking about what life would have been like back in the '60s and early '70s if my parents could have reached me any hour of the day or night by cell phone, as I can with my children, and if they had resembled the obsessive, meddlesome, intrusive, logorrheic parents of the present era, who are determined to be best friends with their progeny, insisting on nonstop telephone contact, as I do.

Dad: Hey, dude. What's happening?

Me: Well, Friday I've got tickets for Emerson, Lake & Palmer and Big Brother & the Holding Company. Then I'm going to hear Crosby, Stills & Nash, Lothar & the Hand People, Country Joe & the Fish, Pacific Gas & Electric, and at least one other band that has an ampersand in its name.

Dad: Far out.

Me: Next Saturday the whole school is going down to Washington to levitate the Pentagon and bring the running capitalist dogs and their boot-licking lackeys to their knees.

Dad: Wish I could be there, if only to see Norman Mailer.

Me: It's really just an excuse for a free trip to Washington. It's more about sex, drugs, and alcohol than politics.

Dad: Okay, I'll send you some money for condoms. And let me know if you score any good reefer. By the way, how's school?

Me: School is groovy. I stayed up all night reading Carlos Castaneda, Frantz Fanon, and Hermann Hesse.

Dad: Funny, we were thinking of buying you *The Teachings of Don Juan* and *The Wretched of the Earth* for Christmas. Guess we'll have to stick with *Soul on Ice*. Let me put your mother on.

Mom: Your father said you're going to levitate the Pentagon this weekend. Aren't you concerned about the pigs?

Me: A little, but an army prepared to kill is no match for an army prepared to die. Besides, if you're not part of the solution, you're part of the problem.

Mom: Power to the people!
Me: Right on.
Mom: Call you tomorrow. If you can't be with the one you love, love the one you're with.

12   That conversation never took place. Nor should it have. The whole point of going to college is to quietly slip out of your parents' orbit forever while surreptitiously extricating as much cash as humanly possible. There is nothing wrong with liking your children, or even with liking your parents. But constantly invading their privacy in an unwholesomely chummy fashion is a sign of emotional stuntedness, perhaps even incipient madness.

13   Occasionally, I think about deep-sixing the cell phone entirely, but then I come to my senses and realize that it is useful in emergencies, like when my son needs my credit card number to buy Final Fantasy XXIII. But I have decided to make a serious effort to limit my calls to essential conversations, and I am encouraging my children to do the same.

14   For example, one Monday in November, shortly before midnight, my son called to express his disbelief that Donovan McNabb had thrown a season-wrecking interception with less than three minutes to go in a pivotal game against the Dallas Cowboys. Shortly thereafter, my daughter called to make sure I still had a pulse.

15   As I said: Only call in case of a real emergency. ◆

CRITICAL THINKING

1. What are "helicopter parents"? Do you have helicopter parents or know someone who does? In your opinion, are such parents helpful, or do they hinder students' ability to become full-fledged adults?
2. Is Queenan a "helicopter parent"? Does he fear he could be?
3. On the one hand, Queenan implies that helicopter parenting is invasive and prevents adult children from separating from parents. On the other, he seems pleased with the connection he has with his own children. What view do you think he has on this issue? What do you think?
4. How involved are your parents in your college experience? Did they help you choose a school? A major? Have they intervened in college disputes or issues? Do you discuss your college experiences with them regularly? Do you ever find them intrusive? Explain.

CRITICAL WRITING

1. *Personal Narrative:* Write about your personal relationship with your parents. How involved were/are they with your personal and academic life? How often do you call them, or they call you? Would you like more or less contact?
2. *Research Writing:* Queenan notes the differences between his relationship with his parents (he didn't have a phone) to that of his relationship with his own kids (who call him daily). How different is the college experience

for students today. Research of the American college system. Select a time period (1950s, 1970s) and research this era of the American college experience in greater depth. Then write an essay comparing the modern system, of which you are a participant, to that of the era you researched. Would you have rather gone to college in the time period you researched? Why or why not?

GROUP PROJECT

1. As a group, research the term "helicopter parent." Discuss what the correct balance should be for parents and their college-age children. While the media seem to be critical of helicopter parents, this form of interaction with children seems to be more prevalent, especially with the connectivity cell-phones and email provide the current generation. There is even some evidence that high-parental involvement may have benefits. Share your own experiences with each other, and then discuss the pros and cons of parental involvement in the lives of college students today.

VIEWPOINTS

► **Welcome to the Fun-Free University**
David Weigel

► ***Animal House* at 30: O Bluto, Where Art Thou?**
Eric Hoover

Many students arrive on campus eager to learn and equally eager to party. This chapter's Viewpoints section explores the issue of personal responsibility on campus. If college students are truly adults, do they need college administrators acting *in loco parentis*—like parents, controlling what they decide to do outside the classroom? With personal freedom comes responsibility. Are students expecting college to be an educational experience that will prepare them for the real world, or are they expecting merely a fun time? The readings in this section consider the nuances of college life—what students might expect and what the university expects in return.

Until the 1960s, the concept of colleges acting in the place of a parent was a generally accepted practice. But many students of the 1960s objected to controls that they felt were unfair violations of their rights as adults. For almost 30 years, colleges allowed students to assume personal responsibility for their actions, but in the wake of alcohol-related student deaths, unhealthy habits, and even medical conditions leading to suicide, many colleges are rethinking their hands-off approach. First, David Weigel challenges that the return of *in loco parentis* is killing student freedom. A new graduate from Northwestern University at the time he wrote this essay in 2004, Weigel wonders if the rights his parents' generation fought so hard for in the 1960s are slowly being whittled away for students today.

In 1998, Congress amended Section 444 of the General Education Provisions Act by adding Section 952, Alcohol or Drug Possession Disclosure: "Nothing in this Act or the Higher Education Act of 1965 shall be construed to prohibit an institution of higher education from disclosing, to a parent or legal guardian of a student, information regarding any violation of any federal, state, or local law, or of any rule or policy of the institution, governing the use or possession of alcohol or a controlled substance. . . ." Referring to this provision, some college administrators warn students that their parents will be contacted if they are caught drinking alcohol or if they are deemed intoxicated by campus security. Does notification reduce alcohol abuse? Eric Hoover explores both sides of this issue in his essay, "*Animal House* at 30: O Bluto, Where Art Thou?".

 # Welcome to the Fun-Free University
*David Weigel**

1   In April 1968, student activists at Columbia University schemed to take over the dean's office as a protest against the Vietnam War and plans to build a new gym. More than 700 students were arrested, and the uprising won national attention. But the school's buttoned-up administrators hadn't wanted to involve the police, and the rioters eventually were allowed to graduate. The mayor of New York, John Lindsay, even arrived in December to address the students and applaud "the urgent, authentically revolutionary work of this generation."

2   How much of that revolution has carried over to the Columbia of 2004? Registered students who occupy a building would get a dialogue with administrators, but the school wouldn't shy from expulsion. According to Ricardo Morales, the school's crime prevention specialist since 1983, nonstudent radicals wouldn't make it into the campus buildings. "If you want to bring a friend over," Morales explains, "you bring him to the lobby and swipe your ID cards. The guest leaves a piece of ID. If he wants to stay for a few days, you can apply for a guest pass."

3   Even when they're not keeping their borders sealed so tight, college administrators have been adopting harsh measures in response to unapproved student behavior. Last fall, students at Southern Methodist University saw their "affirmative action bake sale," a bit of political theater in which prices were determined by the races of buyers, shut down by the student center. They had failed to register with the university as a "protest" or to go to the officially designated "protest zone" on the south stairs outside of the Hughes-Trigg Student Center.

4   Many college administrators throughout the country are taking great pains to keep their students under tight control. Yet in the late 1960s and '70s, whether colleges could rein in students was an open question. Previously, America's universities had operated

*David Weigel, *Reason Magazine*, October 2004; Eric Hoover, *Chronicle of Higher Education*, September 5, 2008

under the doctrine of *in loco parentis* ("in the place of a parent"). By the start of the '70s, thanks to a series of legal rulings and cultural shifts, courts and colleges were tossing out that policy, and universities that had been dealing with students as wards struggled to find a new approach.

Many college administrators throughout the country are taking great pains to keep their students under tight control. Yet in the late 1960s and '70s, whether colleges could rein in students was an open question.

5   That didn't last. *In loco parentis* has been rejuvenated and returned. Administrators have tapped into the devaluation of personal responsibility illustrated by smoking bans and fastfood lawsuits, coupling it with bullish political correctness. The resulting dearth of individual liberties on campuses would have seemed impossible to college students of 25 years ago.

Double-Secret Probation

6   The rights of schools over their pupils were codified before the U.S. Constitution was written. In 1765 the legal scholar Sir William Blackstone wrote that, when sending kids to school, Dad "may also delegate part of his parental authority during his life to the tutor or schoolmaster of the child; who is then *in loco parentis*, and has such a portion of the power of the parents committed to his charge."

7   Blackstone was writing about grammar school students, but 19th-century college administrators liked the idea, too. Wheaton College, five years after its 1861 founding, denied students the right to form a secret society. The students sued, but judges washed their hands of the matter. In *Pratt v. Wheaton College* (1866), the Illinois courts said judges have "no more authority to interfere than [they] have to control the domestic discipline of a father in his family."

8   Courts took this hands-off approach well into the next century. When public or private universities bought land, the state treated them like personal fiefdoms. Students got whatever rights their school administrators saw fit to give. At Harvard in 1951, the Administrative Board could tell reporters that it would increase the punishment for a window smashing—by however much it wanted—"if a student's name is on the police blotter or in the Boston press." That was the power of *in loco parentis*.

9   Not until 1960 did this system begin to break down. That year, six students at the all-black Alabama State College participated in anti-segregation lunch-counter sit-ins. The school's president sent them letters expelling them for "conduct prejudicial to the school." According to Stetson Law School professor Robert Bickel, the students' case cut to the root of *in loco parentis*: "The university actually asserted the right to arbitrarily give some students [due] process and deny it to others." When the students sued, federal courts sided with Alabama State. But in the 1961 decision *Dixon v. Alabama State Board of Education*, the U.S. Court of Appeals for the 5th Circuit rejected the school's claim of omnipotence. Suddenly, college enrollment was a contract between the student and the school. Since kids didn't lose their constitutional rights in their backyard, they couldn't lose them on campus. State universities slackened their grip, and private universities such as Columbia followed suit.

10   During the next few years, *in loco parentis* continued to collapse as courts chipped away at it. In 1974 the U.S. Supreme Court ruled 8–0 in *Scheuer v. Rhodes* that Kent State students had the right to sue the governor of Ohio for damages incurred during the notorious 1970 shooting there. Chief Justice Warren Burger concluded the brief decision this way: "We intimate no evaluation whatever as to the merits of the petitioners' claims or as to whether it will be possible to support them by proof. We hold only that, on the allegations of their respective complaints, they were entitled to have them judicially resolved." Students had been handed the keys to their kingdom.

11   By then, campus revolts were making national headlines, radical groups had been profiled in *Life* and *Esquire*, and undergrads were helping manage George McGovern's presidential campaign. By 1978, when Dean Wormer in *Animal House* threatened his students with "double-secret probation," audiences recognized it as a knowing goof on a dead-and-buried policy. As Stetson's Bickel puts it, "The fall of *in loco parentis* in the 1960s correlated exactly with the rise of student economic power and the rise of student civil rights."

Save the Children

12 In 1969 Sheldon Steinbach arrived at the American Council on Education, the catchall coordinating body for universities, just in time to weather the worst of the campus revolts. Elite schools such as Berkeley, Columbia, and Cornell were acquiescing to radical students and opening up their internal judicial processes. Students won seats on some boards of trustees. Administrators appeared to have lost their grip.

13   "The basic liberal arts education began to crumble," Steinbach says. "That's what it looked like. When the war ended, we could consolidate, sit back, and look at how to save the system."

14   An unexpected boon arrived in 1974, the year of the Kent State decision *Scheuer v. Rhodes*. Sens. John Warner (R–Va.) and James Buckley (Conservative–N.Y.) sponsored the Family Educational Rights and Privacy Act (FERPA) in the hope of empowering parents to keep tabs on their kids' academics. Committees amended the bill into a codification of student privacy rights, and Steinbach got a crack at it before FERPA moved on to the Senate. When the bill passed, parents could peek into the records of their children until their 18th birthday, at which point those rights transferred to the student. But FERPA created exceptions: Schools could release records to providers of financial aid and to "appropriate officials in cases of health and safety emergencies." If a student was hit with a subpoena or legal charge, the school could peek into his criminal records. Yet college administrators and their advisers, Steinbach included, kept the champagne corked. It wasn't immediately clear what effect the law would have, outside of giving parents annual notice of their new rights.

15   "It was a schizophrenic time," Steinbach explains. "We were moving from segregated campuses to co-ed, affirmative action campuses. We didn't have our feet on the floor in 1974."

16   Meanwhile, concern about the state of campuses was spreading. In March 1977, *Newsweek* ran a hand-wringing exposé titled "The End of Expulsion?" which gave the supposed academic apocalypse some context: "In just 10 years, most of the rules that once governed student life *in loco parentis* have simply disappeared. Even serious

scholastic offenses, such as cheating and plagiarism, seldom incur the harsh penalties that were once automatic. Most college administrators admit that they lean over backward to avoid expelling students." The irksome rites of passage that had been mandatory—core curricula, single-gender dorms, class attendance—fell away.

17   In the 1979 case *Bradshaw v. Rawlings*, the U.S. Court of Appeals for the 3rd Circuit spelled out the universities' weakness. When a Delaware Valley College sophomore three years under the Pennsylvania drinking age hitched a ride from a drunk driver and was injured in a car crash, he sued the school. The court shrugged him off. "The modern American college is not an insurer of the safety of its students," it said. "Rights formerly possessed by college administrations have been transferred to students." Expectations were pointless, because "beer drinking by college students is a common experience. That this is true is not to suggest that reality always comports with state law and college rules. It does not."

18   The court's decision reflected the way students lived: They had a new relationship with their deans, who should treat them like the young adults they were.

19   How then, did the contemporary nanny university arise? Administrators who got their degrees in the 1960s had a certain idea of how students should be governed, and they found three tools for regaining control. The first involved intoxicants, including the escalating war on drugs and the mid-'80s change in the drinking age from 18 to 21. The second was an attempt to stave off liability for student mental health problems by intervening with students who were seen at risk of breakdowns. The third and most well known was a rigid enforcement of political correctness that set standards for just how rowdy students could get.

Just Say No

20 University administrators immediately started wringing their hands over the "kids will be kids" philosophy of *Bradshaw v. Rawlings*. When one of their wards was arrested, injured, or killed, whether a lawsuit resulted or not, the school felt a blow to its prestige and sense of community. Unchecked hedonism and recklessness among students increasingly free to skip classes or make their own schedules were perceived as a threat to the institution's reputation.

21   Brett Bokolow, manager of the National Center for Higher Education Risk Management (NCHERM), estimates that colleges have been seeking formulas to keep students out of actionable situations for 20 years. In the 1980s, they were increasingly finding themselves liable for providing services or sponsoring events that involved alcohol. After only a few legal wounds, schools sought methods to put the responsibility for drinking or drug use on the backs of students and fraternities and sororities. Two weapons fell into their laps.

22   As the Department of Education opened for business in 1980, an increasing number of students were turning to government aid and loans to pay for their college bills. From 1970 to 1980, federal aid to college students soared from $600 million to $4.5 billion. In 1978 Congress had passed legislation that entitled all college students to federally insured loans. Suddenly, colleges had leverage to punish students for misusing their leisure time. If they were getting money from taxpayers, they were treated like any other employee found partying on the job. Since students were making use of

their loans every minute of the academic year, all of their fun was suspect, and much of the adult behavior that vexed administrators was happening on the public dime.

23   Colleges became willing and able to shift some burden to Greek organizations, which had grown again after a marked falloff in the Vietnam era. Many schools created incentives for fraternities and sororities to go dry, or at least disincentives for them to stay wet. In one typical action in 1988, Rutgers University, which had just banned bringing kegs into dorms, responded to a student's death by embargoing all Greek events. In 1997, after first-year student Scott Kreuger drank himself to death at a pledge event, MIT banned freshmen from fraternities. More responsibility was shifted to fraternity and sorority members. By the mid-'90s, universities had become so strict that they were rarely found liable for student sins. Instead of threatening to punish their kids if they came home late, schools simply took away the car keys. If kids somehow got themselves into trouble, it was a police matter.

24   Colleges found the rest of their arsenal in 1987, when Congress threatened to withhold federal transportation money from states that allowed anyone below the age of 21 to buy alcohol, with the result that 21 became the de facto national drinking age (see "Age of Propaganda" below). Across the country, the harshness many schools had formerly applied only to drug offenses began to apply to drinking as well, and the war on fraternities was ramped up. Finally, in 1998 FERPA was amended to make one provision clearer: Colleges could sidestep their students' wishes and inform parents whenever a drug or alcohol law was broken. Before that, less than 20 percent of schools had informed parents of such violations. Afterward, most of them did so.

25   In 2001 the *Chronicle of Higher Education* reviewed this phone-home policy and found great success. Reporters spotlighted the story of a University of Delaware freshman who pledged to quit drinking after police stopped him on the street for a Breathalyzer test. After he was caught, his parents began bringing him home each weekend and lecturing him on his mistakes. The student stopped drinking, but not because he worried about the effects of booze. If he was caught again, he would be suspended for a year.

For Your Own Good

26 Keri Krissik transferred to Stonehill College in Easton, Massachusetts, in January 1999, 10 years after she was first diagnosed as anorexic. Krissik survived a heart attack four months after arriving and finished her course work while convalescing. In September the school refused to let her back in because, according to spokesman Martin McGovern, "we couldn't monitor her." If she were allowed back in and was injured, the school could have been liable. Stonehill dearly wanted to avoid the risk.

27   Krissik eventually settled with Stonehill, but the courts neglected to ask why, after they'd relieved colleges of the need to nanny their students, the college wouldn't damn the consequences and let her study. The lawsuit provides an answer.

28   Just as colleges have calculated the legal risks of letting students get away with drinking or recreational drugs, they remain in danger of being held responsible when students face mental collapse or attempt suicide. If administrators had moved on and handed their wards more lifestyle freedom after *in loco parentis* ended, they'd have room to dodge these bullets. But since they had accepted responsibility for keeping

kids off the bottle, it was easy for lawyers to make them responsible for the rest of the pressures of campus life.

29   Schools started this battle with a handicap. During the last decade, more and more students have been diagnosed as overstressed or treated for depression while still in high school. In February 2003, after tracking student complaints from 1989 to 2001, researchers at the University of Kansas found that the number of students diagnosed with depression had doubled while the number of "suicidal" students had tripled. The proportion of students taking psychiatric medication rose from 10 percent to 25 percent.

30   In response to such trends, college administrators started making pharmaceuticals and therapy sessions more readily available on campus. Elite universities have been able to provide the most buffers against mental illness claims. According to the May 2002 issue of *Psychology Today*, 2,000 Harvard students had sought counseling in one year. Fully half of them walked away with a prescription for antidepressants. Students who lived on campus had access to free massages and an ever-expanding mental health center.

31   The overarching goal of these programs is not to eliminate stress or wean students off medication. It's to stop lawsuits, and the ugliest lawsuits of the last decade have concerned students who killed themselves while enrolled, even though studies (including one conducted by the MIT task force appointed after Scott Kreuger's death from alcohol poisoning) have shown that most students who commit suicide never seek counseling.

    At the University of Illinois, counselors work with residential assistants to mon-
32 itor students who attempt or seriously consider suicide. Such students are ordered into four weeks of assessment sessions under the university's watch. Those who refuse get the Keri Krissik treatment—they're no longer students. The *New York Times Magazine* called Illinois' approach "a highly successful, model plan" for colleges that want to keep their undergrads under control.

How to Think

33 As the protective mind-set returned, it jibed with administrators' desires to make their campuses placid in every possible way. Alcohol and drug policies had emerged in a national context, justified by laws beyond the university's control, while mental health policies were driven largely by the threat of lawsuits. But administrators didn't need anyone to force their hands to insert speech standards and "hate crime" prohibitions into campus life. In 1987 the University of Michigan responded to a handful of anonymous racist fliers with new campus regulations aimed at suppressing offensive speech. The speech code, the first to end up in court, prohibited "any behavior, verbal or physical, that stigmatizes or victimizes an individual on the basis of race, ethnicity, religion, sex, sexual orientation, creed, national origin, ancestry, age, marital status, handicap, or Vietnam-era veteran status." A university pamphlet, soon withdrawn, explained that such "harassment" would include hanging a Confederate flag on your dorm room door or being part of a student group that "sponsors entertainment that includes a comedian who slurs Hispanics."

34   Ironically, a one-time member of Berkeley's Free Speech movement seized on this approach when she became an administrator. Annette Kolodny, a dean of the University of Arizona's College of Humanities, used her 1998 book *Failing the*

Future to explain why colleges needed to regulate what students said. In concert with other administrators, Kolodny had stiffened penalties for offensive speech and created workshops in which new students could have their values certified or corrected. Her bogeyman was "antifeminist intellectual harassment," and her policies were designed to bring contrary speech out into the open, so it could be "readily recognized and effectively contained."

35   By the start of the 1990s, Kolodny's view of campus speech was the norm. Harvard law professor Randall Kennedy told the *New York Times* in 1991 that speech codes made sense, and that their opponents were just warring against 1960s values. Journalists had gotten some taste of universities' strange speech standards through the *Dartmouth Review*, a conservative newspaper whose editors were punished for articles that would have been protected anywhere else in New Hampshire. But they didn't comprehend how strict the standards were until codes at Stanford, the University of Wisconsin, and George Mason University were challenged in court and overturned. Based on these cases, schools learned how to design speech restrictions that were more likely to pass legal muster.

36   The speech codes, increasingly unpopular but largely still in effect, contain more than a whiff of the omnipotence administrators enjoyed under *in loco parentis*. Students are not treated as the adults that Dixon made them out to be. Instead they're young minds that need shaping. In most cases the bodies formed to govern speech—student judicial boards, special committees—are uniquely able to adjudicate without explaining their standards for punishment.

37   Universities' speech restrictions, unlike their recreational policies, do more to attract lawsuits than to repel them. NCHERM offers a seminar on how administrators can thwart the Foundation for Individual Rights in Education and the American Civil Liberties Union. But there hasn't been any measurable trend toward saving face by scrapping these rules. They're seen as too important to ditch—and that's illustrative of the way universities view their students.

Back in Control

38 Four decades after *in loco parentis* started to stagger, college students would be hard pressed to name their new personal liberties. Yes, they no longer fear "double-secret probation." And when administrators crack down, they will almost always at least provide a reason. But today's students may be punished just as hard as their predecessors—often harder. They've discovered that social engineers have a hard time turning down the opportunity to control things.

39   The expanding control over college students has had repercussions in the rest of America. Campuses are proving grounds for make-nice public programs. They've provided laboratories to test speech codes and small, designated "free speech zones" for protests. (Such zones marginalize and effectively silence dissent, which is one reason they've been adopted by the major political parties for their national conventions.) The stiffening of campus law also illustrates the trend toward greater control of adults' personal behavior.

40   *In loco parentis* could be overturned only once. After 1974, students should have had an arsenal of new rights. But parents never stopped believing that

universities were responsible for shaping their kids, and schools have nervously assumed that too much freedom will bring about the system's collapse.

41   It won't. College students will drink, despair, play loose with hygiene, make dirty jokes. Before *in loco parentis* made its comeback, they were thriving. Meanwhile, the changes that really worried academics in the 1970s—demands for new disciplines, shrinking core curricula—are settling into permanence. It's the most enjoyable effect of the '60s student revolts that's being whittled away.

Animal House at 30: O Bluto, Where Art Thou?
Eric Hoover

1   A gentleman does not steal horses, spit food across the table, or pee on people's shoes. By that definition, John "Bluto" Blutarsky is not a gentleman, but something more extraordinary.

2   The fictional antihero of *National Lampoon's Animal House,* Bluto is a slovenly symbol of irreverence, a bloated personification of the id. Bored by the past and future, he lives to party in an endless now. Alas, even icons must turn 30.

3   *Animal House,* the most infamous movie ever made about college, first hit theaters in the summer of 1978. Since then it has inspired three decades of big-screen imitations soaked in booze, rebellion, and sophomoric gags. It remains a keg of cultural references.

4   Thirty, however, is always an ambiguous milestone. Although *Animal House* continues to shape popular understandings of fraternity life and student culture, the world it caricatured has been transformed.

5   The law has redefined the traditional relationship between students and colleges. Many administrators see themselves no longer as disciplinarians but as partners in student "success" and "wellness." Customer care is the new campus creed. Today's students—ambitious, competitive, diverse—demand all the services they can imagine.

6   Nonetheless, Bluto abides. He still sways to "Louie, Louie" in higher education's collective unconscious. He still lives on dorm-room walls and on the ubiquitous replicas of his "COLLEGE" shirt, advertising not a place but a state of mind.

7   "He's a reminder not to take everything too seriously," says E. Gordon Gee, president of Ohio State University, who has a framed photograph of Bluto above the couch in his office.

8   As the patron saint of parties, the toga-wearing buffoon also represents the enduring appeal of raucous bashes in an era of alcohol prevention and risk management. *Animal House* still reflects a warped, but true, image of higher education's beer-drenched belly. Perhaps that's why people tend to love the movie or curse it.

9   Indifference is impossible when Bluto (John Belushi) first appears on the screen. We watch him stumble around, dazed and drunk, outside the Delta Tau Chi

fraternity house. He relieves himself, then opens the front door for two wide-eyed freshmen.

10   Inside, mayhem rules. Bottles fly and windows break. A guy drives a motorcycle up the stairs. Goldfish swim inside the see-through breasts of a cut-out mermaid at the bar.

11   Should we laugh? Cringe? And wait . . . is Bluto drinking from a goblet?

12   "Come on in," he says. "Grab a brew. Don't cost nothin'."

Out with *In Loco Parentis*

13 For anyone who's been locked in the library since 1978, *Animal House*, directed by John Landis, depicts life at fictional Faber College in 1962. The protagonists are Bluto and his Delta brothers, all misfits with bad grades. They must contend with Dean Vernon Wormer, who yearns to kick them off the campus.

14   Stern and scheming, Wormer (John Vernon) symbolizes the era of *in loco parentis,* when colleges and universities stood "in place of the parent," asserting control over students and their affairs. As legal scholars have noted, *in loco parentis* insulated colleges from litigation. Generally courts gave administrators, like parents, leeway to discipline their charges as they saw fit.

15   At Faber, Wormer is sheriff, judge, and jury. He boasts of putting the Delta House on "double-secret probation." He spouts off like a mad dictator. "The time has come for someone to put his foot down," he says, "and that foot is me."

16   In real life, the administrative heel was long free to stomp. Then, in 1961, the U.S. Court of Appeals for the Fifth Circuit decided *Dixon v. Alabama,* a landmark ruling that presaged a new definition of student rights.

17   The case arose after Alabama State College (now Alabama State University) expelled six black students who had participated in civil-rights demonstrations. In a letter to the students, the college's president wrote that Alabama State had the power to remove them for various offenses, such as "Conduct Prejudicial to the School" or "Insubordination and Insurrection." It was, more or less, double-secret expulsion.

18   The appellate court deemed such rules unconstitutional. A public college, it said, could not remove students without at least minimal due process, such as a hearing they could attend. "This was the first time a court had ever said anything remotely like that," says Peter F. Lake, a law professor at Stetson University.

19   *Dixon* doomed *in loco parentis,* explains Mr. Lake, who directs the Center for Excellence in Higher Education Law and Policy at Stetson. Courts would recast students as adults, or "nonminors," with constitutional rights. Colleges, in turn, would no longer have near-limitless power to govern and punish them.

20   "Today the very concept of discipline is a relic," Mr. Lake says. "We're in a contractual relationship with students."

21   In *Animal House,* the unruly Deltas resist discipline, but their nemeses, in the Omega House, bow to the dean's authority. Privileged and proper, the Omegas cling to tradition. During an arcane initiation ceremony that consecrates "the bond of obedience," an Omega pledge gets on his hands and knees to accept a paddling on the rear. "Thank you, sir," he says after each whack, "may I have another?"

22   By contrast, the Deltas reject tradition and authority alike. Their own half-hearted initiation rite involves reciting an ad-libbed pledge, then getting a nickname and a beer shower. After Dean Wormer expels them from Faber, they refuse to surrender to the rules. Instead they plan a fantastic act of revenge. "Wormer," Bluto declares, "he's a dead man!"

An "Uneasy Truce"

23 C. Arthur Sandeen witnessed the dean's figurative death firsthand. When he began his career in student affairs, at Michigan State University in 1962, his role as a supervisor was clear. Discipline took much of his time. "It was the expectation for a dean," he says.

24   The civil-rights era, however, changed the profession just as it changed colleges. Protests flared. Enrollments grew, and campuses became more diverse. In 1971 the 26th Amendment to the U.S. Constitution lowered the voting age to 18.

25   When *Animal House* arrived, *in loco parentis* was already a fossil. Still, Mr. Sandeen, then vice president for student affairs at the University of Florida, laughed at Dean Wormer for a reason: "Unfortunately, he reminded some of us of ourselves."

26   After the fall of *in loco parentis,* courts repeatedly affirmed that students, as young adults with rights, were beyond the control of colleges. Although such rulings limited colleges' legal liability, they also left administrators unsure of their roles. Where, exactly, did their responsibilities end and student freedoms begin?

27   The uncertainty left students and college officials in an "uneasy truce," Ernest L. Boyer wrote.

28   Mr. Boyer, a former U.S. commissioner of education, described the evolution of campus culture in *College: The Undergraduate Experience in America* (Harper & Row, 1987). As the role of colleges had changed from that of "parent to clinician," he wrote, distance grew between students and administrators: "Students still have almost unlimited freedom in personal and social matters. . . . And yet, administrators are troubled by the limits of their authority, and there is a growing feeling among students that more structure is required."

29   Mr. Sandeen and his contemporaries helped create a new kind of structure. By the time he retired from Florida, in 2004, student affairs had become a giant umbrella, covering a wide range of offerings—academic advising, counseling, career planning, cultural programming, residence-life education, financial assistance, and help for students with disabilities.

30   "One of the healthiest changes was an increased recognition that there were students with different needs," Mr. Sandeen says. "Students used to fail out of school a lot more. Now there's a much bigger emphasis on retention."

31   Perhaps Dean Wormer has given way to Dean Coddler. Administrators from other countries, Mr. Sandeen says, now tease their American counterparts about "babying" their students. On the modern campus, Bluto's bad behavior and failing grades surely would cause administrators, staff members, and resident assistants to intervene long before his cumulative average fell anywhere close to the 0.0 he carries at Faber.

32   Mr. Sandeen believes *Animal House,* though "inaccurate," contains shreds of truth. He counts himself as a fan of the movie. "It's still funny," he says.

33   Margaret J. Barr has yet to laugh. In 1978 she was an assistant dean of students at the University of Texas at Austin. One night she and some colleagues went to see *Animal House* in a packed theater. Afterward they went for coffee. Ms. Barr was steaming.

34   "Incensed," she says. "I had paid good money to see this movie. I saw no humor in it at all."

35   The portrayal of Dean Wormer bothered her the most. After all, she believed in the ideals of her profession. Also, she liked students. And she certainly would never steal from their activities fund, as the dean does in the movie.

36   Years later, as vice president for student affairs at Northwestern University, Ms. Barr usually knew when *Animal House* had played on the campus—toga parties inevitably followed. "It's the only film I ever thought about banning," she says. "It taught them how to misbehave."

37   When she arrived at Northwestern, she urged fraternities to follow their own risk-management policies. "If your policy requires you to have a guest list for parties," she told chapter leaders, "then make sure you use a guest list."

38   At first they looked at her as if she were crazy. The student newspaper said she was trying to ruin social life on the campus. But over time, she says, students accepted more responsibility as they came to understand that she was looking out for them.

> *On many campuses, students now police their own parties and run their own judicial systems. Some colleges have phased out the title "dean of students." And fraternity leaders work closely with student-affairs staff members, who stand between them and high-ranking administrators.*

39   On many campuses, students now police their own parties and run their own judicial systems. Some colleges have phased out the title "dean of students." And fraternity leaders work closely with student-affairs staff members, who stand between them and high-ranking administrators.

40   Ms. Barr, now retired, credits the movie with affirming at least one crucial lesson. "It showed how administrations had to become much better at communicating with students," she says. "You don't just say, Do it because we say so."

Us vs. Them

41   *Animal House* presents a campus of absolutes, a conflict between good and evil. Not by accident, the only lecture we hear at Faber concerns Milton's *Paradise Lost,* the epic poem that recounts Satan's rebellion against Heaven and the Fall of Man—an expulsion for the ages.

42   Professor Dave Jennings (Donald Sutherland) plays the desperate English instructor, who asks, "Was Milton trying to tell us that being bad was more fun than being good?"

43   For the Deltas, bad is always better. At three crucial moments in the movie, when Dean Wormer appears to have doomed them, they rebel by having fun. After learning about their double-secret probation, they throw the toga party. When the dean revokes their charter, they go on a road trip. After he expels them, they prepare to crash Faber's homecoming parade.

44   "They're going to nail us anyway," one Delta brother says. "We might as well have a good time."

45   The recurring premise captures a lingering tension between students and administrators. Nancy E. Tribbensee, general counsel at Arizona State University, believes that *Animal House,* while entertaining, continues to reinforce an us-versus-them mentality. "This polarization is now so ingrained in the campus culture," she says, "it is difficult to overcome in working together to find meaningful ways to improve the campus environment."

46   Some student groups have learned that sitting down with administrators can do more to influence campus policies than a dramatic protest can. "Especially with touchy issues, it's important to talk to administrators first," says Irina Alexander, a junior at the University of Maryland at College Park and chapter vice president of Students for Sensible Drug Policy. "You have to show them you that you actually know what you're talking about, and that you're not just partying and being crazy like in *Animal House."*

47   Graham B. Spanier, president of Pennsylvania State University, recalls watching *Animal House* on the big screen as a young professor. A studious guy, he had never experienced anything like the movie's wild soirees. "It seemed like a gross exaggeration," he says. "But now I realize that for a lot of students, it's a mild exaggeration."

48   For instance, students may not have seen a friend chug a bottle of bourbon in seven seconds to cheer himself up, as Bluto does, but most would recognize the behavior.

49   Kyle A. Pendleton tells students not to just dismiss the movie. He shows the film in the course he teaches on fraternity and sorority leadership on Purdue University's main campus.

50   Students need to understand how the movie reinforces the stereotype that fraternities are only about "chicks, beer, and hazing," says Mr. Pendleton, Purdue's assistant dean of students and a past president of the Association of Fraternity Advisors. "We do still have problems shown in *Animal House,* but at least at this point we're admitting them and trying to address them."

51   He still encounters Blutos, those who join fraternities just to party. Despite their misconceptions, such students often bring enthusiasm to fraternities, he says, and with the right guidance can become mature, valuable members.

52   And if they resist?

53   "In today's world," he says, "you're not going to be Bluto for long."

54   But count Mr. Pendleton among those who see some good in the fictional Deltas. Viewers may remember Delta House as nothing more than a den of depravity, but it also embraces at least some form of diversity. Unlike the über-exclusive Omegas, who exile minority students and other undesirable visitors to a couch in the corner, the Delta House accepts outcasts, including nerds and fat kids.

55   "They had issues," Mr. Pendleton says. "But if you boil down the core of the Delta chapter, it's about tight-knit brotherhood. They're a diamond in the rough."

56   Of the many outrageous moments in *Animal House,* few seem as far-fetched today as when Dean Wormer strolls, uninvited, through the Delta House front door and threatens to close down the chapter. A credible remake of the movie would omit that scene and replace it with a heated discussion between Faber's general counsel and the Deltas' lawyer.

"We're Not Shooting Horses"

57 Today's colleges operate in a litigious era of high-stakes liability. And alcohol, of course, is the main ingredient in numerous lawsuits.

58 In this way, too, *Animal House* is a relic. Set long before the drinking age was 21, the movie plays drunk driving for laughs. Ditto for a Delta brother's internal debate about whether to have sex with a girl who has passed out after guzzling several drinks too many.

59 "In many ways, *Animal House* is a great advertisement for why an institution should invest in risk management," says Alyssa S. Keehan, a risk analyst with United Educators Insurance, a major insurer of colleges. "We know that students engage in risky behavior that is often stranger than any piece of Hollywood fiction."

60 *Animal House* derives from stories that Chris Miller, a 1963 graduate of Dartmouth College, wrote about his fraternity, Alpha Delta Phi. Today that fraternity seems far more respectable than the fictional Delta House does. "We're not shooting horses," says Reed Boeger, a junior, referring to the unfortunate prank in *Animal House.* "As much pride as we take in parties, we take pride in other things, too."

61 Mr. Boeger's fraternity carries a 3.4 grade-point average. One of his brothers was Dartmouth's most recent valedictorian. His chapter sponsors an annual literary contest, with a $1,000 prize. Recently, members built a playground near the campus.

62 Mr. Boeger, who describes himself as an occasional drinker, says his brothers get along with administrators, although he has some complaints. For one, he dislikes that Dartmouth limits the number of kegs a fraternity can have during parties. "It leads to an unbelievable amount of trash," he says. "We're throwing away thousands of cans per week."

63 At times Dartmouth has had rough relationships with its fraternities. In 2000 it considered making them coeducational. One of Alpha Delta's advisers, John Engelman, believes the relationship has since improved. "The administration has come to accept that these organizations are here to stay," says the 1968 Dartmouth graduate, "and that it might as well work with them to make them the best organizations they can be."

64 Bluto has become an obsolete archetype, according to Mr. Engelman. He believes career-minded students have learned to balance fun and responsibility without wrecking themselves or sticking around for seven years. "Kids have more freedom," he says. "So all those opportunities for a rebellious attitude do not exist."

Bluto at 30

65 Or maybe Bluto has just become harder to spot. After all, many students who drink excessively are not "fat, drunk, and stupid," as Dean Wormer describes one Delta brother. They are often clean-cut, high-achieving, and smart.

66 That Bluto's 30th birthday coincides with a renewed debate over the drinking age seems only fitting: The law pits students against administrators like nothing else.

67 Recently more than 120 college presidents signed a letter calling for debate on the issue. Enforcement, they argue, has failed to change the culture of high-risk drinking on campuses: "Alcohol education that mandates abstinence as the only legal option has not resulted in significant constructive behavioral change among

our students," the letter says. It reads like a renunciation of Dean Wormer and his devotion to discipline at all costs.

68   And just look what became of him. In *Animal House*'s symbolic finale, the Delta brothers ruin the homecoming parade by crashing their "Deathmobile" into the grandstand, bringing down the dean, literally and figuratively. Bluto, dressed as a pirate, drives away in a convertible. We learn that the outlaw goes on to become a U.S. senator.

69   Despite its many punchlines, *Animal House* may not resound for another 30 years. The diversity of modern campuses makes the movie's superficial portrayal of women, stereotypical rendering of black people, and images of suppressed homosexuality all seem hopelessly dated. And how well can students relate to a college movie that includes exactly zero parents?

70   Mr. Lake, the Stetson professor, has shown *Animal House* in his classes. The movie's cultural relevance, he believes, has faded as the definition of college has evolved. "Going to college is not the quintessential experience it once was," he says. "For students today it's not this dramatic change of scenery, but a continuation of their experiences. With technology they can create their own societies and go off the grid. They don't need to fight us—they just avoid us."

71   Then again, Bluto teaches us never to count the Deltas out. When his brothers despair for the fraternity's future, he rallies them with a question for the ages: "Was it over," he asks, "when the Germans bombed Pearl Harbor? Hell, no!" ◆

CRITICAL THINKING ──────────────────

1. What reputation do fraternities have regarding alcohol consumption and student responsibility? How has the attitude toward student drinking changed over the last 30 years? How has the attitude changed toward fraternities and sororities?

2. What is each author's take on the issue of student responsibility?

3. Do you think college administrators have the right to contact parents when underage students are caught drinking? Do you think that parental notification would reduce drinking? Would knowing that this could happen to you curtail your own drinking habits? Why or why not?

4. What rights and privileges do you expect to enjoy as a college student? Do you expect to be treated entirely as an adult? Or do you expect the school to ensure certain protections and safeguards as part of your college experience? If so, what is the balance between safety and personal responsibility?

5. How does the history of *in loco parentis* inform the current trend adopted by many colleges and universities to curtail student drinking on campus and enact other policies to ensure student safety?

6. What movie does Hoover base his essay upon? What does the reader need to know about this movie in order to understand his essay?

7. What does Hoover think of the resurrection of *in loco parentis* on college campuses? Identify specific areas where he makes his viewpoint clear.

8. Who is "Bluto" and what does he represent? Does he exist merely in comedy, or is there a real-world equivalent on college campuses around the country today? Explain.

CRITICAL WRITING

1. *Personal Narrative:* Have you ever been in a situation—such as at a party, concert, or sporting event—in which either you or the people around you became unruly because of excessive alcohol consumption? How did college administrators respond? Were parents notified?

2. *Expository Writing:* Hoover's essay recounts moments from the classic college movie, *Animal House*, which centers around fraternity life and alcohol consumption. What role does alcohol play in your life? In your roommates' and friends' lives? How would your college experience be different if there were no alcohol at all? If you attend a "dry campus," describe how you think your college experience may be different. Explain.

3. *Research Writing:* Research the history of *in loco parentis*. If possible, see if you can find out more about your own college's rules and regulations guiding student behavior 20 or 40 years ago. How have things changed? Do you think things are better now or worse? Explain.

4. *Research and Persuasive Writing:* Review your student handbook and summarize your student rights and responsibilities. Do you agree with your college's rules and regulations? Write an essay in which you agree or disagree, in whole or in part, with the rules and regulations guiding student conduct.

GROUP PROJECTS

1. One of the most pressing issues regarding student responsibility is binge drinking. Many of the policies enacted around *in loco parentis* resulted from tragedies connected to binge drinking (defined as four drinks in a row for females and five or six drinks in a row for males). Discuss this definition with your peers and determine whether you feel that it is realistic. Then discuss the seriousness of the issue of drinking at your own campus. What reputation does your school have? Is it considered a "party school" or a "drinking school"? Is it a dry campus? Share your views with the class as part of group discussion.

2. Prepare a short questionnaire on drinking habits at your school, and administer the survey to at least 50 college students from different majors and years. When writing your survey, think about the data you wish to collect. For example, do you want to determine whether some majors are more likely to drink? Is drinking more common among fraternity members? Is it more common among seniors or freshmen? Should college administrators implement measures to curtail college students' drinking? After administering the survey, collect the data and discuss the results. Prepare a short report analyzing the information you gathered.

Perspectives: Binge Drinking

Brain Fairrington, *The Arizona Republic*, April 15, 2002

THINKING CRITICALLY

1. What is happening in this cartoon? How can you tell who the people are in the cartoon? Explain.
2. Do you think this cartoon presents a stereotype of college life? Is it fair? Explain.
3. If you drink alcohol, how many drinks do you think are reasonable to ingest in an evening? Does it depend on the situation? Describe the different situations that influence how many drinks you have and why you believe the number you cited is a reasonable one for you.
4. Have you or someone you know ever faced a dangerous situation because of alcohol? What role did alcohol play in the situation? Explain.
5. In response to increasingly unruly alcohol-related behavior on campus, Michigan State cut short its "welcome week," the week that allows freshman to learn about the campus before the rest of the student body arrives. Does your school have a welcome week for first-year students? If it does, what did you do during your welcome week experience? Did you drink or attend any parties? Explain.

CHAPTER
9

Domestic Affairs
The Family in Flux

The American family is always in a state of change. How we perceive the very concept of family is based largely on where we come from and what values we share. We have a tendency to base our views on traditional constructs—models that are generations old and perpetuated by media archetypes. As a result, sociologists tell us, our vision of family is usually not based on realistic examples but on political ideals and media images. Yet the traditional family is obviously changing. Stepfamilies, same-sex relationships, single-parent households, and extended families with several generations living in one home all force us to redefine, or at least reexamine, our traditional definitions of family.

From traditional models of a nuclear family—with a husband, wife, and children—to same-sex unions, this chapter takes a look at how our concept of marriage and family has changed over the last several decades. Divorce, for example, is a widely accepted reality of life that is no longer viewed as a deviation from the norm. Single motherhood is no longer ascribed the social stigma it had 30 or 40 years ago. Some states have legalized same-sex marriage. A census report issued in 2007 revealed that only 24 percent of households are made up of what many politicians refer to as the "model family" of husband, wife, and children. Clearly, the American family unit has changed, and with it our expectations and social collective consciousness have changed.

We open the chapter with an examination of family from an academic perspective. In "Family: Idea, Institution, and Controversy," Betty G. Farrell discusses the social and political structures that influence our concept of family, and how the institution of family is firmly entrenched in our cultural consciousness. She also explores the concept of the family in transition and why we seem to fear change when it comes to family structures, which are based more on nostalgia than on reality.

The next piece, "Numbers Drop for the Married-with-Children," features an article and interview with reporter Blaine Harden, who reports that the more educated and affluent you are, the more likely you are to get married. Marriage is in sharp decline, however, among the lower middle class and the poor, where more people are bearing children out of wedlock and possibly perpetuating cycles of poverty.

Not everyone agrees that marriage is best, however. Sociologist Stephanie Coontz challenges the idea that marriage should be a goal. There is no way, she contends, that marriage can be reestablished as the main site of family and interpersonal relationships in our modern world, a view she defends in "For Better, For Worse." Then, Dorian Solot argues that marriage is an unnecessary institution altogether in "On Not Saying 'I Do.'" Solot wonders if she missed the day in preschool when they told the little girls that the happiest day of their lives would be their wedding day?

Dennis Prager questions such views, however, in his editorial, "Five Non-Religious Arguments for Marriage." Prager argues that living together simply represents an underlying unwillingness to fully commit to another person, and anyone who says marriage is "just a piece of paper" isn't telling the whole truth.

The instability of American marriage is often cited as the source of many childhood problems. Most of us have heard the statistics—over half of all U.S. marriages end in divorce. The next essay, by Lowell Putnam, explains that children of divorce may not be as scarred by the experience as politicians and the media seem to think.

Having lived most of his life as a child of divorce, Putnam wonders, "Did I Miss Something?"

This chapter's Viewpoints section addresses the issue of gay marriage. The issue has been hotly argued for the past few years, as some states have banned and others have allowed same-sex marriage. In California, the debate has reached a crescendo—in July of 2008, same-sex marriage was sanctioned by the courts, but just four months later, voters banned the practice. Is marriage an inalienable right? The authors in this section give different views on why same-sex marriage should be permitted—or not.

Family: Idea, Institution, and Controversy

Betty G. Farrell*

Although the family has always been in a state of transition, many politicians expound that the family is not just in a state of change, it is in a state of decline—to the detriment of society. And whether this is true or not, it seems that many people agree that most of society's ills are directly connected to the decline of the family. The truth is, the American family is more than an icon in our culture. It is an American institution, subject to intense scrutiny and criticism. Professor Betty G. Farrell explores the importance of the institution of family in American culture and how this importance is inextricably linked to our social and political consciousness.

1   Q: What did Eve say to Adam on being expelled from the Garden of Eden?

2   A: "I think we're in a time of transition."

3   The irony of this joke is not lost as we begin a new century, and anxieties about social change seem rife. The implication of this message, covering the first of many subsequent periods of transition, is that change is normal; there is, in fact, no era or society in which change is not a permanent feature of the social landscape. Yet, on the eve of the twenty-first century, the pace of change in the United States feels particularly intense, and a state of "permanent transition" hardly seems a contradiction in terms at all. To many, it is an apt description of the economic fluctuations, political uncertainties, social and cultural upheaval, and fluidity of personal relationships that characterize the times. For a large segment of the population, however, these transitions are tinged with an acute sense of loss and nostalgia. Moral values, communities, even the American way of life seem in decline. And at the core of that decline is the family.

4   In a nationwide poll conducted by the *Los Angeles Times* [. . .], 78 percent of respondents said they were dissatisfied with today's moral values, and nearly half of that group identified divorce, working parents, and undisciplined children as the key

---

* Betty Farrell, *Family: The Making of an Idea, an Institution, and a Controversy in American Culture,* 1999

problems. Only 11 percent of the respondents believed that their own behavior had contributed to the moral problems in the United States, and a resounding 96 percent believed that they were personally doing an excellent or good job of teaching moral values to their children. Conversely, 93 percent thought that other parents were to blame for the inadequate moral upbringing of their children. The sense of loss and decline many Americans feel today is filled with such contradictions. Americans want their families to offer unconditional love yet also to enforce and uphold strict moral values. They want flexibility, mobility, and autonomy in their personal lives but yearn for traditional communities and permanently stable families. When the substance of the debate over families is this ambiguous and contradictory, it is important to look more closely at the underlying issues in this time of transition.

5   For most people in most eras, change seems anything but normal. Periods of social change can evoke much social anxiety, because the unknown is inherently unsettling and because many people are stakeholders in the status quo. Those who seek change generally want to effect a shift in the relations of power, either for themselves or for others. But such shifts are always unpredictable, and they can seem treacherous to those who hold the reins of power, as well as to those who feel their social, economic, or political power eroding. The groups with eroding power are the ones most likely to resist, through active strategies and passive resistance, the ideas, values, symbols, and behaviors associated with change. This describes such groups in the contemporary United States as militias who see minorities, foreigners, and new cultural values as a threat to the American way of life; whites who see blacks, Latinos, and Asians as challenging their privileges and claim on limited resources in a zero-sum game; pro-life advocates who see pro-choice supporters as threatening traditionally defined family roles; and antigay pro-ponents who see gays and lesbians as subverting the gendered social order. Although social structural forces are ultimately responsible for the realignment of prestige and power among social groups in any society, these forces are always complex, abstract, intangible, and invisible. So those who symbolize or represent the forces of the new—women, minorities, immigrants, the poor, and other marginalized groups—tend to be singled out and blamed for the disruptions and upheaval associated with change. Social psychologists identify this process as scapegoating, the act of displacing generalized anxiety onto a conveniently visible and available target. Scapegoats have been identified in every era; but in periods in which the pace of change is particularly fast and a sense of unsettling disruption is acute, those social newcomers who challenge established values and behavior can all too readily become the targets of the rage, fear, and ambivalence of people feeling the earthquake tremors of social change.

Popular Perspectives on the Family

6 The family values debate has been generated against just such a backdrop in the late-twentieth-century United States. Fundamental changes in the expectations, meanings, and practices defining American family life have characterized much of the twentieth century, but especially the final 30 years. Consequently, concern about the family has moved to the center of the political arena. Threats to the family on the one hand and salvation through the family on the other are the two most prominent

themes in the recent family politics discourse. That the American family is broken and in need of repair is a common assumption of many social observers. Its complement is that families are worth fixing, because making them strong (again) is the key to solving most of society's ills. Neither of these assumptions has been subject to much critical scrutiny, nor has the historical image of the strong, vital, central family institution of the past on which they rest. Longing for order is one of the impulses behind the current turn to family politics in the United States; and feminists, gays and lesbians, single-parent mothers, absent fathers, pregnant teenagers, and gang-oriented youth, among others, have all at one time or another been made the scapegoats for family decline in the United States.

7   Longing for a more orderly, mythic past is most commonly associated with the conservative position on the family politics spectrum, and it would be easy to caricature the nostalgia for a family modeled on the classic 1950s television sitcom as the sum total of this side of the family values debate. But if we assume that concerns about The Family, writ large, are only those of conservative politicians attempting to manipulate public sentiment, we would overlook the vast reservoir of social anxiety about contemporary family life that is also being tapped by many others from a variety of political and social perspectives: working moth-

> *That the American family is broken and in need of repair is a common assumption of many social observers. Its complement is that families are worth fixing, because making them strong (again) is the key to solving most of society's ills.*

ers who are consumed with worry about child care; white Christian men who, by the tens of thousands in the late 1990s, attended Promise Keepers revivals that focused on renewing their traditional roles as husbands and fathers; adolescents seeking the emotional attachment of family ties among peers and in gangs when it is found lacking in their own homes; committed gay and lesbian couples fighting for inclusion in the legal definition of family even as they retain a skeptical stance toward this fundamentally heterosexual institution. Why such concern about the family? One reason is that the metaphor evoked by family is a powerful one. A family is defined not so much by a particular set of people as by the quality of relationships that bind them together. What seems to many to be the constant feature of family life is not a specific form or structure but the meanings and the set of personal, intimate relationships families provide against the backdrop of the impersonal, bureaucratized world of modern society.

8   The core sentiments of family life that define the nature and meaning of this social institution for most Americans are unconditional love, attachment, nurturance, and dependability. The hope that these qualities are common to family relationships accounts for the shock with which we react to reports of violence, abuse, and neglect occurring inside the sanctuary of the private home. In popular culture, as in real life, stories of families beset by jealousy, envy, lust, and hatred rather than by the ideals of love, loyalty, and commitment provide an endless source of titillation and fascination. Family stories are not only the stuff of life we construct through our daily experience but the narrative form used to entice us as consumers

into a marketplace adept at presenting all sorts of products as invested with emotional qualities and social relationships.

9   The widely promoted "Reach Out and Touch Someone" advertising campaign developed by AT&T in 1978 was a prototype of this genre. In this set of ads, a powerful multinational company hoped to pull at the heartstrings and the pocketbooks of the consuming public by promoting itself as the crucial communication link between family members separated by great global distances. The copy in the print advertisements told heartwarming personal tales of mothers and sons, uncles and nephews, and grandmothers and grandchildren reunited by AT&T's implied commitment to family values, albeit at long distance phone rates. The family metaphor works as an advertising ploy because there is widespread sentimentality in American society about family life. What makes families so compelling for those of us who actively choose to live in them, as well as for those of us who just as actively reject them as oppressively confining, is that families reside at the intersection of our most personal experience and our social lives. They are institutions we make, yet they are in no small part also constructed by cultural myths and social forces beyond any individual's control.

10   A desire for the kind of care and connection provided by the ideal family cuts across class, race, and ethnic lines in the United States. A commitment to family seems to be so widely shared across groups of all kinds in the hybrid mix that makes up American culture as to be nearly universal. It therefore comes as some surprise that the qualities many accept as natural components of family ties today—unconditional love, warmth, enduring attachment—were not the same expectations most American families had until 150 years ago. The historical variations in family life challenge the claim that the family, even within the same culture, has had the same meaning or has offered the same timeless experiences to its members.

11   Assumptions about American family life in the past are widely shared. These include the beliefs that families were large and extended, with most people living in multigenerational households; that marriages occurred at an early age and were based on permanent, unwavering commitment between spouses; that the ties between kin were stronger and closer than those experienced today; and that family life in the past was more stable and predictable than it is currently. These assumptions about the family of the past have collectively produced an image that one sociologist has called "the Classical Family of Western Nostalgia." It is the image upon which politicians and advertisers, among others, routinely draw as they explain contemporary social problems by reference to family breakdown or as they tap consumer desires by associating a product with positive family values and warm family feeling. The family is a potent symbol in contemporary American society, because it touches our emotional needs for both intimate personal attachments and a sense of embeddedness in a larger community.

12   Is there truth to the fears that family values are weaker today than in the past—that children are more vulnerable, adolescents more intractable, adults less dependable, and the elderly more needy? In both popular culture and political discourse, sentimentality and nostalgia about the family have often prevailed, and a social and historical context for framing the issues has largely been missing. It is important to challenge the popular understanding of the family as an institution that is biologically

based, immutable, and predictable with a more culturally variable and historically grounded view. Because families are central to the way we talk about ourselves and about our social and political lives, they deserve to be studied in their fullest scope, attached to a real past as well as a present and future.

Academic Perspectives on the Family

13 Assumptions about the nature of the family abound not only in popular culture but in social science as well. The disciplines of anthropology, sociology, history, and psychology all have particular orientations to the institution of the family that define their theoretical positions and research agendas. Among sociologists and anthropologists, for example, a starting premise about the family has been that it is one of the central organizing institutions of society. Its centrality comes from having the capacity to organize social life quite effectively by regulating sexuality, controlling reproduction, and ensuring the socialization of children who are born within the family unit. Many social science disciplines start with the question "How is society possible?" and they recognize that the organization of individuals into family units is a very effective means of providing social regulation and continuity. Through the institution of the family, individuals are joined together and given the social and legal sanction to perpetuate their name and traditions through their offspring. Whole societies are replenished with future generations of leaders and workers.

14 In the early twentieth century, the anthropologist Bronislaw Malinowski made the argument that the most universal characteristic of family life in all cultures and all time periods was the "principle of legitimacy." He had noted that the rules for sexual behavior varied widely across cultures but that control over reproduction was a common feature of every social order. Every society made the distinction between those children (legitimate) born to parents who had been culturally and legally sanctioned to reproduce and those children (illegitimate) whose parents were not accorded this sanction. The function of the principle of legitimacy, according to Malinowski, was to ensure that a child born into a society had both an identifiable mother and father. The father might, in fact, not be biologically related to the child, but his recognized sociological status as father was the affiliation that gave the child a set of kin and a social placement in that social order.

15 In addition to being the only sanctioned setting for reproduction, families are important sources of social continuity, because they are most often the setting in which children are cared for and raised. The power of social forces is such that parents normally can be counted on to provide long-term care for their dependent children, because the emotional closeness of family bonds makes them want to do so. Families are therefore particularly effective institutions, because they press people into service for their kin by the dual imperatives of love and obligation. Although it is possible that food, shelter, physical care, and emotional nurturance could be provided through alternative means by the state or other centrally administered bureaucratic agencies, it would require considerable societal resources and effort to ensure that these needs were effectively met for a majority of individuals in a society. What families seem to provide naturally, societies would otherwise have to coordinate and regulate at great cost.

16   To argue that families are effective or efficient as social institutions is not, however, to claim that they are necessary or inevitable. One common fallacy that some sociologists have promoted in studying the family at the societal level is the equation of its prevalence with the idea that it is functionally necessary. The assumption that societies "need" families in order to continue, based on the observation that some form of family exists in all known societies, ignores the range of variation in or the exceptions to this institution. Individuals and subgroups within all societies have constructed alternative arrangements to the traditional family of parents and their children. But the very fact that they are considered alternatives or experimental social organizations suggests how powerful the dominant family norm continues to be.

17   Another assumption that is shared across several social science disciplines is that family harmony and stability constitute the basis for order and control in the larger society. From this perspective, the family is a microcosm of the larger society, and social regulation in the domestic sphere helps promote order and control at all social levels. Individual social analysts might alternatively celebrate or lament the kind of control, regulation, and social order that was understood to begin in the family and radiate outward to the larger society; but the assumption that society was built on the foundation of the family was rarely challenged.

18   As a microcosm or a miniature society of the rulers and the ruled who are bound together by reciprocal rights and obligations, the family helps maintain social order first by its capacity to place people in the social system. It does so by providing them with identifiable kin and establishing the lines of legitimate succession and inheritance that mark their economic, political, and social position in society. Because individuals are located in an established social hierarchy by their birth or adoption into a particular family group, the nature of power and access to resources in a society remain largely intact from one generation to the next. Thus, one meaning of the family as a central institution of the social order is that it reinforces the political and economic status quo. Families ensure that the distribution of resources both to the advantaged and disadvantaged will remain relatively stable, since the transmission of wealth, property, status, and opportunity is channeled along the lines of kinship.

19   In another important way, families help to regulate the social order. Family life, according to both law and custom, prescribes roles for men, women, and children. Although these roles are really the products of social and cultural forces, rather than biological imperatives, and are therefore highly fluid in times of change, they appear to most people to be prescribed by stable and immutable rules governing everyday life. The meaning of "traditional" family life is that people are conscripted into established roles. Everyone knows his or her place and tends to keep to it by the pressures of community norms and social sanctions. But such traditional family roles exact a toll as well. What promotes social harmony and order to the advantage of some produces severe constraints on others. Women and children, whose roles in the family have traditionally been subordinate to those of men, have sometimes resisted such prescriptive expectations and have led the charge for social change in both overt and covert ways. It is not surprising that in times of rapid social change the family has been identified as an inherently conservative institution, one that not

only helps to perpetuate the status quo but is perceived as being oppressively restrictive to many of its own members.

20   Although many changes have characterized American family life over time, we should be mindful of important continuities as well. The most striking continuity is the importance that the family holds for so many people. The reasons that the family is important have varied historically, but there is no doubt that it has been a central institution, one on which people have pinned all manner of beliefs, values, and prejudices, as well as fears about and hopes for the future. Families reside at the intersection of private and public experience. We are all experts, since most of us have lived within one or more families at some point in our lives. Families can house both our highest hopes and our greatest disappointments, and their fragility or resilience therefore carries great personal meaning, in addition to social significance. The novelist Amos Oz has called the family "the most mysterious, most secret institution in the world." Its mysteries and secrets are not fully revealed in the social and historical record, but in reconstructing some of the patterns of family life, we can begin to understand why it has continued to play such a central role in American culture, as an organizing social institution, a lived experience, and a powerful metaphor. ◆

CRITICAL THINKING

1. Social scientists and family historians often comment that the American family is in a "state of transition." What do they mean? What is *transition*? Is it a positive or negative thing?
2. Farrell notes that in a poll on moral values, 78 percent of respondents said that they were dissatisfied with today's moral values, but that only 11 percent believed that their own behavior had contributed to this moral decline. What is your own opinion about today's moral values, and how does your own behavior fit in with these values?
3. Evaluate Farrell's opening joke about Adam and Eve. How does it connect to her material? Is it an effective means of drawing in readers and orienting them to her topic?
4. Farrell notes that Americans want their families to "offer unconditional love yet also to enforce and uphold strict moral values. They want flexibility, mobility, and autonomy . . . but yearn for traditional communities and permanently stable families" (paragraph 4). What, according to the author, is problematic with this yearning? Do you agree? Explain.
5. In her fifth paragraph, Farrell discusses our social fear of change. How does our fear of change connect to the practice of scapegoating? Identify some social scapegoats of the last century. For what were they blamed and why? Who "represents the forces of the new" today?
6. Farrell comments that our social concern for "The Family" is rooted in the "metaphor evoked by family" (paragraph 7). What does she mean? How does she define *family* in this paragraph, and how does this definition connect to our social concerns about the decay of the family in general? Explain.

7. How do we construct the institution of the family? What cultural myths and social forces contribute to our construction of this institution? How does nostalgia influence our view? Explain.

8. According to Farrell, what assumptions about family span many academic disciplines, such as anthropology, sociology, history, and psychology? How do these assumptions form the basis for the theoretical approaches of these disciplines? Explain.

9. How do families "help to regulate the social order" (paragraph 19)? How can this regulation "exact a toll" on certain members of society? Do you agree or disagree with Farrell's assessment? Explain.

CRITICAL WRITING

1. *Exploratory Writing:* At the end of her essay, Farrell quotes novelist Amos Oz, who calls the family "the most mysterious, most secret institution in the world." Write an essay in which you explore this idea. How is the family "secret"? If almost everyone has a family and understands what the term implies, how can it be "mysterious"? Support your position with information from Farrell's article as well as your own personal perspective.

2. *Research and Analysis:* If you are a practicing member of an organized religious faith, research your religion's beliefs about family. If you are not a member of an organized religion, select one to research. Be sure to include references from news sources, journals, theologians, religious texts, and spiritual leaders of the faith. If possible, interview a religious leader for a summary of beliefs. Write an essay in which you describe the position the religious faith has on family and how these beliefs are "institutionalized" in the religion.

3. *Exploratory Writing:* In a letter to a politician or public figure of your choice, discuss the current state of the family as it applies to the concept of family as an institution in American culture. In your letter, you should make specific references to the politician's own stance on the state of the family.

GROUP PROJECTS

1. Design and administer a poll to people outside your class. Ask for opinions on the health of the American family versus its decline, the ideal role each family member should play in family structure, the desirability of day care, and so on. Also ask for anonymous information about each participant's age, economic status, education, political affiliation, religion, and race. After you have assembled the data you collected as a group, analyze the results. Do any groups seem more or less optimistic about the state of the American family? If so, in what ways? Are some groups more traditional? Explain.

2. Farrell notes that although politicians and social conservatives attribute social ills to failings within the institution of family, there are other forces that help formulate popular opinion about the family. Visit the American Family Association (AFA) Web site at http://www.AFA.net and evaluate its social and political stance on family. What conventions does it embrace, and how does it view nontraditional family structures? What outside forces, according to the AFA, threaten today's families? Explain.

Perspectives: The New American Family

"This is our daughter, my son from my first marriage, John's daughter from his second marriage, and I've no idea who the one on the end is."

www.roystonrobertson.co.uk

THINKING CRITICALLY

1. What is happening in this cartoon? Who are the people in the picture, and what are they discussing?
2. What social or cultural situation does this cartoon depict? Can you relate? Explain.
3. What unique challenges do children of blended families face? Explain.

Numbers Drop for the Married-with-Children
*Blaine Harden**

Many conservatives connect the decline of the American family to the liberal and feminist influences of the 1960s and 1970s. But the erosion of the "traditional family unit" of husband, wife, and children living together under one roof may have less to do with the progressive nature of these decades and more to do with finances. In the next article and interview that follow, reporter Blaine Harden explains that marriage is becoming an institution for the educated and the affluent. Is the working class being pushed out of marriage? And if so, what will that mean for the American family in years to come?

1 Punctuating a fundamental change in American family life, married couples with children now occupy fewer than one in every four households—a share that has been slashed in half since 1960 and is the lowest ever recorded by the census.

2 As marriage with children becomes an exception rather than the norm, social scientists say it is also becoming the self-selected province of the college-educated and the affluent. The working class and the poor, meanwhile, increasingly steer away from marriage, while living together and bearing children out of wedlock.

3 "The culture is shifting, and marriage has almost become a luxury item, one that only the well educated and well paid are interested in," said Isabel V. Sawhill, an expert on marriage and a senior fellow at the Brookings Institution.

4 Marriage has declined across all income groups, but it has declined far less among couples who make the most money and have the best education. These couples are also less likely to divorce. Many demographers peg the rise of a class-based marriage gap to the erosion since 1970 of the broad-based economic prosperity that followed World War II.

5 "We seem to be reverting to a much older pattern, when elites marry and a great many others live together and have kids," said Peter Francese, demographic trends analyst for Ogilvy and Mather, an advertising firm.

6 In recent years, the marrying kind have been empowered by college degrees and bankrolled by dual incomes. They are also older and choosier. College-educated men and women are increasingly less likely to "marry down"—that is, to choose mates who have less education and professional standing than they do.

7 Married couples living with their own children younger than 18 are also helping to drive a well-documented increase in income inequality. Compared with all households, they are twice as likely to be in the top

> *"The culture is shifting, and marriage has almost become a luxury item, one that only the well educated and well paid are interested in."*

20 percent of income. Their income has increased 59 percent in the past three decades, compared with 44 percent for all households, according to the census.

* Blaine Harden, *Washington Post*, March 4, 2007

8   As cohabitation and out-of-wedlock births increase among the broader population, social scientists predict that marriage with children will continue its decades-
long retreat into relatively high-income exclusivity.

9   Jim and Michelle Fitzhenry live with their 5-year-old son, John Robert, in a
four-bedroom house in a gated community high in the wooded hills west of Portland. Sixteen years ago, when Jim met Michelle, they fell in love because they liked
each other's looks—and loved each other's values.

10   "What attracted me to Michelle was her kindness and her honesty, but also her
discipline, ambition, and achievement," said Jim, who has a law degree and an
MBA. He is a senior vice president at FLIR Systems, a Portland company that
makes night-vision equipment.

11   Those same personality traits, Michelle said, drew her to Jim. She has a bachelor's degree in business administration and worked for a decade as an executive at
Plum Creek Timber Company in Seattle. The Fitzhenrys, who married 10 years ago,
are an example of what sociologists call "assortative mating," the increasing tendency of educated, affluent people to unite in marriage.

12   When the Fitzhenrys married (he was 42, she was 32), it changed the way they
managed their finances, which Jim said had been in a "death spiral" when they were
single. Michelle quickly paid off $20,000 in credit-card debt. Jim cut up most of his
credit cards and got rid of a BMW convertible.

13   Among its many benefits, marriage raises the earnings of men and motivates
them to work more hours. It also reduces by two-thirds the likelihood that a family
will live in poverty, researchers have learned.

14   "Although we didn't plan it that way, and we certainly didn't marry for money,
it turned out that a by-product of the values we both care about has been financial
success," said Michelle, who places the couple's annual earnings between $350,000
and $400,000, much of which is invested conservatively.

15   The marital unions of high earners are a significant factor in the growth of
income inequality since the 1970s, according to Gary Burtless, an economist at
Brookings. His research attributes 13 percent of the increase in the nation's income
inequality to such couples.

16   The Fitzhenrys said they had no idea marriage with children was becoming an elite
institution. "By getting married and having a kid, we just assumed we were doing what
everyone else in the country was doing," Jim said. "We thought we were normal."

17   As far as marriage with children is concerned, the post–World War II version of
normal began to fall apart around 1970.

18   "Before then, if you looked at families across the income spectrum, they all
looked the same: a mother, father, kids, and a dog named Spot," said Sawhill, of the
Brookings Institution.

19   Around that time, rates of divorce and cohabitation were rising sharply—and
widely publicized.

20   "What I don't think the public knew then or knows now is that well-educated,
upper-middle-class professionals did not engage in these activities nearly as much
as less advantaged families," Sawhill said.

21   College-educated women, whose numbers have risen sharply since 1980, often
live with a partner and postpone marriage. But in most cases, they eventually marry

and have children and divorce at about half the rate of women who do not finish high school.

22   While the marriage gap appears to be driven primarily by education and income, it does have a racial dimension.

23   Marriage and childbearing seem to be more "de-coupled" among black people than white people, with about a third of first births among white women coming before marriage, compared with three-quarters among black women, according to a recent review of research on cohabitation. As for children, the review found that 55 percent of blacks, 40 percent of Hispanics, and 30 percent of whites spend some of their childhood with cohabiting parents.

24   Class, though, is a much better tool than race for predicting whether Americans will marry or cohabit, said Pamela Smock, coauthor of the review and a University of Michigan sociology professor.

25   "The poor aren't entering into marriage very much at all," said Smock, who has interviewed more than 100 cohabitating couples. She said young people from these backgrounds often do not think they can afford marriage.

26   Arguments that marriage can mean stability do not seem to change their attitudes, Smock said, noting that many of them have parents with troubled marriages.

27   Victoria Miller and Cameron Roach, who have been living together for 18 months, are two such people, and they say they cannot imagine getting married.

28   She is 22 and manages a Burger King in Seattle. He is 24 and works part time testing software in the Seattle suburb of Redmond. Together, they earn less than $20,000 a year and are living with Roach's father. They cannot afford to live anywhere else.

29   "Marriage ruins life," Roach said. "I saw how much my parents fought. I saw how miserable they made each other."

30   Miller, who was pressured by her Mormon parents to marry when she was 17 and pregnant, said her short, failed marriage and her parents' long, failed marriage have convinced her that the institution is often bad for children. Shuttled between her mom and dad, she moved eight times before she was 16.

31   "With my parents, when their marriage started breaking down, my dad started to have trouble at work and we spent years on government assistance," Miller said.

32   Her two young sons live with their father.

33   "For most Americans, cohabitation will continue to increase over the coming decades, and the percentage of children born outside of marriage is also going to increase," Smock said. ◆

Online Interview with Blaine Harden

One-quarter of U.S. households are traditional married-with-children families, the most recent census found—down from half of households in the 1960s. *Washington Post* writer Blaine Harden was online Monday, March 5, 2007 to discuss his article about the trend, which has overwhelmingly affected the poor, as marriage almost has become—as one expert put it—"a luxury item."

1   **Blaine Harden:** Hi, this is Blaine Harden out in Seattle, delighted to talk about marriage with children.

2   *Bowie, MD: Fascinating article. Important question that wasn't clearly addressed: Are there behavioral differences between the married and unmarried parents, aside from income levels?*

3   **Blaine Harden:** What researchers and demographers have increasingly found since the 1970s is that people who tend to get married also tend to have a higher education. They say that with that education comes higher income, better housing, better schools, better knowledge about nutrition, and lower rates of divorce and child abuse.

4   *Gaithersburg, MD: What is believed to be the root cause for this shift from married-with-children being the norm to less than 25 percent of today's households living in a married-with-children status? The article seems to suggest it's a matter of economics—I'm inclined to believe there is much, much more to it than that. . . .*

5   **Blaine Harden:** You are right, it is more than a matter of economics. Researchers who have spent hundreds of hours talking with cohabitating young people—mostly from working-class and lower-middle-class backgrounds—have learned that many of them do not see marriage as an enviable model. They have seen marriages that have ended in divorce or have been soured by endless fighting, and they see upper-middle-class marriage—as portrayed on TV and in the movies—as beyond their means. Researchers say that many young people view marriage as a kind of pie-in-the-sky ideal, something they will attain when they pay off their car, get rid of credit card debt, or get a promotion. They often are not persuaded by fact-based arguments that point out how marriage has a way of increasing financial stability.

6   *"Marriage Is For White People" was the name/catch-phrase of an article the* Washington Post *ran a few months back, dealing with the low number of marriages in the black community. I coupled your article with that one and others from the "Being a Black Man" series, where the issue of fatherhood was brought up. The fathers in the articles were not married to the children's mother and appeared to be of the uneducated/lower socioeconomic class. They all appeared not to have a flattering outlook/opinion of marriage. As a married black father of two young daughters myself, I am concerned—did your research find more men, in general terms, than women with such negative outlooks of marriage?*

7   **Blaine Harden:** Class, not race, is probably the best filter for guessing who will marry in America. That is the conclusion of most of the researchers who have been studying the data. Because income and education continue to skew higher for whites than blacks, there is a higher marriage rate for whites and a considerably lower rate of out-of-wedlock birth. But as time goes by, the researchers are finding, cohabitation for whites and all other races is becoming a norm for people who don't go to college. The national rate for out-of-wedlock birth is 37 percent. That means that a huge part of the population—black and white and all races, as well as men and women—is defining normal behavior much differently than in the years after World War II.

8   *Washington: It seems to me that if marriage is one of the ways one preserves and increases one's wealth, then perhaps those who are choosing instead to live together or reject marriage ought to rethink that choice if they value their economic well-being. In other words, if you want to be wealthy, don't do what poor people do.*

9   **Blaine Harden:** What you say is logical. A good student of demography and economic well-being would choose marriage for a better life, more money in the bank, better housing, and probably better health. But decisions about who you live with and when you have kids are usually not driven by a shrewd understanding of economic/demographic trends—much more powerful in shaping those decisions is the culture and what peers are doing. As cohabitation and out-of-wedlock births become increasingly common, marriage no longer seems to have the same allure— that is, of course, except for people with college educations and high income. Researchers find that while the college-educated postpone marriage and often do cohabitate, they continue to see marriage as desirable and valuable for children—at rates that are much higher than for the population as a whole.

10   *Laurel, MD: I realize you're a reporter, not an activist, so you're not going to take a stand on this, but this illustrates to me the outright hypocrisy of the Republican party: They long for a return of the family-orientation of the post-war period (roughly 1950–65) while rejecting the economic leveling that made it possible. The fact that the period experienced a record marriage rate and baby boom is inextricably tied up with its job security. When a sensible person decides whether to start a family, "Do I have reasonable expectation of steady income for 20 years?" is an important datum, but today's Republican party wants a free-agent economy that discourages family formation and community roots. I strongly suspect their "profamily" orientation is just a cover for the fact that they know their economic priorities are bad for families and communities, so "if the people had family values, poverty wouldn't cause crime" is how they escape responsibility.*

11   **Blaine Harden:** Partisan politics aside, I think it is fascinating that marriage with kids became the overwhelming norm in the United States after World War II, during a phenomenal time of widespread prosperity—and that marriage with kids has gone into a long, downward slide that roughly coincides with the rise of income inequality. This is a subject that deserves a lot of research. There are some other factors at work, however, in the relative decline in the United States of households occupied by parents with kids. Most important are demographic trends—people living longer (so they raise kids who leave and occupy empty-nester households) and the increasing age at which people marry (from the low 20s to the high 20s).

12   *U.S.: So young adults now think that marriage is too expensive, causes fighting, and divorce is messy—but they're still having kids with each other. Having kids can be expensive and cause fighting, and I would hope that leaving someone who has your child is messy, not just "See ya." So do we just need to provide Depo Provera to these people—as their birth control isn't what it should be—or are they choosing to have kids but not applying the same logic to that choice, which is a much bigger choice? After all, a marriage is entered into by two consenting parties. The kids don't get a choice.*

13   **Blaine Harden:** Not sure if that is a question. Marriage with kids, of course, can be horrible—at any income level. Researchers are careful to point out that kids growing up with biological parents in a family where there is domestic violence or chronic psychological abuse usually are better off elsewhere.

14   *St. Mary's City, MD: Among young people, is there a difference between genders in attitudes about marriage? Until the 1960s, marriage largely was a*

patriarchal institution. I suspect that before the women's movement, many married men didn't put much work or thought into being a good husband, because they took their "head of household" position for granted. Likewise, many married women may have assumed that it was their lot in life to be saddled with bad husbands. My perception is that today's young women feel more empowered, rightly believing that marriage should be a partnership between equals, but today's young men still may be behind in their attitudes, but in an infantile way, where they expect wives to be substitute mommies. I'm thinking particularly of the recent phenomenon of many young men living at home until age 30 or so. Is this accurate?

15   **Blaine Harden:** This is a great question and I am afraid I don't know enough to give a complete answer. Here's a partial stab at it: For women, rising rates of college education (there are more women in college now than men) has given them economic independence, allowed them to postpone marriage, and allowed them to be much pickier when it comes to husbands. By and large, though, these educated, independent women do want to have kids and they tend to see marriage to a suitable partner as the best, most secure way to go about it, according to a wide body of research. As I mentioned in my story, this has helped push a powerful trend in marriage of like-marrying-like. Lawyers do not as frequently marry secretaries or doctors marry nurses—it is lawyers merging with lawyers and doctors with other doctors. I think this means that these women are finding men who will do more to hold up their end of the bargain when it comes to household chores and child-rearing duties.

16   *Vienna, Va.: Out-of-wedlock births may be more common, but is that really a good thing? Don't most studies suggest that children born in an intact marriage are more likely to go to college, less likely to commit crime, et cetera? But as in your answer earlier, people don't make these decisions based on demographic data. The story makes me sad—it clearly is not in anyone's long-term economic interest to live together instead of marry, and especially not to create a child out of that relationship. Yet more people persist in doing so, with none of the social stigma that those decisions used to bring on.*

17   **Blaine Harden:** It is a sad trend from the perspective of what is best, on average, for children. There are some exceptions, though. Given sufficient income and education levels, raising kids outside of marriage is less likely to have poor results. But of course, the whole point of my story is that it is the best educated and the best paid who are most likely to see marriage as essential for raising kids.

18   *New York: In looking at low-income marriage rates 50 years ago versus today, that negates your almost Marxist theory of economics determining marriage trends. Why not look at the cultural shift in the past 35 years of perceptions of marriage, morality, and values? I have tutored young adults in the inner city, and any aversion to marriage has nothing to do with economics, but rather a firm belief that is almost the opposite of the values and morals of the previous generations—not because of economics, but because of a self-centered and openly antitraditional way of thinking.*

19   **Blaine Harden:** I can state without fear or favor that I am not Marxist. And you are right that cultural norms play a huge role. I was just pointing out that it is interesting that marriage has declined as economic inequality has risen. But it is also interesting to examine who *wants* to get married in modern America and who does not. Lots of social science research—as well as my interviews with married and cohabiting couples—suggests that people tend to imitate in their own lives what

they experience growing up. As marriage becomes the province of the affluent and educated, it is likely that affluent and educated young people will see marriage as valuable. On the other hand, those growing up in a world of cohabitation will tend to see marriage as something for the privileged. Researchers who have conducted interviews over time with hundreds of cohabitating young people often are told that marriage is for doctors and lawyers.

20   ***Kingston, RI:*** *What are the trends in number of people per household?*

21   **Blaine Harden:** The number of people per household has declined pretty steadily since the 1960s. Not much of a surprise. Over that time, the percentage of households that are married with kids has been cut in half.

22   ***Bowie, MD:*** *How much of the rejection of marriage is due to men's fear that "an ex-wife is a luxury I can't afford"?*

23   **Blaine Harden:** Your question is very insightful. Young people who have witnessed their parents' wrenching divorces—a father complaining bitterly for years about money—have good reason to be fearful of marriage. On this point, it is interesting to note that divorce rates are considerably lower among people who have higher-than-average education and incomes. This means that, across the U.S. population, there are going to be relatively more low-income, low-education people with sour images of marriage/divorce. Presumably, these feed into the trend of marriage becoming a class-based institution.

24   ***Silver Spring, MD:*** *We know that divorce rates are higher among the lower-educated and less economically secure (on top of the fact that they are less likely to marry). Is there any reason to believe that an increase in marriage would provide more stability for these couples and their children?*

25   **Blaine Harden:** This is the $64,000 question in the marriage debate. The Bush administration has tried to promote marriage, arguing that is good for kids, for parents, and for society as a whole. But there is very little evidence, at least so far, that a desire to marry and stay married can be taught. . . . Thanks very much for the chat. ◆

CRITICAL THINKING

1. Many of Harden's readers refer to the family unit of the 1950s and 1960s. To what are they referring? What was the established family structure, and how was this structure conveyed in cultural media at the time?

2. A reader from St. Mary's City, Maryland, comments on the possible role of feminism on the changing structure of the family. What does this reader think is the problem? What is your opinion of this viewpoint?

3. Harden notes that marriage seems to have become the social norm for the educated and, therefore, more likely the affluent. What factors have contributed to this phenomenon?

4. As a student likely to be part of the educated group of people Harden connects to marriage, what is your personal viewpoint on his observations? Are you more likely to marry a college-educated person? Do you intend to ever get married? How does your social view compare to friends or acquaintances who are not pursuing a college education? Explain.

5. What are the long-term consequences of the decline of marriage among the working poor?
6. Does the fact that Harden is a reporter and not a politician or social expert make him more or less credible in the article and subsequent interview? Explain.
7. What is Harden's position on the issue of marriage and family? Identify areas of his article and interview in which he reveals his viewpoint.
8. What other factors, besides the financial constraints the author describes, could be contributing to the apparent decline in marriage and married-with-children households?

CRITICAL WRITING

1. *Exploratory Writing:* If you are a parent, or if you are thinking about marriage and children in your future, do you feel that marriage is an important consideration for you? What factors influence your decision to marry or not to marry? Explore your perspective in a well-considered essay.
2. *Personal Narrative:* Write a personal narrative in which you describe the structure of your family during your childhood. How does your family compare to the family situations described in this article? Are you more or less likely to follow the marriage and family patterns set by your parents? Explain.

GROUP PROJECTS

1. Working in small groups, discuss and compare the structures of families within your own experiences. Think about the families you grew up in, the families you know well, and the families you may have started. Evaluate the kinds of families you find. These may include two-earner families, traditional families, families with no children, blended families with stepparents and children, children raised by other relatives, and other groupings. Compare notes with your group.
2. Working in small groups, interview several people who have children under the age of 18. Describe the family unit of the people you interviewed. Are they married with children, or are they living in a different family arrangement? What circumstances led to their family situations? Finally, how satisfied are they with their family arrangements, and what are their hopes for the future? After completing your interviews, compare your interviews with those of the rest of the group and write a short article reporting your results.
3. Visit the Coalition for Marriage, Family, and Couples Education Web site at http://www.SmartMarriages.com/articles.html and review some of the statistical and research information posted there. On the coalition's Web site, pick a topic related to marriage that interests you and research it using the information on the site and additional Web resources. Write a short research report on your topic, connecting it to the subject of trends in marriage in the twenty-first century.

CULTURE SHOCK

Marriage Trends in the United States

Several authors in this section note that marriage is on the decline in the United States. This graph below, based on 2004–2005 U.S. Census data, provides a detailed look at the numbers.

Percentage of All Persons Age 15 and Older Who Were Married, by Sex and Race, 1960–2005 United States[a]

	Males			Females		
	Total	Black	White	Total	Black	White
1960	69.3	60.9	70.2	65.9	59.8	66.6
1970	66.7	56.9	68.0	61.9	54.1	62.8
1980	63.2	48.8	65.0	58.9	44.6	60.7
1990	60.7	45.1	62.8	56.9	40.2	59.1
2000	57.9	42.8	60.0	54.7	36.2	57.4
2005[b]	55.0	37.9	57.5	51.5	30.2	54.6

[a] Includes races other than black and white
[b] In 2003, the U.S. Census Bureau expanded its racial categories to permit respondents to identify themselves as belonging to more than one race. This means that racial data computations begining in 2004 may not be strictly comparable to those of prior years.

Source: U.S. Bureau of the Census. Current Population Reports, Series P20–506; *America's Families and Living Arrangements: March 2000* and earlier reports; and data calculated from the Current Population Surveys, March 2005 Supplement

THINKING CRITICALLY

1. Is marriage an archaic institution, no longer practically functional in today's society?
2. What cultural factors could have influenced the numbers in this table? For example, do you think women's improved economic role outside the home has influenced their feelings about marriage? Could the social acceptance of divorce have influenced these numbers? Explain.
3. Are you more optimistic or less optimistic about the prospect of marriage after viewing this graph? Explain.
4. In your opinion, what is the long-term outlook for marriage? How do you fit into the outlook shown in the table?
5. If you could live together with a partner and enjoy the same benefits afforded to married couples, such as health insurance, inheritance rights, and retirement benefits, would you still get married? Why?
6. What cultural and social trends can you infer influenced the data in the table? Explain. If you were a social scientist, what predictions might you be able to make based on the data provided?

On Not Saying "I Do"

*Dorian Solot**

> Several of the essays in this chapter lament the decline of marriage as an inevitable—and regrettable—reality. The author of the next reading argues that marriage isn't all it is cracked up to be. In fact, people can exist in meaningful and rewarding relationships without marriage, and children can grow up in nurturing and emotionally stable homes. In the next essay, a personal narrative, Dorian Solot wonders why such a fuss is made about getting married.

1   I must have missed the day in nursery school when they lined up all the little girls and injected them with the powerful serum that made them dream of wearing a white wedding dress.

2   From that day onward, it seemed, most little girls played bridal dress-up, drew pictures of brides, gazed in magazines at the latest bridal fashions, and eagerly anticipated their Prince Charming popping the question. More than anything, they dreamed of walking down the aisle and living happily ever after. I dreamed mostly of the cats, dogs, and horses I'd get to adopt when I grew up. When I was old enough to walk around town on my own, I remember my best friend stopping in front of a bridal shop window to point out which dress she'd like to wear someday, and she asked me to pick mine. I told her honestly that I didn't like any of them, aware even then that she would probably think I was weird, because that wasn't what girls were supposed to say.

3   In my early twenties, about three years into my relationship with my partner, Marshall, the occasional subtle hints that my family and friends were ready for an engagement announcement became decidedly less subtle. To keep their hopes in check, I announced what had seemed clear to me for a long time: I did not intend to get married. Ever. Be in love, sure. Share my life with this wonderful man, absolutely. But walk down the aisle and exchange rings—the tradition baffles me.

4   I didn't expect my small refusal to matter much to anyone. But I have quickly learned that in a society in which 90 percent of people get married sometime in their lives, lacking the desire to do so appears in the "barely acceptable" category.

5   Not being married to my partner has meant ending the conversation with a potential landlord after his first three questions: How many people? Are you married? When are you getting married? It's meant paying an extra fee—the unmarried surcharge, you might call it—to be allowed to drive the same rental car. And it's meant having my partner be denied health insurance through my job when he needed it, even though our four years together exceeded the relationship length of my newlywed coworkers who received joint coverage.

6   It's also meant answering questions that get frustrating. "Do you think you'll change your mind?" is a common one. I want to ask these people, "Do you think you might convert to a new religion? Do you think you might change your mind about the ethics of abortion?" Anything is possible, of course, and I'm not so naïve as to think we all don't change our minds about things over the course of a lifetime. But the

* Dorian Solot, *Nerve.com*, May 27, 2004

frequency with which I'm asked this question makes it less an innocent inquiry about a personal choice and more a suggestion that says, "Your position is so absurd you can't take it seriously for long."

7　　　I've lost track of the number of sympathetic strangers who've shared with me their incorrect assumption that as an unmarried woman in a long-term relationship, my partner must suffer from a severe case of commitment phobia. Women in newspaper

> *I've lost track of the number of sympathetic strangers who've shared with me their incorrect assumption that as an unmarried woman in a long-term relationship, my partner must suffer from a severe case of commitment phobia.*

advice columns and television talk shows are forever strategizing about where to find a man willing to get hitched and debating whether to leave the guys who won't marry them. Interestingly, though, every survey ever conducted on this subject finds that on average, men are more eager to marry than women are. The National Survey of Families and Households, for example, found that 24 percent of unmarried 18–35 year old men said they'd like to get married someday, compared to 16 percent of unmarried women the same age.

8　　　Eventually, frustrated that we couldn't find any group that could provide the support and information we needed, Marshall and I founded the Alternatives to Marriage Project. Judging by the number of emails and phone calls we received after posting a Web site, we weren't alone. There are growing legions of women who, like me, are not interested in assuming the role of wife. Books like *Marriage Shock: The Transformation of Women into Wives* and *Cutting Loose: Why Women Who End Their Marriages Do So Well* quote scores of women who explain how their relationships changed when they got married. Suddenly, they found themselves more likely to be making breakfast and less likely to be talking candidly about sex. As a result of this kind of research, some made the case for more conscious marriages with fewer gendered assumptions, and I think that's a great goal. But if marriage has that much power to change people's behavior, I'd rather invest my energy exploring alternatives, not struggling to reshape an institution that doesn't suit me.

9　　　To me, the issue isn't whether civil marriage should include same-sex couples. Of course it should; that's a fundamental matter of civil and human rights. The issue is the confusing tangle of meanings in the word "marriage," and how they do and don't correspond to real-life relationships and real people's lives. There's religious marriage, conferred by blessings; civil marriage and the legal protections it brings; and social marriage, the support of communities who give special treatment to couples they perceive to be married. (Having just bought a house in a neighborhood where no one knew us before, it's been fascinating to be treated as a married couple, even though our "marriage" is social, not legal.) On top of that, although the concepts of commitment, monogamy, and marriage usually go hand in hand, my work is filled with committed unmarried couples. And we've all read the tabloid headlines about married ones whose commitments don't last all that long. Among both married and unmarried couples, the vast majority chooses monogamy, while smaller numbers choose polyamory or engage in infidelity. We have only one concept—marriage— that is used to divide the world neatly into two groups, married and not married. The real world is a lot messier than that. Our cultural inability to face that complexity leaves us in a state of collective bafflement about the status and future of marriage (Is marriage overvalued? Undervalued? Having a renaissance? Dying out?) and inspires confused debates about same-sex unions. The solution, I believe, is to encourage and support healthy, stable relationships and families in all their forms, instead of linking so many unrelated benefits to the piece of paper we call a marriage license.

10   There are joys to not being married. I love that I am not a wife, with all its hidden meanings and baggage. I love the consciousness of my relationship, day after day of "I choose you" that has now lasted 11 years and counting. I take secret pleasure in watching people wrestle silently when I mention "my partner," trying to ascertain my sexual orientation and marital status—as if it mattered. I love reading the headlines as one by one, companies, universities, cities, and states decide to provide equal benefits to the partners of their employees, regardless of marital status. I feel as if my daily life proves to those who say it can't be done—that unmarried relationships will fall apart when times are hard, that we can never achieve true intimacy, that we are doomed to lives of sin, sadness, or "perpetual adolescence"—that maybe the problem is theirs and not mine. There is an amazing diversity of families in this country; I hope one day society will be courageous enough to recognize and validate all of them.

11   I don't know how I failed to acquire a yearning for marriage. Maybe it's because of my feminist, hippie mom, who played *Free to Be You and Me* while I was in utero and encouraged me to have goals beyond marrying the handsome prince (and who, by the way, considers my handsome prince her son-in-law—or sometimes, affectionately, her son-outlaw). Perhaps it has to do with too many unhappily married people and the divorces I've seen, too many breezily pledged lifetime vows that lose their meaning long before the lifetimes end. Perhaps it has to do with my friends in same-sex relationships who can't legally marry (unless they live in the right city or state on the right day of the week), the fact that I already have a food processor, or my academic background in animal behavior, where I learned how few mammals mate for life. Or perhaps it's because I really was absent that day in nursery school. ◆

CRITICAL THINKING

1. If you decided to live with your significant other, do you think you would feel social pressure to marry after a period of cohabitation? Would your family approve? What are your personal expectations of cohabitation? Explain.

2. The author notes that although living together for a period of time is considered socially acceptable, deciding to maintain such an arrangement with no intention of ever marrying is not. What accounts for this view? If it is okay to live together, why isn't it okay never to get married?

3. Solot jokes that she missed the day the little girls were "injected with serum" that makes them obsessed with being brides and getting married. What does she mean? Explain.

4. What is the reaction of friends and family to Solot's decision not to marry? Do you agree that her decision appears in the "barely acceptable" category?

5. Why did the author decide not to get married? What are the benefits she cites about not being married?

CRITICAL WRITING

1. *Expository Writing:* Solot observes that many people live together before getting married. In your opinion, does this arrangement make sense? Is it better to test out a relationship before making a marriage commitment, or does it just make it easier for people to walk away from a relationship when the going gets rough? Would you live together with a sweetheart before making a commitment of marriage? Explain.

2. *Reader's Response:* Before you read this narrative, did you have any opinion on this issue? Did the essay change your ideas or give you something to think about that you had not considered before? Was Solot successful in persuading you to her point of view, if you did not already agree with it?

GROUP PROJECTS

1. Using free association and writing down anything that comes to mind, brainstorm with your group to develop a list of terms associated with the phrase *living together*. The list could include anything from "noncommitment" to "independent." Once you have developed a list, try and locate the source of the association, such as television, opinion editorials, government, political speeches, religion, and news media. Which sources are grounded in fact and which are not? What role does changing social opinion have on these associations? Explain.

2. Visit the Frontline Web site "Let's Get Married" at http://www.pbs.org/wgbh/pages/frontline/shows/marriage/etc/quiz.html and take the online quiz as a group. Have one person write down your responses before submitting the quiz for scoring. Review your score. Did any of the statistics surprise you? As a class, discuss your results.

Five Non-Religious Arguments for Marriage

*Dennis Prager**

> With the long list of celebrities living together and having children out of wedlock, coupled with a divorce rate at almost 50 percent, it would seem as if marriage is becoming passé. All across the economic spectrum, many couples prefer to live together rather than get married, at least for awhile. In the next essay, author Dennis Prager gives five reasons why he thinks marriage is preferable to living together.

1 I have always believed that there is no comparing living together with marriage. There are enormous differences between being a "husband" or a "wife" and being a "partner," a "friend," or a "significant other"; between a legal commitment and a

---

* Dennis Prager, *TownHall.com*, October 3, 2006

voluntary association; between standing before family and community to publicly announce one's commitment to another person on the one hand and simply living together on the other.

2   But attending the weddings of two of my three children this past summer made the differences far clearer and far more significant.

3   First, no matter what you think when living together, your relationship with your significant other changes the moment you marry. You have now made a commitment to each other as husband and wife in front of almost everyone significant in your life. You now see each other in a different and more serious light.

4   Second, words matter. They deeply affect us and others. Living with your "boyfriend" is not the same as living with your "husband." And living with your "girlfriend," or any other title you give her, is not the same as making a home with your "wife." Likewise, when you introduce that person as your wife or husband to people, you are making a far more important statement of that person's role in your life than you are with any other title.

5   Third, legality matters. Being legally bound to and responsible for another person matters. It is an announcement to him/her and to yourself that you take this relationship with the utmost seriousness. No words of affection or promises of commitment, no matter how sincere, can match the seriousness of legal commitment. Fourth, to better appreciate just how important marriage is to the vast majority of people in your life, consider this: There is no event, no occasion, no moment in your life when so many of the people who matter to you will convene in one place as they will at your wedding. Not the birth of any of your children, not any milestone birthday you may celebrate, not your child's bar-mitzvah or confirmation. The only other time so many of those you care about and who care about you will gather in one place is at your funeral. But by then, unless you die young, nearly all those you love who are older than you will have already died.

6   So this is it. Your wedding will be the greatest gathering of loved ones in your life. There is a reason. It is the biggest moment of your life. No such event will ever happen if you do not have a wedding. Fifth, only with marriage will your man's or your woman's family ever become your family. The two weddings transformed the woman in my son's life into my daughter-in-law and transformed the man in my daughter's life into my son-in-law. And I was instantly transformed from the father of their boyfriend or girlfriend into their father-in-law. This was the most dramatic new realization for me.

7   I was now related to my children's partners. Their siblings and parents became family. Nothing comparable happens when two people live together without getting married. Many women callers to my radio show have told me that the man in their life sees no reason to marry. "It's only a piece of paper," these men (and now some women) argue.

If in fact "it is only a piece of paper," what exactly is he so afraid of? Why does he fear a mere piece of paper? Either he is lying to himself and to his woman or lying only to her, because he knows this piece of paper is far more than "only a piece of paper."

8   There are two answers to this argument. One is that if in fact "it is only a piece of paper," what exactly is he so afraid of? Why does he fear a mere piece of paper?

Either he is lying to himself and to his woman or lying only to her, because he knows this piece of paper is far more than "only a piece of paper."

9   The other response is all that is written above. Getting married means I am now your wife, not your live-in; I am now your husband, not your significant other. It means that we get to have a wedding where, before virtually every person alive who means anything to us, we commit ourselves to each other. It means that we have decided to bring all these people we love into our lives. It means we have legal obligations to one another. It means my family becomes yours and yours becomes mine.

10   Thank God my children, ages 30 and 23, decided to marry. Their partners are now my daughter-in-law and son-in-law. They are therefore now mine to love, not merely two people whom my children love. When you realize all that is attainable by marrying and unattainable by living together without marrying, you have to wonder why anyone would voluntarily choose not to marry the person he or she wishes to live with forever.

11   Unless, of course, one of you really isn't planning on forever. ◆

CRITICAL THINKING

1. Many couples move in together without being married first but eventually marry later. Others never marry. Do you think people should live together before getting married? Should they marry at all? Why or why not?

2. Why do people marry? What values and expectations does marriage carry in our culture? Are the values and expectations that same for couples who live together? Why or why not?

3. Review Prager's second point, "words matter." What importance does he place on words? What words does he mean?

4. According to Prager, when one partner tells the other that marriage "is only a piece of paper," she or he is either lying or doesn't truly believe that the relationship is in fact forever. Do you agree with this assertion? Why does Prager feel it is a false argument against the importance of marriage?

5. In your opinion, which of Prager's five arguments is the strongest one? Which is the weakest? Explain.

6. Even though Prager is personally opposed to gay marriage, could his essay make an argument for legalizing gay marriage? Explain.

CRITICAL WRITING

1. *Persuasive Writing:* Argue the opposite viewpoint; in other words, provide five arguments for living together over getting married.

2. *Expository Writing:* If living together with a partner provided the same legal benefits afforded to traditionally married couples—such as health insurance, inheritance rights, and retirement benefits—would you still get married?

3. *Reader's Response:* Before you read this editorial, did you have any opinion on this issue? Did the essay change your ideas or give you something to think about that you had not considered before? If you did not already agree with him, was Prager successful in persuading you to his point of view?

GROUP PROJECTS

1. With your group, research the state of marriage in the United States today. Then in your own words, define what marriage is. You will have to discuss this as a group to come up with a definition that works for the majority. How easy or difficult was it to arrive at a definition that satisfied everyone?

2. Among the members of your group, describe the structure of your family during your childhood, focusing specifically on the role of marriage in your family. Were your parents married or divorced? Do you think the choices they made affected your outlook on marriage? Did they affect your life in general? How has your past experience influenced your future expectations of family life? Do you think the expectations of college students today about marriage and family differ from those of your parent's generation? Why or why not?

For Better, For Worse
Stephanie Coontz*

As Betty G. Farrell explained in the first essay in this chapter, many Americans feel that the family and marriage in general are in a state of decline. Underlying this feeling is a sense of the loss of "traditional family values" that have contributed to the decay of marriage. How much of this belief is rooted in fact and how much is hype? Stephanie Coontz maintains that the problem is that we are longing for a social construction based on a false memory rather than fact. Culturally, we cannot "go back," and Coontz wonders why we would even want to.

1 [Y]ears ago, Vice President Dan Quayle attacked the producers of TV sitcom *Murphy Brown* for letting her character bear a child out of wedlock, claiming that the show's failure to defend traditional family values was encouraging America's youth to abandon marriage. His speech kicked off more than a decade of outcries against the "collapse of the family." Today, such attacks have given way to a kinder, gentler campaign to promote marriage, with billboards declaring that "Marriage Works" and books making "the case for marriage." What these campaigns have in common is the idea that people are willfully refusing to recognize the value of traditional families and that their behavior will change if we can just enlighten them.

2 But recent changes in marriage are part of a worldwide upheaval in family life that has transformed the way people conduct their personal lives as thoroughly and permanently as the Industrial Revolution transformed their working lives 200 years ago. Marriage is no longer the main way in which societies regulate sexuality and parenting or organize the division of labor between men and women. And although some people hope to turn back the tide by promoting traditional values, making

---
* Stephanie Coontz, *Washington Post*, May 1, 2005

divorce harder, or outlawing gay marriage, they are having to confront a startling irony: The very factors that have made marriage more satisfying in modern times have also made it more optional.

3   The origins of modern marital instability lie largely in the triumph of what many people believe to be marriage's traditional role—providing love, intimacy, fidelity, and mutual fulfillment. The truth is that for centuries, marriage was stable precisely because it was not expected to provide such benefits. As soon as love became the driving force behind marriage, people began to demand the right to remain single if they had not found love or to divorce if they fell out of love.

4   Such demands were raised as early as the 1790s, which prompted conservatives to predict that love would be the death of marriage. For the next 150 years, the inherently destabilizing effects of the love revolution were held in check by women's economic dependence on men, the unreliability of birth control, and the harsh legal treatment of children born out of wedlock, as well as the social ostracism of their mothers. As late as the 1960s, two-thirds of college women in the United States said they would marry a man they didn't love if he met all their other, often economic, criteria. Men also felt compelled to marry if they hoped for promotions at work or for political credibility.

5   All these restraints on individual choice collapsed between 1960 and 1980. Divorce rates had long been rising in Western Europe and the United States, and although they had leveled off following World War II, they climbed at an unprecedented rate in the 1970s, leading some to believe that the introduction of no-fault divorce laws, which meant married couples could divorce if they simply fell out of love, had caused the erosion of marriage.

6   The so-called divorce revolution, however, is just one aspect of the worldwide transformation of marriage. In places where divorce and unwed motherhood are severely stigmatized, the retreat from marriage simply takes another form. In Japan and Italy, for example, women are far more likely to remain single than in the United States. In Thailand, unmarried women now compete for the title of "Miss Spinster Thailand." Singapore's strait-laced government has resorted to sponsoring singles nights in an attempt to raise marriage rates and reverse the birth strike by women.

7   In the United States and Britain, divorce rates fell slightly during the 1990s, but the incidence of cohabitation and unmarried child raising continues to rise, as does the percentage of singles in the population.

8   Both trends reduce the social significance of marriage in the economy and culture. The norms and laws that traditionally penalized unwed mothers and their children have weakened or been overturned, ending centuries of injustice but further reducing

Although some people hope to turn back the tide by promoting traditional values, making divorce harder, or outlawing gay marriage, they are having to confront a startling irony: The very factors that have made marriage more satisfying in modern times have also made it more optional.

marriage's role in determining the course of people's lives. Today, 40 percent of cohabiting couples in the United States have children in the household, almost as high a proportion as the 45 percent of married couples who have kids, according to the 2000 Census. We don't have a TV show about that yet, but it's just a matter of time.

9   The entry of women into the workforce in the last third of the twentieth century was not only a U.S. phenomenon. By the 1970s, women in America and most of Europe could support themselves if they needed to. The 1980s saw an international increase in unmarried women having babies (paving the way for Murphy Brown), as more people gained the ability to say no to shotgun marriages, and humanitarian reforms lowered the penalties for out-of-wedlock births. That decade also saw a big increase in couples living together before marriage.

10   Almost everywhere, women's greater participation in education has raised the marriage age and the incidence of nonmarriage. Even in places where women's lives are still largely organized through marriage, fertility rates have been cut in half and more wives and mothers work outside the home.

11   From Turkey to South Africa to Brazil, countries are having to codify the legal rights and obligations of single individuals and unmarried couples raising children, including same-sex couples. Canada and the Netherlands have joined Scandinavia in legalizing same-sex marriage, and such bastions of tradition as Taiwan and Spain are considering following suit.

12   None of this means that marriage is dead. Indeed, most people have a higher regard for the marital relationship today than when marriage was practically mandatory. Marriage as a private relationship between two individuals is taken more seriously and comes with higher emotional expectations than ever before in history.

13   But marriage as a public institution exerts less power over people's lives now that the majority of Americans spend half their adult lives outside marriage and almost half of all kids spend part of their childhood in a household that does not include their two married biological parents. And unlike in the past, marriage or lack of marriage does not determine people's political and economic rights.

14   Under these conditions, it is hard to believe that we could revive the primacy of marriage by promoting traditional values. People may revere the value of universal marriage in the abstract, but most have adjusted to a different reality. The late Pope John Paul II was enormously respected for his teaching about sex and marriage. Yet during his tenure, premarital sex, contraception use, and divorce continued to rise in almost all countries. In the United States, the Bible Belt has the highest divorce rate in the nation. And although many American teens pledged abstinence during the 1990s, 88 percent ended up breaking that pledge, according to the National Longitudinal Study of Adolescent Youth that was released in March.

15   Although many Americans bemoan the easy accessibility of divorce, few are willing to waive their personal rights. In American states where "covenant" marriage laws allow people to sign away their right to a no-fault divorce, fewer than three percent of couples choose that option. Divorce rates climbed by the same percentage in states that did not allow no-fault divorce as in states that did. By 2000, Belgium, which had not yet adopted no-fault divorce, had the highest divorce rates in Europe outside of Finland and Sweden.

16   Nor does a solution lie in preaching the benefits of marriage to impoverished couples or outlawing unconventional partnerships. A poor single mother often has good reason not to marry her child's father, and poor couples who do wed have

more than twice the divorce risk of more affluent partners in the United States. Banning same-sex marriage would not undo the existence of alternatives to traditional marriage. Five million children are being raised by gay and lesbian couples in this country. Judges everywhere are being forced to apply many principles of marriage law to those families, if only to regulate child custody should the couple part ways.

17   We may personally like or dislike these changes. We may wish to keep some and get rid of others. But there is a certain inevitability to almost all of them.

18   Marriage is no longer the institution where people are initiated into sex. It no longer determines the work men and women do on the job or at home, regulates who has children and who doesn't, or coordinates caregiving for the ill or the aged. For better or worse, marriage has been displaced from its pivotal position in personal and social life and will not regain it short of a Taliban-like counterrevolution.

19   Forget the fantasy of solving the challenges of modern personal life by re-institutionalizing marriage. In today's climate of choice, many people's choices do not involve marriage. We must recognize that there are healthy as well as unhealthy ways to be single or to be divorced, just as there are healthy and unhealthy ways to be married. We cannot afford to construct our social policies, our advice to our own children, and even our own emotional expectations around the illusion that all commitments, sexual activities, and caregiving will take place in a traditional marriage. That series has been canceled. ◆

CRITICAL THINKING

1. Is marriage in danger of becoming an obsolete institution? Why do people marry today?
2. Is marriage a goal for you in your life plan? Why or why not?
3. Coontz's opening paragraph begins with a reference to Dan Quayle and the television sitcom *Murphy Brown*. Why does Coontz start her essay this way? How does this example set up the points she makes in her essay?
4. What, according to Coontz, has contributed to the erosion of marriage?
5. Coontz states, "For better or worse, marriage has been displaced from its pivotal position in personal and social life and will not regain it short of a Taliban-like counterrevolution." Respond to this statement in your own words. Do you agree with her? Is it a generalization or a statement based largely on social fact? Explain.
6. Evaluate Coontz's use of statistics and facts. Do they support her points? Are they relevant to her thesis? Based on these facts, do you find yourself swayed by her argument? Why or why not?
7. Based on her essay, summarize Coontz's view of marriage. Cite specific areas of the text to support your summary.

CRITICAL WRITING

1. *Personal Narrative:* Write a personal narrative in which you describe the structure of your family during your childhood, focusing specifically on

the role of marriage in your family. Were your parents married? Divorced? If you could have changed anything about your parents' marital relationship, what would it have been?

2. *Exploratory Writing:* Coontz notes that as people began to view marriage as more about love and intimacy, the divorce rate soared. Is marriage about love? Is it about family? Children? If a couple has children, but find that they no longer feel the marriage is a loving one, should they stay together anyway? Write an essay in which you describe what you think marriage is and what grounds individuals have to terminate it.

GROUP PROJECTS

1. As a group, make a list of the benefits of marriage Coontz cites in her essay. (Make sure you review the entire essay when compiling this list.) Discuss the list in terms of your own personal experience and perspective. Based on the list, decide whether marriage needs to be made more of a political priority.

2. Coontz asserts that "marriage has been displaced from its pivotal position in personal and social life." Working in small groups, discuss and compare the structure of family and the role of marriage within your own experiences. Think about the family you grew up in, families you have known, and the families you may have started. What marital structures do these families have? Compare your observations with Coontz's statement.

Did I Miss Something?
Lowell Putnam*

Many of the articles in this section cite the increase in the divorce rate as one reason for the decline of marriage and the shifting shape of the American family. Divorce has become an American way of life. Nearly half of all children will see their parents' marriage terminate by the time they turn 18. And although society may shake its collective head at such a statistic, lamenting the loss of the traditional family, not all children of divorce see it as a problem. In this piece, student Lowell Putnam wonders why divorce is still such a taboo topic. Having known no other way of life, children of divorced parents, explains Putnam, simply take such a lifestyle for granted.

1   The subject of divorce turns heads in our society. It is responsible for bitten tongues, lowered voices, and an almost pious reverence saved only for life-threatening illness or uncontrolled catastrophe. Growing up in a "broken home," I am always shocked to be treated as a victim of some social disease. When a class assignment required that I write an essay concerning my feelings about or my personal experiences with divorce, my first reaction was complete surprise. My second was a hope for large

* Lowell Putnam, student essay, 2002

margins. An essay on aspects of my life affected by divorce seems completely superfluous, because I cannot differentiate between the "normal" part of my youth and the

supposed angst and confusion
that apparently comes with all
divorces. The divorce of my parents over 15 years ago (when I
was 3 years old) has either saturated every last pore of my developmental epidermis to a point

---

*Growing up in a "broken home," I am always
shocked to be treated as a victim of some
social disease.*

---

where I cannot sense it or has not affected me at all. Eugene Ehrlich's *Highly Selective
Dictionary for the Extraordinarily Literate* defines divorce as a "breach"; however,
I cannot sense any schism in my life resulting from the event to which other people
seem to attribute so much importance. My parents' divorce is a true part of who I am,
and the only "breach" that could arrive from my present familial arrangement would
be to tear me away from what I consider my normal living conditions.

2   Though there is no doubt in my mind that many unfortunate people have had
their lives torn apart by the divorce of their parents, I do not feel any real sense of
regret for my situation. In my opinion, the paramount role of a parent is to love his or
her child. Providing food, shelter, education, and video games are of course other
necessary elements of successful child rearing, but these secondary concerns branch
out from the most fundamental ideal of parenting, which is love. A loving parent will
be a successful one even if he or she cannot afford to furnish his or her child with the
best clothes or the most sophisticated gourmet delicacies. With love as the driving
force in a parent's mind, he or she will almost invariably make the correct decision.
When my mother and father found that they were no longer in love with each other
after 9 years of a solid marriage, their love for me forced them to take the precipitous
step to separate. The safest environment for me was to be with one happy parent at a
time, instead of two miserable ones all the time. The sacrifice that they both made to
relinquish control over me for half the year was at least as painful for them as it was
for me (and I would bet even more so), but in the end I was not deprived of a parent's
love, but merely of one parent's presence for a few short weeks at a time. My father's
and mother's love for me has not dwindled even slightly over the past 15 years, and
I can hardly imagine a more well-adjusted and contented family.

3   As I reread the first section of this essay, I realize that it is perhaps too optimistic and cheerful regarding my life as a child of divorced parents. In all truthful-
ness, there have been some decidedly negative ramifications stemming from our
family separation. My first memory is actually of a fight between my mother and
father. I vaguely remember standing in the end of the upstairs hallway of our
Philadelphia house, when I was about 3 years old, and seeing shadows moving back
and forth in the light coming from under the door of my father's study, accompanied
by raised voices. It would be naïve of me to say that I have not been at all affected
by divorce, since it has permeated my most primal and basic memories.

4   However, I am grateful that I can only recall one such incident, instead of having parental conflicts become so quotidian that they leave no mark whatsoever on
my mind. Also, I find that having to divide my time equally between both parents
leads to alienation from both sides of my family. Invariably, at every holiday

occasion, there is one half of my family (either my mother's side or my father's) that has to explain that "Lowell is with his [mother/father] this year," while aunts, cousins, and grandparents collectively arch eyebrows or avert eyes. Again, though, I should not be hasty to lament my distance from loved ones, since there are many families with "normal" marriages where the children never even meet their cousins, let alone get to spend every other Thanksgiving with them. Though divorce has certainly thrown some proverbial monkey wrenches into some proverbial gears, in general my otherwise strong familial ties have overshadowed any minor snafus.

5   Perhaps one of the most important reasons for my absence of "trauma" (for lack of a better word) stemming from my parents' divorce is that I am by no means alone in my trials and tribulations. The foreboding statistic that 60 percent of marriages end in divorce is no myth to me, indeed many of my friends come from similar situations. The argument could be made that "birds of a feather flock together" and that my friends and I form a tight support network for each other, but I strongly doubt that any of us needs or looks for that kind of buttress. The fact of the matter is that divorce happens a lot in today's society, and as a result, our culture has evolved to accommodate these new family arrangements, making the overall conditions more hospitable for me and my broken brothers and shattered sisters.

6   I am well aware that divorce can often lead to issues of abandonment and familial proximity among children of separated parents, but in my case I see very little evidence to support the claim that my parents should have stayed married "for the sake of the child." In many ways, my life is enriched by the division of my time with my father and my time with my mother. I get to live in New York City for half of the year and in a small suburb of Boston for the other half. I have friends who envy me, since I get "the best of both worlds." I never get double-teamed by parents during arguments, and I cherish my time with each one more, since it only lasts half the year.

7   In my opinion, there is no such thing as a perfect life or a "normal" life, and any small blips on our karmic radar screen have to be dealt with appropriately but without any trepidation or self-pity. Do I miss my father when I live with my mother (and vice versa)? Of course I do. However, I know young boys and girls who have lost parents to illness or accidental injury, so my pitiable position is relative. As I leave for college in a few short months, I can safely say that my childhood has not been at all marred by having two different houses to call home. ◆

CRITICAL THINKING

1. In this essay, Lowell Putnam notes that people speak of divorce in hushed tones. If half of all marriages end in divorce, why does society still treat it as a taboo topic?

2. Is divorce detrimental to children or simply a way of life? Explain your point of view.

3. Evaluate Putnam's description of the way people discuss divorce in "lowered voices, and an almost pious reverence saved only for life-threatening illness." What accounts for this attitude? Do you agree with his assessment? Explain.

4. At the end of his first paragraph, Putnam comments that "my parents' divorce is a true part of who I am." Why does Putnam associate his personal

identity with his parents' marital status? Discuss how parent relationships influence how children view themselves and their world.

5. Analyze Putnam's definition of what makes a good parent. Do you agree or disagree with this viewpoint?

6. Critics of divorce say it is a selfish act of parents who put their wants before their children's needs. Putnam contends that his parents divorced out of love for him, and their divorce was a kind of sacrifice. Evaluate these two perspectives. Can divorce be a positive event for children?

7. Putnam comments that his parents' love for him has not dwindled as a result of their divorce, and that he "can hardly imagine a more well-adjusted and contented family." Why do you think he uses the singular *family*? Explain. How would his meaning change if he had used the plural form, *families*?

CRITICAL WRITING

1. *Research and Analysis:* Using newspapers and newsmagazines, research a topic related to children and divorce. You might examine the issue of "deadbeat dads," the psychological aspects of divorce on children, or social perspectives of broken families. Write an essay analyzing the results of your research.

2. *Persuasive Writing:* Draft a letter to a pair of married friends with children who are filing for divorce to reconsider their decision, or to support it, considering the impact the new arrangement is likely to have on their children. Assume that both parents are working and they are considering an amicable divorce in which they intend to continue a close relationship with their children.

3. *Personal Narrative:* Putnam's essay is a personal narrative describing his view of how his parents' divorce influenced his life. Write a personal narrative describing how your parents' marriage or divorce has influenced your own life. Can you relate to anything Putnam says in his essay? Explain.

GROUP PROJECTS

1. As a group, design and administer a poll for your classmates to answer anonymously, asking questions about family status (divorce, remarriage, single parenthood, absentee fathers or mothers, etc.). Administer the same poll to a group of people a generation or two older than you, perhaps your professors or college staff members. How do the results compare? Are divorced families more "normal" than non-divorced families? Explain. What structures are more common among the different age groups? Discuss your results with the class.

2. In your group, discuss the effects of divorce on children. Further develop Putnam's idea that it is just another way of life. Compare notes with classmates to assemble a complete list of possible effects. Based on this list, develop your own response about the effects of divorce on children.

VIEWPOINTS

► **How Getting Married Made Me an Activist**
*David Jefferson**

► **Less Shouting, More Talking**
Richard Mouw

► **Why I'm Not Getting Married . . . Again**
David Shneer

This chapter's Viewpoints section addresses the issue of gay marriage with a focus on the controversy in California. Much of the debate hinges on how we define marriage—is it a partnership between two loving, consenting adults or a sanctified or legal union between a man and a woman? Many arguments supporting gay marriage focus on the issue of love—if two people love each other, goes the argument, they should be allowed to marry. Opponents to this view contend that marriage is more than about love—it has traditionally been a legal and social bond between a man and a woman, foremost to support the upbringing of children. To redefine this definition of marriage would be to undermine the institution itself and threaten the family.

Should same-sex couples be afforded the legal right to marry? On May 15, 2008, the California Supreme Court ruled that the statute enacted by Proposition 22 and other statutes that limit marriage to a relationship between a man and a woman violated the Equal Protection clause of the California Constitution. It also held that individuals of the same sex have the right to marry under the California Constitution. A UCLA study estimated that by November 2008, over 18,000 same-sex couples married, at which point the passage of Proposition 8 suspended all further same-sex marriages. Proposition 8 was a California ballot proposition passed November 4, 2008 that changed California's Constitution to restrict the definition of marriage to opposite-sex couples and eliminated same-sex couples' right to marry. The measure added a new section (7.5) to Article I, which reads: "Only marriage between a man and a woman is valid or recognized in California." When this book went to print, Proposition 8 was being challenged in the California Supreme Court.

The first essay describes how *Newsweek* editor David Jefferson's wedding put him in the middle of the culture wars. As he and his spouse wait to see if their marriage is valid, he wonders if history will be on their side. His piece is followed by a short editorial by Richard Mouw, the president of a theological seminary, who explains why he voted for Prop 8. Yes, he explains, he opposes gay marriage, but his reasons are based less on religious principles and more on social ones. The section ends with an essay by history professor David Shneer, who explains why he chose not to marry his partner "again" when same-sex marriage was legally offered in 2008.

---

* David J. Jefferson, *Newsweek*, November 24, 2008; Richard Mouw, *Newsweek*, February 9, 2009; David Shneer, *Huffington Post*, July 3, 2008

How Getting Married Made Me an Activist

David Jefferson

1   Proposition 8 has changed my life. In October 2008, when it looked like the gay marriage ban was winning support here in my home state, I turned to my partner of 7 years and told him we'd better say "I do" before California voters told us "you can't." Immediately, Jeff Bechtloff and I jumped into full "Bridezilla" mode. We ordered a three-tiered mocha-chip wedding cake from the best bakery in Los Angeles (which now carries same-sex cake toppers). We pulled together a soundtrack of Frank Sinatra songs to play in lieu of "Here Comes the Bride." We asked *Newsweek*'s film critic David Ansen and his friend Mary Corey to do a reading from our favorite romantic film, *"Breakfast at Tiffany's."* We went flower shopping with my high school girlfriend, who made the table arrangements and corsages for us.

> *In October 2008, when it looked like the gay marriage ban was winning support here in my home state, I turned to my partner of 7 years and told him we'd better say "I do" before California voters told us "you can't."*

2   Finally, on October 25, Jeff's mother walked him down the aisle, followed by my 86-year-old father and 93-year-old mother, who accompanied me as I bit my lip and fought back unexpected tears. Standing before the judge, I looked out at the audience of 100 familiar faces and saw my tears of joy returned in kind. With such an outpouring of support—and Barack Obama's promises of hope and inclusion gaining traction—I couldn't imagine that voters here on the liberal Left Coast would deem our wedding a threat to "traditional" marriage. But we were living in a bubble. We'd wrongly assumed that because most Americans no longer feel entitled to call us "faggot" to our faces, we had won acceptance.

3   Today, Jeff and I and 18,000 couples like us wait anxiously to see whether our marriages will remain valid. California Attorney General Jerry Brown says yes, but there's a good chance that will be challenged in court by proponents of Proposition 8, which changes the state constitution to read "Only marriage between a man and a woman is valid or recognized in California." The judge who married us is of the opinion that our wedding will stand, since ex post facto, or retroactive, laws are illegal under Article I of the United States Constitution. I can only say that I am grateful the Founding Fathers had the foresight not to make the U.S. Constitution as easily fungible as the state of California's.

4   Like all Americans, I was taught to believe in the promises those Founding Fathers made: you know, "All men are created equal," and that sort of thing. I always felt especially proud when my teachers would invoke the Declaration of Independence, because it was written by a long-lost cousin of mine (look again at my byline). I would only hope that the man who promised me "life, liberty, and the pursuit of happiness" would agree that affairs of the heart should not be determined by popular vote.

5   As luck would have it, the organization that helped my father and me trace that bit of family genealogy is the same one that played a central role in revoking my right to marry this month: the Church of Jesus Christ of Latter Day Saints, whose members donated an estimated $15 million or more—nearly half the Prop 8 war chest—in a state where only 2 percent of the population is Mormon. That's made the Mormon church a prime target as the gay community does its Prop 8 postmortem. Some activists are calling for the IRS to revoke the church's tax-exempt status; others have suggested boycotting companies with Mormon executives who supported the ban and getting Hollywood types to pull out of the Sundance Film Festival in Park City, Utah.

6   But it's becoming clear to me that the main failing may have been our own. Most gay people I know seem to have forgotten—or in many cases never learned—the lessons of our collective history. For what transpired in California is only the latest skirmish in a three-decade battle between the religious right and the gay community in what has come to be known, euphemistically, as the culture wars. Had Prop 8 opponents taken their playbook from the gay-rights battles of the 1970s, I might not be in my current predicament. But most gay people my age and younger have little memory of those battles, in large part because many of the pioneers who fought them succumbed to a virus called HIV before they could teach us. And because gay rights have advanced so far since then—we are protected by nondiscrimination laws, our employers give us domestic-partner benefits, and several states recognize our unions—we probably took for granted that gay marriage was an inevitability.

7   How are we to learn our history? I decided to go back to my high school government teacher for a civics lesson. Robert Garland, now 76, never spoke publicly about his sexual orientation when he was my instructor at Ulysses S. Grant High School in Van Nuys, California, even to the co-workers whom he and his longtime companion Tom Ethington socialized with: it was just understood that they were a couple. This past August 20, on the 50th anniversary of their meeting, Garland finally could call Ethington what he had been all along: his spouse.

8   When Garland first started teaching at Grant in 1967, homosexuals lived in an America where they could be arrested just for being in a gay bar. "We were all closeted then," he recalls. It would be two more years before one such bar raid, at the Stonewall Inn in New York's Greenwich Village, would spark gays to riot, an event that launched the modern-day gay-rights movement. But even after the Stonewall riots, police harassment of homosexuals continued for many years. On Labor Day 1974, San Francisco policemen beat dozens of gay men who were standing outside the popular Toad Hall bar in the city's Castro district after one ignored an officer's order: "Off the street, faggot." The incident helped galvanize the gay community behind a Castro Street camera-store owner who had aspirations of becoming the first openly gay man elected to office in a major U.S. city. His name was Harvey Milk.

9   As part of my gay-history lesson, I went to a preview screening this past week of *Milk*, a new movie being released November 26 that stars Sean Penn as the gay-rights activist. Watching Penn dissolve into the role of the endearingly nebbishy San Francisco city supervisor who urged gays to come out of the closet and flex their political power, I was transported to an era I had lived through but didn't comprehend at the time. I had no idea who Harvey Milk was when I was in junior high (I was more preoccupied with Farrah Fawcett), though even if I had, I would have been too frightened to express any interest in what he was doing for fear someone

might think I was homosexual—something I was loath to admit even to myself back in those days.

10   I had good reason to hide what I was feeling. In 1977, the pleasant redhead I recognized from commercials as the pitchwoman for Florida orange juice was suddenly all over the media, railing against the evils of homosexuality. "Homosexuals cannot reproduce so they must recruit," Anita Bryant declared as she launched a campaign to roll back a gay-rights ordinance that had been enacted just months earlier in Dade County, Florida. "If gays are granted rights, next we'll have to give rights to prostitutes and to people who sleep with St. Bernards." What I didn't know at the time—probably none of us could have comprehended it—was that Bryant had, for the first time, rallied born-again Christians around a specific piece of legislation. And once they tasted victory that June, there was no turning back.

11   Bryant's triumph was a stunning loss for the nascent gay-rights movement. "Gay leaders had made a vast mistake in 1977 by underestimating the intense dedication of the legions of born-again Christians," the late journalist Randy Shilts wrote in his biography of Milk, *The Mayor of Castro Street.* But the loss brought gays together like never before. To shouts of "Two, four, six, eight, separate the church and state," they marched through the streets of San Francisco, with Milk at the lead, shouting on his ever-present bullhorn. Gays weren't about to let it happen again, and they were ready when Bryant and her followers set their sights on California the next year.

12   My teacher Mr. Garland remembers that battle well. "They wanted to fire all the gay teachers," he says, recalling California state Senator John Briggs's ballot initiative to prevent gays and lesbians from working in the public schools. SAVE OUR CHILDREN FROM HOMOSEXUAL TEACHERS, one newspaper ad for the Briggs initiative screamed. (That sentiment was echoed to great effect this fall in a Prop 8 commercial featuring a young girl informing her horrified mother, "Guess what I learned in school today? I learned how a prince married a prince, and I can marry a princess.")

13   Milk and the other gay-rights leaders pulled every string they had with their Democratic allies (President Jimmy Carter even urged Californians to vote "no"), but "the thing that helped to defeat it was Ronald Reagan coming out against it," Garland recalls. "Homosexuality is not a contagious disease like measles," the former California governor wrote in September 1978. "Prevailing scientific opinion is that an individual's sexuality is determined at a very early age and that a child's teachers do not really influence this." Why did Reagan—the man who revived the Republican Party by welcoming into the fold the very forces supporting Briggs and Bryant—go to bat for gays? Briggs said it was because Reagan was part of the "Hollywood crowd," though Shilts, in his Milk biography, reported, "Gay insiders credited Reagan's help to the fact that he had no small number of gays among his top staff."

14   But the gay community's joy over the defeat of Briggs would be short-lived. A few weeks after the election, Milk was assassinated along with San Francisco Mayor George Moscone by Dan White, Milk's conservative nemesis on the Board of Supervisors. When White was convicted in 1979 of manslaughter—not murder—San Francisco gays took to the streets in what became known as the "White Night Riots."

15   So what can the life and times of Harvey Milk teach us now? Dustin Lance Black, the screenwriter of *Milk*, put it this way when the screening audience asked him why he'd made the film: "I felt like we were making the same mistakes again,"

said Black, who is gay and was raised a devout Mormon. (Black got his break in Hollywood writing for *Big Love*, the HBO series about a polygamist family in Utah.) Before Milk, most gay leaders were content to let their straight allies fight their political battles for them—rather than take to the streets and demand their rights—because they feared a backlash if gays appeared too "uppity." Milk argued that the only way to win civil rights is to demand and take them—as Thomas Jefferson, Martin Luther King Jr., Gloria Steinem, and all the others did—rather than wait for them to be granted.

16   History has repeatedly favored Milk in this debate. Thousands of gay men died waiting for the government to respond to AIDS in the early 1980s, but no one paid much attention until Larry Kramer and his ACT UP activists took to the streets and demanded more funding for HIV therapies; by 1996, those drugs had hit the market, and the course of the epidemic changed. In contrast, when gays and lesbians counted on Bill Clinton to let them serve openly in the military and to promote the burgeoning gay-marriage movement, they wound up with "don't ask, don't tell" and the Defense of Marriage Act of 1996, which outlaws the federal government from recognizing same-sex marriage.

17   Fast-forward to this year's battle. Gay leaders cried foul when the Prop 8 campaign targeted African Americans with ads quoting Obama as saying he opposes gay marriage, since Obama had, in fact, come out in opposition to Prop 8. What the gay leadership failed to do was to press Obama on the obvious question: how can you say that you oppose gay marriage but also oppose banning it? (With mixed messages like that from Obama, gays shouldn't blame African Americans—many of whom don't approve of same-sex marriage for religious reasons—for voting 70 percent in favor of banning it.) In the interest of getting a Democrat into the White House, gays gave Obama a free pass.

18   Likewise, gay leaders decided that the best way to fight Prop 8 was to downplay the "gay angle" so as not to offend the undecideds. That's right: no gay people allowed in the commercials defending gay marriage. Instead, we got Senator Dianne Feinstein and other well-meaning straight folk talking about the danger of eliminating "fundamental rights" and stretching credulity by comparing the ballot initiative to the internment of Japanese Americans during World War II. If I was offended by the disingenuousness of these ads, I can only imagine what Milk would have thought.

19   At least he would have been encouraged by what he's seeing now. Just as the victory of Christian conservatives with Anita Bryant's initiative got gays to fight for their rights, so too has the passage of Prop 8 mobilized a new generation of activists. "The community's defeat on marriage equality has energized a whole group of young people who took for granted the civil rights of gay people," says the Los Angeles Gay and Lesbian Center's Jim Key. The center brought together a group of young leaders who formed FAIR (Freedom. Action. Inclusion. Rights.) to channel all this new energy. Its motto is "From street to strategy."

20   Watching this revitalization of the gay-rights movement, I've come to realize that what Jeff and I did may not have been in vain after all. Even as same-sex couples in California stopped marrying, Connecticut gays and lesbians began walking down the aisle last week. By standing at the altar, Jeff and I made a commitment—to pledge our devotion to one another; to show our family and friends (and even

those who oppose us) that we're all more alike than we are different; and to refuse to stand silently by while others try to take away our rights. This past week, Jeff and I decided to get our wedding rings engraved as a declaration of our newfound independence. They now say "MAKING HISTORY OCT. 25, 2008." For that, I think Thomas Jefferson and Harvey Milk would be proud.

 ## Less Shouting, More Talking

Richard Mouw

1   On the morning of November 4, I saw an angry confrontation between two groups at an intersection in my California town. Both sides were carrying signs: one set supporting Proposition 8—the ban on same-sex marriage—and the other opposing it. The two groups were angrily shouting and gesturing at each other as I passed by. That's when the tears welled up.

2   I voted for the ban. As an evangelical, I subscribe to the "traditional" definition of a marriage, and I do not want to see the definition changed.

3   Does that mean I want to impose my personal convictions on the broader population? No. I celebrate the fact that we live in a pluralistic society, with many different worldviews and lifestyles. I support the democratic process and believe that civil society is at its best when people with different perspectives engage in a mutually respectful dialogue. And that's why the tears welled up on Election Day morning. The angry sign wavers on opposite corners symbolized the way this whole disagreement over same-sex marriage has gone. Angry shouts. Shaking fists. It makes me sad.

4   This is something that happens on occasion in an intimate relationship. People who care deeply about each other start arguing about some touchy issue. As temperatures rise, so does the rhetoric. Mean-spirited things get said. The situation seems hopeless.

5   That is why I want to issue this plea to my fellow citizens on both sides of this divide over sexuality: Can we talk?

6   I ask this as someone who has been one of the angry ones—angry about things that have been said about people like me. I've been on talk shows where people phone in to call me a fascist or equate me with those who burned accused witches at the stake. One remark that hit especially close to home was made by the editor of *Newsweek* magazine. He wrote that anyone—anyone!—who tries to make a scriptural case against same-sex marriage is guilty of "the worst kind of fundamentalism."

7   That hurt. I have spent several decades of my life trying to spell out an evangelical alternative to "the worst kind of fundamentalism." My friends and I have argued that the Bible supports racial justice, gender equality, peacemaking, and care for the environment—views that often draw the ire of the worst kind of fundamentalists. But none of that seems to matter to folks who don't like our views about same-sex relations. Because we also believe that the Bible frowns on sexual intimacy outside of marriage between a man and a woman, we are being relegated to the margins of the civil dialogue.

8   I refuse to go to the margins. As my fellow citizens in a pluralistic society, gays and lesbians have a right to ask me what my sincerely held convictions mean for how they pursue their way of lives.

9   While my views about sexuality are shaped by my religious convictions, I know that I cannot simply quote the Bible in arguing for public policy. Not every sin ought to be made illegal. But in this case, the issues go deep. For many of us, "normalizing" same-sex marriage comes down to deep concerns about the raising of our children and grandchildren. What will they be taught about sexual and family values in our schools? How will they be affected by the ways the entertainment media portray people with our kinds of views? And will we even be allowed to counter these influences in our homes and churches without being accused of "hate speech"?

10   And, fair or unfair, "slippery slope" concerns loom large. Are there limits to what we can be asked to tolerate when it concerns matters that violate our convictions? If we were to accept mutual consent and deeply felt convictions as a sufficient basis for allowing the legalization of same-sex relationships, what would keep us from extending marriage to a three-partner arrangement?

> *And, fair or unfair, "slippery slope" concerns loom large. Are there limits to what we can be asked to tolerate when it concerns matters that violate our convictions?*

11   But I also want to hear from folks who worry about my views. What is it about people like me that frightens you so much? What would you need to hear from us that would reduce your anxiety? What is your vision of a flourishing pluralistic society? Where do people like me fit into that kind of society?

12   Maybe I am unrealistic in thinking we can have this national conversation. But the alternatives are frightening. Posing this question has worked at other times when people seemed hopelessly at odds. So let's try asking it now as a nation, and in a gentle tone: Can we talk?

Why I'm Not Getting Married . . . Again
David Shneer

1   Twelve years ago, on June 23, 1996, my husband (sic) and I got married under a Jewish wedding canopy, known as a *huppah*, surrounded by 120 friends and family in the hills above Berkeley, California. It was a perfect day of singing, celebration, and, in quintessential California fashion, organic food prepared by our friends. It was an affair of love and done on a shoestring $4000 budget. An artist friend of ours, Helene Fischman, made our *ketubah*, the wedding contract that spells out the terms of the agreement, and this Jewishly legal contract hangs in our dining room, serving as a reminder of the commitment we made.

2   A few years later, we found ourselves in Toronto, Canada, just after Canada legalized same-sex marriage; so we decided, why not have a piece of paper that might come in handy some day? The Canadians took everything very seriously with music, poetry,

and a very earnest justice of the peace, but I honestly don't remember the date, or even which year it was, because we were, of course, already married before we signed the documents in Canada. But now we had the religious and the civil documents in hand.

3   About one month ago, friends and family started asking when we were coming to California to participate in the biggest party of the year—California's legal same-sex weddings. They reiterated that this privilege extended by the state could be taken away in November when "the people of California" have their say. Rabbi and pastor friends of ours were suddenly booked months out to perform weddings, and everyone it seemed knew someone or was someone getting hitched. I received one Evite to a wedding celebration (Okay, not the most formal affair, but it's the thought that counts), the fifth one that she and her wife had done. I'm awed by their fortitude to get married five different times to meet five different religious and civil bodies' requirements for marriage.

4   But when asked about our plans, I recoiled at the suggestion that my husband and I should come to California to get married. "We've been married for 12 years." "Yeah, I know David, but it's legal now. You can take advantage of all of the benefits."

> *But when asked about our plans, I recoiled at the suggestion that my husband and I should come to California to get married. "We've been married for 12 years." "Yeah, I know David, but it's legal now. You can take advantage of all of the benefits."*

5   I have had this conversation no fewer than five times in the past month, since California took the bold step of both allowing same-sex marriage and not having a residency requirement for the happy couple. Articles about the economic benefits to the state flooded cyberspace, pictures of happy couples adorned Web sites, newspapers, and television broadcasts around the world. So why was I being such a party pooper?

6   Mind you, I'm married, which is proof that I'm not a radical anti-marriage advocate. I understand the arguments of the anti-marriage camp, sympathize with them, but I'm just not that radical. I liked having had an awesome religious experience to show ourselves and our community the depth of our commitment to one another. And I like having a stunning piece of art that is our wedding contract hanging in the hearth of our home.

7   I'm not going to California to get married, because I am already married, and from my vantage point, the repeated requests for me to finally "get married" continually chip away at the powerful edifice that is my relationship. Those who are asking if I am getting married, most of them gay and lesbian themselves, do so out of a place of love and hope, but they are unwittingly articulating to me and to themselves that they never saw my marriage as real. Yes, it was beautiful; yes we were a couple, but in their eyes, we were not married until a state blessed our relationship. How did marriage become so detached from spiritual connection and so embedded in mundane social relations that our big fat Jewish wedding with all of the smells and bells of Judaism (including the not-so-traditional opera singer!) just did not count?

8   Now, the excited question about when we're coming to California was the benign, sweet articulation of the fact that marriage today in the United States has little to do with spirit and everything to do with civil society. But the question about proving and documenting our relationship constantly is also a source of disrespect and discrimination toward us.

9   I recently accepted a job at the University of Colorado in Boulder, a liberal, hippy-dippy university in a state that is home to Marilyn Musgrave and *Focus on the Family*. It makes for a fun political environment. Two years ago, the university's regents graciously decided to extend employment benefits to same-sex domestic partners, something that had been debated and rejected several times previously. These benefits, however, came with a serious condition—same-sex couples would have to document their relationships to the university in not one but two extra ways. First, unlike legally married straight couples, who do not have to document their relationship in any way to the university, we had to sign an affidavit in front of a notary proving that we live together, have joint bank accounts, and other rather intimate details. What if we, like many academic couples, didn't live together or didn't have joint bank accounts? We wouldn't have counted. Luckily we could sign the affidavit honestly, because we do share our household together. We faxed that in, and then HR called requesting "proof of your registration of your domestic partnership with the City of Boulder or Denver." "But I just faxed you an affidavit legally attesting to my relationship." "I'm sorry, but we need that documentation." "But I registered my relationship in the City of Oakland where I used to live and have a marriage license from Canada. Why would I have renewed my vows for the City of Boulder?" "I'm sorry, but the Regents require both a signed affidavit and a copy of your registration with the city." Note that this city registration costs $25 and requires my husband and I to go to City Hall, stand in front of a clerk, and, once again, attest to our relationship.

10   So here I was, once again being asked to renew my vows to please a state body, this time out of clear spite for same-sex couples, as there is no legal reason to require the documentation. How could the university be allowed to get away with this? I began investigating what other same-sex couples at Boulder did in response to this injustice. I heard something like the following from several faculty and staff, "We're just grateful to have benefits at all, David." I was so sad that the experience of these same-sex couples had been so difficult that the separate-and-clearly-not-equal status was something they were okay living with. In fact, most on campus had no idea how many hoops the university required same-sex couples to go through and apologized profusely. The HR staff person who delivered the bad news to me that my Jewish wedding, City of Oakland registration, Canadian marriage, and signed affidavit were not sufficient proof of my relationship apologized but reiterated that "this is a state decision over which we do not have control." As I hung up the phone, without thinking I said to myself, "I wish I were in California right now," and realized why so many people wanted me to come get remarried in California. At that moment, I recognized the power of the state to undermine and bless our relationships. I saw that whether we like it or not, our religious institutions have very little power over our lives in comparison with the power the state has to deny my husband the health care he depends on. Should we go to California?

11   And yet, if my Jewish wedding, Canadian marriage certificate, City of Oakland DP registration, and signed Colorado affidavit aren't enough for the university, a California marriage license would be as worthless. So instead of running off to the next state, municipality, or federal government that has finally woken up to the reality of our lives, of my life, and asking that state to sanctify our relationship, we decided to have dinner in our dining room and reread the text of our ketubah that spells out the real commitment of our relationship that we made 12 years ago. ◆

CRITICAL THINKING

1. In your opinion, should same-sex couples be permitted to legally marry? Are you likely to be swayed by hearing different points of view on the subject? Why or why not?

2. Identify the primary points of argument Jefferson uses to support his case. Make a list of his reasons, and respond to each one. How do you think Mouw would respond to Jefferson's points in an editorial?

3. According to Jefferson, why do homosexual couples want to marry? What motivates them? Do heterosexual couples marry for the same reasons as gay couples?

4. Mouw explains that he upholds a "traditional view of marriage." What is the traditional view? Explain.

5. Evaluate Mouw's allusion to "slippery slope" arguments that support same-sex marriage. How do you think Jefferson and Shneer would respond?

6. Evaluate the argument that same-sex marriage would undermine the institution of marriage itself, to the detriment of society.

7. What challenges could society face if gay marriage were indeed to undermine the cultural value of marriage as an institution? Explain.

8. Who was Harvey Milk? Why does he figure so prominently in Jefferson's argument and his decision not to marry in California?

9. What reasons does Shneer give for choosing not to marry his partner "again"? How do you think Jefferson would respond?

CRITICAL WRITING

1. *Persuasive Writing:* Write a letter to a minister, rabbi, or other religious leader. Explain why you think he or she should agree to perform a marriage ceremony celebrating the commitment of two of your best friends—a gay couple. Assume that this leader has not given much thought to gay marriage. Use comments made by authors in this section as support for your case. Alternatively, you may write a letter arguing against such a marriage. Assume that you care about your friends, and know that your opinions can cause them pain, but that you still must advise against such a union.

2. *Exploratory Writing:* Gay couples have been more prominent in the media over the past few years. What images of gay life has television presented to its viewers? How do the images correspond to claims that many gay men and women just want what marriage affords: social stability, anchors in relationships, and family and financial security? Write an essay in which you explore the portrayal of gay relationships in the media and how this portrayal may or may not influence public opinion on the issue of gay marriage.

3. *Persuasive Writing:* Will legalizing gay marriage increase or decrease the problems gay men and women now encounter in America in gaining social acceptance? What benefits might all gay people receive, whether or

not they choose to marry? Do you think that a legal change in marriage will help to change the beliefs of people who now disapprove of homosexuality? Why or why not? Explain.

4. Most of the arguments supporting gay marriage note that many gay couples are in committed, loving relationships and wish to legitimize their relationship with a marriage license. Can you think of other, less idealistic reasons why people marry? Based on these other reasons, including the practical and the shady, could these reasons undermine the movement legalizing homosexual marriage? For example, what if two female heterosexual friends, one employed the other not, wished to marry for health insurance? Could such alliances be avoided if same-sex marriage were legal? Explain.

GROUP PROJECTS

1. Working as a team using Internet resources, see what information you can find about same sex-marriages in California and in the United States over all. Assemble a list of resources and compare it with other groups in your class then select a more narrow topic for each group to research online. Prepare a brief description of what Internet users might find at each site. What cultural and social conclusions about gay marriage can you make based on your research? Explain.

2. Should marriage be a public and political institution? Should it be a religious, private, and moral institution? Should it have features of both? List the qualities that a marriage draws from each of these realms. After you have compiled your list, discuss with your group what marriage should be and for whom.

3. Design a survey that you will administer anonymously, to other members of your class or students in the student union, asking for opinions on gay marriage. Design your survey to allow people to formulate opinions and express their views while incorporating some of the ideas presented in this Viewpoints section. Collect the surveys and discuss the results. How do the responses connect to the arguments presented in this section? Explain.

Photo Credits

Text Credits

Ben Adler. "Are Cows Worse than Cars?" from *The American Prospect*, December 3, 2008. Reprinted with permission.

"Annika Sorenstam Has Another Remarkable Year For A Lady," from The Onion.com, December 1, 2005. Reprinted with permission.

Margaret Atwood. "Debtor's Prism," from *The Wall Street Journal,* September 20, 2008. Reprinted with permission.

Jeffrey Ball. "Six Products, Six Carbon Footprints," from *The Wall Street Journal*, March 1, 2009. Reprinted with permission.

Meredith Blake. "The Strange Life and Impending Death of Jane Goody." This article first appeared in Salon.com on February 19, 2009. An online version remains in the Salon archives. Reprinted with permission.

Karlyn Bowman. "The College Track: Onward and Upward," from *The American,* October 13, 2008. Reprinted with permission.

Jake Brennan. "Has Male Bashing Gone Too Far?" from AskMen.com, August 13, 2007. Reprinted with permission.

David Brooks. "People Like Us," From *The Atlantic Monthly*, September 2003. Reprinted with permission of the author.

Lakshmi Chaudry. "Mirror, Mirror on the Web," from *The Nation*, January 11, 2007. Reprinted with permission.

John Cloud. "Never Too Buff," from *TIME* Magazine, April 24, 2000. Copyright © Time Inc. Reprinted with permission.

Stephanie Coontz. "For Better, For Worse," *The Washington Post*, May 1, 2005. Reprinted with permission of the author.

Jennifer Davidson, "My Carbon Footprint: A Documentary, a Daughter, and All that Is Dear," from *NewsReview*, March 8, 2007. Reprinted with permission.

William Deresiewicz. "The Disadvantages of an Elite Education." Reprinted from *The American Scholar,* Volume 77, No. 3, Summer 2008. Copyright © 2008 by the author.

Stephanie Dolgoff. "Tattoo Me Again—and Again." From *SELF,* September 2007. Reprinted with permission.

Tamara Draut. "Strapped," an excerpt from *Strapped*: *Why America's 20- and 30-Somethings Can't Get Ahead,* by Tamara Draut. Copyright © 2005 by Tamara Draut. Used by permission of Doubleday, a division of Random House, Inc.

Gregg Easterbrook. "Global Warming: Who Loses—and Who Wins," *The Atlantic Monthly*, April 2007. Reprinted by permission of the author.

Roger Ebert. "Death to Film Critics! Hail to the CelebCult!" from *Chicago-Sun Times*, November 26, 2008. Reprinted with permission.

Joseph Epstein. "The Culture of Celebrity," from *The Weekly Standard*, October 17, 2005. Reprinted with permission.

Amitai Etzioni. "Leaving Race Behind." Reprinted from *The American Scholar*, Volume 75, No. 3, Spring 2006. Copyright © 2006 by the author.

Betty G. Farrell. "Family: Idea, Institution, and Controversy." Reprinted by permission of Westview Press, a member of Perseus Books Group.

Laura Fokkena. "Are You a Terrorist, or Do You Play One on TV?" from *PopPolitics,* November 20, 2002. Reprinted with permission from the author.

Garance Franke-Ruta, "The Natural Beauty Myth," from *The Wall Street Journal*, December 15, 2006. Copyright © *The Wall Street Journal*. Reprinted with permission.

Al Gore. "Nobel Lecture on Global Warming," delivered in Oslo upon acceptance of The Nobel Peace Prize, December 10, 2007. Copyright © Nobel Foundation, 2007. Reprinted with permission.

Daniel Gross. "Will Your Recession Be Tall, Grande, or Venti?" From *Slate,* October 20, 2008. Reprinted with permission.

Lev Grossman. "Grow Up? Not so Fast." From *TIME* Magazine, January 16, 2005. Reprinted with permission of *TIME* Inc.

James Hannaham. "Our Biracial President." This article first appeared in Salon.com, at http://salon.com. An online version remains in the Salon archives. Reprinted with permission.

Blaine Harden. "Numbers Drop for the Married with Children," *The Washington Post*, March 4, 2007. Reprinted with permission of the author.

Jeffrey Hart. "How to Get a College Education," *from The National Review,* September 29, 1996. Copyright © 1996 by National Review, Inc, 215 Lexington Avenue, New York, NY 10016, Reprinted by permission.

Graham Hays. "Why Men Don't Watch Women's Sports," ESPN.com, August 22, 2003. Reprinted with permission.

Ryan Healy. "Twentysomething: Be Responsible, Go Back Home After College," from *Employee Evolution* blog, http://www.employeeevolution.com/archives/2007/09/04/be-responsible-go-back-home-after-college/, September 4, 2007. Reprinted with permission.

Caroline Heldman. "Out-of-Body Image," from *Ms. Magazine*, Spring 2008. Reprinted by permission of *Ms. Magazine*, © 2008.

Michael Hirschorn. "The Case for Reality TV," from *The Atlantic,* May 2007. Reprinted with permission.

Eric Hoover. "'Animal House' at 30: O Bluto, Where Art Thou?" Copyright 2008, The Chronicle of Higher Education. Reprinted with permission.

Hua Hsu. "The End of White America?" from *The Atlantic*, February/March 2009. Reprinted with permission.

Kay S. Hymowitz. "The New Girl Order," from *City Journal*, Autumn 2007. Reprinted with permission.

Independent Television Service, "Masculinity," Public Broadcasting Service-Independent Lens, http://www.pbs.org/independentlens/hiphop/masculinity.htm. Text written by Lisa Ko.

Niranjana Iyer, "Weight of the World," from *Smithsonian Magazine,* August 2006. Reprinted with permission of author.

Beth Janes. "Why I Rue My Tattoo," from *MSNBC*, October 4, 2007 http://www.msnbc.msn.com. Reprinted with permission.

David Jefferson. "How Getting Married Made Me an Activist," From *Newsweek*, November 24, 2008. *Newsweek*, Inc. All rights reserved. Used by permission and protected by the copyright laws of the United States. The printing, copying, redistribution, or retransmission of the material without express written permission is prohibited.

Allen Jenkins. "Inequality, Race and Remedy," from *The American Prospect*, Volume 18, Number 5: May 4, 2007. The American Prospect, 2000 L Street NW, Suite 717, Washington, DC 20036. All rights reserved. Reprinted with permission.

Charles Johnson. "The End of the Black American Narrative," from *The American Scholar*, Summer 2008. Reprinted with permission.

Liz Jones. "What I Think of the Fashion World," *You* Magazine, April 15, 2001. Copyright © *You* Magazine. Reprinted with permission.

Anya Kamenetz. "Generation Debt," an excerpt from book by the same title, Riverhead Books, 2006. Reprinted with permission.

Gary Kamiya. "Black vs. Black." This article first appeared in Salon.com, at http://salon.com. An online version remains in the Salon archives. Reprinted with permission.

Madeleine Begun Kane. "My Most Attractive Adversary," *PopPolitics,* December 2000. Reprinted with permission of the author.

Jennifer L. Knight and Traci A. Giuliano. "He's a Laker; She's a 'Looker,'" an excerpt from "He's a Laker; She's a 'Looker:' "The Consequences of Gender-Stereotypical Portrayals of Male and Female Athletes by the Print Media," *Sex Roles, August 2001.* Reprinted with permission.

Elizabeth Larkin. "Reality TV: Should We Really Watch?" from About.com, 2004. Reprinted with permission.

William Lutz. "With These Words I Can Sell You Anything," from *Doublespeak,* 1989. Blond Bear, Inc. Reprinted by permission of the author.

John H. McWhorter. "Why I'm Black and Not African American," from *Los Angeles Times*, September 8, 2004. Reprinted by permission of the author.

Richard Mouw. "Less Shouting, More Talking," from *Newsweek,* February 9, 2009. Reprinted with permission.

Charles O'Neill. "The Language of Advertising." Reprinted with the permission of the author.

Peggy Orenstein. "What's Wrong With Cinderella?" from *The New York Times Magazine,* December 24, 2006. Reprinted with permission of the author.

Steven Pinker. "The Science of Difference," from *The New Republic*, February 7, 2005. Copyright © *The New Republic*. Reprinted with permission.

Dennis Prager. "Five Non-Religious Arguments for Marriage over Living Together," from TownHall Online, October 3, 2006. Reprinted with permission.

Lowell Putnam. "Did I Miss Something?" Reprinted with permission of the author.

Joe Queenan. "Just Let Go Already," from *The New York Times*, January 8, 2006. Reprinted with permission.

Christine Rosen, "Virtual Friendship and the New Narcissism." *The New Atlantis,* Summer 2007 (No 17). Reprinted with permission. For more information, visit www.TheNewAtlantis.com.

Douglas Rushkoff. "A Brand by Any Other Name," from the *London Times,* April 30, 2000. Reprinted with permission of the author.

Witold Rybczynski. "Can Cities Save the Planet?" from *Slate,* December 17, 2008. Reprinted with permission.

Scott Russell Sanders. "The Men We Carry in Our Minds," Copyright © 1984 by Scott Russell Sanders; *Milkweed Chronicle*; from *The Paradise of Bombs*; reprinted by permission of the author and the author's agents, the Virginia Kidd Agency, Inc.

Danny Schechter. "Investigating the Nation's Exploding Credit Squeeze," from *Neiman Reports,* Spring *2006.* Reprinted with permission.

James D. Scurlock. "Maxed Out: Hard Times in the Age of Easy Credit," an excerpt from *Maxed Out* by James D. Scurlock. Copyright © 2007 James D. Scurlock. Reprinted with permission of Scribner, a Division of Simon & Schuster.

Alicia C. Shepard. "A's for Everyone!" from *The Washington Post*, June 5, 2005. Copyright © 2005, by the author.

David Shneer. "Why I'm Not Getting Married . . . Again," from *The Huffington Post*, July 3, 2008. Reprinted with permission.

Dorian Solat. "On Not Saying 'I Do.'" Posted on www.nerve.com, May 27, 2004. Reprinted with permission of author.

Michael Specter, "Big Foot," from *The New Yorker,* February 25, 2008. Reprinted with permission.

Ted Spiker. "How Men Really Feel About Their Bodies," from *O, the Oprah Magazine,* August 2003. Reprinted with permission.

E.M. Swift. "Gender Inequality," from SI.com (*Sports Illustrated*), October 10, 2006. Copyright © 2006. Time Inc. All rights reserved. Reprinted with permission.

Rebecca Traister, "Return of the Brainless Hussier." This article first appeared in Salon.com, at http://www.salon.com. An online version remains in the Salon archives. Reprinted by permission.

Index